human relations

STRATEGIES FOR SUCCESS

Seventh Edition

Lowell H. Lamberton

Leslie Minor

Demitrius Zeigler

Mc Graw Hill

HUMAN RELATIONS
Published by McGraw Hill LLC, 1325 Avenue of the Americas, New York, NY 10121.

This book is printed on acid-free paper.

5 6 7 8 9 CPI 26 25 24 23

ISBN 978-1-264-58930-2
MHID 1-264-58930-1

Cover Image: *elenabsl/Shutterstock*

All credits appearing on page or at the end of the book are considered to be an extension of the copyright page.

mheducation.com/highered

authors

Lowell Lamberton is an emeritus business professor with an extensive background in both writing and business. He has worked as an expert consultant to many businesses, especially in the area of human behavior, specializing in organizational behavior and management. Prof. Lamberton has had many years of experience teaching management, human relations, and business communications classes at Central Oregon Community College and at Linfield College. He lives in Bend, Oregon, with his wife, Ruth, who is an artist.

He holds two degrees in English, one from Walla Walla University and the other from the University of Nebraska. He also holds an MBA and an advanced professional certificate (APC) in management from Suffolk University in Boston, Massachusetts.

Besides this textbook, he has also coauthored *Working with People: A Human Relations Guide* with Leslie Minor.

©Lowell Lamberton

Leslie Minor is a social psychologist and sociologist with a bachelor's degree in psychology from the University of Washington (Seattle), and MA and PhD degrees from the School of Social Ecology at the University of California (Irvine). Her teaching career spans more than 20 years, with teaching experience at large and small colleges, public and private, rural and urban, two-year and four-year institutions, in online and traditional formats, in the United States and in Singapore. She also has several years of experience in college administration in the roles of Department Chair, Dean, and Vice President. Dr. Minor believes that her most rigorous and satisfying on-the-job training in teaching and administration has come from rearing her three sons.

©Leslie Minor

Demitrius Zeigler is a freelance project manager and small business owner in in Long Beach, California. He earned a BS in Urban and Regional Planning from Cornell University and a Master's degree from the University of Southern California. Demitrius has worked in various roles including urban planner, middle school teacher, and urban farmer, among other things. But his favorite role is as project manager for his rambunctious young daughter.

©Demitrius Zeigler

preface

Throughout our years of teaching, administration, running small businesses, and consulting in the fields of social science and organizational behavior, we have become increasingly aware of the need for a textbook that is down to earth, experience based, and grounded in sound research and theory. We believe strongly in the importance of understanding the relationship between self-awareness and human relations, and, by extension, the relationship between human relations skills and ongoing career success. We encourage building self-awareness, growth, and success skills inside the context of the real world. What realistic strategies and techniques can we teach our students to encourage their growth in human relations success, on and off the job site? How can students tap into the power that comes from working well in one-on-one situations, in groups, and in organizations large and small?

Human Relations: Strategies for Success attempts to provide answers to these questions and guidance in developing human relations skills that transfer from the classroom to the real world of work. Our commitment to the creation of a book that is at once interesting to read, motivating to study, and relevant to a wide variety of students has been the driving force behind *Human Relations: Strategies for Success.*

This text covers research-based social science and management principles, as well as newer ideas in human relations drawn from management theory, group theory, personality theory, and relationship theory. Business applications of these theories are included in this text to bring attention to current best practices in these fields. More than ever, effective human relations skills are crucial to business success when organizations grow and compete in a global business environment, or when they arise from small-scale entrepreneurial enterprises. Employees must have the knowledge and skill to adapt to a workplace where change is as frequent as it is inevitable.

FEATURES OF THE SEVENTH EDITION

This seventh edition features the following changes from previous editions:

Chapter 1

- Improved discussion on employers' and managers' responsibilities in creating a work environment that respects the dignity and rights of workers
- Updated research, demographic data, sources, figures, and business applications to reflect current trends and issues
- Expanded discussion on current challenges in human relations and the modern workplace, and other concepts
- New, more contemporary "Case Studies" to reinforce Chapter 1 themes
- Added TED Talk reference and discussion questions to reinforce chapter concepts

Chapter 2

- Inclusion of more recent scholarship on self-concept and achieving a "growth mindset"
- Updated sources, with text revisions throughout the chapter to update concepts and their applications to business settings
- Added "More About" examples to reinforce course concepts
- Updated "working it out" exercise to focus on growth mindset
- Added TED Talk reference and discussion questions to reinforce chapter concepts

Chapter 3

- Enhanced discussion on the topic of self-disclosure, including the benefits and risk factors of disclosure in the workplace
- Inclusion of more recent scholarship, plus updated sources and business applications
- Updates throughout the chapter to provide a fresh look at core concepts and their applications to business settings
- New and updated "Real World Examples" for modern context
- Added TED Talk reference and discussion questions to reinforce chapter concepts

Chapter 4

- New opening vignette to emphasize contemporary workplace issues
- Revised and updated research findings on happiness, United States and international comparisons, and the down side to happiness
- New section on introverts, and a new "working it out" exercise focused on introversion
- Enhanced research on attitudes and values related to job satisfaction
- Updated information on values in corporate culture and corporate cheating
- New "Real World" examples and relevant quotations to reinforce student learning
- Text revisions throughout the chapter to update concepts and their applications to business settings
- Two new "Case Studies" focus on positive workplace attitudes and workplace values conflicts
- Added TED Talk reference and discussion questions to reinforce chapter concepts

Chapter 5

- New and updated sources for scholarship on the topics of motivation and self-esteem

- Revisions throughout the chapter to promote understanding and clarity of the material
- New demographic data added, and figures provided to illustrate changing demographic and workplace realities
- Text edits throughout the chapter to update sources and business applications of concepts
- Added TED Talk reference and discussion questions to reinforce chapter concepts

Chapter 6

- New opening vignette to reflect modern workplace scenario
- New and updated "Real World" examples to illustrate course concepts
- Expanded discussion of specific strategies to improve active listening skills
- Revisions and updates throughout the chapter to include more contemporary sources and applications of concepts
- New section on listening skills and delivering verbal messages
- Updated information and sources on international and intercultural communication
- New "working it out" exercise on cross-cultural aspects of marketing
- New "Case Studies" addressing difficult communication situations in the workplace
- Added TED Talk reference and discussion questions to reinforce chapter concepts

Chapter 7

- Chapter has been overhauled with major updates and revisions to better reflect contemporary workplace issues
- Inclusion of more current scholarship around the ideas of group and team work in the workplace
- Enhanced discussion on leadership and organizational culture/ climate
- New team development and team building strategies added to text
- New, improved activities to support the concepts in the chapter
- Added TED Talk reference and discussion questions to reinforce chapter concepts

Chapter 8

- New opening vignette to illustrate course concepts
- Updated discussion on Gardner's theory of multiple intelligences, including critique of theory

- Added section on Sternberg's theory of triarchic intelligence
- Added concepts and applications in strong emotions including aggression and passivity
- New "More About" examples to illustrate course concepts
- Text revisions throughout the chapter to promote understanding and clarity
- Text edits throughout the chapter to update sources and business applications of concepts
- Added "working it out" exercise on emotional intelligence
- New "Case Study" addressing the inner saboteurs
- Added TED Talk reference and discussion questions to reinforce chapter concepts

Chapter 9

- Greater, more detailed discussion on how technology is shaping our personal lives, and our roles in the modern workplace
- Newer research, and more up-to-date scholarship related to the concepts
- New figures, exhibits, and photos to connect readers' learning
- "Managing Life Changes" section revised to offer clear, straightforward advice for self-care during times of stress
- Discussion on Organizational Change Models has been updated to reflect more current thinking and scholarship on the topic
- Greater emphasis on stress reduction strategies to deal with changes in our personal and professional lives
- New "Real World Examples" to connect the concepts of the chapter with contemporary issues
- Added TED Talk reference and discussion questions to reinforce chapter concepts

Chapter 10

- Expanded discussion of creativity in the workplace, health effects, and characteristics of creativity
- Revisions throughout the chapter to update contemporary sources and applications of concepts
- New, more contemporary "More About" examples
- New "Real World" material on developing creativity
- Added material on the creativity strategy of reverse brainstorming
- New "working it out" exercise on creativity
- Added TED Talk reference and discussion questions to reinforce chapter concepts

Chapter 11

- New opening vignette to help students connect real-world example with learning material in the chapter
- Expanded analysis on conflict in the workplace guides students toward successful strategies such as "BATNA"
- Updated data sets for workplace employment
- Edits throughout the chapter to update contemporary sources and business applications of concepts
- Added TED Talk reference and discussion questions to reinforce chapter concepts

Chapter 12

- New, clearly presented information to help students identify and manage stress in their personal and professional lives
- Inclusion of new data and scholarship on the physical effects of stress, workplace productivity and stress, and technology effects
- New "More About" examples to illustrate course concepts
- Revisions and edits throughout the chapter to update contemporary understanding of issues and their applications to the workplace
- Updated survey research summarizing sources of stress in the United States
- Holmes and Rahe Stress Scale has been moved to this chapter to better place it with the topic
- Added TED Talk reference and discussion questions to reinforce chapter concepts

Chapter 13

- New opening vignette on the importance of good service
- Updated research and references to reflect contemporary scholarship and ideas around improving customer service in the workplace
- New "More About" sections to guide learning toward creating empathy in the workplace
- Edits throughout the chapter to update contemporary understanding of issues
- New "Case Study" on internal/external customer relations
- Added TED Talk reference and discussion questions to reinforce chapter concepts

Chapter 14

- New opening vignette to present workplace experiences of diversity

- Updated demographic data and statistics on diversity in the United States
- Text revisions throughout the chapter to reflect changing U.S. economic and political climate
- New figures provided to illustrate changing demographic and employment trends
- Text edits throughout the chapter to update contemporary understanding of issues
- New section illustrating the benefits to employers and employees of workplace diversity
- Expanded section on LGBTQ issues and sexual harassment in the workplace
- New "More About" examples to illustrate course concepts
- New section on cultural intelligence
- New "Case Study" on workplace discrimination
- Added TED Talk reference and discussion questions to reinforce chapter concepts

Chapter 15

- Updated opening vignette to help students connect with the material in the chapter
- New and updated information on contemporary issues such as the spread of disinformation, cyberbullying, and a growing digital divide
- The Global Ethics Issues section and others have been updated to reflect current trends and more recent scholarship around the topic of ethics and social responsibility
- Added TED Talk reference and discussion questions to reinforce chapter concepts

Chapter 16

- Revisions throughout the chapter to update contemporary sources and applications of concepts
- Enhanced information on improving employee morale, and on reducing procrastination
- Updated research and statistics on substance abuse and its effects, and on the workplace response to substance abuse
- New "working it out" exercises on practicing interview skills and on career planning
- Added TED Talk reference and discussion questions to reinforce chapter concepts

TEXTBOOK-WIDE FEATURES

Each chapter includes the following pedagogical features to facilitate student comprehension and to show how chapter concepts apply to the real world:

Strategies for Success. To highlight the connection between human relations theories and their real-world applications, this textbook contains a unique series of strategies that are integrated into all of the chapters. These strategies offer concrete guidance on how to use human relations skills to address situations that all people face.

Opening Vignettes. Each chapter opens with a short vignette to set the tone of the chapter. These vignettes use the narrative approach to make the chapter concepts more real to students at the outset, before they begin to absorb concepts and terms.

Key Terms. Important terms are highlighted within the text and called out in the margin. They are also listed at the end of each chapter and are defined in the glossary.

Review Questions and Critical Thinking Questions. Each chapter closes with thought-provoking questions. These questions call on students to go beyond simply reading the chapter, by asking them to consider its implications for their lives in the classroom and beyond. Many questions tap students' creativity and problem-solving abilities as they encourage students to think beyond the boundaries of the book.

Case Studies. Two realistic, job-based case studies (each with questions) are presented in every chapter. These classroom-tested case studies are drawn from familiar experiences in a wide variety of workplace settings. These cases allow students to resolve realistic human relations problems for which there is usually more than one viable solution. Each case study can be used as a springboard for classroom discussion and group problem-solving activities.

"working it out" exercises. For most students, active participation is motivating, rewarding, and crucial to reinforcing learning. In a variety of classroom-tested working it out exercises, students are encouraged to build on their human relations skills as they role-play, interview each other, assess their own and each others' strengths and weaknesses, work on setting goals and developing strategies, practice giving and receiving feedback, and explore other applications of chapter topics.

acknowledgments

This edition marks 25 years since the first edition of the textbook was published. We could not have achieved this milestone alone; many people were involved in the writing and production of this book. We especially would like to thank Laura Hurst Spell, our associate portfolio manager from McGraw-Hill Higher Education, and our editor Sarah Blasco, for their help, kindness, and patience. Many reviewers provided valuable feedback that strengthened the content in this edition. At home, too many students to mention have offered suggestions and help since the last edition.

We would also like to thank our colleagues and co-workers, friends, and family members for the help they have offered by presenting real-life situations involving human relations issues. This real-life material has been incorporated into opening vignettes, Real World examples, and some of the case studies. A special thanks goes out as well to our families who provided ongoing support and assistance: Lowell's wife, Ruth Lamberton; Leslie's sons, who have now planted roots on the east and west coasts but stay close virtually and in real life; and Demitrius' daughter, who is always ready to contribute a critical artistic or editorial eye in the writing process.

Solid previous editions have made this one possible. In the first edition, Betty Morgan, our adjunct editor, created the "Strategies" approach, for which we are extremely grateful. Heather Lamberton spent many hours doing research for nearly all of the chapters. And without Carla Tishler, our first editor, we would never have completed the project. In the second edition, we were helped greatly by Cheryl Adams, adjunct editor for Glencoe/McGraw-Hill. Tammy Higham was invaluable in the creation of the third edition. Of course, the instructors and students who have used the textbook over the past two and a half decades have a special place in our hearts as well.

We would also like to thank the following people for their feedback and guidance as reviewers of this edition of the manuscript:

- Irene Church, Muskegon Community College
- Kim Fox-Marchetti, Lone Star College System
- Philip Mathew, Olympic College
- Lori Merlak, Kirkwood Community College
- Karen Overton, Houston Community College
- Matthew Clayton Reynolds, College of Southern Idaho
- Eric B. Terry, Miami Dade College
- Juliett Tracey, Palm Beach State College

Mc Graw Hill **connect**®

FOR INSTRUCTORS

You're in the driver's seat.

Want to build your own course? No problem. Prefer to use our turnkey, prebuilt course? Easy. Want to make changes throughout the semester? Sure. And you'll save time with Connect's auto-grading too.

65%

Less Time Grading

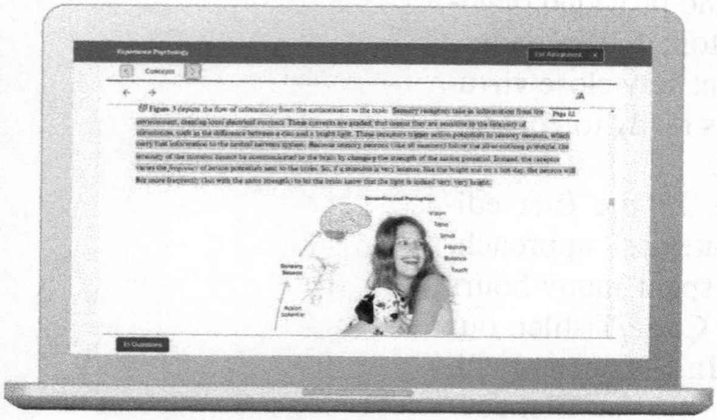

Laptop: McGraw-Hill; Woman/dog: George Doyle/Getty Images

They'll thank you for it.

Adaptive study resources like SmartBook® 2.0 help your students be better prepared in less time. You can transform your class time from dull definitions to dynamic debates. Find out more about the powerful personalized learning experience available in SmartBook 2.0 at **www.mheducation.com/highered/connect/smartbook**

Make it simple, make it affordable.

Connect makes it easy with seamless integration using any of the major Learning Management Systems—Blackboard®, Canvas, and D2L, among others—to let you organize your course in one convenient location. Give your students access to digital materials at a discount with our inclusive access program. Ask your McGraw-Hill representative for more information.

Padlock: Jobalou/Getty Images

Solutions for your challenges.

A product isn't a solution. Real solutions are affordable, reliable, and come with training and ongoing support when you need it and how you want it. Our Customer Experience Group can also help you troubleshoot tech problems—although Connect's 99% uptime means you might not need to call them. See for yourself at **status.mheducation.com**

Checkmark: Jobalou/Getty Images

FOR STUDENTS

Effective, efficient studying.

Connect helps you be more productive with your study time and get better grades using tools like SmartBook 2.0, which highlights key concepts and creates a personalized study plan. Connect sets you up for success, so you walk into class with confidence and walk out with better grades.

Study anytime, anywhere.

Download the free ReadAnywhere app and access your online eBook or SmartBook 2.0 assignments when it's convenient, even if you're offline. And since the app automatically syncs with your eBook and SmartBook 2.0 assignments in Connect, all of your work is available every time you open it. Find out more at **www.mheducation.com/readanywhere**

"I really liked this app—it made it easy to study when you don't have your text-book in front of you."

- Jordan Cunningham,
Eastern Washington University

Calendar: owattaphotos/Getty Images

No surprises.

The Connect Calendar and Reports tools keep you on track with the work you need to get done and your assignment scores. Life gets busy; Connect tools help you keep learning through it all.

Learning for everyone.

McGraw-Hill works directly with Accessibility Services Departments and faculty to meet the learning needs of all students. Please contact your Accessibility Services office and ask them to email accessibility@mheducation.com, or visit **www.mheducation.com/about/accessibility** for more information.

Top: Jenner Images/Getty Images, Left: Hero Images/Getty Images, Right: Hero Images/Getty Images

brief contents

« part 1

Human Relations and You

contents

Chapter Ten

Chapter Eleven

Chapter Twelve

Chapter Sixteen

482 A Productive Workplace and Success

PART ONE

«« human relations and you

1 Human Relations: A Background

2 Self-Concept and Self-Esteem in Human Relations

3 Self-Awareness and Self-Disclosure

4 Attitudes and Values in Human Relations

5 Motivation: Increasing Productivity

In Part One, we'll explore the foundations of human relations skills. Specifically, how does each one of us develop the necessary tools to work well together at home, in school, and on the job? What aspects of our personality contribute to our success at human relations? Are there strategies we can use to build human relations skills?

Chapters 1 through 5 define human relations, then look closely at the relationship between self-understanding and communication. These chapters will test your ability to ask questions about personal and global values, and help you discover how to tap motivational strategies for yourself and others. These are important first steps to develop the human relations skills you need for success in your personal life and in the world of work. »»

CHAPTER ONE

1

HUMAN RELATIONS
A Background

LEARNING OBJECTIVES

After studying this chapter, you will be able to:

LO 1-1 Define human relations.

LO 1-2 Explain the importance of human relations in business.

LO 1-3 Discuss the challenges of human relations as these factors affect success in business.

LO 1-4 Identify what the study of human relations does *not* include.

LO 1-5 Describe the areas of emphasis for human relations in today's workplace.

LO 1-6 Discuss a short history of the study of human relations.

STRATEGIES FOR SUCCESS

Strategy 1.1 Develop Mutual Respect

Strategy 1.2 Build Your Communication Skills

Social Media Meltdown

SITUATION

KieferPix/Shutterstock

It had been a long day for Kelly, the kind where she felt the universe was conspiring against her. In her job as an administrative assistant at the county's Small Business and Entrepreneurship Program, she dealt with dozens of people each day, often at a dizzying pace. Now that the work day was ending, she felt frazzled, tired, and angry. The last client of the day had been rude and insulting to her. The client, Mr. Petrov, blamed Kelly for problems with his new business. He wouldn't listen when Kelly tried to explain that she was there as clerical support, not as a consultant; that she could not give him business advice; and that she was not responsible for his business failure. Voices were raised as tempers flared on both sides.

As a public employee, Kelly had signed confidentiality and ethics agreements with her employer agreeing that she would not disclose private information related to the program, and that she would not make public statements that put the organization in a bad light. But this terrible, horrible day ending with Mr. Petrov made her forget about all that. Later that evening, she logged into her Twitter account and started venting. She posted a quick series of tweets about her frustrations with the difficult client, called out other clients who had treated her badly, her supervisors, and had a few choice words for county administration in general. She really let 'em have it.

The next morning as she arrived at work, her supervisor immediately called Kelly into her office and closed the door. "Kelly," she began, "as a public agency, we hold high standards for our office. We work hard to keep our community's trust. With your venting session on your social media page, you violated confidentiality and ethical behavior policies, and tore down the basic integrity of our work here that has taken years to build. Just this morning, I have heard from more than a dozen people who saw your tweets and called to complain. I'm going to have to ask for your resignation."

Kelly was in complete shock. She felt sick, and could barely speak. "But. . ." she stammered, "those were my private opinions from my own, personal account! I have free speech rights, don't I? Those weren't meant to be public statements, and I didn't really mean what I said, I was just very upset!"

DISCOVERY

As Kelly gathered her belongings and prepared to leave, the seriousness of the situation began to sink in. There was no way she could explain away what she had posted. She had mocked Mr. Petrov, his business, and even his accent. She had made sarcastic and hostile remarks about other clients and county administrators by name, and in detail.

Kelly felt terrible about what she had said. The bitter irony was that she was proud to work for an organization that helped people work toward achieving their dreams. She was filled with remorse and regret. She wished she could apologize to everyone, on the spot.

"It's going to take a miracle for me to make this right with everyone," Kelly thought to herself. Kelly's impulsive behavior had become a human relations nightmare for the organization, clients, staff and administrators, and Kelly herself.

THINK ABOUT IT

Consider the situation Kelly now finds herself in—at what point did her situation became problematic?

As you read through Chapter 1, ask yourself, "Which of the areas of major emphasis in human relations arise with Kelly's situation?"

How can human relations knowledge and skills be used to resolve this situation?

» WHAT IS HUMAN RELATIONS?

The importance of human relations in our personal and work lives cannot be exaggerated. The skills that are necessary for good relations with others are the most important skills anyone can learn in life. Human relations decisions may not involve life-or-death outcomes, but they can have very serious impacts.

human relations
The skill or ability to work effectively through and with other people.

Human relations is the skill or ability to *work effectively through and with other people.* Human relations includes a desire to understand others, their needs and weaknesses, and their talents and abilities. For anyone in a workplace setting, human relations also involves an understanding of how people work together in groups, satisfying both individual needs and group objectives. If an organization is to succeed, the relationships among the people in that organization must be monitored and maintained.

In all aspects of life, you will deal with other people. No matter what you do for a living or how well you do it, your relationship with others is the key to your success or failure. Even when someone is otherwise only average at a job, good human relations skills can usually make that person seem better to others. Sadly, the opposite is also true: Poor human relations skills can make an otherwise able person seem like a poor performer. A doctor who respects patients, a lawyer who listens carefully to clients, a manager who gets along well with others in the workplace—all of these people will most likely be thought of by others as successful.

» THE IMPORTANCE OF HUMAN RELATIONS SKILLS

The ability to create and maintain effective relationships with others is the most important reason to understand human relations. Other reasons for studying human relations include the following:

more about. . .

Internal customers can be defined as a department's employees, or as employees in other departments within an organization.

1. **Human rights.** Today, managers in the workplace have a greater awareness of their responsibilities to safeguard the rights of employees, who for their part have come to expect dignity, respect, equity, and fairness from their managers and other employees in the workplace environment. This awareness calls for more skillful relations among employees, using tact, **trust**, and diplomacy with greater skill. In today's workplace, the term *internal customer* is often used to describe stakeholders or employees within the company, who may be grouped into different departments or groups (such as IT, HR, front vs. back office, and similar employee-to-employee relationships). Addressing the needs of the *internal customer* can help promote human rights within the workplace by creating a culture of mutual respect among employees and managers, where the rights of all—including outside customers and competitors—are safeguarded.

trust
Firm belief in the reliability, truth, ability, or strength of someone or something.

2. **The global marketplace.** While most people in other countries tend to view the United States favorably, global opinion of Americans can vary in some countries–even countries we had long considered to be our friends.[1] When anti-American stories are told, they tend to invoke the metaphorical "ugly American" and involve stories of Americans using poor human relations skills when doing business with or communicating with people from other cultures. Improving interpersonal skills (the skills associated with getting along with others) can be a factor in promoting an image that Americans do respect individual liberties both at home and abroad, and remain competitive in the global marketplace.

Group work is a necessity in today's workforce.
GaudiLab/Shutterstock

3. **Emphasis on people as human resources.** Decades ago, forecasters predicted that by this time in history, strong computer skills would be the number one factor in the workplace. However, managers and corporate planners are now placing great emphasis on the human factor *in addition to* technical or occupational skills. In the age of automation, successful job applicants are now being sought for their additional business "soft skills," such as effective communication, responsibility, teamwork, problem-solving, leadership, time management, problem-solving, emotional competence, and an "ethical compass."[2]
4. **Renewed emphasis on working groups.** Today's employees tend to enjoy working as teams and being involved in making decisions as a group. Helping groups work well together in such endeavors (as either a team member or leader) requires a great deal of human relations skill. Both managers and employees need to understand the dynamic of group interaction if such participation is to be effective.
5. **Increasing diversity in the workplace.** Few countries on earth contain the diversity of race, religion, and culture that exists in the United States. For example, the Census Bureau estimates foreign-born residents made up 13.7 percent of the U.S. population in 2018. Likewise, the number of women in the workplace has also dramatically grown globally in recent decades. And older Americans now contribute to an increasing share of adults in the workplace, with an increasing number of employees staying in the workplace past typical retirement age.[3] In fact, looking ahead to the future, the participation rate for workers age 65 years and older is expected to increase to 23.3 percent by 2028.[4] The point of these data: A deep understanding of how diversity strengthens an organization is one of the most important skills in human relations.

Human Relations and You

The study of human relations can help you in several ways. Human relations skills can help you get a job, enjoy your work, be more productive at it, and stay there longer with better chances for advancement. An understanding of yourself and others can help you be happier and more productive in all areas of your life.

You, the Manager

A percentage of students who read this book will one day become managers. For a manager, no skill area is more important than the ability to relate to, and communicate with, other employees in the company. A manager with good human relations skills will retain employees longer, be more productive and help the organization to be more productive, and provide employees with the type of positive engagement that promotes a more enjoyable workplace environment.[5]

more about. . .

An **entrepreneur** is someone who organizes and assumes the risks and rewards of beginning a business enterprise.

You, the Entrepreneur

In the 21st century, an increasing number of today's students leave college to enter an exciting realm of entrepreneurship: owning their own businesses. When you are the owner and operator of a business, your people skills—or human relations—are among the most important factors in your success. In an e-commerce business, although there is less face-to-face contact with customers and suppliers, the ability to communicate with people and to fulfill their needs is as crucial to success as choosing the right e-commerce platform or maximizing the use of social media.[6] Even in an e-commerce business, human relations skills matter immensely.

In a larger sense, your knowledge of human relations helps the work you do—or the business you own—provide fulfillment. Famed Russian author Fyodor Dostoyevsky wrote in the 1800s, "If it were desired to reduce a man to nothingness, it would be necessary only to give his work a character of uselessness."[7] Many entrepreneurs become business owners to escape the feeling of uselessness associated with their former jobs. The entrepreneur is in the position of being able to control the human climate of the business he or she owns and operates.

You, the Engaged Employee

For modern businesses, employee engagement is key, with employee engagement leading to reduced turnover, higher productivity, and increased profitability.[8] Being uninvolved, unapproachable, or pessimistic about your work can be reasons for failure at a job. Staying engaged and practicing good communication with your superiors, clients, and other co-workers will set you on a good track.

» CURRENT CHALLENGES IN HUMAN RELATIONS

From the executive boardroom to the shop floor, businesses function in a dynamic way with the world economy. For example, changes in economic policy, or changes to the means of production can provide a challenge to human relations in the workplace. Similarly, changes in the social structure or in the social or economic priorities of people in a society cause unanticipated workplace challenges. These forces can also work in reverse: changes and challenges at the individual level can influence changes at the professional level.

Young Millennials and those from Generation Z entering the job market for the first time can find that good, sustainable-wage jobs are hard to come by, and that advancement can be difficult at first. The problems faced by this group, and by the slightly older Generation X, are often blamed on the Baby Boomers, the late-middle-aged people who are mostly in management positions above them. Although a generation gap is nothing new in the American workplace, the potential friction between up-and-coming Millennials, Generation Zers, and not-yet-ready-to-retire Baby Boomers is one that may have a direct and profound effect on relations in the workplace.[9] You will learn more about this topic in Chapter 14, which discusses issues of workplace diversity.

more about. . .

Baby Boomers are the largest cohort of Americans living today. Those of the Baby Boomer generation were born during the years 1946 to 1964.

Generation X is the generation of Americans born between 1965 and 1980. "Gen X" is the generation that follows the Baby Boomers.

Millennials generally refers to Americans born between 1981 and 1996. Sometimes also called "Generation Y," the term Millennials especially applies to the generation that follows Generation X.

Generation Z, or those born between the years 1997 and 2012, is the emergent generation of the next economy. Also thought of as the "Post-millennial generation," Gen Z will navigate a vastly different business workplace than their Baby Boomer grandparents.

Increased Competition in the Workplace

Competitiveness reaches into all geographic areas—urban, suburban, and rural—and affects all businesses, large and small. Small businesses may feel pressure to meet the high international standards of the foreign market and of the huge multinational companies that dominate the economy. When a chain retailer such as Walmart moves into a small town, the competition felt by local business owners is very real. Likewise, the increasing expectation among consumers that they should be able to get most of what they need online has created a source of major competition for both established and emerging businesses.

Secure, well-paid jobs are more competitive than ever before. Having a college degree is no longer a ticket to a meaningful career, as it was just a generation ago. This new reality causes a great deal of frustration for many people in the workplace, and many human relations problems can result.

Another important factor increasing competition is the continued economic strength of some of America's global trading partners, especially China, which leverages an ever-increasing share of the world economy. For example, China—which is the world's largest economy in 2020, with the United States the second largest—had an average annual growth rate of 9.69 percent from 1989 until 2017.[10] Contrast that with an average annual growth rate of less than 4 percent in United States during the same time period, and it becomes easier to understand American workers' general anxiety about their role in an increasingly competitive "global workplace." Other countries are also seen as emerging markets, including India and other nations around the world. Will all of them become large enough to become a strong competitor? Time will tell. Worldwide issues such as wars, widespread illness such as the global pandemic, new technology, trade wars, changing international

DIVORCE
Divorce often has a heavy impact on employees' lives.
Aleksandr Davydov/Alamy Stock Photo

trade agreements, and the global political landscape are among many of the factors that affect the global economy and the global workplace.

Family Work Dynamics Changing

Most families or households now need income from more than one adult member to survive comfortably. With both adults in a family working, this can place a strain on the family and its members–a strain that can be felt in the workplace in a number of ways. For example, additional financial pressures at home can cause workplace stress. And the time needed for the everyday realities of child rearing–such as visits to the family doctor and transportation to and from school–can create difficulties for everyone involved.

Even with an increasing trend toward two-income households, two important factors have contributed to the existence of a higher number of single parents than was prevalent among the Baby Boomer or earlier generations: (1) a high divorce rate and (2) an increase in the number of never-married parents. The single parent must be the provider, taxi service, spiritual guide, and emotional support source. These many roles often result in a spillover effect of frustration and stress in the workplace. This type of worker can be truly overloaded.

A divorced or newly single person typically has to go through a period of emotional recovery, during which many emotional issues can form. Such issues can negatively affect job performance and attitudes and can harm relationships with co-workers, bosses, and fellow employees. Newly divorced or single workers may also be dealing with issues of self-worth and self-esteem related to the dissolution of their relationship.

"Sandwich Generation" Getting Cheesed

People are living longer now than in previous decades. In fact, life expectancy nearly doubled during the 20th century with a ten-fold increase in the number of Americans age 65 or older.[11] This rise in life expectancy–when combined with fewer high-income jobs for senior citizens and cuts to pension funds and post-retirement health insurance–means that many middle-aged adults now find themselves supporting their aging parents and parents-in-law, while raising their own children, at the same time.

These middle-aged adults who find themselves squeezed for time and finances are often referred to as the "sandwich generation" (think of the elderly, dependent parents as one piece of bread, and the dependent children as the other, with the middle-aged adults in the middle). The added responsibilities exist when parents or in-laws live with the adult children and their families, but also when elderly parents live alone or in retirement homes. The emotional impact affects all involved, including the dependent parents, who usually would prefer self-sufficiency.

» WHAT HUMAN RELATIONS IS *NOT*

To achieve a thorough understanding of the study of human relations is, it is wise to look at some characteristics it *does not* have. First, human relations is not a study in understanding human behavior in order to manipulate others. Good human relations means being authentic, positive, and honest. Practicing effective human relations means *being yourself at your very best.*

Second, learning better human relations skills is not a cure-all. Nor is it a quick fix for deep and ongoing personal problems. The skills you will learn in this book are skills to be built upon, developed, and tried out whenever you can as part of your own experience on the job and throughout your life.

Last, human relations is not just *common sense.* This argument is often used by people who think a book like this in unnecessary. "Common sense," they may say, "will carry you through!" In the area of human relations, however, common sense (meaning ordinary good sense and judgment) is all too *un*common. The abuses of many workers on the job today, the misunderstandings that cost thousands of companies millions of dollars every year, the unhappiness of many workers with the jobs they have: all of these factors illustrate the need for a strong foundation in human relations—even if much of it seems like simple common sense.

Despite all of the progress in human relations during the past decades, the 21st century has produced some surprising examples of lack of forward progress. Companies in the ride-sharing industry, for example, have shaken off past lessons of successful workplace models in favor of newer, "disruptive" models that can ignore many of the basic worker rights gained through the 20th century, such as regular breaks, paid time-off, and vacations. Some of these companies have even resisted calling the people who staff their businesses "employees" so that they are not obligated to provide normal compensation such as standard employee wages and benefits. And it is widely understood of these ride-share businesses that good human relations among employees is directly *in*compatible with the ultimate business goals of some segments of the auto industry—to replace human drivers with robotic driverless cars.

The evolving market sectors we see emerging today challenge our notions of organizational structures, as well as basic human relations in a workplace setting. Legal challenges as they arise in response to workplace changes remind us to pay attention to an evolving workplace landscape in which common sense and assumptions about what to expect in the workplace are not enough to maintain a healthy and productive work setting. One such legal change is Assembly Bill 5 in California, in effect in 2020, which requires many independent contractors to be reclassified as employees entitled to benefits.[12] In a changing economy, it is more important than ever to remember to practice good human relations.

more about...

Assembly Bill 5, California, 2020, and Contract Work

AB 5 went into effect in California in 2020. This law requires companies to pay salary and benefits to people who work for them in positions in which they had previously been defined as contractors. As contractors, companies are not required to pay these workers benefits. Major companies including Uber, Lyft, and Postmates said they would not comply with the new law, as it would be too expensive for them to absorb. In November 2020, Proposition 22 was passed by voters, allowing ride-share and delivery companies to continue to classify their workers in the state as independent contractors rather than employees. Legal challenges may continue to take some time to resolve.

» AREAS OF MAJOR EMPHASIS

In the broadest sense, the study of human relations has two goals: personal development and growth, and achievement of an organization's objectives. (See Figure 1.1.) All of the following areas of emphasis take both of those goals into consideration. You will notice that each of the areas is further developed in the following chapters of this book. Most of them overlap, and some are dependent upon others. Those relationships will become clearer as you read further.

Self-Esteem

self-esteem

The regard in which an individual holds himself or herself.

Self-esteem is your feeling of confidence and worth as a person. Psychological research has shown that lower self-esteem is related to a variety of mental health problems, including alcoholism, anxiety, and depression–all of which cause problems on the job. Higher self-esteem, on the other hand, improves attitudes, job morale, and overall quality of life. In the workplace, healthy self-esteem and self-awareness are key to top performance and high-quality work–especially when the work directly affects other people. Chapter 2 deals more with this important subject.

Mutual Respect

mutual respect

The positive consideration or regard that two people have for each other.

Notice that this isn't simply respect, but *mutual* respect. **Mutual respect**, the positive consideration or regard that two people have for each other, can exist only when your self-esteem is stable. If your self-esteem is too fragile, you will have little energy left for cultivating mutual respect. Also, without trust, mutual respect is meaningless. Many human relations specialists rate trust as one of the key elements of successful employee–manager relationship and consider it the single most important element in human relations.[13] People at all levels of an organization need trust and mutual respect to perform at their best.

figure 1.1

MAJOR GOALS AND EMPHASIS AREAS OF HUMAN RELATIONS

Which of these areas do you personally consider most important to effective human relations?

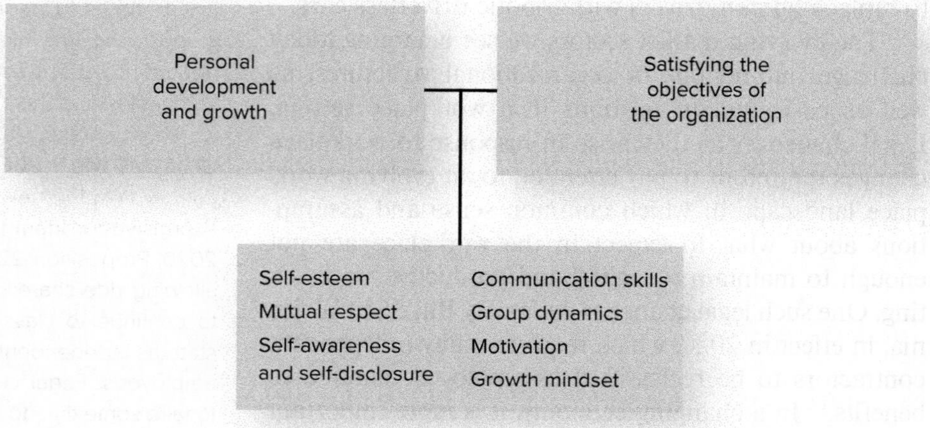

Self-Awareness and Self-Disclosure

These two concepts are interconnected. **Self-awareness** is the knowledge of how you are being perceived by others. **Self-disclosure** is the process of letting other people know what you are really thinking and feeling. Self-awareness allows one to know what in one's own behavior is being perceived as real by other people; self-disclosure involves "being real" or authentic with others. In *The Seven Habits of Highly Effective People,* author Stephen Covey said, "Until we take how we see ourselves (and how we see others) into account, we will be unable to understand how others see and feel about themselves and their world."[14] Self-disclosure, on the other hand, reflects the positive side of human relations: By allowing others to see what feelings and thoughts you really have in a given instance, you can promote genuineness and authenticity in the other person. A positive side effect is that your relationship with the other person is likely to become closer.

self-awareness
The knowledge of how you are being perceived by others.

self-disclosure
The process of letting other people know what you are really thinking and feeling.

more about...

Stephen Covey (1932–2012), author of numerous books, was known globally for his emphasis on personal and professional integrity. He co-founded the Franklin Covey Company, which is the largest leadership development organization in the world.

Communication Skills

Communication is the process of sending ideas, thoughts, and feelings from one individual or group to another, and having them received in the way you intended.[15] The communication process is at the heart of all managerial functions, and it is directly related to success or failure at the managerial level. It is also a vital part of all personal interactions. When a human relations problem emerges, miscommunication is usually involved.

If you are to grow either as an individual or in groups, *effective* communication is essential.[16] Much of your success depends on your ability to express ideas and concepts precisely. Part of that ability is based on your listening level, which includes listening for feelings and emotions as well as for objective content.

communication
The giving and receiving of ideas, feelings, and information among people.

Group Dynamics

Whenever two or more people form a relationship, there is, in effect, a group. Once a group is formed, it immediately requires understanding, planning, and organizational tactics appropriate to groups. Thus, understanding **group dynamics**—the ways in which groups operate—is a cornerstone in the study of human relations.[17]

Individuality is an important part of Americans' identities. But the nature of business work often involves collaboration, and it is through group efforts that the important things in life are achieved (think development of electric and autonomous vehicles, or co-teaching in the classroom, for example). A pioneer in the field, management expert Peter Drucker, once said, "Management is about human beings. Its task is to make people capable of *joint performance,* to make their strengths effective and their weaknesses irrelevant."[18] For success, people learn how to make group processes more effective.

group dynamics
The set of interpersonal relationships within a group that determine how group members relate to one another and that influence task performance.

more about. . .

Peter Drucker (1909–2005), a management expert for over 60 years, authored several books that still carry the same strong impact as they did when he was still alive. His first influential work was the 1945 study *The Concept of a Corporation,* which compared his ideal of management with the management of General Motors.

Within the group dynamic, today's teams are different from the teams of the past. Today's teams are far more diverse, often dispersed in different locations, highly digital, and dynamic (with frequent changes in membership).[19] While teams today may face new hurdles in a changing economy, their success still hinges on the fundamental skills emphasized in this section, such as self-esteem, awareness, mutual respect, effective communication, motivation, and maintaining a growth mindset.

Motivation

motivation
The force of the need or desire to act.

People often use the term **motivation** to describe the force that gets them to do their tasks. It is no longer enough to threaten punishment or even to reward a job well done. Motivation derives from the needs of an individual and of a group. It is also a major element in understanding human relations.

Growth Mindset

growth mindset
The belief that our basic abilities can be developed and improved through dedication and hard work.

At its core, a **growth mindset** is the belief that our basic abilities can be developed and improved through dedication and hard work. With this mindset, it is believed that people can break through stagnation or other challenges to achieve the goals they have set for themselves. A mindset tuned to *growth* is thought to be the opposite of a *fixed* mindset, which can decrease self-knowledge and self-awareness, cut off opportunity, and provoke dissatisfaction, disappointment, and a broad range of associated negative feelings.[20] Expand your mind with a growth mindset! Chapter 2 covers more on this important topic.

» A BRIEF HISTORY OF HUMAN RELATIONS

One cannot fully appreciate the present state of human relations without at least a partial understanding of the past. The history of human relations is essential to a thorough understanding of its place in today's world.

Human relations has been important ever since human beings began to live together in groups. These groups, in turn, created structures of power in their communities and regions. Over time, attitudes toward power—especially the sharing of power—have changed across time and places. For example, most modern cultures have moved toward allowing equal power sharing among men and women in society; this is a dynamic issue that continues to evolve. Because of societal changes, the history of human relations problems will be viewed in different ways during different times.

The Early Years

Human relations began to be an issue as we know it today around the early to mid-1800s. Figure 1.2 gives a thumbnail view of major events in the field.

figure 1.2

A HUMAN RELATIONS TIMELINE

What are the major changes you see in human relations over the years?

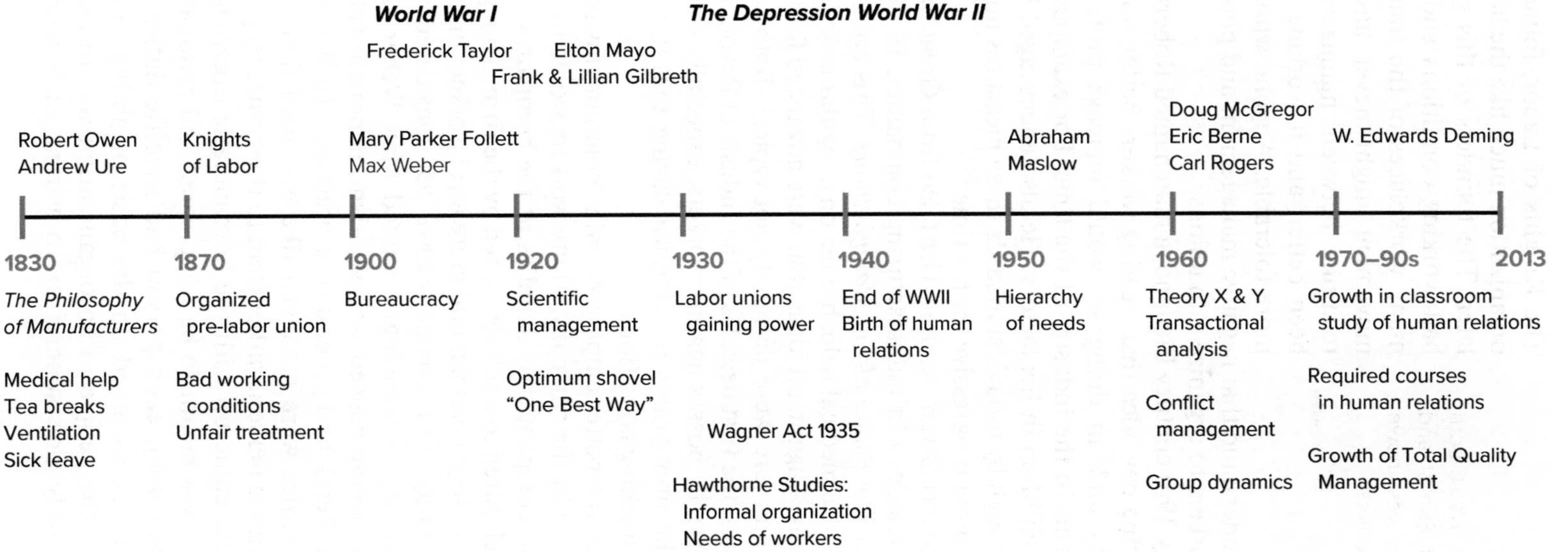

more about. . .

Robert Owen (1771–1858) was a Welsh-born social reformer who influenced both English and American employers. His philosophy was known as "Owenism" and his followers Owenites.

The Knights of Labor, founded in 1869, was an organization much like the labor unions that came later. The founders of this group denounced the bad working conditions and unfair treatment in many workplaces of the time.[21] The labor union movement might never have started if human relations between managers and workers had been better, and if working conditions had been more tolerable. Anyone who is blindly anti-union needs to understand that negative management and poor working conditions pushed workers to organize into unions.

In early 19th-century England, a man named Robert Owen came up with the surprising new idea that treating workers better would actually increase productivity and, in doing so, would increase profits. Owen introduced many reforms in the industry of the time. For example, he stopped employing young children in his factory. He also encouraged his workforce to stay sober. Although by today's standards these measures might seem quite basic, Owen was quite progressive for his time.[22]

Like Robert Owen, Andrew Ure (also from Great Britain) was interested in human relations in manufacturing companies. In 1835, Ure published a book called *The Philosophy of Manufacturers.* This book suggested that workers should have medical help, hot tea on a regular basis, good ventilation, and even sick leave—again, all ideas that were advanced for their time.[23]

Owen and Ure were definitely not typical. Both in Europe and in the United States, the first decades of the Industrial Revolution (1760–1840) were full of abuses by bosses against workers, especially workers with few skills. Many of the immigrants to America during that time were forced to face inhumane working conditions.

Some of the better employers built "company towns." These were settlements, owned by the company, where workers would live in standard housing built by the company, buy supplies at the company-owned store, and even send their children to a school owned by the firm. Though not popular today, this setup produced happier and more loyal workers in many cases, especially when the quality of the company town was considered high.

In Germany, a sociologist named Max Weber saw human relations problems as being caused by favoritism, nepotism (playing favorites with family members), and other unfair practices. In Weber's time, most European companies were managed like extended families. Employees were loyal to a single person, rather than to the company goals or mission statement. Weber came up with the bureaucratic organizations approach,[24] a system that was meant to be impersonal and rational. In Weber's model, called *bureaucracy,* each person had specific duties and responsibilities that were to be assigned on the basis of ability and talent only. Also, the work of the people in an organization was to be done in an orderly way, with only one supervisor to whom each worker must answer.[25]

This approach reduced favoritism and many other unfair practices.

more about . . .

Andrew Ure (1778–1857) was, like many of his time, an avid enthusiast of the Industrial Revolution. He was the first person to write a detailed study of manufacturers and their management processes.

Max Weber (1864–1920), who was a sociologist, philosopher, and political economist, is best known for writing *The Protestant Ethic and the Spirit of Capitalism* (1904).

Human Relations and Bureaucracy

Today the word **bureaucracy** often has a negative connotation. The word is often associated with government inefficiency ("red tape") and paperwork. Bureaucracy actually started out as a method of improving not only efficiency but human relations as well.

Scientific Management

In the early years of the 20th century, Frederick Taylor and others began a movement called **scientific management**. Most people today who have heard of Taylor think of him as an industrial engineer who tried to find the "one best way" to do a job. He is often criticized as someone who cared more about production than about the needs of workers. However, Taylor is important to the history of human relations because he showed how crucial the human element is in the performance of any organization.[26]

bureaucracy
A formal organization in which each person has specific duties and responsibilities and is assigned to only one supervisor.

scientific management
A system based upon scientific and engineering principles.

Like others in the scientific management movement, Taylor was concerned with increasing efficiency while getting as much work as possible out of employees. Taylor's approach contained two major features:

1. Managers should carefully select and train workers for specific tasks.
2. Managers should try to motivate workers to increase productivity.

Careful hiring and in-depth training do not seem very earthshaking today, but Taylor was among the first to recognize the importance of both. Also, in Taylor's time, motivation was believed to be induced only through increased pay. Though short-sighted and a bit simplistic, his view of motivation at least focused attention on the issue. Increased pay was likely a larger incentive during Taylor's time than it is today. Today's workers tend to value humane treatment and increased job satisfaction more than was the case a few generations ago.

One of Taylor's best-known theories was the invention of the *optimum shovel.* At an eastern steel mill, Taylor watched men shoveling coal for the large smelters. Using the same shovel, these men would also load cinders into waste containers. After carefully studying both processes, Taylor came up with two shovels: a much larger shovel for the light cinders and a smaller shovel for the heavier coal. This shovel was exactly the right size and weight to allow the maximum work without the need for frequent rest periods. The productivity of the steel mill rose immediately, making Taylor and scientific management both very popular.[27]

more about . . .

Frederick Winslow Taylor (1856–1915) was also renowned as an inventor; the optimum shovel is perhaps his best-known invention. By experimenting with different materials, he was able to design shovels that would permit workers to shovel for the whole day.

FRANK AND LILLIAN GILBRETH
Pioneers in scientific management, especially time and motion study, in the late 1800s and early 1900s.
George Rinhart/Corbis/Getty Images

Frank and Lillian Gilbreth

Living around the same time period as Taylor, Frank and Lillian Gilbreth were a married couple who were both industrial engineers–and scientific managers. The Gilbreths became especially well-known for their research study of bricklayers. Frank Gilbreth identified 18 different motions that had been used by bricklayers, apparently for as long as people had been laying bricks. By inventing some labor-saving devices and by changing the basic routine, the Gilbreths reduced those 18 motions to 5. The result was a system of bricklaying with more than double the productivity of the old system.

Lillian Gilbreth was especially interested in studying workers and their reactions to working under stressful conditions. She taught the importance of standard work days, relaxed and regular lunch breaks, and periodic rest periods. Her life's work helped influence the U.S. Congress to pass the first child labor laws in 1918 and 1922. The mother of 12 children, Lillian was among the first women in America to receive a PhD in psychology. In her later life, she became known as "The First Lady of Management." She was an important early force in the human relations movement as well.[28]

more about. . .

Frank Gilbreth (1868–1924) and **Lillian Gilbreth** (1878–1972) were pioneers in time and motion study. Besides their early work refining the bricklaying process, they had a great impact on medicine by significantly reducing the amount of time patients had to spend on the surgical table. In this way, the Gilbreths were also responsible for saving many people's lives.

Source: Daniel A. Wren, *The Evolution of Management Thought,* 2nd ed. (New York: Wiley, 1979), p. 171.

Mary Parker Follett

In the early years of the 20th century, Mary Parker Follett became known for her lectures and writings on what we would now call human relations issues. Follett was a member of the upper class–not someone with a work-related background. She lectured widely on issues of human relations among workers, however, and was quite influential.

Follett taught three concepts that were ahead of their time. First, she held that workers should be allowed to be involved in decisions affecting them. To her it was logical that the people closest to the action could make the best decisions. Second, she stressed that the workplace is dynamic—that is, constantly changing. She felt that inflexible, static rules were potentially harmful to maintaining a productive workforce. Finally, Mary Parker Follett believed that the main job of managers at all levels was to maintain positive relationships with workers. Happy workers with a sense of belonging, she said, would end up making more money for the company and would remain at the same job for a longer time. These three concepts define Follett as a very important early pioneer of the human relations movement, and definitely ahead of her time.[29]

more about. . .

Mary Parker Follett (1868–1933) attended the college known today as Radcliffe. She studied philosophy and political science but became deeply interested in management. Always the advocate of humanizing the workplace, she stressed people over technology. One of her pieces of advice to engineers was "Don't hug your blueprints!"

Source: Henry Metcalf and Lyndall Urwick, eds., *Dynamic Administration: The Collected Papers of Mary Parker Follett* (New York: Harper & Row, 1940).

The Hawthorne Experiment

In the late 1920s, a group of scientific management scholars went to a factory in Hawthorne, Illinois, to study the effects of physical factors on workers and their productivity. Each time they would try an experiment, productivity would go up. However, when they reversed the experiment, productivity would still increase. The most popular of these experiments was with lighting. When the lights in this Western Electric assembly plant were brightened, productivity increased. However, when the lights were dimmed, productivity went up again.

more about. . .

Elton Mayo (1880–1940) was born in Australia and relocated to the United States in 1922. He was the driving force behind the Hawthorne Studies, and translations of his work appeared in German, Spanish, Italian, Japanese, Arabic, and other languages.

The researchers were really confused. Why would workers work even harder under such poor conditions as very dim lighting? The problem confronting these scientific management scholars attracted the attention of Elton Mayo, a social psychologist from Harvard University. He traveled to Hawthorne and stayed. For nearly five years, from 1927 to 1932, he and his Harvard colleagues studied the **Hawthorne Experiment**.[30]

Two important discoveries came from this five-year study. First, Mayo showed that the workers at Hawthorne performed better because someone was paying attention to them. This attention was more than they had been accustomed to receiving at work, and they responded with higher motivation. Second, Mayo found that the relationships that had formed naturally in the workplace made up what he called the **informal organization**. On days when a worker would not be as motivated as usual, the expectations of the group would make up the difference, and productivity would remain high.

Hawthorne Experiment
A five-year study conducted at the Western Electric plant in Hawthorne, Illinois, that showed that workers performed better when someone was paying attention to them.

informal organization
The ever-changing set of relationships and interactions that are not formally put together; they form naturally in the workplace.

Recent research has suggested that the Hawthorne workers were very likely motivated by fear as well as by attention. Whether or not this new interpretation is true, the findings of Elton Mayo influenced decades of thought on the role of human relations on the job. Whether reacting to fear or attention, human relations issues are still the driving force in the workers' behavior. Much of what has been written and practiced since Hawthorne has been influenced by what Mayo himself concluded–and although the findings have been reexamined, the original shape of those findings still influences people today.[31]

Human Relations and Management

Probably the most important improvement Elton Mayo brought about was to change the way management looked at workers. Rather than seeing workers mostly as people who need wages, managers now began to understand that the complex needs of workers include a unique combination of values, attitudes, and desires.

more about. . .

The Wagner Act, also called the National Labor Relations Act, made it illegal for employers to use scare tactics or other techniques to prevent employees from forming or joining unions.

Source: "The Wagner Act," Digital History (2019), http://www.digitalhistory.uh.edu/disp_textbook.cfm?smtid=2&psid=3445 (retrieved March 11, 2020).

By the time Elton Mayo left Hawthorne, the Great Depression was several years old. Although the interest in human relations still existed, the stubborn fact was that a ruthless manager could mistreat workers now without much fear of losing them. After all, jobs were very hard to find.

During the Great Depression, labor unions began to gain power. Congress passed the Wagner Act in 1935, giving unions and union members more rights than they had enjoyed before. For example, businesses were now forced to negotiate contracts with union representatives.[32] Although this new union activity was good for workers, it did not necessarily mean that human relations issues were being emphasized. Many managers still had the attitude that one needed only to "fire the problems and hire the solutions." Unions usually emphasized salary and benefits for workers rather than the more abstract issues of employee treatment and workplace morale.

The Great Depression
This was an era of human relations setbacks.
Franklin D. Roosevelt Presidential Library & Museum, Hyde Park, New York

By the time the Japanese bombed Pearl Harbor in 1941, the Depression was showing some signs of lifting. Once the country began gearing up its manufacturing sector for World War II, the workplace was affected drastically. With hundreds of thousands of young workers going overseas to fight, employers were forced to hire nearly anybody who would work. With the onset of World War II, managers knew their employees would be very hard to replace, so treatment of workers temporarily improved. However, cases of sexism, racism, and sexual harassment became common once again, as the wartime economic boom receded over time.

Throughout the war, and in the years immediately following, many studies were being done on human relations factors. One of the most important outcomes of these studies was by the noted psychologist Abraham Maslow, who devised a "hierarchy of needs." Maslow's hierarchy of needs teaches that people tend to satisfy their needs in a certain order. More attention is give to this topic in Chapter 5.

more about. . .

Douglas McGregor (1906–1964) was a pioneer in industrial relations. His concepts of Theory X and Theory Y allowed management to understand their influence on employee morale and productivity. Although well-respected in his lifetime, his peak popularity did not come until the 1990s, 30 years after his death.

Studies related to human relations continued through the 20th century. In 1960, psychologist Douglas McGregor wrote *The Human Side of Enterprise,* considered by some to be among the most important book on human relations ever written.

McGregor introduced the concepts of **Theory X** *and* **Theory Y**. These two theories are held by different types of managers, based on their ways of looking at workers. Theory X managers see workers as lacking ambition, disliking work, and wanting job security above all else. Theory Y managers, on the other hand, see workers as happy to work, able to assume responsibility, and overall quite creative. These two theories—especially Theory Y—have influenced thinking in both management and human relations since the year of their creation.

Theories X and Y

Theory X managers see workers as lacking ambition, disliking work, and wanting security above all else. Theory Y managers see workers as enjoying work, able to assume responsibility, and being creative.

Human Relations, History, and the Individual

The second half of the 20th century brought a great deal of attention to the study of the workplace from psychologists and other social scientists. In the early 1960s, Eric Berne had created his famous *Transactional Analysis* method of understanding interpersonal communication. Carl Rogers published his findings on the development of the personality, group dynamics, and conflict management. Some managers began experimenting with participative decision making and other human relations-based management.

By the late 1960s, an era had started that would affect human relations for years. A new emphasis was placed on the rights and needs of the individual person. For the first time, it was popular in this culture to "do your own thing." Perhaps even more importantly, other people were allowed to do their own thing as well. Also new was the revolutionary attitude toward success as having to do with people, rather than just with money. Many managers and executives in recent years were members of an emerging youth subculture at that time, sometimes referred to as hippies. As those young people grew into leadership roles, influence from that era grew and influenced their leadership styles for years to come, often adopted by the next leaders as the earlier leaders retired or left the workforce.

By 1980, the concept of **Total Quality Management (TQM)** had been introduced in the United States after being adopted three decades earlier in Japan. The man responsible for this new movement was an American named W. Edwards Deming. This important school of thought held that the *process* of whatever happens in an organization is more important than the *product.* Doing away with targets, "zero defects" programs, and slogans, those practicing TQM concentrated on the process—which inevitably includes people and relationships. The work that was pioneered by Elton Mayo and others

Total Quality Management (TQM)

A management organizational philosophy that was very influential in the 1980s and 1990s, which stated that quality must be present in the product or the service produced, and in the process itself of producing the goods or service. **See quality movement.**

became refocused with a process emphasis. People in organizations participated at work to an extent unimagined before. Working conditions had come to be seen as the most important single issue in many companies.[33]

By the late 1980s, Total Quality Management had changed industry both in the United States and abroad. From the mid-1990s to the present, the label "TQM" has been heard less frequently. However, the process of TQM survives under other names—sometimes simply "quality"—and remains an important part of many successful organizations. There must be quality in the process itself, as well as in the final product. Of course, TQM covers many other organizational issues besides human relations, but the positive effect of the quality movement on human relations promises to be lasting.

One of today's influential researchers is George Ritzer, a sociologist who studies topics such as globalization, buying and consumption patterns, and meta-theory (examining theories themselves). His most well-known theory is what he calls the McDonaldization of society.[34] This theory, made public in the 1990s, is an extension of Max Weber's ideas. McDonaldization is the idea that corporate culture is based on *efficiency* (the least cost to the company for the most product produced), *calculability* (products are standardized and calculated), *predictability* (customers recognize the same processes and products at all locations), and *control* (specialized tasks for each employee, much like an assembly line). The name itself comes from the highly efficient and recognizable business model of McDonald's fast food restaurants. While this model provides efficiency and profitability to companies, its down side is the alienation that Max Weber had earlier described. People who work in companies with these business models tend to feel more like machines and less human and humane. They develop fewer human connections, and feel more like a cog in a well-oiled machine.

The 1970s through the 2000s saw a tremendous growth in the academic study of human relations. Today, an increasing number of college business and industrial education departments require courses in human relations. This trend reflects the growing awareness of the importance of understanding, and working with, others effectively. As the global economy continues to develop, human relations assumes a broader significance.

« STRATEGIES FOR SUCCESS

Strategy 1.1 **Develop Mutual Respect**

1. Develop your self-esteem.
2. Develop your self-awareness.
3. Develop trust.
4. Learn to self-disclose.
5. Cultivate mutual respect.

Although these are big tasks, they can be achieved by anyone with a clear understanding of human relations.

1. **Develop your self-esteem.** First, you must develop your self-esteem. Self-esteem can be encouraged or damaged very early in life, and some people who have self-esteem problems do not even realize it. However, no matter what your age or self-esteem level, you can always learn to like yourself more. Chapter 2 will cover self-esteem in great detail and provide tips on how you can build your own self-esteem.
2. **Develop your self-awareness.** Without self-awareness, you will find it hard to develop self-esteem or any of the other issues that are important to successful human relations. This is because you must know yourself before you can value yourself highly and express yourself honestly to others. You will learn more about how to develop self-awareness in Chapter 3.
3. **Develop trust.** Without adequate self-esteem, you will find it difficult to trust. With trust, however, you will find that your relationships will grow deep and meaningful, and that you will be able to tell other people what's in your "gut" without unnecessary fear. Trust is developed when we are honest with others, follow through, include others, admit when we are wrong, and communicate openly. Say what you'll do, and do what you say. Remember that trust takes time to build.
4. **Learn to self-disclose.** As you develop trust, you will be able to disclose more about yourself. Self-disclosure and trust are areas that you can develop simultaneously: As you learn to self-disclose appropriately, you will develop deeper trust in your relationships. Chapter 3 will cover self-disclosure in greater detail.
5. **Cultivate mutual respect.** Developing trust and self-disclosing, as addressed in Chapter 3, will lead to mutual respect as you forge relationships that are based on honesty and an appreciation for others. This includes understanding and appreciating the diversity we find in our colleagues, as discussed in this chapter. Treating others in the way that you would like to be treated builds respect, which strengthens workplace relationships.

« STRATEGIES FOR SUCCESS

Strategy 1.2 Build Your Communication Skills

1. Learn to communicate honestly.
2. Learn what effective communication is and how to develop this skill.
3. Know what you are communicating to others by increasing your self-awareness.
4. Know what you are communicating to others by your nonverbal signals.
5. Learn to deal effectively with conflict.

1. **Learn to communicate honestly.** When you communicate honestly by learning to say what you feel, by establishing trust, and by using effective and appropriate self-disclosure, your listeners will learn to respect and trust you more.
2. **Learn what effective communication is and how to develop this skill.** Effective communication is communicating so that your listener receives the message you intended to send. When you use honesty and appropriate self-disclosure, and state your message in a clear way that shows high self-esteem, you will send your message more effectively. Chapter 6 discusses communication in more detail.
3. **Know what you are communicating to others by increasing your self-awareness.** If you have low self-awareness, you may communicate so that your true meaning is unclear. By working on your self-awareness, you will improve your communication skill. Learn more about self-awareness in Chapter 3.

4. **Know what you are communicating to others by your nonverbal signals.** If you give nonverbal signals that are unintended, your message will be different from what you expect. This can lead to confusion and mistrust. Nonverbal communication is covered in more detail in Chapter 6.
5. **Learn to deal effectively with conflict.** Effective communication skill involves the ability to deal with conflict. Chapter 11 will show you how to deal with conflict to restore trust and mutual respect.

CHAPTER ONE SUMMARY

Chapter Summary by Learning Objectives

LO 1-1 Define human relations. Whatever direction your life takes—whether you become a manager, an entrepreneur, or an employee—you will always have to deal with other people, and human relations skills will be essential. Human relations is the skill or ability to work effectively with and through other people.

LO 1-2 Explain the importance of human relations in business. Human relations skills are especially important today for several reasons: greater awareness of human rights, current fluctuations in international markets, growing emphasis on the human resource in companies, current emphasis on teamwork, and increased diversity in the workplace.

LO 1-3 Discuss the challenges of human relations as these factors affect success in business. Today's problems make workplace survival an even greater challenge. Increased workplace competition, the rise of the dual-career family, the divorce rate, and the problem of two generations of dependents: All of these factors increase personal stress and complicate the issues of human relations.

LO 1-4 Identify what the study of human relations does *not* include. Skill in human relations does not mean being phony or manipulative. It is neither a quick fix nor a cure-all, and it is not just common sense. It is a skill area that is learnable, though growth continues for a lifetime. Changing business practices challenge human relations.

LO 1-5 Describe the areas of emphasis for human relations in today's workplace. The main areas of human relations are self-esteem, mutual respect, self-awareness and self-disclosure, communication skill, group dynamics, motivation, and a growth mindset.

LO 1-6 Discuss a short history of the study of human relations. Starting with the scientific managers in the early part of this century, and finding a focal point in the Hawthorne Experiment, the human relations movement began in the 1800s and spanned the entire 20th century. Names to remember include Robert Owen, Andrew Ure, Max Weber, Frederick Taylor, Frank and Lillian Gilbreth, Mary Parker Follett, and Elton Mayo. In 1960 Douglas McGregor wrote about

Theory X and Theory Y managers, showing the latter as both more effective and more humane. George Ritzer is known for his examination of efficiency that reduces human relations impact, known as the McDonaldization of society.

key terms

review questions

1. In your own words, write a one- or two-sentence definition of human relations as you would have defined it before reading this chapter. Then, assuming your definition has changed a bit, write a new one.
2. Consider the importance of Elton Mayo and his work in the Hawthorne Studies to the history of human relations. Fear was noted as a possible driver for productivity in the studies. Do you think fear is a good long-term motivator for employees? Why or why not? How would human relations skills affect a fear motivation?
3. How can the development of human relations skills help you on the job as a manager? As an entrepreneur? As an employee who reports to a manager?
4. Consider the information on Theory X and Theory Y. Which theory do you think is more useful, and why? If you chose Theory X, why do you think some people who win the lottery continue to work afterward, or do volunteer work? If you chose Theory Y, why do you think some employees seem unhappy with working no matter what they are doing?
5. List three reasons why human relations issues are more important today than ever before.
6. Why is self-esteem important to the development of human relation skills?
7. List the seven "areas of emphasis" in the study of human relations and explain each one briefly.
8. Why did the human relations movement not make much progress during the Great Depression? Discuss the relevance that experience might have to today's workplace.

9. Have you worked in a position that fit with George Ritzer's McDonaldization model? If yes, describe the system and your experience in it. If no, describe places you have been a customer that seem McDonaldized and imagine how you would feel there as an employee.

critical thinking questions

1. Explain the importance of the work of Frederick Taylor and Frank and Lillian Gilbreth and the scientific management movement to the development of modern industry.
2. What are the problems of today's society that cause greater stress on the job, which increases the need for human relations skills? List and explain the importance of each.
3. Consider Peter Drucker's statement that "Management is about human beings. Its task is to make people capable of joint performance, to make their strengths effective and their weaknesses irrelevant." Can you think of examples in your own life where a leader helped facilitate this for a group you were part of (whether or not you were the leader)? Did this help you feel more motivated to complete the task your group was working on? Why or why not?

working it out 1.1

COMMUNICATING WITH A SUPERVISOR

School-to-Work Connection: Interpersonal Skills, Thinking Skills, and Personal Qualities Skills

Situation: Doris Johnston is the president of Elko Manufacturing Company. Workers are in short supply in the town where Elko is located. Doris noticed that the turnover rate has been extremely high in one department. The supervisor in this department, Janet Kent, has been having problems relating to her workers. Janet has become known as someone who abuses her power by intimidating her workers and purposely conducting herself in a way that makes them constantly concerned that they will lose their jobs. Many workers never voice their complaints and simply find work elsewhere.

Doris has asked Janet six times during the past five months why the turnover is so high in her department. She also tells Janet that she has overheard workers complain about the way Janet treats them. Janet answers that the workers leave because they can't handle her demands and maintains that she is "tough, that's all, not unreasonable."

Instructions: Four volunteers should play Doris and Janet in two separate role plays. The first will present how Doris should *not* confront Janet with her concerns. Then, without class discussion, play the second role play, showing a better way that Doris can communicate her concerns with Janet. Finally, the class should discuss both role plays, sharing what they have learned from the process.

a. How could those differences create human relations issues?

b. How can effective human relations prevent or solve misunderstandings related to these differences?

working it out 1.2

HISTORY TODAY

This exercise can be completed individually or in small groups.

Situation: Suppose you are the chief executive officer(s) of a large international manufacturing firm that produces pet food. Profits have been down recently, and your shareholders and investors are pushing you to increase profits.

Instructions: Select any two of the historical figures you read about in this chapter: Robert Owen, Andrew Ure, Max Weber, Frederick Taylor, Frank Gilbreth, Lillian Gilbreth, Mary Parker Follett, Elton Mayo, or George Ritzer.

Explain how each of them would work to meet the goals of increased profits for your pet food company. What pitfalls would they need to avoid? What other factors would need to be taken into consideration?

Report your ideas back to the group.

working it out 1.3

SOLVING THE WORKFORCE CRISIS OF 2030

Watch the TED Talk with human resources expert Rainer Strack, titled "The Workforce Crisis of 2030 and How to Start Solving it Now," and then answer the following questions.

1. What is the workforce crisis that the speaker is describing? What caused it?
2. What outcomes can we expect if the crisis unfolds as the speaker suggests? How can we improve the situation?
3. How do the speaker's main points fit with the ideas in this chapter?
4. Think about the interconnectedness of the world's economies. As a global marketplace, do his concerns fit with the U.S. economy?
5. If you were in charge of setting policy for the U.S., how would you address these issues to maintain or improve productivity?

The video can be found here: www.ted.com/talks/rainer_strack_the_workforce_crisis_of_2030_and_how_to_start_solving_it_now?

case study 1.1

The Fighting Carpenters

Of all the units in the construction company, Alan's remodeling division was showing the lowest profit margin. Yesterday, his boss had called him from a job outside of town. "Alan," his boss shouted into his phone, "I drove out here to double-check on the sheet rock work, and I found a big fight going on between your carpenters. They are about three days behind schedule on this job, and they're holding up other subcontractors who are now all complaining about you–and the company. Get over here and straighten things out!"

The boss wasn't telling Alan anything he didn't already know. Alan knew what the problem was. The question was what to do about it. He had two groups in his crew who kept sabotaging each other's work and hurling insults at each other. Last week, a fistfight had broken out between the leaders of the two groups, and now, apparently, the same people were at it again. Alan immediately jumped into his truck and left for the job site.

As he drove to the job site, Alan's mind was preoccupied with his sick child. As a single dad, he had spent the morning arranging childcare so that he could handle his duties at work. Now, when he had arrived at the job site, the fight had ended, but the atmosphere was still very tense. Alan was frankly alarmed about what would happen next. If only he could solve his human relations problem, it seemed like his other problems would be much more easily solved. He was not sure he had the bandwidth to handle everything at once.

"I'll drive out there and get hold of the situation right away," he told his manager.

"You'd better," the manager snapped back. "The company can't keep losing subcontractors because your crews would rather fight than work."

Case Study Questions

1. Which emphasis areas of human relations does this case mostly address?
2. What steps should Alan take to solve the conflict in his department?
3. Could Alan have done anything to prevent this problem from occurring in the first place? If so, what?

case study 1.2

The Buzz in Bakersfield

While Jenny was a sophomore at her college in Bakersfield, she started her own business: a food delivery service. She had started out by working with one of the established food delivery companies and then had branched out on her own. She started her new business delivering sandwiches, cookies, drinks, and fruit from sandwich shops in town to office workers in local businesses. From there, the business had grown by word of mouth as the lunch crowd asked if she could deliver restaurant dinner orders to their homes.

At first, business was good and she could handle the orders on her own. Jenny found herself spending long hours taking orders, delivering food of all types, doing some marketing, and managing accounts. She had been getting by with a few part-time workers, but as the business began to grow, she was feeling the growing pains of too much to do as one full-time person. The business had succeeded largely because Jenny had a great relationship with the restaurants and with the office employees and the families she met on her delivery runs. Her personal touch made all the difference in the success of the business.

Now, with five new people she had hired, that element of a personal touch was often missing. In fact, she began to get messages from well-established clients that they had been "treated rudely" by her new hires. One day, Jenny walked into her new downtown office to hear one of her employees in a heated argument with a restaurant manager over a delivery error. As it turned out, the food had been delivered to the wrong address, and the office that ordered it had not even received it.

"Henry," she said to the employee, "we need to talk."

Case Study Questions

1. What should Jenny say to this employee during her talk with him?
2. What steps could Jenny take to improve relationships among her staff and their clients? If she calls a meeting of all the employees, what issues should she address?
3. What could Jenny have been done to prevent this from happening in the first place?

CHAPTER TWO

2

SELF-CONCEPT AND SELF-ESTEEM IN HUMAN RELATIONS

LEARNING OBJECTIVES

After studying this chapter, you will be able to:

LO 2-1 Define self-concept.

LO 2-2 Identify the four areas of the self-concept.

LO 2-3 Describe the real and ideal selves.

LO 2-4 Explain the importance of pleasing yourself and others.

LO 2-5 Define self-esteem.

LO 2-6 Discuss the relationship between self-esteem and work performance.

LO 2-7 Distinguish among different types of self-esteem.

LO 2-8 Explain the origins of your self-esteem.

LO 2-9 Discuss suggestions for achieving higher self-esteem.

LO 2-10 Explain the growth mindset and how to build it.

STRATEGIES FOR SUCCESS

Strategy 2.1 Steps toward Combating Low Self-Esteem

Strategy 2.2 Build Your Growth Mindset

In the Workplace: First-Day Jitters

SITUATION

Renee was excited about starting as an intern in a cooperative work experience opportunity at her college. As a student finishing up a two-year program in robotics, she needed two more credit hours to have a full-time student load, and she thought the work experience hours would be a perfect fit. Her instructors had told students many times that companies often wound up hiring their cooperative work experience students after they completed their programs. Renee had appointments this afternoon with three companies close to the college. Her goal was to get an offer from one of these companies for cooperative work experience, with the cooperative work experience hopefully then leading to a job after graduation.

Daniel Ernst/Getty Images

As Renee made her way to the parking lot to drive to her first appointment, she began to have some doubts. "What was I thinking?" she asked herself. "I don't know what I'm doing. Some of those other students in my class have been doing robotics forever, and I just started. Who am I kidding? I can't do this. I'll never get a job." Renee sat in her car and debated whether she should even go to the scheduled appointments.

DISCOVERY

Renee knew that if she kept thinking of herself as incompetent and unprepared for an internship, she would not do well in the interview. However she felt about herself would come through in an interview. If she seemed unsure of herself, the interviewers would not ask her to come back and she would lose out on an internship and a possible future job.

Renee decided to behave as though she was competent and confident, and to present herself in such a way that interviewers would see her as competent, too. She began to focus on the things she could do well. She was a strong student and had done especially well in her electronics and programming classes. She also liked her welding classes and had great fun with the machines she made as her project assignments. If the interviewers asked her to talk about her strengths, she could talk about those classes. She began to make a list of other activities, and to think of these as her strengths: she was an officer in the Robotics and Mechatronics Club at her school, she had volunteered for the Sustainability Committee fundraiser, and she had helped form a study group for her applied math classes. She could use these examples to show her strengths as a leader and as a team player.

Renee began to feel much better about the upcoming interviews and about putting her knowledge of robotics to good use in the manufacturing industry. She realized that she had a lot to offer a company, and she was determined to present herself in a way that showed she knew her stuff. She had a bright future. With those thoughts in mind, she headed off to her first interview.

THINK ABOUT IT

How can your opinion of yourself and your competence affect your self-esteem?

How much does your view of yourself affect the way that other people react to you?

Think about former first lady Eleanor Roosevelt's famous quote, "No one can make you feel inferior without your consent." What does this mean? Do you agree or disagree?

REAL WORLD EXAMPLE 2.1

Rosa yelled at her co-worker Gail in front of everyone in the office for not filling up the paper tray in the printer. Several print jobs were backed up, and Rosa was going to have to wait a while for the document she had hoped to quickly print. Later in the day, Rosa felt bad about yelling at Gail. As she reflected on the way she had treated her colleague, her self-concept changed and she began to realize that perhaps she had become the unprofessional and irritable employee she did not much respect. This self-realization made her feel awkward around Gail and others in the office, which then reduced her positive self-concept even more. She had to figure out how to break this cycle. But first, she needed to find Gail and apologize.

» WHAT IS SELF-CONCEPT?

self-concept

The way you picture yourself to be.

Self-concept is the way you *conceive* of (or see) yourself; this view of yourself is the foundation of all your thoughts about yourself, including your self-esteem. Our concepts of who we are can affect our relationships, our work, and nearly every part of our lives. Most of what you do is controlled by your self-concept—the way you picture yourself to be. For example, you may say to yourself, "Other people are always asking me for help in setting up their research projects. I must be pretty good at that." You have a good self-concept when it comes to this skill. This good self-concept then increases your opinion of yourself.

Your everyday actions also tend to affect your self-concept; in turn, your self-concept affects the things you do. When the things you do make you feel bad about yourself, and your self-concept is threatened or changed in a negative way, you wind up in a vicious cycle. Once this cycle gets started, it is difficult to stop. You will need to take some definite action to break it, or your life and your relationships with others won't be as fulfilling or successful as they could be. Once the cycle has begun, trying to analyze who started it—who is to blame—is nearly always pointless. Instead, you need to examine ways of stopping it, or at least minimizing the effects of the vicious cycle.

» THE FOUR PARTS OF THE SELF-CONCEPT

The self-concept can be divided into four parts (as shown in Figure 2.1).[1]

In a perfect world, all four shapes in the self-concept diagram would be one single circle. However, the most realistic way of viewing the diagram is with the goal of pushing all four shapes closer together, knowing that they will probably never completely coincide—but may occasionally.

Ideal Self

This is your vision of your future self. Everyone has some notion of what he or she would like to become. People may see themselves in the ideal as the best possible parent, a successful entrepreneur, or a compassionate and

REAL WORLD EXAMPLE 2.2

All the while Danica was growing up, her parents told her, "We expect you to become a dentist and join our dental practice. It's a family tradition." This statement told Danica that she *must* plan her life around becoming a dentist. She feels obligated to excel in science classes while in school and to plan her classes around preparing for dental school. She knows that she doesn't have the interest and passion that her classmates have in these courses. She wonders what she is missing in other areas of study. But because she has accepted her parents' message of what her ideal self *should* be, this continues to motivate her and affect her self-concept and her self-esteem.

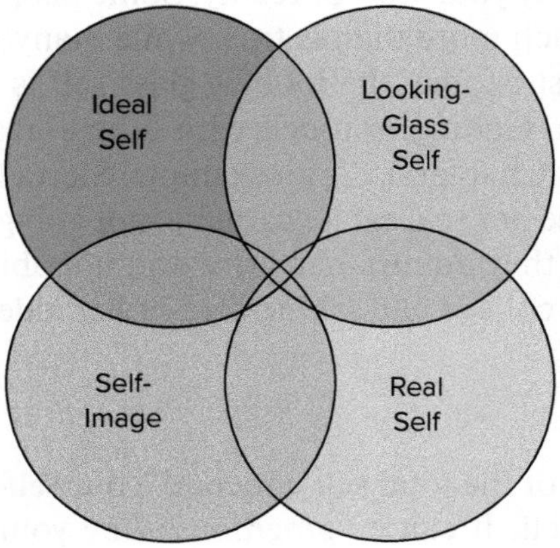

figure 2.1

THE FOUR PARTS OF THE SELF-CONCEPT

Self-concept can be divided into four parts. *How can you bring all four of these selves closer together?*

supportive friend all of the time. For some people, the image of the **ideal self** is sharp and clear; they know the changes they need in their lives and what they must do to make them happen. Many people, though, have a less clear picture of their ideal self, and still others have an unrealistic idea of what they want to become. One common mistake is to think that you have already reached your ideal, when actually you still have a long way to go. Another error is to create an ideal self that is unrealistic and unattainable. The ideal self is not the same over the course of our lives; we will have a different ideal self in childhood or adolescence than we do in adulthood.[2]

ideal self

The way you would like to be or plan to become.

Some parents present their children with a picture of how the children must act to win approval. Such parents are said to hold *conditional positive regard* for their children, whereby positive regard, praise, and approval depend upon certain conditions their children must meet, behaving in ways that the parents think are correct. Under those conditions, children may grow up either rejecting the parents' plans for them completely, becoming depressed and giving up, or falsely believing that they have already become their parents' ideal and do not have to go any further to grow as a person.[3] As a child, you may have known classmates whose parents punished them or rejected them for low grades, and were happy with them and accepting only when their grades were high. In this case, parents' acceptance of their children was based on the *condition* they received high grades.

REAL WORLD EXAMPLE 2.3

Sarah, a college student, may think of herself as an A student in her ideal self. Then she gets her first graded exam back from her instructor, and the grade at the top of the paper is a D. This information about her real self is very different from her ideal self. This difference results in a change in her self-concept and lowered self-esteem.

Looking-Glass Self

looking-glass self
The self you assume others see when they look at you.

The **looking-glass self** is the self that you *assume* others see when they look at you. It is also affected by your view of reality. Some people assume that others think well of them much more than is true, while many more tend to assume the opposite. For most people, the looking-glass self is much more negative than it deserves to be. Getting in touch with others' real feelings about you will also be covered in Chapter 3. As an example, Sierra thinks her friends see her as a failure because her real estate career is not going as well as she would have liked. In reality, they admire her drive and her ability to have started a career while finishing college and taking care of her elderly grandparents.

Self-Image

self-image
The way you honestly see yourself.

Self-image is one part of the total self concept. Your **self-image** is the way you truly feel about yourself. It can be *programmed* by your day-to-day behavior and by the things you say to yourself or others. If you say (even to yourself) that you are a loser, a failure, a bumbling idiot, or whatever other negative description you might use, your self-image will automatically memorize that message for future use. Fortunately, the opposite is also true: if you use positive words and phrases to describe yourself, those messages will also become a part of your memory, helping you to achieve your goals and increase your level of happiness.[4] You will learn more about this growth process later in this chapter. In brief, believing that you cannot do something can make it real. In a conversation with his family, Jay told them, "I want to get an MBA, but I know it will be too hard for me." In reality, he was already doing the work of others in his office who had an MBA, and his grades in college showed that he was a good student who would do well in a graduate program. However, because of his self-defeating beliefs, he never applied for graduate school.

real self
The way you really are when nobody is around to approve or disapprove.

more about. . .

Self Image

"The past is not simply the past, but a prism through which the subject filters his own changing self-image."

—Doris Kearns Goodwin, Pulitzer prize winner

https://www.brainyquote.com

Real Self

The **real self** is you as you really are, when nobody is around to approve or disapprove of your actions. Often this part of the self-concept is something that has to be discovered. Just as with the ideal self, what you think of yourself or what you present to others is not necessarily what is real; discovering your real self might take months, even years.

This process, known as developing your *self-awareness,* is discussed in more detail in Chapter 3. Gita loves to draw and create designs whenever she wants to relax. She doesn't share these with her family or friends because she thinks it is a silly waste of time, not a talent. She is actually quite a talented artist.

» FOCUSING ON THE REAL AND IDEAL SELVES

Carl Rogers, a well-known psychologist, developed ideas about the self-concept in the mid- to late-1900s that are still in use today. He said that your ideal self comes from the messages you receive from your parents and people around you about what you *should* be like.[5]

more about...

Self Concept

"I'm not perfect . . . But I'm enough."

—Carl Rogers (1902–1987)

The ideal self may be quite far apart from the real self, or the two may overlap to some extent. Rogers believed that people get little bits of information all the time about their real selves from their experiences in the world.

When the real self and ideal self are not very close, people feel bad about themselves. They can become depressed and unhappy and can have a lowered opinion of themselves. Rogers believed that in order to have a healthy self-concept, people need to work on making the ideal and real selves much closer. This can be done by paying more attention to messages about one's real self, adjusting one's ideal self to fit the reality, and working up to a more realistic and attainable ideal.

BALANCING YOUR NEEDS AND OTHERS' NEEDS

A crucial factor to a healthy self-concept is balancing your needs with the needs of others. In a culture that values selflessness, and in jobs that require frequent caregiving, this can be a challenge. *What are ways to maintain healthy self-esteem while caring for others' needs?*

Realistic Reflections

» BALANCING YOUR NEEDS AND THE NEEDS OF OTHERS

Many people derive purpose from taking care of others. In American society, women often fall into this pattern of behavior even more than men, in a way that does not allow them to meet their full potential. According to psychologist and author Mary Pipher, girls often grow up in American culture surrounded by media messages that they are valued for their physical appearance, while their intelligence, talents, and skills are seen as less important. Girls then blame themselves for not being pretty or desirable enough, and their self-concept can be damaged in the process, sometimes keeping them from reaching their full potential.[6]

Having a healthy self-concept means not allowing yourself to be captive to other people's opinions. On the other hand, maybe you've known someone who honestly didn't care about what others thought of him or her. This individual was probably a bit hard to get used to. You may find it a bit uncomfortable to be around people who don't *need* anyone to approve of them, perhaps because most people would expect others to share their need for acceptance. While some people might appear not to need others, or care what others

REAL WORLD EXAMPLE 2.4

Facebook and Self-Esteem

Is there any connection between self-esteem and use of social networking sites such as Instagram or Facebook? If so, what is it? After many years of study by researchers around the world, we can scientifically describe the link between self-esteem and Facebook and, like so many relationships . . . "It's complicated." Some general findings that have held up are that these sites provide a great way to connect with others, but overuse is often linked to those who are insecure or have low self-esteem; and comparing oneself with others who are seen as more successful can reduce self-esteem. Researchers suggest that using Facebook to edit profiles or post pictures activates the "ideal self" rather than the "real self," resulting in a boost to self-esteem, especially when positive feedback is then received from others. So to boost self-esteem, the message seems to be: go ahead and post good news about yourself, avoid comparing yourself unfavorably to others, and don't spend all your time Facebooking.[12]

think, humans are social animals and this kind of apathy, or not caring, can actually cause communication problems at home and in the workplace due to misunderstandings.

It is important to strike a balance between caring for yourself, and considering other people's expectations, when seeking acceptance and approval in our personal and professional lives. When your self-concept is stable at a comfortable level, you will find that understanding yourself and taking care of the "real you" will feel very natural without threatening others' sense of self.[7]

» WHAT IS SELF-ESTEEM?

self-esteem
The regard in which an individual holds himself or herself.

Self-esteem can be defined as the extent to which an individual believes him- or herself to be capable, sufficient, and worthy.[8] It is the regard people hold for themselves as part of their self-concept. Self-esteem can be thought of as a measure of how much each of us "values, approves of, appreciates, prizes, or likes him or herself."[9]

Self-concept is closely tied to self-esteem; however, they don't mean exactly the same thing. Anyone in a situation such as Renee's in the opening vignette may discover two important concepts. First, many people don't feel as good about themselves as they should. Second, most individuals respond better to situations and to other people who help, rather than hurt, the good feelings they have about themselves–feelings that people need to function well in business and in life.[10] You may have had a similar experience in planning or starting a new job or social situation: as you are getting to know people there, you find yourself leaning toward those who are supportive of you. Everyone has probably felt this way at one time or another!

Have you ever met someone you just did not like, no matter how long you knew him or her? Most people have. If you were to look carefully, you would probably see one of two reasons for this dislike. Either you and the problem person had a real *personality clash* in which your personality characteristics are just incompatible, or that person simply *did not like himself or herself.* Disliking oneself is an indication of low self-esteem. Messages of low self-esteem or dislike of self can come in the form of being extremely sensitive to any type of criticism, being hostile toward others, or being preoccupied with one's own personal problems, among other signs.[11]

Liking and accepting yourself is one of the most important skills you can learn in life. All of the relationships you have with other people are affected by the way you see yourself, accept or reject yourself, and assume others feel about you. All of these factors combine to create your self-esteem and feelings of self-worth.

Research shows that low self-esteem is common and that people with lower self-esteem have more emotional and related problems than others do, including depression, anxiety, addiction, and poor relationships.[13] When people compare themselves with others, they sometimes feel they don't *measure up* to their own—or their perception of society's—standards. You may feel this way at times, and you may think that you are the only one—but after asking others, you will find that this feeling of not measuring up is quite common.

You might wonder why some people brag about themselves. Most people who always need to talk about their accomplishments are actually **compensating** in some way for low self-esteem. Another form of compensating is when people focus on a single strength (such as good looks, mental ability, or athletic skills) to make up for their overall bad feelings about themselves. These feelings are also due to **lower self-worth**. No matter how hard most people work at exercising those special abilities, many find that after months and years of trying, they still have lower self-worth.

In other words, these people are motivated by their own **lower self-esteem**. They work to excel in one or more areas of their lives in an unsuccessful attempt to overcome their low self-worth and find happiness. Wouldn't it feel better, though, to be motivated by something positive instead? People who have healthy feelings about themselves, or **higher self-esteem**, are more likely to succeed at their personal goals, career goals, and even more important, at *life goals*. They are not motivated by a need to compensate, but by a desire to see their dreams and goals achieved. People with higher self-esteem believe in themselves and believe they can reach these goals. No matter what your occupational experiences are or how your career goals change, with a healthy self-perception and sense of self-worth, the experiences will be worthwhile and reaching desired goals is more likely to be successful.[14]

Self-esteem is usually described as high or low. But the reality is that our self-esteem falls along a scale, from high to moderate to low. Higher self-esteem is healthier self-esteem. Because low self-esteem poses the biggest problem for human relations both in the workplace and in personal life, the rest of this chapter focuses mostly on how to raise low self-esteem and how to build a growth mindset.

compensating
The use of a strength to make up for a real or perceived weakness.

lower self-worth
When individuals believe they have little value to offer the world.

lower self-esteem
When individuals are unable to see themselves as capable, sufficient, or worthy.

higher self-esteem
When individuals have healthy feelings about themselves and are therefore more likely to succeed in personal and career goals.

more about. . .

Compensating is a psychological defense mechanism people may use to reduce embarrassment, shame, anxiety, guilt, or other negative emotions that arise internally when facing unpleasant truths; either by displaying, or by working toward, excellence or gratification in a different area or behavior.

more about. . .

Be Comfortable with Yourself

"The worst loneliness is to not be comfortable with yourself."

—Mark Twain (1835–1910)

SELF-ESTEEM AT WORK

Customers and co-workers can detect high or low self-esteem in employees. If your self-esteem is higher, it will show in your body language, communication skills, and ability to handle setbacks and criticism. *How can you develop higher self-esteem?*

paulaphoto/Shutterstock

» SELF-ESTEEM AND WORK PERFORMANCE

Business success depends greatly on the confidence and self-perception people bring to the experience. Both customers and employees can quickly sense a businessperson's level of self-esteem. A healthier self-esteem is often the key factor that separates success from failure. If you believe you are *good enough to succeed,* your chances of success are much stronger than they would be without such a belief.[15] Research on work performance and confidence finds that those with lower self-esteem earn less on average, as much as $28,000 per year less. They are also less likely to become entrepreneurs, and less likely to take risks such as setting ambitious goals or asking for promotions or jobs, which can result in lower earnings and less job satisfaction. Perhaps even worse is how people with lower self-esteem are perceived by others: Lower self-esteem and lack of confidence can be mistaken for apathy and incompetence.[16]

Success in the workplace is also linked to personality characteristics and behaviors. Psychological research finds that people with lower self-esteem are more likely to experience anxiety and depression and are also more vulnerable to eating disorders and substance abuse. They are also more prone to irritability, aggression, feelings of resentment and alienation, unhappiness, insomnia, and other problems.[17] When people are experiencing these conditions, their work performance is bound to suffer.

People with lower self-esteem also may feel awkward in social settings, including the workplace, and may feel self-conscious and vulnerable to rejection. Lower self-esteem is also associated with low job satisfaction and has even been linked to a higher likelihood of unemployment. People with lower self-esteem often work with little enthusiasm or commitment. In contrast, when an employee feels positive about his or her ability to compete and make a worthwhile contribution, work performance is usually higher.[18]

A person with healthier self-esteem will be open and ready for new experiences. On the job, this readiness translates into usefulness and adaptability. When such people tackle problems, they tend to be more objective and constructive because they do not fear that their ideas will be rejected. Because employees with higher self-esteem are more comfortable with themselves, they can more readily accept their co-workers and take criticism from others in their work team. All of these qualities make the person with healthier self-esteem a more valuable—and more satisfied—employee.[19]

REAL WORLD EXAMPLE 2.5

Bob feels that he is not very intelligent, and he has a hard time keeping up with the new technology in his job and his daily life. This causes him to feel lower self-worth overall. At the same time, he just designed (on paper, without the help of a computer) and built a beautiful cedar deck for his home. He tells his wife, "You and the kids may be good on the computer, but I'm good at building things we need. I'll do the 'hands' stuff, and you can do the 'head' stuff." Bob feels high self-efficacy for his woodworking skills, even though he may feel lower self-worth overall.

TYPES OF SELF-ESTEEM

Currently, researchers describe two different types of self-esteem: (1) feelings, either positive or negative, about self-worth, and (2) confidence in the ability to deal with problems when they happen, often called **self-efficacy**. The first type has to do with how you feel about yourself when you are alone. The second type has to do with actions, problem solving, and the ability to succeed at particular tasks. Your self-perception may be stronger in one of these areas than in others.[20]

self-efficacy
The confidence an individual has in his or her ability to deal with problems when they occur and to achieve goals.

ORIGINS OF SELF-ESTEEM

Where does your self-esteem come from? As with nearly all of the major influences in life, it starts to develop in early childhood from messages we receive from parents and others around us. According to psychologist Carl Rogers, the sense of self is a guiding principle that structures the personality. Though internal, the sense of self is shaped by many outside forces. In young children, self-esteem is just a reflection of the esteem that parents and others have for the child; it develops as children react to the ways that important people treat them. During childhood, parents are the most important people among those shaping self-esteem. Older children and adolescents are also influenced by teachers, coaches, friends, classmates, siblings, neighbors, and others who build up (or damage) their self-esteem.[21]

more about. . .

Carl Rogers (1902–1987) revolutionized the way psychologists thought of therapy. He believed clients understood their own problems and experiences, and that the therapist's role was that of a consultant in assisting client treatment.

When your parents and other important people show you **unconditional positive regard**, or accept you no matter what your behavior may be at the moment, then you are likely to develop a healthy self-esteem. For example, a parent shows unconditional positive regard when he says, "Ashley, I want you to know that I love you and I'm proud of you, but the way you were teasing that little girl on the playground just now was not okay with me."

unconditional positive regard
The acceptance of individuals as worthy and valuable regardless of their behavior, usually applied to parental acceptance of children.

REAL WORLD EXAMPLE 2.6

A four-year-old girl spends 20 minutes in the bathroom, using her mother's best makeup trying to make herself as beautiful as her mommy. When her mother discovers her, though, she is anything but happy. "Emmy, no! Why are you getting into my things?" she yells. "You're a bad girl!" When Emmy cries, she does so from fear of her mother's anger, and confusion at her mother's reaction to what she thought was a great idea. Her self-esteem and confidence deflate.

figure 2.2

THE ORIGINS OF SELF-ESTEEM

Psychologist Carl Rogers believed that the self-esteem of a child depends on the acceptance by the parents. *How can a parent influence a child's self-esteem?*

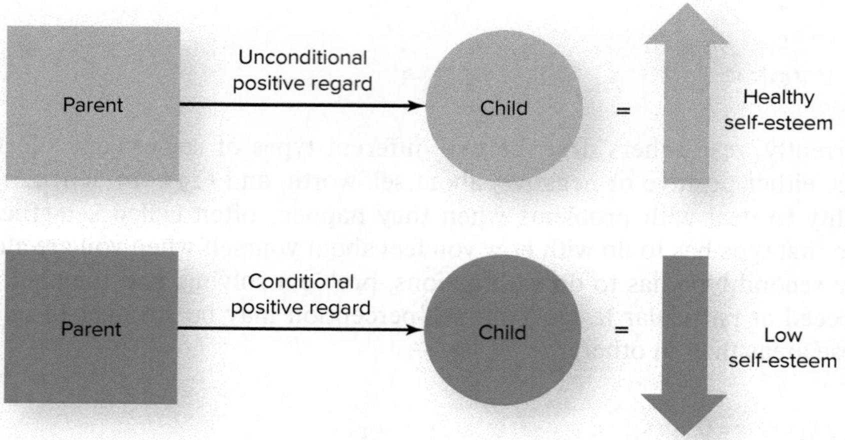

conditional positive regard

Acceptance of individuals as worthy only when they behave in a certain way.

When parents show children **conditional positive regard**, accepting their children only when they behave the way they want, then children may not develop a healthy self-esteem. Children may have a hard time understanding just what parents want from them, and they may end up believing that they are bad people who can't do anything right. See Figure 2.2. Using the example in the previous paragraph, a parent who scolds in an annoyed voice, "Ashley! You're a bad girl!" does not give enough information for Ashley to understand what it was that she did wrong. She may feel she is a bad person overall, but does not realize that teasing other children is unacceptable.

Parents frequently remind children that they aren't perfect and they aren't what they should be. With the best of intentions, they attempt to improve their children's behavior by comparing them with others. What happens is that these children find out that there are other children who do things better than they can, who in some way please adults more. From childhood onward, then, people learn to compare themselves with others and adapt their behavior around others' reactions to them–and react to the ways that all of this affects their self-esteem.

You may have had employers or supervisors who treated you with this same conditional positive regard: only treating you kindly or respectfully when you acted in the way that pleased them. They may have scolded you (even in front of others), or compared you disapprovingly with another, "better" employee. In Adler's theory, we hear messages throughout our lives from others that we then add to our existing self-concept, sometimes raising self-esteem, sometimes reducing it. For others who are especially influential or important to us, these messages have even more impact.

This idea of the origins of self-esteem was first put forward by psychologist Alfred Adler, who (like Carl Rogers) was another pioneer in the area of self and personality. Adler believed that the main motivation for everything people do, including efforts toward a successful career, is to get away from a deep childhood-based feeling that they are not as good as they should be—that they are not perfect. "In comparison with unattainable ideal perfection," he wrote, "the individual is continuously filled by an inferiority feeling and motivated by it."[22] Again, this is compensating for low self-worth by trying to succeed in other areas of life. An even more dramatic statement by Adler, who coined the term *inferiority complex,* is: "To be a human being means to feel oneself inferior."[23]

If Adler is even partly right, you can see just how important self-esteem must be to every part of life. While you read the rest of this book, keep in mind this important idea: *If you can improve in just one area—maintaining a healthy concept of self—you can improve in all other areas of human relations.* With a healthy self-concept and higher self-esteem, you can become an effective manager of other people; in any area of life, you can become someone whom others listen to and respect. Most important, you can become a happier, more contented person who is able to reduce harmful stress and solve problems.

more about. . .

Alfred Adler (1870–1937) developed theories about the inferiority complex and about compensation for feelings of deficiency compared with others. He also coined the term *lifestyle* (a style of life in which people strive to succeed in their strengths).

» ACHIEVING HIGHER SELF-ESTEEM

A quick Internet search for boosting self-esteem will likely return hundreds of thousands of results. The sheer number of results can be overwhelming. The good news is that many of the suggestions come from psychological research and are similar to each other. Some of these results are summarized here. They include suggestions to accept yourself, develop an internal locus of control, develop an interest or skill, study confident people in real life or biographies, list your talents, stop procrastinating, find a mentor or role model, use positive self-talk, don't forget the needs of others, and avoid excessively high self-esteem. We will explore each of these suggestions.

Learn to accept yourself. Don't feel that you have to be like someone else. Don't dwell on the past, but instead remember that the past does not determine the future. Avoid thinking that you should become your ideal self right now. That ideal is something to work toward for the future. Here, in the present, you are okay.[24] Self-acceptance means learning to believe that you are valuable and that your differences from others are more a plus than a minus. Differences are what make everyone so interesting!

locus of control

The perceived location of the control you feel you have over events that happen to you; this control is perceived to be located within the individual (internal locus of control) or is attributed to external factors (external locus of control).

internal locus of control

When people feel they are in control of the events in their own lives.

external locus of control

When people feel they have no control over the events in their lives.

self-respect

Positive self-image with high self-esteem.

Develop an internal locus of control. Julian Rotter, an influential psychologist, described the **locus of control** as the perceived center of control over the events in people's lives. People with an **internal locus of control** feel that they are in control of events in their own lives and have more of a *take-charge* attitude. Rotter and others also believe that an internal locus of control is related to both higher self-esteem and better physical health.[25] On the other hand, people with an **external locus of control** feel that the world and events in their lives are happening *to* them, and that they have no control over the processes or outcomes of these events.

To go back to the earlier example of Sarah, the student in Real World Example 2.3 with a low exam score, if she has an *internal* locus of control, she might say, "I should have studied instead of playing video games all night with my roommates. Next time I'll do better." If she has an *external* locus of control, she might say, "Those questions were all too tricky. I can't help it if all the questions came from the chapters that I didn't understand. Anyway, the instructor is probably just out to get me. I don't think she likes me."

Develop an interest or skill. If you have a special hobby or interest, spend some time cultivating that skill. Developing these abilities puts focus on your positive qualities and takes focus away from the negative. This adds to your self-efficacy. Also, developing one area will teach you to focus on achievements, which is necessary for growth. And success in one area often spills over into other areas. It may build your confidence *and* build your career skills. Finally, you'll begin to feel more **self-respect**. Don't let a day go by without doing something that you can do very well.[26]

more about. . .

Julian Rotter and Locus of Control

Julian Rotter (1916–2014) refined social learning theory to say that personality comes from an interaction of the individual with his or her environment. People develop internal or external explanations for control because of their life experiences.

Study confident people in real life or through biographies. Study those who seem to have strong self-esteem. Watch for things you could do to raise your confidence. Such behaviors might include ways of dealing with negative responses from other people, daily habits, or even ways of looking at others while talking. Remember the suggestion in the first paragraph of this section. You do not need to be *just like* anyone else; in fact, losing your identity can destroy your self-esteem. However, you can learn skills from others that you can apply to your own life. Notice any misfortunes the successful person had to overcome. Try to put yourself in the situation and see yourself meeting the challenge.

While you are following the success stories of others, try not to get carried away in just admiring them. Start to think of healthy self-esteem as something that you already have. You *do* have it; it may just be out of focus, or you may be out of touch with it. See yourself when reading or watching biographies as discovering a lost treasure—your self-worth.[27]

Make a list of your talents. If you draw a blank, ask someone close to you—a friend, family member, or significant other—to help you start the list. Others will often see your good points, talents, and abilities more clearly

Source: Library of Congress Prints and Photographs Division [LC-USZ62-117124]

Source: U.S. National Archives and Records Administration [6802718]

Source: Library of Congress Prints and Photographs Division [LC-DIG-ggbain-06354]

LOOK TO HISTORY

John F. Kennedy, Jackie Robinson, and Marie Curie are three great examples of admirable people in history. *Whom do you admire that you would like to learn more about?*

than you see them. Once you have written the list, consider each talent as a section of your new self-concept. Put the talents you can develop with the least effort at the top of the list. This step builds your self-confidence.[28]

Stop procrastinating. If you honestly feel that you never put off tasks too long, you can skip this section. Most people, though, tend to procrastinate. When you are not working toward goals, this can easily bring your self-esteem even lower. Procrastination will be addressed again in Chapter 16.

Some people think of procrastinators as lazy people. Other people see procrastination as a controlled decision. Actually, many very hard workers are terrible procrastinators. To overcome this common problem, identify the emotions that are blocking you from action. Although several emotions are often involved, among the most important ones are fear and pain—or fear *of* pain—associated in some way with putting off the task. Once you realize that fear and avoidance of pain are involved, you can look more closely at the task and figure out what it is about it that seems to be blocking you from completing the tasks. Getting tasks completed will give you a feeling of being "on top of things," which is very important to high self-esteem. If you've been meaning to do something about your procrastinating, don't put that off, too![29]

PROCRASTINATION IS A TIME KILLER

Many people have the best of intentions, but putting off tasks is often an easy thing to do. *What strategies can you use to avoid the procrastination trap?*

PBNJ Productions/Getty Images

Find a mentor. A **mentor** is someone who will walk you through experiences that are new to you, but that he or she has already been through. True mentoring involves two people communicating well, one mostly teaching and the other mostly learning. If you find someone who will work with you in this way, you've discovered an excellent method of building self-esteem. Mentors, though, are not always available. The next best person is a **role model.** A role model is someone you can look to for guidance by example, but who

mentor

A person who acts as a guide or teacher for another, leading that person through experiences.

role model

A person to whom an individual can look for guidance by example, but who isn't necessarily actively interacting with the individual.

positive self-talk

A method of building self-esteem by thinking and speaking positively about yourself.

self-fulfilling prophecy

The tendency for a prediction to actually occur once it is believed; for example, when a victim believes that prejudice against him or her is true, then fulfills these negative expectations.

isn't necessarily actively interacting with you. Such a person can help you, although you are doing most or all of the work. Remember that both role models and mentors are people who will help you be a better you. Once again, don't lose your identity in the process of adopting their habits. You need to find success on your own strengths.[30]

Use positive self-talk. For generations, schoolchildren have used the proverb: "Sticks and stones may break my bones, but words can never hurt me." Teachers and parents have also taught this saying to children to help them overcome the bad feelings caused by name-calling and teasing. The sad truth, though, is that words *can* and *do* hurt, and they even cause permanent damage. The flip side is that words are also powerful healers. The way you talk to others and to yourself about yourself can be a strong force for change in your life. **Positive self-talk** means telling your subconscious mind that you are a good person and doing fine.[31]

When using positive self-talk, avoid using sentences like, "I want to be a great success." You might ask, why not? Doesn't that statement sound positive? Although it's much better than "I want to be a big failure," it can be improved in two ways. First, change "great success" to "great success at self-control," or "great success at my retail sales job," or "great success at bowling," or whatever specific goal you have. In other words, be specific rather than general. Second, use a present tense verb form. Say, "I am a successful bowler," or whatever you specifically want to improve. (See Figure 2.3.) These affirmations, or positive statements about one's self, reinforce positive attitudes.[32]

Why does this work? Because of what psychologists call the **self-fulfilling prophecy**, also referred to as the *power of self-suggestion*. This means that when you believe something strongly enough, it becomes a reality: by your beliefs and the actions that follow, you fulfill the prophecy or expectation you hold about your future behavior. Whenever you have a success in your journey toward better self-esteem, take pride in your achievement. Reward yourself. Acknowledge your progress without fear of exaggerating it. If it was a big deal to you, then it was a big deal! No one else's judgment of your progress is more important than your own, but don't allow your current and past achievements to be enough. If you make that mistake, you'll stop trying

figure 2.3

SELF-ESTEEM AFFIRMATIONS

Why is it important for affirmations to be as specific as possible?

Source: Adapted from Patricia A. Doherty, "Affirmations for Self-Esteem," 1998.

Positive Self-Talk: Self-Esteem Affirmations

- I am effective because I have high self-esteem.
- I influence my own future by planning and taking action to meet my goals.
- I am a success at many things, such as: (insert your own list here).
- I share my strengths with others.
- I am responsible for my own choices.
- I accept my feelings and manage them effectively.
- I overcome obstacles to meet my goals.
- I succeed because I am persistent.
- I can achieve goals I set for myself or decide when to revise them.
- I alone decide what success means to me.

to improve yourself, and the daily trying is what will make your self-esteem grow in the long run.[33]

Self-fulfilling prophecies can come from your beliefs about yourself, and also from your "buy-in" or taking as fact the beliefs that others hold about you. The self-fulfilling prophecy can also lead to both positive and negative outcomes. Researchers Robert Rosenthal and Lenore Jacobson conducted a research project with schoolchildren in which they told the children's teachers that some of the children were "late bloomers" who would increase their performance significantly over the year. The children were never told of these positive expectations their teachers had for them. Over the course of the year, these children, who had been selected at random from the classroom, did in fact blossom and soar in their performance. Their increased performance was due to the different treatment they received from their teachers, who expected the best from them.[34] Many adults also allow others' opinions of them to affect their behavior. The stronger or higher a person's self-esteem is, the weaker the effect other people's negative statements will have on his or her behavior.

Don't forget the needs of others. Competitiveness can keep people from allowing others to achieve the same things they are achieving. If you have this level of competitiveness, get rid of it. When you are a manager or in any other position of leadership, remember the power you have—for both good and bad—over the person who works for you. (Don't go overboard, though, in giving in to others' needs.)

With all this discussion about boosting one's own self-esteem with positive self-talk, it may be a natural assumption that we can easily boost the self-esteem of others just by saying positive things to them. After researchers found a link between self-esteem and academic achievement in schoolchildren, schools all over the United States set up self-esteem programs, believing that boosting a child's self-esteem would also boost grades. But do admiring teachers and strings of gold stars really have this effect? Perhaps the high self-esteem arose *after* the high achievement; in other words, maybe successes lead to greater self-esteem, rather than high self-esteem leading to achievement.

So, should we say positive things to others in an attempt to help build their self-esteem? Many of the self-esteem-building programs in past years asked teachers to give out any praise, even when children had not succeeded or put in much effort. These programs tend not to be very successful. Children can usually tell the difference between hollow praise, and genuine approval for a job well done or effort put forward toward a difficult task. Genuine positive feedback *does* seem to have the effect of boosting self-esteem. Insincere praise, however, may backfire and result in children not trusting adults to tell the truth. Most teachers (and other experts) today would encourage giving authentic praise, that is, only when it is deserved, rather than lavishing undeserved praise at

more about. . .

Praise

"The wrong kind of praise creates self-defeating behavior. The right kind motivates students to learn."

—Carol Dweck, American psychologist

every opportunity.[35] Adults as well as children can usually tell the difference between insincere flattery and sincere praise. So, if you're going to say positive things in an effort to help boost self-esteem, the bottom line is to mean what you say![36]

Beware of excessively high self-esteem. After so much attention to the positives of high self-esteem, it is worth noting that there is a dark side to excessively high self-esteem. Healthy self-esteem does not go overboard in the perception of the self. The person whose self-esteem is excessive runs the risk of narcissism and a belief that he or she is the most important person in the world. Excessively high self-esteem is not an accurate understanding of the real self. Those with excessive self-esteem may think they are too good for the work they need to do. They may be arrogant, have a huge ego, feel a sense of entitlement, and may be incapable of learning from their mistakes. This set of beliefs causes problems in personal relationships and in the workplace.[37] A healthy self-esteem finds a balance between extremes of too high and too low. As with most things in life, a balance is key.

STRATEGIES FOR SUCCESS

Strategy 2.1 Steps toward Combating Low Self-Esteem by Defeating the Inner Critic

1. Listen for the inner critic.
2. Take notes on the critic and separate "I" from "you."
3. Recognize the origin of the inner critic's voice.
4. Respond to the inner critic and challenge the message.
5. Recognize when the inner critic leads you to action.
6. Change your behavior.

inner critic
An inner voice that attacks people and negatively judges their worth.

Psychologists Lisa Firestone and Robert Firestone believe that most people have a negative inner voice that attacks and negatively judges their worth. They call this voice the critical inner voice or **inner critic**. This critic comes from the "should" and "should not" messages that parents and other adults give children while they are young. You listen to the critic because it helps shape your identity and, ironically, can make you feel somewhat better in the short run because it gives you some direction (even though unhelpful and often painful) about how to behave in situations. In the long run, though, the critic does a great deal of damage.[38]

The inner critic knows that people have basic needs. Nearly everyone needs to feel that they are accepted by others they care about, and everyone needs to feel a sense of basic worth. People with lower self-esteem tend to fulfill these needs in totally different ways than people with higher self-esteem, and they will use the inner critic as a method of dealing with negative situations. Since this is an *easy way out*, relying on the critic can become a lifelong habit.[39]

Knowing that this critic exists is the first step in toning it down. Really knowing the critic requires that you are skilled at recognizing when it invades your mind. You should be especially aware of what sort of touchy situations bring it out of hiding.

Follow these steps below to begin silencing the inner critic that is damaging your self-esteem and your experiences in the world.

1. **Listen for the inner critic.** Take note of the inner critic, being mindful of what it is saying. Sometimes we listen to it without even realizing what we are listening to, similar to listening to soothing music that fades into the background. Although the inner critic often says mean and insulting things such as "you are incompetent" or "you're a mess," it often says calming things too. A message such as "Just stay home, sleep in, nobody will notice you didn't make it to work" is another way the inner critic sabotages you and brings you down.[40]
2. **Take notes on the critic and separate "I" from "you."** Listen to the specifics of the inner critic's messages. Writing down the messages you hear can be the first step of a powerful process. After writing down the messages the inner critic is saying to you, such as "I am terrible at my job," or "I am lazy," re-write them into the second person. "You are bad at your job" or "You are lazy" separates the message from your inner critic to the real you, allowing you to see the inner critic as the enemy.[41]
3. **Recognize the origin of the inner critic's voice.** Recall from an earlier section in this chapter the importance of conditional, and unconditional, positive regard on the development of the self. Infants and children are like sponges, constantly absorbing all messages around them. These messages affect how we see ourselves, and how others see us. Rejection, criticism, and negative experiences build up the inner critic's voice. Listen to the content of the messages and try to recognize where they came from: a teacher in elementary school? a parent? a coach? an older sibling? Understanding where the inner critic comes from can help you begin to push it away, and separate it from your real self.
4. **Respond to the inner critic and challenge the message.** When we are feeling down, it can be easy to let the inner critic take over our thoughts. Responding to the inner critic and challenging the messages it gives may be the most important step to silencing this voice. Be realistic, and yet compassionate, with your responses. Challenge the messages that come as "I" statements from the inner critic by re-writing them to more positive statements. Treat yourself with respect. Shut down the negative messages. Change "I am a failure" to "I do many things very well. I am a loving person. I work hard at my job." Commit to continuing to write positive statements about yourself.
5. **Recognize when the inner critic leads you to action.** Whether the inner critic is loud and rude, or subtle yet suggestive, pay attention to the behavior it leads you to do. "Don't go for a walk after work, nobody cares if you do or not," or "You are not going to develop heart disease, if you do it will be 40 years from now, who cares," or "Just do that report tomorrow, everyone knows you always miss deadlines anyway" are examples of unhelpful behavior your inner critic encourages. Sometimes behavior occurs without conscious thought: have you snapped at a loved one? Shut down your emotions and walked away from a situation? Try to recognize patterns of your behavior that come from the inner critic's direction.
6. **Change your behavior.** After recognizing the behavior your inner critic has encouraged or directed, begin a mindful and deliberate counter-behavior. Is your inner critic telling you to take a nap instead of studying? To yell at the dog? To ignore the e-mail from your boss? Tell yourself that you will not give in to your inner critic, that you recognize the inner critic is trying to make you act in unhelpful ways. Stand up and stretch, then get ready for your study time. Let the dog outside rather than yelling at it to stop bothering you. Answer the supervisor's e-mail, even if it will mean more work for you. Changing behavior will be difficult in the beginning, and may make you feel uncomfortable. But the more you can recognize, detach from, and challenge these negative internal messages, the easier it will become over time. You will begin to feel better about yourself, and become more productive, which in turn will make you feel even more positive about yourself.

» BUILDING SELF-CONCEPT: GROWTH MINDSET

growth mindset

The belief that abilities can be developed with work and practice.

fixed mindset

The belief that talents and abilities are inborn and unchangeable.

One of the most dynamic and influential concepts in recent years related to self-concept is Carol Dweck's work with the **growth mindset**. The growth mindset happens when we believe that our skills, talents, and abilities can be developed and strengthened through hard work and determination. The efforts that we make to improve our skills can occur only when our self-concept is healthy enough that we believe in ourselves and are willing to make the effort.

While a growth mindset promotes personal growth, a **fixed mindset** prevents it. In Dweck's words, "In a *fixed* mindset, people believe their basic qualities, like their intelligence or talent, are simply fixed traits. They spend their time documenting their intelligence or talent instead of developing them. They also believe that talent alone creates success–without effort."[42] This does not mean that anyone can achieve anything they want by working hard at it, however. We all have a fixed (or stable) mindset for impossible superhuman abilities such as flying or becoming invisible (and rightfully so). In Dweck's theory, the main reason people fail is because they talk themselves out of reaching their goals–an extreme example of negative self-talk. We do enter the world with a genetic encoding for some abilities and some aspects of intelligence, but in Dweck's view, what we then do with those genetic traits is just a starting point for what we can achieve. With a *fixed* mindset, you believe you are limited to the hand you are dealt. If you have heard someone (perhaps including yourself?) saying things like "I'm just not good at math," or "I'm not much of an artist," or "I'm not planning to go college, I'm just not smart enough," then you are hearing messages from a fixed mindset.

So how do we escape the negative, self-fulfilling prophecy of a fixed mindset? Develop a growth mindset! "In a growth mindset, people believe that their most basic abilities can be developed through dedication and hard work–brains and talent are just the starting point. This view creates a love of learning and a resilience that is essential for great accomplishment."[43]

Research on the growth mindset theories has mostly focused on students in elementary through high school, although adults have also been studied. A study of students transitioning to high school included nearly 12,500 ninth-graders in urban, suburban, and rural public high schools and found that two sessions of a 25-minute online task at the start of freshman year could boost their academic performance.[44] In another study, ninth-graders who had experienced growth mindset training did much better in their math classes over two years than their peers who did not have the training.[45] In a third study, 535 college students trained in the growth mindset learned better from their mistakes, and showed more brain activity when processing information.[46] For children and teens, parents and teachers are key in helping to promote a growth mindset with successful results.[47] What about adults? Can coaches train this belief in athletes? The answer seems to be yes, for both amateur and professional athletes. In a study with race car drivers, those who received the training had better racing times in driving laps.[48]

You may not be a race car driver or a ninth-grade student, but there have been many studies across age groups and social statuses that support these positive results of developing a growth mindset. You may not have a teacher or coach training with you to develop a growth mindset, but you can do it on your own. It is never too late to develop a growth mindset.

more about. . .

Growth Mindset

"The passion for stretching yourself and sticking to it, even (or especially) when it's not going well, is the hallmark of the growth mindset."

—Carol Dweck

STRATEGIES FOR SUCCESS

Strategy 2.2 Build Your Growth Mindset

According to Carol Dweck, "Growth mindset assumes that intelligence and other qualities, abilities, and talents can be developed with effort, learning, and dedication."[49] Having the self-confidence to push toward a growth mindset depends in large part on having a healthy self-concept.

Our mindset comes from the powerful beliefs about ourselves that we develop over time. When these beliefs no longer help us reach our goals, it is time to change them. These beliefs are life-defining. In Dweck's words, "The view you adopt for yourself profoundly affects the way you lead your life."[50]

Strategies to work toward a growth mindset include:

1. Create a new powerful belief.
2. Look at failure differently.
3. Boost your self-awareness.
4. Increase your curiosity and learn.
5. See challenges as your new best friend.
6. Love what you do.
7. Be tenacious.
8. Be inspired by others.

Be willing to make the commitment to change your beliefs and behavior toward self-growth. Start now.

1. **Create a new powerful belief.** Choose a path to mastering long-held skills and new interests. Get rid of the fixed mindset that says you don't have the talent, skills, or intelligence to do the things you want to do. Know that you *can* meet your goals, with practice, determination, and effort.
2. **Look at failure differently.** Don't let failure define you. Begin to see failure as not meeting your goals . . . *yet.* Keep working toward them. Failure is not a defeat—it as a challenge. Avoid falling into the trap of the "tyranny of now," or the false belief that we need to meet our goals now, or not at all. Failure means it is time to apply extra effort to meet your goals.
3. **Boost your self-awareness.** A necessary ingredient to changing from a fixed mindset to a growth mindset is self-awareness. You will need to be able to recognize the situations that trigger your fixed mindset in order to avoid falling into it. Become aware of your gifts, talents, abilities, and skills. Ask for feedback from friends and family to get multiple perspectives of your key strengths and weaknesses.

4. **Increase your curiosity and learn.** Act the way a child does on a daily basis, being open to discovery and wonder. Ask questions and focus on learning and growing. Be curious without judgment. Know that others you meet on your journey of discovery have things to teach you.
5. **See challenges as your new best friend.** See challenges as the fuel to your fire of discovery. Don't be overwhelmed by challenges—view them from different perspectives to see all the angles. Value the challenge, and once you have mastered it, move on to the next level of challenges.
6. **Love what you do.** Find the joy in the questions you ask as you meet your challenges. Don't wait for approval from others; take on the adventure of the work that you have chosen to focus on. Speed is not important in mastering the challenge you have chosen.
7. **Be tenacious.** Don't give up easily. Stay with a task until you have resolved the questions within it. Be unstoppable. Do not stop, do not give up. Know that with practice and willpower you can achieve more than you thought you could. Turn negative defeating thoughts into positive self-talk.
8. **Be inspired by others.** Observe others who approach their lives with a growth mindset. Take delight in their successes and their growth. Allow their success to create excitement for you as you turn toward your own challenges. Learn from them.[51]

CHAPTER TWO SUMMARY

Chapter Summary by Learning Objectives

LO 2-1 **Define self-concept.** Self-concept is the way you *conceive* of (or see) yourself; this view of yourself is the foundation of all your thoughts about yourself, including your self-esteem.

LO 2-2 **Identify the four areas of the self-concept.** The self-concept is divided into four parts: the ideal self, looking-glass self, self-image, and real self. In a perfect world, all four would be one; in reality, they are distinct and separate, and people work to get the four together as much as possible.

LO 2-3 **Describe the real and ideal selves.** The real self is you as you really are, when nobody is around to approve or disapprove of your actions. Often this part of the self-concept is something that has to be discovered. The ideal self is your vision of your future self. When the real self and ideal self are not very close, people feel bad about themselves. They can become depressed and unhappy and can have a lowered opinion of themselves.

LO 2-4 **Explain the importance of pleasing yourself and others.** Balancing a need to nurture yourself with other people's needs to be accepted and liked is very important. When your self-concept is set and stable at a comfortable level, you will find that knowing and taking care of the "real you" will be quite possible without threatening others.

LO 2-5 **Define self-esteem.** Self-esteem can be defined as the extent to which an individual believes him- or herself to be capable, sufficient, and worthy. It is the regard people hold for themselves as part of their self-concept.

LO 2-6 Discuss the relationship between self-esteem and work performance. In the workplace, high self-esteem usually separates success from failure. If you believe you are *capable enough to succeed,* your chances of success are much higher. Work performance and outcomes are linked to self-esteem and self-confidence.

LO 2-7 Distinguish among different types of self-esteem. The art of liking and accepting yourself is one of the most important things you can learn in life. Current self-esteem researchers have identified two types of self-esteem: self-worth–the value you place on yourself, and self-efficacy–your confidence in your own ability to deal with problems or tasks as they arise.

LO 2-8 Explain the origins of your self-esteem. According to Carl Rogers, an inborn sense of self structures the personality from earliest childhood; this is affected by parents' unconditional or conditional positive regard. Alfred Adler said that everyone feels inferior to some degree, and people are motivated to do nearly all the things they do because of that common feeling.

LO 2-9 Discuss suggestions for achieving higher self-esteem. Suggestions for boosting self-esteem include: accept yourself, develop an internal locus of control, develop an interest or skill, study confident people in real life or biographies, list your talents, stop procrastinating, find a mentor or role model, use positive self-talk, don't forget the needs of others, and avoid excessively high self-esteem.

LO 2-10 Explain the growth mindset and how to build it. In a growth mindset people believe that they can apply work and effort to meet challenges. In a fixed mindset people believe that the qualities, skills, and intelligence they are born with in not changeable. The most important way to change one's mindset is to change one's self-concept.

key terms

compensating 35
conditional positive regard 38
external locus of control 40
fixed mindset 46
growth mindset 46
higher self-esteem 35
ideal self 31
inner critic 44
internal locus of control 40
locus of control 40
looking-glass self 32
lower self-esteem 35
lower self-worth 35
mentor 41
positive self-talk 42
real self 32
role model 41
self-concept 30
self-efficacy 37
self-esteem 34
self-fulfilling prophecy 42
self-image 32
self-respect 40
unconditional positive regard 37

review questions

1. What are the differences among self-concept, self-respect, and self-efficacy? Provide an example of each.
2. You are certain that your co-workers see you as a cranky, reclusive hermit. Actually, they think of you as a shy person who is quiet but nice to be around. How can this difference between self-concept and others' opinions exist side by side regarding the same person? Explain, using concepts from this chapter.
3. Imagine yourself back in the third grade. Your teacher is yelling at you for accidentally knocking over a full trash can: "Look at what you've done! You're such a bad student! Go back to your seat!" If you could explain the work of Carl Rogers to your teacher using this example, what would you say?
4. Do you ever find yourself compensating for a weakness you feel you have? For what behaviors are you compensating? Do you notice when other people compensate? Describe.
5. What specific skill or area of your self-concept needs work? Think of some examples of positive self-talk you could use to boost your self-esteem in this area.
6. Which would you rather have in your current job or profession, a mentor or a role model? Why? If you were mentoring a new employee in your field, what kinds of things would you say and do?
7. Two employees who are learning a new accounting system are talking about it. "It's no use," says the first. "Management is always dumping these new things on me that I can't learn." The second one replies, "We can learn this; it will just take a little practice. Come on, let's try it." According to Rotter, which employee has an *internal* locus of control, and which employee has an *external* locus of control? How will this likely affect each one's ability to learn the new system?
8. You are waiting for your appointment for an important job interview. A voice inside you shouts, "You're so stupid and lazy! You'll never get this job!" Who is this voice? Why is it sending you these messages? What will you do to stop it?
9. Explain the difference between a growth mindset and a fixed mindset. Which of these do you see in yourself? Do you believe you have any changes to make to improve your outcomes? Explain.

critical thinking questions

1. Is an internal locus of control good to have in *all* situations? Can you think of a situation in which it would *not* be helpful to feel in complete control of your life? For example, when something truly terrible happens, such as a natural disaster or other tragedy, are you really in control of events? If you are not in control of events, what are you in control of in such a situation?
2. Some people say that when they were children, their parents lacked confidence in them and treated them with conditional (instead of unconditional) positive regard—and this treatment, rather than reducing their self-esteem, challenged them to work harder and succeed. Do you agree that such treatment, then, might be *good* instead of damaging to people's developing self-esteem? Explain.
3. Millions of people worldwide regularly enjoy the use of social networking sites such as Twitter, WhatsApp, TikTok, and many more. But when does active participation in social networking sites risk damage to a person's self-esteem? Discuss examples from the news or current online postings that illustrate extreme effects or minor damage related to online social networking sites.

working it out 2.1

EXPLORING YOUR SELF-ESTEEM

School-to-Work Connection: Personal Qualities Skills
This scale was developed by Dr. Morris Rosenberg.
Instructions: Following is a list of statements dealing with your general feelings about yourself. Place a check mark under the answer with which you most agree.

	Strongly Agree	Agree	Disagree	Strongly Disagree
1. On the whole I am satisfied with myself.	______	______	______	______
2. At times I think I am no good at all.	______	______	______	______
3. I feel that I have a number of good qualities.	______	______	______	______
4. I am able to do things as well as most other people.	______	______	______	______
5. I feel I do not have much to be proud of.	______	______	______	______
6. I certainly feel useless at times.	______	______	______	______

7. I feel that I'm a person of worth, at least on an equal plane with others. ______ ______ ______ ______
8. I wish I could have more respect for myself. ______ ______ ______ ______
9. All in all, I am inclined to feel that I am a failure. ______ ______ ______ ______
10. I take a positive attitude toward myself. ______ ______ ______ ______

To score these items, give yourself one point if you answered "Strongly Agree" or "Agree" for 1, 3, 4, 7, or 10. Give yourself one point if you answered "Disagree" or "Strongly Disagree" for 2, 5, 6, 8, or 9. Total your score. Ten indicates high self-esteem answers, while zero indicates low self-esteem answers.

Source: Morris Rosenberg, *Society and the Adolescent Self-Image* (Princeton, NJ: Princeton University Press, 1965). See also: Rich Crandal, "The Measurement of Self-Esteem and Related Constructs," in J. P. Robinson and P. R. Shaver, eds., *Measures of Social Psychological Attitudes,* rev. ed. (Ann Arbor: ISR, 1973); Earle Silber and Jean Tippett, "Self-Esteem: Clinical Assessment and Measurement Validation," *Psychological Reports* 16 (1965), pp. 1017–1071; and Ruth C. Wylie, *The Self-Concept,* rev. ed. (Lincoln, NE: University of Nebraska Press, 1974).

working it out 2.2

TESTING YOUR LOCUS OF CONTROL

School-to-Work Connection: Interpersonal Skills

Instructions: Test whether your own locus of control is more internal or external by answering the following questions.

1. Do you believe that some people are just born lucky, while others are just born losers and there is nothing these people can do to change their lot in life? ____ yes ____ no
2. Do you believe that skill and hard work are more important than luck? ____ yes ____ no
3. Do you keep a good luck charm or have a good luck ritual? ____ yes ____ no
4. When bad things happen to you, do you look for a cause and try to prevent the event from happening again? ____ yes ____ no
5. Do you believe that good things happen to good people, while bad things happen to bad people? ____ yes ____ no
6. Do you believe that if you try hard enough, things will turn out right? ____ yes ____ no
7. Do you believe that fate determines what will happen, regardless of any planning for the future? ____ yes ____ no
8. Do you believe that in the long run, people get the respect they deserve in the world? ____ yes ____ no
9. Do you believe that no matter how hard you try, some things just never turn out right? ____ yes ____ no
10. Do you believe that making a well-founded decision for the future is more important than believing in fate? ____ yes ____ no

Scoring: If you answered "yes" to most odd-numbered questions and "no" to most even-numbered questions, you lean toward an external locus of control. If you answered no to most odd-numbered questions and yes to most even-numbered questions, you lean toward having an internal locus of control. Remember, though, that an internal/external locus of control cannot always be defined in black and white. Many people have a combination of these two that changes depending on the situation.

working it out 2.3

BUILD YOUR GROWTH MINDSET

Watch the TED Talk with psychologist Carol Dweck, titled "The Power of Yet," and then answer the following questions.

1. What is the "power of yet" described by the speaker? Why is this important?
2. What is the difference between a *fixed mindset* and a *growth mindset*? Which do you believe you use more often?
3. The speaker describes research with school-aged children. How do you predict the results would fit with adults? Does the "effect of praise" that she describes work for adults as well as for children?
4. How does brain activity change within a fixed mindset and a growth mindset at work?
5. After watching this video, what will you do differently in order to move beyond the "tyranny of now" and develop a growth mindset?

The video can be found here: www.youtube.com/watch?v = J-swZaKN2Ic&vl = en.

case study 2.1

Stage Fright

Julio Garcia was a new manager for a retail store who had done very well with a business degree from a two-year college. Although he often felt overshadowed by his peers at the other store locations, Julio seemed to get along well unless he was asked to give an oral presentation. In the past couple of weeks, he had been asked—no, told—to give two 15-minute presentations at their annual training meetings.

As the day of torment approached, Julio found it increasingly difficult to sleep. When he finally did drop off to sleep, he woke up often, sometimes with his head pounding. During the wakeful times, he would imagine himself during the presentation, becoming tongue-tied and being forced to sit down because he couldn't go on. Then, the aftermath he pictured was even worse. He imagined the people he worked with laughing behind his back and losing all respect for him. In another of his often-repeated wide-awake nightmares, he did manage to get through the talk, but everyone thought it was simpleminded and boring. He could hear the voices of his colleagues as he walked through the halls at work. In his mind he had become the butt of their favorite jokes.

Finally, the week before the presentations, Julio decided to talk to a counselor recommended by his company's Human Resources Department through their Employee Assistance Program. Although he felt ridiculous admitting what was happening to him, he realized that he needed to act or the worst would actually happen. The counselor was really understanding. Julio found that just talking the problem out with her helped calm him down a bit. He was greatly relieved when she told him that dozens of people in his situation had come to her with the same problem. She advised him to practice the speeches in front of a mirror, and then with family or friends, multiple times, until he felt comfortable. He took her advice.

When Julio finally stood up to speak, he did so with more confidence than he thought he had. Although his presentation wasn't flawless, his hands didn't shake, and he kept the interest of the audience throughout the speech. When Julio sat down, he felt a sense of relief and the beginnings of self-confidence. Somehow, he knew that his future public speaking experiences would never be as uncomfortable as they had been before.

Case Study Questions

1. Let's say that you were Julio's counselor. What additional advice would you give him? Why?
2. Explain the role self-esteem played in this case.
3. If you get stage fright, what steps do you take to minimize its effects?

Jill, Self-Esteem, and the Job Search

Jill was unhappy with her job as a customer service representative for a company that did follow-up survey calls to customers who had recently purchased cars and other large consumer items. Many of her clients immediately assumed that she was a telemarketer as soon as they answered the phone—if they answered the phone at all. The negative reactions were getting her down. Worst of all, she had been letting the negativity affect her sense of self worth. She began to take clients' negative reactions about their purchasing experiences personally, and her self-concept began to drop.

As long as she could remember, Jill had wanted to do something creative in the field of marketing. She was especially interested in advertising and brand management. Although her friends would encourage her and express a belief in her abilities, Jill kept hearing from a part of herself that seemed to be telling her, "You can't do it. You don't have enough creative talent; your ideas are worthless . . ." and on and on.

Anita, one of Jill's best friends, was a successful advertising executive, working for a mid-sized company that specialized in online advertising. One day, Anita invited Jill to lunch supposedly to "talk about business." Anita had picked up on both Jill's ambitions and her self-doubt. "You know, Jill," she offered, "I've been concerned about that job of yours for quite a while. I see it taking you nowhere, when you have some real creative talents that a job like that just doesn't cultivate."

"Well, what do you think about digital advertising as a job for me? I'm a pretty fair artist, and I seem to have a sense of what appeals to customers; that's one thing I've learned from the dead-end job I have." Anita's answer was definite: "Jill, I think you'd be doing yourself and others a disservice if you didn't get out there and at least give your dreams a try!"

Jill returned to work with a new perspective—and with some real optimism. Those persistent negative feelings were not so strong. That very week, she started searching for an opening as an advertising account executive. Within a month, she had landed a job with a local agency—and at a salary higher than she had been getting at her old job. The most important change in Jill was her newfound motivation to succeed; she was no longer prevented by fear and negative self-perception.

Case Study Questions

1. Discuss the relationship of Anita's "pep talk" and the self-fulfilling prophecy.
2. What was the source of the negative thoughts Jill had been fighting?
3. What steps does Jill need to take to make this new reality a permanent part of her life?
4. Do you see parallels to Jill's situation and similar situations in your own life? What steps might you take to change your situation for the better?

CHAPTER THREE

SELF-AWARENESS AND SELF-DISCLOSURE

LEARNING OBJECTIVES

After studying this chapter, you will be able to:

- LO 3-1 Define self-awareness.
- LO 3-2 Explain how awareness-related barriers impact human relations.
- LO 3-3 Use the Johari Window as a tool for self-understanding.
- LO 3-4 Define self-disclosure.
- LO 3-5 List the outcomes of failing to self-disclose.
- LO 3-6 Understand the five major levels of communication as they relate to disclosure.
- LO 3-7 Discuss the impact of making assumptions regarding other people.
- LO 3-8 Explain the risk factor of disclosure.

STRATEGIES FOR SUCCESS

- Strategy 3.1 Know When to Stop
- Strategy 3.2 Pay Attention to Differences
- Strategy 3.3 Facing Fear of Self-Disclosure

In the Workplace: Campus Espresso

SITUATION

Jen and Laura were about to celebrate their fifth year in business. Their gourmet coffee shop had become a very popular hangout for the undergraduate crowd in their small college town. As the anniversary approached, it became more and more obvious to Jen that she and Laura, though longtime friends, were seeing two different coffee shops when they arrived early each morning. Lauren's vision of the shop, in her mind, was finally complete. She had fulfilled her long-time goal of becoming a successful business owner, and felt the business was doing great operating just as it was. Jen, on the other hand, wanted to expand the business, adding a full lunch menu, maybe moving into a larger location or even adding a second shop across town. She feared that if Starbucks or another of the big chains were to come to town, Campus Espresso would struggle to stay alive. As time passed, Jen felt like she was dropping more and more hints about her vision, but Laura just wasn't "getting it."

DISCOVERY

"Why don't you just tell her exactly how you feel—in detail?" Jen's boyfriend asked one night.

"What would that do?" Jen replied. "Laura and I have known each other for years and, besides, we're usually on the same page with these things. What she doesn't see is the *intensity* of how I feel. Why can't she see how much she is stressing me out?"

"Jen, you need to have a talk with her right away."

"Yes, I'll talk to her first thing tomorrow morning. I just don't understand why my dearest friend isn't responding to my feelings."

THINK ABOUT IT

Do you know anyone like Jen, who can't understand why others fail to read her feelings, or like Laura, who isn't receiving messages that other people are convinced they are sending?

» WHAT IS SELF-AWARENESS?

self-awareness

The knowledge of how you are being perceived by others.

self-disclosure

The process of letting other people know what you are really thinking and feeling.

The key issues between Jen and Laura are **self-awareness** and **self-disclosure**—two of the most important elements in human relations. Chapter 2 established the need that people have to be themselves. This means that people need to act in a way that is consistent with their true thoughts and feelings. Often, people refuse to reveal what is true and real about themselves, instead revealing only as much as feels comfortable. A goal of this chapter is to show how people can learn to be, and express, their genuine selves. Being self-aware is one important factor in improving communication, which improves the workplace overall.

Chapter 2 introduced the *looking-glass self* as part of the self-concept. Simply put: better self-awareness means roughly the same thing as *developing a better looking-glass self.* Without self-awareness, you will be unable to show your true self or expect others to do the same.

» AWARENESS-RELATED BARRIERS TO EFFECTIVE HUMAN RELATIONS

Many people spend much of their lives unconsciously building walls. They develop traits such as privacy, secrecy, dishonesty, or other defenses to prevent people from determining their true thoughts and motives. They may tailor online personas that are different from their true selves in order to promote a social or professional image that they want others to believe.

These people may worry that if these walls are not there, catastrophes such as rejection and loneliness will result. Once these barriers are firmly in place, the person who builds them can struggle to reconcile his or her true self with the "walled off" in-person or online identity. Without self-awareness, people may wonder why others often misunderstand them.[1]

more about...

"**Self-awareness** involves knowing how your values, beliefs, assumptions, attitudes, and preferences affect your behavior."

—Robert E. Levasseur

Source: Robert E. Levasseur, "People Skills: Self-Awareness—A Critical Skill for MS/OR Professionals," *Interfaces,* vol. 21, January/February 1991, pp. 130–131.

Do you know anyone like Juanita in the Real World Example 3.1? Do you know people who are currently pursuing goals to impress others or to please parents? What could you say to people like Juanita that would increase their self-awareness?

» THE JOHARI WINDOW

Have you ever said a key word or phrase that asked a disturbing question, or simply touched another person's sense of humor? Suddenly, you saw a frown, rolled eyes, or a chuckle–some reaction that showed a side of the other person that you had never seen before. Everyone has these different parts, or selves. If you are like most people, you are one person to your boss,

REAL WORLD EXAMPLE 3.1

Juanita's parents—especially her father—wanted badly for Juanita to become a medical doctor, preferably a pediatrician like her mother. Without knowing they were doing it, they gave nonverbal cues throughout childhood, letting her know how important their choice for her career was to be. And of course, they let her know in more direct ways as well. Juanita went along with her parents' wishes, excelling in science courses, and eventually entering medical school. But it seemed that the closer Juanita came to her goal, the more frustrated she became with her choices. Finally one day, she admitted to herself that she wanted to be a wildlife biologist, and that this field fascinated her vastly more than medicine did. When she finally entered that field and experienced the subsequent satisfaction, she became aware of the extent to which she had been allowing someone else to make her important life choices for her.

another to your family, another to your close friends, and still another to strangers. Which one is the *real* you?

Everyone shares four ways of relating to others: the open (or public) side, the blind side, the hidden side, and the unknown side. These are illustrated by the panes in the **Johari Window** (see Figures 3.1 and 3.2). These separate responses deal with two factors: people's understanding of themselves and the way they interact with others based on that level of understanding.[2] A larger size pane means that the area, or way of relating, is predominant, Different people have different sizes of each pane, and none of these panes will necessarily remain the same size for all relationships or interpersonal encounters.

Johari Window

A composite of four panes that shows you ways of relating to others: the open, blind, hidden, and unknown panes.

The Open Pane

This upper-left pane of the Johari Window contains information that you know about yourself and have no reason to hide from most people. This pane will become larger as a friendship develops. You will likely show more and more of yourself to the other person until the **open pane** begins to resemble the one in Figure 3.2. If you become friends with someone and she tells you her personal history and the way she views things, she is enlarging her open pane–at least in her relationship with you. The pane size increases with your desire to be known and understood.

open pane

The pane in the Johari Window that contains information that you know about yourself and that you have no reason to hide.

Sometimes the act of showing more and more of your inner feelings can be done unwisely, as you will read later in this chapter. Usually, though, the more information that you mutually share with a friend, the more productively that relationship is likely to develop.

The Hidden Pane

The **hidden pane** of the Johari Window contains information and feelings that you are aware of but hide from other people. People possess a great deal of private information, including information that they are ashamed of or afraid to share with others, such as things they regret or consider failures. If you

hidden pane

The pane in the Johari Window that contains information and feelings that you are hiding from other people.

figure 3.1

THE JOHARI WINDOW

This figure illustrates four ways people relate to one another. The Johari Window is divided into four "panes": the open pane, the blind pane, the hidden pane, and the unknown pane. It includes both our understanding of ourselves and the way we interact with others. *Does everyone have all four of these "panes" of perception? Do you?*

Source: Joseph Luft, *Group Process: Introduction to Group Dynamics* (Palo Alto, CA: National Press, 1970).

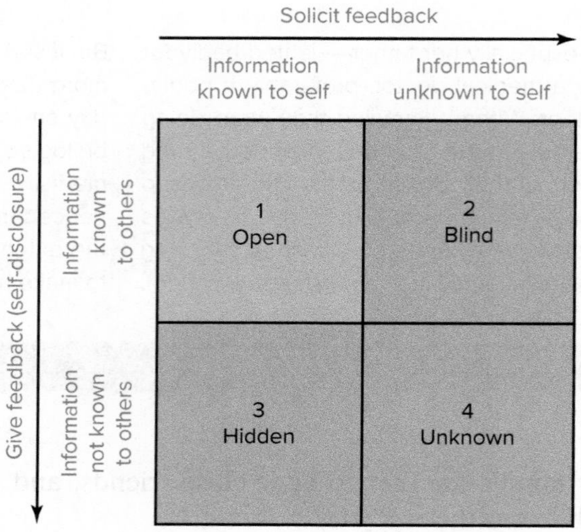

figure 3.2

THE JOHARI WINDOW AFTER ESTABLISHED RELATIONSHIP

The Johari Window allows for sharing personal information. *How does the open pane expand?*

Source: Joseph Luft, *Group Process: Introduction to Group Dynamics* (Palo Alto, CA: National Press, 1970).

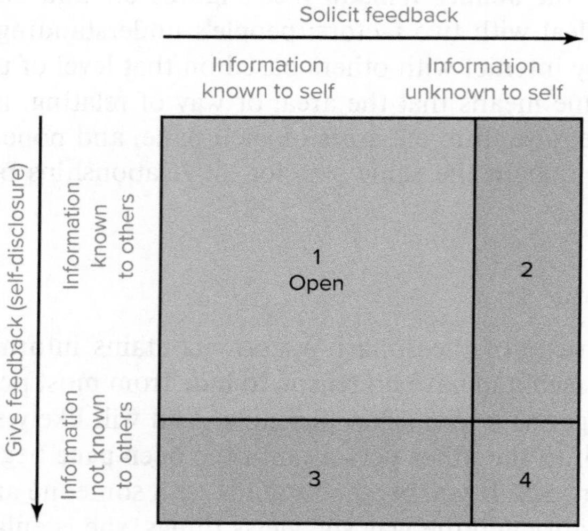

are secretive or very shy, your hidden pane might be quite large. As a close relationship develops and the open pane grows bigger, the hidden pane will become smaller. Increased trust in someone will help you decrease the size of the hidden pane. You will withhold fewer and fewer details about yourself.

The Blind Pane

This pane contains everything about you that other people can see—but you cannot. This pane can be surprising or possibly disturbing to people who choose not to believe what others say about them. Not realizing your own issues could prove problematic in the workplace, emphasizing why listening to feedback is so important.

The **blind pane** can hide good qualities in people as well as bad traits. This pane can shrink if you listen to another person's encouragement and allow yourself to look into your blind areas to a greater extent.

blind pane
The pane in the Johari Window that contains everything other people can see about you, but you can't see yourself.

The Unknown Pane

If the blind pane can be frightening, the **unknown pane** is probably even more so because it focuses on areas that nobody–yourself, your friends, or your family–can see. The unknown pane can include childhood memories that people block out for various reasons. In this pane, people also retain the unspoken attitudes and prejudices of their parents–feelings that they may have acted out but never actually said.[3] This pane contains all of the experiences, feelings, fantasies, and possibilities that people **repress**. It can be reduced in size by developing close friendships or relationships that allow for constructive feedback and self-discovery.

unknown pane
The pane in the Johari Window that contains unknown talents, abilities, and attitudes, as well as forgotten and repressed experiences, emotions, and possibilities.

repress
To block off memories that may cause pain, embarrassment, or guilt.

For the same reason, this can be an even more exciting pane than the blind pane. Information and emotions that are repressed may come out in dreams, fantasies, and even slips of the tongue. Once these desires or fears are recognized, the person can then open avenues of self-knowledge and make changes in his or her life.

According to famous psychoanalyst Sigmund Freud, dreams and slips of the tongue allow your underlying thoughts to leak out. But these are not the only ways to learn about your underlying thoughts: the unknown pane can also be made smaller by a developing friendship or relationship. Feedback from the right person can trigger information that has been unexamined. The process can be painful, but it is usually rewarding if you communicate with friends who truly care about you. Sincere friendships or relationships can help with self-awareness at any level.

» WHAT IS SELF-DISCLOSURE?

Self-disclosure is letting another person know your real thoughts, desires, and feelings. When people say that someone seems *authentic* or *real* (or seems genuine, or legitimate), they are usually saying that the person is good at self-disclosure. Being seen as "phony" or inauthentic is seen as a negative, both in the workplace and in interpersonal relationships. Positive outcomes can result when we practice self-disclosure in our social circles and professional environments.

Self-disclosure allows people to know themselves and those around them better. Openness and honesty become especially important in the workplace. Since most people spend the majority of their days at work, they need to understand themselves and others with whom they interact so those hours are meaningful and productive.

SELF-DISCLOSURE IS A PART OF EVERY RELATIONSHIP
How much we choose to disclose influences the closeness of our relationships. *How does your disclosure differ depending on the people in your life?*
George Rudy/Shutterstock

REAL WORLD EXAMPLE 3.2

Malcolm loved music, and his playlist proved it: from opera to country, hipster to trip-hop, he would play almost anything that made his feet move. The problem was, when Malcolm watched himself dance in the mirror, he saw more Fred Rogers than Fred Astaire. This made him a little shy about dancing in public, so he usually avoided those types of scenes.

When Malcolm's roommate, Clovis, invited Malcolm to check out a couple of live bands with some friends, Malcolm briefly hesitated before agreeing, since he always looked forward to hearing some new music. Turns out, the bands were to Malcolm's liking and he had a great time! Later in the evening, Clovis commented on some of Malcolm's moves at the edge of the dancing area. "Malcolm, you've got some moves, I see! Where have you been hiding those?!" The next few times the group went out, Malcolm ventured further and further out into the main dancing area . . . he had arrived!

Malcolm let out a small chuckle as he remembered back to his original hesitation about going out that first night. The feedback from his roommate had reduced the size of Malcolm's blind pane, opening him to the new experience.

Why do people pull back from letting others know what they are like—the "real" them? People justify withholding the truth in social and professional circles for different reasons, some of them legitimate, others less so. Perhaps a person may feel that withholding certain parts of their feelings or belief systems will help them get along better with others. Another person might avoid telling his friends or colleagues the truth to protect other people's feelings. Some people avoid disclosure due to fear—a fear of rejection, fear of abandonment, fear of being made fun of, or fear the person will use information against us.[4]

Willfully withholding information can have negative effects on happiness, productivity, and interpersonal relationships. There are many reasons why people may withhold information about themselves, most of them negative. Withholding information may allow someone to feel more powerful, or feel they are superior to those around them. Withholding information allows us to avoid listening to disapproval, avoid being challenged, and avoid embarrassment. Such withholding also allows people to deny they have problems or might be at fault, and avoid feeling inadequate. Think about a time when you were just getting to know someone and found yourself holding back some personal information that could have helped build a stronger connection. Did your decision not to share information fit with one of these reasons?

Other reasons people avoid disclosure may stem from childhood experiences. Many people learn very early to shut away large parts of themselves in the hidden pane. Were you ever shamed or punished during childhood for showing anger, too much pride, or some other emotion? You may have been taught to hide strong emotions from others. If a young child's emotions or opinions are silenced, those emotions can remain hidden.

Personal relationships are not the only relationships at risk when people are not comfortable disclosing. In the workplace, creativity suffers when people are not willing to disclose their thoughts. You may have found yourself in a workplace situation or a college class in which you were asked to come up with new and creative ideas. Were you able to do so, or did you feel uncomfortable and decide to keep quiet about your ideas? If you kept your creative ideas to yourself, were the reasons similar to those above? That is, did you keep quiet as a way to avoid possible embarrassment, inadequacy, or disapproval, for example? Because of this unwillingness that many of us have to share our creative ideas, productivity in the workplace is reduced.[5]

For years, psychologists have shown that most people in this culture tend to adapt their behavior to the audience or listener they are communicating with. Also, our opinions, beliefs, and actions often wind up conforming to the group. But why do we do this? Adapting to others around us allows us to feel accepted, and it reduces possible conflict. Following the norms of a group becomes a shortcut to help us understand and act in a particular situation. In ancient times, banding with others gave us a better chance at survival. Conforming today has its benefits, but if we remain silent when we disagree with the group, we are not being true to ourselves.[6]

Whichever our approach to self-disclosure, whether we are comfortable sharing a lot or uncomfortable sharing even a little, we should strive to represent our true selves. In business settings in particular we should strive for authenticity and we should, according to the *Harvard Business Review,* be ourselves . . . but carefully.

In representing our authentic selves, we should be careful not to *overdisclose.* It is best to avoid, or tread wisely through, topics such as religion, politics, or non-work-related topics that are better left out of the workplace. Other topics to address prudently with colleagues include things like deep family issues, sexual experiences, or certain lifestyle choices that might offend others. The term *political correctness* is irrelevant here: there are certain norms of conduct that persist in American workplaces, and our business communication should reflect the professional values of the workplace or industry.

We can arrive at an authentic, effective style of self disclosure by *following these five steps:*[7]

1. **Build a foundation of self-knowledge**. You can learn about yourself in many ways, but the best approach is to ask for honest feedback from friends and co-workers. Consider your upbringing, your work experiences, and new situations, such as volunteer opportunities, that test your comfort zone and force you to reflect on your values. Considering these things can help you choose which stories are most appropriate to share with others.
2. **Consider relevance to the task**. Your goal in revealing yourself at work should be to build trust and promote better collaboration and teamwork, not to make friends (though that may happen!). So before you share personal information, ask yourself whether it will help you do your job. Is it relevant to the situation? If not, you might want to save the story for a coffee date with friends.

REAL WORLD EXAMPLE 3.3

Curly Fries and Mozart: You Are What You "Like"

What do you disclose about yourself on Facebook? Are you revealing more than you realize? Research on nearly 60,000 Facebook users has found that we are what we "like." That is, results emerging from the pattern of "likes" we submit are consistent with results from standard personality and intelligence tests. Researchers analyzing "likes" can quite accurately predict age, gender, ethnicity, religion, political party, interests, and hobbies, in addition to personality, intelligence, and many other factors about a person. By the way, "likes" for curly fries, science, and Mozart were predictors of intelligence.[8]

more about...

Self-Disclosure

Psychologist Frederick Perls (1893–1970) wrote that the purpose of **self-disclosure** is to own one's own feelings, claiming one's own secrets in a way that allows people to be aware of them and content in them.

Source: Fritz Perls, Ralph Hefferline, and Paul Goodman, *Gestalt Therapy* (New York: Random House, 1988), p. 1120.

3. **Keep revelations genuine**. Tell the truth when self-disclosing with colleagues. This one is easy. People will respect you more when you are genuine. Also, as a bonus, telling the truth is much easier than remembering details of fabricated stories.
4. **Understand the organizational and cultural context**. Considerable research has shown that people from individualistic societies, such as the United States and Australia, are more likely to disclose information about themselves and expect others to do the same than people from collectivist societies, such as China and Japan. Look for cues such as eye contact and others' attempts to share or solicit stories with you. Share things that will help the team with a specific task at hand, don't share things to promote yourself.
5. **Delay or avoid very personal disclosures.** Sharing too much personal information too quickly can make one appear awkward or needy. This doesn't mean you have to wait years before telling colleagues anything about your personal life—just enough to develop a foundation of trust. In some workplaces you will eventually find it safe and helpful to share; in others you'll realize it's extremely unwise to do so.

more about...

Reasons to Self-Disclose

"Secrets diminish self-respect; they foster paranoia, and they make it impossible to have honest and open communication."

Source: Karen Casey and Martha Vanceburg, *The Promise of a New Day* (San Francisco: Harper & Row, 1985), p. 243.

» OUTCOMES OF FAILING TO SELF-DISCLOSE

To understand why people should self-disclose, you can examine the *negative* things that can happen to you when you *don't.* Has a deep, dark secret ever gotten the better of you? You might have thought

REAL WORLD EXAMPLE 3.4

A few years ago, Marisol found herself in a dilemma: she could enter a full-time MBA program at a high-ranking university or accept a job offer from a local respected company. Although she liked the idea of getting an MBA early in her career, she was unsure about giving up the security of the job offer. She knew that her family would criticize her if she did. She was reluctant to disclose her true feelings to her family.

At the same time, she started having dreams of boredom and a feeling of imprisonment. Marisol then knew that her deepest fear—job unhappiness—was surfacing because of this dilemma. She made up her mind and entered the MBA program, later graduating with honors. In an ironic twist, she was offered a job at the same local company as before, *supervising* the position she was originally offered. Marisol experienced personal growth and a better relationship with her family once she was able to talk openly about her fears, her own goals, and ideas of the future.

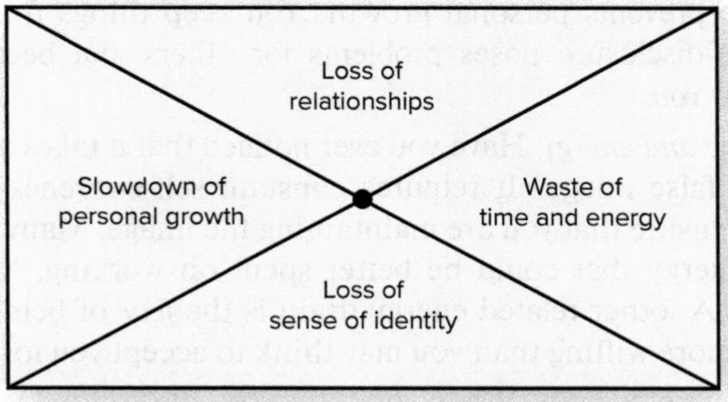

figure 3.3

FOUR OUTCOMES OF FAILING TO SELF-DISCLOSE

Failing to self-disclose may result in the loss of relationships with others, the slowdown of personal growth, the waste of time and energy, and the loss of a sense of identity. *How can your identity be affected when you refuse to self-disclose?*

John Powell, *Why Am I Afraid to Tell You Who I Am?* (Allen, TX: Argus Communications, 1969), pp. 50–62; revised 1990.

that the secret was causing you pain, but perhaps the pain was coming from the effort of holding it inside.

Author John Powell was well known for his writings on self-disclosure. Although it has been decades since his original work, he is still often seen today as an expert on these ideas. According to Powell, there are several common results of failing to self-disclose These are shown in Figure 3.3 and include the following:[9]

1. *Loss of relationships with others.* When you withhold important parts of yourself, you untie the common thread that binds you to others, creating an "isolation booth" for yourself. When the basic human need to interrelate with others is gone, loneliness and isolation are often the result. When you share something about yourself, a relationship grows a little at a time. When there is little or no self-disclosure, the relationships you develop are usually not deep ones. The result is an acquaintanceship rather than a friendship, a crush rather than a romance, or a superficial association rather than a deep and meaningful one. Carefully thought-out self-disclosure allows co-workers to understand each other better and promotes a smooth-running operation.
2. *The slowdown of personal growth.* One of the most positive by-products of self-disclosure is the personal growth it promotes. In contrast, failure to

REAL WORLD EXAMPLE 3.5

Tyrone's lack of self-disclosure created increasing problems as his personal relationships failed and friendships grew stale. Finally, his sister approached him at a family gathering and asked what was wrong. He brushed her off, but she persisted, and finally he admitted that he felt depressed about his ongoing problem with credit card debt. He felt embarrassed to admit it to his friends and girlfriend, all of whom were successful and perceived him as successful, too. It seemed like it was easier to let relationships go rather than admit his problem to others.

As they talked and he disclosed more of his feelings, Tyrone realized that his habit of secrecy had made the problem worse because it allowed him to avoid dealing with it. After talking with his sister, he entered debt counseling and soon found that his debt problems, along with his self-esteem, began to recover.

self-disclose prevents personal growth. You keep things from others not because self-disclosure poses problems for others, but because it poses problems for *you*.

3. *Waste of time and energy.* Have you ever noticed that it takes a lot of energy to create a false image? It requires constant self-awareness and a good memory to ensure that you are maintaining the image. Many people waste time and energy that could be better spent on working, loving, or just having fun. Another related energy drain is the *fear* of being discovered. People are more willing than you may think to accept you for who you are.
4. *Loss of a sense of identity.* When you refuse to self-disclose, you're denying important parts of your personality. You are also keeping others from appreciating who you are. Since much of your self knowledge comes through close, genuine contacts with others, your sense of identity can be threatened when that contact is either damaged or lost. Failure to self-disclose may hinder one's self-acceptance and assertiveness.

more about...

Self-Disclosure

"Why am I afraid to tell you who I am? I am afraid to tell you who I am, because, if I tell you who I am, you may not like who I am, and it's all that I have . . ."

—John Powell (1925–2009)

John Powell (1999) *Why Am I Afraid To Tell You Who I Am?* London: Fount.

People who refuse to self-disclose at work can lose their sense of identity on the job and end up relying too heavily on family, friends, and outside organizations for social contact. People who rely too much on their workplace to make friends and plan social activities are in an opposite version of the same danger, since in effect they never leave the office. To retain a sense of who you are, strive to self-disclose and be genuine in all aspects of your life without over-disclosing.

» LEVELS OF COMMUNICATION AS THEY RELATE TO DISCLOSURE

To enhance your self-awareness and self-disclosure skills, you need to better understand the levels of disclosure you use. Author John Powell identified

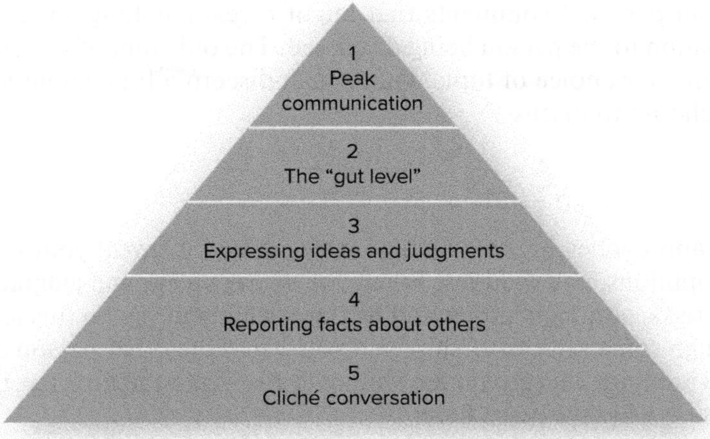

figure 3.4

LEVELS OF SELF-DISCLOSURE

The five levels of communication are also the five levels of self-disclosure: what you communicate is what you disclose. These levels range from everyday cliché conversation to peak communication, which happens in times of great change, turmoil, or self-discovery. *On which level do you feel you are having "real" conversation and disclosure?*

Source: John Powell, *Why Am I Afraid to Tell You Who I Am?* (Allen, TX: Argus Communications, 1969), pp. 50–62; revised 1999.

five general levels of self-disclosure. These five levels of communication are helpful in understanding the amount of self-disclosure taking place. (See Figure 3.4.) The following list begins with the very lowest level of self-disclosure and concludes at the highest level.[10]

Level 5: Cliché Conversation

This is the level that most people rely upon during part of every day. **Cliché conversation** includes niceties, such as:

- "Nice morning, isn't it?"
- "How is your family?"
- "How's the weather up your way?"

cliché conversation
The level of communication with the least amount of self-disclosure, including niceties such as, "Have a nice day."

The most common of these, repeated throughout the workday, is some variation of "How are you?" The primary purposes of such niceties are to acknowledge the other person's presence and, especially in the case of strangers, to present oneself as nonthreatening.

This is **nonconversation** in a real sense. It is dialogue said at a laundromat and at a supermarket checkout line. As speaker, you are called upon to disclose very little, and you ask little of the other person in return. Everyone remains emotionally safe. Nobody will challenge or threaten you, but then nobody receives any real rewards, either.

nonconversation
A way to describe the amount of actual conversation in cliché conversation.

Level 4: Reporting the Facts about Others

On this level, people move beyond clichés, although no real self-disclosure takes place yet. This level stays on a "what so-and-so has been doing" basis,

CLICHÉ CONVERSATIONS Cliché conversations are a part of life. While they may not be rewarding, they are oftentimes necessary. *Are there any benefits of cliché conversation?*
Ian Lishman/Juice Images/Corbis

excluding all personal comments that might reveal anything about the self, even in relation to the person being discussed. The only hint of self-disclosure comes from your choice of topic. Others can discern a little about you from what you choose to discuss.

Level 3: Expressing Ideas and Judgments

This level approaches honest expression because you reveal your conscious thoughts, opinions, and theories. When you express **ideas and judgments**, you take more risks, although undemanding ones: what you say on this level is filtered through some self-censorship, and you watch the other person carefully before you jump in. Unless you are willing to rise up to the next level, no real self-disclosure will take place here.

ideas and judgments
Expressed through conscious thoughts, opinions, and theories in this level of communication.

Level 2: Expressing Feelings and Emotions on the "Gut Level"

If you really want someone to understand who you are, you must tell the person what's in your "gut." Powell explained how you need to be honest about who you are when he said, "If I am a Republican or a Democrat by persuasion, I have a lot of company. If I am for or against space exploration, there will be others who support me in my conviction. But the feelings that lie under my ideas, judgments, and convictions are uniquely mine. . . . It is these feelings, on this level of communication, which I must share with you if I am to tell you who I really am."[11]

Your uniqueness, then, is what you communicate when you risk taking communication to the second level—**gut-level communication**. At this point you are beginning to apply genuine self-disclosure.

gut-level communication
Level of communication in which feelings are expressed honestly.

Level 1: Peak Communication

All deep and lasting relationships are based on complete openness and honest self-disclosure. Level 1 is based on the *peak experience* concept developed by Abraham Maslow, the first social scientist to study peak experiences. Maslow stated that the spiritual, emotional, and aesthetic high points in people's lives do not happen very often, but when they do, they create memories that help sustain them during ordinary non-peak times.[12]

Powell translated this idea into communication. Like Maslow's peak experience, a **peak communication** experience does not occur very often. When it does, though, as Powell suggested, "The two persons will feel an almost perfect and mutual empathy."[13] The more often Level 1 self-disclosure takes place, the more you invite close relationships that can lead to enhanced opportunities for peak communication.

peak communication
Communication characterized by complete openness and honest self-disclosure. It happens rarely.

Nobody should expect peak communication to happen regularly. Such experiences can be triggered by unexpected events. For instance, enduring a death in the family, winning the lottery, or experiencing an automobile accident could all create similar intensity of responses in how you communicate with others. In cases like these, self-disclosure is often not a choice, but an automatic response. In other words, self disclosure is essential to responding to a given situation and your feelings about it in a healthy way, and for regaining a sense of balance afterward.

more about...

Abraham Maslow (1908–1970) was a founder of humanistic psychology in the 1960s, along with Carl Rogers and others. Their movement provided an alternative to the traditional beliefs of psychoanalysis which had been prominent in psychology up to that time.

A Key to Improved Human Relations–Level 2

Making gut-level communication work for you is a key step in the process of learning to self-disclose. When people communicate on this level, human relationships grow, people understand themselves better, and conflict is reduced. In work environments, such benefits translate into greater efficiency and productivity throughout the organization.

The primary benefits include the following:

1. *Improving relationships.* The most important benefit to communicating on the gut level is that relationships often grow stronger. Powell believed that silence tends to promote involvement only in *fraudulent relationships,* which have little benefit for the individual or company.[14]

   With Level 2 communication, genuine emotions and viewpoints are shared, giving each person a stronger sense of identity. If you communicate your true thoughts and feelings, the things you have in common with others will become increasingly obvious. This can happen only when both sides are making an effort. Powell theorized, "I will understand only as much of myself as I have been willing to communicate to another,"[15] because it is through self-disclosure that you are able to define your beliefs.

2. *Growing toward maturity.* When you are relating to others on a gut level, you may begin to notice patterns in the way you react that might reveal your weaknesses. Gut-level sharing can expose those reaction patterns, so that you can examine them–and, if necessary, change them. Perhaps your feelings get hurt too easily. You may conclude that you are taking matters too personally, or that you overreact to certain situations. You may get negative responses when offering your opinion. Perhaps your gut-level sharing is too confrontational. When a pattern like that becomes clear, you can (and probably will) change. You will never be able to explore your strengths and weaknesses unless you learn to communicate on a gut level.

3. *Bringing out the honesty of others.* The third advantage of gut-level disclosure is that it encourages openness and honesty in others. If you want someone to communicate more openly with you, try self-disclosing first. When you are bold enough to *break the ice,* the other person may be reassured and inspired to do the same.[16]

JANE AND JOE'S CONFLICT
Oftentimes, conflict results from a breakdown in communication. *Can you think of a time when this has been true in your life?*
Tetra Images/Getty Images

» MAKING ASSUMPTIONS ABOUT OTHER PEOPLE

Another dimension of both self-awareness and self-disclosure is the way so many people operate on perceptions or hunches they have about each other. Consider this scenario. In a small company, Brandon meets Kathy, a worker in his own department. Brandon likes Kathy, but is unaware that she likes him, too. Kathy is also unaware that Brandon likes her. In fact, she is quite certain that he dislikes her, because he seems often to ignore her. However, Brandon ignores Kathy because he doesn't want her to think that he likes her romantically; he wants only to be her friend—at least for now. As you can see, the situation becomes more and more complicated simply because both people are operating on hunches, rather than on real information.

Psychologist R. D. Laing (1927–1989) became well known for his work in this area of behavior. Laing said that assumptions or hunches we have about others keep us from operating in the real world. Here is an example that Laing often used:[17]

Jane's Internal Conversation	Joe's Internal Conversation
She thinks: I'm really upset!	He thinks: Jane seems upset.
She says: "I had an awful day!"	He says: "Sorry you had a bad day; let's have a nice evening."
She thinks: He doesn't understand; I'll tell him about everything that happened.	He thinks: She needs to forget about work. I'll get her mind off her work problems.
She thinks: Joe seems so unconcerned about my problems.	He thinks: I'll help her by staying calm and relaxed.
She thinks: If Joe really cared about me, he would get upset about this, too.	He thinks: She's getting more upset. I'll try to stay *very* calm.
She thinks: He knows I'm really upset!	
She says: "Hey, why are you so uncaring!"	He thinks: Hey, is Jane accusing me of hurting her? What's happening here?
She thinks: He knows that acting indifferent upsets me; he must want to hurt me.	He thinks: I'm only trying to help! He says: "Why are you on my case?"
She thinks: No real friend would act so unconcerned; it just wouldn't happen.	He thinks: Man, she's really ticked off! What's wrong with her, anyway?
She says: "Joe, you're very mean. I really hate talking to you."	He says: "Jane, you're neurotic! I give up."

Remember to clear up hunches both by working on your own self-awareness and self-disclosure and by encouraging self-disclosure from others. Though this last example is not from the workplace per se, this same type of misunderstanding often takes place on the job, as well. Don't rely on your assumptions about others. Check them out.

REAL WORLD EXAMPLE 3.6

When Adina went to her first job interview after graduation, she felt extremely nervous and was unable to relax. She attempted to make small talk as the interview began, but this backfired as she began blurting out inappropriate personal facts about her family, husband, and fears about not getting the job. She realized that she was embarrassing herself and tried to make a joke out of it by saying, "Well, this is my first interview," but then felt worse for admitting how inexperienced she was. She did not get the job, nor was she confident enough to go on another interview for almost a month. Adina found herself over-disclosing without having tried to do so.

» THE RISK FACTOR OF DISCLOSURE

As with virtually any worthwhile change in your life, choosing to self-disclose involves risks. These risks may occur on a personal or a relationship level, or a professional level. No matter the level, the perceived risk may include facing something unpleasant within yourself and losing self-respect. The risk may be appearing to others to be inferior or even being rejected or being belittled. On a personal and relationship level, a particular risk may be the feeling of losing control, that is, giving the other person information they may later use against you. On a professional level, the same type of risk can occur, as (for example) a politician or other professional losing votes or losing power after disclosing treatment for a drug or alcohol addiction or a mental health issue. Employees may find themselves facing demotion, dismissal, or social exclusion after disclosing unpleasant personal information. Remember that whatever is disclosed cannot be taken back. As the old saying goes, "You cannot unring a bell." The best course is to disclose, but not over-disclose, and be aware of the context–especially in a professional setting.[18]

The first step in dealing with fear is *to look at exactly what you are afraid of.* If your fear is not on this list, you need to identify it and then decide how to respond to it.

In her book *Feel the Fear and Do It Anyway,* Dr. Susan Jeffers shows that eliminating your fears is not necessary for you to change your life. In a way, the title of her book says it all: everybody feels fear, although most fears are unfounded. You do not need to wait until your fears are gone to begin to improve yourself.

more about...

Dealing with Fear

"Fear is the mind-killer. Fear is the little death that brings total obliteration. I will face my fear. I will permit it to pass over me and through me. And when it has gone past . . . Only I will remain."

—Frank Herbert (1920–1986)

Source: Frank Herbert, "Bene Gesserit Litany Against Fear," *Dune*, Chilton Books 1965 (1st Edition).

« STRATEGIES FOR SUCCESS

Strategy 3.1 **Know When to Stop**

1. Understand that self-disclosure can be difficult and awkward at first.
2. Be aware that you can over-disclose unintentionally.

3. Learn how to avoid over-disclosure, especially with strangers or in the workplace.
4. Learn how to self-disclose comfortably and appropriately.

Knowing the limits of your own self-disclosure is an important dimension of interpersonal experience. Use these four tips to help evaluate your own attempt at achieving appropriate and balanced self-disclosure.

1. **Understand that self-disclosure can be difficult and awkward at first.** Self-disclosure can be difficult and even uncomfortable, especially if you are not used to it. Prepare yourself and don't beat yourself up for feeling awkward.
2. **Be aware that you can over-disclose unintentionally.** Over-disclosing often happens when a person feels socially awkward and is trying to make conversation. Problems occur when someone goes too far in self-disclosing. A person who over-discloses may be seen as insecure, and may be judged as acting inappropriately. Being aware of over-disclosure will help you avoid falling into this situation.
3. **Learn how to avoid over-disclosure, especially with strangers or in the workplace.** Over-disclosing personal information can make others around you feel uncomfortable. Avoid over-disclosing by watching for nonverbal signs of withdrawal, discomfort, negativity, or even rejection by those to whom you are disclosing.
4. **Learn how to self-disclose comfortably and appropriately.** Take self-disclosure one step at a time, at whatever speed is most comfortable for you. Most people will appreciate your efforts and respond to them.

STRATEGIES FOR SUCCESS

Strategy 3.2 Pay Attention to Differences

1. Know how much to disclose and how soon.
2. Remember: Different cultures, different disclosure.
3. Allow for the other person to take the lead.
4. Factor in gender, race or ethnicity, and social position.
5. Pay attention to the other person's level of openness.

The information on self-disclosure in this chapter will be helpful only if it can be applied wisely in different situations and in interaction with different types of people. These five tips will help you in dealing with the often complex differences that self-disclosure can present.

1. **Know how much to disclose and how soon.** This often depends on many factors, including the specific circumstances and situation. People need to consider the other person's cultural, ethnic, religious, and even geographic background.
2. **Remember: Different cultures, different disclosure.** Always remember that people from different regions and countries and cultural backgrounds respond differently because they approach self-disclosure with widely divergent expectations.
3. **Allow for the other person to take the lead.** Nevertheless, under all circumstances, you can minimize your uncertainty by allowing the other person to take the lead. By staying within the self-disclosure limits exhibited by the other person, you will be less likely to over- or under-disclose, especially when meeting someone for the first time.
4. **Factor in gender, race or ethnicity, and social position.** Other points that should be factored in include gender, race, and social position. Generally, people tend to disclose things to members of their own sex that they may withhold from the opposite sex. Also, different ethnic groups may hold varying attitudes toward self-disclosure, as

do people from different regions of this country. Finally, socioeconomic position often influences how much disclosure is considered appropriate.

5. **Pay attention to the other person's level of openness.** Remain focused and interested in the other person with whom you are speaking. When you receive messages warning you that any self-disclosure would be unwelcome, you may want to avoid self-disclosure altogether, or you might try to ask nonthreatening questions. Be responsive and, above all, patient.

STRATEGIES FOR SUCCESS

Strategy 3.3 Facing Fear of Self-Disclosure

1. Start with the worst possible scenario.
2. Prepare yourself to accept the worst possible outcome.
3. Proceed with a plan.

Business success expert Dale Carnegie (1888–1955) offered three suggestions for moving ahead even when fear is present. These suggestions can be applied to fears in any area of your life, not just to self-disclosure.[19]

1. **Start with the worst possible scenario.** This means imagining the very worst thing that could happen if you self-disclose. You'll find that often the worst thing that could happen is something you can live with. Then remind yourself that it will not happen unless everything goes wrong, which is unlikely.
2. **Prepare yourself to accept the worst possible outcome.** Be willing to accept the worst possible outcome. Consider whether you're feeling strong enough to survive the worst that could happen. Adopt the frame of mind that you are ready for whatever happens, and you will not let it get you down. Prepare yourself for the fact that anxiety might overtake you during some moments, but try not to let fear discourage you.
3. **Proceed with a plan.** Using the worst case scenario as a safety valve, map out a plan that you can realistically put into action. Remind yourself that the worst possible scenario most likely won't happen, plan to succeed, and don't let temporary setbacks discourage you. Allow your subconscious mind to absorb the plan by thinking about it as often as possible, then view it as a challenge—one you can meet.

Anticipate that not everyone may like what you have to say when you self-disclose. Be prepared for a variety of possible responses. Remind yourself that your reasons for self-disclosure are self-generated and prepare yourself for the fact that your honesty may invite honest reactions in return. If a relationship changes as a result of your self-disclosure, it may be time to reevaluate it. Any relationship based on reality and honesty can withstand more of the same.

CHAPTER THREE SUMMARY

Chapter Summary by Learning Objectives

LO 3-1 **Define self-awareness.** Self-awareness is the ability to see yourself realistically, without a great deal of difference between what you are and how you assume others see you. Better self-awareness means roughly the same thing as *developing a better looking-glass self.*

LO 3-2 **Explain how awareness-related barriers impact human relations.** Many people spend their lives unconsciously building walls around themselves to keep others from seeing them, but these walls also keep them from learning about themselves. As an individual, you need to grow, develop, and be open to change. To develop a meaningful life, you must learn more about yourself and those around you.

LO 3-3 **Use the Johari Window as a tool for self-understanding.** Everyone has at least four areas of self-understanding. The Johari Window shows these with four *panes:* open, hidden, blind, and unknown. To understand what areas you need to develop within relationships, you need to examine all four panes.

LO 3-4 **Define self-disclosure.** Self-disclosure is letting another person know your real thoughts, desires, and feelings.

LO 3-5 **List the outcomes of failing to self-disclose.** Often, people avoid letting others know what they think and feel. When individuals fail to disclose they risk losing relationships with others, slowing down personal growth, wasting time and energy, or losing their sense of identity.

LO 3-6 **Understand the five major levels of communication as they relate to disclosure.** Of the five levels of communication, which are related to the five levels of self-disclosure, the highest level you can achieve most of the time is the gut level. The advantages of communicating on the gut level include improving relationships, growing toward maturity, and bringing out honesty in others.

LO 3-7 **Discuss the impact of making assumptions regarding other people.** Assumptions or hunches we have about others keep us from operating in the real world. Working on your own self-awareness and self-disclosure and encouraging self-disclosure from others will help you avoid misunderstandings and conflict at work and in your personal life.

LO 3-8 **Explain the risk factor of disclosure.** The final barrier in your path is fear. You can feel the fear but should go ahead anyway. Dale Carnegie offered three suggestions for pressing forward even when the fear is present: start with the worst possible scenario, prepare yourself to accept this worst possible outcome, and proceed with a plan.

key terms

review questions

1. What does the term *self-awareness* mean to you after reading this chapter? Use an illustration from your own experience to clarify your definition.
2. Why do people often withhold from others their true selves—or parts of who they really are?
3. How can a lack of appropriate self-disclosure be a barrier to effective relations with others? Specifically, how can a failure to disclose affect your position in the workplace?
4. Briefly explain each of the four panes of the Johari Window. How can this model help you understand yourself better by understanding your relationships with others?
5. Think of an incident in your life when someone over-disclosed to you or someone else. How did the incident affect the relationship? What steps can you take to avoid over-disclosing?
6. How might self-disclosure help you in your relationship with your manager? With co-workers? Can you think of examples that illustrate either negative or positive effects of self-disclosure in the workplace?
7. Of John Powell's five levels of communication, what is the best one for everyday use? Explain why.
8. Discuss Dale Carnegie's three rules for reducing fear. Would any of them work for you when self-disclosure is the issue? Why or why not?

critical thinking questions

1. Have you ever experienced differences in people's level of self-disclosure based on where they live (in another country or a region of your country, for example)? What did you observe, if anything?
2. Most anything you post on the Internet exists forever, even after you delete it. What kinds of information have you disclosed about yourself online? Are there items that you regret posting, or information you regret revealing? If a local newspaper wrote a headline about you based on your Internet postings, especially those to social networking sites, what would the headline say? How would this differ from what you would want it to say? What levels of communication in self-disclosure do you typically find online?
3. Are you as self-aware as you would like to be? If not, what steps can you take to allow yourself to reach a higher level of self-awareness?
4. After reading this chapter, how will you change your approach when faced with fear of self-disclosure? What if not everyone likes what you have to say?

working it out 3.1

THE "OPENER SCALE" QUESTIONNAIRE

School-to-Work Connection: Personal Qualities Skills

Instructions: For each statement below, indicate your level of agreement or disagreement, using the following scale. Record your responses in the spaces on the left.

4 = I strongly agree
3 = I slightly agree
2 = I am uncertain
1 = I slightly disagree
0 = I strongly disagree

________ 1. People frequently tell me about themselves.
________ 2. I have been told that I am a good listener.
________ 3. I am very accepting of others.
________ 4. People trust me with their secrets.
________ 5. I can easily get people to "open up."
________ 6. People feel relaxed around me.
________ 7. I enjoy listening to people.
________ 8. I am sympathetic to people's problems.
________ 9. I encourage people to tell me how they're feeling.
________10. I can keep people from talking about themselves.

This test measures your perception of your ability to get others to "open up" to you, their reactions to you, your desire to listen, and some of your other interpersonal skills.

To score, add up the numbers that you have recorded in the spaces on the left. The total is your score. In studies with this test, women tend to score a little higher because of society's higher tolerance of emotional expression in women. Here are average scores for others who have taken this test: High "opener" ability is 35–40 for women, 33–40 for men; this can indicate a higher level of honesty in communication, but it can also indicate a tendency to over-disclose. An intermediate score is 26–34 for women, 23–32 for men; this likely indicates people who do not jump into conversations *feet first,* but are comfortable with self-disclosure. A low score is 0–25 for women, 0–22 for men; this can indicate either a desire to self-disclose more selectively or an inability to do so.[20]

working it out 3.2

YOUR FEELINGS ABOUT SELF-DISCLOSURE

School-to-Work Connection: Personal Qualities Skills
Purpose: This exercise is designed to make you think about your self-disclosing behavior.
Instructions: Begin by finishing the following incomplete sentences. Go through the sentences fairly quickly; don't think about your responses too long. There are no right or wrong answers.

____ 1. I dislike people who ____
____

____ 2. Those who really know me ____
____

____ 3. When I let someone know something I don't like about myself ___
____

____ 4. When I'm in a group of strangers ____
____

____ 5. I envy ____

____ 6. I feel emotionally hurt when ____
____

____ 7. I daydream about ____
____

____ 8. Few people know that I ____
____

____ 9. One thing I really dislike about myself is ____
____

____ 10. When I share my values with someone ____
____

Based on your responses to these incomplete sentences, do you feel that you engage in the right amount of self-disclosure? Too little? Too much? In general, what prevents you from engaging in self-disclosure? Are there particular topics on which you find it difficult to be self-disclosing? Do you receive much self-disclosure from others, or do people have difficulty opening up to you?[21] ____
____

working it out 3.3

EXPRESSIONS OF SELF AWARENESS

"When I discover who I am, I'll be free."

–Ralph Ellison, *Invisible Man*

"Everything that irritates us about others can lead us to an understanding of ourselves."

–C. G. Jung

"Your visions will become clear only when you can look into your own heart. Who looks outside, dreams; who looks inside, awakes."

–C. G. Jung

"Oh, would some power the gift give us, To see ourselves as others see us. It would from many a blunder free us."

–Robert Burns, 'To a Louse'

"To say 'I love you' one must know first how to say the 'I'."

–Ayn Rand, *The Fountainhead*

"There comes a time when you look into the mirror and you realize that what you see is all that you will ever be. And then you accept it. Or you kill yourself. Or you stop looking in mirrors."

–Tennessee Williams

"Part of the problem with the word 'disabilities' is that it immediately suggests an inability to see or hear or walk or do other things that many of us take for granted. But what of people who can't feel? Or talk about their feelings? Or manage their feelings in constructive ways? What of people who aren't able to form close and strong relationships? And people who cannot find fulfillment in their lives, or those who have lost hope, who live in disappointment and bitterness and find in life no joy, no love? These, it seems to me, are the real disabilities."

–Fred Rogers, *The World According to Mister Rogers: Important Things to Remember*

"I have been and still am a seeker, but I have ceased to question stars and books; I have begun to listen to the teaching my blood whispers to me."

–Hermann Hesse, *Demian: Die Geschichte von Emil Sinclairs Jugend*

"You can't get away from yourself by moving from one place to another."

–Ernest Hemingway, *The Sun Also Rises*

"At the center of your being
you have the answer;
you know who you are
and you know what you want."

–Lao Tzu

"An unexamined life is not worth living."

–Plato, *Apologies*

"To be aware of a single shortcoming in oneself is more useful than to be aware of a thousand in someone else."

–Dalai Lama

QUESTIONS:

1. Which two or three of these quotes resonates with you, and why?
2. How do the quotes you've chosen fit in with the concept of "self-awareness"?

working it out 3.4

INCREASE YOUR SELF-AWARENESS

Watch the TED Talk by organizational psychologist Tasha Eurich, titled "Increase your Self-Awareness with One Simple Fix," and then answer the following questions.

1. What are the benefits of self-awareness?
2. What is the one simple fix described by the speaker?
3. What is the difference between introspection and self-awareness, according to the speaker? Why does she suggest that we are "doing it wrong" with introspection?
4. What are self-awareness unicorns? Should you be one?
5. What is the difference between the "why" and the "what" questions we ask ourselves, according to the author? Give an example. Which type of question is more helpful? Explain.

The video can be found here: www.ted.com/talks/tasha_eurich_increase_your_self_awareness_ with_one_simple_fix?

case study 3.1

Silent Sydney

Sydney Schoenberg had always been on the quiet side, and had never felt comfortable "spilling her guts" to others, as she put it. She was not accustomed to confiding her inner thoughts to other people, but didn't see this as a problem. In fact, when she was younger, family members and teachers had complimented her for being mature and free of "unnecessary drama," as her aunt described it.

In her hiring interview for her current job as a scheduling supervisor at McCharles Air Services, a "below-wing" contractor for major airlines, the company CEO had said she appreciated Sydney's professionalism as shown in her quiet, calm attitude. After a few months on the job, the company CEO praised Sydney for not wasting time socializing, gossiping, or going into detail about her personal life with co-workers.

Sydney's co-workers, on the other hand, were not praising her. Behind her back they referred to her as "Silent Sydney" and described her as stuck-up, and thinking she was better than they were. It must be because she was a scheduling supervisor, while they were employees who reported to her, they decided. The truth was, Sydney was introverted to the point of being shy, and she had chosen a professional style that included little meaningful self-disclosure.

On a particular day when Sydney found herself especially busy, two co-workers approached her. In their view, she was not busy, she was just avoiding them.

"What's the matter with you, anyway, Sydney? Why are you always avoiding us? Is there something wrong with us?" asked Mehdi.

Sydney was surprised, and stammered that she was not trying to avoid them.

"Then why won't you talk to us? We don't even know where you're from, what you like to do, if you have pets, or anything else about your personal life," stated Julie.

In a confused voice, Sydney responded, "But those things don't have anything to do with work. Why would I want to talk to you about that kind of thing?"

In exasperation, Mehdi and Julie walked away, with Julie saying over her shoulder to Sydney, "Fine, have it your own way."

Sydney sat with her thoughts and wondered if she should share more with her colleagues at work, or continue to keep to herself as she had always been more comfortable doing. She asked herself, "would sharing more about my personal life make me more successful at work, or would it be better to keep my focus strictly on the job at hand?"

Case Study Questions

1. How did self-disclosure affect the situation that Sydney and her co-workers experienced?
2. Were Sydney or her co-workers doing anything wrong in the situation described? Explain.
3. How could the discomfort in this situation between Sydney and others at her company have been avoided?

case study 3.2

Fred Lincoln

Fred Lincoln, a popular administrator at a local college, was well-liked and well-known around campus for two things. The first was that he was an avid technology buff who stayed current on all the latest gadgets, from the newest phones and wearable technologies to his desktop 3D printer. The second was that Fred was also known for the amusing fact that he was *always* on his phone. There was no doubt that he was talking business, but the fact that he would talk loudly in public places, talk while ordering food, talk while with friends in social situations . . . was problematic.

People liked Fred. They would forgive him when he would smile warmly and famously hold up his "I'm on the phone" finger at them. But these same people found it tricky to communicate fully with Fred when they had questions or needed help with something. And because Fred was so nice and otherwise caring about his colleagues and students, no one felt particularly compelled to confront him about the fact that his incessant phone chatter made him a little difficult to approach.

Case Study Questions

1. How self-aware is Fred? On what do you base your assessment?
2. How might Fred's always-on-the-phone habit affect his work at the college?
3. How would you approach Fred about his problematic cellphone usage?

CHAPTER FOUR

4

ATTITUDES AND VALUES IN HUMAN RELATIONS

LEARNING OBJECTIVES

After studying this chapter, you will be able to:

LO 4-1 Define an attitude.

LO 4-2 Examine what makes a good attitude.

LO 4-3 Discuss what goes into changing an existing attitude.

LO 4-4 Find details regarding the link between positive attitudes and job satisfaction.

LO 4-5 Define values, and show how they differ from attitudes.

LO 4-6 Explain the origin of your values.

LO 4-7 Identify strategies for coping with values conflict.

LO 4-8 Apply values in a global context.

STRATEGIES FOR SUCCESS

Strategy 4.1 Changing Pessimism to Optimism

Strategy 4.2 Building Positive Attitudes at Work

Strategy 4.3 Redefining Your Personal Values: The Rath Test

In The Workplace: Payroll Panic

SITUATION

sakkmesterke/123RF

In her role as a payroll clerk, one of Anh's duties was to validate each month's payroll data to make sure the benefits were being calculated correctly. The hospital where she worked had many different classifications of employees, and each classification had a different benefits package. The hospital used a computerized payroll system and had several employees in the business office. Several other employees in the business office were involved in data entry.

At her desk one morning, Anh thought she must be misreading the data reports. She then realized with a growing sense of disbelief that payroll had been coded incorrectly. The temporary nurses paid on per diem shifts had been given full benefits, while the permanent staff nurses had not received any benefits.

Anh reported the error to her supervisor, and it did not take long for the news to spread. Back at her desk, Anh could hear several angry voices coming through the wall from her supervisor's office. Nurses had left their shifts to come to the business office to complain about their paycheck errors.

DISCOVERY

Anh did not know if she was expected to take sides between the nurses and management, and if so, which side to take. She did not know if she should take the blame for the error, or pass the blame to the data entry clerks. Perhaps most upsetting was that she had wanted to work at a hospital where she assumed everyone's first priority was helping others. She began to feel angry that the nurses were putting their paychecks above helping patients.

THINK ABOUT IT

How do you react to situations where you may be confused, or angry? What do you think are the reasons behind it? How might negative attitudes escalate this situation? Did values also play a role in this situation?

» WHAT IS AN ATTITUDE?

attitude

An evaluation of people, ideas, issues, situations, or objects.

An **attitude** is an evaluation of people, ideas, issues, situations, or objects. An attitude has three parts: thoughts, feelings, and actions. For example, you may have a negative attitude toward eating leafy green vegetables such as kale. You *think* that the kale will not taste good. You *feel* dislike or disdain when you think of kale. Your *action* is to choose a different vegetable when at a grocery store or restaurant. These three parts of an attitude are so intertwined that you probably do not even notice them as separate components. Your attitudes toward everything, including people, are the result of the beliefs and feelings you have about yourself and about other people, and attitudes directly affect your treatment of others as well as your own actions you choose for yourself.

more about...

Work Attitudes

Regarding work attitudes, American psychologist Martin Seligman advises, "How you handle adversity in the workplace tends to have much more impact on your career than how you handle the good stuff. The people who know how to overcome adversity are the ones who rise to the top of the organization."

Source: Heath Row, "Coping—Martin Seligman," *Fast Company*, December 1998.

Attitudes range along a scale from positive to negative, or they may be neutral. They may be strong and intense or even weak, and they usually don't change very much over time. Your attitudes have a lot to do with how you relate to others and to the world. Attitudes can make or break your relationships with others. Many people are unaware of how strongly their attitudes affect those around them.

» WHAT MAKES A GOOD ATTITUDE?

positive attitude

A position resulting from healthy self-esteem, optimism, extraversion, and personal control.

Happiness is an attitude–one that most people strive for. Many studies have shown that you can actively work toward, or even *choose* to have a happy or **positive attitude**. Whether or not you are happy has little to do with the traditional factors people usually connect with happiness. Happiness doesn't seem to have much to do with a person's age, gender, occupation, or wealth. Instead, more important factors to achieve joy include healthy social relationships, finding meaningful work or a purpose to work toward, and maintaining healthy daily habits. Experiences, rather than objects, lead to longer lasting happiness. Feeling happy, content, or joyful is not a destination to work toward in the future or a commodity we can purchase, it is more of a daily personal experience.[1]

What makes for a happy, positive attitude? Psychologist and happiness expert David Myers lists four characteristics that happy people *do* all seem to have in common.[2]

1. *Healthy self-esteem.* Start liking yourself more and you will be happier. Sounds simple, doesn't it? The point is that whatever works to increase your self-esteem–such as the strategies you've read in previous chapters–will be the same strategies that will improve your overall attitude of happiness.

Test Your Optimism

Measuring optimism is one way to measure a person's likelihood of success, according to psychologists. How you handle setbacks is a good indicator of how well you will succeed in school, sports, and work. The following test shows you some examples of questions psychologists might ask to find out whether or not you are able to bounce back from a setback such as a poor grade or an unsuccessful sale. For each of the following situations, pick the response that more closely matches your own, and rate your optimism. (a = 10 points; b = 20 points)

1. **Your credit card statement shows a $200 charge you did not make. What would you do?**
   A. Pay the bill and do nothing about it because you feel it would be a waste of time, and the credit card company wouldn't believe you anyway. It's a big hassle.
   B. Think they made an error, call the company to notify them of the mistake, and tell them that you won't be paying that portion of the bill.
2. **Your vacation week begins tomorrow, and you have a special trip planned, but you feel like you might be getting sick. What would you do?**
   A. Assume that your vacation is ruined, because this is just your luck. You call your travel agent and cancel the trip, forfeiting your airfare and prepaid hotel reservations.
   B. Take some vitamins and get to bed early with the expectation that you will feel better in the morning.
3. **On your way to work, you get a flat tire. What would you do?**
   A. Panic while you're driving and barely miss hitting another car as you pull over to the curb, feeling sure that you will get in trouble at work for being late.
   B. Tell yourself to keep calm, slow down, pull over to the curb, and proceed to change your tire if you know how, or call for assistance. You tell yourself these things happen to everybody.
4. **Your home computer crashes, and you have a final paper due the very next morning. What would you do?**
   A. Kick your computer and then get depressed, knowing that your instructor will not understand and will probably give you an F.
   B. Call a friend to see if you can use his or her computer to finish your paper. If that isn't possible, you plan to ask your instructor for an extension of the deadline until you can use another computer at school, realizing that this situation was not your fault.
5. **You've just been interviewed for a job, and you have all the necessary skills the company requires. What do you expect will happen?**
   A. You are sure you won't get the job, because the interviewer didn't respond well to you when you fumbled while answering one of the questions.
   B. You believe you have a good chance of getting the job, because even though the interviewer doesn't know you well, you are qualified and you answered all the questions reasonably well.

What was your score? If it was 80 to 100 points, you are probably able to handle setbacks and rejections. People who see setbacks as permanent and pervasive are more pessimistic, more likely to feel helpless, and more likely to give up without resolving a problem.

figure 4.1

HOW OPTIMISTIC ARE YOU?

Your level of optimism will indicate your ability to "bounce back" from obstacles, even catastrophes—and will increase your likelihood of success. *How optimistic are you?*

more about...

A Positive Attitude

Studies from the National Institute on Aging and many other sources have found that regardless of changes in occupation, marital status, or location, people who were happy at the beginning of studies were also happy years later, and also had better physical health outcomes. Interestingly, researchers have also found that happiness in a person's spouse or romantic partners is also associated with better health in oneself.[6]

2. *Optimism.* Happy people are hope-filled. Several studies have shown that optimistic people are both happier and physically healthier than less optimistic people. Optimists are more likely to cope with their problems better than pessimists, and are less likely to become ill.[3] In fact, researchers have found that traits like optimism and hope have been associated with higher levels of happiness and satisfaction with one's life, and are linked with longer life and reductions in the risk of heart disease and stroke.[4]

Optimists tend to try to find solutions to their problems; they rely on social support from others to help them through rough times; and they look for positives in problem situations. Where pessimists see problems, optimists see possibilities. Optimists more often take a longer term perspective and focus on a solution and not the immediate negative effects of the situation.[5]

In contrast with optimists, pessimists do not seem to cope with problems as well. They tend to deny that problems exist, but if they do recognize problems, they conclude that solutions don't exist, things will only get worse, or solutions are out of their control. They then tend to focus on their negative feelings instead of on solving their problems.[7]

Evidence over many years suggests that pessimism is related to poor health. In an early study that has stood the test of time, Harvard graduates who were rated the most pessimistic when interviewed in 1946 were also the least healthy people of those interviewed 34 years later. Other studies have found higher risk for cardiovascular disease and lower immune system response to fight infections and injuries in those with lower self-reported happiness.[8] In several studies of optimism and health, researchers found the most affirming result of all: people who report higher levels of happiness live longer, while pessimism predicts poorer health and higher death rates.[9]

The most dangerous kind of pessimism is hopelessness. Feeling hopeless leads to feeling helpless, which leads to giving up. Hopelessness can even be deadly. In one study, men who reported feeling moderately hopeless or very hopeless had a death rate two to three times higher than men who reported feeling little or no hopelessness.[10]

Imagine that you have just been told that your position at work is going to be eliminated. How do you feel? After the shock wears off, you probably feel angry and frustrated, but then what? You may begin to feel depressed, hopeless, and helpless. While you are feeling this way, on what are you focused? Most likely, your focus is on yourself and your negative emotions, and not on what to do about losing your job. Your self-esteem may suffer as a result of your negative feelings. You may internalize these feelings instead of looking for productive ways to find another job.

It's not surprising that people with this negative focus on their feelings begin to have physical symptoms of illness and stress. Chapter 14 will examine stress and the body's reaction to stress in greater detail.

3. *Extraversion.* The third component of a good attitude is **extraversion**. An extravert is an outgoing person–one whose behavior is directed outward toward others. As the famous psychiatrist Carl Jung said, the behavior of extraverts is directed to the *objects in the external world.*[11] Notice, though, that this factor is also very directly related to one's level of self-esteem. People who feel comfortable in new situations and who feel certain that others will accept them are usually people with relatively high self-esteem. These people will most likely be relatively happy and satisfied at work and in their personal lives.

extraversion
Characteristic of a happy attitude in which a person's behavior is directed outward, toward others.

The secrets to effectiveness and happiness at work may very well be as simple as *purpose, engagement, resilience,* and *kindness,* according to research from psychology, neuroscience, and management studies.[12] Finding *purpose* means identifying work that is meaningful to you and valuable to the company. Being *engaged* means taking an active part of decisions being made at work and being able to feel creative. *Resilience* is the ability to bounce back after a setback. *Kindness* is just as it sounds– treating others with genuine respect, dignity, and empathy. When we are happy, it ripples well beyond our colleagues at work or inner circle of friends and family. And as we age, having regular interactions with a wide circle of friends has a significant impact on psychological well-being well into our middle years.[13]

Some might wonder about the benefits of extraversion on the Internet. Does having a large number of "online friends" through social networking websites such as Facebook, LinkedIn, and others improve our psychological well-being in the same way that friends do in person? Surprisingly, researchers studying a sample of 5,000 Canadians found that friends we are connected to in real life interactions have a very *large impact* on one's level of happiness, while there is *no great impact from the size of one's online network;* further, the researchers found that doubling the number of real-life friends has an effect on well-being equivalent to a 50 percent increase in income.[14] The conclusion: interaction with real-life friends makes you happier than interaction with online friends. People who have a public profile on many platforms tend to feel a higher sense of negativity as they compare themselves to others who seem to be more successful. Retaining some anonymity is linked to less negativity. For those who are isolated and may not have as much access to friends in person, though, online friendships can be very important.[15]

personal control
The power people perceive they have over their destinies.

4. *Personal control.* The fourth component of a good attitude is a feeling of **personal control**. In Chapter 2, you learned about an *internal* and *external locus of control.* This is the idea that you believe either that

more about...

Extrovert or Extravert?

Many people spell extrovert with an "o," but the "a" spelling was originally used by the renowned psychoanalyst Carl Jung (1875–1961), who coined both extravert and introvert. Because of this book's focus on his teachings, his spellings will be used.

Ronnie Kaufman/Larry Hirshowitz

you are responsible for your own situations and life events (internal locus of control); or that *other people, luck, chance, or fate* are in charge of the events in your life (external locus of control). A person with a positive attitude is more likely to have an internal locus of control. Happy people control their own destinies. They control their own futures. They plan and manage their time well. When someone else controls your choices, either large or small, your happiness will probably diminish.

Image Source

Health psychologist Judith Rodin conducted research with nursing home residents on control and choices over many years, with results that have been replicated by other researchers. Rodin found that those who were able to make their own choices about simple things, such as decorating their rooms with plants, were sick less often and actually lived longer than residents who had less control over their lives.[16]

The characteristics of happy, positive people are helpful to know, but beyond just knowing about these attributes, there are specific actions you can take to achieve a more positive attitude. Dr. David G. Myers says that by acting happy, you can actually help yourself become happier. Does that sound too simple? When things happen to you, as they do every day—things over which you have no control—you *choose* how to react.

Many people are quick to blame the other person, the situation, or their own physical condition when things go wrong. People make the *choice* of the reactions they feel. Myers is simply suggesting that making the choice to act happy, and doing so on a regular basis, will go a long way to improving your overall attitude.[17]

You may wonder, is there a "dark side" to a positive attitude, or happiness? Yes, say psychologists. Extreme happiness can lead to ignoring reality, not paying attention to details, and taking unnecessary risks. When a person's happiness is based on vanity or narcissism (extreme self-centeredness), these feelings can lead to devaluing and being aggressive toward others—a definite negative in outcomes.[18]

We have been discussing happiness and positive attitudes so far as just an issue for individuals and an area of expertise more for psychologists than other researchers. But happiness can also be compared among societies, cultures, and nations. Economists and political scientists along with sociologists also have found similar results among

more about...

Happiness

Happiness is not just a modern topic. Consider that the United States Declaration of Independence of 1776 speaks of our rights to "life, liberty, and the pursuit of happiness."

Author Robert Louis Stevenson (1850–1894) in the 1800s stated that "The habit of being happy enables one to be freed, or largely freed, from the domination of outward conditions."

groups as are found for individuals. That is, a happy society is not just one that is economically wealthy. A happy society is one in which people feel they have close social relationships, a sense of freedom, and trust for each other.[19]

more about...

Are Americans Happy?

Is happiness in the United States declining? According to the annual World Happiness Report for 156 countries, it is. Americans ranked 19th in happiness in the world in the most recent report. This is the lowest ranking since the survey began, and the third year in a row of decline. In fact, the United States has not yet made it into the top 10. The survey measures "GDP per capita, healthy life expectancy, the freedom to make life choices, social support, generosity, and perceptions of corruption." Analysts do not know the cause of this happiness decline, but suggest that widespread drug addiction may play a part, along with loss of trust in politicians and public figures, as well as higher anxiety overall. And the top five ranked countries? Finland, Denmark, Norway, Iceland, and the Netherlands.[20]

» CHANGING EXISTING ATTITUDES

Most likely, at some time you will be in a position where you can (and should) work to change the attitude of a co-worker or employee. If you are in a management position, you might find yourself with an employee whose attitude must change if the employee is to stay with the company. You might be a member of a work group or a committee where the attitude of one or more members is getting in the way of productivity. However, changing a person's attitude is not always possible. At times, you will simply have to face the fact that some people will be happier in a different company and must leave their current position.

Angry, bored, or resentful employees present a tough case. They probably won't want to accept the rationale from their supervisors, or different points of view. Luckily, not all employees have this attitude. Often, people with negative attitudes need only to be shown how destructive their attitudes are before a change takes place. The key is **feedback**—everyone needs feedback. Literally, feedback means "returning a part of the output . . . to the input."[21] Here, the person with the bad attitude is the input source; he or she needs some of that output returned, with comments. When feedback is successful in changing people's attitudes, others who are developing attitudes about a new situation or a new workplace can take a more positive view and ultimately become more successful at work.

feedback

Information given to people either on how well they are performing a task, or on how clearly they are being understood.

When giving attitude-improving feedback, be sure to deal with facts rather than opinions, and descriptions rather than judgments. Instead of saying something confrontational like, "Why don't you try a little positive attitude for a change?" co-workers can describe some ways to improve or focus on smaller and more manageable issues one at a time. The co-worker could go even further and describe specifically what these actions would do to improve overall job attitude and success within an organization.

The giver of feedback should also try to strike a balance between negative and positive feedback. Some authorities on this subject suggest giving two positive messages for every negative one, while others suggest that a ratio of 5:1, that is, five positive messages to one negative message, is more effective; and still others promote a ratio of 10:1 positive to negative messages.[22] Regardless of the exact ratio, using good feedback to balance any

REAL WORLD EXAMPLE 4.1

Patty was in her first full-time job as a grocery store cashier. She hoped to move up in the store to a management position and felt that a firm and businesslike attitude with customers would show management that she was the right person for a leadership promotion.

Her attitude, however, was not working out the way she had hoped. Customers were complaining that she was unfriendly and even rude. She noticed that some regular customers avoided her line and went to other cashiers.

One day, Patty's supervisor Araceli pulled her aside and had a serious talk with her about her attitude.

"But customers should see that I am not being unfriendly, just serious and businesslike!" said Patty.

"Unfortunately," said Araceli, "that is not how they are reading it. Customers want a friendly face, someone they feel comfortable enough with to ask questions and talk about products."

Patty thought about what she said, and then her attitude underwent some subtle changes. She still had a competent attitude but added in more courtesy and an open attitude. People grew warmer and friendlier to her, and she ended up enjoying her job more than before.

negative feedback can positively change attitudes and behavior in the workplace and in our personal relationships.

In thinking about changing attitudes, should we change the attitudes of introverts into extraverts? Research and theories on positive attitudes seem to promote the idea that extraversion is good and introversion is bad. But is that the case? In recent years, attention has been paid to the attitudes of those who are not shy or isolated, but introverted. Traits of introversion include being more calm, observant, thoughtful, and feeling more comfortable in a small group than a large one. Rather than feeling energized by taking part in activities in a large group, introverts often need solitude to recharge after being in a large group.

In the workplace, introverts are often the self-starters and innovators who can create and produce ideas without waiting for external praise. They are likely to take thoughtfully calculated risks, after planning and assessing the options. Many of our most influential inventors and leaders (e.g., Albert Einstein, Bill Gates, Elon Musk, Eleanor Roosevelt, Warren Buffet) would describe themselves as introverts. For an effective workplace, consider pairing an introvert with an extravert to create a dynamic and productive team. Don't overlook introverts as valuable contributors, even when they are not the loudest members of the group.[23] If you are an introvert, you are not alone—estimates are that one-third to one-half of employees are introverts.

» ATTITUDES AND JOB SATISFACTION

What do you find satisfying about your job? Since needs and desires vary from person to person, it is difficult to generalize about job satisfaction, but it is clear that a person's satisfaction with work is directly related to attitude. The degree of satisfaction any employee feels is based on the

REAL WORLD EXAMPLE 4.2

"This job is mind numbing," said Gina. "I don't know why I stay here."

Instead of the sympathetic nods she expected from her co-workers, though, she got a little wake-up call.

"So why don't you find something else, then?" said Chandra. "I mean, everywhere I go, I see 'help wanted' signs. There are plenty of jobs out there right now. Plus, all this negativity is getting old."

As Gina looked around the room she could see that others agreed with what Chandra was saying. Gina had not really been serious, she had just been venting. But on her way home from work, Gina began to think more seriously about what Chandra had said. Maybe Chandra was right, and it was time to find a place where she felt valued and her work was satisfying to her.

Working Conditions That Help Job Attitudes

1. Mentally challenging work with which the individual can cope successfully.
2. Personal interest in the work itself.
3. Work that is not too physically tiring.
4. Rewards for performance that are fair, informative, and in line with the individual's personal ambitions.
5. Working conditions that are compatible with the individual's physical needs and help toward the accomplishment of his or her work goals.
6. High self-esteem on the part of the employee.
7. Agents in the workplace who help the employee to gain job values, such as interesting work, pay, and promotions; whose basic values are similar to his or her own; and who keep conflicts to a minimum.

figure 4.2

CHANGING ATTITUDES

Sometimes a co-worker, an employee, or a supervisor needs to change his or her attitude in order to communicate better with the rest of your work team. By opening communication and giving constructive feedback, you can help others overcome difficult communication problems. *What are some ways that you can give constructive feedback?*

extent to which the job and benefits associated with it fulfill that employee's needs and desires.

Not very long ago, business experts assumed that if managers could provide good working conditions for employees, every other measure of the job would also be good. Experts are now becoming aware that the connections between job satisfaction and employee turnover, absenteeism, and overall performance are not so simple. Recent studies showing connections among these factors have not been as conclusive as expected.[24]

We can draw two definite conclusions, though. First, when job satisfaction is very high, employees are less likely to be absent for unexcused reasons.[25] Second, job performance leads to job satisfaction, rather than vice versa. In other words, the successful performance of a series of tasks will often lead to feelings of satisfaction and well-being, which in turn will motivate the employee to complete other tasks that bring about an even higher level of satisfaction (see Figure 4.2). Managers need to be in touch with the type of tasks—and rewards—that cause high satisfaction in employees.[26]

Recently, a number of research studies have focused on what is called **organizational citizenship behavior**. This is really an attitude—an attitude of willingness to go above and beyond the behaviors that are generally associated

organizational citizenship behavior

An attitude of willingness to go above and beyond the behaviors that are generally associated with life in the workplace.

more about...

Job Satisfaction

Studies done over the past 25 years about the job satisfaction of human resource managers and employees have consistently demonstrated that job satisfaction is more important to employees *than any other factor*, including pay level or job security. Factors mentioned most often as part of satisfaction on the job include respect and trust from management, job security, a healthy environment, possibility for career growth, and pay.[28]

with life in the workplace.[27] Organizational citizenship behaviors are voluntary, and they contribute to the overall effectiveness of the organization. Here are some examples:

- Sally, an employee, finds several wads of wet paper towels in one of the hallways of her company. Fearing that someone might slip on the towels and suffer an injury, she removes the towels quietly and returns to work.
- Jose, a new employee, helps a fellow worker in another department with the translation of a document from Spanish to English.
- Sylvia, who is not an accountant but who did well in college accounting, helps a fellow employee understand how the new tax laws affect her department.

A detailed management study at Indiana University, Bloomington, showed how critically important organizational citizenship behavior is to the productivity–in terms of both quantity and quality–of any organization or work group.[29] As teams become increasingly important in today's workplace, organization citizenship behavior is likely to be studied–and promoted–more and more.

values

The worth or importance you attach to different factors in your life.

value systems

Frameworks people use in developing beliefs about themselves, others, and how they should be treated.

organizational or corporate culture

An organization's network that includes the shared values and assumptions within it.

» WHAT ARE VALUES?

Values are the worth or importance you attach to different factors in your life. Values include both cognitive (thoughts) and emotional (feelings) components, and may lead to actions.[30] These three components of values are very similar to the components of attitudes. Values, however, are considered more deeply held than attitudes, and are strong enough to drive behavior and important choices we make in our lives. Values can be thought of as standards that define the larger, long-term goals we believe in and work toward.

Values usually come in a list of priorities that we are not fully consciously aware of at the time when value judgments take place. All of your values taken together are called a **value system**–the set of standards by which you have chosen to live. Values exist not only within individuals but in organizations as well. A **corporate culture** is a system of shared values throughout any given company or other organization. Some organizations may value service to others (Doctors without Borders, for example, or ReachAnother Foundation). Other organizations may value a profit margin over anything else.

fizkes/Shutterstock

Values are especially important to understanding human behavior. Conflicts between employees, as well as between managers and employees, often are based on differences in values. When you seem to be at odds with another person, take a look at how your basic values differ. When you seem to be in conflict with your company, examine the company's value system against your own. When the corporate culture clashes with your own values system, it may be time for you to examine your priorities and consider finding another company that better fits your values.

more about...

Values may be *tangible* (something real in the physical sense, such as material goods) or *intangible* (something that is not real to the touch, but exists in connection to something else), or both. For example, a wedding ring has a cash value (tangible), but it also signifies the value a person holds toward the commitment of marriage (intangible).

Values versus Attitudes

If you ask the average person what the difference is between attitudes and values, he or she might say that they are the same. They are not. Attitudes are often affected by values, and values conflicts with other people certainly involve attitude problems—but values are a deeper and in some ways more important part of everyone's lives and organizations.

more about...

Values are also interpreted differently by people from different generations, religions, political systems, cultures, and ethnic or racial groups. This is true when comparing cultures around the globe, but also in specific groups in the United States.

» WHERE YOUR VALUES COME FROM

Personal values are formed in early childhood and are affected strongly by the values of parents and the child's environment. The place and time period of the first few years of most people's lives have a great effect on the formation of values. Statistics expert Daniel Yankelovich (1924–2017) believed that middle-class values give Americans a feeling of self-worth, a fairly clear idea of who they are, and especially a belief that somehow their personal lives make a positive impact on the lives of others. He identified three value patterns that emerged after the 1970s. First, the nature of a person's paid job is now much more significant. Second, leisure time is more valued, mostly because it has become a rarer commodity. Third, Americans now insist much more strongly that jobs become less impersonal and more human and humane.[31]

These three value areas have created more emphasis on individual freedom of choice, a movement away from rigid organizational and work systems, and a desire to live more closely with both nature and community.[32]

Since the classic Yankelovich study in the 1970s, many political scientists, social scientists, and people in general have asked if our values are stable or changing. And if changing, are they changing for the better or for the worse? A recent *NBC News/The Wall Street Journal* survey compared values of Americans in 2018 with responses from 1998. The results were somewhat surprising. Over that 20-year period, fewer Americans found religion to be important (62 percent down to 50 percent). Fewer place a high value on having children (down from 59 percent to 43 percent). Fewer consider patriotism

A BUYER'S MARKET

Since the beginning of online shopping, consumer values have shifted to an increasing demand for personalized service and more specialized products. *Do you feel that your needs are better met by online shopping than by traditional shopping?*

Hero/Corbis/Glow Images

to be important to them (down from 70 percent to 61 percent). While we do not know exactly how to interpret these findings, and we don't know what they mean for the long term, there is some good news. Americans still believe in the value of hard work. This value in itself has been considered part of our work ethic over many generations and forms one of the bases for traditional American values.[33]

Technology also shapes our values and our lives. In the past couple of decades, the human experience has seen a shift toward the Internet that is profoundly changing the focus of people's values. Consumers are now demanding to be treated as equals to those who sell products and services. Many online companies now allow customers to name their prices, giving customers unprecedented power in the transaction process. In many other ways, widespread use of the Internet signals a change of even the most traditional values, including the nature of our interpersonal relationships, how we value privacy, and more.

During the past few years, many nationally publicized scandals have caught our attention. A number of corporations have been hurt greatly by allowing themselves to be involved in activities that show questionable values. In fact, the decisions and actions of many large corporations, such as automakers and large banks, have recently had detrimental effects on wider society.

more about...

Values and Corporations: Corporate Cheating Scandals

Corporations as well as individuals can fall into the trap of cheating. Wells Fargo Bank has been at the center of investigations for bank fraud since 2016. By the end of 2018, the bank faced civil and criminal suits reaching an estimated $2.7 billion. The fraudulent activities were undertaken by thousands of employees, and 5,300 employees were fired.

In other scandals in recent years, Volkswagen, Fiat Chrysler, Daimler, Mitsubishi, Nissan, Subaru, Suzuki, Mazda, and Yamaha have all faced legal action based on cheating of one sort or another. Included were falsifying records, taking unsafe shortcuts, using inferior products, and more.

Do the actions of banks and automakers reflect a cheating culture? Or, instead, do they help to create and encourage one? Or, are these just unusual situations that have nothing to do with values or with a broader corporate culture?

Source: Matt Egon, "US Government Fines Wells Fargo $3 Billion for Its 'Staggering' Fake-Accounts Scandal," *CNN*, February 24,2020.

Another disturbing area of social values change has been in high school and college student cheating. *Who's Who among American High School Students* published results of a large national survey that showed 80 percent of students featured in that publication admitted to having cheated at some point in their schooling. In this widely cited study, nearly half the same students said that they didn't consider cheating to be "always wrong." Overall rates of self-reported cheating have shown some recent decline since the *Who's Who* survey, but more than half of high school students in recent years still report cheating.[34] Even elite Ivy League institutions such as Harvard have grappled with cheating on a wide scale. In early 2013, nearly half of all students in a 279-student Harvard "Intro to Congress" class were caught in a wide-ranging cheating scandal that ultimately forced dozens of students to withdraw from the university.[35]

In a book called *The Cheating Culture,* author David Callahan shows that American students are being taught "bottom-line economy" thinking. This mindset makes it more likely than in the past that such students will carry their questionable behavior into the workplace after they have

REAL WORLD EXAMPLE 4.3

You may know (or possibly be) someone who grew up in the 1960s, that period of rebellion against authority, fighting for rights for disadvantaged groups, and anti-war protests. Whatever else has happened to the members of that generation, most of them still have definite ideas about maintaining social justice, questioning people in authority, and "doing their own thing" (or pursuing their own interests in careers and personal life). Many of those who have become conservative and less anti-establishment will even admit that the strongly held values of the 1960s affected their desire for a change in point of view. Influences on our values are difficult, if not impossible, to ignore.

finished school. If they do, the workplace of the very near future is likely to feel the impact. We may be seeing this with scandals in major corporations that come to light.[36] The material both in this chapter and in Chapter 15 (on ethics) will deal with ways of understanding your own values and the values of other people with whom you study and work.

Historic periods in past decades have likewise affected the values of those who lived through them. If you knew people who grew up during the Great Depression of the 1930s, you may have noticed that their values were probably affected a great deal by that experience. They knew poverty once, and they have never forgotten the values that experience taught them. Likewise, the Great Recession of the 2000s is still shaping the values of those who were directly or indirectly affected by the national and global economic downturn. The economic impacts of the global pandemic will undoubtedly have similar effects.

more about...

The Great Depression (1929–1941), which was triggered by the Wall Street crash of 1929, resulted in millions of Americans losing their jobs, farms, and homes. It did not officially end until the United States entered World War II in December 1941.

The Great Recession (2007–2009), began with a liquidity crisis among financial institutions that resulted from the collapse of the housing market (or "bubble") in late 2006, which quickly spread economic pain around the globe. According to the U.S. National Bureau of Economic Research (the official authority of U.S. recessions), the recession began in December 2007 and ended in June 2009, although the negative impacts of this global economic contraction continue, with the lingering effects of job loss, home foreclosures, and other serious outcomes.

Other important factors that help form values are religion, political views, parental influence, socioeconomic class, exposure to education, and mass media including television, the Internet, and other sources (see Figure 4.3). Often one generation may judge (sometimes harshly) the values of another generation. Perhaps you have heard someone complain about expressions of violence or the portrayal of sexuality in our modern music, film, and other forms of mass media. This may be a generational complaint. At some point in one's growth, an individual must examine those values to see if they are really his or her own values.

Sometimes people might have certain values without real awareness of them. It might not occur to us to question those values until they are challenged.

Values can be placed in two categories. **Terminal values** (or endpoint ideal values) are likely to maintain a high priority throughout your life. These will often be related to long-term goals that you want to accomplish during

terminal values

Values likely to maintain a high priority throughout your life.

figure 4.3

SOCIAL FACTORS OF A GENERATION

Each generation has been affected by several social factors, which in turn help shape their values. *How do you see these differences in your own generation?*

THE INFLUENCE OF CERTAIN FACTORS AS THEY HAVE AFFECTED VALUES			
Areas of Change	**Pre-Baby Boomers (born 1920–45)**	**Baby Boomers (born 1946–64)**	**Gen X, Millenials (born 1965–2000s)**
Mass Media	Radio networks	Television	Internet
Comedians	Bob Hope, George Burns	George Carlin, Jerry Seinfeld	Amy Schumer, Dave Chappelle
Wars & Disasters	Depression, World War II	Vietnam War, Civil rights unrest and protests	Iraq and Afghanistan conflicts, 9/11 terror attack
New Technologies	Radar, Atomic power	Space technology	Digital technologies
Villains	Adolf Hitler, Joseph Stalin	Nikita Khrushchev, Idi Amin	Kim Jong-un, Vladimir Putin
Musical Choices	Jazz, Swing	Rock 'n' Roll, Motown	Hip hop, Rap, Alternative rock
Fears	Poverty, Total warfare	Atomic warfare	Terrorism, Global warfare, Pandemics

instrumental values

Values that reflect the ways you prefer to behave leading toward larger life goals.

your lifetime. **Instrumental values** (or everyday action-directed attitudes), on the other hand, reflect the ways you prefer to behave. They are based on your actions and attitudes.[37] One could say that instrumental values help you reach your goals, while terminal values *are* those goals. See Figure 4.4 for examples of terminal and instrumental values.

» VALUES CONFLICTS

values conflict

Conflict that occurs when one set of values clashes with another and a decision has to be made.

It is not uncommon—especially in the workplace—to find oneself in the middle of a **values conflict**. This commonly happens when one set of values clashes with another, and a decision has to be made—sometimes very quickly. These conflicts happen surprisingly often in most people's lives.

Interpersonal Values Conflicts

All people come from differing backgrounds, where they have learned various value systems. When they are thrown together in the workplace, they often must work with others whose values differ greatly from their own. A certain amount of conflict from interpersonal values is nearly unavoidable. To deal with such potential problems, you are often called upon to look closely at your own values, trying whenever possible to understand and accept the values of others without compromising your personal integrity. Also, you will often find it necessary to discover common ground where you can agree with others on what is important to both the workplace and the goals that everyone needs to achieve.

Instrumental Values	Terminal Values
Ambition	A comfortable and prosperous life
Open-mindedness	An exciting, stimulating, and active life
Capability, effectiveness	A sense of accomplishment or lasting contribution
Cheerfulness	A world at peace, free of war and conflict
Cleanliness	A world of beauty, nature, and art
Courage	Equality, brotherhood, and equal opportunity
Forgiveness	Family security, taking care of loved ones
Helpfulness	Freedom, independence, and free choice
Honesty	Happiness and contentment
Imagination	Inner harmony and freedom from inner conflict
Independence	Mature love, sexual and spiritual intimacy
Intelligence	National security
Logic	An enjoyable life
Love and tenderness	Salvation and eternal life
Obedience, respect	Self-respect and high self-esteem
Politeness	Social respect and admiration
Responsibility	True friendship
Self-control	Wisdom in understanding life

figure 4.4

EXAMPLES OF TERMINAL AND INSTRUMENTAL VALUES

Instrumental values are those you use in your everyday life to achieve your terminal or endpoint values; that is, values directly related to your long-term goals and dreams. *Can you think of an instrumental value of yours that is helping you achieve a terminal value?*

Source: Based on M. Rokeach, *The Nature of Human Values* (New York: Free Press, 1973), pp. 5–12.

CONFLICTING VALUES HAPPEN EVERYWHERE

Even though our values are often shaped by our families, values conflicts can happen in any household. Conflicting values are not restricted to the workplace. *Would your handling of values conflicts differ depending on the environment?*

Comstock Images/Getty Images

Personal versus Group Values

Values conflicts also often involve a clash between the individual and the group. Case Study 4.2 at the end of this chapter deals with such a

REAL WORLD EXAMPLE 4.4

In a small Midwestern college, four deans ran the institution's instructional wing. One was a Christian, one was Jewish, one agnostic, and the other a Zen Buddhist. People who saw this unusual assortment predicted chaos, but the period of time when they worked together was actually very productive, with little negative conflict. When asked how they managed to work so well together, they all gave similar answers. "We spent our energy on the goals of the college, a college we all love and want the best for; that gave us a unity that surpassed the values differences we might have had in other areas of life."

more about...

Cognitive dissonance can also refer to the stress that is caused by holding two contradictory values or beliefs at the same time, such as when you like a friend for having certain traits but dislike him or her for having others.

situation, where the culture of the organization can work against an individual's values to the point of distress. If you are outnumbered greatly, as in the example, changing the group values is possible but very unlikely. When this happens, you usually must decide whether or not to stay in such a job.

Internal Values Conflicts

INTERNAL VALUES CONFLICTS CAN HAPPEN TO ANYONE

Internal values conflicts are normal. Oftentimes, we find that we want conflicting things. *What are the best strategies for resolving internal values conflicts?*

Purestock/SuperStock

Still another type of values conflict is one that is waged inside of you. People sometimes find themselves wanting two different outcomes that contradict each other. In some cases, you might want something that, if it is achieved, will eliminate the possibility of another outcome that is also very desirable. For example, a college student wants to buy a car and has the money to buy it; however, once the money is spent on the car, none will be left for tuition and college expenses. In this case, achieving/choosing one would contradict the value of the other. Interpersonal and internal conflicts often result in **cognitive dissonance**: the emotional state that results from acting in ways that contradict one's beliefs or other actions.[38]

When early American leaders proclaimed that "all men are created equal," many of them owned slaves. The cognitive dissonance, or difference, between practice and values became increasingly stronger, until finally slavery was abolished. In a more personal example, Garth believes that cheating on his income tax is wrong; doing so violates some basic values he has in defining his own integrity. Yet every April, he finds himself *fudging* a little. This contradictory behavior causes cognitive dissonance in his own life. How can Garth take care of this internal conflict?

cognitive dissonance
The emotional state that results from acting in ways that contradict one's beliefs or other actions.

Most people have a certain amount of such dissonance in their behaviors. If the issues are small and create little compromise to people's values and attitudes, people usually live with the mild discomfort that dissonance can create. However, if what is being compromised is an important value,

REAL WORLD EXAMPLE 4.5

As a salesperson in a car dealership, Halina found herself within a value system among the other salespeople that put a great emphasis on attending social gatherings, usually parties. She found that they always involved staying up until 2 or 3 a.m., even on weeknights. When she tried twice to excuse herself early, she was labeled a "party pooper." Since Halina valued both her health and her alertness, she finally decided she had to find another job, even though she was making very good money at auto sales. The value she placed on health—which included getting adequate sleep—outweighed the values of the group.

people will usually take one of four possible actions–they will change their original beliefs, use denial, or self-justify, or change their behavior.

Imagine that you are in a job in which you resent the management system. You have said that you hate all managers. Suddenly, a supervisor tells you she is being promoted and wants you to take her place. She has cleared the move with her superiors. It is now cognitive dissonance time! What can you do? Here are the major choices you have, according to the cognitive dissonance theory:

1. *You can change your original beliefs about management.* "You know, I was probably overreacting a bit," you could say. "Managers are really important in any organization. I should have been more open-minded."
2. *You can use* ***denial***. This can be defined as a failure to confront your problem. "I didn't really mean all of those things I said before. The things I said were so extreme, anybody could see I wasn't really serious."
3. *You can use* ***self-justification***. In other words, you can explain your behavior so that you feel it is correct, by saying something like, "Yes, managers are mostly oppressive jerks, but I can show everybody that you don't have to be a jerk to be an effective manager."
4. *You can change your own behavior.* You might say, "As a manager, I can treat people with respect and create a positive work environment."[39]

denial

Failure to confront your problem; characteristic response by an alcoholic.

self-justification

Explaining your behavior so that you feel it is correct.

When you experience cognitive dissonance, you don't necessarily move toward trying to make actions consistent with values and beliefs. Instead, you might use any of these methods to make them appear more consistent and to lessen the stress caused by cognitive dissonance. All humans seem to need to justify their actions and make consistent sense out of their own contradictions. This process often happens instantly and without much deliberate thought–so it should not be surprising that it has been found to occur in four-year-old children, in patients with amnesia, and even in Capuchin monkeys.[40]

REAL WORLD EXAMPLE 4.6

JoBeth, a college student, was a politically active Libertarian. She campaigned for Libertarian candidates and expressed a great deal of enthusiasm for the Libertarian political party. One day, a fellow student who was a Democrat asked her to explain why being a Libertarian was so valuable to her. The best answer JoBeth could come up with was that she loved her dad and that had always been his party. She had never closely examined the beliefs and practices of the Libertarian party to decide whether it represented a political philosophy that she personally agreed with. In this case, one could say that her political beliefs were really based on someone else's values—not necessarily JoBeth's.

more about...

Values from Another Culture's Eyes

People from other cultures will define your values by your behavior, so other areas of human relations, including nonverbal communication such as eye contact, tone of voice, and body language will influence their interpretation of your value system.

» VALUES IN AN INTERNATIONAL ECONOMY

As the world gets smaller due to globalization in travel and industry, international differences in values need to be understood. Today's business world is now dealing with people from many different religions, political systems, languages, cultural backgrounds, and ethnic groups. Many citizens of the United States tend to think that the value system in their own nation is the best among all countries, but they need to understand that people in every other country have the same tendency–to think their own national and cultural values are the best or are correct. For example, the value system in the United States stresses "rugged individualism" and speaking out assertively. Traditional Asian cultures, however, usually value the strength of the group over the strength of the individual. An American businessperson would be wise to understand such differences and adapt to them when necessary. Every year, more members of differing ethnic cultures join the American workforce. In addition, a growing number of American companies are doing business around the world. Because of this, people of all cultures need to become increasingly sensitive to the values of others, which may not necessarily be their own.

When you are working with people from other cultures, you will tend to find four major areas of difference in values–and in perception of the values of others.

1. *Views of power and authority.* In many emerging countries, the prevailing attitude is that what a manager says must be followed without question. The practices of power sharing and group decision making in the United States may seem strange and unfamiliar to many people of other cultures. They may follow the traditional values of the top-down organization and often must be urged to participate in decision making, even in decisions that affect them personally.

REAL WORLD EXAMPLE 4.7

When Jasper Arasco arrived in the United States from Panama, he was surprised that his manager asked for his advice in making several important decisions. Jasper's first reaction was to suspect that his manager was not very good at his job; in Panama, only someone very unsure of his or her job would take such an approach. After living in the United States for several months, Jasper began to understand that this was a style of management to which he needed to become more accustomed. He realized that asking for advice was a way of sharing in decision making. However, when Jasper returned to a new job in Panama, he was forced to readjust back to his traditional ways of thinking about power sharing and decision making.

2. *Views of the individual versus the group.* Americans have been taught to value individualism and the individual effort. In many other countries, the group is seen as considerably more important than any of its individual members. In these cultures, taking individual credit for an accomplishment that the group did together would be considered extremely selfish and rude. The group is usually valued more highly than the individual. Our competitive culture tends to encourage and reward individual achievement. This can lead to a stronger focus on individual accomplishments, rather than on group successes.

TOLERATING UNCERTAINTY

Different cultures have different ways of handling uncertainty. *What is your tolerance level for uncertainty?*

Dave and Les Jacobs/Blend Images/Getty Images

3. *Tolerance for uncertainty.* The early history of the United States is a story of people who sailed here with little certainty of what lay ahead. Later, pioneers in covered wagons traveled to new territories south and west. They had to have, or develop, the ability to live with the prospect of the unknown. Other cultures may view uncertainty as recklessness and lack of planning. Within many cultures, maximizing certainty is a value that should be respected by members of other cultures.
4. *The value of punctuality.* In the United States, people are often judged by their promptness and punctuality. Westerners, especially North Americans, often value people less when they are late for appointments. In many other cultures, time urgency is not a value at all. In fact, North Americans are often seen by others as impatient, judgmental, and overly stressed because of the time factor. When dealing with less time-focused cultures, North Americans could learn to relax and behave in the others' time context. They especially need to examine the high value they place on time. These differences can help you understand the values misunderstandings that North Americans might have with members of other cultures.

REAL WORLD EXAMPLE 4.8

When Takara Nishi took a job in California after having worked in her native Japan, she was asked at a planning meeting if she would head a work team, since she had headed a successful one in Japan. Her reply was "I have always worked well with my team; I would welcome an opportunity to do so again." Since her American managers expected her to "sell" herself more assertively, her response was misinterpreted as showing a lack of confidence. When a manager asked why she hadn't sounded more persuasive, she answered, "I didn't want the members of my team to think that I was taking too much credit. That would make it difficult for us to work together." In her culture, Takara had been taught that the group effort is much more important than any individual effort.

STRATEGIES FOR SUCCESS

Strategy 4.1 Changing Pessimism to Optimism

In his book *The Optimistic Child,* Dr. Martin Seligman describes a program for parents who want to change their children's pessimistic beliefs to optimistic ones.[41] He believes that by using this strategy, parents can reduce depression in their children and help them bounce back after facing problems. Using Seligman's strategy for changing pessimism to optimism in families, you can use a similar strategy to help yourself recover quickly from problem situations in the workplace.

Imagine a horrible situation that you are facing at work, one that you believe is a problem building up to a disaster. Using Dr. Seligman's strategy, go through the following steps to reduce the emotional impact this disaster will have on you.

1. Describe the situation.
2. What is the worst possible outcome of this situation, and is there anything you could do to prevent this outcome?
3. What is the best outcome that could occur in this situation, and is there anything you could do to make the best outcome occur?
4. What do you see as the most likely outcome, and what will you do to cope if the most likely outcome occurs?

Now try these steps yourself. Let's say that the Internet retail company you recently began working for is not doing well financially, and you have heard rumors that there will be massive layoffs. Again, by using the four steps of Dr. Seligman's strategy, you might come up with something similar to this:

1. *"People may be laid off at work."*
2. *"The company is going under! They're going to call me into the human resources office and tell me I have ten minutes to pack up my belongings and get out. There would be nothing I could do about that!"*
3. *"They're going to lay off other people and reorganize, giving me a big fat promotion. I'll keep working really hard so that they will keep me on."*
4. *"A lot of technology and start-up companies have financial problems, so there may be layoffs—including me. I'll get my résumé ready and start looking at job announcements."*

Seligman believes that if you stop and ask yourself questions such as these each time you find yourself feeling pessimistic, depressed, hopeless, and helpless, you can stop turning problems into catastrophes. When problems become just situations to handle and not catastrophes, you can figure out reasonable solutions to

REAL WORLD EXAMPLE 4.9

A U.S. company opened a branch in Taiwan. Once they formed a management team, made up of both Americans and Taiwanese, the American top managers called a meeting to brainstorm ideas for entering markets with a new product. The Taiwanese members of the group found this method frustrating, especially when they suggested ideas that were added to, changed, or dismissed by the group. The problem came from differences between the two cultures in their respective levels of tolerance to uncertainty.

these problems instead of dwelling on them and failing to resolve them. In the process of getting rid of catastrophes, you become more optimistic and cope better with your problems.

An important point to remember is that using this strategy is not going to be second nature. It is something you will have to practice. Just like any new skill, it will become easier over time.[42]

STRATEGIES FOR SUCCESS

Strategy 4.2 Building Positive Attitudes at Work

Tips for Positivity:

1. Surround yourself with positive people.
2. Be encouraging in your words and behaviors.
3. Avoid assumptions, ask questions.

How can you keep a positive attitude when you are tempted to be discouraged? What if the environment around you is negative? What about those days when all you have is problem after problem? Here are some suggestions that should help, whatever the situation.[43]

1. **Surround yourself with positive people.** Attitudes are contagious. If you spend your workday with negative people, you will find yourself "catching" the negativity. If you have been assigned to a work team or office area that is full of negativity, see if you can change to another team or space. Don't get trapped by the negativity of others.
2. **Be encouraging in your words and behaviors.** It is easy to talk about being positive, but it is not always easy to do. Act and speak in a positive tone and it will become a habit. Treat others with empathy and consideration. Stop complaining, and start noticing and speaking up about things that are going well. Look for the good in others and in the organization, and comment on it.
3. **Avoid assumptions, ask questions.** When something happens at work that threatens your self-esteem or makes you feel that you have not performed well, ask why. Ask yourself if you are taking things personally when you do not need to. Ask the other person for clarification of the situation. Often, miscommunication is the culprit. Avoid retaliating against a person you think has not treated you well.

REAL WORLD EXAMPLE 4.10

Bethany sells radio and television advertising. One of her customers is the Warm Springs Reservation in Oregon, a thriving Native American reservation. Bethany soon found that she was dealing with a culture that has different attitudes toward time than she does. She has learned not to expect absolute punctuality from some of her Warm Springs clients, because in their culture the "value" of time is viewed much differently than the way American culture views it. She has learned to be more patient and tolerant in her business dealings, and has by now done a large amount of successful business with members of the local Native American community. Bethany has also come to realize that her Warm Springs clients were very patient with her, making allowances for her culture, as well.

STRATEGIES FOR SUCCESS

Strategy 4.3 Redefining Your Personal Values: The Rath Test

Strategies for Success

Questions to ask yourself:

1. Did I choose this value freely, with no outside pressure?
2. Did I choose this value from several alternatives?
3. Did I consider the consequences of my choice?
4. Do I like and respect this value?
5. Will I defend this value publicly?
6. Will I base my behavior on this value?
7. Do I find this value persistent throughout my life?

One of the biggest problems with defining your values and who you really are is that most people have a tendency to be less than honest with themselves. Your ideal self often wants to believe that the values you feel you *should* have are the ones you *do* have. One revealing question to ask yourself is "Do my values change depending on where I am and who I'm with?" If your answer is yes, are they not really your values?

Rath Test

Finds out if the values you think you have are the ones you truly have.

Louis Rath, a well-known expert on values, has put together the **Rath Test,** which you can use to find out if the values you think you have are the ones you truly have. Take any values you consider important in your life and ask these seven questions:

1. **Did I choose this value freely, with no outside pressure?** Or did someone else—such as a parent, group, or religion—provide this value to you? The source of the value isn't the real issue; if it did originate somewhere else, did it later become your own value?
2. **Did I choose this value from several alternatives?** In other words, did you even notice that other values were possible, or did you just accept the value and look in no other direction?
3. **Did I consider the consequences of my choice?** Strong belief in a value is likely to have consequences in your life—not all of them positive. Did you take a good look at the cause-effect sequence of holding this value?
4. **Do I like and respect this value?** If a value really is your own, you will prize it, care for it, and be motivated by it.

5. **Will I defend this value publicly?** This may be the most important question in the Rath Test. If you value something others hate, will you defend that value in front of people who might dislike you because of such a stand?
6. **Will I base my behavior on this value?** It is one thing to say something is valuable to you, but will you make it a part of the way you act in everyday life?
7. **Do I find this value persistent throughout my life?** If it is really your value, you should be able to see it affecting all areas of your life throughout the years of your life. It should have a lasting, long-term effect on you.[44]

The values you have already expressed can now be tested against these questions. This approach will help you separate the real values from the ones you thought were strong in your life.

CHAPTER FOUR SUMMARY

Chapter Summary by Learning Objectives

LO 4-1 **Define an attitude.** You have learned about attitudes: what they are, where they come from, and why they are important. The healthiest attitude is one that is happy, positive, or optimistic.

LO 4-2 **Examine what makes a good attitude.** Ingredients for a positive attitude include healthy self-esteem, optimism, extraversion, and personal control of your life. You should not let situations push you around or control your attitudes. Instead, you should become goal-oriented and increase your internal locus of control. Because your reaction to problems or situations is a choice, you can choose to be happy and maintain a positive attitude.

LO 4-3 **Discuss what goes into changing an existing attitude.** People who have less than positive attitudes sometimes need to receive feedback to be shown how destructive their attitudes are; then a change can take place. The key is feedback.

LO 4-4 **Find details regarding the link between positive attitudes and job satisfaction.** Job satisfaction is also related to attitudes. Job performance leads to job satisfaction, not the other way around. Understand the recently discovered role of organizational citizenship behavior in the effectiveness of the workplace.

LO 4-5 **Define values, and show how they differ from attitudes.** Values are the worth or importance that people attach to different factors of their lives. These factors include objects, activities, or frames of mind that you consider very important. A corporate culture is a system of shared values throughout any organization. Values are deeper than attitudes, and are generally longer-lasting and more important than attitudes in driving life choices. Also, unlike attitudes, values come in a partially unconscious list of priorities.

LO 4-6 Explain the origin of your values. Personal values are formed in early childhood and are strongly influenced by the values of parents and the child's environment. The place and time period of the first few years of most people's lives have a great effect on the formation of values.

LO 4-7 Identify strategies for coping with values conflict. All people come from differing backgrounds, where they have learned various value systems. When they are thrown together in the workplace, they often must work with others whose values differ greatly from their own. When individuals experience cognitive dissonance (the emotional state that results from acting in ways that contradict one's beliefs or other actions), they don't necessarily try to make their actions consistent with their values and beliefs. Instead, they might use one of the following: changing their original beliefs, using denial, self-justifying, or changing their own behavior.

LO 4-8 Apply values in a global context. In an international economy, everyone must deal with members of other cultures who might not share the same values. The chief values differences are differing views of power and authority, of the roles of the individual versus the group, of tolerance for uncertainty, and of punctuality.

key terms

review questions

1. Where do attitudes come from? When in people's lives do they develop? Provide examples of attitudes that you hold and describe their possible origins.
2. How do positive attitudes affect the workplace? How can negative attitudes hurt the success of a business? How do these two workplace environments feel different?
3. Can a person obtain a happy attitude just by desiring to do so? How can circumstances bring happiness into one's life? Explain your answer.

4. Can an employee's attitudes and role in a company make him or her someone with *organizational citizenship behavior*? In your own life, do you function as a worker or manager, and/or as a citizen of your organization? Explain.
5. How do values develop during the early part of people's lives?
6. What is the difference between *terminal* and *instrumental* values? Give examples of each, including examples of each that you hold.
7. How can you be sure that the values that you think you hold are really your own?
8. What is a values conflict? Have you ever been involved in a conflict that involved values differences? If so, what was the focus of the conflict? Was it interpersonal? Did it seem that it was you (or someone else) against the group?

critical thinking questions

1. Bad things do happen to everyone at one time or another. Is it always possible to maintain a positive attitude? Is it always necessary? Can you think of examples in which maintaining a positive attitude (at least temporarily) is impossible and unnecessary? Include an example of something you can't change in the workplace and in your personal life that fits this situation.
2. Have you ever experienced cognitive dissonance in your own life? (More than likely, you have experienced it many times.) Provide an example. How did you react? What strategies did you use to lessen the impact of the dissonance in your life?
3. Can values found in other cultures that are very different from yours be "wrong" or are they just different? How do you respond to others in a clash of cultures?

working it out 4.1

ATTITUDES AND JOB OUTCOMES

School-to-Work Connection: Interpersonal Skills

Purpose: How important are employees' general attitudes on the job when they are being considered for a promotion, or being hired?

Instructions: Role-play different job attitudes in applicants interviewing for a job, and discuss the most likely outcomes in each situation. Each student acting as applicant should present similar credentials for the job. In the first role-play, the student acting as job applicant should act somewhat bored and disinterested. In the second role-play, the student acting as job applicant should act neutral, neither positive nor negative. In the third role-play, the student acting as job applicant should act positive and enthusiastic about the job. Take note of how others respond to these different attitudes.

Discuss your own and others' emotions during these enacted interviews—were you frustrated, relaxed, or some other emotion? Did the positive applicant seem the best for the job?

working it out 4.2

VALUES AND YOUR CAREER CHOICE

School-to-Work Connection: Personal Qualities Skills

Purpose: Your present values are very important to your future success in the career you choose. In your search for the right career, which of the following value factors will you look for?

Instructions: Check the appropriate *terminal* values:

_____ 1. Lifelong learning

_____ 2. Eliminating suffering and hunger

_____ 3. Achieving world peace

_____ 4. Raising a family

_____ 5. Variety of experience

_____ 6. Artistic expression

_____ 7. Achieving recognition

_____ 8. Security

_____ 9. Adventure and excitement

_____ 10. Serving God or fulfilling spiritual/religious beliefs

_____ 11. Serving country

_____ 12. Other _______________

Next, check the specific factors you will look for in the career you choose. The majority of these will be *instrumental* values for most people.

_____ 1. High salary

_____ 2. Great amount of freedom

_____ 3. Nice people to work with

_____ 4. Physical exercise on the job

_____ 5. Mental challenges

_____ 6. Opportunities for advancement

_____ 7. Fairness in the workplace (freedom from prejudice)

_____ 8. Ability to work without being around others

_____ 9. Ability to work in groups with others

_____ 10. Good vacation time

_____ 11. Flexible working hours

_____ 12. Freedom to plan your own job

_____ 13. Freedom to use leadership skills and abilities

_____ 14. Ability to be trained as you work

_____ 15. Freedom to work at home

_____ 16. Freedom to work outdoors

_____ 17. Other _______________

Keep this list and refer to it in the future when job hunting. If you have already chosen a career, use this test to see how many of your values are affected by that choice. Consider the possible impacts on you in the long term if the organization's values conflict with your personal values.

working it out 4.3

ARE YOU HAPPY AT WORK?

Purpose: Employee engagement and happiness at work are important to employee productivity and to the overall financial health of companies. Thinking of your current workplace or a future ideal workplace, what factors are most important to you? How important are they?

Instructions: The following are some of the common questions asked in happiness at work or employee engagement surveys. Discuss these in a group, or reflect individually. There are no right or wrong answers here. These questions are meant to prompt your thoughts about your work values, attitudes, and corporate cultures that are a good fit for you.

- Are you happy at work? How happy, on a scale of 1 to 10?
- Are you engaged at work? That is, do you feel passionate about what you do, committed to the work, and believe you put in your best effort? How engaged are you, on a scale of 1 to 10?
- How would you rate your work–life balance, on a scale of 1 to 10?
- How satisfied are you with your job overall, on a scale of 1 to 10?

- How comfortable are you giving honest feedback to others at work, on a scale of 1 to 10?
- Do you have what you need to do your job, on a scale of 1 to 10?
- Are you clear about what your job requires of you, on a scale of 1 to 10?
- How valued do you feel at work, on a scale of 1 to 10?
- Do you believe in your company's values/vision/mission?
- Do you believe your contribution at work is valuable?
- When you need training to do your job well, is it available?
- Do you have the opportunity to grow and advance in your company?
- Do you feel hopeful about your future in your company?
- Considering all of the different areas at the company, do you have the opportunity to do what you do best at work?

Source: Celine Sugay, "How to Measure Happiness With Tests and Surveys (+ Quizzes)," *PositivePsychology.com*, November 11, 2019, https://positivepsychology.com/measure-happiness-tests-surveys (retrieved March 7, 2020).

working it out 4.4

ARE YOU AN INTROVERT?

Did you find yourself identifying with the description of introverts in this chapter? Can you relate to the experiences of introverts? Or, do you prefer the more outgoing nature of extraverts?

Watch the TED Talk by Susan Cain, titled "The Power of Introverts," and then answer the following questions.

1. What does Susan Cain identify as the "power" of introverts?
2. Define introverts, extraverts, and ambiverts, in your own words. Give examples of how each one might act in a specific context such as a party.
3. Identify an influential person in your life (e.g., teacher, coach, boss, mentor) who was an introvert. What made him or her effective?
4. Why does the speaker believe our culture has a bias against introverts? What evidence does she suggest? Do you agree or disagree with her? Explain.
5. How do you view American culture as a whole: more introverted or more extraverted? How do you think the rest of the world sees American culture? Explain.

The video can be found here: www.ted.com/talks/susan_cain_the_power_of_introverts

You Own Your Attitude

Adam and Ella both worked as speech pathologists for a large school district. Both had started three years ago, and both had been very excited and optimistic when they first started their jobs. But now, the rosy glow they started with had become dim. "Ugh," said Ella, "if one more kid spits or sneezes or spills their juice on me, I am going to scream. Why did I think it would be fun working with children? I feel like I'm just a glorified babysitter. Why can't they learn anything? I should have gone to law school or something instead. I need a new job," she complained.

The more she complained, the more Adam could feel his good mood sinking. "You might be right, I guess this isn't really what I expected, either. Do you think I should look for a different job?" he asked. Her response was instant. "Yes!" she said, "We both can do so much better than this."

By the time he got home, Adam was feeling irritable and dejected. When his wife asked him what was wrong, he told her, "I was in a great mood today until Ella made me feel really negative."

"Wait," his wife said, "how can anyone "make' your mood for you?"

Case Study Questions

1. What is the basic problem leading to Adam and Ella's attitudes?
2. Who is responsible for the attitudes each person is displaying? At this stage, how can each of them build a more positive attitude?
3. Are values and attitudes both involved here? Explain.
4. What are some possible long-term outcomes if they do not change their attitudes?

case study 4.2

The Relationships in Human Relations

Jamar supervised a crew of 15 employees for a moving company. He had been working there for several years and had seen many changes in management during that time. Most recently, he had found himself trying to understand what really bothered him about his newest supervisor.

Jamar prided himself on having one of the highest performing crews at the company–the fewest complaints, and the fewest claims for breakage or loss. But his newest manager, Charles, was not satisfied.

"I don't really care about loss claims," he told Jamar at the weekly logistics meeting. "Your crew needs to pick up the pace. We need to get more work orders done, and faster."

Jamar protested, "But that means more mistakes! A tired crew, more claims, and worse, complaints from families who just want to get their stuff moved to a new place. I have a good crew, we work together well, and they deserve respect just like the families that we move deserve it."

Charles just shook his head at Jamar. "Speed it up, or I'll find another crew. You can all be replaced, you know."

Case Study Questions

1. Would you identify the conflict in this case as a values conflict or as a difference in attitudes? Explain.
2. If you see this as a values conflict, is it interpersonal, personal versus group, or internal? Explain. What should Jamar do to resolve any conflict in this situation?
3. What instrumental and terminal values can you identify for Jamar? For Charles?

CHAPTER FIVE

MOTIVATION: INCREASING PRODUCTIVITY

LEARNING OBJECTIVES

After studying this chapter, you will be able to:

LO 5-1 Define motivation.

LO 5-2 Explain need-based theories of motivation.

LO 5-3 Explain behavior-based theories of motivation.

LO 5-4 Discuss the relationship between self-esteem and motivation.

STRATEGIES FOR SUCCESS

Strategy 5.1 Applying McClelland's Theory

Strategy 5.2 Changing Your Behavior

In the Workplace: Motivated . . . or Not?

SITUATION

Dmitry Kalinovsky/Shutterstock

For months now, Miller had been out of work. Although he did his best to remain optimistic, jobs were scarce in his region, and the economic realities in his state had made finding meaningful work tough for everyone—including him and lots of other people he knew. Finally, he landed a job—and one that paid several dollars an hour more than he had expected to make.

"My new job involves working outside in the cold weather, but just watch me laugh all the way to the bank!" he told his family. "With that kind of money, who is gonna care? Not this guy." His family all remarked on how happy and motivated he was. "I've never seen you so excited about anything, Miller," one of his closest friends remarked.

DISCOVERY

Only two months later, Miller was telling a different kind of story. Not wanting to admit how grim his job really was, he told only a few of his closest friends how discouraged he had become. "I never thought I'd say this," he confided to his best friend one day, "but I'm not getting paid enough for the grief I have to put up with. My supervisor yells at me all the time, for no good reason. He shouts out unclear instructions on how to do a job and then loses his temper when I don't do what he thinks he told me to do. As soon as I can find another job, I'm out of here."

"I'd give anything to make that kind of money," his friend countered.

"You just don't get it," Miller replied. "I'm finding out that it's really not about the money. If you had this job, you'd understand what I mean."

THINK ABOUT IT

Why did Miller lose motivation so quickly? Why did money become less and less important to him as time went by? What other aspects of a job provide motivation? Would the money in his job be enough to motivate you, or would you find stronger motivation from something else?

motivation
The force of the need or desire to act.

organizational climate
The emotional weather within an organization that reflects the norms and attitudes of the organization's culture and affects worker morale, attitudes, stress levels, and communication.

morale
Overall mood of an individual or group, based on attitudes and satisfaction.

» WHAT IS MOTIVATION?

What motivates people? You are reading this textbook, which means you are probably completing the assigned reading for class. Why aren't you watching a movie right now, listening to music with friends, or doing whatever sport or activity you like best? You are obviously motivated to be studying. What motivates you? Is everyone motivated in the same way?

Questions like these have puzzled scholars and managers for many years. **Motivation** is the willingness to make an effort toward accomplishment. To be truly motivated means feeling a desire to do whatever task needs to be accomplished to reach a goal or purpose. Management guru Peter Drucker said, "The purpose of an organization is to enable common men [and women] to do uncommon things."[1] High motivation makes people want to do those uncommon things.

There are many theories about what motivates individuals in their personal and professional lives, although there is no definitive, unified theory; in fact, some theories even contradict each other. As a student of motivation you should try to see both positive and negative positions taken by experts. As you study this material, see if you can choose the theory that makes the most sense to you.

MANAGERS AND ORGANIZATIONAL CLIMATE

The ability to listen to employee needs is a key component for the successful manager. *What are some other skills you can use to improve organizational climate?*

John A Rizzo/Pixtal/SuperStock

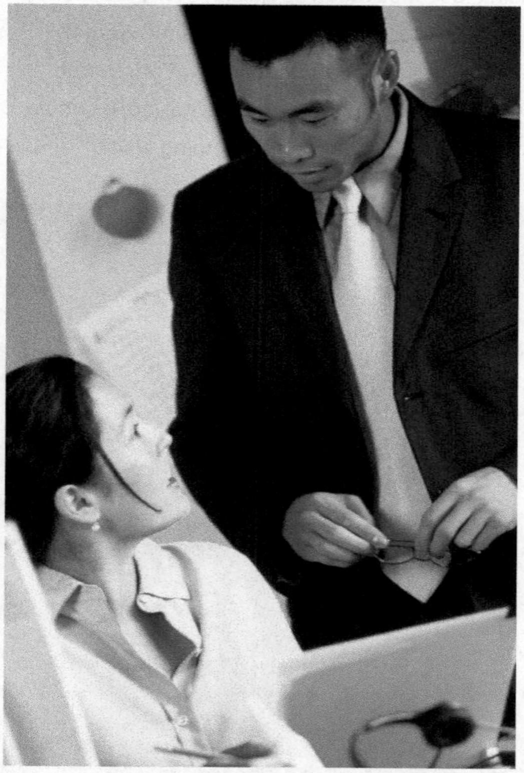

Organizational Climate and Morale

A large motivating factor on the job is the **organizational climate**. The climate within an organization can be compared with the physical climate outdoors, and it can also be described as warm or cold. Organizational climate affects the way employees feel and act because it is the "emotional weather" within an organization; it affects employee morale. Organizational climate is also largely affected by an organization's corporate culture, introduced in the discussion of values in Chapter 4. Think of corporate culture as the expectations about beliefs and behaviors that are set by a particular organization in terms of how they interact with each other and outside organizations. These beliefs and behaviors may be spoken or just implied, and they can strengthen or change over time.

Morale is the overall mood of a group of people and is based on employees' attitudes and feelings of satisfaction. Today most agree that organizational climate, corporate culture, and staff morale must work together for a company to function at its best. When the climate of a workplace is comfortable, the corporate culture is accepting and morale is good, then high motivation levels are much more likely. Few factors can hurt productivity and job performance worse than low morale issues.

A good climate is much more than just people getting along well. An effective climate allows people to work to their full potential without becoming a threat to others. It encourages competent and efficient completion of tasks within deadlines. It also allows employees to feel comfortable: employees in a positive and comfortable work climate can be themselves without feeling threatened.

Many methods can be used to improve the climate of an organization. Though managers are in the key position for making change, individual employees can also accomplish a great deal. They can listen to others carefully. They can step in and help with a task without complaints. And they can maintain a positive attitude with their colleagues. In many workplaces, employees have opportunities to suggest changes. If you are an employee in a negative or uncomfortable climate, take a look at the situation and see what you can do to improve elements under your control. If you are a manager, start with your own attitude toward employees and the tasks at hand. Then look to see where changes should be made in the physical environment, job assignments, and procedures. Institute an open-door policy, if such a thing is practical. Remember that organizational climate is directly related to motivation.

more about...

"Magic happens when you connect people. I credit much of my success to always making it a point to truly get to know people and help them whenever I can. It's become the backbone of our firm's success."

Consider this quote from **Susan McPherson**, who is the founder and CEO of McPherson Strategies, a communications consultancy to corporations, NGOs, and social enterprises. What does this quote suggest in terms of the importance of positive **organizational climates**?

For some workers, motivation seems to work automatically; for most of us, it is not something we usually think about before beginning each task. These general theories of motivation are ways of looking at how motivation relates to people and their behavior. Please remember that these are only theories. No single theory completely explains human motivation. Why? Because social scientists still have much to discover about this complex topic (see Figure 5.1).

Need-Based Theories

Hierarchy of Needs: *Abraham Maslow*

ERG Theory: *Clayton Alderfer*

McClelland's Needs: *David McClelland*

Two-Factor: *Frederick Herzberg*

Job Enrichment: *Hackman and Oldham*

Gamification

Behavior-Based Theories

Expectancy: *Victor Vroom*

Reinforcement/Behavior Modification: *B. F. Skinner*

figure 5.1

MAJOR THEORIES OF MOTIVATION (AND THEIR CREATORS)

The main theories of motivation are listed here. As you learn about each theory, think about which one you feel is the most useful. *Which theory seems most accurate to you, or most applicable to your life?*

figure 5.2

TYPICAL INTRINSIC AND EXTRINSIC REWARDS

Intrinsic rewards come from within and motivate you to excel at your job. Extrinsic rewards come from outside sources, such as managers, co-workers, clients, and the company itself. *Which rewards do you feel are more valuable?*

Examples of Additional Intrinsic and Extrinsic Rewards

Intrinsic Rewards	Extrinsic Rewards
Increased responsibility	Performance bonuses
Opportunities for personal growth	Profit-sharing programs
Ability to participate in decision making	Impressive titles
Variety of job activities	Pay raises
More job freedom	Preferred office furnishings and lunch hours
	Longer vacations

more about...

If Employees Don't Want Money, What DO They Want?

In his book, *Drive: The Surprising Truth About What Motivates Us,* author Daniel Pink describes three main factors that lead employees to better performance, higher motivation, and personal satisfaction.

1. **Autonomy.** This refers to the urge to direct one's own life. Having a say in, or the ability to control what, when, and how we work, and who we work with, motivates us to complete a task. Autonomy allows workers to be creative.
2. **Mastery.** An important element of intrinsic motivation, mastery is described as the desire to get better at something that matters. Most of us have the desire to get better at the things that we do. This is why learning new skills can be so frustrating—because we aren't good at them yet.
3. **Purpose.** Perhaps the greatest motivator of the three, a sense of purpose gives an employee the chance to connect to something larger than themselves. Employees are driven and energized when they feel that their work contributes to the greater good, and when they are connected to something larger than themselves—to other people, their mission, and their values.

Source: Daniel Pink, *Drive: The Surprising Truth About What Motivates* (Riverhead Books, April 5, 2011).

Intrinsic and Extrinsic Rewards

For most people, there is one main reason to work—to make money. Economic need is the primary motivator toward work. Working allows you to pay your bills, collect employee benefits, and build financial security for your retirement—allowing you to work in the present without worrying too much about the future. These are all **extrinsic motivators**. Working can also allow you to satisfy your intrinsic motives. (See Figure 5.2.)

Intrinsic motivators or intrinsic rewards are the internal feelings of satisfaction you get from your job. These often provide more powerful motives than the extrinsic factors do. For example, as part of the "2019 Deloitte Millennial Survey," researchers report that Millennials and Generation Z say they are unhappy with traditional social institutions, mass media, and the lack of social progress. They are uneasy and pessimistic about their lives, their careers, and the world around them. Millennials are also reluctant to trust leaders, particularly those who run companies that are not aligned with Millennials' values or political views.[2] It is not surprising, given these reasons, that Millennials and Generation Z are more likely to quit their jobs for *intrinsic* reasons, such as differences in values or philosophy, than for *extrinsic* reasons, such as money, popularity, or flexible hours.

Employees tend to be motivated when they feel appreciated. And while the nature of work can vary across industries, we can use some common techniques to show appreciation for others in the workplace:[3]

> **more about...**
>
> Dennis Bakke, a motivation author and business management entrepreneur, says this about **motivation and workers:** "I am convinced that the next form of discrimination that needs to be overturned is the second-class treatment [of] working men and women."
>
> Source: Dennis W. Bakke, *Joy at Work* (Seattle, WA: PVG, 2014), eBook.

1. **Words of affirmation.** Express genuine appreciation to co-workers and staff. Encouraging words can help a person feel more wanted, more needed, and more invested in their work. Be generous with praise, but make sure it is genuine. False praise will backfire in motivating employees.
2. **Quality time.** One-on-one interaction between colleagues can lead to higher levels of engagement and motivation. This type of interaction between manager and employee can help to remove any communication barriers that exist, promote understanding, and increase employee satisfaction. Regular check-ins with employees by a supervisor or team lead can go a long way toward helping an employee feel valued.
3. **Tangible gifts.** Giving your co-worker a small token gift (such as their favorite chocolate, an extra coffee, or a nice note) to show your appreciation can boost morale, reduce cynicism, and contribute to a positive workplace environment. Managers who take a difficult employee to lunch, for example, can build reciprocal trust with the employee, and help make the workplace more positive for all. Before doing so, make sure you are not violating any company policies.
4. **Acts of service.** Working collaboratively with your colleagues can help promote a sense of teamwork in the office, which, in turn, can boost morale and motivation. Similarly, rolling up your sleeves to help a colleague complete an important assignment on time can help the colleague to feel appreciated—and more motivated.
5. **Physical touch.** Convey the language of praise through appropriate physical touch when acceptable to the employee, such as a congratulatory handshake, an "elbow-bump," or even an emphatic high-five (or simulated "air high-five"). These will all do the trick!

extrinsic motivators
Those motivators that come from outside sources, such as money and fame.

Intrinsic motivators or intrinsic rewards
In *expectancy theory,* the internal factors related to the value of work, including the amount of creativity allowed, the degree of responsibility, and the satisfaction of helping others.

Whichever techniques you feel might be right for you, remember that empathy and respect drive people to be their best.

» NEED-BASED THEORIES OF MOTIVATION

Many psychologists agree that people are motivated by their *needs.* Recall from Chapter 1 that in the "scientific management" school of thought in the early 20th century, it was believed that money could satisfy all of a worker's needs. Money was considered to be the main motivator for employees. In today's workplace culture, inner needs are often seen as just as important as external needs, like money. This chapter briefly captures different theories on the needs and motivations of humans in the workplace.

Abraham Maslow's Hierarchy of Needs

An original heavyweight in the field, psychologist Abraham Maslow (1908–1970) developed one of the most influential and well-known theories in human behavior that we can still use today to understand motivation. He believed that most people are motivated to fulfill their needs in a certain order. Before you can bloom into your full potential, you must take these steps of **Maslow's hierarchy of needs** typically in the order that follows.[4] (See Figure 5.3.)

1. **Physiological needs** include necessities for life such as air, food, warmth, and water. These needs are often referred to as primary needs because they are necessary in order to stay alive. After these needs are met, you can move on.
2. **Safety and security needs** include physical safety from harm and the elements, as well as financial security. These are the next most important needs in the hierarchy. They include everything from having a danger-free and orderly way of life to buying health insurance. After meeting these needs, you can move on.
3. **Love and belongingness needs** include acceptance from family or friends. Everyone needs to feel love and affection, and these needs drive people to seek out others for meaningful relationships. Finding companionship and friendship are very important on this level. Then you can move on.

Maslow's hierarchy of needs
Model that shows that people tend to satisfy their needs in a certain order: first, physiological needs; then safety and security, belongingness and love, esteem; and finally, self-actualization.

physiological needs
The most basic level of Maslow's hierarchy of needs; includes the satisfaction of physical needs, including food and shelter.

safety and security needs
Second level of Maslow's hierarchy of needs; includes physical safety from harm and the elements as well as financial security.

love and belongingness needs
Third level of Maslow's hierarchy of needs; includes complete acceptance from family and friends.

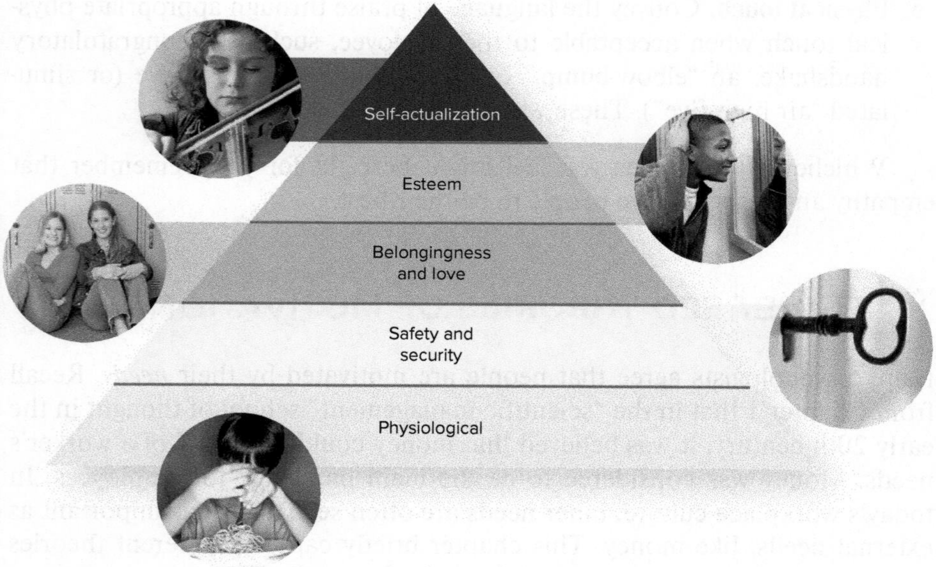

figure 5.3

MASLOW'S HIERARCHY OF NEEDS

Maslow's theory states that people must satisfy basic needs before moving on to higher levels. *At which level do you see yourself right now? Do you see yourself in more than one level at once?*

Source: "Hierarchy of Needs" from *Motivation and Personality*, 3rd ed., by Abraham H. Maslow. Revised by Robert Frager, James Faiman, Cynthia McReynolds, and Ruth Cox. Girl playing violin: Mel Curtis/Getty Images; Two friends sitting against lockers: Andersen Ross/Getty Images; African-American boy checking reflection in mirror: Ken Karp/McGraw Hill; skeleton key in door: Ryan McVay/Photodisc/Getty Images; boy twirling spaghetti: Brooke Fasani/Corbis

4. **Esteem needs** include recognition from peers and colleagues. The development of self-confidence and a healthy self-concept at this level builds self-esteem. At this level you experience some success and a feeling of having achieved something worthwhile. You begin to appreciate yourself. Then you can move on.
5. **Self-actualization** means reaching one's full potential. This is the highest level of the hierarchy. If you reach this level, you will have fulfilled your own inborn potential as a creative, unique person. Maslow believed that not all people would get to this level, but since people are all different, there are different areas in which they might feel self-actualized. Maslow himself made a list of suggestions to increase your self-actualization (see Figure 5.4).

esteem needs
Fourth level of Maslow's hierarchy of needs; includes recognition from peers and colleagues.

self-actualization
Highest level of Maslow's hierarchy of needs; occurs when one has fulfilled his or her potential.

Maslow's theory makes the following assumptions:

1. Needs that are not yet satisfied will motivate or influence a person's behavior.
2. When a need has been satisfied, it will no longer motivate the person's behavior—at least not nearly as strongly.
3. Needs are arranged by order of importance.
4. A need in the hierarchy will not be a motivator until those below it are already satisfied.

- Experience life fully: Be alive and absorbed with what you are doing at the moment.
- Learn to trust your own judgment and feelings in making life choices, such as marriage and career.
- Be honest with yourself and take responsibility for what you do.
- Whenever possible, choose growth rather than safety or security.
- Recognize your defenses and illusions, then work to give them up.
- Even though peak experiences are temporary, keep the aspiration of these moments of self-actualization alive in your everyday thoughts and actions.
- Remember that self-actualization is a continual process; it is never fully achieved.
- Commit yourself to concerns and causes outside yourself, because self-actualization comes more as a byproduct of developing your capacities fully than by the self-focused pursuit of growth itself.

figure 5.4

HOW TO INCREASE YOUR SELF-ACTUALIZATION

Maslow offers several helpful suggestions for finding out what you want and how to get it. *What is holding you back in your progress toward self-actualization?*

Source: Abraham Maslow, *The Further Reaches of Human Nature* (New York: Viking Press, 1971).

REAL WORLD EXAMPLE 5.1

Randall's organization works with the County to provide mental health services to local residents. Recently, one of its largest sources of funding from the state was not renewed, and Randall was told that his job as a mental health technician may not be guaranteed into the future. Randall is finding it increasingly difficult to relax and enjoy leisure time with his family and friends, and the stress is affecting his self-esteem. Using Maslow's hierarchy of needs, we can understand his reduced belongingness and esteem needs as resulting from his need to meet his safety and security needs.

How can Randall's organization help its employees face job loss or uncertainty? According to business leadership expert Robert Tanner, employers must act humanely and maintain open communication, working to create stability so that employees are *as productive as possible* and *less likely to seek jobs elsewhere*.[6]

According to this theory, a starving person might willingly give up the need for self-respect just to stay alive. However, once a person's basic needs have been met, that person is likely to look to higher needs. These higher needs will now motivate the individual to move forward, to move upwards—to achieve the next level.

As straightforward as he makes it seem, applying the principles of Maslow's theory in our own lives can be more complicated. Maslow himself pointed out that what *seems* to be motivating someone *might not be* what really is motivating that person at all.[5] He also pointed out that while his hierarchy of needs applies to humans universally, people are still motivated by very personal and by very culturally specific factors.

But the order and flow within Maslow's hierarchy is not set in stone. A person might move around on the hierarchy ladder, trying to meet several needs at a time. A person may go out of order, for example, if their need for esteem and recognition are more important to them than their need for love and belongingness. In addition, there are cognitive and aesthetic needs—needs for learning and for beauty—that some people possess in great amounts. Maslow agreed that these needs are very important for some people, but admitted that they didn't fit neatly into his "hierarchy of needs."

For workers, an honest self-appraisal will help to better understand what needs have been met and what needs will next motivate behavior. New employees are more likely to be working to meet security and safety needs, for example, while more established senior employees are likely motivated by esteem needs. Those with high needs for belongingness may be less concerned with either paychecks or building esteem for individual accomplishments.

For managers, Maslow's main lesson on motivation is to notice the needs level of employees. When a manager is in touch with the employees' basic needs, he or she can be much more effective in getting employees to perform work tasks at an optimal level. For example, an employee might be at the level of esteem needs. The manager might make positive statements to build the employee's self-esteem; in turn, the employee will feel better about job performance and will work more effectively. In needs theory, people are more interested in the internal or intrinsic factors that make someone perform well.

REAL WORLD EXAMPLE 5.2

Rony had taken many years to get to his current position within the company. Starting in the mail room, Rony had worked his way up the corporate ladder, taking classes and receiving certifications along the way, to ultimately become the head of IT at the company. One day, Rony's corporate bosses held a meeting to tell everyone that the company would be selling itself to a foreign firm because of a major downturn in the economy. After more than 15 years of dedication to the company, Rony suddenly found himself facing the loss of his job. He did his best to identify and look for another, similar high-level position, but he just could not get a toe-hold in the market at the same salary level, or with the responsibilities he'd grown into during his career at the company.

Adding to the pain, Rony re-entered the job market at a tough time of the year, when most employers had already made job offers to new employees. Dejected, but faced with the very real possibility of being jobless, Rony decided to stop looking for work at the high level at which he'd been employed, and wound up taking a position with responsibilities very similar to the entry-level job at which he'd started at his former company more than 15 years earlier. While being conflicted about working below his skill level, the basis for Rony's choice was clear: although he had imagined retiring with his former company, there in that town, he would now be willing to move across town, or even across state, in order to achieve some level of job security—even though it meant a much lower paycheck.

Alderfer's ERG Theory

Another important pioneer in the field, a scholar named Clayton Alderfer (1940–2015), created a theory that is based on Maslow's hierarchy, but with important distinctions. Instead of Maslow's five levels, **ERG theory** has only three areas: existence, relatedness, and growth.

1. *Existence needs* are the needs that have to do with making your way in life in a physical sense. Your physical well-being as a human is the issue.
2. *Relatedness needs* refer to what Maslow called "belongingness" needs and the part of esteem needs that are external, or socially fulfilling.
3. *Growth needs* are the more internal esteem needs that we all have, along with what Maslow called self-actualization.[7]

ERG theory presents three very important differences from Maslow's famous hierarchy. All three should be noted when applying this theory.

First, unlike Maslow's theory that includes the same order of progression for all people, ERG theory explains that the order in which you progress through the three stages can be different for different people. This makes the theory more flexible and more generally useful. Second, some people can even approach these needs steps simultaneously; in other words, some people might be progressing in all three need areas at the same time.

Most important, ERG theory features the **frustration-regression principle**. According to this principle, someone who fails to reach a higher need level will sometimes become frustrated and regress (go back) to a lower need level, and stay there for some time–perhaps forever. For example, someone who has been attempting to fulfill growth needs might decide to settle for just making a living when frustrated in the attempt at career growth.

ERG theory
A modification of Maslow's hierarchy that includes only three needs areas: existence (mostly physical needs); relatedness (needs linked to relationships); and growth (internal esteem needs and self-actualization).

frustration-regression principles
A principle that says that someone who fails to reach a higher need level will sometimes become frustrated and regress (go back) to a lower need level, and stay there for some time—perhaps forever.

manifest needs theory
Developed by David McClelland to show that all people have needs that motivate them in life and on the job. These three needs include power needs, affiliation needs, and achievement needs.

power needs
Desired by individuals who want to control and influence other people.

affiliation needs
Occur in people who want to be accepted and liked by others.

achievement needs
Occur in people who are goal oriented and take personal responsibility for achievements.

Both of these needs theories—Maslow's Hierarchy and Alderfer's ERG Theory—are useful in that they illustrate the importance of workers getting involved with such factors as participative decision making, in which employees have a say in decisions and problem solving; increased worker freedom; and personalized work space. If you are a worker, they help you understand your own development; if you are a manager, they help you ask the correct questions about the needs level of the workers.

McClelland's Manifest Needs Theory

Like Maslow, human relations pioneer David McClelland (1917–1998) believed that all people have certain needs that motivate them, both in life and on the job. Unlike some needs theories, McClelland's **manifest needs theory** isn't a hierarchy. McClelland, a prominent psychology professor during his career, found through years of research that all people have three basic coexisting needs: **power needs**, **affiliation needs** (the need to interact with others), and **achievement needs**. Every person has all three needs, but everyone has them in different amounts and combinations; nearly everyone will feel one need more strongly than the other two needs.[8]

more about...

The Manifest Needs Theory

McClelland's **manifest needs theory** makes no judgment about whether any particular need is better or worse than others; instead, the focus is simply on which needs are the primary sources of motivation in people's lives. McClelland abbreviated the needs as the need for achievement, or nAch; need for affiliation, or nAff; and need for power, or nPow.

Power Needs

When McClelland first started his research on motivation, he saw power as a basically negative force. Later he determined that power, like the other two needs, can be either positive or negative, depending on how it is used. According to McClelland, a manager without a need for power will generally be less effective than one with a strong power need.[9] A person who has a strong need for power wants to control and influence other people. This person is also competitive and wants to win. This type of person also usually likes conflict—even confronting others and being confronted.

Affiliation Needs

Most people need to be with other people, to develop friendships and acquaintances. According to McClelland, some people have this need so strongly that it motivates them to go to work every day. These people often have an intense desire to be accepted and liked by other people. They usually like parties and other social activities, and they tend to join clubs and other groups. McClelland felt that someone with a strong affiliation need will generally *not* make the best manager.[10]

Achievement Needs

A person with a high need for achievement is usually very goal-oriented, has a high energy level, and wants to take personal responsibility for achievements.

REAL WORLD EXAMPLE 5.3

Is becoming an entrepreneur or being your own boss a dream for you? After reading about McClelland's Manifest Needs Theory, it might not surprise you that people with a high need for achievement (nAch) are more likely to become entrepreneurs. And in cultures that promote exploration and reward achievement, entrepreneurship and innovation are more likely to flourish.

Researchers Wu and Dagher conducted research on the relationship between a need for achievement and persistence in starting one's own business. They found that persistence in entrepreneurship, or sticking it out to be successful, is related to need for achievement rather than other needs. So, if your business goal is to become an entrepreneur, the Manifest Needs Theory would advise you to strengthen your "need for achievement" muscle.[13]

This type of person tends to be attracted to careers such as sales and business ownership and likes to have some type of concrete feedback on how much he or she is achieving. If the work doesn't contain enough challenges, he or she may try to find a challenge elsewhere.

more about...

Developing Your Motivational Needs

David McClelland (1917–1998) said that a need is like a muscle; it will develop and grow when it is exercised.

More research has been done on the achievement need than the other two needs. High achievers have been found to differ from low achievers in several ways. People with a high need for achievement usually set goals that are moderately challenging. These goals present a challenge but are not impossible. They are neither too easy nor too difficult. Both high-risk and no-risk situations are seen as a waste of time. A businessperson with a high need for achievement would become successful taking a moderate risk that is more likely to pay off than a high risk that has little chance of success. McClelland believed that successful entrepreneurs are driven more by a high need for achievement than by the profit margin.

High achievers are more likely to credit their successes to their own hard work, ability, talent, and persistence. When they fail, they do not place blame on others, on bad luck, or on fate; they look to their own behavior for an explanation. On the other hand, people with low achievement needs seem to be motivated more by a fear of failure than an expectation of success. They set impossibly high goals or very low, simple goals. They tend to blame their failures on their own lack of ability, on bad luck, or on fate.[11]

Although McClelland did not recommend developing one of these needs and ignoring the other two, recent researchers have found that a high or low need for achievement can become a consistent personality trait. This is generally good news for high achievers who more often excel in school and in their careers, but the news is less happy for low achievers. Low achievers in school are less likely to finish college, maintain a job, or stay married.[12]

According to McClelland, these three manifest needs are not factors that people are simply born with. They are developed through life experiences. If, later in life, you wish to develop more in one of the three areas, you can make that happen. To McClelland, a need is like a muscle; with exercise, it will grow.

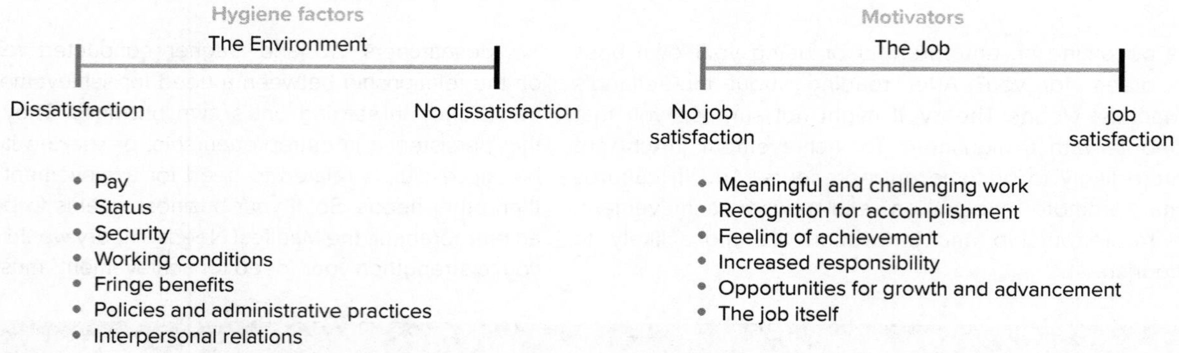

figure 5.5

HERZBERG'S TWO-FACTOR THEORY

Herzberg's Two-Factor Theory

Psychologist Frederick Herzberg (1923–2000) was one of the most influential theorists in business management during his time and is credited with creating the Two-Factor Theory. In his two-factor theory, he described two forces that are often confused with each other. He called them **hygienes** and **motivators**. *Hygienes* are factors connected with a job that make working there better. They are factors that workers don't want to go without. If someone were to take any of them away, workers would be unhappy—even to the point of quitting the job. However, even though people feel that way about them, hygienes—in themselves—do not motivate. They are not what get you up in the morning and out into traffic (see Figure 5.5).

hygienes

(also called "dissatisfiers") The qualities in the workplace that are outside the job itself (examples: company benefits, policies, job security). When these factors are weak or missing, motivation will fall; however, when they are high, motivation will not be strong or long term.

motivators

(also called "satisfiers") The factors in Herzberg's theory that cause real, long-term motivation, usually containing *intrinsic* motivation factors (examples: interesting and challenging tasks, advancement, achievement, growth).

Some examples of hygienes are cafeterias with other amenities, attractive carpeting and furnishings, a good health plan, or good relations with the supervisor. According to Herzberg, factors such as these will keep workers from becoming dissatisfied; for that reason they are also called dissatisfiers. But they *won't* be the factors that make you feel "pumped up" and ready to give the job your all—especially not over a long time period.

The factors on the job that really do motivate workers are called, appropriately, *motivators,* or satisfiers. These are factors that are intrinsic—that is, they are found either within the work itself or within the worker. They include feelings of accomplishment, of worth, of a job well done, or of doing meaningful and interesting work. For example, if an experienced engineer is doing the work that any draftsperson could do, then the pay, the fringe benefits, humane treatment, and pleasant working conditions, although perhaps very real, will not be enough to motivate the engineer. He or she will simply not be getting a sense of meaning or accomplishment from the job. This theory is based on a belief that employees find self-fulfillment in work and are motivated by it.

For motivation to take place, according to Herzberg, *both* the hygienes and the motivators must be used. First, the hygienes have to be in place; then the motivators can take over. If you have meaningful, fulfilling work, but the building where you work is damp and uncomfortable, the motivators won't be as strong as they otherwise would be. You might even quit, if

REAL WORLD EXAMPLE 5.4

Thomas was revved up. He had just traded in his Honda for a sleek but sensible Mercedes-Benz. His job as a food scientist at an international nutrition supplement company had provided him with the means to rent a new apartment in a fun part of town. He worked long hours, but found the working conditions to be acceptable and not too stressful. He also enjoyed some of the formal and informal perks of the job, such as the award-winning cafeteria at the site and the ability to leave early on Fridays. He had settled into a comfortable routine . . . that he slowly started to dread. But why?

Thomas reflected on his own professional growth at the company. He began to feel that the management had not truly recognized his capabilities and that they were slow to recognize his skills or offer him a real path toward a leadership role on the team. When Thomas' immediate supervisor approached him one day and told him, "Thomas, I like you, and I'll help you get *any* job in the company you might want, or in *any* other department that you'd like—but you can't have *my job,*" Thomas read between the lines and saw the ceiling that was being placed over him. Despite his salary and the perks, he knew that his days at the global nutrition supplement company were limited. He would start to look for a new job soon. In Thomas' case, the motivators were not enough to keep his job satisfaction high, even though the hygienes were in place.

you find a job with a more comfortable environment and an equal sense of accomplishment.

Hygienes include a person's desire to avoid unpleasant working conditions in both the physical and the psychological environment. For example, many businesses who lay off workers have found that as morale becomes lower, even employees who were not going to be laid off sometimes decide to resign because the work environment has become too unpleasant.[14]

Herzberg believed that if management cannot make a job more interesting or rewarding, it should be eliminated or automated. According to Herzberg, then, making jobs more challenging and fulfilling is the *only* appropriate approach to meaningful motivation. It remains to be seen how Herzberg's theory will prove out as many former human jobs are mechanized in the current American and world economies. Today, the era of robotics and other technological developments have made the choice to automate jobs much more likely, a condition that will persist as economies change and develop around the world.[15]

Job Enrichment: Hackman and Oldham

In 1980, J. Richard Hackman and Gerg Oldham published their work building on job enrichment concepts.

If your work isn't meaningful, what can be done to change the situation? You could find another position with a different set of tasks–maybe. If you are the manager, you could think about upgrading the job–that is, adding elements to the job that might make it more enjoyable, meaningful, and fulfilling. Upgrading the task, or **job enrichment**, may be the only real way to motivate a previously unmotivated worker for any long period of time.

job enrichment

The upgrading of a job that makes it more interesting, meaningful, or rewarding and provides long-term motivation.

To enrich a job often means complete restructuring of the tasks related to the job, to make them more meaningful and fulfilling–giving the job more

figure 5.6

HACKMAN-OLDHAM JOB ENRICHMENT MODEL

Source: J. Richard Hackman and Greg R. Oldham, *Work Redesign* (Reading, MA: Addison-Wesley Publishing Company, Inc., 1980), p. 90.

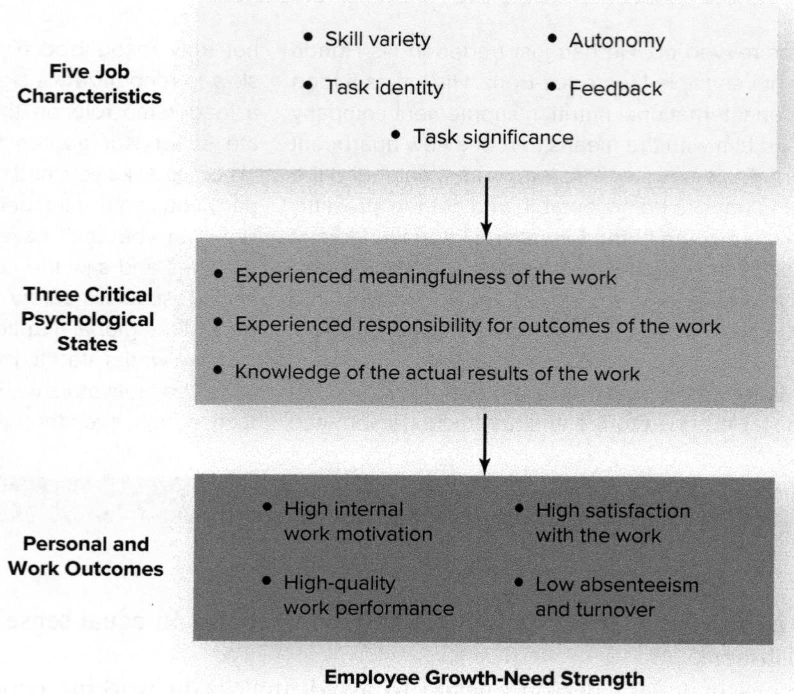

intrinsic motivators. Several factors are necessary for job enrichment to be effective. These are skill variety, task identity, task significance, autonomy, and feedback.[16] Figure 5.6 describes job enrichment in greater detail.

Skill Variety and Task Identity

If you work at a job where you have to use a number of different skills, you are much more likely to be motivated to work hard. You are also more likely to take pride in the job you do. Also, if you are able to start a job and see it through to its completion, the job will seem much more meaningful to you. If you have ever worked at a job on a factory assembly line or in any other situation that calls on only one skill, you probably know how important **skill variety** and **task identity** can be. Those who make career changes often do so because they are looking for a job that is more meaningful to them.

skill variety
The opportunity and ability to use numerous different skills in one's position at work.

task identity
The worker's perception of the meaningfulness of a job, often based upon the worker's permission to start a job and see it through to completion.

Task Significance

Most people are motivated more by a job that seems to make a difference to other people or to the physical environment. If the work directly affects other people's work or lives, the job is said to contain **task significance**. Career choices such as the Peace Corps or AmeriCorps continue to be popular, even with low pay, because of this important quality. One former executive of a large company explained why he had voluntarily quit a high-salaried position. As he put it, "Every product they made could have been dumped into the

task significance
A worker's perception that the task directly affects other people's work or lives.

REAL WORLD EXAMPLE 5.5

Damien is a small business owner who has started a landscaping business. His job is high in skill variety (he oversees all aspects of the business), high in task identity (he sees each job through from beginning to end), somewhat high in task significance (homeowners pride themselves on the appearance of their property), high in autonomy (he is his own boss), and high in feedback (his clients tell him immediately whether or not they are satisfied with his work). After many years working in a cubicle drafting site plans alongside other colleagues doing exactly the same thing, this new business is very motivating, and it is a perfect fit for Damien.

ocean, and humanity would have been improved, not damaged." Although salary had motivated him for several years, the lack of task significance had reduced its motivational strength. Some people who start their own businesses do so because they feel that their own business will allow them to affect others more directly; it is a more task-significant environment.

Autonomy

Autonomy means the freedom to choose one's tasks and methods of work. When workers are given a great deal of autonomy, they feel ownership of the job and of the tasks it involves. They are more likely to feel responsible for—and motivated by—the success or failure of a project. Autonomy can also refer to freedom within timelines. When a worker is given a flexible schedule, with deadlines mostly self-imposed, both job satisfaction and motivation usually increase.

autonomy
Independence, the ability to act and make decisions on one's own without undue interference from management.

Feedback

When a job allows individuals to know how well they are performing, the job is enriched considerably. No matter how much autonomy a worker has, feedback is still essential. Knowing results of one's work can help someone who has some autonomy decide which tasks to emphasize. If a worker has performed poorly on a project, for example, he or she can take steps to improve performance the next time such a task is attempted.

By enriching jobs with these five elements, motivation can be increased greatly. The manager who is redesigning jobs should look carefully at the worker's talents, needs, abilities, and desires. All the job characteristics listed here will not be very motivating if the match between the job and the worker is poor.[17] Job enrichment is essential. If your workplace is one where workers have a voice in major decisions, you don't need to be a manager to help design jobs that are enriched, making them more motivating.

A New Motivational Strategy: Gamification

There has been a growing trend in workplace motivation recently known as *gamification*. The term was coined by computer programmer Nick Pelling around 2002, with the movement gaining popularity around 2010.[18]

Gamification refers to the use of mechanics and design techniques found in video games to motivate and engage employees in work tasks. Game developer and researcher Jane McGonigal points out that "in today's society, computer and video games are fulfilling genuine human needs that the real world is currently unable to satisfy."[19] Many companies–including Nike, DirecTV, IBM, NTT Data, and more–have begun using gamification techniques to motivate employees.[20] Advocates of gamification, such as McGonigal, believe that the use of gamification techniques can make work more fulfilling for employees, as well as help enact real, positive personal and social changes in the real world.

One real-world example of gamification in the workplace is Target's setup for their cashiers. The gamification system within Target's cash register program rates the cashiers based on transaction speed and accuracy, giving scores in "red," "yellow," and "green"–red being a low score and green being a high score.[21] This is used as a means of positive reinforcement for the cashiers, as seeing immediate feedback on one's performance (as we see often in video games) is more motivating than delayed feedback. This allows a person to continually improve performance.

Jane McGonigal argues that humans crave and enjoy work that feels meaningful to us, and that games give us opportunities to do work within them that feels more rewarding and meaningful than the work we encounter in our daily lives.[22] She and other gamification advocates want to see these aspects of games applied to everyday life–in the workplace, and beyond. It is believed that this will lead to happier and more fulfilled lives for everyone.

This rising trend has led to the following questions: *How much time do people spend playing video games? What motivates them to do so? What elements of the game(s) would be helpful for motivating people in the workplace, as well? Is there a dark side to gamifying work?* Researchers and game developers continue to find answers to these questions and are using the results of such research to find new and effective ways to increase workplace motivation.[23]

» BEHAVIOR-BASED THEORIES OF MOTIVATION

Expectancy Theory

expectancy theory

Developed by Victor Vroom to explain human behavior in terms of people's goals, choices, and the expectation that goals will be reached.

Expectancy theory brings several classic human relations ideas together, and different versions of this theory have become popular over the years. Victor Vroom originally developed expectancy theory in the 1960s to explain human behavior in terms of people's goals and choices and the expectation that goals will be reached.[24] Its main concepts are expectancy, instrumentality, and valence.

expectancy

In *expectancy theory*, the likelihood that if a person tried, the result would be better performance.

Expectancy describes the likelihood that if a person tries to perform better, that will really be the result. For example, Carla can easily see that if she takes shorter breaks and works harder, a great deal more work will get done. Vroom would say that Carla thus has high expectancy.

REAL WORLD EXAMPLE 5.6

"Sometimes a jelly doughnut or a handshake is as effective as a monetary bonus," says author and healthcare worker Hina Raheel. Expectancy theory reminds us that any reward system put into place must keep in mind the *individuality of the employees.* People work harder for motivators that are of more value to them.

Raheel finds in her work that some of the intrinsic motivators that are powerful enough to motivate specific individuals include:

- a manager spending time with employees;
- managers providing employees resources to expand their knowledge, skills, and abilities;
- establishing goals collaboratively that are realistic, meaningful, and attainable;
- showing appreciation for work done;
- providing variety to work tasks;
- encouraging self-evaluation of work;
- allowing employees to make more choices about work tasks;
- facilitating team work;
- encouraging continuous improvement in work tasks; and
- showing employees the significance of the work in which they engage.[25]

Instrumentality refers to the likelihood that something good (or bad) will come from an increase in effort. If Carla can also see that her supervisor will reward her with a bonus when her output is greater, Vroom would say that her instrumentality is high. High instrumentality also implies trust in a company and its managers. Can an employee be confident that the company will actually deliver on a promised reward?

Valence is the value a person places on a reward. Valence has a great deal to do with each person's values. A reward with no value to the worker will not be motivating.

more about...

Victor Vroom (1932–), a professor in the School of Management at Yale University, introduced expectancy theory in his book *Work and Motivation.* He has also written *Leadership and Decision Making* and *The New Leadership: Managing Participation in Organizations.*

instrumentality
The likelihood that something good (or bad) will come from an increase in effort.

valence
The value a person places on a reward.

Reinforcement Theory and Behavior Modification

The ideas of reinforcement theory have become popular in businesses today, with the work of psychologist B. F. Skinner as the basis for most of these ideas. **Reinforcement theory** explains human behavior in terms of the results–both good and bad–that have occurred under similar conditions in the past. When something good happens as the result of what you did, you are more likely to repeat that behavior. When you do something and there is no result, or an undesirable result, you will probably not repeat what you did.[26] This process of changing behavior because of a reward, or a lack of reward, is called **behavior modification**.

This concept is not Skinner's alone. An earlier psychologist, Edward Thorndike, tested what he called the Law of Effect more than a hundred years ago, in 1898. To quote Thorndike, "Responses that produce a satisfying effect in a particular situation become more likely to occur again in that situation,

reinforcement theory
Explains human behavior in terms of repetition. Behavior that is rewarded enough times will be repeated, whereas behavior that repeatedly receives no reward will probably discontinue.

behavior modification
The process of changing behavior because of a reward or lack of a reward.

REAL WORLD EXAMPLE 5.7

David worked in sales at an insurance company based in Cody, Wyoming. For years, he tried to get transferred to a larger metropolitan area. He loved big cities and was tired of the wide open spaces of Wyoming and nearby states. He was ready for a change. Finally, he landed a job in Los Angeles. He was happy with his new job and excited about living in a city with so much to offer. The first sales contest the Los Angeles company held offered the prize of a week-long fishing trip to Colorado. Needless to say, David wasn't motivated to win. He never cared for fishing and he wasn't interested in leaving Los Angeles. Although both the expectancy and the instrumentality seemed to be in place, the valence was very low. A prize as simple as a family ticket to an amusement park or tickets to a concert would have involved a higher level of valence for this urban-loving salesperson.

and responses that produce a discomforting effect become less likely to occur again in that situation."[27] In Real World Example 5.8, Janie was getting reinforced for her good performance. Management author and professor Michael LeBoeuf calls this "the greatest management principle in the world," or to summarize in his words: "Things that get rewarded get done."[28]

B. F. Skinner believed that you can help shape and mold people without making them feel that their freedom and dignity are threatened.[29] The method consists of positive reinforcement–reward the behavior that you like, and ignore the behavior that you don't like. Punishment can be very effective in changing someone's behavior, but this theory teaches that punishment has so many negative side effects that it will usually backfire on the manager. Positive reinforcement can be just as effective as negative reinforcement, and it has fewer unwanted side effects.

more about...

B. F. Skinner (1904–1990) was a behavioral psychologist who specialized in behavior modification. His ideas on positive reinforcement can be applied to reward and punishment systems within organizations. He is considered one of the most influential psychologists to date.

A manager trying to motivate employees should use sincere and frequent praise, letters of commendation, and other forms of recognition. To be effective, rewards must be given as soon as the desired behavior has happened. Even negative comments, if a manager must use them, can be reinforcing when tactfully worded and told to an employee in a timely way.

reinforcers
Incentives such as awards, bonuses, promotions, gifts, and even compliments.

Examples of effective **reinforcers** (or incentives) overlap considerably with examples of extrinsic rewards, since they are essentially the same thing. Examples include bonuses, awards, time off, praise, better office space, public posting of performance ratings, promotions, gifts or trips, and impressive titles.

Goal Setting

goal setting
Employees set their own goals.

To make reinforcers or incentives more effective, the employees involved should have the opportunity for **goal setting**. Telling people to *do their best* is not as effective in reaching higher performance levels as setting specific goals

REAL WORLD EXAMPLE 5.8

Janie, a bicycle delivery person, is told by her boss every time she makes a fast and efficient delivery, "You're doing a great job; keep it up." The more often those words are spoken, the more high-quality work she performs. Then her boss leaves and is replaced by a manager who doesn't praise Janie when she does a good job. After a few weeks, Janie's performance is only average.

that are moderately difficult. Goals should be challenging, but not impossible to attain. Organizations can increase their employees' commitment to goals when they follow these four suggestions:

1. Have employees participate in the goal-setting process.
2. Make goals challenging but attainable, specific, and attractive.
3. Provide feedback on how the employees are doing in meeting the goals.
4. Reward employees for reaching their goals.[30]

Reinforcement, Values, and Self-Esteem

Self-esteem is basic to the success of a behavioral modification program of any kind. Much of what the reinforcer is doing is improving the feelings of value and worth that the employee has–or perhaps hasn't–felt before. If you are the reinforcer, be sure to make the praise and recognition sincere. Employees can see through shallow reinforcers that suggest, "I'm doing this because I'm supposed to, not because I care." Also, be sure to clearly identify what you are reinforcing.

One supervisor would periodically tell each of his workers, "You're a heck of a worker." That type of praise is too general to be reinforcing. Soon the employees came to distrust the supervisor's sincerity because his comments did very little to build their self worth, and the comments gave no information on which of the employees' behaviors were being praised–employees did not know what to continue doing or discontinue doing on the job.

Choosing the right type of reward is important, too. Just as valence is important in expectancy theory, reinforcement theory requires giving rewards that are valuable to the person getting them. As in some of the other theories, there must be a direct cause and effect between the reward and the action it is rewarding for that value to be effective.

Perhaps you have heard some of the criticisms of behavior modification: some people see it as unfeeling and inhumane because it manipulates people into doing what the reinforcer wants them to do; others see it as bribery.

THE POWER OF A COMPLIMENT

A sincere and specific compliment to an employee for a job well done can motivate him or her immensely. *How can positive reinforcement help motivate employees?*

Caiaimage/Paul Bradbury/Getty Images

REAL WORLD EXAMPLE 5.9

Researchers Wei and Yazdanifard have found that many organizations are successfully using positive reinforcement to increase work output. Companies including the United States Postal Service, the Ritz-Carlton Hotel Company, and Google (Alphabet Inc.), use positive reinforcement with their employees, most often through *extrinsic* motivators such as bonus pay for performance, added fringe benefits, chances for promotions, job security, and more freedom in the office.

Google, considered by *Fortune* to be top among the best companies to work for in the United States, also motivated employees with free cafeteria food, child care on site, health care, laundry services, shuttles to work, sports facilities, added paid holidays, and even foreign language lessons.

Many organizations will also use *intrinsic* motivators with their employees, such as acknowledgment for work done well, delegation of duties, giving more responsibility or authority, and verbal praise. The researchers in this study remind organizations to consider cultural factors such as race or ethnicity, age, education level, and gender when selecting and implementing reinforcements to motivate behavior.[31]

But rather than seeing it as manipulation or bribery, we should consider it just for what it is: *a reward or recognition for effort or a job well done.*

» MOTIVATION AND SELF-ESTEEM

As studies of motivational theories show, the desire to feel better about yourself is a main motivator in the workplace. In the same way, you are also motivated *not* to perform tasks that threaten your self-esteem. This attempt to maintain self-esteem on the job is important in understanding your motivation to do a task at all.

The role you play at work is probably a basic part of your self-concept. In other words, the way you feel about yourself on the job is a very important part of the way you feel about yourself overall. In Chapter 2 you learned about the importance of self-efficacy to self-esteem. Recall that self-efficacy is your feeling that you are competent enough to succeed in specific tasks and in life.

Let's say that you are new on the job in a company where you know absolutely nobody. How likely are you to ask other people for help? The answer to that question will depend in large part on how high your self-esteem level is. When self-esteem is low, asking for help may make you feel dependent or incompetent.

Self-Esteem and Job Performance

There are two more ways that self-esteem ties in with overall performance on the job. First, if the job calls for creativity in decision making, low self-esteem may keep an individual from making risky decisions. Mediocre decisions might be made instead of exciting and challenging ones. Second, a person with low self-esteem may perform at exactly the level where others expect performance to be, so as not to threaten others' values.[32] This is another side of the self-fulfilling prophecy that you studied earlier.

When your self-esteem is stable, you can throw yourself heartily into your work. When your self-esteem is healthy, you will be higher on Maslow's hierarchy—maybe even working near level five, self-actualization. You will feel good about asking for what you want, and you will find it easier to visualize the results that can come to a truly motivated person.[33] High self-esteem can be the greatest motivator of all.

Perhaps now you can explain the lack of motivation in Miller, whose story you read about at the beginning of this chapter. His good feelings about his new work were threatened by the supervisor who yelled at him and didn't take time to communicate with him properly. Also, the extrinsic reward of money wasn't enough of a motivator to keep him on the job for a long time. McClelland, Maslow, and Alderfer might all say that Miller's needs were not being fulfilled, though Maslow or Alderfer might point out that as soon as his basic or existence needs were met, Miller was no longer motivated by the same needs. Skinner might say that the reinforcer was poorly chosen for the response that management wanted from Miller. Vroom would say that pay, as a valence, was simply too weak.

All of these theories can be used to discover a different aspect of motivation. No single theory explains motivation completely, but all of them together can help you learn how to motivate yourself and those who work for you. If you can see the relationship of motivation to self-esteem, nearly any motivational problem can be better understood.

« STRATEGIES FOR SUCCESS

Strategy 5.1 Applying McClelland's Theory

1. Take a look at your needs.
2. Take a look at what you want in life.
3. Take a look at how the need areas apply in the workplace.

How can you apply McClelland's needs theory to daily life? First, take a look at your own needs profile. Usually, if you examine your daydreams, you will find a pattern that centers on one or two of the three need areas: power, achievement, or affiliation.

1. **Take a look at your needs.** Ask each other in class what you would do if you became instant billionaires. Some might say that they would buy a small island and rule over it (power needs); some might say that they would throw frequent parties (affiliation needs). Others might say that they would train themselves in some way to discover the cure for cancer, to prevent pandemics, or to end world hunger or poverty (achievement needs). Endless variations on answers are possible, but they usually reveal people's general needs areas.
2. **Take a look at what you want in life.** When you know what your needs profile is, take a look at your current job or the career you want. Does your career choice fit your needs? For example, if you are training to be a sales representative but are weak in the achievement need, it might be good either to take a new look at your goals or begin exercising the need area that fits better with your career choice.

3. **Take a look at how the need areas apply in the workplace.** If you are a manager, take a look at how the work you supervise fits the needs of each of the employees you supervise. For example, are you assigning heavy responsibilities to an employee with a very weak power or achievement need? Are you asking an employee with high affiliation needs to work alone? Sensitivity to employee needs can help everyone become more motivated. Higher motivation at work creates a better work environment for everyone, and this spills over into personal life motivation and satisfaction.

STRATEGIES FOR SUCCESS

Strategy 5.2 Changing Your Behavior

1. Identify a behavior or bad habit you want to change.
2. Take small steps to reach your goal.
3. Find a small reward to motivate you.
4. Reward yourself to reinforce the desired behavior.

Is there a particular behavior you have, a bad habit perhaps, that you would like to change? Using Skinner's principles, you can set up a behavior modification program for yourself.

1. **Identify a behavior or bad habit you want to change.** Think of a behavior that you would like to change. Let's say you don't like talking to people at work or in class, but you don't like your reputation as being standoffish, either, so you would like to become friendlier with your co-workers.
2. **Take small steps to reach your goal.** Using Skinner's idea of *shaping,* or taking small steps gradually toward the goal you are trying to reach, you can reward yourself along the way until you have completed your goal. Set up a series of small steps that you are willing to take, which can lead you toward your eventual goal.
3. **Find a small reward to motivate you.** Before you begin, figure out what small rewards you will give yourself for meeting these goals. What rewards would motivate you? A hot fudge sundae? Leaving the dirty dishes until tomorrow? Watching the televised playoff game after work? When you have chosen your small reward, you can begin your plan.
4. **Reward yourself to reinforce the desired behavior.** Let's say you plan to smile at two people the first day. You do so successfully. Now reward yourself! The second day, you smile at two new people in addition to the two from yesterday. Reward yourself. The third day, say, "Hi, how are you?" to one new person. Reward yourself again. See how easy this can be? (Just watch out for those extra calories from all those hot fudge sundaes! Maybe you can go jogging with your new friends from work to burn them off.)

CHAPTER FIVE SUMMARY

Chapter Summary by Learning Objectives

LO 5-1 Define motivation. Motivation is the willingness to move toward reaching a goal. Motivation can be intrinsic (internal) or extrinsic (external). Motivation can be kept high through an understanding of needs and behavior reinforcement.

LO 5-2 **Explain need-based theories of motivation.** Of the theories based on needs, Maslow's is the earliest. The five needs in his theory are based on a hierarchy. A need will not motivate behavior until the one just before it has been satisfied. Alderfer's ERG theory has only three needs: existence, relatedness, and growth. McClelland's needs theory teaches that we all have needs for achievement, power, and affiliation, but in different amounts. Herzberg's two-factor theory shows the differences between hygienes (dissatisfiers) and motivators (satisfiers). Only the motivators make people look forward to going to work and keep them satisfied over the long term. The hygienes must exist, too, or workers will become dissatisfied, perhaps to the point of quitting. Hackman and Oldham teach that job enrichment is the only constructive method a manager can use to motivate an otherwise unmotivated worker. To qualify as being enriched, a job must include skill variety, task identity, task significance, and feedback. Gamification strategies provide motivation by structuring some tasks to be similar to video games.

LO 5-3 **Explain behavior-based theories of motivation.** Two behavior-based theories are expectancy theory and behavior modification. Vroom's expectancy theory brings several ideas together and shows three forces that affect the strength of motivation in any person: instrumentality, valence, and expectancy. All three of these areas must be strong. If even one is weak or nonexistent, motivational strength will lessen greatly. Skinner's reinforcement and behavior modification theory is technically a behavior-based theory of motivation, like Vroom's. However, Skinner's approach also involves the use of specific and sincere praise, as a form of reinforcement. Skinner's theory deals with the nature of rewards and their effect on continued performance of behaviors that can bring them about.

LO 5-4 **Discuss the relationship between self-esteem and motivation.** When self-esteem is weak, motivation to work productively will often be affected negatively. Conversely, when self-esteem—especially self-efficacy—is strong, motivation is usually stronger.

key terms

achievement needs 124
affiliation needs 124
autonomy 129
behavior modification 131
ERG theory 123
esteem needs 121
expectancy 130
expectancy theory 130
extrinsic motivators 118
frustration-regression principle 123
goal setting 132
hygienes (dissatisfiers) 126
instrumentality 131
intrinsic motivators or intrinsic rewards 118
job enrichment 127
love and belongingness needs 120
manifest needs theory 124
Maslow's hierarchy of needs 120

morale 116
motivation 116
motivators (satisfiers) 126
organizational climate 116
physiological needs 120
power needs 124
reinforcement theory 131
reinforcers 132
safety and security needs 120
self-actualization 121
skill variety 128
task identity 128
task significance 128
valence 131

review questions

1. Which of the motivation theories that you've just learned about best explains why Miller's experience in the opening story ends the way it does? Why?
2. What can employees and managers do to improve an organizational climate? How is the corporate culture related to organizational climate and to morale? How does morale affect the workplace?
3. What is a needs theory? Considering Maslow's hierarchy of needs, where do you see yourself on this hierarchy? What do you need in order to become self-actualized?
4. Which of the three needs in McClelland's manifest needs theory (power, affiliation, or achievement), motivates you the most? Give examples from your own life.
5. Do you identify the hygienes—or dissatisfiers—in Herzberg's chart as hygienes in your own motivation? If not, why not? Is money a motivator or a hygiene for you? Whatever your answer, do you think it has always been that way for you? Will it likely be that way later in your life?
6. Which motivates you more, intrinsic rewards or extrinsic rewards? When you imagine getting an "A" in your Human Relations class, are you more motivated by the tangible rewards of a higher GPA or by the self-satisfaction of a job well done? Explain.
7. Why does positive reinforcement seem to work? Can you think of examples in your life where positive reinforcement was used successfully? Unsuccessfully?
8. Overall, which motivation theory do you think best explains motivation? Why?

critical thinking questions

1. Some people believe that trying to find a way to motivate others is somewhat unethical or manipulative. What are your views? Has there been a time when you have felt this was happening to you?

2. Alderfer's ERG theory proposes that when we feel frustrated by an inability to meet a need, we may regress to a lower-level need. If you are leading a work team, would it be important to have your team members motivated by growth rather than regression? Would you expect this difference in motivation to make a difference in their effort, morale, or overall efficiency? What could you do to reduce frustration that might lead to regression among team members?
3. Consider the growing trend of gamification in the workplace, as discussed earlier in the chapter. How can gamification techniques relate to the rest of the concepts discussed in the chapter? How does it work as a form of job enrichment? Do you think it helps fulfill needs, as Jane McGonigal claims it does? If so, under which needs theory do you think it best applies? How does it relate to the behavior-based theories of motivation?

working it out 5.1

WHAT CAREER MOTIVATES YOU?

School-to-Work Connection: Interpersonal Skills

Purpose: In this exercise, you will be picking a career that interests you and doing research to find out more information about it.

Instructions: Think about what it is that motivated you to select this career. Interview someone in the field. Summarize your findings using the following outline.

1. *The nature of the work.* What are the duties and responsibilities on a day-to-day basis?
2. *Working conditions.* Is the working environment pleasant or unpleasant, low-key or high-pressure?
3. *Job entry requirements.* What kind of education and training are required to break into this occupational area?
4. *Potential earnings.* What are the entry-level salaries, and how much can you hope to earn if you are successful in this field?
5. *Opportunities for advancement.* How do you move up in this field? Are there adequate opportunities for promotion and advancement?
6. *Intrinsic job satisfactions.* What can you gain in the way of personal satisfaction from this job?
7. *Future outlook.* How is supply and demand projected to shape up in the future for this occupational area?

Source: Wayne Weiten, Margaret Loyd, and Robin Lashley, *Psychology Applied to Modern Life,* 3rd ed. (Pacific Grove, CA: Brooks/Cole Publishing, 1991, Wadsworth, Inc.)

working it out 5.2

IS EDUCATION A GOOD INVESTMENT? YES!

School-to-Work Connection: Information

Purpose: One of the reasons students give for their motivation in attending college is a better job prospect. But does college really pay off? Yes, according to the U.S. Bureau of Labor. Education pays in higher earnings and lower unemployment rates.

The federal government regularly analyzes statistics on education and employment. It is important to note that these are overall statistics. They will vary by region and will change as the national economy changes. Rather than seeing this chart as a guarantee of your future earnings, look for general trends in the relationship between education and income.

Instructions: Compute the difference in weekly average salary you are likely to make after completing your current education activity (e.g., associate's degree, bachelor's degree), with the average weekly salary for a high school graduate (or less, if you did not complete high school). Compute the difference in weekly salary over a year. How much does this add up to over 10 years? Now compare the average unemployment rate for your current education activity with the unemployment rate for a high school graduate (or less, if you did not complete high school). What is the percent difference?

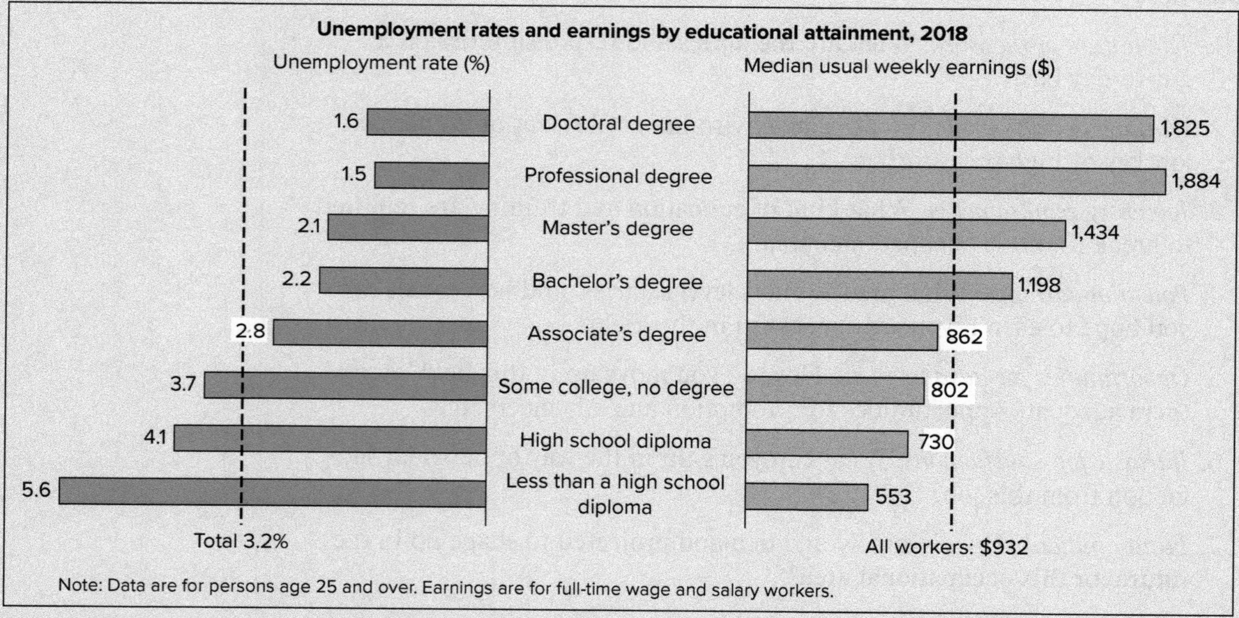

Source: Bureau of Labor Statistics, "Employment Projections," https://www.bls.gov/emp/chart-unemployment-earnings-education.htm (data retrieved March 2020).

working it out 5.3

PUTTING IT ALL TOGETHER: INTEGRATING PART 1

School-to-Work Connection: Information and Thinking Skills

Think about what you have learned in Part One of this textbook. How would you explain why some occupations are growing faster than others? How do you think the major theories of motivation (need-based and behavior-based theories) affect people's choice of occupations? Do these particular occupations interest you?

The U.S. Department of Labor, through its Bureau of Labor Statistics, maintains up-to-date information on specific careers with the future outlook for these careers. Check their website at www.bls.gov/careeroutlook for more information.

OCCUPATION	GROWTH RATE, 2018–2028 (projected)	2018 MEDIAN PAY
Solar Photovoltaic Installers	63%	$42,680 per year
Wind Turbine Service Technicians	57%	$54,370 per year
Home Health Aides	37%	$24,200 per year
Personal Care Aides	36%	$24,020 per year
Occupational Therapy Assistants	33%	$60,220 per year
Information Security Analysts	32%	$98,350 per year
Physician Assistants	31%	$108,610 per year
Statisticians	31%	$87,780 per year
Nurse Practitioners	28%	$107,030 per year
Speech-Language Pathologists	27%	$77,510 per year
Physical Therapist Assistants	27%	$58,040 per year
Genetic Counselors	27%	$80,370 per year
Mathematicians	26%	$101,900 per year
Operations Research Analysts	26%	$83,390 per year
Software Developers, Applications	26%	$103,620 per year
Forest Fire Inspectors and Prevention Specialists	24%	$39,600 per year
Health Specialties Teachers, Postsecondary	23%	$97,370 per year
Phlebotomists	23%	$34,480 per year
Physical Therapist Aides	23%	$26,240 per year
Medical Assistants	23%	$33,610 per year

Source: Bureau of Labor Statistics, *Occupational Outlook Handbook,* updated September 4, 2019. @ https://www.bls.gov/ooh/fastest-growing.htm.

working it out 5.4

THE PUZZLE OF MOTIVATION

Watch the TED Talk by author, attorney, political speechwriter, and career analyst Dan Pink, titled "The Puzzle of Motivation," and then answer the following questions.

1. How would you have solved "the candle problem" seen in the video, before seeing the solution?
2. Why do rewards narrow our results and restrict our possibilities, according to the author? What is his evidence?
3. What types of tasks are best to offer rewards, according to the speaker?
4. If the "highest rewards led to the worst performance," then how do we get better performance in the workplace?
5. Define *intrinsic motivation* and *autonomy* in your own words. Why are they important to productivity? Describe a time in your own life when these have motivated you.

The video can be found here: www.ciphr.com/advice/12-ted-talks-to-inspire-and-motivate.

Maria Chen, Classroom Aide

Maria Chen was working as an educational aide for a third-grade class while taking a human relations course at night. She was especially intrigued by the chapter in her textbook on motivation, since she had quite a number of underachievers in the class. She spent a couple of hours each day working with this small group of students. Working with them was frustrating, since nothing she said or did seemed to motivate them.

For example, Stacy sat like a stone all during their small group time. Jamal and Mike squirmed and giggled with each other every time she tried to work with them. Ayako complained that everything was "too hard." Quinn just looked out the window, yawning with boredom. Recess, however, was a different story; they each had a different routine. Stacy always wanted to eat her lunch early, during morning recess. By lunch time she was asking the other children for their leftover food. Ayako clung to Maria's hand during the entire recess, pleading with Maria to stay with her.

Jamal and Mike tried hard almost every day to get into the soccer game with a big group of kids, but usually to no avail. Quinn showed off his skills at baseball, calling out the whole time, "Ms. Chen! Ms. Chen! Look at me!"

"This is so weird," thought Maria one day, "it's almost like the hierarchy of needs model. They all seem to want—well, that is to *need*—something different. I wonder if Maslow could lead me to some motivational tools to use with these kids."

Case Study Questions

1. Is Maria right? Does it seem that Stacy, Ayako, Quinn, Mike, and Jamal are on different levels of Maslow's hierarchy of needs? On what level would you place each of them?
2. How can Maria use this theory to motivate the children in their school work?
3. Compare Maslow's needs model with McClelland's. Which of McClelland's needs seems to be important for each child?

case study 5.2

What's the Matter with These People?

When Ron took over as supervisor at Midway Machine Works, he had no idea what was facing him. He had inherited a group of workers who were producing at a capacity that he estimated was at least 50 percent below what was reasonable compared to the industry standard. Ron decided on a systematic interviewing procedure in which he would ask the same questions each week of every employee he had. His questions included, "Do you feel your co-workers are working as effectively and as hard as they could?" and "Do you feel *you* are working up to your capabilities?"

Ron was surprised at the consistency of the answers. Nearly all the workers expressed the feeling that "Nobody cares anyway, why should we work hard when nobody else cares?" Also, nearly all the workers believed that those around them didn't work as hard as they easily could have. Fewer of those interviewed said such things about themselves, but all of them acknowledged that, whatever else could be said about their performance, they could be putting forth considerably more energy without wearing themselves out.

Ron was shaking his head in discouragement one morning when Tyler walked into his office. Tyler was the leader of a group in the plating department. "You want us to work harder?" Tyler asked. "Why don't you try making what we do more important? I have a two-year degree in computer-assisted drafting and design. But what am I doing? Working at the same plating machine for almost the whole eight hours when I'm here. Of course, not everybody down there has my background, but they all have the same kind of problem with this place that I have: they don't think anybody appreciates their abilities—or even gives them any credit for having any brains at all."

"I really appreciate your being frank and open with me, Tyler," Ron replied. "If what you're saying is really the problem, it could explain a whole lot of things about this place."

Ron spent the next two days asking the workers some new questions about how they felt their abilities were being used at Midway. He found Tyler's message was accurate. Nearly every employee he spoke with expressed a frustration with being "underutilized."

"Well," Ron reflected on the way home from work, "I think I know what the problem is. My next step is to figure out how to start fixing it."

Case Study Questions

1. If you were Ron, where would you begin in creating a program to increase motivation at Midway Machine Works?
2. Analyze the motivation problems at Midway Machine Works using Skinner's behavior modification theory and Vroom's expectancy theory.
3. Knowing what you now know about employee motivation, how would you describe the organizational climate at Midway? What about the corporate culture? The morale? What would you do to improve each of these?

PART TWO

human relations in groups

People spend a good deal of time interacting with others one-on-one and in groups. Every day brings a series of interactions, from the morning when you greet your family or roommates, during class or work time, until evening. Communication skills and relationship skills are key strengths for human relations.

Part Two takes a look at human relations in groups. Chapter 6 examines ways in which communication can be directed toward better understanding between sender and receiver. Chapter 7 considers communication in group settings. In Chapter 8 we examine the concept of EI (emotional intelligence) in terms of its role in interpersonal relationships.

CHAPTER SIX

COMMUNICATION AND HUMAN RELATIONS

LEARNING OBJECTIVES

After studying this chapter, you will be able to:

LO 6-1 Explain the crucial role of communication at work and what occurs when miscommunications happen.

LO 6-2 Compare and contrast successful and unsuccessful listening skills.

LO 6-3 Explain the importance of timing with regard to messages.

LO 6-4 Examine the role of nonverbal communication.

LO 6-5 Identify the functions of nonverbal communication.

LO 6-6 Outline strategies for communication within an organization.

LO 6-7 Explain the importance of intercultural communication in today's professional world.

STRATEGIES FOR SUCCESS

Strategy 6.1 Become a Better Listener

Strategy 6.2 Practice High-Context Communication

In the Workplace: Caroline's Communication Setback

SITUATION

Image Source, all rights reserved.

Caroline had been working for nearly 10 years at a company that trained security guards and then contracted the trained security staff to work at outside companies. Her job as an administrative assistant to the company's president meant that she often had to decide on the spot when people arrived at her office to see the president whether she should make an appointment for them for a later time or rearrange the president's schedule so the president could see them immediately.

As she hurried to her office on a particular Monday morning, she was already stressed. She had left her home early to arrive at work early, since this week's work was going to be heavy and she had a lot of preparation to do. On the way to work, she had run over a nail and had gotten a flat tire. Taking care of the flat tire had taken much of the morning. So now, instead of being early, she was late to work.

As she came around the corner in sight of her office, she saw a commotion in progress. One of the security guard trainers, Derrick, seemed to be arguing with one of the newest guards, William, in front of her office. Their voices were loud and they both seemed agitated.

When Caroline saw them, she acted quickly to take control of the situation. She interpreted William's behavior as out of control, since she had known Derrick for years and knew that he was calm under pressure.

"William!" she shouted. "Get out! We cannot hire guards who start arguments with our training staff or our supervisors, you are finished here!" William looked stunned as he walked away.

"What are you doing?" asked Derrick. "William was here to give us an update on the chemical spill and evacuation at his location that occurred overnight. It's been on the news all morning, haven't you heard about it?"

DISCOVERY

"Oh, no!" exclaimed Caroline. "That is not what I thought was going on at all. I didn't hear anything about the chemical spill! If I leave right now, I may be able to catch William before he leaves," she said as she headed to the building exit.

THINK ABOUT IT

Have you ever misinterpreted something that you observed? Have you ever been misunderstood? What were the results?

REAL WORLD EXAMPLE 6.1

Miscommunication and ineffective communication can come in many forms. One of those is a mismatch between words and nonverbal behaviors.

The IT manager at a large company announced that any time employees had problems with computer equipment or software, if the rest of her staff was unavailable she would work with them directly and immediately. But when they did call her, she sounded annoyed and often took an hour or two to get to the staff member's office.

With her first statement about being open and available, compared with her actual behavior when employees do approach her, the manager has sent two messages: one of openness, another of irritation. She has made the false assumption that only the first message was communicated to staff members, when in fact both were very clear—and contradictory. Which message is coming through to employees more strongly?

» COMMUNICATION AND MISCOMMUNICATION

Effective communication is essential in the workplace. In the opening story, Caroline *assumed* that she understood what she saw and heard. Making false assumptions about what is being communicated can be a crucial problem in miscommunication, and this can damage personal relationships and business effectiveness. Many factors play into effective or ineffective communication, as we will see in this chapter. (See Figure 6.1.)

False assumptions such as Caroline's often lie at the heart of miscommunication. How many times have you noticed that people were sending you messages without being aware of it? Do you believe you may do the same?

As discussed in Chapter 1, communication can be defined as the giving and receiving of ideas, feelings, and information among people. Note the words *and receiving.* Communication includes listening as well as speaking. In fact, good listening skills and effective communication are critical to success in work. This chapter examines the process of successful communication. Why is this important at work? Without effective communication, no workplace can function properly. Miscommunication not only strains relationships and wastes time, but it also wastes billions of dollars a year in American industry.

figure 6.1

FACTORS OF COMMUNICATION

Several factors go into communication. Major factors include attitudes and values, conscious and unconscious communication, and timing. *Who do you think plays a more important role in effective communication—the sender or the receiver?*

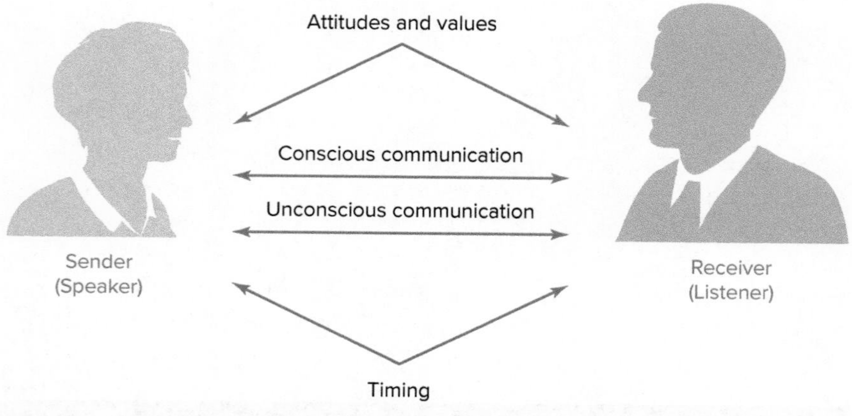

REAL WORLD EXAMPLE 6.2

In 2018, Facebook's CEO, Mark Zuckerberg, took out full page ads in 10 British and American newspapers to clarify some of the details of the Cambridge Analytica data privacy scandal that had made news headlines around the world. In this data privacy leak, information for as many as 50 million users was sold to data mining and marketing operations, in violation of Facebook's privacy rules. Shocking to most people was that Facebook had known about the issue since 2014 and had decided to keep quiet about it.

As many critics noted, the full-page ads did not actually use the word "sorry" or sound like an apology. After many silent days, Zuckerberg did eventually apologize during a television interview. Individual users were also notified that their data was "improperly obtained."

Facebook remains the most widely used social media site in the world, and Facebook now owns other popular social media applications including Instagram and WhatsApp. Facebook's reputation, however, has been damaged by the lack of communication with the public and with users about the privacy leaks, and Facebook is now faced with ongoing multiple lawsuits, governmental investigations, a user boycott campaign, and a drop in share price that cost the organization nearly $50 billion. Effective communication could have prevented some of these negative effects of the data breach.

The importance of communication in the business world cannot be overstated. In Real World Example 6.2, a CEO of a major corporation was not transparent or forthcoming in communicating his company's actions, and his regret, over a major incident. The timing and tone of his message fell short, causing irreparable damage to his professional reputation and that of his company, making them the frequent target of late-night comedians in addition to the lawsuits and investigations.

The ability to communicate well with others in your professional role is perhaps the most important universal job skill for employees. Everything else about a specific job can be taught. This means that being able to speak well and to listen well are probably the most important assets you—or anyone—can bring to a job.

Online Communication

Connecting with others quickly, and more often, is the hallmark of online communication. In our society we are able to freely share our ideas about culture and business through e-mail and instant messaging apps. Online communication is an indispensable business tool for both internal and external communication.

This type of electronic messaging allows users to communicate with one another from nearly any location, at any hour, eliminating the barriers of time and distance (though cultural or other barriers may persist!). And online communication can encourage more flexibility for workers, who may use communications technology when working in the field, or may have the option of "telecommuting" from home periodically during the workweek.

The use of e-mail and social messaging apps to share ideas, feelings, and information has likewise grown tremendously in recent years. Ideas that were

Epic Communication Failures

1. **Nepal Tragedy:** In 2018, a crash landing of an airline carrying 71 passengers resulted in the deaths of 49 people in the nation of Nepal. While this accident is still under investigation, the cause seems to be confusion in the cockpit between the crew and the air traffic controllers on the ground regarding which runway to use in landing.
2. **The Worst Airline Disaster in Aviation History:** The worst airline disaster in modern aviation history occurred in Tenerife, Spain in 1977. Two passenger jets collided on a runway after the cockpit crew in one of the planes misunderstood the air traffic controller's communications about take-off. The accident resulted in the deaths of 583 people.
3. **Lost in Space:** Somewhere in space, the remains of a $125 million spacecraft may be orbiting, due to a miscommunication among experts in aeronautics. In 1998, NASA launched the Mars Climate Orbiter whose mission was to study the atmosphere of Mars. But two teams working on the project, NASA and Lockheed, were using different measurement units (NASA using the metric system and Lockheed using U.S. customary units). The project failed due to a miscommunication among their two systems.

once exchanged in person or in small groups are now sent digitally to co-workers, friends, and family members via computers and wireless devices. Watch the length in e-mail messages you are sending, however, so that you do not get a response back of "tl;dr" (too long; didn't read).

But the same things that make online communication so popular, such as the speed and efficiency, can sometimes become problematic for the sender or receiver. For example, a note may be sent too soon, before it is checked for mistakes, and lead to unnecessary confusion and delays. Another potential problem is that the personalization and "tone" of messages can get lost in brief e-mail or text messages, which can cause misunderstandings and time lost in clearing up confusion. The tone of online messages can be misunderstood accidentally. Using ALL CAPS (all capital letters), for example, can be misunderstood as shouting. Also, technical glitches and human error can delay messages, or reroute them to unintended recipients. Miscues in online communication can lead to major and minor misunderstandings and can cost a person or company valuable time and resources.

When using electronic communication, a great strategy for success is to maintain *self-discipline* in your responses. This self-discipline includes reading, waiting—and re-reading—e-mails or text messages rather than just typing out a response and sending it right away. It requires a professional mindset, and sharp focus on the topic at hand. Likewise, successful online business communication requires that we remain professional, and try to reserve our personal opinions. Ask yourself if the message you are ready to send is professional enough in tone and content to be forwarded to anyone in the company or to the general public, knowing that messages are often forwarded. And finally, we must have the self-discipline to decide when and how to convey information: do the people with whom you're communicating all require the exact same information? Does everyone have the appropriate information that he or she needs to complete his or her job? And does everyone need to be cc'd (copied on the message), or should the message be more targeted?

» LISTENING—AND HOW IT CAN FAIL

What do you really want when you communicate with someone else at work? You might need a question answered or someone to confirm that a job is being done correctly. Maybe you just want to be heard. This tremendous need to be listened to is a primary need among humans, and it is crucial in human relations at work. Most people have a very strong need to have others hear them, understand them, and process the information they receive. This need is so strong that when listening is purposely withheld, the speaker's self-esteem can suffer.

Everyone needs to know they can be heard. You might be amazed at the results you can get once you become tuned in to other people and their needs. The need to be a good listener to others is often ignored by people who consider themselves good communicators.

In the *Harvard Business Review,* author Steve Glaveski said, "Our brains quickly forget what we don't use," which translates to forgetting about 75 percent or more of what we hear after a week.[1] This idea is widely shared in the corporate world and educational settings, and memory strategies are now receiving attention to combat what is known as "the forgetting curve." But what makes people miss so much of what they hear?

more about...

Research on memory and forgetting has been going on for more than 135 years. The "**Ebbinghaus Curve of Forgetting,**" or the "Ebbinghaus Curve," developed by Herman Ebbinghaus (1850–1909), shows that we remember less than half of what we've heard after an hour and about one-fourth after two months. Recent studies have replicated these original findings.

Source: H. E. Ebbinghaus, *Memory: A Contribution to Experimental Psychology* (H. A. Ruger and C. E. Bussenius, Trans.) (New York: Dover, 1964). (From original work published 1885.) See also: Jaap Murre and Joeri Dros. Replication and Analysis of Ebbinghaus' Forgetting Curve. (2015) PloS one. 10. e0120644. 10.1371/journal.pone.0120644.

Selective Listening

There are some legitimate reasons for poor listening. For instance, in modern society everyone is constantly bombarded with messages. No one could possibly give full attention to every message, so many people practice **selective listening**, which is when we deliberately choose what we want to hear. In a personal environment with more demands on our attention, the problem is even greater. For example, picture a home with young children chattering and constantly trying to get attention; or a busy office with phones ringing, people talking, and keyboards clattering; or a crowded subway with traffic and city noise all around you. In these circumstances, people often become selective listeners by default. The main cause of selective listening is **information overload**. Another form of information overload has increasingly come from our own fast-paced tech-driven culture. For example, with a person's smartphone now

selective listening
The type of listening that happens when a listener deliberately chooses what he or she wants to pay attention to.

information overload
The type of listening that happens when a listener is overwhelmed with incoming information and has to decide which information will be processed and remembered; this is a common cause of poor listening skills.

REAL WORLD EXAMPLE 6.3

Norberto was explaining to Heather, for what seemed the hundredth time, how to input work hours on the new online time clock. Meanwhile, Heather seemed to be mentally somewhere else.

"Are you listening to me?" Norberto asked bluntly. "No," she replied, "if I'm honest, I was thinking of the next thing I was going to say to you to defend myself when you ask me what part I don't understand."

serving as the conduit for all calls, e-mails, texts, social media platforms, calendar alerts, news, information, and more, it can be difficult to choose when, and on what, to focus one's attention. Sometimes better listening may simply be a matter of taking a break from technology–by going "offline" and refocusing on face-to-face communication. With information overload, we find ourselves overwhelmed with incoming information and must decide which information will be processed and remembered, and this can lead to poor listening skills.

In addition to turning off technology in order to listen more effectively, some of us may need to remember to turn off our own responses while the other person is still talking. *Rearranging the letters of the word "silent" gives us the word "listen."* Take time to hear the other person out in order to reduce miscommunication.

Many other reasons for poor listening come from bad communication habits. For example, when many people assume a subject will be too difficult for them to understand, they fail to listen. If they had listened, they may have seen how clear and understandable the subject was, or they could have narrowed down the difficulty with the subject. The opposite often happens, too. A listener might reject a speaker or a message because the message seems too basic and beneath the listener's level of knowledge. In either case, the message is lost.

When you are in a group, listening to a single speaker, you can easily allow your mind to wander. If you are attending a business meeting or conference, the success of the meeting can be destroyed by this habit. One reason for this tendency is that most humans have a capacity for listening at a speed that far exceeds the ability of the fastest speaker. You *could* listen and comprehend up to 500 words per minute; the average public speaker travels through a message at about 125 words per minute.[2] How you spend that extra time and energy often determines your effectiveness as a listener. If you can keep your focus on the speaker and use the free time to take notes or think about what is being said, you will hear more and remember more.

FAILURE TO COMMUNICATE

Actions on the part of the listener can contribute to miscommunication. *What are some of the causes of poor listening?*

wavebreakmedia/Shutterstock

REAL WORLD EXAMPLE 6.4

Angelo was proud of being offered the first job he applied for after finishing his college degree. He was also proud of his efficient communication style and hoped to show his older co-workers how to modernize their communication styles, too. The efficiency in communication that Angelo was encouraging consisted of sending e-mail messages in the same format and spelling that he used in texting his friends.

Unfortunately for Angelo, clients and co-workers soon complained to his supervisor that his e-mails (written as a phone text) seemed too casual, informal, and hard to understand. After a long conversation with his supervisor, Angelo began to agree that not everyone appreciated his informal style and that employees' communication format should be consistent across the company. He agreed to work with a mentor to learn to make his communication sound more professional at work and to keep his texting, or TXT, just for personal communications.

Tuning Out

Some people may refuse to listen to co-workers or other people due to **prejudice**; such people may elevate their bias to the point where they refuse to listen to someone from the other gender, or to people from different ethnic backgrounds or social classes, or from different parts of the world. Prejudice can be more subtle than these examples, though, and it can also overlap with envy or resentment. Some people won't listen to a speaker who seems to act a little superior or a bit too perfect. These perceptions can, of course, be flat-out wrong. Others, as in the Real World Example 6.3, may tune out others when they feel defensive. Successful business communicators should observe their personal listening habits to ensure that they are not hampered by personal biases or prejudice. Prejudice will be covered more fully in Chapter 14.

prejudice
The outcome of prejudging a person. Prejudice in communication is the unwillingness to listen to members of groups the listener believes are inferior, such as other ethnic groups or women; it can also take more subtle forms; how you feel as a result of the stereotypes you believe in.

Red flag words and expressions are those that bring an immediate reaction (usually negative) from the listener, generally because of strong beliefs on the subject, or because the words bring up strong emotions. Some red flag words have implied meanings beyond their literal meaning. Words such as *terrorist* or *economic recession* or *pandemic* might begin a flood of emotions that would prevent some people from hearing the rest of your message. The word *sex* might get similar results, although the emotions may be different and more varied.[3]

red flag words
Words that bring an immediate emotional response (usually negative) from the listener, generally because of strong beliefs on the subject.

In choosing their words, speakers may not consider the power of language itself to be important. Even though many of us learned as children that "sticks and stones may break my bones, but words can never hurt me," words, in fact, can be hurtful. Not just red flag words, but the message content itself can have real impacts on how a message is received. Civility, respect, and common courtesy are much more likely to result in effective communication. Language that sounds disrespectful reduces trust and damages relationships. This can damage the internal workings of a business and external business dealings. In thinking about some of the reasons that people "tune out" a message, language used in a message is one reason.

People do not hear what their co-workers really say for a variety of reasons. In addition to those we have already discussed, another major reason for tuning out messages is poor listening habits. Listening expert Anthony Allesandra says that from childhood, most people have been taught that talking requires energy, attention, and organization, but that listening is a passive, compliant behavior. Starting from kindergarten, children in Western society are taught to be assertive and to express themselves effectively. Until recently, though, little has been done to teach what Dr. Allesandra calls **active listening**, which is listening with greater concentration, less tolerance for distractions, and more feedback to the speaker.[4]

active listening
Listening with greater concentration, less tolerance for distractions, and more feedback to the speaker.

To be an active listener, first, pay attention. Listen for the words being spoken and the cues you gain from tone, facial expressions, eye contact, and body language. Wait for the speaker to complete a thought without interrupting or talking over the top of other speakers. Repeat back, or summarize, or paraphrase what you have heard to make sure you understand. Ask questions. Make eye contact (but do not overdo this by staring). Avoid offering solutions unless you are asked. Avoid being judgmental, keep an open mind. Be patient, do not fill in pauses or rush the speaker. Give nonverbal and verbal cues to show you are following the message. Think of active listening as the opposite of passive hearing.

When you improve your listening skills, as you can learn more about in Strategy for Success 6.1 you will find that you learn more effectively. You will also gain more speakers' respect as someone who understands their messages and cares enough to actively listen.

» THE TIMING OF MESSAGES

Many other factors can explain poor communication. Some are psychological, and others depend on the listening situation and circumstances. Timing can be a major factor when a message becomes distorted and misunderstood.

TIMING IS EVERYTHING
Good communication depends on making sure that your audience is listening. *How can you make sure that you are communicating your ideas to a receptive listener?*
Erik Isakson/Blend Images LLC

Emotional Timing

Emotional timing refers to the emotional readiness of the listener to hear a message. Sometimes a message gets to the receiver when the mood is inappropriate. "Time talks," wrote anthropologist Edward Hall in *The Silent Language*.[5] Have you ever received a phone call in the middle of the night? People who hear the phone ring at 2:00 a.m. may feel dread before picking up the phone. "The message must be urgent," they think, "otherwise the phone wouldn't ring at this hour."

REAL WORLD EXAMPLE 6.5

Alyssa had just presented her proposal for the new summer roll-out to her supervisor and the other managers. This proposal had taken months to put together, and she was extremely nervous. After she finished, the managers thanked her and moved on to another meeting item. She felt deflated, and thought their response was not appropriate and not enough. In the sense of "relevance timing," it was.[6] This could create further miscommunication if she feels (right or wrong) that the managers disliked something she said, or she had done a poor job in delivering the proposal, or they thought the talk was not important enough to mention.

The amount of time you take to return calls also communicates a message. For example, when a manager fails to answer a message until three days later, the employee who left the message may feel that the manager is either inefficient or is showing off power or status. This situation is not universal. As mentioned in Chapter 4, people in different cultures maintain different attitudes toward time. Americans sometimes forget this and make false assumptions when dealing with people from another culture.

Situational Timing

Situational timing refers to the listener's situation when a message is received. Privacy is usually a key element. For example, most people wouldn't want to discuss intimate details of their lives in a crowded bus or subway. If two people are enjoying an emotional reunion, they will probably put off the more intimate parts of the meeting until they are alone. Often, communication that would be totally appropriate in one situation is out of place in another. Because of this, a listener usually can't fully hear the message unless the situation is appropriate.

Bad situational timing can also ruin an otherwise good business undertaking. For example, a crowded elevator would be a poor setting for introducing an important new idea to your boss. Your idea would require careful and focused listening that your boss would not be able to give in an elevator.

Relevance Timing

Relevance timing is similar to situational timing. It simply means that communication should fit the other topics being discussed. If a corporate manager in a weekly planning meeting veers from the listed agenda items to talk about company landscaping updates, the relevance will be lost. If an important topic is dismissed, relevance timing is affected.

more about...

Filtering works both ways. It reflects both what a person decides to *hear* and what he or she decides to *say.* In communicating to others, be sure that your filtering is appropriate and that you are not sharing too much or too little.

REAL WORLD EXAMPLE 6.6

Jacob's performance review was not positive. His supervisor tried to soften the negative evaluation statements by finding some positive things to say, while maintaining the facts about the negatives. In truth, she was preparing to place him on a performance improvement plan. If his job performance did not improve, he was at risk of being removed from his job. Without realizing it, she was filtering her outgoing message.

Jacob filtered out the negative statements about his performance review to such an extent that he did not process them. When his office mate asked him how the evaluation meeting went, he said (and believed) it was "just fine."

Filtering

filtering

A method listeners use to *hear only what they want to hear,* which may result in failing to receive messages correctly.

When listeners engage in **filtering**, they may fail to receive messages correctly because they are *hearing only what they want to hear.* Sometimes the listener wants something to be true so badly that he or she interprets the message to make it true. Filtering occurs with speakers and with listeners.

» COMMUNICATING WITHOUT WORDS

nonverbals

Ways of communicating without speaking, such as gestures, body language, and facial expressions.

Nonverbal communication is also related to communication skills. Much of what people say is expressed by **nonverbals**—which are ways of communicating without speaking, such as gestures, body language, and facial expressions—rather than words. Next time you attend a class, either in person or an online video conference format, look around the classroom to see if you can interpret the nonverbal communication around you. Notice the way your fellow students dress, the way they look at each other and the instructor, and the amount of interest they seem to have in the course. These factors send messages that can be read by nearly anyone around them.

In the Real World Example 6.7, note the nonverbal cues that Kiran picked up on as she was assessing her own performance. Even though she hadn't yet received any written or verbal comments on her ideas, she was convinced that what she'd presented had been well-received. But how could she know? Through her reading of nonverbal behaviors and gestures that her team members exhibited as she spoke, the responses seemed clear. Had she been less prepared, or given a poor presentation, nonverbal responses to her would have been notably different. Have you ever found yourself encouraged, or discouraged, by nonverbal cues directed at you? What did you perceive, and what was the outcome?

REAL WORLD EXAMPLE 6.7

Kiran was excited. She had just finished presenting the latest design module to her software development team, which today included team leaders and a senior designer. She found herself smiling as the group concluded its discussion and everyone went back to their desks. Kiran felt the presentation and subsequent Q & A discussion had gone well.

Since starting in her new job six months earlier, Kiran had studied the communication style and "culture" of her new office environment, and had worked tirelessly to learn all she could about the design module she'd been assigned to create. Now that she'd shared her design and ideas with her colleagues, she felt a certain satisfaction. Well, she hadn't *actually spoken* with any of her colleagues in the brief moments since the presentation ended, but she still *knew* it had been received well. For example, she had seen the senior engineer nod vigorously when she reached her important conclusions (which he was known to do when he was pleased), and she had seen several of her colleagues smile broadly and give her the *real* thumbs up—not the fake one—as she drew to a close.

When she called her mother later that night to share the good news, her mother asked what kind of feedback she had received—what had they said about her presentation that showed her they valued her ideas? "Well, mom, they didn't actually say anything. I can't quite explain . . . I just know it. Everyone paid such close attention, and you could tell by the looks on their faces as I was talking, and their nods and smiles. I'll probably get some written feedback tomorrow, but I'm feeling real good about it, mom!"

» FUNCTIONS OF NONVERBAL MESSAGES

What is the purpose of nonverbal communication? Basically, nonverbal messages reflect the *relationship* between speaker and listener. Nonverbal messages can reinforce, contradict, or substitute for verbal language. These messages can regulate the flow of a conversation or influence others. Nonverbal messages:

1. **Show the Speaker's Attitudes and Emotions**

   The words you choose can say a great deal about the way you feel. However, nonverbal signals in this area tend to be both more powerful and more honest. If a speaker's nonverbal signals disagree with the words being said, which do you believe? Which *should* you believe? Both questions have the same answer–the nonverbal ones.

   Understand your feelings and emotions. They will show themselves when you communicate with others, since much of what you communicate is done unconsciously. People often communicate feelings and opinions to others without any awareness they are doing so. And sometimes, people will communicate feelings and opinions that they didn't even consciously realize exist. These feelings may be buried somewhere beneath the consciousness, but can appear clearly in nonverbal signals. When you communicate unconsciously, your *internal climate*–the way you feel within yourself–is likely to give you away. Self-esteem is one key

REAL WORLD EXAMPLE 6.8

In her telemarketing sales training, Hua was told to actually smile while talking to customers on the phone. She was encouraged to keep a mirror at her desk so that she could practice smiling while preparing to make a call. Can a smile come through in a phone conversation? Your voice conveys your emotions—angry, happy, bored, frustrated, and so on; and your attitudes toward the conversation. Smiling and feeling relaxed on the phone comes through to the person at the other end of the conversation.

to internal climate. If you are feeling bad about yourself, it will show. If you are feeling good about yourself, that too will show. If you have other issues on your mind, your lack of complete attention could get in the way of real communication.

2. **Convey Meaning**

   Nonverbal gestures can be very meaningful and brutally honest. When a gladiator lost in the Roman arena, a thumbs down from the emperor signaled his demise. In sports like baseball, entire plays are scripted through brief nonverbal gestures.

3. **Clarify Messages Between and Among People**

   When used together with *verbal* communication, **nonverbal communication** allows you to understand and interpret meaning in context. **Context** is a point of reference, a place from which to begin.

   Have you ever had to ask for directions in an unfamiliar city? If the person were to give you only verbal signals, without offering any nonverbal cues like pointing and gesturing "that way" or "left over there around the corner," your brain might not fully process the directions, and you might even feel slighted by the direction-giver. You may be more likely to get the directions wrong. When a direction-giver points the way using gestures, along with an adequate verbal explanation, the two-way communication should be more successful.

nonverbal communication

Communication that allows you to understand and interpret meaning in context.

context

A point of reference (or a place from which to begin) when communicating.

4. **Show the Speaker's Reactions to the Listener**

   Watch someone walk down a hallway, greeting people along the way. You might be surprised at how many different ways there are of saying things as simple as "Hi" or "How are you?" Although the words are the same, variations in facial expression, tone and pitch of the voice, amount of time spent in the greeting, and eye contact are all likely to show at least some differences in emotional reaction. These differences include variations in acceptance, approval, and comfort level.

   If you were to say, "Nice to meet you" to someone in a fairly neutral tone of voice, that statement could easily be taken as something casual. However, try speaking more enthusiastically while adding a big smile to the same person while saying, "Nice to meet you!" The difference in intensity

REAL WORLD EXAMPLE 6.9

Shirley walked into the office slowly, looking at the floor, speaking softly in a low tone. What message do her behaviors send? Suppose this is not typical behavior for her. What do these nonverbal behaviors say about her current state of mind? Most of us would come to consistent conclusions, based on our shared cultural understanding of nonverbal communication within our own societies. In Shirley's case, a family member had recently passed away, and the difference from her usual behavior was noticeable to everyone who knew her.

alone would be quite obvious, and the message would be interpreted differently by the receiver. **Intensity**, the degree to which you show serious concentration or emotion, is another dimension of nonverbal communication.[7]

intensity
The degree to which an individual shows serious concentration or emotion; another dimension of nonverbal communication.

Over the years, many people have commented that the English language should have a least a dozen different words to express various types and intensities of love. For example, "I love chocolate" certainly means something totally different from "I love my mother." Because of gaps such as this in the English language, nonverbal expressions are often necessary to help communicate feelings more completely. Is it possible to express nonverbals over text messages or e-mail? Yes, with the use of all capital letters versus lowercase letters, punctuation marks, and emoticons (emotional expressions made from keyboard combinations, such as an equal sign and open or closed parentheses to show a smile or frown) or an emoji (small pictures depicting emotional expressions inserted into the message). Emojis are a very popular way of expressing emotion, with more than 3,000 emojis widely used today.

Nonverbal Messages about Self-Esteem

Nonverbal communication can also signal your self-esteem level. Does this mean you should try to act in ways that cover up low self-esteem? When attempting to make a good first impression, such a tactic might be useful. Many experts believe that while we usually act the way we feel, we can also feel the way we act. Also, nonverbal communication that signals an apparent low regard for self can trigger reactions in other people that might actually reduce your self-regard. When your self-regard and confidence are high, this will be evident in your nonverbal behavior. You will be listened to more effectively, and the overall communication process will be more effective.

Thomas Barwick/Getty Images

Gestures and Their Meanings

What about gestures–the movements you make with your arms, legs, hands, fingers, feet, face, and shoulders? By observing gestures, you can tell a great deal about how open or closed people are in their attitudes. Gestures can also indicate the true leader of a group, how open a person is to physical contact, and more.[8] Another way of looking at gestures is to divide them into four categories. Every gesture you use falls into one of these four categories:

illustrators
Gestures that are used to clarify a point, such as pointing when giving directions.

regulators
Gestures that are used to control the flow of communication; eye contact is a common type of regulator.

displays
Gestures that are used like nonverbal punctuation marks, such as pounding your fist on the table.

emblems
Gestures that are used in a specific manner because they have a specific meaning, usually one understood by both sender and receiver; the peace sign is an example.

- **Illustrators** are gestures people use to clarify a point they might be making. Pointing the way down the street when giving directions, and pounding a fist to emphasize a point, are both illustrators.
- **Regulators** are used to control the flow of communication. When you raise your hand in class to get the instructor's attention, you are using a regulator. Perhaps you have seen someone point to someone else who hasn't been allowed to speak. With proper eye contact, the message is: "Please let this person say something." Regulators can also include raised eyebrows, head nods, or any other nonverbal indications that say, "Please let me (or this other person) into–or out of–this discussion."
- **Displays** are gestures that are used like nonverbal punctuation marks. These are gestures that show the emotions going on inside a person, and they effectively reveal just how strongly people mean what they say. Clenched fists displayed during a committee meeting would likely indicate emotional tension. Displays usually augment another type of nonverbal behavior, such as facial expressions and general body movements. If someone is saying, "Yes, that's a pretty good idea," yet the displays don't agree (arms are crossed, the speaker is frowning), the listener will likely not believe what the speaker is saying.
- **Emblems** are gestures used in a specific manner because they have a specific meaning, usually one understood by both sender and receiver. The peace sign used by war protesters in the 1960s would be one example. Another would be the "O" formed by the thumb and forefinger, which means (in mainstream American culture), "Everything is okay." Several obscene gestures would also fall into this category of emblems, as well. Remember, though, that emblems are culture-specific: an emblem we assume is universal can easily mean something quite different in another culture. This is especially important to remember when traveling and doing business in different parts of the world; many embarrassing blunders have occurred when travelers did not know the local meanings of nonverbal gestures.[9] In Figure 6.2, see if you can determine what the gestures indicate.

Distance Between Speakers

distancing
The distance of physical space you maintain between other people and yourself.

Another area of nonverbal communication is called *proxemics,* or **distancing**, which can be defined as the distance of physical space that you maintain between other people and yourself. Most people carry around a *bubble of space,* or several bubbles. These are illustrated in Figure 6.3. The first bubble is reserved for intimate relationships, such as with mates, romantic partners,

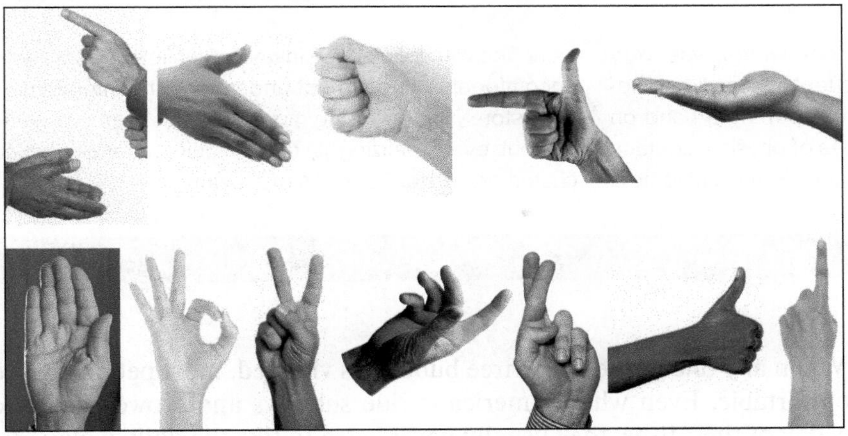

figure 6.2

WHAT DO THESE GESTURES MEAN?

Look at these gestures. *How would you interpret each gesture?*

Source: John Stewart and Carole Logan, *Together: Communicating Interpersonally* (New York: McGraw-Hill, 1993), p. 167.
JGI/Blend Images LLC, Di Studio/Shutterstock, Mark Dierker/McGraw Hill, Ingram Publishing/Alamy Stock Photo, George Doyle/Stockbyte/Getty Images, JGI/Blend Images LLC, ILYA AKINSHIN/Shutterstock, Grant Terry/Shutterstock, Ingram Publishing/Alamy Stock Photo, Barbara Penoyar/Getty Images, Matthias G. Ziegler/Shutterstock, geargodz/123RF

and children. It extends from physical contact out to 18 inches or so. The next, from about 18 inches out to 4 feet, is the area saved for close friends. The third bubble, from about 4 to 12 feet, is used for communicating with business contacts and casual acquaintances. The term "social distancing" in relation to safety measures taken during the coronavirus pandemic is usually set at 6 feet, falling within the social distance space bubble. The last one, from 12 feet on out, is often used for the general public. The amount of space a person takes also signals power, not just the type of familiarity or relationship between people. Note in business settings how much larger the CEO's office is than an entry-level employee, for example.[10]

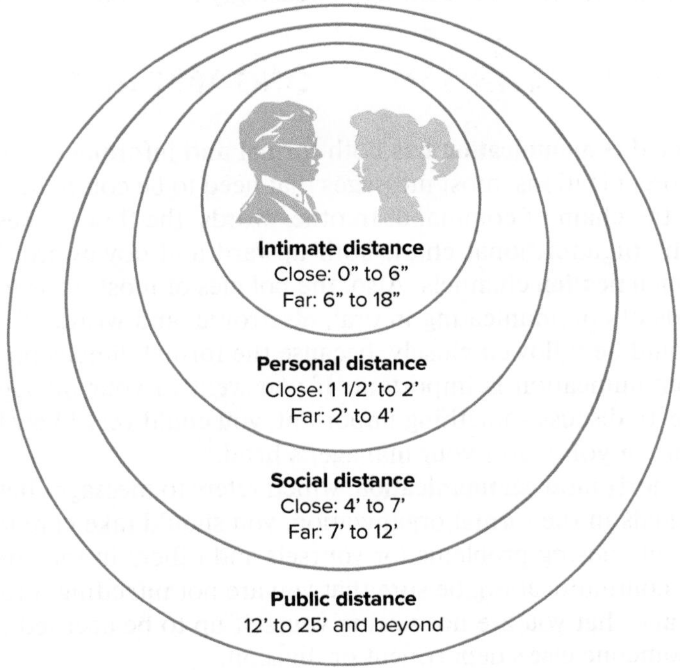

figure 6.3

THE ZONES OF DISTANCING

Everyone has different zones to communicate with different people in their lives. These four zones—intimate, personal, social, and public—can vary, depending on the person and the culture. *Which is the most common zone for you?*

REAL WORLD EXAMPLE 6.10

In a small bookstore, one of the co-owners was very friendly and tried to make customers feel at ease by standing very close to them and sometimes putting a hand on their arm or making other similar types of physical contact. Repeat customers were offered a hug. Some customers were fine with this "space invasion" while others were very uncomfortable and did not understand the intentions. The bookstore may be losing more business than it is gaining, without even realizing it, due to unintentionally violating customers' distance zones of proximity.

When any one of the first three bubbles is violated, most people feel very uncomfortable. Even when Americans ride subways and crowded elevators every day of their lives, they usually never learn to like the daily violations of their personal space. Next time you are in a crowded public vehicle or elevator, notice your fellow passengers' facial expressions. On most of their faces you will see looks of resignation, or else they are showing an unemotional mask–which both show that they have accepted this invasion of their space as necessary, although they don't like it.

This distancing issue varies geographically. In some cultures, being very close to another person is much more acceptable than in the United States or in many European cultures. In most Middle Eastern countries, two business colleagues may typically stand about 18 inches from each other while talking. Most people in East Asian and Southeast Asian societies also feel more comfortable at closer distances with strangers than most Americans do. As the world becomes more and more an international community, learning the norms of other societies is becoming increasingly important.

» COMMUNICATING IN AN ORGANIZATION

organizational communication

Oral and written communication in an organization. It has formal and informal dimensions and travels vertically and horizontally.

vertical communication

Messages that are communicated according to an organization's chain of command by flowing both upward and downward.

horizontal communication

Messages that are communicated between you and your equals in the formal organization.

Organizational communication has both formal and informal dimensions. In traditional organizations, most messages that need to be communicated must go through the chain of command. In other words, the flow of messages has to follow the organizational chart, both upward and downward. These are **vertical communication** channels. Also, the policies of most firms include formal methods of communicating in oral, electronic, and written form. These policies should be followed closely, because the formal dimension of organizational communication is important. If you went to your manager's boss, for example, to discuss something important, you could very likely be seen as jumping rank or going over your manager's head.[11]

Even in **horizontal communication**, which refers to messages between you and your equals in the formal organization, you should take care to communicate without causing problems for yourself and others in the company. In this type of communication, be sure that you are not intruding into someone else's area, and that you are not setting yourself up to be accused of causing trouble in someone else's department or division.

REAL WORLD EXAMPLE 6.11

Berta could not understand why Susan was not completing the report for their joint report to the Board in a couple of days. She had been asking for days, and Susan kept putting her off. Finally, Berta confronted Susan. Susan told her that the reason she had not written the report was because Berta was not in her department, Susan's supervisor had not asked her to work on it, and it was not a priority for her department. Susan had only agreed to work on it as a favor to Berta. Berta was flabbergasted: she thought they were good enough friends that Susan would just do the report to help her out. Now Berta had to scramble to get it done before the Board meeting. Berta had made the mistake of assigning work in another department where she did not have authority.

Grapevines

Probably even more important than a formal organization is the informal organization within it. When communication takes place in an informal context, the rules are less formal but still very real. Every company that has employees contains an informal organization. The informal organization is made up of friendships and friendly relationships that establish themselves naturally in any situation. You may have joined groups like this when you were in elementary school or middle school; the more exclusive ones were known informally as cliques. This can continue through high school and college right into the workplace. Informal groups may be something humans never outgrow.

The informal organization is made up of small groups based on particular interests, beliefs, and activities. These groups tend to communicate among themselves and with each other through a network known as the **grapevine**. The grapevine is not exactly the same thing as the **rumor mill**, which is a gossip network that produces mostly false information. When the informal organization communicates *incomplete* but somewhat accurate information, it is called the grapevine.[12]

grapevine

A network within the informal organization that communicates incomplete, but usually somewhat accurate information.

rumor mill

A gossip network that produces mostly false information.

You can learn a great deal by staying in touch with the grapevine. One of the most important characteristics of grapevines is that they are often selective: everyone doesn't always get all of the information, and everyone doesn't always get the same information. If you are a supervisor, the grapevine might leave you out of touch with information about your employees. If you are an employee, you might not hear what is happening in the world of the managers.

When companies have very poor formal lines of communication, the informal grapevine becomes even more important. Employees often complain that if it weren't for the grapevine, they would have no idea about what was happening. Grapevines are also usually slanted in one way or another in the beliefs on which they are based. Often, a grapevine will tend to be pro-employee, pro-manager, or in some other way biased, especially when other forms of communication are poor.[13] It is wise, then, to keep these

COMMUNICATION IN INFORMAL NETWORKS

The rumor mill and grapevine are two types of networking you may find in a work environment. *What can you learn by joining either network?*

Frank and Helena/Getty Images

more about...

Hooked Up to the Grapevine

By forming friendships with people on various formal levels of your firm, you can get an expanded version of the grapevine and you might be able to get a more accurate picture of what is really happening in your organization. Be clear on the difference between the grapevine and rumor mill or office gossip, however, as these can contain greatly distorted information.

biases in mind when listening to a grapevine; this will help you determine what to believe.

Speaking Effectively

You may be asked to speak to a small or large group as part of your work assignment. When speaking, miscommunication can occur as a result of your rate of speech. A slow rate of speech may signal sadness, seriousness, or confusion on a topic. A fast rate may signal urgency, excitement, nervousness, anger, or other high emotion. A fast rate may be more difficult for your audience to understand. Complex ideas are more easily understood when presented more slowly, and pauses allow the audience to absorb and comprehend the material. In order to slow your speech rate, you may want to practice by reading out loud, or use a metronome to pace your speech. Be sure that you understand complex material you may be presenting so that you sound competent and confident. Listen to speeches of people you admire to get a sense of pacing, and experiment with pacing your own speeches. Practice ahead of time in front of a mirror your complete presentation.[14]

How often does poor communications in the workplace affect productivity? A study by the Project Management Institute finds that about one third of the time, miscommunication leads to project failure. About half of the time, when projects do not fail, they are negatively impacted by ineffective communications. Effective communication does not just happen on its own, it requires planning and the right tools.[15]

» INTERNATIONAL AND INTERCULTURAL COMMUNICATION

As the global economy has continued its expansion that began after World War II, the economies of countries all over the world have become increasingly integrated. This means that, at some point, you may find yourself in a profession that is touched by, or participates in, the global economy. This international web of business has created many changes in the American workplace.

Despite all of the changes to the global marketplace, the average American is not well equipped to communicate with people from other cultures. Do you know your profession's key terms or lingo in Italian, Spanish, German, Tagalog, Hindi, Arabic, or Mandarin Chinese? Are you aware of the nonverbal cues and messages you may be sending to a colleague from a different culture, with different communication interpretations and expectations? Here are some common body-language suggestions to consider when communicating with others from a different culture:

- **Avoid pointing the sole of your shoe at someone.** In many Middle Eastern and Asian cultures, the bottom of your foot is regarded as the lowest part of your body, and it is rude to show the bottom of your foot. *Solution: Keep your feet flat on the floor during business meetings and avoid crossing your leg onto your knee. Best to tuck your feet underneath you if sitting on the floor.*

- **Be careful not to come on too strong in initial meetings.** In Western business culture, we have traditionally valued a strong handshake combined with direct eye contact. We usually do these to signify a certain level of trust and self-confidence, particularly when we first meet someone. But depending on the specific country, these measures may be seen as overly aggressive, overpowering, or dominating. *Solution: Relax your eye contact and soften your handshake when meeting someone from other cultures for the first time.*
- **Be aware of personal space.** During conversation between two or more people, speakers in Western cultures tend to need a large amount of space around them to feel comfortable when talking to others. In the United States, the United Kingdom, Western Europe, and Canada, this distance is usually an arm's length. However, this distance in Asian, Latin American, or African nations is often much closer. When traveling to or interacting with people from those regions, standing a full arm's length away is probably too far. *Solution: Consider the region you are visiting. Close the gap and stand a little closer, or widen the gap and stand a little farther away, depending on the people you are meeting with, to allow them to feel more comfortable connecting with you.*
- **Avoid using your index finger to point out people.** In the United States and some other Western cultures, pointing someone or something out with the index finger is a natural gesture. However, in some other cultures, pointing to an object or a person with your index finger is seen as overly direct and blunt, and can be quite offensive. *Solution: Use an open palm with all of your fingers grouped together when gesturing toward the object or person.*[16]

In his article "15 International Business Customs that could Make or Break a Deal," author Adam Uzialko describes specific suggestions for international business success. Here are some of those. In South Korea, be prepared to sing karaoke as a part of conducting business. Before doing business in France, learn some French phrases and be prepared for business dinners that take a couple of hours. German business talk is more blunt and less casual, so leave the jokes behind. Business deals in Italy will require getting to know your business partners over a period of time before the real business discussions begin. In Australia, punctuality is important, so be early or right on time in order to not lose the deal. When doing business in Russia, however, your business partners may arrive when they think it is appropriate, not the time at which the meeting is scheduled. Chinese business partners may accept a gift, but do not be surprised if they refuse it three times before accepting it. Japanese business partners will expect you to bring business cards and

more about...

Punctuality: A Global Issue

Many people from European and Asian countries value punctuality as much as, or even more than, people from the United States. In Germany, being on time means being 10 minutes early. In cities such as Hong Kong, Seoul, and Tokyo, the trains are famous for always being on time, and people often show up early for appointments rather than risk being late. In countries such as Saudi Arabia, Malaysia, and Nigeria, being punctual is not a priority. In Brazil, punctuality is more likely to occur if the appointment is set for "English time."[18]

accept them with both hands, treating the card in itself with respect. In Finland, a hot and relaxing sauna is a common business tradition.[17]

Anthropologist Edward T. Hall identified different cultures as being high context and low context (see Figure 6.4). The differences between high-context and low-context cultures are not absolute, and individuals within them are not opposites. A more realistic way to view high-context and low-context cultures is along a continuum based on the importance of the *context* (the circumstances or setting) of the communication message. Elements of the communication in addition to context include those we have introduced here:

figure 6.4

HIGH- AND LOW-CONTEXT CULTURE EXAMPLES

Cultural anthropologist Edward T. Hall (1914–2009) illustrated how high- and low-context cultures are different, as well as their reasons for being this way. *Is the United States a low-context culture or a high-context culture? Why?*

Source: Edward T. Hall, "How Cultures Collide," *Psychology Today* 10 (July 1976), pp. 66–74.

These excerpts are from "How Cultures Collide," an article by Edward T. Hall:

"In some cultures, messages are explicit; the words carry most of the information. In other cultures, such as China or Japan or the Arab cultures, less information is contained in the verbal part of the message, since more is in the context. That's why American businessmen often complain that their Japanese counterparts never get to the point. The Japanese wouldn't dream of spelling the whole thing out. To do so would be a put–down; it's like doing your thinking for you."

"Several years ago I was traveling in Crete and wanted to visit the ruins at Knossos. My traveling companion, who was from low-context, fast-moving New York, took charge of the arrangements. He bargained with a taxi driver, agreed on a price, and a deal was made. We would take his taxi. Without warning, just as we were entering the cab, he stopped, got out and asked another driver if he would take us for less money. Since the other driver was willing, my friend said, 'Let's go.' The first taxi driver felt he had been cheated. We had made a verbal agreement, and it had been violated. But my friend, from a low-context opportunistic culture, felt no moral obligation at all. He had saved the equivalent of 75¢. I can still see the shocked and horrified look on the face of the first driver."

verbal messages, nonverbal messages, and gestures. Perhaps most important in the context is the interpersonal relationship between the sender and the receiver of the message.

In a **low-context culture**, a written agreement, such as a contract, can be taken at face value, and should be direct, detailed, and explicit. In other words, one can assume that the contract means what it says and that it is in itself binding. Relationships between the sender and receiver of the message (or the business partners) are not very important. Business partners would not need to know the family backgrounds, for example, of those with whom they do business. These cultures would not need to take long periods of time, then, to build relationships and build trust with business partners. Decisions on making a business deal would be expected to happen more quickly in a low-context than in a high-context culture. Low-context cultures include German and Scandinavian cultures. Canadian and American cultures tend to lean heavily toward the low-context end of the continuum.

low-context culture
A culture in which a written agreement, such as a contract, can be taken at face value.

In a **high-context culture**, on the other hand, the *social context* surrounding the communication is far more important than the business agreement itself. In a high-context culture, one must be alert and aware of cultural norms and values, nonverbal behaviors on both sides, other social cues, and any factors that affect the overall atmosphere of the communication. It would be expected in a high-context culture that potential business partners would take time to know the family background of those with whom they are doing business, for example. The wording of a contract is not as important in a high-context culture as it is in a low-context culture. More important is the building of relationships and trust over time. Notice in Figure 6.5 which countries have the highest- and lowest-context cultures. Do any of them surprise you?

high-context culture
A culture in which the *social context* surrounding a written document is far more important than the document itself. One must be very careful about cultural norms, nonverbal behaviors on both sides, and anything else involving the overall atmosphere of the communication.

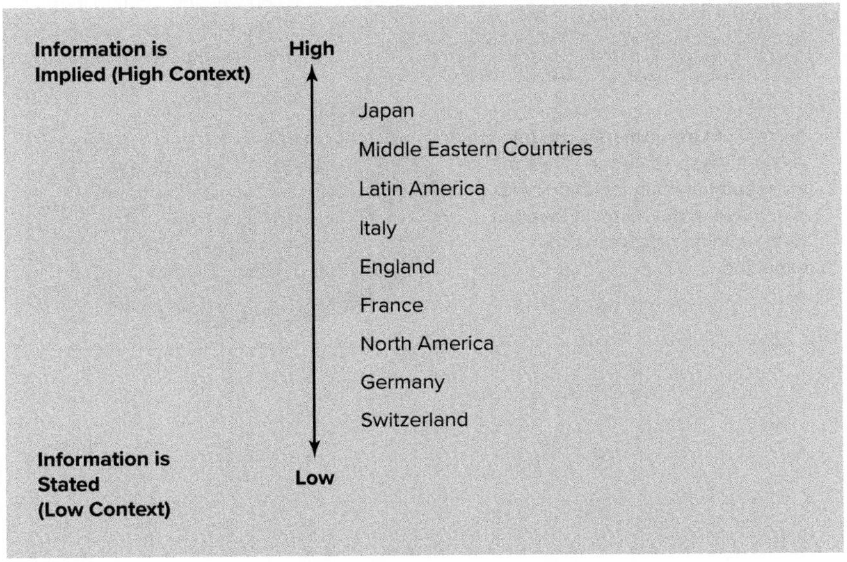

figure 6.5

HIGH- TO LOW-CONTEXT CULTURES

WORKING WITH PEOPLE IN HIGH-CONTEXT CULTURES

Americans who work in high-context cultures have to understand that success with their clients will depend on several factors other than the products or services being offered. *What makes a high-context culture different from a low-context one?*

Rawpixel.com/Shutterstock

Figures 6.4 and 6.6 show examples of communication problems that take place when high- and low-context cultures collide.[19] Those doing business internationally in lower-context countries with other lower-context countries are not likely to have the same considerations in communication when they are communicating together. It will still be important to know about international norms, social cues, and nonverbal communications.

figure 6.6

INTERNATIONAL COMMUNICATION TRAPS

Every culture is different. What is okay in Mexico may be considered rude in Saudi Arabia. When traveling or working abroad, it might be best to prepare oneself beforehand, by learning about the country's norms and customs. If that is not possible, then one should still enter with an open-mind, without expectations that norms and behaviors are the same everywhere. *Is there any other rule for doing business in differing cultures?*

Source: Lennie Copeland, "Training Americans to Do Business Overseas," *Training* (July 1983), p. 12.

International Communication Traps—Some Examples

In **Japan**, the practice of giving small gifts is nearly an obligation in most business situations. In **China**, on the other hand, gift-giving to an individual in a business situation is strictly forbidden.

In the **United States**, "tabling" an agenda item means putting it off until later. In **England**, "tabling" means "putting it on the table" right now and discussing it immediately.

In most of **Latin America**, no offense is taken when someone is late for an appointment. In fact, tardiness is somewhat the norm. In **Sweden**, to-the-minute promptness is expected.

In **Mexico**, it is courteous to ask about the spouse and family of a customer. In **Saudi Arabia**, you should never ask about such things.

STRATEGIES FOR SUCCESS

Strategy 6.1 Become a Better Listener

1. Stop talking.
2. Get rid of distractions.
3. Empathize with the speaker.
4. Avoid judgments and red-flag reactions.
5. Listen for main ideas.
6. Give feedback.
7. Listen for feelings as well as for facts.
8. Encourage others to talk.
9. Be aware of your body language.

What can you do to become an active listener? With time and effort, you can change your listening habits!

1. **Stop talking.** If you are talking, time and opportunity to talk are being taken away from the other person or people. In many ways, this is the most important rule. Remember that most humans have a strong need to be heard—to be listened to. Use pauses in the conversation to reflect on what the speaker has said.
2. **Get rid of distractions.** Distractions can be external (such as noise, or electronic devices), or internal (such as your thoughts and emotions). Move closer to the speaker, change your physical position so that you face the speaker directly, put away your phone, and put any nagging personal problems out of your mind. In a web conference, it is even easier to become distracted, so these points are more important. All of these steps will help eliminate distractions.
3. **Empathize with the speaker.** Even before beginning to listen, prepare yourself to enter the world of the speaker. Consider their perspective. If the conversation is one-on-one, while you are listening *try to make your own needs temporarily less important than those of the other person.* Understand that the other person has very real needs. With a public speaker, listen and watch for clues about the speaker's perspective.
4. **Avoid judgments and red-flag reactions.** Your personal life history can affect your evaluations, or judgments, of others and can raise emotional reactions to specific words. Avoid judging others' appearance or accent, for example, and listen for content. Be aware of words that raise an emotional reaction for you, and work to interpret them in the speaker's meaning.
5. **Listen for main ideas.** When listening to a public speaker, jot down key words and phrases. Try as early as possible to see the outline headings the speaker is using. When talking one-on-one, make sure you understand each point made by the speaker. In many cases, this involves asking questions to make certain you have understood. Keep mental notes of what is being said and how ideas connect.
6. **Give feedback.** Many people mistakenly think of feedback only as communication in a one-on-one situation. Eye contact and facial expressions are also examples of feedback. When talking with another person, respond with "I" statements. This way, it is clear that you are expressing your feelings, not placing blame. Rather than saying, "Your ideas on this project are hard to understand," try saying "I'm having trouble understanding your point here; could you explain it to me again?"
7. **Listen for feelings as well as for facts.** Watch for nonverbal messages that communicate how the speaker *feels* about the subject. Eye and body movements, vocal tone, and posture are examples. By listening for feelings, you will also become more aware of your own feelings about what you're hearing.
8. **Encourage others to talk.** Encouraging others to explain their ideas in more detail can make you more responsible for what you say yourself. In a public speaking situation,

this means allowing others to be involved when the speaker calls for questions and listening carefully to both sides.

9. **Be aware of your body language.** Fidgeting, yawning, looking away, looking at your phone, and other behaviors tell the listener that you are not engaged. Make eye contact, and respond with appropriate facial expressions. Avoid overdoing this, however, so that you do not stare at the speaker or make exaggerated nonverbal responses, as these can seem artificial.

Notice how many of these steps involve being self-aware and comfortable with yourself. People who are comfortable within themselves tend to be better listeners. This is because they are less likely to need attention and can listen to others without an excessive need to be heard.

« STRATEGIES FOR SUCCESS

Strategy 6.2 Practice High-Context Communication

1. Recognize that people in high-context cultures need to know how to put *you* into context.
2. Speak slowly and clearly, and be direct.
3. Use words and expressions from your listener's native language—but know what they mean and know how to pronounce them.
4. Be thoughtful and aware of your nonverbal signals.
5. Practice active listening.

1. **Recognize that people in high-context cultures need to know how to put *you* into context.** This will help them understand you better. They need to know not only about you, but also about the company or organization that you represent. Without that knowledge, any agreement could be meaningless.
2. **Speak slowly and clearly, and be direct.** Stay away from American jargon, slang, clichés, and too many idioms. When nonnative speakers learn English, they often learn a textbook version of the language. Expressions such as, "Let's get all of our ducks in a row" will likely be lost on them. Since Americans use a great deal of informal language, expressions like this slip out even when you are careful.
3. **Use words and expressions from your listener's native language—but know what they mean and how to pronounce them.** In nearly all language groups, it is considered to be good manners to learn some of the other person's language. Such an attempt shows the listener that you care and are interested enough to do a little learning. Of course, you must be sure you understand the meaning before using such phrases, and be careful not to mispronounce the words and phrases—at least not beyond recognition.
4. **Be thoughtful and aware of your nonverbal signals.** If you are communicating through a translator and the listeners are listening to you for periods of time without understanding your words, your listeners are even more likely than usual to pick up on gestures, tone of voice, facial expressions, physical proximity, and all of the other nonverbal cues.
5. **Practice active listening.** Pay attention to the other person, and focus on what you are hearing. Avoid making judgments and keep an open mind about what you are hearing. Summarize or paraphrase what you hear to clarify that you understand. Share your own views and experiences to build trust.[20]

These suggestions should help you when working and doing business in high-context situations. Most of these suggestions would also be valuable when working with people from any other cultures. Even when context is low, thoughtfulness always pays off.

CHAPTER SIX SUMMARY

Chapter Summary by Learning Objectives

LO 6-1 Explain the crucial role of communication at work and what occurs when miscommunications happen. Communication takes place even when speakers and listeners do not realize that it is happening. When people communicate unconsciously, feelings are projected outward. Emotions you are feeling will show. When miscommunication happens, the results include bad decisions, damaged feelings, and loss of productivity.

LO 6-2 Compare and contrast successful and unsuccessful listening skills. Listening skills are important for anyone who wants to communicate effectively. Reasons for poor listening include selective listening, information overload, perceived difficulty of the subject, prejudice, daydreaming, red flag words, and the misunderstanding of listening as a passive position. Good listening is an active process. It is also a matter of priorities. People who understand themselves and understand the importance of good listening tend to be better listeners.

LO 6-3 Explain the importance of timing with regard to messages. Messages need not only to be carefully planned in terms of content, but in terms of timing. A message that would otherwise be clear and well received can be destroyed when it is delivered at a bad time. The areas of possible timing mistakes include emotional, situational, and relevance timing.

LO 6-4 Examine the role of nonverbal communication. Without nonverbal communication, effective exchange of ideas and thoughts is more difficult. Gestures are an important part of the communication process. They include illustrators, regulators, displays, and emblems. Proxemics, or the study of distancing, states that people carry around several bubbles of space. When any of the first three bubbles is violated, the violated person feels uncomfortable. Social distances are affected by culture.

LO 6-5 Identify the functions of nonverbal communication. Nonverbal messages exhibit attitudes and emotions, help clarify the verbal message, and show something about the emotional reactions of speaker and listener.

LO 6-6 Outline strategies for communication within an organization. In any organization, communication has both formal and informal dimensions. Everyone who works in an organization also needs to understand the different requirements of vertical and horizontal communication channels. Within the informal organization, the grapevine is the informal channel of information. It includes information that is largely accurate, but incomplete. When the information is distorted, the channel is called the rumor mill.

LO 6-7 Explain the importance of intercultural communication in today's professional world. International and intercultural communication become more important as the world becomes smaller. One can see international cultures as placed along a continuum of high-context to low-context. Doing effective business with other cultures requires some knowledge of context expectations.

key terms

active listening 154
context 158
displays 160
distancing 160
emblems 160
filtering 156
grapevine 163
high-context culture 167
horizontal communication 162
illustrators 160
information overload 151
intensity 159
low-context culture 167
nonverbals 156
nonverbal communication 158
organizational communication 162
prejudice 153
red flag words 153
regulators 160
rumor mill 163
selective listening 151
vertical communication 162

review questions

1. What is communication? In your definition, use an example of daily communication from your own life.
2. Explain the importance of self-awareness to the communication process. Include examples for when being comfortable with oneself is especially important.
3. Are you usually an active listener? If not, do you know anyone who is? What qualities set an active listener apart from other people?
4. Think of people you have been around who are poor listeners. Do they all have certain qualities in common? If so, what are they?
5. How does nonverbal communication help people understand each other? How can nonverbal cues be negative, especially in the workplace?
6. What are the main differences between communication in the formal organization and in the informal organization? What cautions should you be aware of in each area?

7. What is meant by filtering? Do you ever find yourself filtering a message being sent to you? Have you filtered a message you have sent? How can one reduce the filtering of messages in the workplace?
8. What are the major differences between a high-context culture and a low-context culture? What steps could you take to prevent misunderstandings when dealing with a culture that is different in context from your own?

critical thinking questions

1. Do a brief self-evaluation. Ask yourself, "How effective am I at communicating with people from cultures that are higher-context or lower-context than my own?" Were you able to identify areas of improvement? If so, what were you doing that could be done more effectively?
2. Think of an incident in your life when someone you were listening to was sending nonverbal messages that seemed to contradict the verbal message. Was it in person, or a public setting, or electronic media? Describe the situation. What was your reaction to the mixed message?
3. Consider communication in an organization. Which do you find more important, horizontal or vertical communication channels? When delivering an important message in a business organization, should one come before the other? Are there some types of messages that are more appropriate for the horizontal or the vertical channels?

working it out 6.1

GRAPEVINE OR RUMOR MILL?

School-to-Work Connection: Information Skills

Purpose: This exercise graphically illustrates how quickly distortions of facts can take place, even when they are communicated in a controlled environment.

Instructions: This exercise requires seven volunteers from the class. Six of the volunteers must leave the classroom, taking their places in the hallway. The other volunteer will remain in the classroom. The instructor will choose a very short story that contains several characters and a bit of action. The instructor first reads the story to the entire class, including the first volunteer. When the reading is finished, the second volunteer will be allowed to enter the room.

Volunteer number one will then retell the story he or she has just been read, without any coaching from either the instructor or the rest of the class.

Then, one by one, each volunteer will be ushered into the room to hear the story retold by the last person who heard it. When volunteer number seven has heard the story, he or she must retell it to the rest of the class. Finally, the instructor will ask the seventh volunteer to read aloud the story in its original form, for the benefit of the volunteers who have gotten only distorted versions of it.

Although degrees of distortion will vary from class to class, you will readily see how messages become muddled, sometimes to ridiculous extremes. If most of the facts are correct, but the story is incomplete, the class has created a grapevine example. A rumor mill example that includes gross distortions is much more likely.

Note: This exercise has also been done successfully with a photograph or drawing that contains many different elements and/or people to remember. The picture should be shown on a screen or copies should be distributed to all class members—except six of the seven participants. Let the first participant have one minute to observe the picture; follow the same procedure as for the story.

This exercise can also be done in a web conference classroom where the volunteers hear the story told in a separate breakout room, or after turning off their audio while the story is told to others.

working it out 6.2

THE IMPORTANCE OF FEEDBACK

School-to-Work Connection: Information Skills
Purpose: This exercise illustrates the importance of two-way communication that includes feedback from all communicators.

Instructions: A volunteer from the class will study a geometrical figure provided by the authors of this textbook to the instructor. (The other class members will not be allowed to see the figure.) Then, with the student's back to the class, he or she will describe the figure exactly enough so that each class member can reconstruct it on a piece of notebook paper. Fifteen minutes will be allowed for this portion of the exercise. During this phase, only the volunteer will be allowed to speak. No questions are allowed, except for one request to repeat each instruction. The volunteer is not allowed to explain any single descriptive instruction more than twice, and the second time is allowed only if requested by a class member.

The same volunteer will face the class and will describe the geometric figure, while classmates start over with another sheet of notebook paper. This time, the members of the class are allowed to ask questions. They may ask any question that will help clarify an accurate drawing of the figure. After 15 minutes, compare the results from the two phases. You will very likely see a vast improvement in the second part of the exercise. This is probably because the person who gave the instructions was able to provide helpful nonverbal clues while facing the class. Did the first exercise—with the student facing away—cause any frustration or confusion? If so, give specific examples.

Perhaps the more complex instructions left a lot of people unsure the first time, but were somehow easier to comprehend the second time.

To the instructor: The geometrical pattern can be found in the *Instructor's Manual.*

Note: This exercise can also be done in a web conference classroom when the volunteer stops their video during the first description rather than facing away from the class.

working it out 6.3

MARKETING ACROSS CULTURES

School-to-Work Connection: Information Skills

Purpose: In this exercise, you will practice creating two sets of advertising material, one targeted specifically to a high-context culture audience, and one targeted to a low-context culture audience.

Instructions: Working in pairs or a small group, select any product (real or invented) to advertise to your two culture-specific audiences. The advertisements can include both verbal descriptions and visual depictions. What will you need to take into consideration for your two audiences?

After creating your ads, prepare to explain the differences you created in the colors used, wording used, whether you used more words or more pictures, product placement, image of the product, direct descriptions or less direct associations, celebrity endorsements, facts or images, calls to action, and more. Present your ads to the class along with your explanations.

working it out 6.4

HAVE A BETTER CONVERSATION AT WORK

Watch the TED Talk by Celeste Headlee, titled "10 Ways to Have a Better Conversation," and then answer the following questions.

1. How did the ability to hold conversations decline, according to the author?
2. Which three of the 10 suggestions seemed the most valuable to you? Explain.
3. Which of the speaker's ideas would be difficult for you to use? Explain.
4. Why is it important to learn to have a good conversation? How does this skill add value in the workplace?
5. What suggestion does the speaker say is the most important? Do you agree? Explain.

The video can be found here: www.ted.com/talks/celeste_headlee_10_ways_to_have_a_better_conversation

case study 6.1

Economic Upheaval

When each of the staff members began to arrive at work at the fitness center on Monday morning, they noticed two strange cars in the parking lot. The director, Neela, was obviously in a meeting because they could hear voices coming from behind the closed door. This was starting out to be a very unusual morning.

For the rest of the day, Neela's meetings continued. Neela and the others involved in the meetings looked serious and did not make eye contact with the rest of the staff. Meanwhile, the staff grew increasingly nervous, imagining all sorts of reasons for the closed-door meetings, none of them good. One of the trainers, Ajay, pulled out his cell phone and began searching through business news sites to see if there was any news about their fitness center.

"Oh no, I found something!" exclaimed Ajay. He had found an article about the corporation that owned the fitness center. According to the article, the corporation was in serious financial problems. The fitness center chain was trying to avoid bankruptcy by going into receivership. Whether or not they could return to financial health was unknown.

The next morning, Neela held a briefing with all of the staff. She explained everything that had been going on and told them she would do her best to keep the fitness center open. Most of her 14 employees were skeptical and very frustrated. They found it hard to understand why they hadn't been told the truth from the start. Within a few weeks, the top fitness trainers had left for other companies. Three others admitted that they had also considered looking for work elsewhere. The morale at the fitness center was severely reduced, and loyalty dropped among employees and clients.

Case Study Questions

1. How could the fitness center director and owners have handled this situation differently? What principles of effective communication have been broken in this case?
2. If you were Neela, what would be your next step in communicating with your staff? Why?
3. If the fitness center's owners do decide to change ownership, how should they communicate this to the staff and to the public?

Customer Service or Customer Disservice?

"What happened to customer service?" thought Gisele to herself as she waited for someone, anyone, at the drive-through fast food restaurant to notice that she was waiting to give her order. Five minutes passed . . . she honked her horn. Nobody showed up at the window. She honked again. Ten minutes passed . . . still nobody. "Oh well," she thought, "at least I had time to answer a few e-mails."

Finally, fully exasperated, she pulled through the drive-through lane, parked her car, and went inside. She found a nearly empty fast food place with two employees at the front counter, chatting, laughing, and both with cell phones in hand.

Trying to hold back a very frustrated tone, she said, "I have been waiting for more than 10 minutes in the drive-through. Didn't you hear me honk? Don't you have anyone checking the drive-through? Is it closed or something?"

One of the two counter employees said, "Oh, I didn't hear you. We've been really busy." His tone, facial expression, and demeanor were exactly opposite of his words. He seemed completely bored and disinterested. And while she expected an apology, she did not get one. "So can I take your order now?" he asked, still with a bored expression.

"Never mind," said Gisele, "I'll go somewhere else."

The counter employee just shrugged and turned away. "Come back again soon," he said in an automatic and flat tone, while looking at his phone.

Case Study Questions

1. What is each message channel (verbal or nonverbal) saying in this situation, and which will you most likely believe? Why?
2. How would *you* respond to the nonverbal behaviors you interpret here? What advice would you give to the counter employee to improve communication? How would you convince him that his communication needed improving? Be specific.
3. Gisele's expression, tone, and words may not have been intense enough to give the message she was feeling. If you were Gisele, would you have sent the message in the same way? What listening failures occurred? Explain.

CHAPTER SEVEN

TEAMWORK AND LEADERSHIP

LEARNING OBJECTIVES

After studying this chapter, you will be able to:

LO 7-1 Discuss the characteristics and purposes of groups and teams.

LO 7-2 Discuss team development.

LO 7-3 Explain the steps in team building.

LO 7-4 Examine barriers to group effectiveness and their resolutions.

LO 7-5 Define leadership, leadership styles, and types of power.

LO 7-6 Improve the organizational climate of the workplace.

LO 7-7 Understand the new organizational or corporate culture.

STRATEGIES FOR SUCCESS

Strategy 7.1 Watching for Hidden Agendas

Strategy 7.2 Building a Successful Team

In the Workplace: To Team or Not?

SOLO OR TEAM?

Caiaimage/Glow Images

Pete had been doing great design work for the company since the early days, when the start-up had grown out of a converted garage. For years, he had worked mostly alone on projects, since the staffing had been too lean to rely on others. Recently, his company expanded and bought out a local rival in the same field. Because they respected his past work and his value to the company, his bosses asked him if he wanted to continue to work on projects by himself, or join one of the new permanent work teams that were being created as part of the company's restructuring.

Pete chose to continue to work alone. He just didn't see the value in wasting time talking to other people about getting something done. He figured he could just do it himself and get finished a lot faster. Besides, what if he didn't like the team members he was assigned to work with? Then he would be miserable, he thought, caught in a bad situation.

DISCOVERY

But today as he looked around the office, he wondered if he'd made the right choice. He was stuck on how to finish an individual project and he didn't know whom to ask. The others in his original office staff had all joined work teams. He listened in as Amy and her team were brainstorming ideas and coming up with a lot more creative possibilities than Pete could have thought of alone. His new colleague Jasmine and her team were deciding how to divide up the project tasks; they would have their individual tasks—and the project—done in no time. Haruto's team was in deep discussion on the progress of the second phase of their work. Now, the idea of a team seemed to Pete both more efficient and more pleasant. As he struggled with his project, he wondered if it was too late to reconsider the teamwork idea.

THINK ABOUT IT

Can you think of a time when you worked alone on a work or school project, when a team approach would have been more successful? Have you worked with assigned teams? If so, what unexpected and expected outcomes did you experience?

» GROUPS AND TEAMS

What Makes a Group?

group
A collection of two or more individuals who interact, share certain characteristics, and coordinate their participation in the group around some shared idea or goal.

In the social sciences, a **group** is defined as a collection of two or more individuals who interact, share certain characteristics, and coordinate their participation in the group around some shared idea or goal. It is a broad term that finds its way into the language of the workplace, at school, and in our extracurricular activities.

Groups can form for many different reasons. We organize ourselves into groups by where we live and work, the school and classes we attend, what we like and don't like (see Figure 7.1). Groups even form through our online personas, where we can connect with groups both small (think local book clubs or study groups) and large (such as online communities of art lovers, fan clubs, or social media groups). Groups of friends in "real life" may even

figure 7.1

TEENS, FRIENDSHIPS, AND ONLINE GROUPS

Which online groups do teens prefer?
Source: Monica Anderson and JingJing Jiang, "Teens, Friendships and Online Groups," *Pew Research Center,* November 28, 2018, https://www.pewresearch.org/internet/2018/11/28/teens-friendships-and-online-groups.

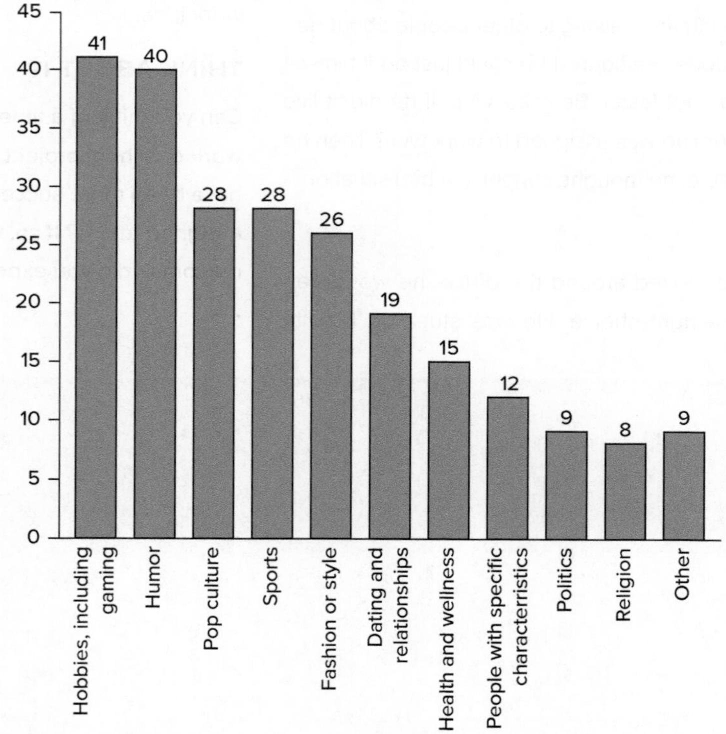

Note: For "people with specific characteristics," question wording is "people with specific characteristics (e.g., LGBT, people of color)." Respondents were allowed to select multiple options. Those who did not give an answer are not shown.
Source: Survey conducted March 7–April 10, 2018.
"Teens' Social Media Habits and Experiences"

GROUPS IN THE WORKPLACE

Groups help people to work more effectively and find satisfaction through interaction. *What are some of the ways that groups form in the workplace?*

Guerilla/Alamy Stock Photo

gather together at virtual hangouts without being in the same physical space, changing up the scene from one online platform to another as the mood of the group changes. Groups—whether formed online or in the workplace—can connect you with new people from different backgrounds and experiences and can make you feel welcomed and accepted.[1]

As you consider the role of the group in society, ask yourself: to which groups do you belong in your life—personal, professional, or otherwise? And, why did you join that group?

Groups at Work: Teams

When talking about organized groups in the workplace, the term **team** is commonly used to describe the relationship among employees with different skill sets who work together to create value for a business or organization. The workplace team might be created for short-term or for long-term interaction. Teams designed for short-term action might include a team put together for training or "on-boarding" a new hire; an employee wellness committee tasked with planning the office's participation in an upcoming marathon; or one that may form to resolve some type of conflict within the organization, such as internal tensions between employees or supply chain problems with a manufacturer.

team

The relationship among employees with different skill sets who work together to create value for a business or organization. Workplace teams can be short term or have a long-range purpose.

Some examples of long-range teams could be the marketing team charged with building the company's brand against its competitors; an executive leadership team dedicated to the long-range promotion of internal talent; or the human resources team, which may be tasked with training workers, maintaining interoffice relationships, and interpreting employment laws.

Why Teams?

Effective teamwork promotes cooperation and the exchange of ideas among co-workers. This positive interaction can, in turn, give individual employees a greater sense of fulfillment in their daily jobs and can help build trust among co-workers. These elements—positive interaction, sense of fulfillment,

more about...

Groups

The following is a list of the largest online groups in the world, by number of members:

- Facebook 2.38 × 10
- Twitter 500,000,000
- LinkedIn 450,000,000
- Duolingo 300,000,000
- Sina Weibo 300,000,000
- Habbo 268,000,000
- Vkontakte 208,833,674
- Renren 160,000,000
- Bebo 117,000,000
- Tagged 100,000,000
- Netlog 95,000,000
- Friendster 90,000,000
- hi5 80,000,000
- Flixster 63,000,000
- MyLife 51,000,000
- Edmodo 50,000,000+
- Classmates.com 50,000,000
- Plaxo 50,000,000
- Sonico.com 50,000,000
- Douban 46,850,000
- Odnoklassniki 45,000,000
- Reddit 36,000,000
- Viadeo 35,000,000

How does the popularity of these websites fit with your own view of them? What do the massive membership numbers in these online groups say about our society?

Source: "List of Virtual communities," Wikipedia, https://en.wikipedia.org/wiki/List_of_virtual_communities_with_more_than_1_million_users (retrieved April 7, 2020).

and trust–create a healthy setting for teams and can mean engaged employees and a vibrant workplace.[2] Ultimately, these factors are likely to have a positive impact on the bottom line.

When operating well, an effective team can work faster and more efficiently than an individual alone. Consider the example of Pete in the introduction. He began to question his preference for working alone as he saw his colleagues thriving in their respective team work. Which approach do you prefer? What strengths do you bring to the teams in your professional or personal life?

» TEAM DEVELOPMENT

Teamwork does not happen on its own. Building a successful team in the workplace can take time, and it is an active, participatory process. Once formed around a specific purpose, the team must be maintained and managed well. On effective teams, individual members feel fulfilled and engaged in their tasks, working collaboratively with team members to complete the team's goals and creating value for the organization.

The Five Stages of Team Development

Teams are at their best when they have predetermined their goals and are formed around the most capable people to accomplish those goals. And the team's effectiveness is enhanced by its commitment to ongoing evaluation of its effectiveness.[3]

Every team goes through five stages of development. The most commonly used framework for looking at team development comes from the work of Bruce W. Tuckman in the mid-1960s, in which his descriptions of *Forming, Storming, Norming and Performing* provide a framework for looking at teams in the workplace. His framework has proven useful over the years, with researchers and experts retooling it, and adding their own context to Tuckman's.

By now, Tuckman's four stages of team development have been expanded to five, with many agreeing to the addition of *Adjourning* as the fifth element.

Each stage of team development has its own recognizable feelings and behaviors; understanding *why* things are happening in certain ways on a team can be an important part of the self-evaluation process.[4] The five stages are described as follows.

Stage 1: Forming

When the team first comes together, this is the "Forming" stage. In this stage, team members meet for the first time and share information about their backgrounds, interests and experience, and form first impressions of each other. Team members may have a lot of questions about one another and may express uncertainty or anxiety about their place on the new team. At this point, the team leader and group agree on norms and procedures. During this initial Forming stage, much of the team's energy is focused on defining protocols for the team, or ground rules, which means that there will be little accomplished by way of tasks in this first stage.

Stage 2: Storming

As they start working together, members of the team move into the "Storming" stage. This stage is unavoidable; every team will go through this stage, in which members may discover that the team does not live up to all of their early expectations and excitement from the first, Forming stage.

During the Storming stage, members are trying to see how the team will respond to differences and how it will handle conflict. In this stage, team members may compete among themselves for status or for acceptance of their ideas. A good team leader is important in this stage to ensure that team members follow protocols for communication laid down in Stage 1. This stage begins to come to a close when the individual members of the group become more accepting of one another, and begin working together in a more cohesive way. At this point, the team leader can begin to step back and let the group lead more of the decision making. As he or she transitions to allow more independence and decision making from the team, he or she will stay involved to quickly resolve any conflicts.

It is in this stage, Storming, that many teams get stuck and never emerge. These failing teams struggle to move beyond this stage, and the project interaction can be marked with conflict, low morale, and reduced motivation, making it difficult to get the project completed. Teams that are comprised of members who are professionally immature in particular have trouble getting past this stage.

Stage 3: Norming

The third stage, "Norming" is when the team starts to "gel" and work more effectively as a team. Team members at this stage feel more comfortable in their roles on the team, with individual goals and motivations losing importance to the collective team's goals, its processes, and mission. In this stage, members feel more comfortable expressing their real feelings, become more accepting of their teammates, and appreciate the value others bring to the team. Trust among members can increase in this stage, and collaboration becomes easier as team members make significant progress on their common team goals.[5] In this stage, team members strive to communicate effectively and take on more collective decision making, if there is still a group leader facilitating.

Stage 4: Performing

By the fourth stage, "Performing," members of the team are feeling satisfied with the way the team operates. They are comfortable with their input into the project and appreciate their colleagues' contributions. At the Performing Stage, team members have gotten to know each other, trust each other, and rely on one another. Most decisions are made by the team without relying on the decisions of a team leader, at this stage. The team leader is still involved, although their role is more to celebrate accomplishments and achievements, and to provide a gateway to higher-up executives if higher level decisions are to be made about the team's direction. Successful teams may remain the Performing Stage indefinitely as old goals are accomplished and new goals set.

Many teams do not make it to the Performing Stage and get stuck at Stage 2 or 3. Or they may revert back to an earlier stage if a member of the team decides to start doing things alone without consensus, or if a member of the team leaves or is replaced. In this case, a team may need to regroup at the Forming stage before proceeding with new members.

Stage 5: Adjourning

While not part of Tuckman's original model, which had four stages, this is widely seen as the termination, or ending, phase for most teams. In the "Adjourning" stage, work has been completed, or the organization's needs may have changed. While some long-term teams may exist for years, most teams will find themselves in the Adjourning stage as they reach their goals or their mission comes to an end. At this time, the team leader helps facilitate an assessment of the team's accomplishments and celebrates their successes, and the team evaluates its work to determine best practices for the future.

As the team is dissolved, members may feel a mix of emotions as they move on to other tasks and team work. Sadness or anxiety may occur from knowing that you will not be interacting and participating with the same people, although this is often balanced by a positive sense of satisfaction as members recall their accomplishments with the team. In any case, the team should acknowledge the upcoming transition, including the variety of ways that individuals and the team may be feeling about the team's impending dissolution. During this stage, the team should focus on three tasks:

1. Completion of any "deliverables" (products, processes, or plans created) and closure on any remaining team work.

2. Evaluation of the team's process and product, with a particular focus on identifying "lessons learned" and passing these on to the sponsor for future teams to use.
3. Creating a closing celebration that acknowledges the contributions of individuals and the accomplishments of the team and that formally ends this particular team's existence.[6]

» TEAM BUILDING

In the more traditional approach to management, companies are run in a traditional "top down" management style–often with no pretense about groups and work teams. The traditional manager is more like the dictatorial captain of a ship than the player-captain of a basketball or football team.

Groups and teams in an organization can improve their performance through what is known as **team building**. With sustained, conscious effort, a skilled manager can build a team of employees who will function effectively as a unit and achieve the company or organization's goals. Building a **work team** can be a difficult, time-consuming process that requires effort from everyone involved.

team building
The process of creating and encouraging a group of employees to work together toward achieving group goals and increased productivity.

work team
A group of employees with shared goals who join forces on a work project.

Despite the difficulty and time, many organizations are willing to put the necessary effort into building the efficiency of work teams. There are many good reasons to do so, but from the position of management, the best reason to make any improvement is the "bottom line." Effective teams save companies money by reducing the need for middle management, increasing productivity, doing work that individuals or normal work groups can't do, and making better use of resources.[7] And in the growing digital economy where our colleagues may be in a satellite office across town or across the globe, people located in different parts of the world are increasingly "teaming up" to get an idea into production and into consumers' hands.

Some employees, including Pete in our opening vignette, are not sold on the idea of work teams; they may even be downright hostile to the idea. They may see working in teams as a challenge to their individual expertise or abilities. Some employees may not want to do things in a "new" way; others think teamwork causes a duplication of effort or a waste of time. But these fears are not borne out by research on effective work teams.

Work teams actually allow individuals to have more say in their jobs, because they can discuss ideas with peers rather than just following instructions from a supervisor. Job satisfaction is then improved. When job satisfaction is improved, morale and productivity rise. Most people who work in teams say they would not want to go back to the "old" way of doing business. The use of work teams typically improves the company's "bottom line" while producing a higher-quality workplace atmosphere for employees.

Implementation

When a team is first forming, or wants to improve its efficiency, a good place to start is to ask the members the following questions:

1. What do you want from this team? What can your membership in this group do for you personally–what do you want it to do?
2. What skills, abilities, or talents do you bring to this team?

These questions will often be asked in writing. From the answers, the team builder, or leader, can learn a great deal about the needs and concerns of the people who will make up the team. The answers to these questions will determine the complexity of the task of building the team. Suppose, for example, that several people responded to the first question, "I want the team to leave me alone and let me do my work." This might have been the answer given by Pete in the opening vignette. Those members would require some selling on the idea of team building before any real progress could be made.

BUILDING TRUST

Trust among team members is essential for a team to be successful. *What are some of the consequences of lack of trust among team members?*

Andersen Ross/Blend Images LLC

Trust

Building trust is one of the first steps in creating a team. Without trust, there can be no team building. Imagine a basketball team whose members didn't trust each other enough to pass the ball. Whoever had the ball would only dribble and shoot. Winning games in this way is unlikely. Often, a great deal of group interaction must take place for a beginning level of trust to develop. Whatever method of trust building is used, it must get members' feelings out in the open so issues of trust can be resolved.

Goals

Finally, the team needs to review and agree upon goals, both individually and collectively. Establishing and refining goals can be aided by using two questions: "What do you want the team to accomplish, and what can you give?" Goals must be clear and attainable, and they must be considered important by all members of the team.

» COMMUNICATION IN TEAMS

Communicating effectively in teams is critical to productivity. The basics of meeting etiquette apply whether you are meeting in person or in a web conference. In either case, the message you are sending in the meeting is one of professionalism and respect. While communication is covered in detail in Chapter 5, some tips for communication in meetings and teams is important to add here.

Meeting Etiquette

In order to be an effective team, each member must actively participate in each meeting. Here are some best practices to ensure the meeting runs smoothly:

- *Be on time.* Punctuality is especially important when others are waiting for you in order to start the meeting.
- *Put your phone away.* Unless you are using the phone to attend or access data for the meeting, turn off the sounds and put it away. To take calls or be distracted by notifications or texts during a meeting is distracting not just to you, but to everyone in the meeting. The signal you send to others is that checking your phone is more important than what they are saying.
- *Make eye contact and listen to what others are saying.* Engage with what is happening in the meeting. If you have a habit of doodling during meetings, try taking a few notes on the important points of the meeting instead.
- *Do your homework.* If you have been assigned work to bring to the meeting, be sure to do it, and be prepared to present it.
- If you are in charge of the meeting, *make introductions* so that meeting attendees understand who has what role at the meeting.
- *Create a meaningful agenda* so that you do not waste anyone's time having a meeting just for the sake of having a meeting. Effective meetings can make or break productivity in the workplace.

Tips for Online "Virtual" Meetings

Online web conferences or meetings are increasingly common in the workplace and in education. Many platforms exist for these meetings, including GoToMeeting, Skype, Zoom, Webex Meetings, BlueJeans, and Cisco, to name just a few. Online meetings save travel time and costs, allowing people from anywhere in the world to attend. Files and data are easy to share, access, and present during an online meeting.

However, communication in online meetings creates some issues to be aware of. In addition to the previous suggestions for effective meetings, a few more criteria apply for online meetings. Since not everyone is comfortable using technology for meetings, participants will need to take time ahead of the meetings to learn to use the software. As with any technology, transmission failure and interruptions can occur, so have a back-up "lower tech" plan to use, just in case.

Security to protect passwords and sensitive information will need to be in place ahead of time as well. Short attention spans can mean participants drift away to non-productive activities, so participants will need to focus effectively. Nonverbal signals are more difficult to see online, so meeting participants will have to pay even more attention.[8] Online meetings, education, and web conferencing are here to stay. The most effective organizations and teams will take advantage of the flexibility and opportunity that virtual meetings provide.

» BARRIERS TO TEAM EFFECTIVENESS

Many barriers to a team's effectiveness can arise from its members' interactions. Status differences between specific team members may create divisiveness or negativity. Team members may not understand their colleagues'–or their own–roles on the team. Some members of the team may seem less invested in its success, or resistant to changes that others feel would make the team more successful. And yet another barrier might be the reaction of some members of the team to its domination by one or more members. A team's effectiveness may even suffer from the phenomenon known as **groupthink**, where over-conforming can discourage creativity and/or personal responsibility. Besides the previous examples, there are many potential pitfalls, or barriers, to a team or group's success. By studying these barriers we can better identify and remove them.

groupthink

A problematic type of thinking that results from group members who are overly willing to agree with one another because of time pressure, stress, and low collective self-esteem.

When team norms have been established and status issues have been sorted out, conformity becomes an issue. **Conformity** is acting in coordination and agreement with one's team. One reason members of teams conform is to avoid pressure or rejection by the rest of the team. Other reasons may include a desire to meet the team's shared objectives, or to be rewarded for their work. For a team to function effectively, a certain amount of conformity is necessary. You may have heard the expression "it's like herding cats" used to refer to the difficulty of getting people in a particular team to conform to team norms and act as a unified team. This expression reminds us how difficult it can be to coordinate tasks within the team without its members conforming to the team.

conformity

Behaving in a way that meets a specified standard, in coordination with a group.

Conformity also has an ugly side. Too much conformity can kill creativity and discourage people from saying what is really on their minds. Groupthink is a type of well-intended, but ultimately warped thinking that results from groups and teams "getting along too well." Likewise, groupthink gives members the illusion that the team is based on what is good and moral. "We're the good guys; who has the right to oppose us?"

Picture a team in which members know each other very well and are used to working together closely. When a well-liked leader of the team offers an idea for discussion that you immediately recognize as unworkable, yet you notice polite nods and smiles around the table, you may hesitate to offer your critical opinion out of fear of not being a team player. When groupthink invades a team or project, otherwise critical or incisive members of the team may say nothing at all.

Status is the rank an individual holds within a team. It comes from a variety of different sources, some based on formal factors and others on informal ones. Sources of status include a person's formal position in a company, effective interpersonal skills, personal charm or charisma, educational level, physical appearance, persuasive ability, and other values shared by the team. Team members with high status will usually have a high impact on the team's morale, and on its output.

status

The rank an individual holds within a group.

REAL WORLD EXAMPLE 7.1

Epic Groupthink Fiascoes

Psychologist Irving Janis (1918-1990) created the concept of groupthink. He believed groupthink affects a group or team's decision making to the point that loyalty to the group or its values overrides realistic and necessary points of view. When working in a team setting, actions made through groupthink can have grave consequences. Consider the following ill-fated examples.

PEARL HARBOR

When American intelligence services intercepted Japanese secret messages indicating that an attack in the western Pacific was imminent, Navy and Army leaders ruled out Hawaii as the target, rationalizing the decision with a number of questionable assumptions. On December 7, 1941, the Japanese attacked Pearl Harbor, catching the American military unprepared to respond. Postwar studies have concluded that the American military overestimated its strength in the region; that it stereotyped the Japanese military as being too weak or scared to carry out such an attack; and the military's culture of conformity meant that different opinions of lower generals regarding risk assessment may not have been evaluated robustly.[9]

SPACE SHUTTLE CHALLENGER DISASTER

After the loss of Challenger and its crew in 1986, the official inquiry into the disaster found that the direct cause was the malfunction of an O-ring seal on the right solid-rocket booster, which caused the shuttle to explode 73 seconds after launching. The commission also found "a serious flaw in the decision-making process leading up to the launch," noting that prior to the launch there had been questions about the O-ring seal's safety, but after months of internal discussion about the product's safety "NASA appeared to be requiring a contractor to prove that it was not safe to launch, rather than proving it was safe."[10] In this case, NASA's remarkable earlier achievements in space exploration had caused it to dismiss its own engineers and data regarding the likelihood of failure. This defective decision-making doomed the mission.

PENN STATE SANDUSKY SCANDAL

Former Penn State president Graham Spanier, former vice president Gary Schultz, and the University's former athletic director Tim Curley were sentenced to jail in 2017 for their role in the scandal at the university in which they and the former head football coach covered up multiple accounts of child sexual abuse committed by a former assistant football coach, Jerry Sandusky.

Among other reasons, the tragedy has been explained by the groupthink phenomenon, whereby sound decision making was impaired by the bigger concern of unity and preservation. The tragedy of this case study was amplified by the officials in charge, who became complicit by doing, and saying, nothing.[11]

An important related factor is degree of *status acceptance.* If you have lower status in a team than you feel you deserve, then your own morale, and in turn, the team's morale, may be badly affected. Even the opposite—giving people more status than they deserve or feel they deserve—can cause problems such as resentment from other team members, or guilty feelings in the person with higher status than is deserved. People with healthy and accurate self-concepts may be more content with the status level the team has given them, and they may attain higher status than others whose self-concept is low or whose self-perceptions are clouded.

Making Teams More Effective

Three steps can help improve a team's effectiveness:

1. *Changing ineffective norms.* A **norm** is a typical or normal way to behave, or an agreed upon behavior. Making a team more effective can be done

norm
A standard of behavior expected of group members.

REAL WORLD EXAMPLE 7.2

The student government body at a small community college was made up of seven students, all of whom wanted to be student body president. The group was ineffective because everyone wanted to be a leader, and no one wanted to work as equals on a team. Not until most of the members either graduated or quit was the student government body replenished with a more balanced composition. Then the group could identify and pursue its goals.

most efficiently by changing its norms. Since most teams haven't ever discussed their norms, examining norms is the first step. The team leader must get the team to agree on the purpose for the team's existence, the role each member can play in achieving that purpose, and why a specific norm needs to be changed. In the case of specific barriers to team effectiveness, the team will need to set norms for an environment that does not allow for continued conflict, where creativity is fostered, all members are expected to participate, and change is encouraged. Additional suggested norms for effective teamwork include avoiding office politics, setting an expectation of high-quality reports and presentations, having small enough meetings so that people can fully participate, allowing both silences and questions, celebrating successes, honoring the expertise in the team, and limiting technology so that people are fully engaged.[12]

2. *Identifying problems.* Try to identify problems the group is facing so that members can discuss ways to solve them. Is one person dominating the discussion? Are some group members in conflict over status differences? Are members resisting change and new ideas? Are they conforming too much, without questioning goals or process? Once the specific problem is identified, group members or the group leader can bring attention to the problem, then create a solution to address it. The solution should be designed so that it uses the full potential of each group member. New job assignments given to members may make them feel they are contributing in a more useful way to the project, using their individual talents and abilities in the process. Open communication and discussion can help to identify and resolve problems.
3. *Improving the composition of the team.* Some teams are ineffective because their composition is poor. For example, they may have members whose abilities, interests, or personalities clash, or simply do not meet the needs for which the team was formed. The team may include members who actively resist change, or those who insist on dominating the team; and are not willing to change their behavior. They may have members who do not have the right mix of expertise to solve a problem they are assigned. The team itself may be too large or too small for the task. In these cases, team leaders should try to change the team's composition, if possible, to make it more effective. The leader should look for a balance of skills and knowledge to allow the team to be effective. Whenever a

REAL WORLD EXAMPLE 7.3

Kerry joins committees and teams and attends their meetings for only one reason—she wants to get to be known by the people on each committee so she will have political power in the managers' association to which she belongs. Her hidden agenda is to network and look good to others, and she doesn't truly care about any of the goals of the different committees. When team leaders and members can identify and confront hidden agendas, the strength and integrity of the team can increase.

team's composition is changed, it will again go through the team process stages described earlier. The team will improve, but this growth toward improvement won't happen without some "growing pains." The leader must be ready to help in the readjustment that will be necessary when team composition changes.[13]

Hidden Agendas

Have you ever been part of a team where nothing seemed to be getting done? **Hidden agendas** may have been part of the problem. Hidden agendas are individual members' secret wishes, hopes, desires, and assumptions that they don't want to share with the team, although they will work hard to accomplish them without being discovered. In other words, people with hidden agendas are out for themselves. Often, people try to get these agendas accomplished even as they pretend to care more about the goals of the team. They might also try to persuade the team to make its agenda fit their own. As with other barriers to team effectiveness, hidden agendas may be uncovered and reduced through good communication, good group composition, and creation of norms that discourage them. If you are the team member with the hidden agenda, ask yourself if your hidden agenda is really more important than the group's goals. Can you attain your goal in another way?

hidden agendas

The secret wishes, hopes, desires, and assumptions hidden from the group. People often try to accomplish hidden agendas while pretending to care about the group goals.

Additional strategies to reduce hidden agendas in teamwork include:

- Understand that hidden agendas exist almost everywhere.
- Talk with key influencers before group work begins to make a connection with them.
- Ask each person what outcomes they would like to see for their teamwork.
- Address all the needs you hear so that people know you are interested.
- Listen.
- Ask good questions. Start with easy questions first, them dig deeper.
- Avoid putting individuals on the spot with uncomfortable questions.
- Check for facts so that you are not imagining a hidden agenda.
- Pay attention to what people say and do to check for a hidden agenda.[14]

LEADERSHIP STYLES
Leaders may interact with others differently depending on their leadership styles. *Which style of leader would you prefer?*
mentatdgt/Shutterstock

leadership
The ability to influence others to work toward the goals of an organization.

autocratic leaders
Leaders who make all the decisions and use authority and material rewards to motivate followers.

consultative leaders
Leaders who tend to delegate authority and confer with others in making decisions, but who makes the actual decisions independently.

participative leaders
Leaders who encourage the group to work together toward shared goals.

persuasive leader
Leaders who make the final decision but are open to persuasion.

free-rein leaders
Leaders who set performance standards, then allow followers to work creatively to meet standards.

» LEADERSHIP: WHAT IT IS AND WHAT IT REQUIRES

Leadership is broadly defined as the ability to influence people toward the attainment of goals.[15] Effective leaders in business exhibit characteristics of honesty, integrity, trustworthiness, and ethics while leading their group toward successful fulfillment of the group's goals. Leadership is a critical factor in the study of human relations.

Leadership versus Management

In his popular books on leadership, management expert Warren Bennis distinguished between a manager and a leader. According to Bennis, good managers *do things right,* whereas effective leaders *do the right things.*[16] The manager who is also a leader is the most effective of managers. Bennis (1925–2014) is widely regarded as a founder of modern leadership studies.

There are different thoughts as to what exactly makes a leader effective. Some argue that leaders are simply born with *traits* that make them effective. Others argue that leaders have mastered different sets of *skills* that nearly anyone can develop. Still others emphasize the *situation* in which a leader finds himself or herself. Which position do you agree with?

more about...

Leadership

"If your actions inspire others to dream more, learn more, do more and become more, you are a *leader.*"

—Pres. John Quincy Adams

"Leadership is about integrity, honesty and accountability. All components of trust."

—Simon Sinek

» LEADERSHIP STYLES

One popular method of understanding leadership is to examine five common styles used by most leaders. These styles are based mostly on the extent to which the leader includes others in the process of making decisions. They are usually called *autocratic, consultative, participative, persuasive,* and *free-rein.*[17]

Autocratic leaders make it very clear that they are in charge. The power and authority autocratic leaders have from their position in the organization are important to them, and followers usually have little or no freedom to disagree or to disobey. Although this style sounds arrogant and dehumanizing, autocratic leaders are often neither. Many operate in an environment where the climate is pleasant enough, but the expectation is that the leader is not questioned.

Consultative leaders will often spend a great deal of time and energy consulting with followers to get information about what decisions should be made for the good of the organization. This behavior sets the consultative leader apart from the autocratic leader. However, when the actual decision is to be made, the consultative leader makes it alone, usually accepting responsibility for the decision regardless of how much input on that decision has been provided by others. Consultative leaders are comfortable delegating authority.

Participative leaders have both concern for people and concern for getting the job done. This type of leadership invites subordinates to share power with the leader. This style is very popular in organizations that rely on teamwork and team building. Although a participative leader encourages others to help make decisions, he or she can and will act decisively, even when not receiving the amount or quality of participation asked for. The effective participative leader will hold company needs equally with group morale, placing emphasis on both factors.

Persuasive leaders are similar to autocratic managers. A persuasive leader keeps control over the final decision. The final decisions, though, are made on how well the leader can persuade the work team toward a position, or the work team can persuade the leader toward a decision. This style works well when managers want information, but are open to discussion. The level of influence is somewhere between consultative and participative. This style works best when employees trust and support management and are invested in the decisions being made.

Free-rein leaders often have subordinates who don't complain about the leadership; however, these leaders are not really leading at all in any strict sense. This "hands off" approach is often called *laissez-faire leadership.* Laissez-faire is a French term that means "allow them to do as they will." In other words, let workers do as they please. This type of leader usually acts as a

more about...

Famous Leaders

Leadership expert Peter Drucker once wrote that "Leadership is lifting a person's vision to high sights, the raising of a person's performance to a higher standard, the building of a personality beyond its normal limitations." Consider the following famous leaders.

Abraham Lincoln

The 16th president of the United States, a towering figure in U.S. history, kept the Union together during the American Civil War, and he effectively ended slavery in the United States by signing the Emancipation Proclamation. His greatest traits were his determination, persistence, beliefs, and courage.

Nelson Mandela

Nelson Mandela was the first South African president elected in fully democratic elections after decades of apartheid in the racially divided country. Mandela served nearly 30 years in prison for his political views, becoming an international hero for his tireless work to dismantle South Africa's apartheid regime, which created a system of institutionalized racial segregation and discrimination. Mandela's main characteristics were his determination, persistence, focus, and will.

Mahatma Gandhi

Mohandas Karamchand Gandhi, better known as Mahatma Gandhi, is considered to be the father of India because of his efforts to end the British occupation of India. Born in 1869, Gandhi pioneered the nonviolent resistance movement, and he inspired civil right movements for equality and freedom across the planet. His main characteristics were resilience, knowledge, people skills, motivational approach, and leading by example.

Do you identify with any of these historical figures? Why? Who are some people, past and present, who have leadership qualities that you admire?

Source: Patrick Alain, "Leadership and 10 Great Leaders from History," *Industry Leaders Magazine*, April 15, 2012.

REAL WORLD EXAMPLE 7.4

Leadership and Major Uber Problems

The story of Uber is not unlike many Silicon Valley success stories. As a ride-sharing pioneer that upended the traditional taxi cab business when it was introduced in 2012, Uber quickly emerged as a leader in the new "gig" or "shared" economy.

Uber experienced exponential growth in its first few years, with stock prices exceeding analysts' expectations. But Uber's first several years in business were also rocky even by start-up standards, and marred by scandals both internal and external. Uber found itself in trouble not only with regulators for its aggressive business practices in new markets, but also for its dysfunctional corporate culture that seems to have permitted, or turned a blind eye to, the harassment of female employees and sometimes clients, and lower pay for females and targeted groups of ethnic minority drivers. After a wide-sweeping audit by former United States Attorney General Eric Holder in early 2017, numerous changes to the company's business practices were recommended, particularly changes at the company's top leadership positions.

It has been widely believed that Uber's corporate culture reflected the notions of its embattled founder, Travis Kalanick, who, by mid-2017, stepped down from his role as CEO because of the widening scandal and mounting dissatisfaction with the corporate culture he had built. In Uber's case, the CEO's leadership style colored the company's early success, but also contributed to major, systemic flaws that threatened the fledgling company's very existence.

more about...

Laissez-faire also refers to a system of government in which industries and other economic influences are controlled very little. The term translates from French as "allow to do," or allowing events to happen as they will, or let people do what they choose.

representative for the group members, while allowing them to plan, control, and complete their tasks as they wish. For success with this leadership style, followers must be self-directed and motivated to act without intervention, and have a clear vision of goals and how to accomplish them.

Which of these four styles of leadership is best? That depends on two variables. First, the *situation* will usually determine the most effective style. High-ranking military personnel may expect a consultative style, making decisions based on incoming shared information. A large orchestra will more likely expect the autocratic approach with the conductor as leader. College and university professors, on the other hand, will often expect either a free-rein approach (since they expect to be treated as independent professionals) or the participative style in their work environments.

Thinking about your college classes, are there some that work better in particular management styles? Your chemistry class, for example, may work better in an autocratic styles in which the professor gives specific instructions. Your ceramics class may work better in a free-rein style in which you work on your own, while your history class may run better in a persuasive or participatory style.

The situation determines, in part, which management style will be more effective. The second determinant focuses on the *personality and skill level* of the leader. Many managers seem unable to use more than one type of leadership style. This often has to do with the flexibility of the leader. Even when the situation calls for a different style, the leader will "default" to the style he or she is accustomed to, sometimes with negative results.

DIFFERENT WAYS TO LEAD

There are several different leadership styles. *What are some of the factors that determine the success of a particular style?*

Baranq/Shutterstock

Leaders and the Use of Power and Authority

The effectiveness of a leader also depends greatly on the leader's attitude toward power. **Power** can be defined as the ability of one person to influence another. This is not to be confused with **authority**, which is the power vested in a specific position within an organization.[18] Some leaders have authority, but little or no power. Other people–sometimes not even designated leaders–have power despite having very little authority.

power
The ability of one person to influence another.

authority
The vested power to influence or command within an organization.

Sources of Power

The way followers respond to power largely determines its effectiveness. How a leader's power is received can depend on where the power comes from.[19] Power is derived at least in part on the position of the person using it. Therefore, there are different forms of position power, as follows:

- **Legitimate power:** This source of power is based on the position the person holds in the organization. This type of power is effective only when followers believe in the legitimacy of the leader's position.
- **Reward power:** This type of power comes from the user's ability to control or influence others with something of value to them, such as praise or a promotion. The reward must be obtainable, and the potential receiver of the reward must believe in the other person's ability to bestow it.
- **Coercive power:** Coercive power depends on the threat of possible punishments, and is commonly used to enforce policies and regulations. When a leader has a great ability to intimidate followers, this type of power is often used.
- **Networking power:** This source of power is sometimes also called "connection power." You have probably heard the expression "It's not what you know; it's who you know." Gaining contacts to help influence others allows a leader to use this power source in many different situations. Often, other people's perception that a leader has that connection or network of connections is just as powerful as the fact itself.

legitimate power
Power based on the position a person holds in an organization that is effective only when followers believe in the structure that produces this power.

reward power
Power that comes from the user's ability to control or influence others with something of value to them.

coercive power
Power that depends on the threat of possible punishment.

networking power
Power that is attained by gaining contact and knowing the right people.

REAL WORLD EXAMPLE 7.5

Tanna quit her job as a systems analyst at a small manufacturing company because of sexism, expressed as significantly lower pay than her male co-workers received. After frantically searching for a replacement, they hired her back as a systems consultant. Now, the company was forced to pay her nearly three times what she had been paid before she quit. They had underestimated the strength of this woman's *expert power.*

expert power

Power that comes from a person's knowledge or skill in areas that are critical to the success of the firm.

charismatic power

Power that is based on the attractiveness a person has to others.

- **Expert power:** Expert power comes from a person's knowledge or skill in areas that are critical to the success of the firm. The employee or manager with expert power has a power source that can often be amazingly strong.
- **Charismatic power:** This power source is based on the attractiveness a person has to others. To produce genuine power, though, the user of charismatic power must also be respected and have characteristics that others admire. Someone with a great deal of charismatic power can often compel others to do favors simply on the basis of positive personal response.[20]

STRENGTHENING YOUR NETWORK POWER.

This source of power comes from gaining contacts. *Can networking help you strengthen other areas of power?*

Dave and Les Jacobs/Blend Images LLC

» ORGANIZATIONAL CLIMATE: THE WEATHER OF THE WORKPLACE

The interaction of groups within the workplace aids in the formation of **organizational climate**, a term introduced in Chapter 5 and reviewed in Chapter 16. Recall that climate in the workplace has some qualities in common with climate in the context of weather. Climate can change rapidly, without warning. A manager with a negative attitude can change a positive climate to a stressful one just by walking into the room. Climate in the workplace can be influenced by environmental factors such as the color of the room, the noise level, and the way people dress. It also affects–and is affected by–the attitudes, stress levels, and communication of the people in the organization.

organizational climate

The emotional weather within an organization that reflects the norms and attitudes of the organization's culture and affects worker morale, attitudes, stress levels, and communication.

Major Qualities of Organizational Climate

The way people see things as individuals, their interactions, and the way an organization is put together produce the climate that all perceive with similar eyes. *Perception* is a very important part of organizational climate, as are *structure* and *interaction.*[21] Organizational climate involves the way members of an organization see it in terms of trust, recognition, freedom to create, fairness, and independence. The climate is produced by the way members relate to each other. It reflects the norms and attitudes of the organization's culture. It also influences and helps to shape the behavior of individuals. Perhaps most

REAL WORLD EXAMPLE 7.6

The large hospital where Farid works is old and noisy. Everyone who works there wears the same type of uniform. The walls are painted standard pale green, and the floors are covered with a dreary gray linoleum. The institution's employee policies have not been changed in decades. It is no wonder than Farid finds the hospital to be an oppressive and stressful place to work. Patients have the same reactions. There are no plants in the waiting room, and the attitudes of the employees are stiff and cold, just like the hospital and its organizational climate.

important, organizational climate is a basis for understanding any situation in the organization.[22]

A manager carries responsibility to lead the organization in a way that will produce a good, or positive, organizational climate. Everyone in the workplace can affect the climate, but the manager's position allows more influence than managers themselves often realize. As an employee, though, do not underestimate the impact that you have as an individual to affect the climate.

more about...

Climate Changes in the Office

Dani, Beto, and Jane have worked together for years in the same small office. They have similar calm personalities, and when they disagree, they quietly talk things out. They are known in their large corporation as the smoothest running division in the company. But twice a month, Gilly, who works in a branch office, spends a day in their office for regular planning meetings. Their supervisor, Lily, can tell the day before Gilly's shared meeting days that she is expected in the office: tempers are short and mistakes get made. Gilly is loud, likes to spend time interrupting the staff to gossip about office politics, takes loud personal conversations on the phone in the office, and just generally disrupts the normal work flow.

One person can greatly change the organizational climate of an office.

Maintaining a Climate

What is a good organizational climate? The best organizational climate is one that allows the highest efficiency and productivity over the longest period of time. That type of climate will almost always include qualities such as high trust levels, a reasonable level of freedom or autonomy in work tasks, high standards of fairness, and appropriate recognition for the work of each person, The best way to communicate these qualities is to set a conscious example. A good place to begin is just basic respect, civility, courtesy, and ethical treatment. A manager can also show appreciation to individual employees for work done well, while allowing them the time and freedom to be creative.

» ORGANIZATIONAL OR CORPORATE CULTURE: SHARED VALUES

How does an organization's *culture* differ from its organizational climate? Organizational culture refers to the collection of deeply held values and assumptions a group of people share. Climate is different in that it reflects the day-to-day norms and attitudes of the organization's culture, i.e., how it "feels" to be in the office. Culture is found in every type of organization,

REAL WORLD EXAMPLE 7.7

Huge transformations are occurring in the American workplace. Companies are taking more serious looks at employee satisfaction as business leaders have come to understand its direct correlation to job performance and the bottom line. Of any company, Alphabet, Inc. (parent company of Google) has been one of the most successful large companies in addressing employee happiness, as well as fostering a distinctly creative, competitive, productive business environment for its workforce.

One of the principal ways Google is able to maintain its success with employee satisfaction is by reinforcing its core values to employees as new hires, and in subsequent training. It also provides generous perks to employees, with free chef-made, organic meals throughout the day; onsite physicians and masseuses; nap pods; free dry cleaning; free haircuts, and more. By meeting their employees' material *hygiene* needs, Google feels that it will attract top talent and lead to happier, more productive employees who will stay longer with the company.

But even Google is not immune to the challenges that all businesses, large and small, face when creating and implementing the corporate values, or culture of the organization. After a male employee wrote an opinion piece contending that women are underrepresented in technology jobs because of psychological differences between men and women, Google fired the employee, then faced a storm of strong opinions from those supporting and those criticizing the company's decision.[28]

from small individual companies to large, multinational corporations. Some industries have their own corporate culture regardless of geography, so that a person working as a medical assistant, programmer, or veterinary technician, for example, would know what to expect in a career field if they moved from one region to another.

organizational or corporate culture
An organization's network that includes the shared values and assumptions within it.

Organizational or corporate culture is the system of shared values and beliefs in an organization. Values are more deep-seated than attitudes. As mentioned in Chapter 4, values also tend to involve a rank order. In other words, the very nature of values places them naturally in a list of varying importance. The values of an organization will set a pattern for its activities, opinions, and actions. Look for a company's culture to be reflected in its dress code, hours of operation, office setup, benefits, hiring and recruitment decisions, client treatment and satisfaction, and every other aspect of how the business operates. The way the company reacts to crises at work, divides up limited resources, trains and coaches employees—all of these actions tell employees what is important to the person in charge. In a well-run organization, these will all be consistent with the company's formally stated mission and philosophy or paradigms—which in itself is a public summary of its culture and values.[26] The trend today is to build a strong, positive culture that motivates employees to work harder, to feel greater loyalty, and to stay with the company and remain productive.

Corporate culture is determined in part by the size of the company and the products it makes. An organization's culture is not just determined by the choices a company's management makes, but also by national traditions and cultures, trends in the economy, and its involvement in global trade. Some aspects of corporate culture are created intentionally, and others grow on their own or are shaped by outside forces, but they all speak to the core of the company's ideology and behaviors and every other aspect of a business.[27]

While every organization has a culture, sometimes it is difficult to see, especially if you look at it from the outside. Some cultures are loyal to management; some are loyal to the union. Some are very close-knit, with a great number of culture stories or myths inspiring loyalty and enthusiasm. Others are weaker, and lack the togetherness and team spirit enjoyed by the stronger cultures. Any culture, be it a corporation, a nation, or a family, is preserved and defined by *oral history* or *culture stories.* **Culture stories** are miniature myths. The culture of an organization can be understood more fully by listening to these stories and finding common themes in them.

more about...

Culture Stories

Culture stories are often shared through videos, in addition to being shared orally. To see some videos created to portray company culture stories, visit https://storiesincorporated.com/7-best-company-culture-videos. There you will find culture story videos for Dell Technologies, Bamboo HR, BAE Systems Inc., Patagonia, Loews Hotels, and Cirrus Logic Inc.

Source: "7 of the Best Company Culture Videos," Stories Incorporated, https://storiesincorporated.com/7-best-company-culture-videos (retrieved April 4, 2020).

Today's Organizational or Corporate Culture: A Focus on Fairness

Many companies today are developing an organizational or corporate culture that is more humane, more closely knit, and above all, more profitable and productive than in the past. This type of corporate culture is made up of a set of newer assumptions about how people should be treated. Much of this thinking is based on a deeper understanding of the importance of employee self-worth on the job. This is moving well beyond the early findings of Elton Mayo, discussed in Chapter 1, which influenced decades of thought on the role of human relations, and have since been re-examined.

culture stories
Stories that illustrate the values of the people who make an organization work.

A strong corporate culture must contain a sense of trust, consistency, truth, clear expectations, equity, influence, justice, respect, and overall fairness in its treatment of people. Figure 7.2 is part of a questionnaire that has been used to study the fairness level of an organization.

Trust in the workplace is the main tool for employees' confidence in management, and management's confidence in employees. One's actions provide a record of trustworthiness. Building trust can be difficult, especially where there has been a record of unfairness or other untrustworthy behavior.

Consistency means remaining predictable and fair. Stability is threatened when there are apparent contradictions in the behaviors of people whom others are depending on, especially managers. With unpredictability and lack of stability come high stress levels.

Truth is one of the most greatest necessities for fairness. Yet the temptation can be great to tell "white lies," withhold information, and tell people what they want to hear.

Integrity is a way of describing the extent to which managers and others are truly willing to put the shared values and expectations of a culture into action. It also means maintaining an ethical code—which is basic to all cultures, as well as to organizations.

more about...

Fairness

"In all people, without exception, there lives some instinct for truth, some attraction toward justice."

—Former U.S. President Franklin D. Roosevelt

figure 7.2

MEASURING FAIRNESS

Factors such as trust, consistency, and honesty—among many others—shape the overall fairness of an organization, and in turn shape that organization's climate. *Which factor do you consider most important?*

Source: Marshall Sashkin and Richard L. Williams, "Does Fairness Make a Difference?" *Organizational Dynamics,* Autumn 1990, pp. 56–71.

Measuring the Fairness Level of an Organization

Check which sentences apply to you. Does your selection reveal what kind of climate you have at work?

Trust

☐ My manager follows through on and carries out promises.

☐ My manager often hides his or her true feelings from others.

Consistency

☐ My manager tells the same story no matter who is asking.

☐ My manager acts inconsistently.

Truthfulness

☐ My manager sometimes tells white lies to help others.

☐ My manager does not change facts in order to look better.

Integrity

☐ My manager keeps his or her word when he or she has made an agreement to do something.

☐ My manager is concerned more with watching out for himself or herself than with helping others.

Expectations

☐ My manager has clear ideas about expectations of employees.

☐ My manager makes sure employees know what is expected of them.

Equity

☐ It is obvious by my manager's actions that he or she has definite favorites among employees.

☐ My manager takes a person's work contributions into account when giving praise recognition.

Influence

☐ My manager makes sure that those who have a "stake" also have a "say."

☐ When an employee is capable of dealing with a job independently, my manager delegates appropriately.

Justice

☐ My manager administers rewards and discipline that fit the situation.

☐ My manager does not give rewards that are out of proportion or inappropriate.

Respect

☐ My manager shows with actions that he or she really cares about employees.

☐ My manager recognizes the strengths and contributions of employees.

Overall Fairness

☐ My manager is fair in how he or she treats employees.

☐ My manager always deals with employees equally.

Expectations, as used here, refer to those that come from management. Through their clear expectations, managers allow the employees to know exactly what is expected of them both individually and in groups.

Equity means treating everyone with the same rules. If a culture has both consistency and equity, all are treated in a way that is fair and just, under all conditions.

Influence means allowing each member of the organization to have a stake in a wide range of activities, including goal setting, problem solving, and helping to make changes.

Justice means that the reward must fit the achievement; the punishment must fit the crime. The two extremes in violation of this quality are overkill (strict zero tolerance, while looking for infractions to punish) and "looking the other way" by ignoring the situation when an infraction occurs.

Respect, or a deep sense of high regard for people, is the basis of all fairness. When you believe that others truly value you, you tend to consider their actions to be fair. Nonverbal signals, such as looking away or walking away while the other person is talking, often show lack of respect for others.

Overall fairness means much more than simply treating people nicely. Fairness is a central issue in the **psychological contract** between managers and subordinates. This contract is not a piece of paper; it is a sometimes unconscious, usually unspoken, agreement between two people to behave in certain ways toward each other.

psychological contract
An agreement that is not written or spoken but is understood between people.

Psychological contracts are a part of all cultures. Although they may not be written down or discussed, they are understood between people. When fairness is implied by managers, employees expect such behaviors from them. Without fairness, the employee usually feels betrayed. A healthy organization will not violate employees' psychological contracts; rather it will respect agreements and expectations set up among management and staff.

more about...

"The violation of a **psychological contract** is the most obvious and painful violation of the principles of fairness."

Source: Marshall Sashkin and Richard L. Williams, "Does Fairness Make a Difference?" *Organizational Dynamics,* Autumn 1990, pp. 56–71.

STRATEGIES FOR SUCCESS

Strategy 7.1 Watching for Hidden Agendas

1. Be aware of strong emotions in other members.
2. Note contradictions between verbal and nonverbal signals.
3. Pay attention to themes that keep coming up, perhaps disguised, even after the formal topic has been changed.
4. Recognize agenda conflicts that involve a group member's self-esteem.

The first key to eliminating hidden agendas from work teams is self-knowledge. Before you join a group, ask yourself, "Am I too focused on what I personally want from this group? Do I know how to keep personal needs from blocking my judgment?"

A tougher problem is dealing with the agendas of other group members. When you are a team leader, you have the power to prevent people's agendas from hurting the group. Even as a member, you can help by watching your behaviors and those of other group members. Important signals include the following:

1. **Be aware of strong emotions in other members.** A hidden agenda will often go beyond the immediate problem. What are those emotions based on, and how appropriate are they? Are they based on a prejudice against the group's real agenda? On fear? On jealousy? On a desire to intimidate other members? On a need for power or dominance?
2. **Note contradictions between verbal and nonverbal signals.** Group members may show hidden agendas through gestures, eye contact (or lack of it), head nods, frowning, and other body movements.
3. **Pay attention to themes that keep coming up, perhaps disguised, even after the formal topic has been changed.** If it's a deeply personal agenda, it could become an underlying issue in any discussion. Note discussions that keep coming back to a topic that someone in the group has brought forward that was not favorably received.
4. **Recognize agenda conflicts that involve a group member's self-esteem.** Often, these are the easiest to spot. Self-esteem issues are behind many agenda issue in a group. The issue is often personal self-esteem versus the esteem of the group as a whole. Note decisions that go against what a particular group member advocated, that seem to be taken personally by the group member.

« STRATEGIES FOR SUCCESS

Strategy 7.2 Building a Successful Team

1. Train the team.
2. Manage the team as a team.
3. Delegate authority specifically.
4. Be a clarifier.
5. Be a communicator.

As is any new method of dealing with people, team building is full of possible areas of error. These possible errors should be examined carefully by anyone attempting team building before the first implementation step is attempted. Each of the following steps will help avoid common pitfalls in the team-building process.

1. **Train the team.** An untrained team might be an informal group; it may be several other things, but it is not a work team. By definition, a work team must be aware of the steps that are to be taken, and the members must be sold on the idea of team building. Often a would-be "team" will feel victimized by management unless each member receives training and understands the role he or she is expected to play.
2. **Manage the team as a team.** The manager has to allow the group to be managed as a team. Any traditional manager will be tempted to continue many of the management functions on an individual basis. Some managers may not be able to break the habit of calling each team member into their office privately to discuss major group problems that arise. They will need to work harder at using cooperative coaching as their model, addressing the group as a whole.
3. **Delegate authority specifically.** The team leader needs to make it very clear what parts of the management responsibilities are to be given over to the group and which are to be retained. The team builder often makes the mistake of thinking that since the team is in place, the leader needs only to sit back and watch.

4. **Be a clarifier.** A major role of the team leader is to clarify the nature of a task and the implementation of the solution. A particular manager, thinking he or she is a team leader, will tell the team to "work out the details" of plans and goals. The team leader needs to be attuned to details, allowing the group to work together but coordinating those efforts through careful monitoring and direction.
5. **Be a communicator.** Whether you are the team leader or a member, you need to listen, write, and speak carefully. Of the three skills, listening is the most important.

To appreciate the usefulness of a successful work team, one needs only to examine a company that has made the concept work. Morale is high, turnover is less, and productivity is higher.

CHAPTER SEVEN SUMMARY

Chapter Summary by Learning Objectives

LO 7-1 **Discuss the characteristics and purposes of groups and teams**. People join groups for many reasons, including affiliation, attraction, activities, assistance, or proximity. Formal groups are created for a specific purpose, while informal groups come together on their own and are more voluntary and fluid in their membership. A group is two or more people who interact with each other, are governed by norms, maintain stable role relationships, and form subgroups.

LO 7-2 **Discuss team development**. Usually, four stages of team development occur, in a specific order: forming, redefining, coordinating, and formalizing. A fifth stage is adjourning.

LO 7-3 **Explain the steps in team building**. Effective team building requires time and effort. Trust building and identification of goals are necessary steps. Implementation and purpose must be defined. Good communication and clarity are essential.

LO 7-4 **Examine barriers to group effectiveness and their resolutions**. Groupthink, status differences, hidden agendas, one-person domination, resistance to change, continued conflict, and lack of creativity can all lead to an ineffective group. Strategies to resolve barriers include changing the group's norms, identifying the specific problems, and changing the group's composition.

LO 7-5 **Define leadership, leadership styles, and types of power**. Leaders are able to influence others toward attaining goals. Leadership styles include autocratic, consultative, persuasive, participative, and free-rein. Sources of power among leaders include legitimate, reward, coercive, networking, expert, and charismatic power.

LO 7-6 **Improve the organizational climate of the workplace**. The climate of a workplace is the tone of its day-to-day functioning. Climate includes physical environment of the workplace, attitudes of managers, communication between employees, and norms of the organization.

LO 7-7 **Understand the new organizational or corporate culture.** Every organization and corporate entity has a culture. Culture includes deeply held values that are used to set goals. Culture stories help transmit and describe the culture. Today's organizational or corporate culture focuses on trust, consistency, truth, integrity, clear expectations, equity, influence, justice, respect, and overall fairness. This type of culture promotes a more productive workplace with higher morale.

key terms

authority 195
autocratic leaders 192
charismatic power 196
coercive power 195
conformity 188
consultative leaders 193
culture stories 199
expert power 196
free-rein leaders 193
group 180
groupthink 188
hidden agendas 191
leadership 192
legitimate power 195
networking power 195
norm 189
organizational climate 196
organizational or corporate culture 198
participative leaders 193
persuasive leaders 193
power 195
psychological contract 201
reward power 195
status 188
team 181
team building 185
work team 185

review questions

1. Think of groups you have joined, both formally and informally. What were the benefits you expected to receive upon joining? Were those expectations fulfilled?
2. Recall a team to which you have belonged, and identify the path the team followed. What did you notice about how the team functioned at first, and near the end of their task?
3. Recalling groups to which you have belonged, how did they assign status in the group? Was it easy to see who had higher and lower status in the group? Did you agree with the statuses that seemed to be assigned within the group? Explain.
4. Recall a leader whose direction you once followed. Do you recognize that leader's style as autocratic, consultative, persuasive, participative, or

free-rein? Provide examples of behaviors that showed that style. Explain whether you liked or disliked this style of leadership.

5. Imagine a leader in any setting with whom you have worked using more than one of the styles of leadership explained in this chapter. Would this improve his or her abilities as a leader? How can flexibility influence a leader? Are there any drawbacks to flexibility?
6. Think of an ideal version, in your opinion, of a perfect organizational climate. What characteristics would be included? Why?
7. Fairness is an important quality of a positive, or warm, organizational climate and culture. What qualities are necessary for a perception of fairness to exist throughout an organization?
8. Explain the expectations for today's organizational or corporate culture. In your opinion, would this type of culture lead toward success for America as an international competitor? Why or why not?
9. At a national conference attended by one of your authors, a facilitator introduced a workshop topic as "How to Work in Teams, and Other Raising-Morale Crap." The audience reaction included dismay and surprise at the speaker's negativity toward the announced topic. Based on information from this chapter, what type of corporate culture would you guess this facilitator worked in? How well does it fit with today's corporate culture?
10. Imagine yourself as (a) a ship captain and (b) a football team player and captain. How would you describe the advantages and disadvantages of each? Considering these advantages and disadvantages, why do you suppose that the team captain, rather than the ship captain, is a more popular analogy for management styles today in the United States?

critical thinking questions

1. Which of the leadership styles is yours or would most likely be yours? Why did you choose this particular style? Does your profession of choice match with this style? How does this leadership style reflect your personality?
2. Is an organizational or corporate culture necessary? That is, can we all just go to work and get our tasks done in an organization that does not have a shared culture? How important is it for an organization to have a shared corporate culture? Why is this such a common—practically universal—phenomenon? Think about an organization that has no corporate culture: What would that be like? Would people get as much accomplished?
3. Describe an organizational climate that would be described as cold. Now, describe an organizational climate that would be described as warm.

working it out 7.1

HOW IS THE "WEATHER" IN YOUR ORGANIZATIONAL CLIMATE?

School-to-Work Connection: Resource Skills, System Skills, and Interpersonal Skills

Organizations have a pleasant or unpleasant climate, whether it is stated or not, whether it is admitted or not. The corporate culture that may be captured in a company's mission statement can sometimes give you clues about the organizational climate. Even though an organization may formally state its climate goals, and these are then agreed upon by an organization as a whole, the intended organizational climate may be interpreted in different ways by different members of the organization.

In this exercise, think about three different offices you have visited within the same organization (your own workplace, or somewhere else), or think about three different instructors' offices at the college you are attending. What differences do you note in pleasantness or unpleasantness of the organizational climate?

Consider these factors in your descriptions of each of the three offices:

1. How is the furniture arranged? Does the desk act as a barrier between the office occupant's chair and the visitor's chair? (Are there even any chairs for visitors?)
2. Is the office stark or inviting? Are there personal effects in the office, such as plants, pictures of family members, or artwork?
3. Is the office cluttered and disorganized, or neatly arranged?
4. How is your interaction with the office occupant? Does he or she make eye contact, or avoid it? Does the person do other tasks while talking with you—take phone calls, look at his or her watch or cell phone while talking—or give you full attention? Does the person smile and act inviting, or frown and act annoyed to see you?

Compare your evaluations of the three offices and discuss your findings in a small group of classmates. What does this exercise tell you about how you will set up, or modify, your own office to fit your view of the desired organizational climate?

working it out 7.2

ROLE-PLAY

School-to-Work Connection: Interpersonal Skills

Procedure: Break the class into groups of five or fewer. One person will be the team leader, and the others will be the team members. The team leader will read the following script while the team members respond where they think appropriate, correcting the team leader on his or her misunderstood concepts of work teams.

Scenario: You are working in a company that has just now enthusiastically embraced the idea of work teams. Your former supervisor, now "Team Leader," hasn't been to the team leader training yet, but really likes the idea of working as a team. The team leader delivers the following pep talk on teamwork one Monday morning.

As you listen, decide what your response will be whenever you think your team leader is saying the wrong thing. Try not to interrupt the team leader as he or she speaks.

"Hey, Group! Team of mine! Good morning! Wow, we're all together again after a great weekend! Hey, how about that Seahawks-Giants game? So, this morning we're going to start working as a team, just like the Golden State Warriors. You all know what to do, you know your parts, so get out there and play ball! I'm going to be calling each one of you into my office, one at a time, to talk about this team thing. Now, when I call you in, bring in a pad and pencil, because I'm going to be giving you all the team directions. Don't worry about thinking up stuff to say or making any decisions, I've got it all figured out how this is going to run. In the meantime, if you need me, I'll be in my office; but try to make an appointment, because I'll be doing my regular administrative stuff. Okay? Then here we go, team! *Go team, go!*"

When the team leader is finished with the pep talk you may do the following:

1. Ask any questions you have about the pep talk.
2. (Gently!) Correct his or her misconceptions about working as a team.

working it out 7.3

TEAM-BUILDING ACTIVITY: MAGAZINE COVER

Objective: Promote teamwork and creativity.

Materials needed: Paper, poster paper, pens, markers, scissors, magazines, any arts and crafts supplies.

Duration: 60 minutes.

To begin: Divide the class into teams of 3 to 5.

Each team will create a (fictional) magazine cover story featuring a successful team project or business achievement. The magazine cover will include (a) the magazine cover, (b) images (drawings or magazine photos) for the magazine cover, (c) headline for the cover story, (d) quotes from team members and (fictional) quotes from business leaders, and (e) sidebar highlights about the project or the business achievement.

Each team will present their magazine cover to the class.

De-brief: Discuss with the class how well the teams worked together. What was successful in working on the magazine cover? What was challenging? What would they do the same, or differently, next time?

Optional: The class chooses the best magazine cover.

Source: Esther Cohen, "35 Team Building Activities Your Team Will Actually Love," Workamajig, June 11, 2019, https://www.workamajig.com/blog/team-building-activities (retrieved April 4, 2020).

working it out 7.4

TEAMWORK: GETTING RID OF THE PECKING ORDER

Watch the TED Talk by business leader and entrepreneur Margaret Heffernan, titled "Why It's Time to Forget the Pecking Order at Work," and then answer the following questions.

1. What is a "pecking" order in the workplace? Why is it called that (in relation to actual chickens)?
2. What is a "super-chicken," according to the speaker? Is this a good thing or a bad thing in the workplace?
3. How does getting rid of a pecking order increase group cohesion and productivity?
4. What are the three characteristics found in the most successful groups, as described by the speaker? Thinking about successful and unsuccessful groups or teams you have worked with, do these ideas fit with your experience?
5. Why is social capital the most important characteristic for group success, according to the speaker? Have you found this to be the case in your own experience?

The video can be found here: www.youtube.com/watch?v=Vyn_xLrtZaY.

case study 7.1

Mariko's Promotion

Part of Mariko Koide's promotion in the advertising firm where she worked was a transfer to another division of the company. The promotion seemed like a totally positive experience for her, and she was very happy—at least initially. Her first day in the new division was one of handshaking, smiles, and welcoming comments. Things looked really positive.

However, after a few weeks had passed, it became apparent to Mariko that this division had a different "feeling" to it. In her old office, her fellow employees had spent a great deal of time on what they called "idea creation." Some nights, when ideas were a bit slow in coming, everyone would work two or three hours late. Throughout the process, everyone had seemed positive and upbeat and not at all resentful of the long sessions.

The new division was not like that at all. It seemed that a great deal of conflict was always going on. One worker was always complaining about what a "jerk" someone else was. Overtime sessions were rare, and when they happened, they were resented and typically resulted in dozens of oral and written complaints. The walls of the restrooms had insulting caricatures of some of the managers on the walls, with equally insulting comments written beneath them.

Also, all of the employees seemed to be heavily involved in outside activities that had nothing to do with company business, or even with the talents needed to work there. The very idea of working late *voluntarily* was laughable.

Mariko began wondering whether she should have accepted the promotion. Instead of being excited and happy, she began finding it difficult to get up in the morning and drive to work. "I wonder if I could get back to the other division," she found herself thinking one day.

Case Study Questions

1. If you knew Mariko as a friend, what would you advise her to do at this point?
2. Is Mariko helpless in her new position? If you don't think so, suggest some courses of action she could take.
3. Evaluate Mariko's situation in terms of norms and status.

case study 7.2

Through the Ranks

Daura had been promoted through the ranks of her company to her present supervisory position in management. The president of the company recently asked her to create another administrative position—one that would report directly to Daura—which would be filled internally. The president was aware that a lot of recent conflict between administration and nonadministrative staff members had led to low morale and high employee turnover, and she had decided one way to reduce this was to create the new position to bridge the gap between these two employee groups. Seven people applied for the newly created position, and Daura sent each of them an e-mail saying that she would be interviewing only the top three candidates.

Soon, grumbling among applicants and other employees interested in the process began to be heard, based mainly on the decision to interview only a few candidates. Since interviews for seven applicants could be managed pretty easily, and employee morale was already low, they reasoned, *all* applicants deserved at least a "courtesy interview." Before the final candidates were announced, Daura's administrative assistant approached her and asked her if it would be possible to schedule interviews for all seven candidates as a way to reduce growing resentment among employees.

Daura's response was straight to the point as she snapped: "If they don't like the process, they can quit. They'd better be happy I even agreed to go along with the decision to open this position. I'm in charge here, and none of you had better forget it. Anyone who wants to stand up to me on this had better do it now, so I know who the troublemakers are and I can make sure they don't get promoted."

Case Study Questions

1. What leadership style does Daura seem to be using?
2. What are Daura's sources of power? Are these the most appropriate ones she should be using in this situation?
3. If you were Daura's manager, would you try to change behaviors in her leadership methods? Which ones? Why?

CHAPTER EIGHT

8

ACHIEVING EMOTIONAL CONTROL

LEARNING OBJECTIVES

After studying this chapter, you will be able to:

LO 8-1 Identify the eight forms of intelligence.

LO 8-2 Describe the theory of triarchic intelligence and contrast it with multiple intelligence theory.

LO 8-3 Explain the significance of emotional intelligence and how it compares with earlier theories of measuring intelligence.

LO 8-4 Describe how to apply emotional intelligence.

LO 8-5 List ways to deal with strong emotions, including anger.

LO 8-6 Compare and contrast assertiveness, aggression, and passivity.

LO 8-7 Give examples of defensive behaviors and how they affect the workplace.

LO 8-8 Explain the importance of positive intelligence and how inner saboteurs can reduce our effectiveness.

LO 8-9 Distinguish among the various scripts that influence our actions.

LO 8-10 Explain why people "play games" in the workplace, and how to deal with games.

STRATEGIES FOR SUCCESS

Strategy 8.1 Defeating Your Inner Saboteurs

Strategy 8.2 Stopping Games before They Start

In the Workplace: Emotions out of Control

SITUATION

After a very long wait in the sales line at the department store, Carmen finally made it to the checkout counter, only to see—too late—the hand-printed notice on the cashier stand that said "This line cash only, no cards."

Bignai/Shutterstock

Carmen apologized to the sales clerk, saying "I'm sorry I didn't see the sign. I don't have any cash, but here is my debit card."

The sales clerk replied, with a disinterested shrug, "The card reader isn't working, I can only take cash. That is clear from the notice I posted. You'll have to get back in line and wait for another clerk."

Carmen was incredulous. "Seriously? But I already waited long enough! Are you trying to drive away business?" Carmen felt herself becoming more and more angry. "I don't even like this store! I only stopped here because it was on my way and I'm in a hurry!"

The sales clerk just shrugged again, looked at the line of customers behind Carmen, and called "Next customer in line."

Carmen dropped her items on the counter and left, her frustration and anger compounded by what she felt was unfair and uncaring treatment. She vowed never to shop at that store again.

DISCOVERY

Carmen was furious about the salesperson's attitude. When she got home, she thought about what she wanted to say and made an angry phone call to the store manager. That gave her some satisfaction, but it didn't change the fact that she didn't get to buy the items she had shopped for. She wished she could have somehow solved the problem on the spot.

THINK ABOUT IT

What were some different ways Carmen could have responded to the salesperson while still in the store?

Could she have addressed the issue afterward in a different manner than contacting the store manager?

What would you have done?

» THE EIGHT FORMS OF INTELLIGENCE

intelligence
Traditionally seen as reasoning ability, as measured by standardized tests.

eight intelligences
Eight separate areas in which people put their perceptiveness and abilities to work.

For many years, people assumed that **intelligence** was a one-dimensional concept of reasoning ability, measured by standardized tests. For example, it was thought a person would either make it through college or fail, based on his or her ability to perform well on college exams. Those who made it through college and graduated were thought to be smart; those who failed were not. In the past several years, though, there has been more agreement among experts that intelligence comes in many forms.

Many researchers, such as psychologist Howard Gardner, believe that there is more than one way to be *smart.* Instead of asking, "How smart are you?" Gardner would ask, "*How* are you smart?" He is referring to the **eight intelligences**—eight separate areas in which people put their intellectual capacities to work. (See Figure 8.1.) Examine your talents and abilities to see which of these intelligence categories best describes you: *language* (the ability to put thoughts into words and to understand words), *math and logic, music, spatial reasoning* (understanding the relationship of objects in a space), *movement, interpersonal* intelligence (ability to form relationships with others), *intrapersonal* intelligence (understanding oneself), and/or *naturalist*

figure 8.1

THE EIGHT DIMENSIONS OF INTELLIGENCE

These different types of intelligence are reflected in various talents and skills. You will know your areas of intelligence by the areas in which you excel. *In what areas of intelligence are you strongest?*

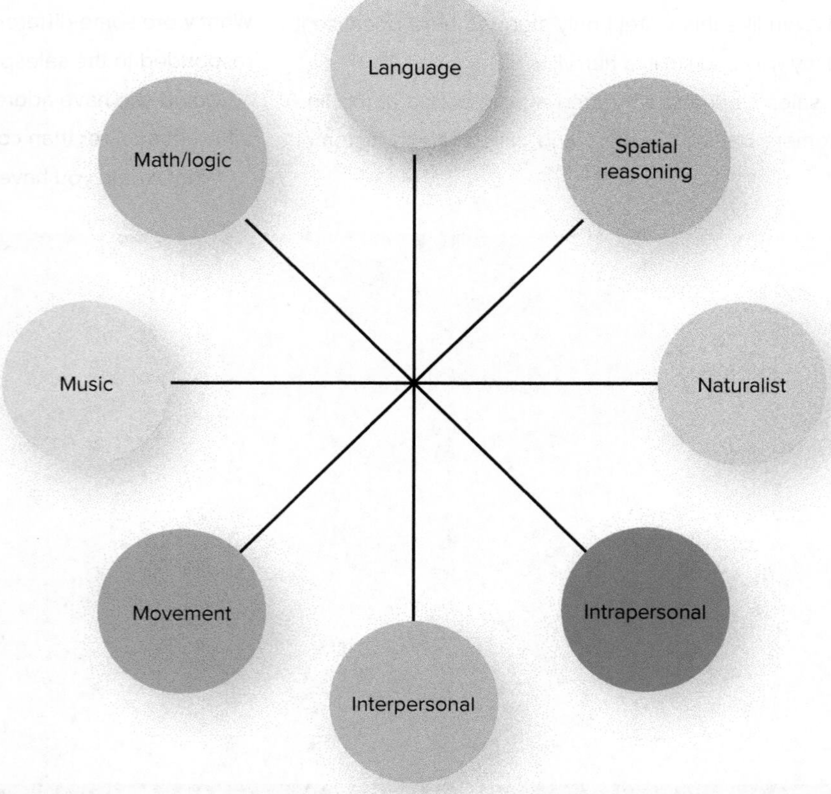

intelligence (relationships with natural surroundings). You may be stronger in one area than others, or a combination of these areas.[1]

Language

People who have verbal or language intelligence are gifted writers, poets, songwriters, and speakers. If you love language and are fascinated by its meanings, expressions, and rhythms, your intelligence falls into this area. Standardized intelligence tests are usually designed to tap into this intelligence in questions on verbal comprehension and vocabulary. Noam Chomsky is a noted linguist who has this talent. Mark Twain, one of America's most celebrated authors; Alice Walker, who won the Pulitzer Prize for fiction in 1983; and Nobel Prize winners Toni Morrison and Bob Dylan are also good examples.

Math and Logic

Scientists and mathematicians find fulfillment in using the logical, reasoning parts of the brain. If you enjoy puzzles of logic or brain teasers, you are strong in this type of intelligence. Those who enjoy reasoning, scientific experimentation, and pattern recognition have this type of intelligence. Most of the standardized intelligence tests measure math and logic ability levels. Albert Einstein is a good example of someone who understood the world through his strength in math and logic. Neil DeGrasse Tyson, Marilyn vos Savant, Manahel Thabet, Terence Tao, Ruth Lawrence, and Stephen Hawking display this intelligence as well.

more about...

Possible Additional Intelligences

Prompted by calls from proponents of multiple intelligence theory to include moral, spiritual, or religious intelligence components, Gardner has suggested that "existential intelligence" and "moral intelligence" may be useful concepts. Those with *existential* intelligence are thought to have the capacity or sensitivity to tackle deep questions about human existence, such as the meaning of life, human consciousness, and why we are born and die. Those with *moral* intelligence have heightened focus on the sanctity of life. Religious and cultural figures such as Buddha, Jesus, Carl Sagan, and the Dalai Lama are thought of as showing traits that would exemplify spiritual and moral intelligences.

While these additional intelligences are accepted by many, Gardner himself is not ready to formally add them to the list—yet. More recently, Gardner suggested a potential *additional* type of intelligence, a teaching-pedagogical intelligence. This intelligence is the ability to teach other people effectively.

Source: Howard Gardner, *Changing Minds: The Art and Science of Changing Our Own and Other People's Minds* (Harvard Business School Press, 2004). See also: Mark Smith, "Howard Gardner, Multiple Intelligences and Education," *Infed*, October 2019, https://infed.org/mobi/howard-gardner-multiple-intelligences-and-education (retrieved March 11, 2020); Howard Gardner, "Intelligence Isn't Black and White: There Are 8 Different Kinds," Big Think, January 12, 2016, https://bigthink.com/videos/howard-gardner-on-the-eight-intelligences, minutes 5:00–5:55 and 8:16.

Music

Most people whose intelligence falls into this category have a relationship with sounds. As children, they may have tried to produce new combinations of sounds on their own. As adults, they may become professional musicians or composers. If you can play, write, or read music with ease and enjoyment, you have this strength. People who are good at understanding music's notes, tones, and structures would fit here. Ludwig van Beethoven, who continued to write music even after he lost his hearing, provides an example of musical intelligence. Your favorite musician or musical group is another example.

more about...

Ludwig van Beethoven (1770–1827), a German composer, was already deaf when he conducted his Ninth Symphony. He had to be turned around to see the ecstatic reaction of the audience.

Spatial Reasoning

A person who excels in this area has a talent for seeing how elements fit together in space. This type of intelligence can be expressed by building structures, completing jigsaw puzzles, or by something as elaborate as perfecting the art of three-dimensional sidewalk chalk drawings. If you can picture how items will look when objects are rearranged, you have this strength. People who are good at interpreting maps, graphs, and charts are high in this intelligence. Spatial reasoning is physical and mechanical, and less tied to ideas and concepts. Michelangelo's understanding of spatial elements in his sculptures provides an example of spatial intelligence. Frank Lloyd Wright's architecture is another example of this strength in his architecture and designs. Other examples include Maya Lin, Leonardo da Vinci, and Zaha Hadid for their architecture and sculpture design talents.

Movement

Most people probably haven't thought of physical movement as a part of intelligence because it is not part of the traditional definition, but the ability to use your body or parts of your body with highly specialized skill is a type of intelligence (also known as kinesthetic intelligence). Athletes and dancers are examples of people who excel in this area. LeBron James, Serena Williams, and Jim Thorpe, a few of the great athletes we have seen in American history, provide examples of kinesthetic intelligence; so does someone like Beyoncé, the celebrated pop star. Simone Biles, considered by many as the greatest female gymnast yet, fits with this intelligence. Another person with kinesthetic intelligence is Olympic athlete Michael Phelps, the most decorated Olympian of all time, who over four Olympic games (2004, 2008, 2012, and 2016) won a total of 28 medals, including 23 gold.

TYPES OF INTELLIGENCE

Recent research suggests that there is more than one way to measure intelligence. *Where do your strengths and skills lie? To which intelligences do they relate most closely?*

Interpersonal Intelligence

This area of intelligence is defined as one's ability to understand and communicate well with other people. It is an essential skill in all aspects of life and is particularly important in business. You may find a person with interpersonal intelligence in a position of power and leadership. These people are often respected by others. They are often skilled at reading nonverbal communication, at seeing situations from different perspectives, and at resolving conflicts. If you have a special skill in communicating with others, or if many people have told you that you are a born leader, then you may have this strength. Eleanor Roosevelt exhibited this strength in her ability to communicate with all types of people. Martin Luther King, Jr., had the ability to create motivation in others. Mahatma Gandi was an attorney and political ethicist who impassioned people in India to work nonviolently for freedom from British rule. Nelson Mandela is remembered throughout the world as a leader who understood others and used his platform on the world stage to speak for their pain and aspirations.

more about...

Aristotle (384–322 B.C.), ancient Greek scientist and philosopher, is one of the Western world's most influential intellectuals. His writings emphasized logic, concrete facts, and deduction. He exemplifies the intelligence of logic.

Intrapersonal Intelligence

Intrapersonal intelligence is described as knowledge of yourself. The person with this type of intelligence is *introspective,* or able to examine his or her own life and experiences. A person with a large amount of this type of intelligence knows his or her own strengths, weaknesses, desires, and fears—and can act on that knowledge realistically. Aristotle, who advised that you should *know thyself,* understood the importance of the introspective process known as intrapersonal intelligence. Sigmund Freud devoted his career to helping people understand themselves. Both have become associated with the idea of intrapersonal intelligence.

Naturalist Intelligence

The person who is high in this type of intelligence has an understanding of nature and natural processes. This person becomes a part of the rhythms and cycles of nature. If you are happiest when you are outdoors and have a natural understanding of the outside world, you have this strength. Jane Goodall, famous for her work with chimpanzees in central Africa, provides an example of this type of intelligence. Dian Fossey, also a primatologist, possessed this intelligence as well. Another example is John Muir, the naturalist, author, and conservationist who founded the Sierra Club.

Fuse/Getty Images

more about...

Changes and Stress

Jane Goodall (1934–), a British naturalist, studied chimpanzee behavior at Gombe Stream Game Reserve in Tanzania for decades. Today she is a leading animal rights activist. She provides an example of strong naturalistic intelligence.

Do some of these intelligences seem a better fit for you than others? If you are an employee, look for opportunities to work in a situation that allows you to utilize the strengths of your intelligences. Working to your strengths adds value and increases productivity in your workplace. If you are a manager, watch for the type of intelligence each of your employees exhibits and learn to use their abilities to the fullest capacity. Such knowledge can help you to significantly raise the level of an organization's creative output. When people are working to their strengths, it becomes easier for them to maintain a sense of purpose, motivation, and emotional control.

Gardner's theory does have its critics. He has not supported his theories with empirical research. Critics say that what he calls intelligences are really closer to talents, skills, or personality traits.[2] Whether you believe that Gardner's theory should definitely replace traditional intelligence theories, or you believe that he is just talking about talents, there is no denying that his ideas have had a big impact in education on how we think about the skills and abilities that people have, and how we all differ from each other.

This theory's impact also comes into play in workplace performance when we assign tasks to others or take on tasks for ourselves that allow us all to work to our strengths.

» TRIARCHIC INTELLIGENCE

triarchic (three arches) theory

Intelligent behavior arising from a balance between analytical, creative, and practical abilities, where these abilities function together to allow people to achieve success within their social and cultural contexts.

Robert Sternberg is known for his **triarchic (three arches) theory** of intelligence. Like Gardner, Sternberg does not believe that intelligence is best explained by a single number or measured by a single test. The triarchic theory of intelligence says that people have three types of abilities in differing amounts: analytical, creative, and practical skills.

Analytical skills are best described as finding the facts. This area of the three abilities is closest to what traditional intelligence tests measure and can be thought of as "book smarts." Typically, a complex problem with one right answer is a good fit to measure this type of ability.

Creative abilities are those that require unique problem solving, putting ideas together in a nontraditional way. Some questions in traditional intelligence tests that are answered in a creative way would be considered incorrect. The ability to see situations in a new perspective is creative ability.

Practical abilities are sometimes known as "street smarts," or the ability to analyze everyday problems and come up with the best solution. Situations that require fast thinking rather than a complex analysis of all the elements in the situation are best managed with practical abilities. These abilities rely on past experience and an understanding of the specific setting.

As you come to understand the three sub-types of intelligence in Sternberg's theory, consider how you would apply them in a workplace setting. As a manager, are there times when your team is stuck and needs a creative solution? Would the creativity intelligence sub-type be effective in specific jobs such as product development or advertising? Where would the analytical subtype best use their strengths in a workplace setting? Perhaps the analytical sub-type is ideal in analyzing a complex price point or a supply chain or in testing manufacturing processes and products. Where do the practical intelligence sub-types come in? When unexpected situations arise that require staff to "think on their feet," this sub-type of intelligence is needed.

Do you see yourself in any of these descriptions? Are you always that way, or does it depend on the situation? Are you a combination of ability types, or strictly one or another? As with Gardner's multiple intelligences theory, not everyone agrees with this description of intelligence. The theory has been criticized for not being empirical or "scientific" enough, and Sternberg's own definitions are not always clear.[3] But that does not mean it is not useful. When we understand ourselves and work to our strengths, our personal and professional lives are more productive.

As with other theories related to intelligences, or skills and abilities, knowing your strengths and how to work to your strengths will help you work to a higher potential. When you work to your strengths and feel

REAL WORLD EXAMPLE 8.1

In his book *Successful Intelligence,* Robert Sternberg tells an apparently true story about two students named Penn and Matt. Penn was very brilliant and creative. The problem was that he was very much aware of his own abilities and acted the part of an incredibly arrogant person. So, in spite of his brilliance, Penn tended to offend people everywhere he went. Of course, he looked fantastic on paper. When he graduated, he had a great number of offers for job interviews. When the interviewing was over, though, Penn ended up with only one real job offer, and it was with a second-rate company.

Matt, on the other hand, wasn't as brilliant academically as Penn. However, his social presence was very positive. People who worked with him really liked him. Matt ended up with seven solid job offers and went on to be successful in his field. Matt had emotional intelligence; Penn didn't.[4]

comfortable with what you are working on in your work team, emotional control is easier.

» EMOTIONAL INTELLIGENCE

Newer ideas of cultural intelligence, such as Howard Gardner's theory of eight intelligences, Robert Sternberg's triarchic intelligence, and other theories, have been received with interest by sociologists, psychologists, and the general public. Another of the more recent approaches to studying intelligence is the concept of **emotional intelligence**, also referred to as EI (emotional intelligence), or EQ (emotional quotient). How often have you observed the life of someone with a very high IQ (a high score on a standard intelligence test) who seems to make mistake after major lifetime mistake? Or have you noticed how often people with high IQs fail to translate their strong ability to learn into other areas of their lives? For a very long time, we had been taught that our traditional idea of intelligence, measured by how well one does on an IQ test, is the most accurate predictor of success. Daniel Goleman, a prominent writer and scholar, has exploded that opinion, showing instead that *emotional* intelligence is a much better predictor of success in nearly every area of life, not always including academic success. He says, "At best, IQ contributes about 20 percent to the factors that determine life success. . . ."[5]

emotional intelligence (EI)
The ability to see and control your own emotions and to understand the emotional states of other people.

Goleman explains emotional intelligence by pointing out that we all have "two minds." First, we have the **rational mind**, which is aware of reality and which allows us to ponder and reflect. The **emotional mind** is another way of knowing. It is powerful, impulsive, and sometimes illogical. As he puts it, "each feeling has its own repertoire of thought, reactions, and even memories."[6] Several dozen definitions of EI have been expressed. In its simplest terms, however, emotional intelligence is the ability to *"recognize, understand and manage our own emotions; and recognize, understand and influence the emotions of others."*[7]

rational mind
An awareness of reality, which allows you to ponder and reflect.

emotional mind
A powerful, impulsive, sometimes illogical awareness; an ability to perceive emotions.

emotional competence
A learned capability based on emotional intelligence; results in outstanding performance at work.

personal competence
The ability to be self-aware, motivated, and self-regulated.

social competence
Empathy for others combined with sensitivity and effective social skills.

Daniel Goleman teaches also that **emotional competence** is an extremely important factor in understanding EI. Emotional competence can be defined as "a learned capability based on emotional intelligence that results in outstanding performance at work."[8] In other words, it is the application of EI use in the workplace.

According to Goleman, there are two types of emotional competence: **personal competence** and **social competence**.[9] These are the ways in which we manage ourselves. If you have effective personal competence, you are self-aware (see Chapter 3), motivated (see Chapter 5), and self-regulated. Being self-regulated means being trustworthy, conscientious, and self-controlled. It also means that you are adaptable and innovative. A worker who constantly procrastinates and who seems unmotivated likely is lacking in the personal competence area.

The socially competent person has empathy for others and has effective social skills. His or her empathy includes a genuine desire to understand other people and to be sensitive to political and social differences of others. Recent studies have isolated four different areas of emotional intelligence based on the set of related EI skills.[10]

1. *Self-awareness.* This is the ability to understand the way you are perceived by other people. In Chapter 3, *healthy* self-awareness was defined as "the ability to see yourself realistically, without a great deal of difference between what you are and how you assume others see you."

   If you have healthy self-awareness you will be able to make decisions that others might describe as "intuitive," when actually you can make such decisions safely because you understand the reactions of other people toward you. A self-aware person will know when he or she is seen as underrating or overrating another person. In other words, such a person will have a clearer view of what other people are really about.
2. *Social awareness.* When you have social awareness in the EI model, you have a set of skills that allows you to understand the politics of your own workplace. You can discern different attitudes from different people toward themselves, the work they are engaged in, and each other. You can also interpret nonverbal communication effectively. You are in tune with facial expressions and body language that disclose the real feelings and political positions of others. You can take others' perspective, and feel empathy.
3. *Self-management.* One of the most important parts of self-management is what we commonly call self-control. It is the ability to hold yourself in check and not overreact when something bothers you. A self-managed person will seldom, if ever, lose his or her temper or get involved in shouting matches with other people. Coming to work with a bad mood from home is another behavior less likely to happen with someone who has this group of skills mastered. Finally, well self-managed people will not allow frustration to get the best of them.

4. *Relationship management.* Someone with effective relationship management skills will be able to settle conflicts and disagreements between groups and between people. This set of EI skills enables the individual to communicate effectively and to build meaningful interpersonal relationships both with individuals and with groups. They can be depended on to settle disputes within a team or other group and have the ability to stay focused on the relevant issues, rather than on the other peripheral things that might be involved.

EMOTIONAL INTELLIGENCE

Social awareness and sensitivity to the emotions of others are just as important for success as your knowledge and abilities. *How do the emotional mind and rational mind function together? Can a lack of emotional intelligence sabotage a person with other types of intelligence?*

Pressmaster/Shutterstock

» LEARNING TO APPLY EMOTIONAL INTELLIGENCE

How can someone with a lower level of emotional intelligence grow and develop into someone with a higher EI? The experts tell us that emotional intelligence *can* be learned. One can learn, for example, to trade one set of responses with another.[11] According to several studies, not only can EI be learned, it can improve over time, often as a lifelong learning process. In one study of business college graduates, continued improvement could be seen as long as seven years after the initial training had taken place.[12]

Motivation expert Richard Boyatzis says that the most common mistake made by people wanting to improve their EI is thinking that knowing more about the issue will make a person's skills better.[13] The trick is learning to *apply* and *use* that knowledge in a practical, real way, rather than just learning about it. Here are a few practical approaches that nearly anyone can take:

1. *Review what you know about self-awareness.* Revisit Chapter 3 of this book, recalling all of the skills one needs to be more self-aware. Next, ask yourself each time you interact with someone whether or not you are tuning in to the manner in which you are coming off during the process. Perhaps you understand what you feel. However, the important issue is *how well does the other person seem to be picking up on those feelings?* Are you hiding them, either purposely or accidentally?
2. *Take note of others whose social competence seems to be high, who have social awareness skills that you don't have but would like to attain.* For example, observe someone who is better able to feel empathy than you are. (Empathy is the ability to identify with the needs and feelings of others.) Watch the person as he or she listens to others; observe the facial expressions used to communicate careful listening; listen carefully to the words used to ask about feelings and needs.[14]
3. *Work actively on improving your self-management skills.* Self-management is an important part of EI. It includes emotional self-control, adaptability,

and optimism, along with other related qualities. Try spending a few extra seconds deciding how you will react whenever something threatening or challenging comes from another person. Those few seconds can make a tremendous difference in how well you self-manage.

4. *Develop relationship management skills.* This is a set of skills identified by Goleman and others to work successfully in groups or teams.[15] Look at others who operate well in the arena of relationships with others. Watch them carefully as they take care of conflicts between people, as they use things people have in common to take care of their differences, as they use humor as a human relations tool.

» HANDLING STRONG EMOTIONS

In a typical workplace setting, where people may spend a third or more of their lives with people whom they did not necessarily choose to be with, it is not unusual for strong negative emotions to arise. These can include anger, envy, frustration, sadness, and others. Of these strong emotions, anger may be one of the strongest and most potentially harmful.

An important aspect of emotional intelligence is the ability to deal with this important area of our personality; in other words, how we manage anger and other strong negative emotions. Many psychologists say that these emotions come more from how we process events than the nature of the events themselves. Emotions become what they are because of "trigger thoughts" about the things that happen around you. These trigger thoughts usually come to the surface when at least one of two things has happened: (1) you are convinced that other people are to blame for deliberately and unnecessarily causing you trouble or (2) you interpret the behavior of other people as breaking the rules of appropriate behavior.[16]

We focus on anger here as one of the most destructive emotions. Anger produces three basic results that are negative and damaging:[17]

IMPROVING YOUR EMOTIONAL INTELLIGENCE

To increase your emotional intelligence, you should take the time to apply the knowledge and perceptions you gain through awareness of yourself and others. *What are some opportunities to improve your EI at your current job, or at the workplace of someone you know?*

Ariel Skelley/Blend Images/ Getty Images

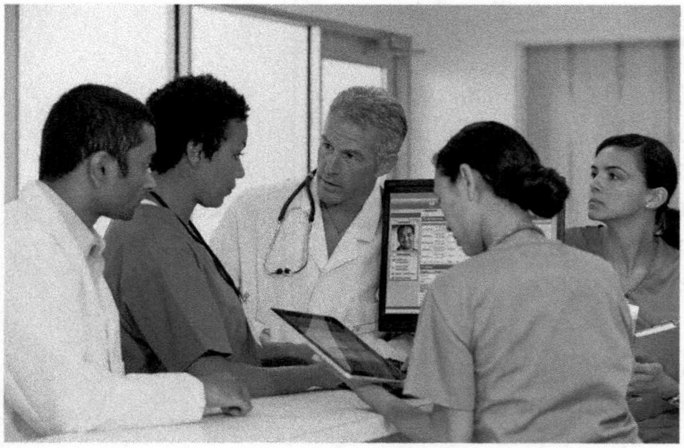

1. *Anger blinds you in several ways.* First, it blinds the individual to other ways of seeing reality. For example, if someone misses a deadline, it is tempting to see the guilty person as irresponsible and uncaring and to be blinded to any other interpretation of the guilty person's behavior. Second, anger blinds the individual to his or her responsibility for what has happened—the fact that someone missed that deadline could possibly be even partly your fault. Third, anger can blind one to other, less painful ways of dealing with the problem.

2. *Left unchecked, anger will grow.* This is how many wars start. Anger is discussed, pondered,

REAL WORLD EXAMPLE 8.2

In his first book on EI, Goleman writes about his early teenage years. "Once when I was about 13, in an angry fit, I walked out of the house, vowing I would never return. It was a beautiful summer day, and I walked far along lovely lanes, till gradually the stillness and beauty calmed and soothed me; and after some hours I returned home repentant and almost melted. Since then, when I'm angry, I do this if I can, and find it the best cure."[18]

and discussed again to the point where the anger turns to aggression, and, almost unavoidably if not stopped in time, to armed conflict.

3. *Anger is often based on fear of some type.* Many types of anger stem from fear. Fear causes apprehension, which in turn causes new layers of pain. Then the pain increases, damaging the people on both sides of the conflict.

Five Steps for Dealing with Anger and Other Strong Emotions

Here are some simple steps that should help anyone who is dealing with the control of anger or other strong negative emotions:

1. *Examine your emotions to find the inner causes.* Instead of focusing on the other person or persons as "the wrongdoers," focus on what it was that triggered your emotions in a given situation.
2. *Learn to recognize your own "flashpoints."* At first, this might seem identical with step 1. This self-examination, though, needs to be ongoing and must examine what it is that usually arouses your negative emotions. These flashpoints might include fatigue, excessive stress, even factors such as excessive alcohol intake.
3. *Examine specifically what damage your emotions have caused.* Examples would be damage to relationships, retaliation from others, or health issues.
4. *Work on developing and using conflict management skills.* For example, work on being assertive, rather than passive or aggressive. (See definitions further in this chapter.)
5. *Get in touch with what types of things help calm you down.* Instead of berating others or lashing out, think about what constructive steps you can take–steps that specifically work for you.[19]

» ASSERTIVE, AGGRESSIVE, PASSIVE

Assertiveness means standing up for your rights without threatening the worth or dignity of the other person. Assertiveness is based on your rights *and* the rights of others. It is important to be assertive when you sense that someone is trying to take advantage of you. Being assertive means expressing what you

assertiveness

Standing up for your rights without threatening the self-esteem of the other person.

believe in or desire. It means being confident and proactive. Actively using assertive communication with others is part of a growth mindset. This type of response fits with higher emotional intelligence. Effective assertiveness demonstrates development in all areas of emotional intelligence: self-awareness, social awareness, self-management, and relationship management.

aggression
Hurting others and putting them on the defensive.

Aggression generally involves hurting others and putting them on the defensive, and it can take many forms. It can be verbal (insulting someone or spreading rumors about them), or even take a physical form (such as slapping or punching). Another form of aggression is workplace bullying. This type of abusive conduct can include verbal abuse, and it is meant to intimidate, threaten, or humiliate the target and can interfere with the target's ability to get their work done.[20] Being able to spot aggressive or bullying behavior, and addressing any of this tendency in your own behavior, can help you avoid the excesses of aggression while maintaining good communication and relations with your colleagues. Developing personal and social competence skills seen in emotional intelligence will provide strategies to defuse anger and aggression in situations of conflict.

passive
Accepting or allowing what happens or what others do, without active response or resistance.

Passive responses are a lack of emotional or behavioral action. You may find yourself at some time being neither assertive nor aggressive, but *passive.* Passivity—not reacting or acting at all—is sometimes a real choice to reduce or avoid conflict. Some people choose passivity because they think they may not be able to control their emotions if they speak out. In the long run, though, people who are frequently passive risk being ignored, not taken seriously, or even taken advantage of. Being able to speak up honestly and assertively will allow you as an individual, and a team member, to improve communication and achieve overall higher levels of success. Applying competence skills as described in emotional intelligence can reduce passivity.

» DEFENSIVE BEHAVIORS

Have you ever felt you were under attack from someone only to discover later that you weren't? When another person is actually physically or emotionally attacking you, reacting to protect or defend yourself might be quite appropriate. However, when the attack is only imagined, not real, such behavior is not only inappropriate, but also often destructive. At its best, it is a waste of time. This is what we mean by **defensiveness**: the inappropriate reaction to another's behavior as though it were an attack.

defensiveness
The inappropriate reaction to another's behavior as though it were an attack.

Defensiveness also can be seen as your body's method of keeping you from being unduly uncomfortable. It usually comes from two sources—negative self-concept and fear.[21] When people feel comfortable with their own value, avoiding defensiveness is much easier for them than it is for an individual who feels low self-worth. Many of us will become defensive from time to time as we work through self-esteem issues, or through different kinds of fears. But must we?

Try to remember the most recent time you yelled or snapped at another person. What happened? What were the basic assumptions you were acting on? What did you say? With what tone of voice? Was something involved in the encounter causing a fear response inside of you?

We all react defensively in different ways, depending on our own personalities, emotional positions, and fear sources. Here is a brief list of the most common defensive reactions used in the workplace:

- *Counterattack.* When we feel under attack, one automatic response is often simply to turn the situation around by going into the attack mode ourselves. This is known as a counterattack. When this happens, you will also be provoking the other person himself or herself to become defensive. When that happens, as it often does, this usually starts a vicious cycle that can continue for a very long time. For example, someone Keith is working with asks, "Why did you decide to approach the project this way?" Perceiving a personal attack, Keith exclaims loudly, "If you have some kind of problem with my approach, you can just do it yourself!" The "attack" has been counterattacked.
- *Passive-aggressive behavior.* The person who uses a passive-aggressive approach seems to be shutting down. Someone not watching closely would not necessarily see the anger or frustration behind the calm behavior. However, by acting in that way, this person will usually be expressing an understated rage. Again, this variety of defensiveness can cause even more negative behavior from both sides. In this case, Keith just stares into space for a while, then says, "Well, okay, if you don't like it, I'm sure I can do something to improve it. It might take a while. I hope you can wait," and so on. What Keith is *really* thinking is just as negative as it was in the counterattack example.
- *Pointless explanations.* This defensive behavior seems to stem from a belief that the other person has been on the attack only because that person "doesn't understand." In this situation, seemingly endless and pointless explanations result, frustrating everyone involved. If he were in this mode, Keith would say, "Well, let me show you what I was thinking when I decided to go this direction. You see, I was thinking not only about product integrity, but also about market acceptance, so I. . . ." (You don't want to hear the rest of his explanation; it is boring and—most important—pointless.)
- *Creating a distraction.* This defensive behavior is sometimes called using a "red herring," because it introduces a point or fact that is irrelevant to the issue at hand. A story about using red colored herring (fish) circulated more than 200 years ago, said to be used to confuse the nostrils of dogs in a fox hunt. In a similar manner, the person who uses this defense brings up something totally unrelated simply to distract attention from the real issue or issues. For example, "Last Thursday at 3 p.m.—no, it was more like 4 p.m., just before closing time—remember that Reina was still here and we were talking about the registration process, did that get fixed? And then you told me that I needed to be involved with this project."

Ending the defensive cycle is actually not difficult for the person who is paying close attention to what others are saying. Defensiveness is like putting on heavy armor, armor that keeps you from functioning as you would normally. Only by shedding that armor, making yourself vulnerable, will you encourage the other person to do the same. Then, once the armor is off the backs of both people—or several people, if it's a group issue—those involved can talk normally and in a more detached and constructive manner.

At some point, one of the people involved in the defensiveness chain needs to stop and challenge the assumptions he or she is using. Assume, for example, that you are *not* under attack and that you are not being threatened personally. Acting on that new set of assumptions can change the situation radically.

Here are some steps one can take in reducing defensiveness and its destructive effects in the workplace:

1. *Back off and cool down.* Give yourself a bit of time to get refocused and let yourself get a renewed perspective. Often just a few minutes makes a great deal of difference. This is especially important in e-mail conversations where your words last forever, and a few moments to reflect before hitting "send" can make a big difference in an outcome.
2. *Use "I statements."* Rather than saying, "You always go out of your way to mess up my schedule with your rescheduling policies," try, "When someone changes my schedule without consulting me, I feel like I'm being treated like a robot instead of as a person." It is unlikely that the other person will come back with, "No, you don't feel that way!"
3. *Avoid absolutes.* Two of the most damaging absolute words are *always* and *never.* Imagine if the employee in the preceding situation said, "You *never* consult me about scheduling decisions; you *always* change my schedule without warning." That type of wording is very likely to produce defensiveness in the other person. Also, remember that it takes only one exception to prove "always" or "never" statements to be wrong. If the supervisor could point to even one time when she consulted the employee about the schedule, a new issue would have come up to cause still more defensiveness.
4. *Make positive assumptions about the other person or persons involved.* We all have faults. However, when you choose to zero in on the positive trait and behaviors rather than the faults, defensiveness becomes less likely—from both sides.
5. *Learn to separate your work from who you are.* When someone criticizes your work performance, do you take that as an attack on you personally? If so, you might be making the mistake of thinking of your job as what you *are,* rather than as what you *do.* This is especially important to remember when you are doing creative work, work that comes from your mind. Just remember that, although it came from your mind, it's not a part of your mind—or of your being. When someone questions your method of doing a part of a task, that person is not necessarily attacking you.

REAL WORLD EXAMPLE 8.3

Ian's supervisor phones him just as he rolls out of bed in the morning. "Ian, I need you to meet a customer downtown and have breakfast with him right away. His new proposal could mean a lot to us. I was going to go, but I'm swamped." The boss's voice sounds like a parent speaking to a child ("please be a good boy and do as I say"). Meeting with clients (especially before work) is not on Ian's job description, and the boss knows it. Besides, if anyone is "swamped," it's Ian. Ian wants to tell his boss, "You need to get off my back. You are always managing your schedule so poorly, don't come to me now to bail you out!" This would have been aggressive. Instead, Ian chooses an assertive stance: "Mr. Tolbey, I have clients scheduled back-to-back all day and am not able to make the breakfast meeting." A passive Ian would have said "OK, Mr. Tolbey, tell me where to meet the client."

» POSITIVE INTELLIGENCE: KNOW YOUR INNER SABOTEUR

One of the sources of our defensiveness, anger, and other self-defeating emotions, according to Stanford and Yale business school professor Shirzad Chamine, is our own mind. "Your mind is your best friend, but it is also your very worst enemy," he says.[22] Chamine has conducted research with thousands of people, including hundreds of Fortune 500 company CEOs and their teams, to better understand how effective teams work together to reach their fullest potential.

Based on his research, he has identified behaviors, or in his words the "**inner saboteurs**" that self-sabotage us. These inner saboteurs distract us from "the Sage," or the voice of authenticity, calm, and positivity, that would otherwise lead us to a more effective outcome. This self-sabotage each of us creates in our mind can be defeated with practice, allowing us to work toward our full potential as individuals, in work teams, and across organizations. Defeating this self-sabotage to create healthy responses to life's challenges strengthens our "Positive Intelligence Quotient," also known as Positivity Quotient or PQ, according to Chamine. He believes that PQ is more important than either standard intelligence (IQ) or emotional intelligence (EI or EQ) in helping us to successfully reach our goals.

inner saboteur

Negative inner voices that form mental habits that sabotage our actions, keeping us from reaching our full potential.

The inner saboteurs Chamine has identified include the Judge (which is the master saboteur), and nine other saboteurs: the Avoider, the Controller, the Hyper-Achiever, the Hyper-Rational, the Hyper-Vigilant, the Pleaser, the Restless, the Stickler, and the Victim (see Figure 8.2). While the names are self-explanatory for the most part, to get a sense of the response of each, imagine that your supervisor has sent you an e-mail saying that the last report you worked on for a month and just turned in was unacceptable. She is asking for your immediate response to her e-mail. How would your inner saboteurs react?

- Judge: "I am a total loser. I should resign right now. I can't do this job."
- Avoider: "This is not such a big problem. I will deal with it later."

figure 8.2

THE INNER SABOTEURS

Ingram Publishing

- Controller: "She is completely wrong. I am going to confront her on this."
- Hyper-Achiever: "I'll re-do the entire report tonight. Everyone will see it."
- Hyper-Rational: "She did not understand the report. She is not capable."
- Hyper-Vigilant: "This is a horrible catastrophe! I am going to get fired!"
- Pleaser: "I'll help Trina with the other report, then they will all like me."
- Restless: "That report was boring anyway, and I have better things to do."
- Stickler: "If I start from the beginning I can re-write it perfectly."
- Victim: "This is not my fault! Peter gave me the wrong data last week!"

Do you see yourself in any of these forms of self-sabotage? Chamine believes that we learn these responses early in our lives and they become almost habitual reactions when we are faced with stressful situations. These behaviors may have been helpful as survival strategies in childhood, and for early humans as adaptive strategies to survive in a threatening world, but today they can lead to negative states of mind that reduce our successful strategies. The self-sabotage behaviors only get strengthened as we continue to use them. Research from neuroscience, psychology, and organizational behavior supports many of Chamine's claims.[23]

Chamine, currently chairman of CTI, the largest coach training organization in the world,

more about...

Defeat your inner saboteurs

"Pretty much all your suffering in life is self-generated by your Saboteurs," says Shirzad Chamine. By strengthening our authentic and original inner Sage, which operates in a positive state of mind, we can reach our goals and our true potential. "Based on my research," says Chamine, "I am convinced that there is an 80 percent probability that you have no idea how truly magnificent you really are."

—Shirzad Chamine

Positive Influence, http://www.positiveintelligence.com.

believes that only about 20 percent of us reach our true potential individually and in teamwork. The 80 percent who do not reach full potential fall victim to self-sabotage. In his research with thousands of people over a 30-year career, results include findings that those with higher PQ:

- Take fewer sick days, and are less likely to resign or report burnout.
- Have healthier immune systems and report less pain, fewer colds, and better sleep habits.
- Have lower rates of hypertension, diabetes, and strokes.
- Show higher work team performance.[24]

The good news is that we can learn to reduce these self-defeating behaviors and beliefs.

STRATEGIES FOR SUCCESS

Strategy 8.1 Defeating Your Inner Saboteurs

Defeat your inner saboteurs by raising your Positive Intelligence Quotient (PQ). Strengthen your "Sage muscles"; that is, focus on the authentic self, or the Sage. Changing the focus to a positive state using repeated intentional actions will, in time, lead to a more automatic set of positive responses, and a reduction of self-sabotage.[25]

Follow these steps to raise PQ and defeat inner saboteurs:

1. **Strengthen the positive.** Just as going to a gym and repeating exercises will strengthen physical muscles, focusing on positive thoughts and repeating them will strengthen a positive state of mind over time. The repeated positive focus acts as exercise repetitions ("reps") to strengthen neural pathways, making the behavior easier and more cemented over time. First, catch saboteurs in the act of self-sabotage. This requires identifying and exposing the self-sabotage. Rather than saying "I am a loser and I failed at writing the report," label that statement as sabotage, and reinterpret the situation as "My inner saboteur is saying that I am a loser and failed in writing a report." While identifying and acknowledging the self-sabotage, focus on breathing, counting, or other calming thoughts. Practice this behavior over several weeks to see a reduction in negativity.
2. **Be patient.** Inner saboteurs are strong. They have directed human behavior from our earliest times, and individual behavior for most of our lives. It is natural for them to want to self-blame and self-accuse when setbacks occur. But be patient with yourself: learn from your mistakes, expect some setbacks, and don't get stuck in a rut of self-sabotage when things do not go exactly as planned. Switch on your Sage inner self, move into a positive state, and go forward.
3. **Focus.** In a fast-paced business setting, taking time to consider a decision may seem like hesitation, or a lack of direction. But taking time to focus will lead to a more thoughtful, well-informed decision. Rather than making a snap decision in a frenzied manner, take a deep breath, calm yourself, consider the alternatives and likely outcomes, and then make your decision or take action. This inner state will also result in more creative outcomes, both for individuals and work teams.
4. **Take risks.** Taking risks by thinking "outside the box" often results in more noticeable mistakes. How do you respond to these mistakes? When you let your inner saboteurs drag you down, you will have more difficulty recovering, and more difficulty moving on to the next decisions or actions. Allow yourself to take risks, knowing that some

mistakes may occur. Acknowledging that risks may result in mistakes, and that mistakes lead to knowledge and growth, will shorten the recovery period over time, and result in more effective and informed risks in the long run.

5. **Become a conversation starter.** Begin a new conversation that is more than just listening and responding to the saboteurs. In this conversation, take a new role in leading a positive, effective interpretation of challenges and issues in your personal life and work hours. Lead a path to your goals, rather than following self-defeating thoughts.

» SCRIPTS

script

In relationship transactions, a psychological script like a movie or theater script, with characters, dialogue, etc., that most people heard as children.

An area of psychology known as "transactional analysis" has created the concept of scripts to explain some important ideas about our behavior as humans. Much of what we do and say in our daily lives is based on scripts that most people heard repeatedly as children. A psychological **script** is very much like a movie or theater script. Like the ones in show business, your scripts have a cast of characters, dialogue, acts, scenes, themes, and plots—but you didn't write them yourself. Instead, they came from parents, other family members, friends, adult role models, the media, teachers–in short, from nearly all human influences during your first years of childhood.[26] You use these same lines (or variations on them) every time you interact with others, including at work.

REWRITING SCRIPTS

If you feel that scripts in your life do not allow you to appreciate life fully, you can rewrite them to help turn yourself into a happier person. *How can you rewrite your own scripts?*

Klaus Tiedge/Blend Images LLC

Although you are also the casting director, you don't necessarily cast yourself into good roles. You could be the villain as easily as the hero of the script. People usually choose their favorite scripted parts during the casting process. Some people who learn to understand scripts get rid of the old ones and write new ones. Most people, though, have some scripts they would be better off without. The information here can help you understand your scripts better, and hopefully can help you throw off those you don't want.

Scripts can be divided into four basic categories. Here are some examples:

- *Cultural scripts* say that Alaskans are tough, Americans are free and rich, and New Englanders are traditional and intelligent.
- *Family scripts* say that the Smiths are honest, the Johnsons are medical people, and the Kennedys enter politics.
- *Religious scripts* are sometimes the strongest: Catholics don't believe in abortion, Jews don't work on Saturday, and Protestants believe in hard work.
- *Gender scripts* tell you how members of your gender should behave: men don't cry, women cook and clean houses, and men should be able to fix cars.[27]

REAL WORLD EXAMPLE 8.4

Whenever Gavin attended a meeting in the government agency where he worked, he would sit at the table looking at the other people and reflect on how much more confident they seemed than he felt. Although he had many years of experience at his job and a good education behind him, he still felt inferior. When asked to speak, he would often stumble over his words, even though he knew what he was talking about. Gavin seems to be stuck in a negative script about his own life.

» GAMES PEOPLE PLAY

Like scripts, the concept of "games" comes from transactional analysis. A **game** can be defined as an encounter between two people that produces a "payoff" for the one who starts the game–at the expense of the other player. Negative game playing can hurt positive relationships. Usually, there is something sneaky or deceitful behind the message or action of the game starter. This definition also implies that both players are playing, willingly or not. The two characteristics that all games have in common are that they include: (1) at least one insincere statement per game and (2) a payoff of some kind to at least one of the players.[28]

game
An encounter between two people that produces a "payoff" for the one who starts the game, at the expense of the other player.

Games are usually emotion-based activities that allow one person to feel "one up" on someone else, or–in some cases–"one down." Although they sometimes seem to help one person gain something of value, games usually don't really help any of the players. Instead, they cause damage to the organization in wasted time, lowered morale, and decreased output. Some games are worse than others, especially in terms of intensity, and can be categorized as first-, second,-, and third-degree games. **First-degree games** are usually quite harmless, whereas a **third-degree game** can result in physical injury. **Second-degree games** verge on being harmful and often cause anger.[29]

first-, second-, and third-degree games
In transactional analysis, categories of games based on intensity of play. First-degree games are relatively harmless; second-degree games are moderately harmful; third-degree games are extremely damaging.

Let's look at some examples of commonly played workplace games. All of the possible games won't fit into this chapter, because there are so many of them.

"Why Don't You . . . Yes, But"

Have you ever been at a committee meeting where the leader asked for constructive suggestions, but never really considered any of them? Have you ever had an instructor who asked students for input on how a class should be run, just to go ahead and do what he or she had planned from the start? The payoff for "Why don't you . . . yes, but" is that the person (acting like a sympathetic parent or adult) reassures both herself or himself and the other individual: "Nobody's going to tell me what to do." It is also sometimes a way that game players can get others to take over their responsibilities for them.

REAL WORLD EXAMPLE 8.5

Why Don't You? Yes, But. . .

Secretary: Stacy, the copier is out of ink, and five people are waiting to print.

Receptionist: Well, why don't you just put in a new cartridge?

Secretary: I would, but I really don't know how.

Receptionist: Well, why don't you call the IT guy?

Secretary: That's a good idea, but he takes so long to get here!

Receptionist: Well, why don't you ask Roger from maintenance to help you?

Secretary: I would, but he's too busy right now. I already asked him for help.

Receptionist: (frustrated) Well, why don't you blow it out your ear!

more about. . .

Office Politics

By understanding defensiveness and game playing, you will be able to answer many puzzling questions about office politics—who does it, what their true motives are, and how you can end its negative effects (at least in relation to yourself).

Wooden Leg

This game is also known as "My Excuses Are Better Than Yours." Excuses are the focus here. Time, illness, and childhood poverty all are useful as excuses for whatever might go wrong. Real reasons for things going wrong exist in many situations, but this game makes an art out of creating excuses. In the end, excuses take the place of a job well done.

Harried (or Harried Executive)

This game is played by someone who uses being "too busy" as an excuse not to interact with others. The reasons for this type of payoff are fairly complex. By not interacting, one does not have to get too personally close with others.

REAL WORLD EXAMPLE 8.6

Wooden Leg

Manager: "What's the matter, John? You're way behind on contacting those companies we were talking about for potential convention business."

Sales executive: "Well, Mr. Ripley, you know how tough it is to make contact with these firms. Monday is out because they're catching up with the weekend accumulation, and you can't call early in the morning because they're trying to wind up the previous day's business. Everyone is super busy mid-week, then by Thursday and Friday they are winding down and they probably leave early."[30]

REAL WORLD EXAMPLE 8.7

Harried

Three co-workers came by Brad's office and invited him to go out to a new BBQ spot for lunch. Brad protests, "I'm just too busy to get away," until they leave him alone. He does this again the next two times they ask, and finally they stop asking. The truth is that he wants to avoid the friendship of his fellow workers. His low opinion of himself warns him that nobody will like him in a social setting. He is playing the game of "Harried" in order to avoid social contact.

But this distance can mask other reasons, such as a negative perceptions of themselves or insecurity of their role at the job. The "too busy, can't talk" person may be actively trying to be seen as working harder than others.

Now I've Got You

This is a game in which one person tries to trap the other in a mistake, a lie, or some other type of negative situation. If the player is successful in trapping the victim, he or she will usually feel justified in harming the person–firing someone, taking back a raise that was offered, damaging the person's reputation in the work group, or simply insulting the victim.[31]

These aren't all of the game categories that exist. The entire experience known as *office politics* can be seen as a large game that contains many combinations of these and other games. If you learn these basic categories well, your knowledge of them should help you identify other games people might attempt to play with you. Most important, you can learn to *stop* playing games, and to stop allowing other people to play them in the workplace. Game playing prevents employees from enjoying open, honest relationships with others, and it wastes company time and money.

PLAYING GAMES IN THE OFFICE

Games in the workplace produce "payoffs" for a few, but ultimately hurt everyone involved and cause damage to the organization itself. *What can you do to prevent or avoid games in the workplace?*

John Lund/Nevada Wier/Blend Images/Getty Images

REAL WORLD EXAMPLE 8.8

Now I've Got You

Anthony, a restaurant manager, spends most of his time checking inventory and other cost-related matters. He looks carefully for any contradictions in his employees' reports. When he finds a discrepancy, he has discovered "proof" of the worthlessness of either whole projects or otherwise very good employees.[32]

STRATEGIES FOR SUCCESS

Strategy 8.2 Stopping Games before They Start

1. Maintain positive self-regard and self-worth.
2. Try to remain rational, regardless of the other person's state of mind.
3. Try to get the other person to be rational and honest.
4. Give positive feedback to other people.
5. De-emphasize the weaknesses of others.

The best way to become aware of games and of the people who play them is to watch for conversations and events that happen repeatedly. People who are major game players tend to play new episodes of the same game over and over again.

You can stop a game at any time by simply refusing to play. Remember that games are made up of messages with double meanings. Just as in any conversation, you can decide whether or not you will play along with something as negative as most games are. Here are some tips on stopping games before you get hooked into them:

1. **Maintain positive self-regard and self-worth.** Low feelings of self-worth are the single most important reason why people both play games and get stuck playing the games of others. You can also get other people to play fewer games by doing and saying things that help maintain *their* self-worth.
2. **Try to remain rational, regardless of the other person's state of mind.** Notice that games are not usually played by people who are trying to be fair and honest. One way to stay fair and honest is by asking *how* questions, rather than *why* questions. Remain logical and calm. Of course, you probably aren't going to succeed in preventing games every time.
3. **Try to get the other person to be rational and honest.** Do everything you can to lead the would-be game player to be reasonable. When the game player starts talking like a selfish child or an attacking critic, say something like, "Please explain that point a bit further; what did you mean by (whatever was said)?"
4. **Give positive feedback to other people.** A great deal of game playing is based on negatives. Getting rid of those negatives is a good method of also getting rid of games.
5. **De-emphasize the weaknesses of others.** All people have weaknesses. By spending more time and energy noticing people's positive points, you can avoid the desire for payoffs—the unhealthy desire that urges people to play games in the first place.

Create a climate at work where people see game playing for what it is: a waste of time. We often play games because we are bored. We can all do a lot to reduce boredom on the job, through job rotation, job enlargement, and job enrichment, for example. Most important, people should be allowed to work up to their full potential, so they can get a sense of fulfillment from their work.

CHAPTER EIGHT SUMMARY

Chapter Summary by Learning Objectives

LO 8-1 Identify the eight forms of intelligence. The eight forms of intelligence refer to intelligence in the following areas: language, spatial reasoning, naturalism, intrapersonal issues, interpersonal issues, movement, music, and math/logic. These replace the old one-dimensional view of IQ. Two additional potential forms of intelligence have been suggested: existential-moral and teaching-pedagogical.

LO 8-2 Describe the theory of triarchic intelligence and contrast it with multiple intelligence theory. The triarchic theory of intelligence states that there are three sub-types of intelligence or ability. The first is analytical intelligence, known as "book smarts," which is a strength in solving complex problems through reasoned analysis. The second is creative intelligence, which is the ability to come up with unique and useful solutions to a situation. The third is practical intelligence, which is thought of as "street smarts" or the ability to find the best solution to everyday problems or events.

LO 8-3 Explain the significance of emotional intelligence and how it compares with earlier theories of measuring intelligence. Emotional intelligence is the ability to see and control one's own emotions and to understand the emotional states of other people. Earlier theories measured ability to comprehend, memorize, and analyze facts only.

LO 8-4 Describe how to apply emotional intelligence. Recent studies have shown that emotional intelligence can be learned. Here are the basic steps toward application: (1) Review what you know about self-awareness; (2) Carefully watch others whose social competence seems to be high, who have social awareness skills that you don't have, but would like to attain; (3) Work actively on improving your self-management skills; (4) Develop relationship management skills.

LO 8-5 List ways to deal with strong emotions, including anger. These are the steps in dealing with the most destructive human emotions: (1) Examine your anger to find the inner causes. (2) Learn to recognize your own "flashpoints." At first, this step might seem identical with #1. However, it refers to the specific areas that trigger anger in you. (3) Examine the damage caused by your anger. (4) Learn to develop and use conflict management skills. (5) Get in touch with the types of things that calm you down.

LO 8-6 Compare and contrast assertion, aggression, and passivity. Assertiveness means standing up for your rights without threatening the other people who are involved. Aggression, on the other hand, involves hurting other people and putting them on the defensive. Passivity is a lack of reaction when one is called for.

LO 8-7 Give examples of defensive behaviors and how they affect the workplace. Defensiveness is the reaction to someone else's behavior as though it were an attack. Defensiveness often brings out further defensiveness and can cause tremendous trouble in any workplace.

LO 8-8 Explain the importance of positive intelligence and how inner saboteurs can reduce our effectiveness. The nine inner saboteurs are controlled by our mind and distract us from the Sage, the inner voice of calm and reason. The inner saboteurs include the Judge, Controller, Hyper-Achiever, Hyper-Rational, Hyper-Vigilant, Pleaser, Restless, Stickler, and Victim. They can be defeated with focus and practice to create new responses.

LO 8-9 Distinguish among the various scripts that influence our actions. A psychological script is like a movie or theater script, with characters, dialogue, and so on. Cultural scripts, family scripts, religious scripts, and gender scripts often determine our behavior.

LO 8-10 Explain why people "play games" in the workplace, and how to deal with games. Games are nearly always played with some type of "payoff" in mind. The payoff is the main reason most games are played. This payoff might be feeling temporarily better about oneself, showing the faults of the other person, or the ability to make excuses for our own failures and weaknesses. Most games are destructive and time-wasting.

key terms

aggression 224
assertiveness 223
defensive behavior/defensiveness 224
eight intelligences 214
emotional competence 220
emotional intelligence (EI) 219
emotional mind 219
first-, second-, and third-degree games 231
game 231
inner saboteur 227
intelligence 214
passive 224
personal competence 220
rational mind 219
script 230
social competence 220
triarchic (three arches) theory 218

review questions

1. Briefly explain each of the "eight intelligences." How are these categories more helpful in understanding the whole idea of intelligence, especially as it impacts the workplace? Provide examples of people who fit into each of the eight categories.

2. What is triarchic intelligence? How is it different from the eight intelligences? What situations would call for the three sub-types of intelligences or abilities in triarchic intelligence?
3. What is emotional intelligence? How does this concept relate to the eight intelligences? Explain the relationship among intrapersonal, interpersonal, and emotional intelligence.
4. Briefly explore each of the four general areas ("clusters") of emotional intelligence. Show how each area can be encouraged to develop.
5. Explain why strong emotions including anger can be so damaging. What are the major effects of anger?
6. What are the five steps for dealing with anger? Which of the five seems the most effective for you personally? Why?
7. Briefly explain the process of defensiveness. List at least two of the four most popular defensive reactions. Have you seen (or used) any of these in your own life?
8. What are the steps one can take to reduce defensiveness? Which of the five seems the most important to you?
9. What is meant by our "inner saboteurs" as they affect our work? How can they be defeated?
10. What specific steps can you take when you suspect that you are dealing with a game player? What steps can you take to prevent yourself from initiating games?

critical thinking questions

1. How can a knowledge of emotional intelligence improve human relations in business situations? How can it help you understand more about your interactions with others?
2. Have you noticed your inner saboteurs affecting your workplace relationships and productivity? How have you reduced their sabotage?
3. Think of a conflict situation you were in recently. Define the terms *assertive, aggressive,* and *passive.* Then answer these questions:
   a. Were you aggressive, assertive, or passive in the situation?
   b. Did the situation work out the way you expected?
   c. Would you act differently if you had to do it again?

working it out 8.1

ANALYZING CONVERSATIONS

School-to-Work Connection: Defensiveness, Emotional Intelligence

Part 1: Rewrite each of the following situations in a way that will eliminate defensive behaviors and use the concepts of emotional intelligence.

1. *Manager:* (calm tone of voice) "Please review the customer surveys and provide me with a summary by the end of the week."

   Employee: "Why are you so focused on me? I always finish my work on time, don't I? Why are you singling me out?"

2. *Employee:* "I'm not sure how to send out these packages. Can you please do them for me this one time so I can hit the road?"

   Manager: "Well, they really do need to go out this afternoon, so I will just have Suze do it."

3. *Customer:* (harsh, critical tone) "You've greeted every person that's come into the store with a hello and asked if you could help them, but I've been standing here for the past 15 minutes, and you haven't even acknowledged me, or looked in my direction. What gives!?"

   Sales Clerk: "Look, lady, you can see I'm busy. I've got regular customers coming in and out, and besides, I didn't even see you there. So go yell at somebody else, will ya? I'm doing the best I can here. If you think somebody else can do a better job, you're free to leave!"

Part 2: Complete the response for each scenario below to display emotional intelligence.

1. *Boss:* "What's wrong with you, are you even capable of arriving on time?"

   Response: ________________________________

2. *Customer:* "Put your manager on the phone. Everyone I've talked to so far at your company is a moron!"

   Response: ________________________________

3. *Wife:* "Why do you always run to your man-cave, or say you're too busy when it's time to go to family counseling? Did it ever occur to you that you might be part of what's wrong with this family?"

   Response: ________________________________

4. *Customer:* "I just purchased this new drill yesterday and it already doesn't work! I am so fed up with your company and you people! I want my money back NOW!"

   Response: ________________________________

5. *Employee:* "Hi Sheri, can you please help me install this new time tracking software on my work computer? I've never been very good with computer stuff, and I'm getting very frustrated."

   Response: ________________________________

working it out 8.2

EXAMINING YOUR EMOTIONAL INTELLIGENCES

Purpose: Consider Howard Gardner's theory of eight multiple intelligences, which include the following: math/logic, language/verbal, visual/spatial, musical, physical body/kinesthetic, interpersonal, intrapersonal, and naturalistic. For this exercise, you may also want to consider the potential intelligences of moral intelligence, existential intelligence, and pedagogical intelligence.

Instructions: Answer each question about yourself honestly. There is no right or wrong answer. Take notes as you answer the questions.

1. What subject in middle school did you like the best?
   - Art
   - Foreign languages
   - Math
   - Physical Education
   - Music
   - Literature
   - Science
2. When you have spare time, which activity are you most likely to do?
   - Pull out a book or e-reader and read
   - Work jigsaw puzzles, Sudoku, or play a game like Jenga
   - Go for a run, bike ride, or a hike
   - Relax and listen to music
   - Volunteer time to help others
   - Draw, paint, or do other creative art project
   - Work in the garden
3. You have agreed to babysit your friend's 8-year-old niece. You don't really know her, but you think it would be really fun if the two of you got to know each other better by:
   - Doing a fun chemistry project you find on YouTube making slime
   - Coloring, drawing, or painting together
   - Going for a walk to do some bird watching
   - Turning on some music and making up silly songs to go with it

- Going to the park to use the outdoor fitness equipment
- Starting journals writing about your innermost thoughts
- Making up funny poems about animals
- Finding other kids her age for a play date with the two of you

4. You stop by a friend's house and find an impromptu party is taking place. What do you do there?
   - Introduce yourself to as many new people as possible
   - Take over the role of picking the best party music
   - Show off your best dance moves
   - Debate current politics with a small group of people
   - Enjoy your friend's outdoor landscaping
   - Volunteer to analyze how many more snacks and drinks are needed from the store
5. You are walking around a large bookstore that sells every type of book. Which area do you head for?
   - Arts and crafts
   - Fitness and exercise
   - Magazines about celebrities
   - Coffee stop where you can visit with other people
   - Music CDs
   - Self-help books
6. You are taking a college drama class. Each student will take responsibility for a role or a task. Which one do you sign up for?
   - Building the sets others have designed
   - Directing characters' emotional portrayals in their roles
   - Memorizing everyone's lines for rehearsals
   - Designing and painting the sets
   - Creating and printing the posters and programs
   - Writing the music and helping the musicians rehearse
   - Analyzing the layout of the stage and the audience spacing
7. You have a big presentation to prepare for at work with your project team. How do you prepare?
   - Memorize the important points by making them into a musical rhyme.
   - Rehearse the presentation in front of your friends.
   - Remember the important parts of the presentation by fitting them with your own experiences.
   - Sketch out a flow chart of how parts of the presentation fit together.

- Outline with bullet points the logic in the points you will make in the presentation.
- Take a walk in the park to clear your head.

Looking at the notes on your responses, what patterns or trends do you see? Do these trends fit with how you see yourself? You may find a pattern that fits one intelligence primarily, or many patterns mixed. According to Gardner's theory, you will want to find employment and leisure activities that build on the strengths of your multiple intelligence(s).

Source: Kendra Cherry, "What Kind of Intelligence Do You Have?" *VeryWellMind,* April 27, 2017, https://www.verywellmind.com/what-kind-of-intelligence-do-you-have-3867398 (retrieved March 11, 2020).

working it out 8.3

YOUR INNER SABOTEURS

Watch the TEDxStanford Talk by corporate CEO and Stanford lecturer Shirzad Chamine, titled "Know Your Inner Saboteurs," and then answer the following questions.

1. What does the speaker mean by an "inner saboteur"?
2. Describe some of the "gang of 9" saboteurs that you most closely recognize in yourself or others. Provide examples.
3. What were some of the findings the speaker discovered in his research work with corporate CEOs and presidents.
4. Who is the Sage? What are the five great Sage powers?
5. What is "positive intelligence" and why is it important? How does this type of intelligence differ from other intelligence theories in this chapter?

The video can be found here: www.youtube.com/watch?v=-zdJ1ubvoXs.

case study 8.1

The Airport Incident

It had been a hectic morning, with bad weather causing delays and short tempers throughout the airport. Heather had just started her shift as an airlines gate agent and was helping to close a flight when a passenger ran up.

"You have to let me on this flight!" she said frantically. "I have a meeting in Denver that I can't miss and I won't make my connection if you don't let me on! This is going to be on your head if I miss this flight!"

"I'm sorry," said Heather as calmly as she could, "The doors have closed, and the flight is preparing for departure. You can talk with our customer service representatives to get re-booked. They are just one gate over."

"No, you have to open the doors NOW! I CANNOT miss this flight! I will sue you personally and this airlines if I miss this flight!" shouted the passenger, "It is NOT my fault that traffic was terrible and the parking lot was practically full!" she continued.

"Ma'am," said Heather, her voice rising, "maybe you should have planned a little better and left a little earlier if you wanted to get your flight. Maybe if you were a little more responsible you would have made it here on time. I am so tired of you passengers blaming everyone but yourself for your own poor planning and bad judgment. You want to sue me? Go ahead. I don't care." With that, Heather walked away and headed toward the break room.

The passenger stared after Heather with her mouth open. Another gate agent who had seen the interaction, Rahim, quickly walked over to the passenger. "Ma'am," he said, "let me walk you to a customer service agent who can help you re-book. With the weather as bad as it is, I wouldn't be surprised if your meeting was postponed anyway."

With that, the passenger walked with Rahim to the customer service agents one gate over.

Case Study Questions

1. What type of emotional response is Heather displaying in this scenario? Explain. If you were to re-write Heather's responses in a way that would calm the situation, what would you say?
2. What type of emotional competence is Rahim displaying? Using first the multiple intelligences theory and then the triarchic intelligence theory, explain what type of intelligence he is displaying.
3. What "inner saboteurs" may be at work in both Heather's and the passenger's statements and responses?

Everybody Is a Critic

The entire restaurant staff was in the conference room today. The order had come down from the corporate headquarters to close all dine-in service and serve customers to-go orders only. Even more alarming were the rumors swirling around that customers would soon not be able to walk in to place orders, but would have to call or order online only for their take-out orders.

Although the change in procedures was necessary to respond to a recent health crisis, the entire staff was upset. All they could think was that the restaurant would close and they would all be out of work soon. The chatter in the conference room included these statements:

"I'm sure everything will be fine," said Ava, "We've gone through tough times before. Don't get so worked up, everyone."

"That is ridiculous! We have to do something about this right now! Come on, everyone, get busy on solutions to this crisis!" shouted Beto.

"You are all so smart and so experienced," said Chloe sweetly, "I'm sure you will figure everything out. I will just say yes to whatever you suggest."

"We will just look at all the variables and come up with a resolution. Keep your unnecessary feelings out of this, it's just an equation to solve. Overreacting is getting us nowhere," said Darcy.

"I'm going to lose my apartment. This is horrible. There is no way out of this. I'll probably wind up starving to death in an alley somewhere," moaned Effie.

"The rest of you can take my shifts. I will work for free. It really is not that big of a deal. I am willing to give up my income so that you can all make some money," said Fiona bravely.

"The rest of you can get back to work, I am the senior waitstaff here so I will take charge. I will let you know once I have a plan together," said Gavin firmly.

"You come up with the overall plan, then. The rest of you should go home and get some sleep. I'll just stay here and take all the orders and get everything ready for tomorrow," said Hakeem.

"I have to get going," said Inga, "you all can keep talking but I am getting bored with all this talk-talk-talk. I am going to go put my applications in at other businesses in the neighborhood before they close for the day."

"This is all my fault," said Jack, "I should have seen it coming. I have been in the food service industry a long time, I should have prevented this from happening here."

With that, and realizing that they were not making much progress, the staff members took a break and agreed to come back together in an hour.

Case Study Questions

1. Identify the critics or inner saboteurs in this conversation.
2. Can our inner saboteurs ever be helpful? Explain.
3. For the various lines in this conversation, how would you flip the script to be more positive and helpful, displaying emotional control?

PART THREE

« « building your human relations skills

In Parts One and Two, you learned about some theories and practices in the field of human relations. In Parts Three and Four, you will examine applied human relations in the business world.

There is an old saying—the more things change, the more they stay the same. Chapter 9 offers strategies for finding constants within change and dealing with the effects on personal and organizational levels. Chapter 10 presents human relations skills that tap your creativity and encourage creativity in others. Chapter 11 gives tools to anticipate and avoid conflicts, and to resolve those that are inevitable. Chapter 12 covers stress and how to recognize, cope, and channel it. Finally, Chapter 13 looks at customer service, a key growth area for all organizations. » »

CHAPTER NINE

INDIVIDUAL AND ORGANIZATIONAL CHANGE

LEARNING OBJECTIVES

After studying this chapter, you will be able to:

LO 9-1 Discuss why change is a fact of life in the 21st century.

LO 9-2 Describe the seven stages of personal change.

LO 9-3 Compare and contrast models of organizational change.

LO 9-4 Give reasons for why employees resist or accept change.

LO 9-5 Provide examples of different approaches to continuous improvement.

LO 9-6 Discuss organizational development.

STRATEGIES FOR SUCCESS

Strategy 9.1 Managing Personal Change in the Workplace

Strategy 9.2 Gaining Acceptance for Change in Your Organization

In the Workplace: Too Much Change

SITUATION

arekmalang/123RF

The gray clouds matched Brandy's mood as she left her parents' home to go to her college Marketing and Accounting classes. Things with her parents were rough: her father had retired early two years ago due to health problems, and her mother was exhausted after recently taking on a second job to pay the medical bills not covered by their insurance. Her mother had just told her that they were probably going to put the house on the market soon—the house where Brandy had grown up—to downsize into a less expensive apartment. Her parents were counting on her to help find an apartment, get the house sold, plan the move, pack up the house . . . the thought of the massive changes for her parents and for herself was dizzying.

She focused her thoughts on school as she made her way to class. Brandy was glad to be able to go to college, but the required management class she had registered for had been cancelled just before school started. This set back her graduation date another semester. Worse than that, Brandy had just learned that her local shopping mall was closing within a year. Brandy had spent countless hours there during middle school and high school—it was the focus of social life for Brandy and her friends. In fact, her decision to get a business degree was based on her goal to start a career in retail management, because she loved being at the mall and was fascinated by business operations of the stores there. She knew that online shopping had reduced the number of shoppers and visitors to the mall, so she had thought a lot about how to increase foot traffic there. She had spent hours sketching out ideas to make the mall a vibrant location for community activities, not just shopping. Now that dream was gone.

DISCOVERY

"I guess my best bet is to stay focused on the things I know I want for myself, while I get used to all these other changes in the best way I can," she resolved. "I still want to focus on marketing and management, but I'll have to figure out a different plan. First, though, I have to help my folks get moved and settled. That is not going to be easy."

THINK ABOUT IT

Does Brandy seem to be responding to her life changes in a positive way? What are some signs that help you form your answer? Would you respond the same way to major changes in your life?

» CHANGE AS A FACT OF LIFE

You may have heard the expression "The only thing constant in life is change," attributed to ancient Greek philosopher Heraclitus more than 2,000 years ago. Change is a reality we all live with, and will continue to live with. Swift, radical changes such as the ones Brandy was going through in this chapter's introduction can be overwhelming. In this chapter, you will look at two different types of change. First, you will take a look at the kind of *emotional personal* changes that Brandy has experienced and that we all may experience. Second, you will examine the type of *necessary, planned changes* that an organization must go through. This chapter also examines how both types of change affect the workplace.

Technical Innovation Creates Change

Since the beginning of the Industrial Revolution in the 1700s and 1800s, rapid change has become a way of life in Western civilization. But centuries ago, it was very likely that you would spend your entire life in the same social class or occupational group–even the same geographic area. Whatever was meaningful to one generation would remain so in the next. The changes that did take place were usually gradual enough that one may not have noticed them.

By the 20th century, the pace of change in all areas of life had become more rapid, a trend that continues today in the 21st century with each new round of technical innovation. In the factories and offices of the past, progress was expressed in terms of *bigger* and *more*. The reality today is that the world has more than ever–more people, more electronic devices, and more information overload. Simply creating more of something is no longer a formula for success. Rather, creating *high-quality and efficient* products and services, and making positive contributions to society, are now driving factors for successful business.

Several additional specific trends in today's workplace drive change. Competition exists to recruit and hire the best talent, especially those with complex skills. The need for mobile technology and a need to work anywhere cause changes both in the abilities of employees and the technology itself. The push to innovate in all areas of business means that change will necessarily occur in order for organizations to remain competitive. Work is now more distributed and less centralized in structures, practices, and locations. This changes employees' roles and even their identities at work. Sustainability is now an issue that causes changes as organizations move to reduce their carbon footprint to save energy costs and to meet LEED (Leadership in Energy and Environmental Design) requirements, the most widely used environmental efficiency rating system in the world.[1]

Recognizing Stress, Managing Change

Stress can make a person's life feel more difficult. It can interfere with your career progress, and it can take a significant toll on your physical health.

Learning how to manage these changes can give us the coping mechanisms to deal effectively with the stress they cause. You owe it to yourself to manage your stress in a healthy way. You can't ever eliminate it completely from your life, but learning to reduce it and manage it effectively can lead to a higher quality of life.

more about...

Life Choices, Control, and Stress

"Doing something that is productive is a great way to alleviate emotional stress. Get your mind doing something that is productive."

—Ziggy Marley, musician/philanthropist

The stressful life changes that most of us go through at one time or another may be perceived as either positive or negative, yet their impacts may feel similar. The death of a spouse, divorce, marital separation, detention in jail or prison, death of a loved one, major injury or illness, birth of a child, marriage—these types of major events can cause tremendous stress in our lives. It is important to note that while some of these events can happen in an instant, their effects can persist for a long time.[2] Recognizing the source of your stress is one of the first steps toward managing it. More detail on stress effects and managing stress is covered in Chapter 12.

When looking at the major life changes that cause stress in *your* life, know that these can be broadly grouped into seven categories of:

- Loss
- Separation
- Relocation
- A change in relationship
- A change in direction
- A change in health
- Personal growth[3]

seven major life changes
Loss, separation, relocation, a change in relationship, a change in direction, a change in health, and personal growth.

These **seven major life changes** have basic characteristics in common:

- **They happen to everyone.** Although they don't happen *regularly* to everyone, they are all bound to happen at least a few times throughout one's lifetime. They are simply part of being alive. A change in direction, for example, can come in many different forms—a career change, a trauma, a change of religious beliefs, or a change in values brought about by a near tragedy.
- **Many of them seem to happen without your control.** Changes that are beyond your control (or seem to be) are likely to be more stressful and difficult to deal with than those you can affect. People try their best to hold on to things they can control—factors in their lives about which they feel some certainty—but change often comes to them anyway.

MAJOR LIFE CHANGES
Everyone is likely to experience all seven major life changes at least once during their lives. *Which of these changes have happened to you, and how have you managed the stress that came with them?*

Neustockimages/Getty Images

- **Each one of these changes has its own ripple effect.** Significant changes create other changes that go far beyond the original change. Sometimes the most severe trouble comes from the side effects of the major change. For example, a divorce can affect your relationships with your friends, your job, and your extended family, and trigger a move to a new home or a new city.
- **People feel the results of change before, during, and after the event.** You've probably heard someone say that worrying about an event is worse than the event itself. With these seven change areas, that is certainly often the case. After a change, we may continue to grieve a loss that has occurred, or second-guess a decision that led to a change in direction. For extremely serious life events, people may experience post-traumatic stress disorder and would benefit from counseling or support groups to work through the trauma's effects.

» THE SEVEN STAGES OF PERSONAL CHANGE

seven stages of personal change
Emotional standstill, denial, anger, helplessness, bottoming out, experimenting, and completion.

Humans process major transitions through basic, recognizable steps. Figure 9.1 shows a diagram of the **seven stages of personal change** that make up the process of healthy reaction to such change. An emotionally healthy person typically takes each of these steps in order.

Suffering while experiencing personal losses is never abnormal, and admitting to suffering is not a sign of weakness or inability. The truth is that *failing* to go through each of these steps is often more detrimental than skipping steps. If you skip one, you may have to return to it at some time.

1. **Emotional Standstill.** The first reaction someone usually has to the news of a sudden death, for example, is to enter an emotional standstill, or shock. "Oh no!" they say. "How did it happen? When?" In shock there is a gap between rational thinking and emotions.[4] In his now-classic famous

figure 9.1

SEVEN STAGES OF PERSONAL CHANGE

These stages can apply to any serious change in a person's life. It is generally believed that you will adapt to the change with greater speed and ease if you can take each step as it appears. *How can you ensure that you moved through each stage with awareness and ease?*

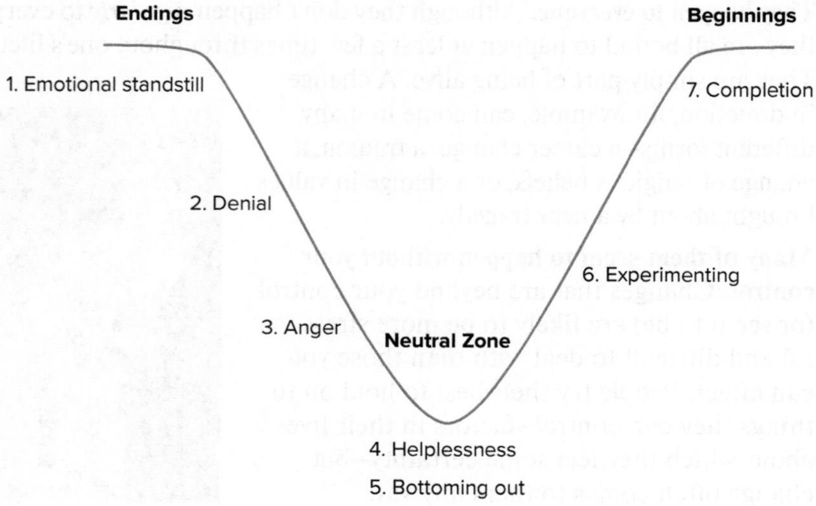

REAL WORLD EXAMPLE 9.1

The mother of a large family died unexpectedly. All eight members of the family—except one—reacted openly, showing the emotions they felt in various ways. However, one of the adult sons in the family remained unemotional, not showing any feelings except the surface statements of sorrow. The other family members were quick to say, "I'm worried about Sui-Toon. He's not letting any feelings out. When they finally come out, he's going to have a rough time." None of them are psychologists, but they were right. They acknowledged that all human beings need to go through certain steps in dealing with a personal loss—steps that cannot and should not be avoided. Even though people may have a delayed or mild reaction to such a loss, they will have to process such a change in some way. Several months later, Sui-Toon broke down and spent several weeks in severe depression.

self-help book *Transitions: Making Sense of Life's Changes,* William Bridges points out that the **beginning** of the personal change process nearly always involves an **ending**. It sounds ironic. In other words, something that was once an integral part of your life is no longer there.[5] For example, many people think of moving to a new city as exciting or stressful because of all the new, strange realities one has to face and learn. Greater stress may come from *what you no longer have,* that is, from the losses you have suffered. This would include your old circle of friends, that familiar grocery store, the family dentist you had grown used to, and dozens of other lost connections.

Even when an event is expected, as in the case of a death after a terminal illness, a separation that ends in divorce, or an expected job loss, an element of shock exists. The reality of the event produces a different mental state, no matter how much advance notice is available.

2. **Denial.** Although many people's *minds* can accept a major change, they often continue to deny it emotionally. This denial can take many different forms. If the loss is a death, bereaved people might not allow themselves to believe the loved one is really gone. In a divorce, it might be the false hope that the marriage will survive. With denial, the mind is keeping the sufferer from accepting reality fully and completely. Ideally, this denial period will be over in a few weeks or months, but it may last as long as a few years. The longer the period lasts, the longer it will take to move through the healing process.[6]
3. **Anger.** Some form of anger usually replaces the emotional vacuum left by denial. The anger felt at this time usually contains a feeling of helplessness–of being a victim who was unable to prevent the change. Most psychologists advise that this anger should be expressed in a way that will not harm others. This is the point where support groups can be helpful: having other people who will listen and empathize with you can help you defuse your anger.
4. **Helplessness.** At this step in the process, the individual is trying but still failing to move forward. In Figure 9.1, the individual is shown as

beginning
The *last* of three general steps in the acceptance of personal loss. This is where "experimenting" and "completion" take place. (See **ending** and **neutral zone.**)

ending
The *first* of three general steps in the acceptance of personal loss. This is where "emotional standstill," "denial," and "anger" take place. (See **neutral zone** and **beginning.**)

denial
Failure to confront your problem; characteristic response by an alcoholic.

REAL WORLD EXAMPLE 9.2

Yuri had been living with his family for five years in a home they rented when the homeowners told them they were putting the home up for sale, and the family would have to move out. Yuri and his family considered buying it, but did not have money saved up for the down payment. Having to find a new home to rent felt overwhelming. Yuri alternated between denial, "This is not happening to me!" and anger, "Those greedy subhumans! How can they just throw my family out on the street like this?" He will need to hit bottom with his emotions and move fully beyond shock, denial, and anger before he can begin the experimenting stage and consider other options for homes to rent.

neutral zone

The *second* of three general steps in the acceptance of personal loss. The neutral zone is the area where "helplessness" and "bottoming out" take place. (See **ending** and **beginning.**)

having entered the **neutral zone**, what William Bridges calls "a gap in the continuity of existence." This is a temporary state of loss that Bridges says "must be endured."[7] The person is still suffering and now is afraid to bottom out into the helpless condition of total despair. In this stage, the individual may make one of two mistakes. Either the suffering person might try to share too much emotion with other people, or the person may retreat into isolation. Both extremes are negative. The first one is a quick way to lose friends or alienate others, and the second is self-destructive.[8] To move through this stage effectively, the individual must be constantly aware of the reality of others—that most friends cannot, and should not, enter into another person's deep sorrow—even when trying to be helpful. The others in the person's life would more appropriately share in small doses of grief.

more about. . .

Sharing Your Grief

Not sure how much is too much? The best thing to do is to talk about it; ask your friends and loved ones to honestly tell you their comfort levels. It is also good to ask yourself, "How much will this sharing of grief really benefit me?"

5. **Bottoming Out.** At this bottom point, for the first time since the event, it becomes possible to let go of the emotional burden. Sometimes a person recognizes this turning point by a peaceful feeling that comes upon awakening one morning. More often, the step is gradual. The overwhelming grief appears less often, and less intensely, over time. Bottoming out means releasing the thoughts, tensions, memories, and emotions that force you to hold on to the past. At this point, you are allowing the life-completing processes to take their course. The shock, denial, and anger are becoming memories.[9]
6. **Experimenting.** Once a person bottoms out, an upturn starts to take place, and the recovery can begin. Normal curiosities and desires come back and new experiences become evident. Notice that Figure 9.1 shows a movement upward—toward healing. If the event was a divorce or death of a spouse, this is the stage where it might become possible to date again or find fulfilling activites with friends and family to enjoy a meaningful life as a single person. If it was a job loss, your experimentation could be with tasks and opportunities that probably weren't previously considered. Emotions left over for other people and other projects are not all being consumed by your recovery.

One thing to remember, though, is that people are sometimes forced into another job out of financial necessity, before they are emotionally ready to adapt. In these cases, the bottoming out and experimenting must be done in different contexts.

7. **Completion.** Some people call this step *rebirth.* Although that term might sound excessively dramatic, it is somewhat accurate. The cycle is complete. This is not to say that the past won't reemerge, nor does it mean there won't be fall-back days. That sort of occasional **regression** is also normal. Now there is a new perspective. You have entered the area of beginnings. You can start anew. Far from being blocked out, the event has become a part of active memory that can be thought about without undue pain.

   However, *regression* often takes place, even in the best of mending cycles. Although your progress has been normal and healthy, you still will likely have bad days now and then—days when it seems the change happened only yesterday. The important thing to know about regression is that it is normal and human and is nothing to be disturbed about.

THE POWER OF DENIAL
Although denial is a normal stage in the change process, dwelling in it for too long will prevent you from adapting to a situation as it really is. *When have you felt yourself dealing with a problem through denial?*
Jon Feingersh/Blend Images LLC

regression
Slipping backward to an earlier stage of growth; it can be either temporary or permanent.

One danger with the seven-step recovery diagram is that people might be tempted to think they should passively let these steps happen to them. The process is a natural process, but sufferers still need to maintain control of their destinies. Going through the steps does require some effort, but millions of people who have never heard of these steps come through them successfully. Knowing what the steps are can help you see that your emotional recovery is both important and normal. It can also help you understand what is happening to you, so that you can evaluate your progress.

» MANAGING LIFE CHANGES

As we have discussed previously, managing major, stressful change in our lives involves recognizing the experiences we are dealing with and adapting a plan to handle the stress that results from that change or event. You may have found that personal change can affect your sense of wellness. In fact, any change that affects something or someone close to you is likely to upset your self-concept, which is your view of who you are. (See Chapter 2.) Healing is the process of returning to a point where you know who you are and feel good about yourself once again. Figure 9.2 contains specific advice on how to do this.

Recall Heraclitus' expression that the only thing constant in life is change. When we experience the inevitable transitions in our work and relationships, have changes in our physical or mental health, or try to keep up with news

figure 9.2

DEALING WITH CHANGE

These six steps can help you move through the seven stages of change and also through any minor, everyday changes you encounter, such as finding a different place to shop after your favorite store goes out of business. *How does this six-step list help you adjust to any change?*

Source: Based on Shad Helmstetter, *You Can Excel in Times of Change* (New York: Pocket Books, 1992).

HELMSTETTER'S SIX STEPS FOR DEALING WITH CHANGE

In his book *You Can Excel in Times of Change,* Shad Helmstetter lists what he calls Six Steps for Dealing with Change. His application is broader than the major changes you just read about. Rather than dealing with only the large-scale changes, he is writing about all changes that directly affect people's lives.

1. **Recognize and understand the change.** Be sure you can identify the change, understanding why it is occurring and the variables surrounding it.
2. **Make the decision to accept or reject the change.** When you include changes over which you might have some control, this is an important decision. When you have no control over the change, it is still good to think in terms of acceptance. The seven-step change process you just learned involves accepting the change and allowing it to become a useful part of your life.
3. **Choose the attitude you are going to have toward the change.** People often make the mistake of seeing themselves as victims, unable to form their own attitudes when outside forces affect them. Remember that the choice of what attitude you are going to have is yours and yours alone.
4. **Choose the style that you are going to use to deal with the change.** Some examples of choices are giving in, partnering with someone else, passively or actively resisting, retreating, and actively accepting.
5. **Choose the action that you are going to take *every day*.** A way of dealing with change is to live one day at a time. Each day needs a new plan. Make sure that each day represents a renewed effort.
6. **Review the steps and evaluate your progress daily.** The best way to make that renewed effort is to do a daily progress check. With some idea of where you're headed, your progress can be both faster and more effective.

events in our local communities and around the globe, these can have profound impacts on our mental and physical health. Dr. Kathleen Smith of Harvard University describes the following healthy practices for increasing your level of resilience and coping with change.[10]

Evaluate Your Level of Control

Don't fixate on events over which you have no power, or people who might never change their actions or attitude. Avoid blaming others or "moving the unmovable"—resilient people set their sights on what they *can* control. Evaluate your level of control over a situation by asking yourself, "What can I take responsibility for in this situation?" Look for opportunities to empower yourself; work toward change that is possible; and you are less likely to feel stuck in difficult situations.

Practice Self-Care After a Loss

Recognize that life's transitions involve losses, deaths, the end of relationships, and other experiences that might feel very negative. Even positive

REAL WORLD EXAMPLE 9.3

When Laurie learned that the real estate company she worked for was downsizing, she refused to believe she would be affected. It was the perfect job with a great salary. When she found out she was one of the many employees who lost their jobs, she became angry. "How could they do this to us?" she said crying as she packed her things. She went home, closed her door, and was unable to do anything that day. The next few days were difficult for Laurie. Over time, she began to accept the job loss and look for new employment. With the support of friends and family, Laurie was able to get through a difficult time in her life.

transitions, like a graduation or a job change, can make you feel a little sad. You may have heard the saying, "stay with your feelings." In other words, don't push away any grief you might feel. Acknowledge the loss; pay attention to what you've learned from the experience; seek support and camaraderie among friends and family; and if you feel you need extra support during the transition, consider speaking with a counselor or other mental health professional.

Check Your Thought Patterns

Take time to examine your thought patterns and assess how rational they are. If you find some irrational thoughts creeping in, nudge your thinking back toward resilience. Slow down your mind by practicing breathing or other relaxation techniques, such as mindfulness. These actions can help bring the mind into balance so that you can more effectively evaluate a major change.

When focusing your mind, remind yourself about transitions and challenges you successfully navigated in the past. List the times you've been resilient and successful in the past, and consider what traits and actions might help you through the current challenge. Focus on your strengths instead of your weaknesses to feel more empowered to meet future challenges that await you.

Be in the Present

Look to the past to find your inner strengths, but do not jump ahead to the future and start worrying about future outcomes, especially those over which you have no control. Stay present and observe your surroundings. Get in tune with your body. Pay attention to what your body is telling you, and note how it responds to stress. Set aside time every day to relax, take some deep breaths, and bring your focus back to the present.

Find Your Priorities

Transitions can be wonderful opportunities. The most resilient people see change as an opportunity, rather than something to fear. Transitions in life allow you to ask yourself essential questions, such as, what are your priorities in life? What things are really important to you? Are you involved with any people or things that waste your time and energy? With a clear sense of your goals and values, you will find your mind and body can be much more resilient when it comes to the stressors of change.[11]

Dr. Smith also recommends prioritizing your mental and physical health, and seeking the support of family, friends, or a support group to share your experiences. Don't be afraid to ask for help when you need it!

» MODELS OF ORGANIZATIONAL CHANGE MANAGEMENT

organizational change
Change that a group of people must learn to accept and implement.

Organizational change often occurs when a business needs to become more productive, when technology or other industry standards force different procedures to be put into place, when external initiatives or laws require a change, or when new management comes in with a different philosophy of how an organization should be run. Organizational change can be challenging and exhausting at times, but can also ignite the spirit of adventure in people. Flexibility and a commitment to the larger goals of the group will make the change process smoother for everyone. Change is a necessary part of doing business, yet members of an organization can get so comfortable with the *status quo* (the way things already are) that it becomes easy to ignore warning signs that something has to change.

more about. . .

Technology and Change

Perhaps the *only* constant factor in business is constant technological advancement, and to thrive in it you must have a high tolerance for uncertainty and for organizational change. How do you feel this fits (or doesn't fit) into American cultural norms? How do technological changes such as globalization and the rise of social media affect organizational change?

The field of change management has grown in recent decades to a point where many American and international colleges and universities offer certificates and even degrees in this area. Organizations have also developed their own proprietary models of managing change, and can act as consultants to other organizations undergoing change. As change is inevitable and progress unstoppable, it is not surprising that this area has gained interest in business schools and the corporate world.

Ultimately, when an organization undergoes change, it is not the *organization* that changes, it is the *people* in the organization who change. Change management requires that leaders in the organization prepare employees for the change, equip their employees to make a change, and support the change in process.[12] The types of change individuals must make will range from workflow and work processes, to use of technology, to organizational structure, to job roles, behaviors, even to their identity in the workforce. Failure on the part of an organization can result in a failed project or even a failed business. Fortunately, humans are pretty resilient, so change can be managed successfully if organizations are prepared for it.

John Paul Kotter, a former professor at Harvard University and established international business leader, has developed an organizational change model that is widely followed today. The steps in this process include:

- Establish a sense of urgency.
- Create the guiding coalition.
- Develop a vision and strategy.
- Communicate the change vision.
- Empower employees for broad-based action.
- Generate short-term wins.
- Consolidate gains and producing more change.
- Anchor new approaches in the culture.[13]

Taking a look at Kotter's steps, it is worth noting the importance of time in creating the need for change and in making certain employees see short-term gains that reinforce the change process. The importance of communication throughout the change process is imperative. And organizations must not forget the impact on everyone involved in the change. As well, all change management leaders must remain aware that organizational change should have the goal of continuous improvement. If organizations are to be successful, they can never stop changing and adapting.

In the following section, three additional ways to view and understand organizational change are introduced, including the Lewin change model, force field analysis, and logical incrementalism. These three models can be used in managing either personal or organizational change.

more about . . .

Leading Change

For more about how you can successfully lead change in your organization, visit John Paul Kotter's website, Leading Change, Kotter International.

According to Kotter, "Because management deals mostly with the status quo and leadership deals mostly with change, in the next century we are going to have to try to become much more skilled at creating leaders."

—John P. Kotter

Source: John P. Kotter, *Leading Change* (Harvard Business Review Press, 2012).

The Lewin Change Model

Once an organization has established the need to change, management must come up with a method. A good beginning point is to examine a *change model,* which outlines the steps one must take to change an organization effectively.

One of the workplace change models used over many years is the **Lewin change model**. Kurt Lewin saw three different levels where any change has to happen. First, the *individuals* who work for a company must be convinced that a change is essential, then guided to the necessary attitudes and behaviors. Second, the *systems* of an organization need to be changed. Systems include work design, information systems, and compensation plans. Third, the *organizational climate* must be adjusted. Essential climate change areas include methods of conflict management and the decision-making processes.[14] (See Figure 9.3.)

Lewin change model

A workplace change model with three steps; unfreezing the status quo, making changes, then refreezing to the previous work mode.

figure 9.3

THE LEWIN CHANGE MODEL

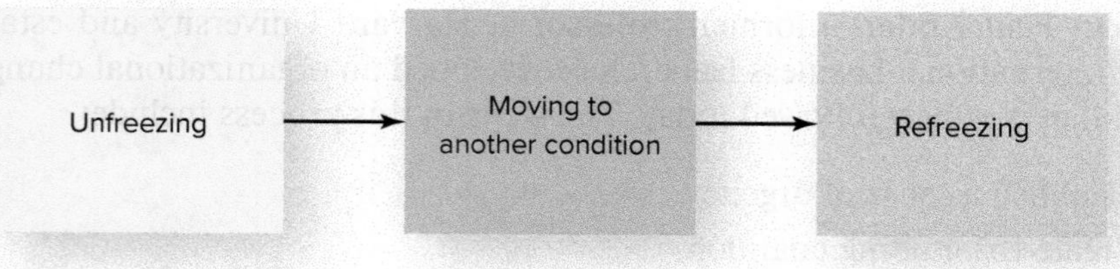

This change model shows that to make change, the status quo must first be "unfrozen." After that, you can make change and then, in some cases, refreeze back to your original working environment. *What is your chief criticism of the Lewin change model?*

Source: Based on Kurt Lewin, "Group Decisions and Social Change," in G. E. Swanson, T. M. Newcomb, and E. I. Hartley (eds.), *Readings in Social Psychology* (New York: Holt, Rinehart & Winston, 1952).

The Lewin change model contains three steps: unfreezing the status quo, moving to a new condition, and refreezing to create a new status quo.[15]

1. *Unfreezing.* In any group change process, people's habits, attitudes, and positions usually have to change to adjust. Sometimes, even personnel must change. On the individual level, this unfreezing could involve promoting employees or letting them go, preparing them for change, or convincing them of the need for the change. On the structural level, redesigning the organization could be the focus of the change effort. On the climate level, the company could create a new open-door policy or begin a data-based feedback system showing how employees are reacting to the proposed changes.[16] In the unfreezing process, *fear* in some form is nearly always one of the major obstacles.
2. *Moving to another condition.* This is the step where the actual changes are made. On the individual level, people should be developing the new skills that are required for the change. On the structural level, you would probably see changes in actual organizational relationships, reward systems, or reporting relationships. On the climate level, there should be more openness and trust, with fewer conflicts.[17]
3. *Refreezing.* Kurt Lewin referred to this final step as being "relatively secure" against change. The refreezing might involve new hiring policies, so that employees hired after the change would be more accepting of the new system. During this stage, the company must ensure that the new behaviors actually become new norms or standards on the job.

more about...

Refreezing in the Rapids?

Management expert Peter Vaill has shown that although the Lewin model worked well in slower times, it is much less useful in today's "white water rapids" business climate.

Source: Peter B. Vaill, *Learning as a Way of Being: Strategies for Survival in a World of Permanent White Water* (San Francisco, CA: Jossey-Bass, 1996).

Current Criticism of Lewin's Change Model

Since the mid-1990s an increasing number of people in the fields of management and organizational behavior have begun to see flaws in this model. The most important criticism has been that refreezing is not a realistic concept in today's business world. The 21st century faces a growing number of change situations, where taking the time to refreeze would simply hinder progress. In the areas of high technology, this scenario seems to be especially accurate. Moreover, nearly every area in today's business world is touched at least indirectly by ever-changing technology. The refreezing step is unrealistic when environmental and technological changes are everyday realities.

The Lewin change model is still useful, however, given this one qualification. In today's world, one must be realistic about the fact that changes take place so rapidly that people don't have the luxury they once had of refreezing, even for a short time, because they may fall behind.[18]

TECHNOLOGY AND THE RATE OF CHANGE
In e-business, traditional companies have had to learn fast what works and what does not. Traditions are often ignored because there are newer, faster, and more efficient ways to do business on the Internet. In this environment you must be ready and willing to accept almost constant change. *How tolerant toward change are you? What are some ways you could increase your tolerance of change?*
Nenetus/Shutterstock

Force Field Analysis

Another approach to change that was developed by Lewin is the concept of **force field analysis** (illustrated in Figure 9.4). According to this model, the status quo is like a battlefield being fought for by two armies–the driving forces and the restraining forces. The driving forces are trying to take over and change the status quo, and the restraining forces are trying to defend it.[19]

In today's world, staying with the status quo is not realistic. As just mentioned, today's world moves too rapidly for that. However, the driving forces generally face the opposition of the restrainers. Much like a real battle, the task is either to build up the driving forces or to decrease the restraining forces in order to win. If driving and restraining forces are equal in strength, no change will take place–only frustration on both sides; and the status quo remains unchanged.

The driving forces can be strengthened in several ways. If resistance arises, more driving forces must be added. Another method is to improve the quality or focus of the driving forces. Diminishing the restraining forces involves persuasion by showing the benefits of change–in short, eliminating the many factors that keep change from happening.

Force field analysis is positive in three ways. First, it requires the changers to *plan* for the change. Second, it allows those who are organizing the change to take a close look at the forces likely to restrain them and put together a strategy to overcome that restraint. Third, analyzing the restraining forces before a conflict starts can often keep the conflict from beginning at all.[20]

force field analysis
A model in which the status quo is like a battlefield being fought for by two armies: the driving force and the restraining force.

Logical Incrementalism

Another useful model of organizational change is **logical incrementalism**. This model acknowledges that bringing about changes in a large organization is usually time-consuming and complicated. Many forces, both inside and outside the firm, can put pressure on those who are involved in the planned change. Management professor James Brian Quinn studied many

more about...

Kurt Lewin (1890–1947) was a social psychologist whose ideas became very influential in management and organizational behavior.

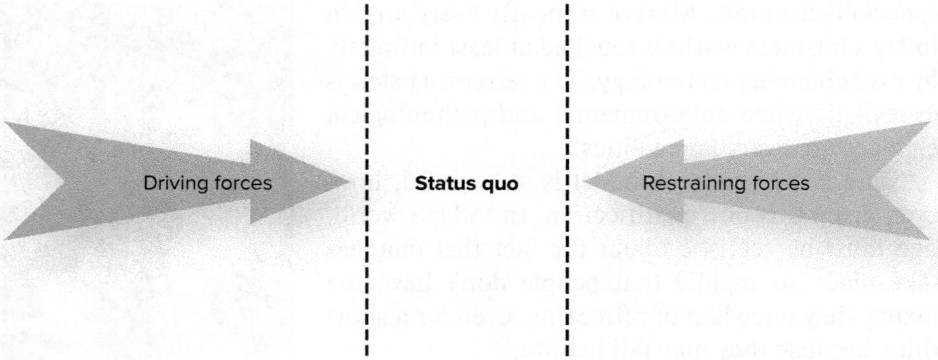

figure 9.4

FORCE FIELD ANALYSIS

This change model compares change with a battlefield, in which some forces attempt to bring change and others attempt to stop it. *What are the positive effects of this change model? How could you use it in planning?*

large organizations involved in important changes and devised a system to address those forces.

logical incrementalism
A model that acknowledges that bringing about changes in a large organization is usually time-consuming and complicated, and presents a method of simplifying the process.

Like the Lewin models, logical incrementalism can address change at the individual or corporate levels. This approach starts on a general level, then moves slowly into the more specific needs for change.[21]

The five stages of logical incrementalism are:

1. *General concern.* A vague feeling or awareness of a threat or opportunity.
2. *Broadcasting a general concern or idea without details.* The new idea is tried out on others in general terms, with details to be filled in later. This procedure is often described as the *trial balloon.*
3. *Development of a formal plan for change.* The new idea is outlined both in terms of its nature, and of the method of making it happen.
4. *Using an opportunity or crisis to begin the change plan.* Something important that gets everyone's attention, such as a crisis that the change plan can solve, can be used to get the ball rolling.
5. *Ongoing adaptation of the plan.* Many managers see logical incrementalism as an accurate description of how change occurs in most successful companies. Thus, the model shows a natural process as it should happen. Critics of logical incrementalism see it as generally ineffective; in fact, when the change plan is poorly defined, the process does fail. Logical incrementalism is most successful when used to bring a well-designed plan into general acceptance.[22]

Additional Organizational Change Models

There are many other strategies and approaches that address change within a business or organization. While not covered in this text, curious readers can research more details about the models as follows:

- *McKinsey 7 S Model.* The seven "s" words that make up this model include structure, strategy, systems, skills, style, staff, and shared values.[23]

EXCUSES FOR RESISTING CHANGE

- We don't have time to do it.
- We've tried something like this before, and it didn't work.
- It's impossible; it just won't work.
- It would have worked years ago, but not now.
- You can't teach an old dog new tricks.
- Let's spend some more time thinking about it.
- It's a good idea; it just won't fit this company.
- It's unrealistic; reality will kill it.
- It's not in my job description.
- We're already too busy to start something new.
- Let's appoint a committee to look at it.
- We're too far along to change now.
- The company is doing fine already; who needs it?
- The union just won't go for it.
- Top management won't accept it.
- I like the job the way it is.
- We don't have the technology to make it work.
- Write a report on it, and I'll take a look later.
- It will cause conflict in the company.
- It will upset our stockholders.
- Our competitors will jump right on it.
- If it fails, we'll lose our jobs.
- Why haven't our competitors already tried it?
- The results just aren't clear to me.
- Too many changes have been made already.

figure 9.5

RESISTING CHANGE

Throughout an organization, people will think of excuses, many similar to those in this list, for resisting change. They may believe in these excuses very strongly and may spend a lot of effort trying to prevent change from occurring. *What can you do when you encounter resistance to change?*

- *Nudge Theory.* This behavioral economics theory focuses on identifying choices for people to nudge them to choose a behavior that is more helpful for them and for the wider interests of a company, society, the environment, or other entities.[24]
- *ADKAR Model.* In this model, people and organizations can achieve lasting change with tangible and concrete outcomes when they include the five characteristics of awareness, desire, knowledge, ability, and reinforcement.[25]
- *Kübler-Ross Five Stage Model.* This five-stage model of reacting to grief or loss includes denial, anger, bargaining, depression, and acceptance.[26]

You can probably think of reasons why people resist change. Some may be valid while others are excuses to cover up resistance to change. Figure 9.5 lists 25 common excuses people make. Most are related to either fear or insecurity related to the change. Those are the two common denominators that seem to unite people who resist organizational change.

» ACCEPTING CHANGE

The major problem with getting organizational change to take place is nearly always the same–human opposition. Before they come to accept it,

REAL WORLD EXAMPLE 9.4

Before Kathleen started college, she had no real sense of what college life would be like. She tried, but she couldn't paint a mental picture of a typical college day and put herself into it. It was frightening because she did not know what to expect. The fear didn't overwhelm her, though, because she went on to college—and found that most of the changes she encountered were pleasant ones.

ACCEPTING CHANGE Before employees come to understand and accept it, they may resist change for several reasons, most of which are based on fear and denial. *How have you seen change resisted in an organization, and what happened?*

Digital Vision/Getty Images

some people can be skeptical or even hostile to change. People resist change for a number of different reasons. For one thing, the status quo is often just too comfortable. Employees ask, "Why should I get out of my comfort zone and try something new?" This is because they are more secure in knowing exactly what they are going to do each day. But how do organizations allow for change?

Among the main reasons people resist change are:[27]

- *Fear of losing job status or job security.* We are not eager to make changes that could threaten our jobs. When administrative or technological changes might mean jobs being eliminated or reduced, resistance to change occurs. The change is seen as harmful to the individual involved and the organization. Especially when the change is forced on to the person, more resistance occurs. A thoughtful and planned approach will reduce turnover and strong resistance.
- *Reward systems that are not rewarding.* You may have heard the saying that managers get what they reward. Employees who do not see any reward in it for them may resist change. In your planning for the change, think about the rewards you can offer, and remember from Chapter 5 that intrinsic (internal) rewards are more powerful motivators than extrinsic (external) rewards.
- *Fear of the unknown or unwelcome surprises.* The more that team members know about a change and how it will impact them, the less anxious and fearful they will be. Do not spring unwelcome surprises on your team or the organization. Remember, too, that communication goes both ways. Listen to fears, answer questions, and help the people involved to be prepared.
- *Peer pressure.* We are all creatures of habit, and we are all members of a team or organization. We look to others for how to respond in a situation. Our need to belong to a group is very powerful, whether we are young or old, introverted or extraverted. We often look to others to see how to respond in an unusual situation. If others are resistant, team members may just follow along. Set an example of acceptance. If

REAL WORLD EXAMPLE 9.5

Prior to the Covid-19 pandemic, many U.S. hospitals had been slow to roll out so-called telemedicine services to patients unable to physically attend an appointment with a health specialist or doctor.[28] These patients, many living in rural areas hundreds of miles away from the nearest hospital, had few healthcare options. And while technology and advances in the medical field have rapidly increased over the past 10 years, lawmakers and doctors remained largely resistant to the idea. State licensing requirements, legislation designed to protect patients' privacy, and other legal and ethical concerns persisted, slowing the roll-out of telehealth services across the country.

Forced to respond to widespread public health concerns, the medical profession began to work closely with legislators and technology experts to quickly increase the number of practitioners involved and improve the quality of care for people remotely via the web.[29] This model has since gained more widespread acceptance, and lessons learned during the pandemic inform the success of telemedicine today.

possible, work with key leaders ahead of time to get their buy-in for the change. They can then lead with acceptance.

- *Mistrust in the corporate climate.* Is the workplace one of trust, or mistrust? In a mistrustful climate, even good planning and preparation may be doomed to failure when organizational changes are necessary. Build up trust before making changes through honest and open communication, and following through with promises made.
- *Office politics.* When office politics are at play, some team members may try to sabotage others or try to keep a power position by questioning the need for change. Staff members may take sides and become divisive without genuinely considering the necessity for the organization's changes. Communication, trust, and equitable treatment of team members may help to downplay office politics.
- *Fear of failure.* As has been stated in this chapter, fear often drives resistance to change. This may be a fear of failing at a new assignment or role, fear of looking incompetent, lacking skill, or just not being up to the task being asked of them. Thoughtful planning in advance for any needed professional development and new training opportunities will help reduce some of this fear.
- *Poor timing or delivery.* Is it *what* is said that creates resistance or *how* it is said? Sometimes it is how the message is delivered that creates resistance. Be aware of the timing and delivery of the message to reduce conflict. Poor times to deliver an organizational change message are in a time that is already stressful and immediately before the change is planned to begin. Remember to be thoughtful, be thorough, and consider all the potential resistance before beginning your organization's changes. Change happens! Be ready for it, and help team members be ready for it, to reduce resistance.

The other extreme of acting too quickly in bringing about change is bringing in the change too slowly. When the pace of change is so sluggish that employees

more about...

Kaizen is founded upon five main elements:

- **Teamwork:** The starting point for *Kaizen* is teamwork. A strong business or corporation is one in which all employees work as a team toward the common goal of improving the company's production. Participants work for the good of their colleagues and the company.
- **Personal Discipline:** For the team to succeed, each member of the team must be strong. Individual team members should have self-discipline in time management and quality assurance, and loyalty to the company and its customers. A lack of personal discipline can negatively affect the employee, and have a negative impact on other employees and clients.
- **Improved Morale:** Employers and managers can encourage strong morale at work by focusing on creating a comfortable, dynamic work environment for their employees, and through motivational strategies such as promotions, bonuses, and paid medical insurance to create an overall sense of belonging and well-being. When morale is high, a business can have an easier time achieving long-term efficiency and productivity.
- **Quality Circles:** Employees and managers share ideas, skills, resources, and technology in group meetings called "quality circles" that allow the business to discuss its quality and performance and brainstorm for ways to improve.
- **Suggestions for Improvement:** The last foundation of the *Kaizen* concept is having an open process for workers to freely provide feedback and suggestions, no matter what their rank in the company. By welcoming and addressing feedback, management can improve morale and address potential problems before they become significant.

Source: Brendan McGuigan, "What Is Kaizen?" published by Conjecture Corporation, November 29, 2012, www.wisegeek.org (retrieved March 17, 2013).

question whether any real change is going to happen, attitudes again are affected negatively. Find a balance in timing: slow enough that people can process the changes, and quickly enough that the necessary changes can occur without damaging productivity.

» APPROACHES TO CONTINUOUS IMPROVEMENT

It can be useful to understand how organizations and businesses change by taking note of different approaches to "continuous improvement." Consider the following approaches that a business or organization can take toward continuous improvement both internally and in the marketplace.

Kaizen

Kaizen is a Japanese term meaning "change for the better" or "continuous improvement." It is an approach that seeks to create continuous improvement within an organization based on the idea that small, ongoing positive changes can reap major improvements. Some examples of large companies that use this approach include:

- *Lockheed Martin:* Through the use of *Kaizen,* Lockheed Martin has been successful in reducing manufacturing costs and inventory and cutting delivery time.
- *Ford Motor Company:* The auto giant was on the brink of bankruptcy when Alan Mulally became CEO of Ford in 2006. Mulally used *Kaizen* to execute one of the most famous corporate turnarounds in history.
- *Pixar Animation Studios:* Pixar has taken a continuous improvement model that reduced risks of expensive movie failure by using quality control checks and iterative processes (repeated cycles of operations toward improvement).[30]

Six Sigma

Six Sigma is a set of techniques and tools made popular by American engineer Bill Smith while he was working for Motorola in 1986. Smith's *Six Sigma* strategies are designed to improve the quality of an organization's output by identifying and removing any causes of defects or other problems in the manufacturing and business processes. A Six Sigma project carried out within an organization follows a defined sequence of steps and has specific value targets, such as to reduce process cycle time, reduce pollution, reduce costs, increase customer satisfaction, and increase profits.[31]

Kaizen

Literally, "to become good through change." The concept of *Kaizen* is one of restructuring and organizing every aspect of a system to ensure optimal efficiency.

quality circles

Process that bring employees and managers together to brainstorm and find ways to improve quality and performance.

Lean

The *Lean* method is focused on eliminating waste. It is designed to provide maximum value to customers with the lowest possible amount of investment. The principles of Lean are complementary to, and often combined with, the *Kaizen* and Six Sigma approaches.

The primary difference between Lean and Six Sigma is that Lean is less focused entirely on manufacturing, with a wider focus on every facet of the entire business.[32]

organizational development (OD)

A planned, companywide, systematic method of achieving change in an organization.

» ORGANIZATIONAL DEVELOPMENT

Organizational development (OD) is a planned, companywide, systematic method of achieving change in an organization. It requires the participation and support of top management. Usually the change agent is an outside consultant who specializes in planned change. This person is called an **OD change agent**. This agent's job is to use **OD interventions**, which are training tools that teach members of the organization how they can solve the problems they are facing.

OD change agent

A company's formal change agent; often an outside consultant who specializes in planned change or organizational development (OD).

OD intervention

Training tools that teach members of the organization how to solve problems they face or make needed changes to organizational development (OD).

OD change agents base their procedures on specific ideals concerning organizations. These specific ideals usually involve the following values:[33]

1. *Participative operations:* The more that employees are involved with a change effort, the stronger their commitment will be to putting that change into effect.
2. *Equality:* Effective organizations must de-emphasize hierarchy and heavy-handed authority.
3. *Respect for others:* Since people are mostly responsible and conscientious, they should be treated accordingly.
4. *Confrontation:* Problems are to be confronted and dealt with immediately, never swept under the carpet.
5. *Trust and mutual support:* A climate of openness and trust is the most productive in any organization.

Pixtal/AGE Fotostock

more about...

OD interventions may include team building, sensitivity training, role playing, and survey feedback. Members of the organization are involved in the implementation process.

Nearly all of the emphasis of organizational development is on changes affecting people and their relationships, making knowledge of human relations central to OD. Today OD is often used as a tool for empowerment. Empowered employees feel that they are in control of their own contributions to the firm. OD interventions can serve another purpose—to help make employees more comfortable and accepting of the new position that empowerment gives them.

STRATEGIES FOR SUCCESS

Strategy 9.1 Managing Personal Change in the Workplace

1. Take care of you.
2. Keep an open mind and stay flexible.
3. Have a positive attitude.
4. Control your life.
5. Be the change agent.

Change is inevitable. When personal changes take place, they are nearly always both unavoidable and energy-consuming. These steps can be helpful in such situations where change is occurring.

1. **Take care of you.** Maintain your physical and emotional health. Get enough sleep, eat well, exercise, and maintain social support. Build in time to relax and follow your interests. The healthier you are, the better able you will be to manage change.
2. **Keep an open mind and stay flexible.** Let go of your expectations that nothing changes and everything will stay the same—and stay comfortable—forever. Things change. Know that your familiar environment may change, your routines may change, and you will have to adapt to a new normal. Flexibility will help you see the multiple perspectives in the situations you are facing. Some of the changes you may be dreading will turn out to be improvements that you couldn't imagine now doing without.
3. **Have a positive attitude.** Remember that you control your reactions to events. Stay positive, let go of negativity and suspicion. Look for the positives in the change that is coming. Choose to be optimistic.
4. **Control your life.** Use critical thinking to examine the changes that are coming. What will you do to make the transition easier? List your options. Consider all angles and approaches to maintain as much control as you can about the upcoming change.
5. **Be the change agent.** Act, don't react. Put yourself in the position of owning and controlling the upcoming change. Step out of the rut and the routines that you allow yourself to feel comfortable within. Look at areas that need improvement and positive change. Prevent the stress and anxiety of the unexpected by being the force of change.

We all need to learn to manage change. Even though it is challenging and we may be resistant to the change, we will have to manage it. Learning to accept change and manage the challenges will go a long way toward reducing stress and making the change more comfortable. Whether the changes are in your personal life or are due to global events, the economy, climate change, or other larger life events, we can still learn and grow from managing change effectively. Remember—nothing stays the same forever!

Source: Adapted from Z. Hereford, "5 Tips to Help You Manage Change," *Essential Life Skills*, https://www.essentiallifeskills.net/change.html (retrieved April 14, 2020).

STRATEGIES FOR SUCCESS

Strategy 9.2 Gaining Acceptance for Change in Your Organization

1. Overcome opposition and create a climate where change is acceptable.
2. Involve everyone in the change effort.
3. Make changes in stages.
4. Communicate effectively.

Resistance to change is often caused by a feeling of being left out of the decision making, a belief that change has been abrupt and maybe unnecessary, and generally poor communication. These factors result in a hazy understanding of the purpose and consequences of the change. They can also reduce trust in management—a barrier to accepting any type of change. What should be done to promote acceptance among employees of positive change within an organization? Remain honest and open. The manager can communicate to employees the entire situation with all of its implications. Usually in a situation that calls for change, the alternative—remaining the same—will produce negative consequences. Employees should know specifically what those consequences will be and how their positions will be affected.

1. **Overcome opposition and create a climate where change is acceptable.** The manager's responsibility is to create a work environment that allows employees to be comfortable with change. This includes educating employees and communicating with them on an ongoing basis. If managers maintain a rigid, inflexible attitude toward new ideas, they create climates that discourage change-oriented thinking. A manager who communicates with employees only when a change is coming misses the power that regular communication brings. Find out what the resistance is based on or what the concerns are. Communicate the changes upcoming, and explain why they are happening. Be truthful, straightforward, and timely with big changes. Help employees see the big picture and understand what is in it for them.
2. **Involve everyone in the change effort.** People who have been involved with the creation of a change will find that change is more difficult to resist. Even when employees don't have the expertise to make technical decisions connected to a change effort, they usually can be involved somewhere in the process. Sometimes top management orders a change, and the supervisor must announce it to employees. Some participation is better than none at all. One note of caution: employees should be told how their input is going to be handled. If their advice will be considered but they will not actually have a vote, this should be clearly stated. Failure to make that point clear can result in very low morale. Whenever possible, ask for feedback. And then listen, listen, listen.
3. **Make changes in stages.** Help employees prepare for the big changes to come. Companies should prepare their employees for the changes to come, share with them the plan for change, and then provide support along the way for all changes that occur. When possible, making changes in stages rather than abruptly will result in less resistance. Reassure employees that the phased changes are happening as planned. Preparation reduces the fear of the unknown, which can be a major barrier in accepting change.
4. **Communicate effectively.** This suggestion cannot be overstated. If people do not understand why something is happening, they will fill in the blanks themselves, even making up their own explanations. Use formal and informal communications channels (see Chapter 6 for reminders on organizational communication). As with any communication issues, timing is important. When employees resist change, it may not be the actual change they are resisting, but the timing and delivery of the message. Be sure to include the vision, goals, and expectation for what is happening with the coming change—and why.

Source: Adapted from "Overcoming Employee Resistance To Change In The Workplace," Paycor, July 17, 2019, https://www.paycor.com/resource-center/change-management-in-the-workplace-why-do-employees-resist-it (retrieved April 11, 2020).

CHAPTER NINE SUMMARY

Chapter Summary by Learning Objectives

LO 9-1 Discuss why change is a fact of life in the 21st century. Since the beginning of the Industrial Revolution, changes have come with increasing speed. When we think about change in today's world, we often think about changing technologies. That is the area of the most obvious change. However, social change is also a common part of 21st century life. Despite all of the changes, individuals and groups at work often fight against change when it is introduced.

LO 9-2 Describe the seven stages of personal change. The normal person requires a process of adjustment to cope realistically with dramatic changes. The process involves emotional standstill, denial, anger, helplessness, bottoming out, experimenting, and completion.

LO 9-3 Compare and contrast models of organizational change. Several models can be used for the process of group change management. They are the Lewin change model, force field analysis, and logical incrementalism. The Lewin change model has been strongly challenged recently because the refreezing step is often unrealistic in today's high-tech environment. All three change models describe the forces of change and deal with human opposition to the change effort.

LO 9-4 Give reasons for why employees resist or accept change. One important reason for employee resistance to change is fear of loss. Another reason is resistance to the speed of the change (either too fast or too slow).

LO 9-5 Provide examples of different approaches to continuous improvement. Companies using a *Kaizen* approach emphasize employees' participation and feedback in operational and change decisions and encourage communication among managers and workers. Six Sigma and Lean are tightly focused on systems and eliminating waste or inefficiency from business and production systems.

LO 9-6 Discuss organizational development. Organizational development is a planned, company-wide, systematic method of change achievement in an organization. It involves employees in implementing humanizing changes that are based on workplace equality and participation.

key terms

review questions

1. Explain the seven steps of personal change management. Why are they all essential?
2. Imagine yourself as a manager with an employee who is going through a painful divorce that is affecting his or her quality of job performance. How could the material in this chapter be helpful to you?
3. Do you agree with the critics of the Lewin change model who say that it is no longer relevant—especially refreezing? Why or why not?
4. Briefly explain how force field analysis can be helpful to someone attempting change in an organization.
5. Someone once said that recognizing the need for change is the most difficult step in the change process. Why would that be true? Explain.
6. Explain the concepts behind logical incrementalism. Make sure to discuss the different steps that organizations go through based on James Brian Quinn's research of meaningful changes within organizations. Do you find this model helpful? Why or why not? Do you think it would ever be helpful in managing change in a smaller company? Why or why not?
7. What do *Kaizen,* Six Sigma, and the Lean methods have in common? One could say that they arose in response to a need in organizations. How would you describe that need?
8. What is organizational development? How is it used in a company that wants change? On what types of change does it usually focus?

critical thinking questions

1. How has change impacted your own life? When you reflect on your past, which changes were positive? Which changes were negative? Did changes that you originally thought would be negative turn out to be positive?
2. In general, do you see change as mostly a positive or negative force? Explain why.
3. Identify organizations you have seen or heard about that resisted change. Why did they resist change? What consequences did such companies suffer, if any?

working it out 9.1

THE RESILIENCY QUIZ

Part One

People bounce back from tragedy, trauma, risks, and stress by having the following "protective" conditions in their lives. The more times you answer yes (below), the greater the chances you can bounce back from your life's problems in a healthy way.

Answer yes or no to the following. Celebrate your "yes" answers and decide how you can change your "no" answers to "yes." (You can also answer "sometimes" if that is more accurate than just "yes" or "no".)

1. **Caring and Support**

   I have several people in my life who give me unconditional love, nonjudgmental listening, and who I know are "there for me."
   I am involved in a school, work, faith, or other group where I feel cared for and valued.
   I treat myself with kindness and compassion, and take time to nurture myself (including eating right and getting enough sleep and exercise).

2. **High Expectations for Success**

   I have several people in my life who let me know they believe in my ability to succeed.
   I get the message "You can succeed," at my work or school.
   I believe in myself most of the time, and generally give myself positive messages about my ability to accomplish my goals—even when I encounter difficulties.

3. **Opportunities for Meaningful Participation**

   My voice (opinion) and choice (what I want) are both heard and valued in my close personal relationships.
   My opinions and ideas are listened to and respected at my work or school.
   I volunteer to help others or a cause in my community, faith organization, or school.

4. **Positive Bonds**

   I am involved in one or more positive after-work or after-school hobbies or activities.
   I participate in one or more groups (such as a club, faith community, or sports team) outside of work or school.
   I feel "close to" most people at my work or school.

5. **Clear and Consistent Boundaries**

   Most of my relationships with friends and family members have clear, healthy boundaries (which include mutual respect, personal autonomy, and each person in the relationship both giving and receiving).

I experience clear, consistent expectations and rules at my work or in my school.

I set and maintain healthy boundaries for myself by standing up for myself, not letting others take advantage of me, and saying "no" when I need to.

6. **Life Skills**

I have (and use) good listening, honest communication, and healthy conflict resolution skills.

I have the training and skills I need to do my job well, or all the skills I need to do well in school.

I know how to set a goal and take the steps to achieve it.

Part Two

People also successfully overcome life difficulties by drawing upon internal qualities that research has shown are particularly helpful when encountering a crisis, major stressor, or trauma.

The following list can be thought of as a "personal resiliency builder" menu. No one has everything on this list. When "the going gets tough" you probably have three or four of these qualities that you use most naturally and most often.

It is helpful to know which are your primary resiliency builders, how you have used them in the past, and how you can use them to overcome the present challenges in your life.

You can also decide to add one or two of these to your "resiliency-builder" menu, if you think they would be useful for you.

Personal Resiliency Builders (Individual Qualities That Facilitate Resiliency)

Put a check mark by the top three or four resiliency builders you use most often. Ask yourself how you have used these in the past or currently use them. Think of how you can best apply these resiliency builders to current life problems, crises, or stressors.

☐ **Relationships**—Sociability/ability to be a friend, ability to form positive relationships

☐ **Service**—Giving of yourself to help other people, animals, organizations, and/or social causes

☐ **Humor**—Having and using a good sense of humor

☐ **Inner Direction**—Basing choices/decisions on internal evaluation (internal locus of control)

☐ **Perceptiveness**—Insightful understanding of people and situations

☐ **Independence**—"Adaptive" distancing from unhealthy people and situations; autonomy

☐ **Positive View of Personal Future**—Optimism; expecting a positive future

☐ **Flexibility**—Can adjust to change; can bend as necessary to positively cope with situations

☐ **Love of Learning**—Capacity for and connection to learning

☐ **Self-Motivation**—Internal initiative and positive motivation from within

☐ **Competence**—Being "good at something"/personal competence

☐ **Self-Worth**—Feelings of self-worth and self-confidence

☐ **Spirituality**—Personal faith in something greater than oneself

☐ **Perseverance**—Keeping on despite difficulty; doesn't give up

☐ **Creativity**—Expressing yourself through artistic endeavor, or through other means of creativity

You can best help yourself or someone else be more resilient by:

1. Communicating the resiliency attitude: "What is right with you is more powerful than anything wrong with you."
2. Focusing on the person's strengths more than problems and weaknesses, and asking "How can these strengths be used to overcome problems?" One way to do this is to help yourself or another person identify and best utilize top personal resiliency builders listed in The Resiliency Quiz Part Two.
3. Providing for yourself or another the conditions listed in The Resiliency Quiz Part One.
4. Having patience . . . successfully bouncing back from a significant trauma or crisis takes time.

Source: The Resiliency Quiz, by Nan Henderson, MSW, Reprinted with permission from www.resiliency.com.

working it out 9.2

FEEL THE CHANGE

Simple changes can bring both discomfort and insight. Complete the following activities that ask you to make some simple changes.

1. **Cross your arms.** Cross your arms in your usual way. Take a few moments to become comfortable. Now, cross them the other way.

   Afterward, discuss: How comfortable, or uncomfortable, was this change? Even though it was basically the same movement, did it feel awkward? How long did it take to get used to this change? Necessary changes may be uncomfortable at first.

2. **Write your name.** Write your name five times with a pen or pencil using your usual, or dominant, hand (right hand if right-handed, left hand if left-handed). Now change hands and write your name again five times.

   Afterward, discuss: Again, as with crossing your arm, this is basically the same action. How uncomfortable did it feel? Did you get used to the change?

3. **Take a seat.** Everyone in class should stand up, stretch, and move to a different seat in the classroom. Get comfortable. After a few minutes, stand up again, and sit wherever you want.

   Afterward, discuss: Where did you sit? Did you go back to "your" seat, that is, the seat you originally took? Do you always sit in the same seat? Why? How quickly do we become comfortable with a specific behavior? Why do we resist changing out of our comfort zone, even with something this slight?

4. **Pretend to be space aliens.** In a small group in class, imagine that you are meeting for lunch. Now, imagine that you are an extra-terrestrial space alien sitting among the Earthlings. Describe the norms, behaviors, and culture of Earth people in your observation. Imagine that you need to report back to your home planet on Earth behaviors.

   Afterward, discuss: How did it feel to think of yourself as the outsider trying to understand the behaviors of a group? Was it awkward to try to describe behavior we take for granted? Now, back in your space alien mode, is there really only one way to do things? Describe a different way to do at least one of the behaviors you noted.

5. **Create mini-companies.** Break into small groups of five. In your groups, come up with a new product: shoes for cats, horse saddles with wings so you can ride and fly, or anything new and creative. Within each group or new "mini-company," there should be at least one designer, one producer, one marketer, and one distributor. Collaborate on a plan for your new product. After 5 to 10 minutes, two people in each mini-company change groups to a new mini-company. Take a few more minutes to prepare a presentation to the class on the new product your mini-company is creating. The class then selects the winning presentation.

Afterward, discuss: How easy was it to be flexible, to communicate, and to change the group's dynamics? What benefits did you note from the new group configuration? After adapting to the change in membership, were you able to work effectively together?

Source: Christopher Smith, "7 Fun and Engaging Change Management Exercises," *Change Management,* September 16, 2018, https://change.walkme.com/7-fun-and-engaging-change-management-exercises (retrieved April 1, 2020).

working it out 9.3

ORGANIZATIONS AND TRANSFORMATION

Watch the TED Talk by business leader Jim Hemerling, titled "5 Ways to Lead in an Era of Constant Change," and then answer the following questions.

1. How does the speaker explain the link between college students studying and organizational transformation?
2. What are the five strategic imperatives for change, in your words?
3. What is the one most important aspect of transformations, according to the speaker? How is this different from transformations you may have experienced?
4. The speaker addresses a "fixed mindset" and a "growth mindset" in his imperatives. How do these ideas (described in Chapter 2) fit with the topic of organizational change?
5. What is inclusive leadership? When have you experienced this in your work or in classes? Explain. What were the positives and negatives of the experience? If you have not experienced it, imagine a large class project running on inclusive leadership to respond to this question.

The video can be found here: www.ted.com/talks/jim_hemerling_5_ways_to_lead_in_an_era_of_constant_change/discussion.

case study 9.1

Making Motors

Jack Monroe is the Director of Marketing for Minor Motors, a small, boutique automobile maker that specializes in the design and limited production of hybrid and electric vehicles. Each June, Minor Motors holds its annual Client Council Conference, at which an independent management consultant listens to candid suggestions from the company's clients. Typically, more than an hour of the morning meeting involves all Minor Motors employees leaving the room while consultants talk with their clients. The thought is that the employees' presence could "interfere" with an open and honest exchange of ideas among the company's clients and the hired management consultant.

For the past two years, much of the discussion at this closed meeting has been aimed at the company's slow pace of technological development, specifically at how Minor Motors has lost ground to larger automakers and newer companies such as Tesla Inc. and Faraday Future. Clients have complained that even Alphabet, Google's parent company, continues to gain ground in their technological innovations with their Waymo automotive technology.

Last year, clients worried (behind closed doors) that Minor Motors was dangerously behind the major automakers in its research and development into self-driving cars that rely on robotic navigation and could, literally, put humans out of the driver's seat. "If we don't speed up our research and development into this important driverless technology, we will get left in the dust–or have to take our business elsewhere," one major client lamented. This year's conference featured the same complaints, but voiced even more loudly. Clients also expressed concerns about the lack of development into solar-powered cars and drone technology.

After the meeting, Jack said to his assistant Don and fiscal manager Dori, "I can't figure out why Hugh and Dean are dragging their feet on getting into the self-driving technology. They've got to know that these customers are right; all of our major competitors are invested in developing this new technology, and we'll get trounced if we don't act fast."

"As the senior partners in this company, Hugh and Dean have the most to lose if they don't get going," said Dori. "What do you think the real problem is on this issue?"

"I don't know what is going on with them," answered Jack. "For some reason, they don't want anything to do with this driverless technology, and they have not been very interested in talking about solar-powered, hydrogen, or all-electric cars, either. And they have told me they have no interest in drones."

"Well, then," replied Dori, "it's our job to get them moving forward. The company's future depends on it. What should we do?"

Case Study Questions

1. What is likely the main issue here with the senior partners and their reluctance toward the new technology? What other factors play into their reluctance?
2. Assume for a moment that fear is at least one issue here. What can Jack, Don, and Dori say, as marketing and fiscal specialists, to attack the fear that seems to be dangerously delaying progress on their company's research and development into important new technologies?
3. Briefly evaluate the Client Council Conference as a tool for obtaining suggestions from major clients. How well does such a strategy work to drive change in an organization such as Minor Motors, in your view? Would such an approach work in other types of organizations? Why or why not?

case study 9.2

The Family Tragedy

It was midafternoon on a busy Friday when everyone in the company learned that Carlos Garcia had been seriously injured in an auto accident. Juanita, Carlos's life partner, was a well-liked agent at Zola Insurance. Carlos himself was a former employee, and was very well known and respected by many in the company. The weekend was to be a long one: doctors immediately placed Carlos in intensive care, and his condition remained critical. Zola Insurance employees swarmed through the hospital, encouraging family members, hoping for the best, and praying in the small chapel near the intensive care unit.

Early on Sunday morning, Carlos lost the fight. With only 24 hours to get back into a working frame of mind, the insurance company employees struggled to make up some badly missed sleep. Needless to say, the situation wasn't exactly business as usual when Monday morning came. Nobody seemed to be working up to speed, and the company was uncharacteristically quiet. Customers who walked unknowingly into the service office invariably asked what was wrong.

Days passed, then weeks. Soon the surface behavior of the employees seemed to return to normal, but more than ever the focus was still on Juanita. She had seemed numb at first, but now her behavior seemed confusing. Some days she acted nonchalantly, denying that she was having a tough time—then she would suddenly show a burst of anger. Few of her co-workers understood exactly why she was acting this way.

Devi Ramasamy, the CEO, decided to bring in a grief counselor. When she described the situation to the counselor, he said, "It seems to me that everybody in the company needs this, not just Juanita."

Case Study Questions

1. How could an understanding of the seven steps of personal change help everyone at Zola Insurance?
2. Explain the grief counselor's statement that everybody at the company needs a grief counselor, not just Juanita.
3. There are some disadvantages to the company in keeping Juanita at work at this time. What are they? What are some advantages of having her remain on the job during her healing process?

CHAPTER TEN

10

CREATIVITY AND HUMAN RELATIONS

LEARNING OBJECTIVES

After studying this chapter, you will be able to:

LO 10-1 Explain the importance of creativity.

LO 10-2 Define creativity.

LO 10-3 Discuss the relationship between perception and creativity.

LO 10-4 List the steps in the creative process.

LO 10-5 Describe creativity in the workplace.

LO 10-6 Compare and contrast creative methods for groups.

LO 10-7 Give examples of ways to solve problems creatively.

STRATEGIES FOR SUCCESS

Strategy 10.1 Increase Your Creativity

Strategy 10.2 Roger von Oech's Ten "Mental Locks"

Strategy 10.3 Use SCAMPER to Solve Problems

In the Workplace: More Than Two Ways

SITUATION

Comstock Images/Alamy Stock Photo

The community college business club held its first annual flea market in the fall. Despite hard work and much planning, the results were turning out to be disappointing. It was an indoor event, but customers wanted to be outdoors on what turned out to be a beautiful autumn day. Also, a similar event was being held nearby—out in the open.

Around lunchtime, the club members met to decide how to salvage the day. One member suggested giving the participants back their table space rental money and taking only 10 percent of their sales, rather than both, as contracted. Someone else suggested the opposite: just keep their rental money, but don't ask for a percentage. Then members took sides on those two approaches and argued. After 20 minutes, the members with the louder voices and greater persuasive ability won. The club then announced to each of the participants that they wouldn't be asked to pay the percentage.

DISCOVERY

When the club adviser, a management instructor, returned from lunch and heard about the decision, she was irate. "What happened to creative problem solving?" she asked. "You've made the old mistake of choosing from two alternatives, while ignoring other creative possibilities." Earlier, the adviser had polled the participants. Only 12 of the 40 had been seriously unhappy with the sales they had made. "With a little creativity, you could have come up with a solution to make everyone happy and still realize a nice profit. I hope you've all learned a lesson from this," she exclaimed. The club later estimated that they had lost over $700 just from one bad, noncreative decision.

THINK ABOUT IT

What could the members of the business club have done to improve their creative process? What would you have suggested if you had been a club member in this situation?

» THE CREATIVITY CONNECTION

creativity

The ability to produce ideas or solutions to problems that are unique, appropriate, and valuable.

The connection between human relations and creativity may not be obvious, but this chapter explores how much **creativity**—the ability to produce ideas or solutions to problems that are unique, appropriate, and valuable—is linked with your perceptions of yourself and your relationships with other people. Having the ability to work creatively with team members is an increasingly important skill in a competitive workplace.

more about...

Creativity

"You can't use up creativity. The more you use, the more you have."

—Maya Angelou (1928–2014)

Creativity is the ability to come up with original and effective solutions in ways that people may call "out of the box thinking." It is an important factor for businesses as they develop, produce, and market their services and products. Consider a small tech startup in Nashville, Tennessee, or a party planning business near Orlando, Florida—the success of each business is strongly influenced by the creativity of the people in an organization.

Whether for someone employed in a traditional workplace, or a self-starter in the new "shared" or "gig" economy, the role of creativity has taken on new meaning and a new urgency. Fundamental changes to the American and global economy are occurring at a dizzying pace, and redefining the type, availability, and meaning of work. These changes have quickly created a new reality for American workers over the past decade: *creativity is the new economy.* But what exactly does that mean? It suggests that employers in traditional workplaces are looking to hire people who can stand out from the crowded field of applicants with their leadership skills and *creativity.*

more about...

Creativity Challenge

For a simple test of creativity, take this challenge. Think of as many creative uses of a paper clip as you can. Take a few minutes. How many did you think of? 10? 50? 100?

To get you started, here are a few ideas: mini imitation trombone, earrings, fingernail cleaner, book mark, cherry pit remover, doll clothes hanger, and zipper fixer. Now, it's your turn!

Creativity is something that no one completely understands. You can usually tell the difference between what seems creative and what does not, but can you really put your finger on creativity in individuals and groups, in terms of what causes it and how to make it happen? In the next sections of this chapter, we will look at some common characteristics held by creative people; the creative process itself; and using creativity in groups for effective problem solving. In learning about the science and application of creativity, think about your own creative processes - and how you can harness it to your benefit.

» WHAT IS CREATIVITY?

Creativity is defined as coming up with unique and useful ideas, but it is more than that. Creativity is more than just thinking, it is *action.* When composers create a new piece of music or engineers propose a new bridge design, the creativity we see is what is more important than their thoughts. In other words, creative ideas have to be paired with action, sometimes repeated action, for a successful outcome. As Albert Einstein once said, "I have tried 99 times and have failed, but on the 100th time came success." Without putting your ideas into action, creativity is meaningless. *Acts* of creativity can enhance the contributions of an individual and can positively influence the productivity of the group or team.

In thinking about what creativity *is,* it is also useful to think about what it is *not.* Creativity is not the same as intelligence. It is not a personality type, and it does not depend on specific products or materials. It is not limited to any type of job, economic status, age, gender, religion, language, or region of the world. Creativity can be developed, and the place to start in developing it is to consider your own interests and passions. What drives your creative energy?

"Flow" and Creativity in Our Everyday Lives

Psychologist Mihalyi Csikszentmihalyi (pronounced "me-high cheek-SENT-me-high") describes creative people as having flexibility and fluency in ideas, with the ability to know a good idea from a bad one.[1] Creative ideas can be used to solve everyday problems (sometimes called "little c" creativity), or can be used to imagine ideas and create products that change our lives (sometimes called big "C" Creativity), such as digital technology and the Internet.

"What makes you happy? Do you love what you do?" Csikszentmihalyi has spent more than 50 years asking precisely these questions to people from all over the world. Over his long career researching creativity and happiness, he conducted more than 8,000 interviews in which he asked people to describe the activities that made them feel happy and more creative, and to describe how they felt when doing those activities. He found similar answers whether he was talking with people in small Thai and Cambodian mountain villages, Navajo towns in the United States, European cities, or South American peasant communities.

Whether people talked about gardening, playing tennis, mountain climbing, or performing surgery, they gave similar answers when they talked about the activity they felt most passionate about. They said they felt totally engaged and absorbed in the activity. Each step of the task seemed to flow into the next, and the task almost always challenged them and kept their full attention.

When people reached their goal, they felt a sense of mastery, but their real pleasure came from the creative process itself, rather than achieving the goal. He called these moments

FLOW
You can find flow nearly anywhere. Flow is one of those concepts that might be hard to define, but you know when you're feeling it. *What are some of the areas of life where you find flow?*
kasto/123RF

optimal experience

The pleasure in performing the process of an activity itself, rather than achieving the goal.

flow

The feeling of oneness with an activity that allows an individual to uniquely experience an event or activity by becoming totally engaged in the process; term was coined by Mihalyi Csikszentmihalyi.

optimal experience. He refers to the process itself as **flow**, to describe the motion in which each step of the task seemed to flow effortlessly into the next.

Optimal experiences are intensely enjoyable and stimulate our creativity, but they are also very demanding. After examining many thousands of people's descriptions of flow, Csikszentmihalyi has found eight components that are usually found in a flow experience:

1. *The activity requires a specific skill and is challenging.* The task is challenging enough to require your full attention, but it is not so difficult that it is impossible or makes you feel defeated.
2. *Attention is completely absorbed by the activity.* You stop being aware of distracting things going on around you, and you seem to become a part of the task itself. The task seems automatic and spontaneous.
3. *The activity has clear goals.* You are working toward a logical end point, and the direction is clear.
4. *Feedback is clear about how you are doing.* You may get feedback from yourself or someone else, or the task itself comes to its natural end.
5. *You are concentrating only on the task itself.* You become unaware of distractions around you.
6. *You achieve a sense of personal control.* You enjoy the feeling of being in charge of the activity, and you enjoy the control you feel over your actions.
7. *You lose a sense of self-awareness.* You are not thinking about yourself or how others are evaluating you. You are lost in the moment, with your attention focused on the activity and your goals.
8. *You lose your sense of time.* Hours can go by like minutes. You are surprised by how much time has passed. The opposite can also happen: you may sometimes feel a small span of time stretch out almost infinitely.

Csikszentmihalyi believes that everyone can incorporate optimal experiences into their everyday lives and, in doing so, become more creative. He believes that one key to personal happiness and life satisfaction is to take responsibility and find out for yourself what makes you feel flow in your work. As an example, many students working in the computer lab say that they are surprised by how much time has gone by while they are surfing the Internet finding information for a class assignment. They get absorbed in the "flow" of the task.

Do you believe that you can experience flow only when you are away from work, enjoying yourself in leisure time? Many people think that flow does not happen much at work. However, this is not what Csikszentmihalyi found. He found that people are *more likely* to feel flow while at work.

more about...

Mihalyi Csikszentmihalyi is the Distinguished Professor of Psychology and Management at Claremont Graduate University in California. His interests "include the study of creativity, especially in art; socialization; the evolution of social and cultural systems; and the study of intrinsically rewarding behavior in work and play settings." His studies of finding happiness in one's work have changed the shape of psychology, and his theories have been adopted by business and government leaders around the world.

REAL WORLD EXAMPLE 10.1

Steve Jobs: Creating "iCulture"

Steve Jobs (1955–2011) was one of the most famous and prolific American inventors and entrepreneurs of our time, known best as the co-founder and CEO of Apple, Inc., established in the mid-1970s. In a speech he gave in 2005 at Stanford University, 20 years after being fired from Apple, Jobs said that being fired was the best thing that could have happened: "The heaviness of being successful was replaced by the lightness of being a beginner again, less sure about everything. It freed me to enter one of the most creative periods of my life." Without his creativity, the computer industry, cell phones, and even the music and movie industries would likely be very different today. And without the divergent thinking made possible by leaving an established corporation to start a new career path on his own again, these inventions may not have come about.

Source: Steve Jobs, "You've Got To Find What You Love," *Stanford Report*, June 14, 2005.

Therefore, people should stop buying into the conventional wisdom that work should be drudgery and that play should be fun, and learn to recognize and enjoy the parts of their jobs that make them feel alive and creative—and feel flow! If you are seeing the similarities between intrinsic motivation and positive attitudes (from Chapters 4 and 5) and creative flow, you are right—a state of flow feels good, and is highly internally motivating.

more about...

Csikszentmihalyi believes that you will be truly happy only when you take personal responsibility for finding out what gives you joy and meaning in life. This joy opens the opportunities for creativity. "**Optimal experience** is thus something that we make happen."

—Mihalyi Csikszentmihalyi

Are intelligence and creativity the same thing? Because people often use the word *genius* when talking about extremely creative people, many make the mistake of linking creativity with traditional intelligence. You have probably heard stories about creative people, such as Thomas Edison and Albert Einstein, who did badly in school. Actually, **intuition**, which is direct perception or insight, has been shown to be much more important to creativity than scholastic ability. "You don't have to have a high IQ to be intuitive," said the late Frank Barren, a psychologist at the University of California at Santa Cruz who studied the "science of creativity" in its emergence during the 20th century. "Intuition depends less on reasoning and verbal comprehension [the main devices used to measure IQ] than it does on feelings and metaphor."[2]

intuition
Direct perception or insight.

How are traditional intelligence and creativity linked? How close to being a genius do you have to be in order to be creative? These questions were asked by Lewis Terman in 1921. Terman was a pioneer in the study of intelligence, intelligence testing, and creativity. Terman followed more than 1,500 academic geniuses throughout their lives and found that they usually excelled in their careers, were socially and personally well adjusted, and were physically healthier than others. They were not, however, likely to be more creative than other people. By 1959, after almost 40 years, not one of them had produced highly creative works or been awarded Pulitzer or Nobel Prizes.[3]

Since Terman's pioneering research, many other psychologists have reported similar findings. Creative people are usually average or above

REAL WORLD EXAMPLE 10.2

A Beam of Light

When Albert Einstein was 16 years old, he asked an interesting question: "What would the world look like," he asked, "if I rode on a beam of light?" He would ponder this question for years, later answering it as an adult with what would become one of the most important theories of all—the principle of relativity. Einstein, who lived from 1879 to 1955, was considered by many to be a creative genius and revolutionary physicist who used his imagination and his creativity to come up with his most famous and elegant equation.[5]

average in intelligence, but being a genius (in the way that traditional intelligence is measured) does not automatically make someone creative. True creativity requires "divergent thinking," or what is referred to in more common terms as "thinking outside the box." Divergent thinking is spontaneous and free-flowing, without constraints, and typically results in many new ideas rather than one solution to a problem. Review Chapter 8 for a more complete treatment of the different types of intelligence.

» PERCEPTION AND CREATIVITY

Researchers who have studied creativity agree that creative people are somehow able to get away from the ordinary, everyday way of seeing things. In his book *The Act of Creation,* Arthur Koestler describes major scientific inventions of the past and shows the creative processes that produced them. Koestler says that *habit* is the stumbling block to creativity. How many people throughout history never tried to invent the airplane because they were in the habit of believing that humans cannot fly?[4] Even Galileo, the great 17th century pioneer astronomer from Italy, fell into this trap. He saw comets through his telescope, but refused to accept them because he was used to believing that all heavenly bodies must move in a circle. Those that didn't move in circles, he decided incorrectly, were optical illusions.

Likewise, groups of people (such as companies, committees, and universities) are often unable to move beyond habits of thinking.[6] Groups often have their own beliefs about *what* should be done and *how* it should be done; these are called **collective habits of thought**. Both individuals and groups need to get past the old, established ways of seeing things if they are going to increase their creativity.

collective habits of thought

Ways of thinking that occur when groups have own beliefs about *what* should be done and *how* it should be done.

Perception is the way in which a person views the world. When you are in a class with 25 other students and your instructor, in a sense, there are 27 different instructors teaching the class. This is because everything that each person sees is filtered through his or her own perceptions. Each person in the room *perceives* the instructor in a slightly different way. And, of course, the instructor perceives herself in a certain way, too.

perception

The way in which a person views the world.

Being able to look at the world from different angles makes a great difference in how creatively you deal with the world and solve problems.

Consider Einstein's question: "What would the world look like if I rode on a beam of light?" Research has shown that highly creative people aren't afraid to ask what might seem to be silly or childish questions. They might ask questions such as: "Why do rivers rarely run north?" or "Why don't spiders get tangled up in their own webs?" The curiosity everyone has as a child, a basic inquisitiveness, is an essential part of the creative process. Most major discoveries would not have been made without curiosity. Whatever you can do to retain or regain some of that childlike curiosity will help you produce more creative ideas.

CURIOSITY AS CREATIVITY

Sometimes your ability to solve problems creatively is limited by your fear of being childish. However, using the "childish" freedom of curiosity is an important way of increasing your creativity. *What kinds of questions can you ask—and answer—by being curious and thinking creatively?*

real444/E+/Getty Images

Abraham Maslow, who is best known for his hierarchy of needs theory (Chapter 5), has also talked about highly creative people. In his words, "They tend to be called childish by their more compulsive colleagues, irresponsible, wild, crazy." His opinion has elements of truth. "It should be stressed," he went on, "that in the early stages of creativeness, you've got to be a bum or a Bohemian or an eccentric."[7] By this remark, Maslow means that by being unduly influenced by conventional society, the way things are done, and the way people think of them, people are likely to become conventional and noncreative. The lesson for businesspeople is to learn to look beyond the conventional business world for ideas that will manifest success.

We all perceive events and situations based on our own experiences, knowledge, and interpretations. Other people's perceptions also have their own life and reality. Both are open to be challenged, reexamined, and reevaluated. But do perceptions have a basis in personality? Interestingly, as we see in Figure 10.1, this may be the case.

more about...

Imagination

"Imagination is more important than knowledge."

—Albert Einstein

Sometimes people's perceptions are blocked or distorted by rules that they think they need to follow. Often, they are rules that actually don't exist. The **nine-dot puzzle** is often used as an example of people's respect for such rules. Participants are told to connect nine dots using only four straight lines, without lifting the pen or pencil from the paper.

Try it. Can you do it? An amazing number of people won't come up with the solution because they are afraid that by going outside of the "square" that is formed by the nine dots, they are breaking a taboo or a rule of some kind. Even some people who solve the puzzle will ask, "Is this cheating?"

As James Adams from Stanford University explains it, all people who live in high-technology societies have developed an unconscious but very strong respect for squares and rectangles. These are shapes that seldom occur with perfect symmetry in nature. Because of this most people are stumped by the puzzle.[8] Solutions to the puzzle are at the end of this chapter.

figure 10.1

PERCEPTIONS AND CREATIVITY

What do your personality traits say about your creativity? Research on personality traits finds that "openness to experience," one of five identified major personality traits, is a good predictor of creativity. How open are you to new ideas and experiences?

Source: Psychology Today (n.d.). "Big 5 Personality Traits," *Psychology Today,* https://www.psychologytoday.com/us/basics/big-5-personality-traits (retrieved July 10, 2020).

Perception and Creativity

One of the most widely used personality theories, the Five Factor model (or Big Five model), says that our personalities are made up of a combination of high, medium, or low amounts of five major personality traits. These include *openness to experience* (open to new ideas, creativity, imagination, curiosity, adventure), *conscientiousness* (organized and detail-oriented), *extraversion* (sociable and outgoing), *agreeableness* (responsible and respectful to others), and *neuroticism* (anxiety and depression). Openness to experience, or openness, is similar to being in the open mode, except that it is a part of someone's personality rather than a temporary state of mind. Most personality theorists believe that personality traits are a long-term part of someone's life, but personality is possible to change.

How do you know whether you are high in openness? If you answer a definite "yes" to the following questions, you will probably score as high in openness on the Five Factor personality traits test.

1. I love adventure.
2. I often come up with interesting ideas.
3. I have a vivid imagination.
4. I find it easy to understand abstract ideas.
5. I am curious about things I don't understand and try to find the answers.
6. I like to try new things.
7. People say my ideas are unusual and creative.

nine-dot puzzle

A puzzle that is used to show people's respect for rules that don't exist. Participants are asked to connect nine dots using only four straight lines, without lifting the pen off the paper. Most fail because they feel the need to stay "inside the box" formed by the nine dots.

intrinsic motivators or intrinsic rewards

Factors that motivate a person from within, such as the joy and excitement of the discovery process.

extrinsic motivators

Those motivators that come from outside sources, such as money and fame.

According to a study of nearly 500 people in careers that require creativity, the following characteristics appeared most often:

1. *Imagination and playfulness, or associative orientation.* Creative people are usually playful and imaginative in their thoughts. They have lots of ideas and also the ability to focus on one. They move easily from fantasy to reality and are less rigid in their thinking. They are curious, questioning, and open to new ideas. Later in this chapter, this idea of being in the *open mode* (open to new ideas) will be explored again.
2. *Flexibility.* Creative thinkers do not get stuck on one idea. They can see different perspectives and come up with varying solutions. This flexibility can also appear as insight, or that "aha!" moment.
3. *Originality.* Creative people are often independent thinkers who prefer to do things their own way. They are non-conformists in their thinking. They are not easily swayed by the opinions of others.
4. *Motivation.* Creative people are motivated, more often by intrinsic than extrinsic motivators. As you learned in Chapter 5, **intrinsic (or internal) motivators** are those that motivate a person from within, such as the joy and excitement of the discovery process. These move people more than **extrinsic (or external) motivators**, which are motivators that come from outside sources, such as money and fame. The motivation found in creative people also translates to hard work and persistence.

REAL WORLD EXAMPLE 10.3

Persistence Pays Off!

There are many well-known stories of creative geniuses finally getting their dues (e.g., Steve Jobs, Albert Einstein, as described here), but what about the other folks who may not have been what we normally consider genius-types but were still able to fulfill their creative visions and contribute to society? For example:

- Michael Jordan was cut from his high school basketball team before becoming a 14-time NBA All-Star and one of the greatest professional basketball players ever, popularizing the NBA and American sports culture around the world.
- A divorced, single mom named J. K. Rowling was severely depressed and nearly penniless when she wrote *Harry Potter.* Rowling's persistence helped her become one of the best-selling fiction authors of all time, in any language.
- Dr. Seuss's first book for kids was rejected by 27 publishers before it was finally published by Vanguard Press in 1937. (American author Jack London was rejected 600 times before his first story was published!)
- NASA experienced 20 failures in its first 28 attempts to send rockets to space.
- Henry Ford recovered from the repeated failure of his early businesses, which left him broke five times before he founded Ford Motor Company.

5. *Ambition.* Creative people enjoy being influential. They attract recognition and attention.
6. *Low emotional stability.* Creative people may experience negative emotions and widely fluctuating emotional states. They may have low self-confidence.
7. *Low sociability.* Creative people may act in ways that seem inconsiderate. They may look for faults in other people or in their ideas. They may not mind working alone.[9]

Of the seven most common characteristics found in creative people, the first two listed–imagination and flexibility–seem to have the highest association with creativity. The remaining five characteristics may be linked to a spark in creativity, but not as much to the actual creative thoughts and actions that arise. Not all of the characteristics seem positive. Some are neutral, and some are less than positive (low sociability, low emotional stability). This is not a bad thing–it just reminds us that there are balances in strengths and abilities in all of us.

» INSIDE THE CREATIVE PROCESS

Even though there is much about creativity that we don't really understand, we can trace the *process* of creativity as it happens in most people. The idea of the **creative process**–the way in which creativity helps you develop ideas and solve problems–has been around since the 1920s. At that time, a creative thinker and public official named Graham Wallas described four basic steps or stages in this process.[10] This model is still in use today by

creative process

The way in which creativity helps you develop ideas and solve problems.

more about...

Carl Sagan's Apple Pie Recipe

Carl Sagan was an American planetary scientist, astronomer, astrophysicist, astrobiologist, and author. How do you interpret his quote below in terms of creativity?

"If you wish to make an apple pie from scratch, you must first invent the universe."

— Carl Sagan (1934-1996)

psychologists to describe the process of creativity. Whether we intend to do so or not, most of us follow some fairly consistent steps whenever we create anything.[11]

Step One: Perception and Preparation

As mentioned earlier, *perception* is the beginning point for creativity. How we perceive things enables us to interpret our ideas differently to others, so that we can offer insight into fresh perspectives and possibilities.[12] The first step in creative thinking is consider the problem, or question to be solved. Recall that the Theory of Relativity, for example, began to take shape when Einstein first tried to picture what it would be like to travel so fast that you caught up with a light beam. If he rode alongside it, he later wrote, "I should observe such a beam of light as an electromagnetic field at rest." In other words, the wave would seem stationary. Because he had ridden bicycles, studied electricity, and experimented with electromagnets, he had useful and real insights into his perception of light and speed.

Another point to remember is that your perception of reality might well be aimed at something that already exists. Your idea might be to adapt, change, or update a concept that is already created. Another scientist, Thomas Edison, once gave this bit of advice to his colleagues: ". . . keep on the lookout for novel and interesting ideas that others have used successfully. Your idea has to be original only in its adaptation to the problem you're currently working on."[13]

EXPERIMENTATION
The second step in the creative process is incubation, which often includes experimentation. *When have you experimented in order to creatively solve a problem?*
dra_schwartz/E+/Getty Images

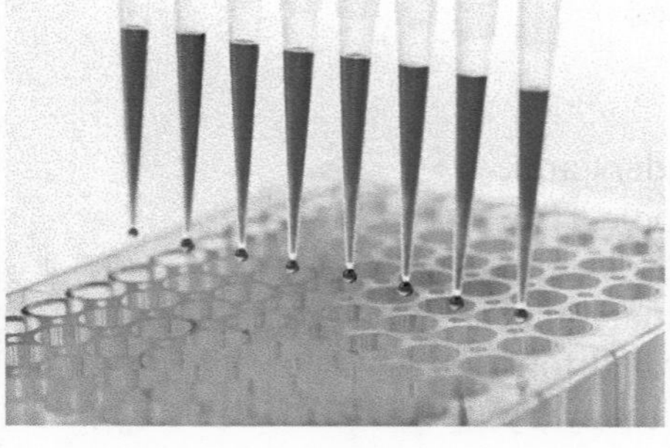

Step Two: Incubation

The metaphor of a bird sitting on a nest of eggs, waiting for the baby birds to hatch, is fitting for the second step in creativity. An "unhatched" idea has come into your perception, and now, something fairly dramatic has to happen, or the creation of the new concept won't take place. The process might take minutes or hours, but it also could take months or even years.

In some creative processes, this step will involve research and experimentation. Depending on the nature of the creation, it could also involve simply turning the ideas over and over in one's mind until the breakthrough finally takes place. In his invention of the light bulb, Thomas Edison's incubation included thousands of experiments with different metal alloys to use as a filament.

Let the problem *sit* while you process the relevant information, turning it over in your mind. Some of this incubating will take place outside of your conscious awareness; this explains why many people think that creative problem solving occurs in a flash of insight.

Step Three: Inspiration

This third step can also be called "illumination." Whatever we choose to call it, it is the stage where the creator yells, "Aha!", "Eureka!", or "That's it!" It is the moment when the incubation and preparedness and action all finally come together, transforming the creative concept into a solid, real concept. This magic moment can happen when we least expect it–such as in the middle of the night, having a drink with friends, or in the shower. However, when it does happen, the person it happens to usually feels rewarded and positive about the next step. Wallas called this step the *happy idea(s).*[14]

ILLUMINATION
The third, and probably most satisfying, step in the creative process is illumination. This is where your mind has processed all of the information it has received, then offers you solutions. Illumination can be summed up by the famous phrase, "Eureka! I've found it!" *How do you recognize when you've reached illumination?*
Don Hammond/Design Pics

Step Four: Verification

Verification is the step where the newly created concept, product, or service is proven to be worthwhile. Now you can transform the new solution to your problem into useful action, and verify your solution.[15]

What does the verification process include? If it's the writing of a book, this is where its publication pays off, whether financially, intellectually, or both. If it's a functioning mechanism of some kind, this is where the test takes place as to whether or not it really "works." This is the point when the Wright brothers test flew their airplane and found that it did, indeed, get airborne.

Whatever you are creating, these four steps will be covered in some way.

» CREATIVITY IN THE WORKPLACE

Managing Creativity

A paradox exists when it comes to managing creativity in the workplace: businesses and organizations will say they promote creativity, but will often reject creative ideas from their employees. Likewise, few external rewards are offered for creative thinking in most companies, with little time allowed for it in daily assignments–despite evidence that creativity can increase internal rewards for employees. Managers are often notorious creativity killers, with a vocabulary of *killer phrases* that are designed to stop creative thoughts before they start. Some common ones are: "It's not in the budget," "Management won't go for it," and "We tried that before, but. . . ."

Researchers examining this paradox found that many people hold an unconscious negative bias against creativity. The researchers' results suggest that people will typically favor what they feel to be more practical and unoriginal options when presented with newer, creative ideas. The key to changing this phenomenon is to shift the emphasis in the workplace from "How do we generate more creative ideas?" to "We must learn to better recognize and accept creativity among our staff."

REAL WORLD EXAMPLE 10.4

Business manager Jane McCarroll believes that creativity will be one of the top three skills that leaders will need most in the current decade and that it is critical in order to keep organizations competitive. The following are her six tips for building creativity and innovation, based on her own experiences:

1. *Focus on small steps.* Rather than waiting until you can make one massive change, pace yourself for continuous improvement. Accumulate these small steps toward larger scale innovation.
2. *Look for creativity everywhere.* Keep a notebook to write down ideas as they occur to you. Don't wait until you get into the office or your work space to begin thinking creative thoughts.
3. *Draw.* In your notebook, sketch (literally) ideas as they occur to you. Some creative thoughts occur in words, and some in pictures.
4. *Get out and about.* Go outside your house, office, or normal environment for inspiration. Walk around. Look at the world with fresh eyes and a new perspective.
5. *Keep the tank full.* The "tank" here refers to your imagination and creative energy. Rather than reaching for your phone first thing in the morning to check messages, instead grab an affirmation, a meditation, your favorite song, a dance around the kitchen, or a blog to kick start the day. As McCarroll says, "Whatever it is, make sure it fuels your imagination—and that it feels good."
6. *Be sociable.* Creative ideas build on other ideas. Talk with others, be friendly and open, share ideas, and innovate together. When everyone creates together, synergy occurs.

Source: Jane McCarroll, "Six Tips for Building Creativity and Innovation," *New Zealand Management,* January 16, 2018, https://management.co.nz/article/six-tips-building-creativity-and-innovation (retrieved April 4, 2020).

The researchers also found that managers who are confident in their own creative capabilities are more likely to encourage creativity in the people around them. By promoting discussion about new ideas or work methods; by being receptive to creative ideas generated by their staff; by avoiding severe criticisms of new ideas; and in striving to find value even in less promising ones, managers can help to facilitate more creativity in the workplace.[16]

Fostering Creativity

At an individual level, creativity, unique problem-solving skills, and the ability to communicate ideas effectively are critical skills that an employee must use to progress through the ranks in any organization. For a creative spirit to emerge from a company or a department, the environment must encourage enthusiasm and commitment from the employee. Work must be made rewarding, challenging, and fulfilling for a creative atmosphere to exist. Figure 10.2 describes several ways that employers such as Google have fostered creativity within their organizations. The use of sometimes unorthodox means can inspire continuous innovation in a business world that is constantly changing.

Additional ideas to promote creativity can be built into the company design. This includes the right physical space. Steve Jobs understood this in the early days at Apple, where he deliberately promoted open work environments in modular sections or pods that *forced* employees to interact with each other throughout their day to collaborate and generate new, creative ideas. Organizing the physical space to promote interaction is the biggest lever to encourage collaboration and creativity.[17]

Many of today's most successful companies, especially those in the technology and other design-related industries, have gravitated toward more employee-friendly workplaces in order to foster creativity and increase productivity. Yelp's Manhattan office offers karaoke and table hockey, while LinkedIn's employees can play a video game or watch a film at work. Kickstarter in Brooklyn offers arcade games and a relaxing rooftop garden. The PayPal and Venmo offices in New York have instruments available for employees to rock out with. Facebook's Manhattan office has virtual reality games available for employees. At the Adobe office in San Jose, employees can use the gym and the gymnastic equipment freely.[18] These types of settings–game lounge, garden, studio, gym–can be places where creative energy is harnessed and used to boost workers' productive output and motivation.

Encouraging play and getting out of the office is not just fun, it increases brain activity. Dr. Stuart Brown, founder of the National Institute for Play and author of *Play: How It Shapes the Brain, Opens the Imagination, and Invigorates the Soul,* tells the audiences at his TED Talks, "What does play do for the brain? Well, a lot. Nothing lights up the brain like play. Three-dimensional play fires up the cerebellum, puts a lot of impulses into the frontal lobe (the executive portion), helps contextual memory to be developed and much more." Likewise, working casually or getting together informally outside of the office can stimulate creative thinking among a work group.[19]

Creativity is not just fostered by workplaces with "extras" as those just described. As the economy continues to shift toward businesses based on ideas, creativity, and innovation, organizations will need to find new ways of incentivizing and rewarding staff. Incentives matter, according to a study of 3,500 employees, 100 HR managers, and 100 IT managers across the UK, France, Germany, the United States, and Japan, conducted by the Future Foundation on behalf of Google. Nearly 6 in 10 employees surveyed said they would already be coming up with more creative ideas for their employers if they were rewarded for them. Financial reward is not the only option, but is the most preferred option (39 percent).[20]

more about...

Managing Creativity: Task Switching

Can we "switch on" creativity in real life? Researchers say yes. Organizations can promote creativity within their ranks by allowing employees more time to alternate back and forth between different tasks. Whereas past research has focused on the downsides of task switching, newer research uncovers a potential upside: increased creativity. In two experiments, researchers showed that task switching can enhance two principal forms of creativity—divergent thinking (Study 1) and convergent thinking (Study 2)—in part because temporarily setting a task aside reduces "cognitive fixation," or being stuck on one right answer, which can lead to reduced productivity.

Participants who continually alternated back and forth between two creativity tasks outperformed both those participants who switched between the tasks at their own schedule *and* those participants who attempted one task for the first half of the allotted time before switching to the other task for the second half. The researchers also found that people in the workplace overwhelmingly did not choose to adopt a continual-switch approach when given incentives to choose a task switching strategy that would maximize their creative performance. These findings provide insights into how individuals can "switch on" creativity when navigating multiple creative tasks.

Source: Jackson G. Lu, Modupe Akinola, and Malia F. Mason, "'Switching On' Creativity: Task Switching Can Increase Creativity by Reducing Cognitive Fixation," *Organizational Behavior and Human Decision Processes* 139(C) (2017), pp. 63–75.

figure 10.2

WORKPLACE CREATIVITY: THE GOOGLE MODEL

Businesses and other organizations can nurture creativity in ways that improve productivity and morale. *How can your workplace benefit from increased creativity? What things might help your workplace become a more "creative environment"?*

Source: Annika Steiber (2014). The Google Model: Managing Continuous Innovation in a Rapidly Changing World (Management for Professionals). New York: Springer Publishing.

Fostering Workplace Creativity—The Google Model

Organizations that foster a workplace culture of creativity are more likely to have happy, motivated employees who are more loyal and more productive. Google is seen as both a pioneer and continued frontrunner in its research into (and application of its findings) harnessing its employees' creativity. Experts point to six key principles that Google seems to get right:

1. **The right people.** Google hires a diverse range of creative, enthusiastic, and sometimes outspoken people to fill its ranks. An office environment of people actively trading ideas, collaborating, and brainstorming can bring great success to a company. Employees are expected to think independently and be flexible in managing new situations as they arise.
2. **Flexibility.** As situations and scenarios change, the company adapts by reassigning engineers to new products. Project integration and movement of staff where needed occurs even when new products in design may challenge the success of existing products. Their dynamic flow of resources allows them to reconfigure easily, to rapidly meet new challenges.
3. **Nimble responses.** The company's ability to respond quickly to change as it arises means it will not lag behind other technology companies. Companies that are always alert in anticipating the need for new ideas and new products will be nimble enough to meet and exceed challenges from competitors. They will more easily see and respond to the needs of their customers.
4. **Being ambidextrous.** We typically think of someone who is ambidextrous as a person who can easily use both their right and left hands. For Google, being ambidextrous means valuing two types of organizational logic: *daily production* and *innovation.* Daily production requires logic, planning, organization, and consistency. Innovation requires experimentation, risk-taking, and independence. In Google's case, their commitment to this type of dexterity is seen in their 70-20-10 rule. Engineers focus on their core business 70 percent of the time, on related projects 20 percent of the time, and on unrelated and new ideas 10 percent of the time.
5. **A systems approach.** This requires working together in an interdependent, interactive style. A systems approach is different from the more traditional linear set-up, in which sub-areas of the corporation work on their own as separate units. In the systems approach, employees understand the larger holistic view of the organization, and see how the parts affect each other and depend on each other.
6. **Integration with surroundings.** Companies that are more involved with the world around them will be more successful than companies more closed to their surroundings. Openness to surroundings means loosening the borders between the world inside the company and the world outside. Actively exploring the need for existing and future products by integrating with surroundings promotes corporate success.

» CREATIVE METHODS FOR GROUPS

In today's workplace, creative problem solving is increasingly done in a group or team setting. A creative idea from an individual may really take flight with input from the group, for example. And if the creative process is structured carefully, the team can usually implement more ideas more efficiently than the individual. For group creativity to be fruitful, the process around it must contain just enough structure to be effective, with enough freedom to remain creative.

more about...

Creativity and Health

Is creativity good for your health? Yes, according to a review of the results of more than a decade of research on the topic. Researchers found that doing activities that required creativity raised people's mood and released endorphins, reduced anxiety and even helped people work through trauma, boosted brain function, and over the long term helped to improve immune function and prevent disease.[21] Creativity is good for your health, and better health promotes more creativity!

Brainstorming

In 1934, a sales manager named Alex Osborne devised a method of sparking creativity in a group situation. He called his idea **brainstorming**, which is a type of spontaneous group discussion to help find multiple solutions for problems. The process starts with a small group of people; groups of five to eight work best. With a leader in front to record their ideas, they begin by addressing a problem. In this first session, nothing is allowed except free-flowing ideas. Everyone is encouraged to speak in phrases rather than in sentences, to *hitchhike* on the ideas of others, and to be as wild and crazy as they can be within the social context. No one is allowed to criticize anyone else's ideas. Statements such as "Get serious!" or "No way!" are forbidden.

brainstorming
A type of spontaneous group discussion to help find multiple solutions to problems.

When this first session is over, the second session begins. In this part of the brainstorming process, the adult part of everybody's personality takes over. The group examines the ideas that have come up, noticing whether any of them duplicate each other. The group can then prioritize the ideas, agreeing together which is the most important, second most important, and so on. (These rules are shown in the following list.) When a group brainstorms, following these rules correctly, an amazing number of high-quality ideas are produced in a fairly short period of time. Note that brainstorming works best for the solving of simple, well-defined problems, although it can be used in nearly any context. Although a lot of shallow, even useless ideas are suggested, there are usually gems among the dust.[22]

First Session

1. Participants speak in phrases.
2. Hitchhiking on others' ideas is encouraged.
3. Criticism is forbidden.
4. Silliness is encouraged.
5. Climate is relaxed.
6. All ideas are recorded.
7. A large quantity of ideas is encouraged.

Second Session

1. Return to rational mode.
2. All ideas are analyzed and prioritized.

3. Idea duplications are eliminated.
4. Ideas are ranked in order of importance.
5. Everyone gives evaluative input, just as all gave creative input in Session One.

After the second session, before putting new ideas into place, the leader may ask some employees to take on the task of researching the new ideas. Refinements may occur at this stage. Finally, after the new ideas are put into place, the group may need to make adjustments or "tweak" the new process depending on follow-up examinations of the results of these new ideas or new processes.

Reverse Brainstorming

reverse brainstorming
A group problem solving method that begins with how to cause a problem, and reverses those ideas to solve the original problem.

You may have used brainstorming techniques in the past, but what about **reverse brainstorming**? This strategy may be effective when solutions are hard to find. Instead of starting with solutions to a problem, reverse the question: "How can I *cause* this problem?"

1. Identify the problem or challenge. Write down the parts of the problem.
2. Reverse from finding a solution to causing a problem: "How could I cause this problem?" or "What should I do to reach the opposite effect?"
3. Follow the brainstorming rules to come up with reverse solution ideas. Let the ideas flow; do not reject any at this stage.
4. Once you have brainstormed all the ideas to solve the reverse problem, then flip those ideas into solution ideas for the original problem or challenge.
5. As with normal brainstorming, evaluate the ideas and decide on the best solutions for the actual (not reversed) problem.

Here is an example of reverse brainstorming. In the growing accounting firm where Sean works, a common complaint is that they are not able to recruit many candidates, and those who apply are often not qualified. In a reverse brainstorming process, Sean asks, "How can we *cause* a poor hiring pool?" Responses from the Human Resources team included expecting people to apply without advertising, writing confusing job descriptions, giving poor instructions on submitting an application, not giving a closing date for applications, taking a very long time from application to interviews, and not communicating with applicants who have submitted an application. Based on an an analysis of how to *cause* a poor hiring pool, the team was able to reverse those suggestions to create a successful system for hiring good applicants.

The Nominal Group Method

nominal group method
An exercise that encourages creativity within a group framework by allowing everyone to offer ideas individually.

The **nominal group method** of group creativity is designed to provide a structure that encourages individual creativity within a group framework. The reason this method is called nominal is because the members are actually a group in name only. The group is basically a tool for voting. Usually, nominal grouping involves six steps:

1. Each employee puts his or her ideas down in writing.
2. The leader lists all of the ideas up on a board or chart where everyone can see them.
3. The leader leads a discussion to clarify the ideas and add new ones.
4. Each group member rates the ideas and votes; the voting eliminates other ideas at this point.
5. After the vote, there is a brief discussion of the voting results. The purpose is to clarify points, not to persuade anyone.
6. The group casts a final vote to select the proposal or proposals that will be used.

The nominal group method can be especially effective when used with people who are shy, unsure of themselves, or simply not used to being assertive in public. The ideas are anonymous; nobody in the group should know who wrote what, unless the writers give themselves away in the discussion.

» CREATIVE PROBLEM SOLVING

As with brainstorming and reverse brainstorming, it is important when solving problems creatively to reward–rather than ridicule–any ideas put forward. In considering how to stimulate ideas, however, rewards are not everything. Even more influential than positive reinforcement from outside is the reward that comes from inside one's self.

In study after study, whether in the field of psychology or the business world, *creativity is found to flourish with intrinsic motivation.* A noted researcher in the field, Dr. Teresa Amabile, finds that intrinsic motivation is more powerful than extrinsic motivation in encouraging creativity–regardless of whether you are talking about rats, children, or scientists. In her explanation, she uses the example of a rat going through a maze to get to the cheese reward (see Real World Example 10.5) to illustrate the concept.

In summary, group creativity has become increasingly important in today's workplace. Creative problem solving–especially in teams and other groups, whether face-to-face or online–is a useful skill all employees will need to develop. Since creative problem solving is critical in today's workplace, new ideas for group creativity continue to be researched and tested. New problem-solving strategies will all have one thing in common: all of them will be attempts to extract the greatest number of quality ideas from a group of people in a short time.

more about...

Teresa Amabile (1950–) has been doing research on creativity and intrinsic motivation for over 35 years. Her main focus is increasing creativity and motivation in work settings. She began a career as a chemist, then earned a PhD in psychology from Stanford University. She is currently a professor in business administration at Harvard Business School and heads their entrepreneurship program. She is also a consultant for businesses and government agencies on team creativity and leadership. Dr. Amabile's current research program focuses on the psychology of everyday work life, creativity, and career transitions.

REAL WORLD EXAMPLE 10.5

Consider rats in a maze. "If you [the rat] are extrinsically motivated, your primary motive is to achieve the extrinsic goal. . . . You have to earn the reward, or win the competition, or get the promotion, or please those who are watching you. You are so single-minded about the goal that you don't take the time to think much about the maze itself. Since you're only interested in getting out as quickly as possible, you will likely take only the most obvious, well-traveled route.

"By contrast, if you are intrinsically motivated, you enjoy being in the maze. You enjoy playing in it, nosing around, trying out different pathways, exploring, thinking things through before blindly plunging ahead. You're not really concentrating on anything else but how much you enjoy the problem itself, how much you like the challenge and the intrigue."[23]

STRATEGIES FOR SUCCESS

Strategy 10.1 Increase Your Creativity

1. Get into the open mode.
2. Think of yourself as a creative person.
3. Learn to see problems as opportunities.
4. Look for more than one or two solutions to a problem.
5. Learn to play the violin.
6. Turn your ideas into action.
7. Don't be afraid to break some rules.
8. Don't be afraid to make mistakes.
9. Spend time with creative people.
10. Capture creative ideas when they happen.

The question, "How can I become more creative?" has no easy answer. However, you can learn some basic steps. Only you know what specific barriers keep you from reaching your own creative potential.

open mode

A state of mind where you are relaxed, expansive, less purposeful, and more fun than in the everyday closed mode.

1. **Get into the open mode.** In the daily routine of work, most people are in a *closed mode*. When most people are working, they feel pressured because they keep thinking about how much they have to do. This everyday mode contains a certain amount of anxiety, not much humor, a lot of stress, and a definite element of fear—but it doesn't contain creativity. The **open mode**, on the other hand, is relaxed, expansive, and less purposeful. Operating in the open mode often involves giving yourself sufficient time. Although you are likely to meet many people who claim that they do their most creative work under time pressure, the truth is that most people produce better when they have given themselves enough time to relax and reflect. In it, people tend to let things come as they may, act more thoughtful, and smile and laugh more often. You can have fun in the open mode!

   Playful is a word that British comedian John Cleese uses when discussing the open mode. In Real World Example 10.6 he tells the story of Alexander Fleming, who discovered penicillin.[24]

   This does not mean that you should stay in the open mode permanently. Important parts of your life require that you stay in the closed mode just so that you can concentrate on a non-creative task. As mentioned, asking childlike questions is important;

REAL WORLD EXAMPLE 10.6

When Alexander Fleming had the thought that led to the discovery of penicillin, he must have been in the open mode. The previous day, he had arranged a number of laboratory dishes so that the cultures would grow in them. On the day in question, he glanced at the dishes and discovered that on one of them no culture had appeared. Now, if he'd been in the closed mode, he would have been so focused upon his need for dishes with cultures grown in them, that when he saw that one dish was of no use for that purpose, he would have simply thrown it away. It was useless to him. . . . But, fortunately, he was in an open mode. He became curious about why the culture had not grown in this particular dish, and that curiosity led him to penicillin. In the closed mode, an uncultured dish is an irrelevance; in the open mode, it's a clue.[25]

answering those questions, though, may involve—and even require—the closed mode.

2. **Think of yourself as a creative person.** One of the biggest stumbling blocks to creativity is the belief that you somehow aren't good enough to create anything worthwhile. Many people carry around a self-image that includes statements like "Oh, I couldn't come up with a new idea if my life depended on it; I'm just not a creative person." This kind of poor self-image causes a person to put creative people on a pedestal.

   The key to this step is **self-perception**, which is what and how you believe yourself to be. Research has shown that people who produce more creative output are different in one major way from those who create less: the more creative people *believe that they are creative*. The others have serious doubts, and this directly hurts their performance. Believe in yourself creatively, and you will have accomplished an important step. Don't let self-doubt reduce your creativity![26]

3. **Learn to see problems as opportunities.** Once you put yourself into an open mode and see yourself as creative, you'll need to get a mindset that doesn't see problems as anything to get frustrated about.

4. **Look for more than one or two solutions to a problem.** A major stumbling block with traditional methods of learning is that people are taught to look for *the one right answer.* Instead of casting about for the many right answers and numerous ways to view a problem, they tend to go after the one surefire answer that will please the teacher or the boss and make them feel they have succeeded. If you think there is only one right answer, you behave accordingly, and stop looking once you have found an answer that works—even if it isn't a perfect fit.[27]

   People settle for the one right answer out of a tendency to grab the first idea that comes to mind. They are more likely to make this error when they feel pressured, frustrated, or afraid they aren't going to succeed in solving the problem. That first idea might be good, but how do you know it's the best? Again, taking some extra time might be the only way to proceed.

   Another common mistake in decision making is called the **either/or fallacy**, which sees only one of two extremes as a possible solution without really looking at the great number of compromises and other creative choices that might exist in between. This was the mistake made by members of the community college business club in the opening story at the beginning of this chapter. When you are in the closed mode, you are much more likely to fall for this mistake. To get beyond this trap, learn to look for the **second right answer**, in other words, get rid of the stumbling block that prevents most people from looking for more than one answer. Think of an idea as a letter in the alphabet. Everything ever written in English was written with the same 26 letters, yet the relationship of those letters to other ones forms words and ideas in a limitless number of possibilities. Get in the habit of finding at least three right answers

self-perception
What and how you believe yourself to be.

either/or fallacy
When you see only one of two extremes as a possible solution, while ignoring the endless number of creative choices that might exist between the extremes.

second right answer
Refers to a method of decision making in which people get rid of the stumbling block that prevents them from looking for more than one solution.

REAL WORLD EXAMPLE 10.7

To file away important documents at work, Jody has more fun filing them in a unique and playful system that she invented, but no one else can find the files when they need them. It is more productive in the long run for everyone at Jody's company if she files them appropriately and carefully, paying attention while performing this task. In this case, the closed mode works better.

more about...

The Second Right Answer

"Nothing is more dangerous than an idea when it is the only one you have."

—Emile Chartier (1868–1951), French philosopher

Source: Eugene Raudsepp, "Overcoming Barriers to Effective Problem Solving," *Supervision* 52 (February 1991), pp. 14–16.

for each problem you encounter. Chances are that once you discover three, you won't stop there.

Many people feel a need to be able to make decisions rapidly. After all, such a reputation is certainly better than one of being uncertain or indecisive. If you are truly decisive, great. If you're not, don't fake it. Instead, examine the alternatives. Try to get at least a few possible solutions before going on to finish solving a problem. Use combinations of ideas other people have thought of, bringing them together for your own creative result. Of course, even in the world of business, one will sometimes encounter a problem that truly has only one right answer. In such a case, methods of discovery still need to be varied, rather than limited.

5. **Learn to play the violin.** Management expert Peter Drucker was once asked how one can become a better manager. "Learn to play the violin" was his reply. He didn't literally mean that learning to play the violin was a solution. His point was that anything that gets people outside of their regular context would force them out of their comfort zone and into different ways of thinking. You are more likely to be creative when you are outside of your comfort zone.[28] As an added bonus, you may get to be really good at the violin, or at crossword puzzles, or at wind surfing—and your enjoyment and self-esteem will grow. That is a bonus that improves your performance in all areas of your life.
6. **Turn your ideas into action.** How many ideas have you thought of, then dismissed, only to find later that someone else who thought of the same idea had put it into action? You may have thought, "That was *my* idea!" Painful, isn't it?

   Creativity doesn't do anyone much good if its products aren't followed through into action. What if all of Robert Frost's poems or Michelangelo's artwork or Marie Curie's scientific breakthroughs had simply remained unexecuted ideas?
7. **Don't be afraid to break some rules.** Whatever the task at hand, most people feel compelled to follow the rules. Many of those rules aren't rules or laws at all, only customs—customs that everyone has been afraid to change. This does not mean that you should break the law or break a rule that will get you fired. Instead, it is a suggestion that you break away from outdated or pointless customs and think creatively. Remember the lesson of the nine-dot puzzle!

   Sometimes rules outlive their usefulness, but people continue to follow them anyway.

   Von Oech calls this problem with rules the **Aslan phenomenon**:

   - People make rules based on reasons that make a lot of sense.
   - They follow those rules.
   - Time passes and situations change.

Aslan phenomenon

A circumstance that exists when people make rules, then follow them even after the situations to which they originally applied no longer exist.

REAL WORLD EXAMPLE 10.8

Nolan Bushnell, one of the inventors of the first video games and a founder of the video game industry, is a good example of just how easy creativity can be. He says that he noticed that people like to watch television and that they also enjoy playing games. He just put the two ideas together.[29]

The original reasons for generating these rules may no longer exist, but the rules are still in place and people continue to follow them (see Real World Example 10.9 for the origin of the Aslan phenomenon).

8. **Don't be afraid to make mistakes.** Most people have two selves—the safekeeping self and the spontaneous self. The safekeeping self keeps you clothed, fed, and out of trouble. The spontaneous self allows you the freedom and fun of doing things without structure and detailed planning. Childhood training warns people not to be too spontaneous or too messy, not to *color outside the lines,* and (most important) not to make fools of themselves. Actually, making mistakes is one of the most effective ways of learning, and being a bit foolish is part of being human. The president of a successful, fast-growing computer company tells his employees, "We're innovators. We're doing things nobody has ever done before. Therefore, we are going to be making mistakes. My advice to you: Make your mistakes, but make them in a hurry."[31]
9. **Spend time with creative people.** Creativity researcher and Harvard professor Teresa Amabile finds that creative people spark creativity in others. Whether the setting is formal or informal, being around others who *think outside the box* helps you to do so, too.[32]
10. **Capture creative ideas when they happen.** Change your routine and do things a little differently. Pay attention to your thought processes and feelings, and when inspiration hits, be ready: have a notebook, sketch pad, audio recorder or smart phone that records audio, or other device ready to capture new ideas as they occur. Creativity has a way of not happening at convenient times![33]

STRATEGIES FOR SUCCESS

Strategy 10.2 Roger von Oech's Ten "Mental Locks" to Avoid

1. Look for the one right answer.
2. That is not logical.
3. Follow the rules.
4. Be practical.
5. Play is frivolous.
6. That isn't my area.
7. Don't be foolish.
8. Avoid ambiguity.
9. To err is wrong.
10. I'm not creative.

REAL WORLD EXAMPLE 10.9

Roger von Oech, creativity guru of California's Silicon Valley, talked about an example of a mental lock he called the Aslan Phenomenon. In his example, he explained that he regularly ran for exercise, and when taking a particular route would often stop near his house to pet a friendly dog named Aslan. Stopping there became a pleasant end to his regular run. But after the owner moved away, he found himself staying with this "obsolete rule" and continuing to stop at the house where Aslan had lived—the Aslan Phenomenon.[30]

ten "mental locks"

Rules or beliefs that keep people from being as creative as they otherwise could be.

According to creativity guru Roger von Oech, **ten "mental locks"** keep people from being as creative as they otherwise could be. Read them over and see how many of them might apply to your life and to your attempts to be more creative.

1. **Look for the one right answer.** When you start out with the assumption that there is only one right answer to a given problem, you have just limited yourself to a very narrow set of possibilities. Von Oech quotes French philosopher Emile Chartier: "Nothing is more dangerous than an idea when it is the only one we have." So learn to look for the second "right answer," and the third, and so on.
2. **That is not logical.** Although logic certainly has an important place in life, one who spends too much time and energy trying to view everything as logical at all times is likely to miss out on the use of intuition—"one of the mind's softest and most valuable creations." Von Oech makes the distinction between "soft" and "hard" parts of reality. Logic is a valuable tool for the "practical phase" of the creative process.
3. **Follow the rules.** If you don't challenge the rules, but just follow them blindly, you will likely either fall prey to the Asian phenomenon (see Real World Example 10.9), or you will get locked into a single approach without seeing other possibilities. Thus you're back to the "one right answer" rut.
4. **Be practical.** Von Oech says we all have an "artist" and a "judge" within us. Both of them are important to the creative process. Most of us have to challenge our judge with "what if" questions.
5. **Play is frivolous.** "Necessity may be the mother of invention, but play is certainly the father" (Roger von Oech). Play is, in fact, not frivolous, but actually essential to the act of creation. "Playing" with a problem is often the best way to solve it. Children are more creative than adults, and ability to play is one of the reasons.
6. **That isn't my area.** Specialization can be a real enemy of creativity. How often could someone who specializes in one area learn to apply a principle or process that is peculiar to another area? So often in companies, someone will say, "Oh, that's an advertising problem," or "That's a customer service problem," when a bit of overlapping between departments was exactly what was necessary.
7. **Don't be foolish.** This statement is mostly about conformity, especially about the human desire not to "stick out" and look weird or different to others. Occasionally, try letting yourself look stupid. Also, learning to laugh at oneself is a helpful exercise. New ideas often look stupid to others.
8. **Avoid ambiguity.** The reason most of us actually follow this lock is because ambiguity can hamper communication with others—because we need to be specific when we communicate. However, in the creative process, being too specific can prevent the flow of new ideas.

REAL WORLD EXAMPLE 10.10

Years ago, Steve completely thought out the idea for what is now called multilevel marketing, but he didn't put it to use. Three years later, the founders of Amway, Inc. put the same idea (which they certainly didn't get from him) into action. Amway is now a billion-dollar corporation, and Steve was left with the regret that he didn't act on his idea sooner.

9. **To err is wrong.** Actually, success can have a negative side. If too many things we try succeed, an anti-creative smugness can stifle creativity. Think of a huge error you made some time in your life. Did something good come out of it in the long run? If not, is there something you could have done to make something positive come from it?
10. **I'm not creative.** This statement usually develops into a self-fulfilling prophecy. We need to let our own creative style develop and to allow ourselves to let go and be creative. Often, people need to give themselves permission to be creative.

Source: Roger von Oech, *A Whack on the Side of the Head: How You Can Be More Creative* (New York: Grand Central Publishing, 2008).

Strategy 10.3 **Use SCAMPER to Solve Problems**

Have you ever found yourself stuck—unable to think of a creative solution to a problem? When the "creativity block" hits you, try Bob Eberle's **SCAMPER**[34] strategy to release your creative mind. Eberle is author of several teacher resource books on increasing creativity in the classroom. Think of a current problem or issue you are having at school, work, or home; or a problem facing your campus, student body, or local community. Once you have identified the issue or topic you want to work on, apply Eberle's SCAMPER strategy to the problem. To do this, ask yourself "To come up with a creative solution, what might I . . .":

- ***S***ubstitute? Is there a person, place, or object that might work better?
- ***C***ombine? Are there ideas, goals, or purposes that could be combined?
- ***A***dapt? Are there parts of the plan or the process I can reshape or fit to this issue?
- ***M***odify? How and what can I alter, revise, enlarge, or shrink to resolve this issue?
- ***P***ut to another use? What can I put to different or new uses to resolve the problem?
- ***E***liminate? What can be omitted, simplified, or removed?
- ***R***earrange? Can I change the order of events, the plan itself, or the desired outcome?

What new solutions did you come up with?

SCAMPER

A strategy, created by Bob Eberle, to release your creative mind.

REAL WORLD EXAMPLE 10.11

Bill Browerman, an athletic coach at the University of Oregon, noticed that his track athletes were having difficulty with sore feet and blisters throughout the season. After examining the shoes his runners were wearing, he decided that he could make a better shoe that would work with nature rather than against it. Using the most lightweight and tough materials he could find, he made a shoe that improved both cushion and traction. Browerman went on to form Nike, which is now a multi-billion-dollar company.[35] He saw the problem as a challenge, and he was able to meet that challenge in a remarkable way.

CHAPTER TEN SUMMARY

Chapter Summary by Learning Objectives

LO 10-1 **Explain the importance of creativity.** Business factors, such as the number and quality of good products created, are affected strongly by the creativity of the people in an organization. Competitiveness depends on creativity, as does success at business or nearly anything else.

LO 10-2 **Define creativity.** Creativity is the ability to produce ideas or solutions to problems that are unique, appropriate, and valuable. It is tied in to our relationships with others. In a nutshell, creativity is thinking up original and useful ideas.

LO 10-3 **Discuss the relationship between perception and creativity.** Whatever model of creativity one uses, perception is nearly always the first step. Perception is one's unique way of seeing the world. If problem solving is the issue, perception also means perceiving the problem correctly.

LO 10-4 **List the steps in the creative process.** The process begins with perception and preparation, and is followed by incubation, inspiration, and verification. Whatever one is creating, these steps will be covered in some way.

LO 10-5 **Describe creativity in the workplace.** The typical workplace of today is not set up to handle creative ideas. More often than not, creativity is stifled by companies of all sizes. The challenge is to transform the workplace into a place where creativity is encouraged and rewarded.

LO 10-6 **Compare and contrast creative methods for groups.** Three major methods of creativity in groups are brainstorming, reverse brainstorming, and the nominal group method. All use techniques to stimulate original thought and to discourage negativity.

REAL WORLD EXAMPLE 10.12

Dr. Spencer Silver, a scientist for the 3M technology corporation, invented an adhesive in 1968 that was considered a failure for the purpose he wanted. Nearly 10 years later, Dr. Art Fry, another 3M scientist, had an idea for Silver's "failed" adhesive: to keep his bookmark from falling out of his church hymnal. From this simple idea, the Post-it note was created, which is now used internationally and one of 3M's more popular office products.[36]

LO 10-7 **Give examples of ways to solve problems creatively.** Get into the "open mode." Also, learn to think of yourself as a creative person and to see problems as opportunities. Learning to look for more than one possible solution to a problem will also help. In addition, try to avoid creativity traps, such as the either/or fallacy. "Learn to play the violin," which is a figurative way of saying that one must be willing to go beyond the company's job description. Turn your ideas into action, and don't be afraid to break some rules or to make some mistakes. Spend time with creative people, and capture creative ideas when they happen. Intrinsic motivation works better than external rewards to stimulate creativity.

key terms

Aslan phenomenon 298
brainstorming 293
collective habits of thought 284
creative process 287
creativity 280
either/or fallacy 297
extrinsic motivators 286
flow 282
intrinsic motivators 286
intuition 283
nine-dot puzzle 285
nominal group method 294
open mode 296
optimal experience 282
perception 284
reverse brainstorming 294
SCAMPER 301
second right answer 297
self-perception 297
ten "mental locks" 300

review questions

1. Is creativity the same as intelligence? How are they related? In what ways are they different?
2. What is "flow" in the creative process? Describe an experience in which you had this experience.

3. Explain the differences among the four steps of the creative process described by Wallas, using examples from your own experience of a problem you have solved.
4. Why do workplaces so often lack creativity? What steps can managers take to increase the quality and quantity of their employees' creative output?
5. What does it mean to be in the open mode? What does this feel like? How can the open mode allow for greater creativity?
6. Explain the difference between brainstorming, reverse brainstorming, and the nominal group method. How would you use these three methods to help produce more creative group results? Provide examples.
7. How many right answers are there to any one problem? What is meant by the *second right answer*? How many right answers should you look for in solving a problem before deciding on a solution to implement?
8. How does the phrase *playing the violin* relate to an increase in creativity? What skill or talent would you like to explore? How would a new skill increase your creativity?
9. Which better promotes creativity: external rewards or intrinsic motivation? Explain.

critical thinking questions

1. Do you think creative geniuses are more likely *born* or *made*? Do you think you could become more creative if you were to work at it?
2. Which type of talent do you think has greater worth to society, creativity or academic intelligence? Why? Do you think one of these is more important than the other?
3. Some of our nation's most creative minds, including Bill Gates, Steve Jobs, Frank Lloyd Wright, Buckminster Fuller, James Cameron, Oprah Winfrey, Ellen DeGeneres, Anna Wintour, Henry Ford, and Mark Zuckerberg, did not finish college. Do you believe this ultimately hurt, or helped, their creative endeavors? Explain your response, applying strategies for creativity discussed in this chapter into your response.

working it out 10.1

FLEX YOUR CREATIVE MUSCLES

School-to-Work Connection: Fostering Creative Thinking Skills

Exercise 1: Think of a problem or challenge you've been dealing with at work or at school. This exercise asks you to use your five senses to inspire yourself with things around you. Look around for objects, analyze their shape, their color, where they are coming from, and other details. Use all of your senses to listen to the sounds of your environment. Touch the objects you're looking at. Note the smells and odors in the room. Now link those elements to your brainstorming session. This should help you to generate new ideas.

Exercise 2: Create a mind map. Consider the same problem or challenge from Exercise 1. Write your problem in the middle of a sheet of paper, and circle it. Next, draw the major topics branching off the center, and continue with subtopics. Keep adding branches to the map as ideas occur to you. At the end of 20 minutes, you should have a solid start to address the problem.

Exercise 3: Again, consider the same problem from Exercise 1. Now go outside, wherever there are strangers and people you barely know, and ask a few people for solutions to your problem. A second, third, or fourth opinion from an objective person can be valuable. You may hear solutions you've never thought of, or even additional problems you'd never even considered!

Source: Adapted from Lorenzo Del Marmol, "Creativity Exercises to Improve Your Lateral Thinking Abilities," World of Digits Blog, December 7, 2015, https://creativecorporateculture.com/creativity-exercises-improve-lateral-thinking.

working it out 10.2

CREATIVITY PUZZLERS

Many tests have been created over the years to measure creativity. Some are just for fun (as the candle test that follows), and others are used in formal testing (as the incomplete figures test below). Complete these puzzlers and see how creative you may be.

1. **The Candle Test**

   This classic test of creative problem solving was developed by psychologist Karl Duncker in 1945. The test challenges our tendency to get "stuck" on one use for a familiar item.

   You have been given a candle, a box of thumbtacks, and a book of matches. Your task is to attach the lit candle to the wall so that it will not drip wax onto the table below. How will you do it?
   The solution is found at the bottom of the page.

2. **Incomplete Figures Test**

   The incomplete figures test was created in 1966 by Ellis Paul Torrance. It is part of a larger Torrance Test of Creative Thinking, which is the most widely used creativity test in the world, that predicts creative achievement better than any other creativity test. The test measures originality, elaboration, flexibility, and other aspects of creativity.

   Take three minutes each to complete the following figures into complete drawings. What did you draw? Describe your completed figures. There is no right or wrong answer.

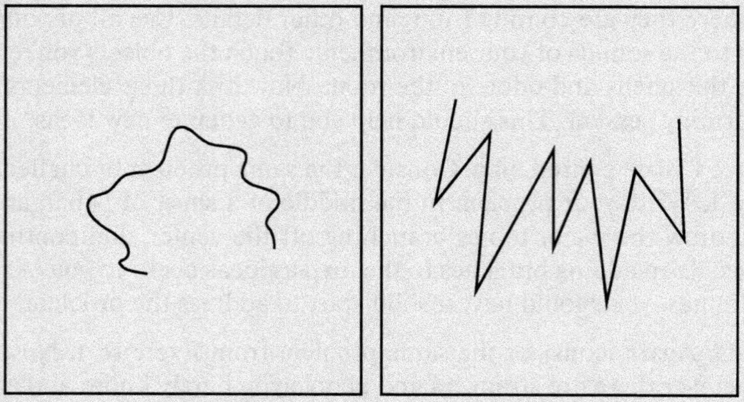

Solution to the Candle Test: Empty the box of thumbtacks. Use the thumbtacks to attach the box to the wall. Put the candle into the empty box. Light the candle with the match.

Source: Creativity-Innovation.EU (Dec. 2017). "Torrance Tests of Creative Thinking," European Interest Group on Creativity and Innovation, https://www.creativity-innovation.eu/torrance-tests-creative-thinking/ (retrieved 7/14/2020).

working it out 10.3

FLOW AND HAPPINESS

Watch the TED Talk by preeminent psychologist Mihaly Csikszentmihalyi, titled "Flow, the Secret to Happiness," and then answer the following questions.

1. What is "flow," according to the speaker? Why is it important?
2. What is the link between income and happiness, according to the speaker?
3. When, or under what conditions, do we find maximum happiness? How does this vary around the world?
4. What is the link between flow and creativity? Describe a time when you have felt flow, as the speaker describes it, that led you to higher creativity.
5. What did the speaker find about flow when he interviewed CEOs of major corporations?

The video can be found here: www.ted.com/talks/mihaly_csikszentmihalyi_flow_the_secret_to_happiness.

Noisy Neighbors/New Nook

"Oh my gosh, I have just about HAD IT!" thought Cybele to herself. How could she *ever* get her work done when her neighbor in the next cubicle, Ken, seemed to chat incessantly with clients over the phone. She needed quiet to get into her creative groove. It didn't seem to matter that she had tried to politely talk to Ken about the volume and tone of his phone calls, but she was reluctant to make waves at work. She decided to try some self-preservation techniques before approaching her boss, such as wearing noise-canceling headphones, and listening to her favorite music station, but these were blocking her off from interacting with her colleagues, and she had missed more than one phone call while jamming out with her headphones. "I've got to talk to the boss," Cybele decided.

Luckily, Cybele's boss, Olivia, was forward-thinking and fair. After listening to her employee's complaint about Ken, Olivia contemplated the situation. There were many angles here. Both were prized employees, very efficient, and generally well-regarded in the office. Olivia valued Cybele for her heads-down approach to getting high-quality work *done*. And while she personally thought Ken's style was a little flamboyant, Olivia knew that some of the company's largest client accounts actually preferred working with Ken due to his outgoing personality and his flair for details of the industry. But Olivia also knew that the bottom line was down a bit lately because, simply put, their competitors had been cashing in on better, fresher ideas than her team had been generating.

After work, Olivia went to the quiet, meditative place in her garden where some of her best ideas occurred. She thought only briefly of her employees, but instead thought more about how some of the larger, successful firms had been changing their office configurations around to promote more collaboration and creative thinking. And she considered how these same offices were providing perks that would have seemed excessive when she was a young hire—perks like gourmet coffee in the break room, game room areas to bring play into the workplace, yoga and meditation rooms—but were now becoming more commonplace.

A few days later Olivia called an office-wide meeting. With a broad smile, she outlined some exciting changes that were coming to the office, including a tear-down of the old cubicles and broad reconfiguration of the work space, which would now include several nooks and a game room. She also announced, to some applause, that the company would be implementing new rules for employees to be able to work outside of the office during the week. And she looked at Cybele, the employee who with her noise complaint had sparked this creative renaissance, as she announced that the old glass-walled conference room would now serve as a quiet area for those needing shelter from the bustle of the office. From across the room Cybele and Ken looked at each other and smiled.

Case Study Questions

1. Imagine you are Cybele. What are some creative ways you might have addressed the "noisy neighbor" issue?
2. How will taking down the old cubicles and changing the office around help the company?
3. Explain how Olivia came up with her new ideas for the office. Using keywords from the chapter, describe her creative process.
4. Did Olivia fail to directly address her employee's noise concern? How will the new configuration address the employee's concern and the wider issue of losing ground to their competitors?

case study 10.2

Smarts, Luck, or Skill?

Carlos sat slumped at his desk, gently banging his head against his keyboard. The blank screen seemed to blink accusingly at him, "Write something! Get busy!" but he just couldn't seem to get started on his piece of the city planning proposal, due later that afternoon. His co-worker, Debi, walked by his office waving a greeting, stopped, backed up, and walked into his office. "What's wrong, Carlos? You don't look like the usual happy camper I see in this office!"

"I just can't do this job, Debi. I'm not smart enough to come up with something creative and original for every different project, week after week after week. I can't do it any more!"

"Wait a minute! What are you saying? You think that smart and creative are the same thing? No way! You don't have to be *smart,* you just have to be *lucky*! Creative ideas pop into people's heads out of nowhere! Isn't that right, Susan?"

They both turned to the vice president, Susan, who had just walked into Carlos's office with a smile. "Actually, you're both wrong. I was just coming to check on that proposal, Carlos, and I'm glad I did. You both need to hear this: creativity is a *skill* that can be practiced and improved on. It's not luck, and it doesn't take a genius. It's a strategy you both would benefit from." She then said thoughtfully, "You know, maybe we should schedule a full office meeting to talk about this creativity thing. I think we could all benefit from it, and I'd like to hear your ideas about this and a few other things."

Case Study Questions

1. Who's right about the definition of creativity—Carlos, Debi, or Susan? Is there more than one right answer to this question?
2. Suppose you are Susan. What kinds of information would you bring to a meeting on creativity? What kind of input would you solicit from your staff?
3. Do you see a link between Carlos's creativity slump and his self-esteem? Please explain.

SOLUTIONS TO THE "NINE-DOT" PUZZLE

(This is the "standard" solution):

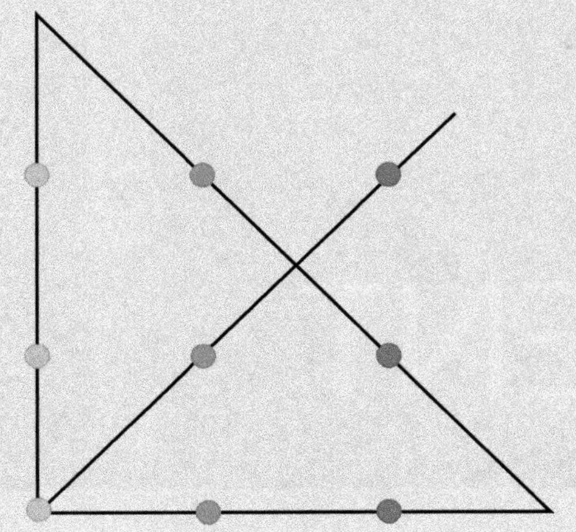

The solution below also works if you don't go through the middle of each dot. Also, it uses only three straight lines:

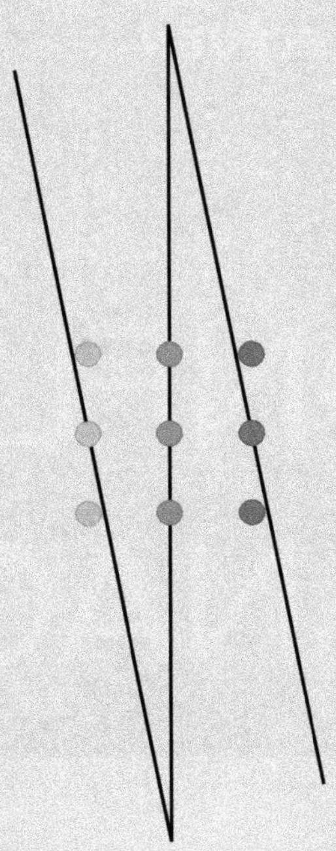

Creative people have come up with several other possible solutions. One is with the edge of a long crayon, connecting all dots using only *one* line!

CHAPTER ELEVEN

11

CONFLICT MANAGEMENT

LEARNING OBJECTIVES

After studying this chapter, you will be able to:

- LO 11-1 Identify the types of conflict.
- LO 11-2 List sources of conflict.
- LO 11-3 Define conflict analysis.
- LO 11-4 Give examples of potential solutions to a conflict.
- LO 11-5 Compare and contrast styles of conflict management.
- LO 11-6 Explain how to deal with special conflict cases.

STRATEGIES FOR SUCCESS

- Strategy 11.1 Negotiate Win–Win Solutions
- Strategy 11.2 Make Collaboration Work
- Strategy 11.3 Stop Conflicts before They Start

Conflict on the Job

SITUATION

zimmytws/Shutterstock

Jorge enjoyed working for his family's business, Mundo Property Management. Like many property managers in the area, Mundo managed the day-to-day operations for local property owners who rented out second homes and apartments they owned. In his job at Mundo, Jorge would ensure that the property was well-maintained for the owners by keeping the landscaping tidy, handling small repairs, and resolving complaints from the tenants. Mundo was well-respected in the area and Jorge was proud to be a part of the business.

After a particularly tough economic downturn, Mundo began to feel the pinch from both sides of the business—owners and renters. Renters who were unable to pay rent were asking the property owners for rent relief, and owners who were unable to pay their mortgages were asking their banks for loan modifications. This meant that Mundo was not getting all the regular percentage payments on these rentals that they had contracted for and, in some cases, was unable to collect any rent at all. While they all expected the economy to recover eventually, no one knew when it would be healthy again.

DISCOVERY

"Well," Jorge said to his father at work one morning, "I think the worst thing about this is the conflict between renters and owners. They both keep putting me in the middle of it. When I'm at the properties, the renters are anxious and frustrated and they tell me I need to 'do something' about the owners asking for rent. When the owners call me, they are upset and they want me to 'do something' to get the renters to pay rent. Meanwhile, we are running out of cash flow to keep up the repairs and landscaping. I am about ready to look for a different job, something more stable," he said with a sigh.

THINK ABOUT IT

Jorge's situation is an illustration of one type of conflict discussed in this chapter. What other sources of conflict can you think of that might exist in a situation like Jorge's? What would you do if you were in Jorge's position in terms of keeping your job, and in terms of keeping the peace between renters and owners as the person stuck in the middle?

» TYPES OF CONFLICT

Wherever there are people, there is conflict. The results of conflict can range from minor inconveniences to major losses—even company failures. In American business, the workplace contains a greater amount of conflict today than in the past, in large part because of the movement of the United States from an agricultural economy to an industrial economy to a service-dominated economy. In a service economy, work tasks depend on successful interactions between people. Jorge's workplace experience in the opening scenario within the service economy is one example of conflict.

Service industries account for roughly 80 percent of employment in the United States overall.[1] With four out of five jobs found in the service sector, employers who want to be successful will need to continue to focus on training employees who communicate effectively. Since conflict nearly always damages productivity, the U.S. workplace is in need of both workers and managers who can manage conflict in a realistic and helpful way.

Several common factors are involved in conflicts:

- Some type of interaction is occurring.
- Opposition or incompatibility exists between the people in conflict.
- The existence of a conflict is perceived by people involved in it or witnessing it.

conflict
Friction or opposition resulting from actual or perceived differences or incompatibilities.

For the purposes of this chapter, **conflict** will be defined as friction or opposition resulting from actual or perceived differences or incompatibilities.[2] Someone might perceive that damage is a possible outcome of the difference, and that perception of possible damage in itself can begin a conflict. The perception of opposition or differences or the belief that damage may occur can refer to ideas, values, or goals, or damage to a person's well-being.

functional conflict
Constructive conflict.

dysfunctional conflict
Destructive conflict.

Conflict is usually seen as a negative factor in the workplace. However, it can be both beneficial and constructive when approached constructively. One way to classify conflicts is by seeing them as either **functional** or **dysfunctional**, that is, either constructive or destructive. For example, when a group of employees meets to make a decision that affects all of them, some conflict can be good because too much unity and agreement can result in a poor decision (groupthink, review in Chapter 7). When people focus more on getting along well than on coming up with creative solutions in decision making, they may not generate as many ideas as they would have otherwise. However, if the same group generates so much conflict that fighting and polarization result, that decision could also be faulty. A manager should try whenever possible to change a dysfunctional (destructive) conflict into a functional (constructive) one.

inner conflict
Conflict within an individual; it might involve values, loyalties, or priorities; the pressure you feel when you are forced to make a choice.

Another way to classify conflict is by the participants in the conflict and where it originates. These classifications include *inner conflict, person-vs.-person conflict, intergroup conflict, intragroup conflict,* and *person-vs.-group conflict.* These are explored further as follows.

Inner conflict is conflict within an individual. It might involve values, loyalties, or priorities. Suppose that your manager wants you to do something

REAL WORLD EXAMPLE 11.1

Ed works as a community health worker. His purpose for working is to help people, and he puts in a lot of time and effort into doing so. Robin also works for the organization, but she spends more time at her desk than interacting with clients. Ed perceives her to be a time waster—someone who doesn't hold the values he holds. Values, personalities, and loyalties could all be involved in the conflict that may occur between Ed and Robin.

that you believe is unethical, and you will feel uncomfortable if you do it. Or suppose your co-workers will call you a "snitch" or informant if you bring the manager's direction out into the open. Or suppose that you have two job offers, both with attractive qualities that pull you in opposite directions.

A **person-versus-person conflict** involves two people who are at odds over personality differences, values conflicts, loyalties, or any number of issues. When only two people are involved in a conflict, the focus tends to be personal on both sides (see Real World Example 11.1).

Intergroup conflict takes place when already-formed groups have conflicts with each other. When this type of conflict takes place, the conflict often becomes widespread. War between two nations provides an extreme example of intergroup conflict.

Intragroup conflict occurs when a conflict arises among group members, and they choose sides and split off into factions within the existing group (see Real World Example 11.2). Sometimes intragroup conflict evolves from person-versus-person conflict because people take sides with the two opposing individuals.[3]

Person-versus-group conflict occurs most often when a member of a group breaks its rules, or norms. It also can involve someone who never was a member of the group, but who opposes it (see Real World Example 11.3).

person-versus-person conflict

Conflict that involves two people who are at odds over personality differences, values conflicts, loyalties, or any number of issues.

intergroup conflict

Conflict that occurs when already-formed groups have conflicts with each other.

intragroup conflict

Conflict that occurs when two groups form and take sides.

person-versus-group conflict

Conflict that occurs most often when a member of a group breaks its rules, or norms.

» SOURCES OF CONFLICT

The preceding four types of conflict describe in general terms *who* is involved in each type, but not *how* conflict starts. No two disagreements are alike; each one starts at a different point over different issues. If you know what type of conflict you are involved in, that knowledge can help you discover how best to resolve it.[4] Figure 11.1 shows the sources of conflict and their potential solutions.

Content Conflict

When disagreements stem from a **content conflict**, they tend to focus on disagreements over what a statement or concept means. The only real issue is whether or not an idea is correct. The correctness of an idea usually focuses on one of two factors–existence or meaning. For example, if the argument is about whether or not there is a Loch Ness monster, the disagreement is over existence.

If the conflict is over existence, it helps to have some way of verifying whether or not something is real. The Loch Ness monster is real to a few

content conflict

Conflict that tends to focus on disagreements over what a statement or concept means.

REAL WORLD EXAMPLE 11.2

Several medieval monks were having a heated discussion about how many teeth a horse has. After the discussion had gone on for nearly an hour, a young monk offered to go out to the post where his horse was tied and count the horse's teeth. He was promptly scolded and called a troublemaker. Because the young monk wanted to solve the debate, he indirectly showed the others that their arguing was pointless—and they were angry with him.

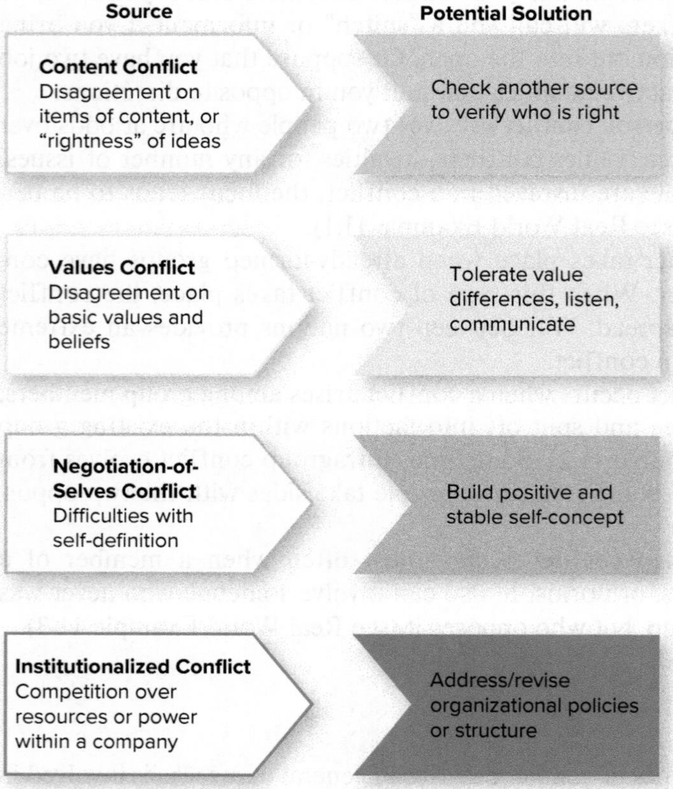

Source
Potential Solution
Content Conflict
Disagreement on items of content, or "rightness" of ideas
Check another source to verify who is right
Values Conflict
Disagreement on basic values and beliefs
Tolerate value differences, listen, communicate
Negotiation-of-Selves Conflict
Difficulties with self-definition
Build positive and stable self-concept
Institutionalized Conflict
Competition over resources or power within a company
Address/revise organizational policies or structure

figure 11.1

SOURCES OF CONFLICT

These are the four basic sources of conflict. *Which of these sources do you feel is easiest to confront and resolve?*

people, so the conflict over its existence still abounds—as it does over the conspiracy theories of President Kennedy's death, the existence of UFOs, and many other issues that are difficult to prove or disprove to everyone's satisfaction. However, when an original or reliable factual source can settle the dispute, arguing is pointless. Many existence issues are more like the number of a horse's teeth. Both sides should wait until proof is available.

More commonly, content conflicts are over meaning and interpretation. If the argument is about whether or not the task you were just assigned is included in the vague wording of your job description, you have probably moved into a disagreement over meaning. You might find a copy of your job description and discover that it contains wording so ambiguous that

REAL WORLD EXAMPLE 11.3

The six mechanics from Nello's Paint & Body Shop had a tradition of shooting pool together at a local bar every Friday evening. After a few years, one of the six quit the body shop and was replaced by Raffi, a non-pool player. The other mechanics regularly asked him to come and shoot pool, and he declined, saying that he was not interested in wasting time and money in a bar or in learning to shoot pool. Person-vs.-group conflicts resulted from Raffi's unintentional breaking of this group norm.

your present task may or may not be appropriate to it, according to different interpretations. Even the interpretation of certain laws by different attorneys would fall in the category of content conflicts over meaning, as Americans can see in the public outcomes of U.S. Supreme Court rulings, for example.

Values Conflict

A **values conflict** usually goes very deep. For example, a Democrat, a Republican, a Green Party member, and a Libertarian Party member would likely disagree on many issues related to politics. In the workplace, managers may have deep disagreements with each other over management practices. These disagreements may be rooted in their values and the basic beliefs they hold about people and how they should be treated.

values conflict
Conflict that occurs when one set of values clashes with another and a decision has to be made.

Values conflicts can be solved, rather than avoided. The solution is that many people need to develop a greater tolerance of values differences. By listening carefully and communicating your values cautiously, you can often create a sense of trust and mutual respect for differences. You will find that if you think carefully about your own values, examining them regularly, you will feel less threatened by someone with values unlike your own. Often that security becomes contagious!

Negotiation-of-Selves Conflicts

This type of conflict erupts over differences in self-definition. Individuals generally define who they are based on their own self-concepts. Many people see themselves as less worthy than they really are, while some see themselves as superior to others. Employees are likely to see themselves differently than the manager sees them; children see themselves differently than their parents see them, and so on.

Many interpersonal conflicts are based on a **negotiation-of-selves conflict**. Part of being human is being constantly involved in the process of defining yourself to others and responding to their implied definitions of themselves. Most of this activity goes on unnoticed. A rude bank loan officer is not likely to say, "Well, I'm responding this way to you because I feel that I'm superior to you," even when he is thinking those thoughts. Even the nonverbal cues in such a case might not deliver the correct message, because people try to play

negotiation-of-selves
Conflict that is involved in the process of defining yourself to others and responding to their implied definitions of themselves.

REAL WORLD EXAMPLE 11.4

A state government agency was planning its annual budget when factions formed behind two rival leaders who were both perceived as powerful, and disliked each other. The conflict continued at a high level until members of the majority "winning" side were running the agency and in charge of the funds. The opposing members gradually quit and found other jobs, or lost interest in the conflict and focused on other tasks of the agency.

CONFLICT ON THE JOB

Conflict comes in more ways than many people imagine. Like Jorge at the beginning of the chapter, you may expect conflict from certain aspects of your job—such as dealing with clients. However, conflict among employees, or between levels of employees, can also be very destructive. *What conflict do you feel is most common in organizations?*

Marcus Clackson/Getty Images

more about. . .

Values Conflicts

Often, many people exaggerate the number of **values conflicts** they have. A conflict may seem to be over values but is actually over the other person's perception of you and your perception of yourself, with neither side identifying the real issue.

the roles that society has constructed. This negotiation of identity of self-identity is something that we do in business relationships and in our personal relationships. It is a way of deciding "who is who" when people come together. A conflict can arise when people do not agree on their status in the "who is who" parts that we play in a conversation or a business relationship. At a simple level, think of a small child telling a parent in frustration, "You are not the boss of me!" In the child's mind, the "who is who" is different from the picture in the parent's mind.

Consider the following real-world negotiations-of-selves conflicts.

Employee: Why is it always my job to take messages? I'm not good at things like that. I get messages wrong and mess up a lot.

Boss: I ask you to take messages because you are, in fact, very good at it.

Mother: What on earth are you thinking, coming home at this ungodly hour? You're not old enough to be trusted out this late.

Daughter: I'm only two years younger than you were when you met Dad. Lighten up. I can take care of myself.

Employee 1: What do you think of this report? I'd really like some input on it.

Employee 2: Don't look to me for approval. I'm not your boss.

All three of the preceding brief exchanges have something in common. They express conflicts that originate from the speakers' self-concept and self-definition. Conflicts such as these can focus on power or authority (as the first two do), on personality traits (as all of them do), or on questions of duty and obligation.

Institutionalized Conflict

Institutionalized conflict occurs when a conflict factor is built into the structure or the policies of the organization. Some organizations encourage conflict, just by the way they are structured. One example of institutionalized conflict is sports at the professional or even high school or college level, where competition for a starting position on the team is built into the organizational structure, and competition among teams is the purpose of the organization. A second example is a sales organization where competition for the most sales is built into the company's policies, with rewards and benefits going to the top sellers.

institutionalized conflict
Conflict that occurs when a conflict factor is built into the structure of the organization.

more about. . .

Conflict and Courage

"Courage is what it takes to stand up and speak. Courage is also what it takes to sit down and listen."

— Author unknown

» CONFLICT ANALYSIS

Anyone wishing to manage a conflict should begin by looking closely at what is really happening. When strong emotions are involved, there is a temptation by conflict managers to jump to conclusions before examining the interests of those in conflict–and their own interests, as well.[5] Instead of making this common mistake, try focusing on these questions:

- **Who is involved?** How many people are taking part in this conflict? How well do they understand the basic issues? Are any of them repeatedly involved in conflicts, or is this a unique situation? By knowing these details, a leader can do a better job of designing a conflict management process that addresses everyone's interests.

- **What is at stake?** Do all or both sides in the dispute agree about what is really at stake? If duties and responsibilities are at stake, does everyone agree on exactly what those issues are? If money is involved, is everyone talking about the same amount? Does the issue center on assigning blame for misconduct, or could the issue be expressed as a desire to define proper conduct for the future? Without this step, the entire issue can become blurred.
- **How important is time?** Does this dispute have to be settled right away? If so, why? Does one side benefit from stalling? Would both sides benefit from a thoughtful, measured analysis of the situation that may take more time? A conflict manager should consider whether the time factor will cool tempers on both sides, or if the passage of time will simply aggravate the issue.
- **What are the tie-ins with other issues?** What relationship does this dispute have with other disputes between the individuals or groups involved? What working relationships will likely be affected by the outcome of the conflict?

After these questions are answered (and assuming you decide that the issue is worth resolving), a solution can be negotiated.

» POTENTIAL SOLUTIONS

Generally speaking, there are three possible solutions to a conflict: win-lose, lose-lose, and win-win. The first two tend to produce a negative, side-taking mentality and are not likely to solve the problem permanently. Yet sometimes, because of time constraints and the other side's unwillingness to work toward a win-win solution, you may be forced to use win-lose or lose-lose tactics.

win-lose strategy
A strategy that allows one side of a conflict to win at the expense of another.

Win-Lose

In negotiating a conflict, both (or all) sides should be working toward a BATNA, or "best alternative to a negotiated agreement."[6] The **win-lose strategy** allows one side of a conflict to win at the expense of the other.[7] It works as a quick-fix conflict solution that sometimes must be chosen when a win-win approach isn't feasible. One win-lose approach is the *democratic vote.* Democracy sounds like a wonderful approach to conflict resolution, and it is the approach on which our political system is based. Unlike a political system, though, most organizations don't contain a series

more about. . .

Win-Lose

The American legal system takes a **win-lose strategy** (also called an *adversarial system*). What are the benefits of this? The drawbacks? Is there a better approach for certain situations?

REAL WORLD EXAMPLE 11.5

In a negotiation of labor union contracts, labor and management had been unable to reach agreement on a new contract for several months. After a grueling six-hour meeting with a neutral external professional negotiator, both sides left the negotiation table smiling. Both sides felt they had won their major points. In a true win–win strategy, a negotiator will find the most critical points of conflict for each side, and work to settle those in a resolution that both sides find acceptable.

of checks and balances, political rallies, or campaigning. In these situations, the majority vote will leave a minority of unhappy people without any real recourse. Especially when a vote is very close, many people on the losing side will potentially be unhappy. These are the people who are likely to bring the problem back, perhaps in another form.

Another win-lose approach is the *arbitrary approach* (arbitration). With this method, the conflict manager decides which side is right and which is wrong, then considers the issue to be resolved. Like the democratic vote, this approach produces a situation in which the losers tend to have hard feelings against both the winning side and the conflict manager. A skillful conflict manager or arbitrator can soften the effect of the arbitrary approach by using persuasive explanations. Usually, however, the gains from win-lose are short-term ones only, and problems will very likely continue.

Lose–Lose

In the **lose-lose strategy**, everyone gives up something. The main approach in lose-lose is compromise. That is, nobody gets what they want, but everyone can live with the decision. Like win-lose, this method usually fails to solve the underlying causes of the conflict. *Unlike* win-lose, the lose-lose strategy produces unhappy people on both sides of the issue. In the lose-lose strategy, the arbitrator typically gives little attention to tracing the development of the conflict, resulting in solutions that are mostly short term.[8]

lose–lose strategy
A strategy in which everyone gives up something, and the focus is on compromise.

Win–Win

A **win-win strategy** is one in which both sides feel they have come out on top. One might ask how both sides in a conflict could end up feeling like winners. The reason is that most conflicts stem from multiple sources and reasons. Because of this complexity, win-win can be accomplished. The key to the success of the win-win strategy is to satisfy as many of each side's needs as possible.[9] People in conflict almost always have more than one reason for being involved in the dispute, and they tend to attach different priorities to each of those reasons. They will, as a rule, be satisfied with less than the entire package if they feel their main goals are achieved. (See Strategy for Success 11.1.)

win–win strategy
A strategy that leads to a solution in which both sides feel they have come out on top.

REAL WORLD EXAMPLE 11.6

Williams Home and Auto Insurance has five departments, all bidding for a portion of a limited company budget. Whatever one department gains, the other four see as a loss. In the end, it is very possible that none of the five will be completely content with the outcome. Conflict, it seems, is built into the way the company allocates funds.

DIFFERENT STYLES OF MANAGING CONFLICT

People have many different styles of managing conflict. They include the competitor, the avoider, the compromiser, the accommodator, and the collaborator. *Why might the collaborator require the most skill and diplomacy of all the styles of managing conflict?*

fizkes/Shutterstock

» STYLES OF CONFLICT MANAGEMENT

Everyone has his or her own style of managing conflicts, often one of five common approaches, discussed in the following list developed by Thomas and Kilmann (also see Figure 11.2).[10] The style you use will have a tremendous impact on the outcome of a conflict and will determine whether it has negative or positive consequences (see Figure 11.3 for effective conflict resolution strategies). Before you read any further, take the Conflict Management Style survey at the end of this chapter in Working It Out 11.1 to find out what your preferred style of conflict management is.

1. A **competitor** is the most likely to try a win–lose approach to conflict resolution, especially if he or she is personally involved in the conflict. The ideals of teamwork are foreign to competitors, and they rarely move to a win-win solution. If the conflict manager (who should be neutral) is a competitor, he or she might use the lose-lose style to resolve the issue. In this role, competitors are afraid of the disruption that could result from other people's conflict, so they work rapidly and energetically to eliminate the potential disruption.
2. An **avoider** would rather not be around conflict at all. Remaining neutral is very important to an avoider. When the avoider is a manager, he or she will often mistakenly assume that if a conflict involves only other people, it should be left only to them. However, if any conflict is causing even the slightest morale problem at work, *it is the manager's business to resolve it.* Some avoiders will say positive things about the conflict if someone else does bring it up; others will pretend that nothing significant has happened. In either situation, though, the avoider often feels great internal stress.
3. A **compromiser** uses his or her skills to blend differences of both sides together and form a workable alternative. Although allowing the issue some real urgency, compromisers tend to see *agreement* as more important than the issue itself. A compromiser generally doesn't feel as much of a need to rush to a solution as a competitor does. If you are a compromiser, watch for the tendency to settle for a lose–lose compromise. Push instead for a win-win solution, following all the steps in that process, so that both sides will feel their main goals have been achieved.

competitor

Someone who is most likely to try a win–lose approach to conflict resolution, especially if he or she is personally involved in the conflict.

avoider

Someone who would rather not be around conflict at all and values neutrality highly.

compromiser

Someone who uses his or her skills to blend differences and form a workable alternative.

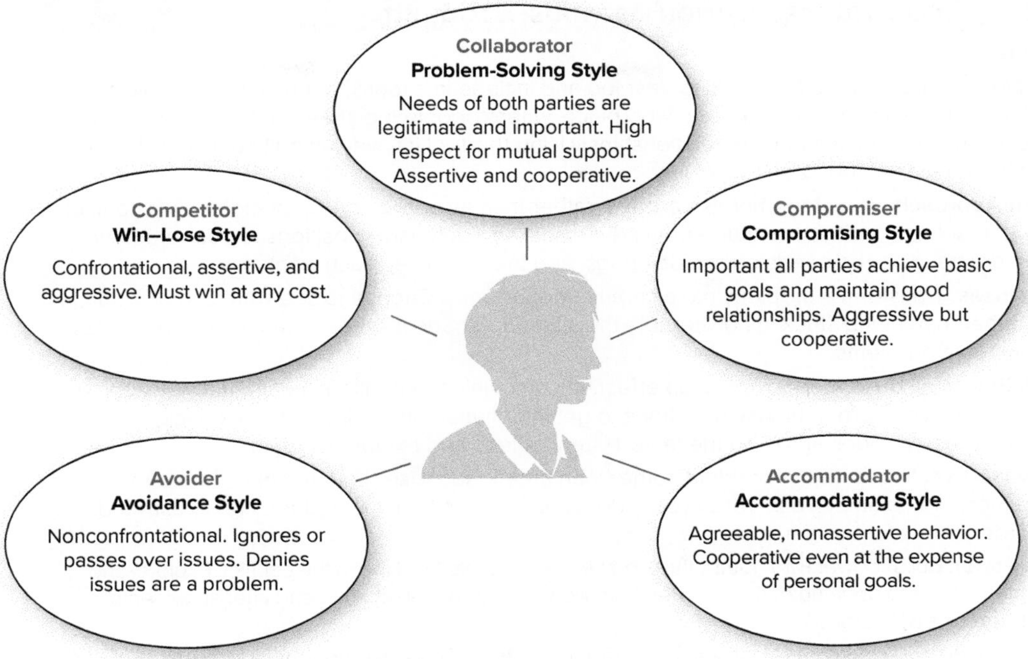
Collaborator
Problem-Solving Style
Needs of both parties are legitimate and important. High respect for mutual support. Assertive and cooperative.
Competitor
Win–Lose Style
Confrontational, assertive, and aggressive. Must win at any cost.
Compromiser
Compromising Style
Important all parties achieve basic goals and maintain good relationships. Aggressive but cooperative.
Avoider
Avoidance Style
Nonconfrontational. Ignores or passes over issues. Denies issues are a problem.
Accommodator
Accommodating Style
Agreeable, nonassertive behavior. Cooperative even at the expense of personal goals.

figure 11.2

THE THOMAS–KILMANN CONFLICT MODEL

These are the five styles of conflict management. Each has a different level of assertiveness and cooperation. *With which style do you identify?*

4. An **accommodator** might tell both parties involved in the conflict, "Don't worry; be happy!" Accommodators want to avoid conflict by positive thinking. They tell people to "count their blessings" or "look on the bright side." Keeping the manager happy is also a top priority. The downside to this is that people involved in the conflict may feel they are not being taken seriously, and the accommodator may not be able (or willing) to get others to fully express their reasons for being angry, which may be counterproductive.
5. The fifth type of conflict management style is collaboration. The **collaborator** brings both sides together for discussion. The collaborative approach is not only the most likely to bring about a win-win solution, but is actually necessary for it. The collaborator opens communication channels and learns about what issues each party feels are most important. Collaboration requires more skill than the other styles of conflict management. For example, it is fairly simple to use the competitive method and force your will on others—so it is easy to see why many conflict managers fall back into that style or one of the simpler methods.

accommodator

Someone who wants to avoid conflict by engaging in positive thinking.

collaborator

Someone who brings both sides together for discussion and not only is most likely to bring about a win–win solution but is actually necessary for it.

WINNING ON BOTH SIDES

With win–win situations, companies and individuals grow. Conflicts are resolved with higher morale than before, and communication stays open. *How can people bring more win–win situations to their work environments?*

Cathy Yeulet/stockbroker/123RF

CONFLICT RESOLUTION METHODS: A TOOL KIT

Conflict Resolution Skills

The *Conflict Resolution Network* has mapped 12 skills to develop and include in a tool kit for resolving conflicts. Effective use of these skills will result in a more cohesive workplace, where people feel they can trust each other and experience more satisfying communication and relationships. Using this tool kit, we can pull out the skills that are appropriate for specific situations. The 12 skills include:

1. **Develop a Win–Win Approach.** Work together as partners, rather than as opponents, to decide how a conflict can be minimized and resolved. Shift your attitude from adversarial and defensive positions to cooperative positions. Start by understanding the needs each side brings, and the outcomes each wants to reach.
2. **Use Creative Responses.** Transform a problem into a creative opportunity. Choose to see what can be done in regard to an issue, rather than being stuck in how terrible the situation is. See issues as learning opportunities, rather than insurmountable problems.
3. **Communicate with Empathy.** Build rapport. Develop effective communication skills including active listening to clarify your understanding of a problem. Ask questions to get information on the issue. Check back, summarize, and make sure both sides agree on the facts. Listen, reflect, and explore for clarity.
4. **Be Appropriately Assertive.** Focus on the problem, rather than the person. Use "I" statements, rather than accusations. Phrase these, for example, as: "When you order your supplies from my budget, ***I*** feel frustrated. ***I*** would like you to order from your budget, not mine."
5. **Create Cooperative Power.** Build "power *with*" rather than "power *over*" others involved in the conflict. Explore, and clarify the details. Ask questions to open up options, rather than allowing the conversation to end after statements about *why* proposed solutions will not work.
6. **Manage Emotions.** Eliminate excessive fear, anger, hurt, and frustration. Express emotions appropriately to identify them without allowing destructive emotions to take over the conflict resolution. This may require disengagement from an escalating situation until emotions cool.
7. **Be Willing to Resolve.** Recognize and set aside personal problems that cloud the picture and keep you from wanting to resolve a conflict. Refuse to allow unresolved personal history to get in the way of a conflict resolution.
8. **Map the Conflict.** Identify common needs and concerns, and define the issues in a way that all can agree. Define the issue or problem area, including who is involved, along with their fears and their needs. Remain neutral so that both sides can agree on the mapping of the conflict.
9. **Develop Options.** Come up with more than one "right" solution to an issue. Break the conflict into smaller pieces, research to find more information, and set goals toward the outcome. Generate more potential solutions through brainstorming and consensus-building.
10. **Negotiate.** Compromise, using effective strategies to reach an agreement that is satisfying to all sides. Be hard on the problems and soft on the person. Focus on needs, not positions. Emphasize common ground. Be inventive about options. Make clear agreements.
11. **Mediate.** Help conflicting parties move toward solutions. Be objective and supportive rather than judgmental. Focus on the process, not the content. Reframe. Respond, rather than react. Refocus on the issue and preserve the relationship. Identify and halt unfair tactics.
12. **Broaden Perspectives.** Respect and value differences in viewpoints. Recognize that a long-term time frame may be needed. Assume a global, rather than an individual, perspective. Calm any resistance to the broader perspective, recognizing that this perspective may make us feel less secure about our own positions. Remain open to the idea of changing and risk-taking. With one step forward, dynamics can change, and new opportunities open up.

figure 11.3

A CONFLICT RESOLUTION TOOL KIT

Good methods for resolving conflict result in better overall morale, communication, workplace relationships, trust, and commitments. *Can you think of other qualities of effective conflict resolution methods?*

Source: 2015 Conflict Resolution Network, PO Box 1016, Chatswood NSW 2057, Australia. www.crnhq.org

REAL WORLD EXAMPLE 11.7

Jim frequently traveled for his job in pharmaceutical sales. While the other salespeople followed a strict set of procedures on travel authorization and reporting, Jim, a low conformer, often traveled without checking in or getting preauthorization for his sales calls. His company tolerated it because customers loved his freewheeling spirit, but his supervisors found it very frustrating.

» SPECIAL CONFLICT CASES

Other conflict issues are caused by the specific behaviors of those identified as *problem people.* Such people are those who for one reason or another aren't living up to the expectations of an organization. Some are involved with alcohol or drug abuse. Others are simply people who don't like to do things the way other people do them. What follows is a description of a few of these different types of problem behaviors, and strategies for dealing with them.

Low Conformers

High conformers are usually easy to work with. They like to fit in, work well in teams, and are generally friendly toward policies and group norms. **Low conformers** are just the opposite: they think independently, solve problems creatively, and often cause some conflict in the process. Working with and managing this type of personality requires a special capacity for patience and goodwill.[11] Here are some suggestions that will make working with low conformers less problematic:[12]

low conformers
Individuals who think independently, solve problems creatively, and often cause some conflict in the process.

- **Learn to tolerate their honesty.** Low conformers are usually straightforward, using less tact and diplomacy than you might be used to. Sometimes the low conformers are also the "class clowns" who ignore the rules and just want to have a good time at work. Although this may be fun for a while, the disruptions take focus away from the work at hand.
- **Continue to calmly ask for information.** Some low conformers are not straightforward; instead they don't feel the need to communicate much with you about what they are doing. If there are procedural or legal requirements they must follow, continue to calmly press for compliance to these behaviors.
- **Accept the low conformer.** Accept them and their firm method of self-expression without labeling it as stubbornness or disloyalty.
- **Support low conformers.** Let them know they have an ally when others are overly critical.
- **Accept their independence.** Don't be offended if they don't ask for advice.
- **Resist the urge to force them to conform.** Trying to force them to do something probably won't work.
- **Give relevant positive reinforcement.** Even when they don't seem to need it, people who are rewarded for behavior you would like them to repeat are more likely to repeat it later.

You won't be able to change the low conformer any more than you're likely to change the high conformer. Both personality types are important to an organization, one balancing the other.

ENVY

Shannon Fagan/Image Source

Envious People

Envy is wanting what another person has, to the extent of feeling ill will toward the person who has it. Envious co-workers cause conflict that can be damaging to morale and productivity and can spread through a department or division like a virus. They can try to undermine your work, leave you out of important decisions, be unwilling to help with the team's work, and invent "evidence" to make you look bad.

The following are several suggestions for dealing with an envious person at work. Some will be more appropriate for you than others, depending on whether you are a manager or an employee. Some may seem to contradict each other, but just remember that they are simply strategies to try. If one doesn't work, go on to the next:

- **Avoid destructive conflict with the envious person.** Keep your focus on your own tasks. Do your best work. If you keep that goal in mind, your actions will be more focused and purposeful. If you need to document your work to show you are doing your best, do that.
- **Confront the envious co-worker.** Some envious people are dealt with best by calling them on their envy, openly and honestly. Once you have called the play, the game usually changes. Because of your approach, you are now perceived as having the power advantage. The envious co-worker will back away and choose someone else as a target (hopefully not another co-worker). One warning: *A vengeful, envious person* often will work even harder behind your back after a confrontation.
- **Avoid excessive contact with the envious person.** Say hello and good-bye, but avoid making prolonged eye contact or starting a conversation. If the other person wants to chat, politely cut the conversation short. Politeness is very important, for you must avoid making the person feel snubbed. Have short conversations, then move on.
- **Discuss the problem with your manager.** This meeting should be a perception check. You're just checking to see if your boss perceives the same attitude that you perceive. Don't turn the discussion into a gripe session; remember that you are trying to avoid open conflict.
- **Build up the envious person's self-esteem.** People often are envious because of low self-worth. Even when other methods fail, this one often reduces the intensity of the envious behavior. But be sure to point out authentic, rather than manufactured, reasons for praise.

REAL WORLD EXAMPLE 11.8

Becca is envious of Matt, whom she sees as having a more impressive work history and a better education. They make the same salary and have the same title, but she perceives him as being held in higher regard. She envies what she perceives as Matt being treated better and admired by others at work. She talks negatively about Matt behind his back and causes conflict between him and others.

Whatever course of action you decide to use, don't play into the other person's game: don't descend to subtle insults and backstabbing. If you wait long enough, the problem will usually pass, and the envy will eventually burn itself out.[13]

Whiners and Complainers

One can readily find people in the workplace who are never happy and who want to discuss their problems constantly with anyone who will listen. Whether you are their manager or co-worker, these steps can help you deal with this common source of conflict:

- **Listen, but not too much.** Whiners and complainers are good at taking advantage of sympathetic listeners. Although you should give honest, relevant complaints an ear when they involve you, learn to pull a rambling gripe session together by asking, "What is it that you need?" or "What are you going to do to solve this?"
- **Do frequent reality checks.** You might be able to call the bluff of the chronic whiner by saying something like, "OK, tell me exactly what the problem is and what you want me to do about it." By forcing the complainer to focus on the purpose for the gripe session, and by stressing the limits of your own power to change things, you can often reduce the complaining.
- **Challenge the word *unfair*.** *Unfair* is one of the most common words used by whiners and complainers. With them, the word often means "I'm not getting what I want." By demanding specific examples of unfairness, and by demanding facts rather than implications or innuendos, you can force the whiners to focus on what they are really saying.
- **Be a team leader or player.** As a manager, you can promote a spirit of teamwork and camaraderie in the workplace. You can stress the possibility of transfer for people who aren't team players. As a team member, you can be the kind of team player who won't tolerate the whiners.
- **Don't enter the drama.** Complainers may escalate into "drama queens" or "drama kings" who thrive on the high emotion and chaos they create. Avoid getting pulled into the drama and becoming part of the performance: remain calm, leave the "stage" of the drama.

REAL WORLD EXAMPLE 11.9

When Joachin was asked to do anything outside of the bare minimum of his tasks at work, his response was always a passive "Will do." The problem was that he seldom completed what he was asked to do. His supervisor was baffled as to how to get him to complete his work. He didn't complain, didn't speak up when she tried to engage him in a conversation, so she usually ended up giving him his task list, and listening to his automatic response, "Will do."

more about...

Complainers and Whiners

This combination is a conflict waiting to start. Learn to recognize the legitimate complaint when you hear it, but don't tolerate this type of chronic behavior. It is counterproductive and causes negative conflict.

more about...

Passive people are often angry people who express their anger silently and indirectly.

Passive, Unresponsive People

Unresponsive people are sometimes the most difficult people to work with because on the surface they often seem agreeable and even easygoing. These personality types react to any confrontation or potential conflict by shutting down.

How can you be sure you are dealing with a passive person? Not all quiet people are passive. Some people don't speak up until they are absolutely sure they have something relevant to say; others are very good at screening out irrelevant material and thus seem somewhat unresponsive.[14] Passive people are different—when you most need a response, they will disappoint you.

Passive people have a variety of different reasons for their behavior. Some people use their absence of response as a way of intimidating—a method of calculated aggression. Others remain quiet because they are afraid of sounding foolish. Still others keep quiet to escape responsibility. Words give a concrete reality to thoughts and feelings. When you speak inner thoughts, you are admitting you have them—a frightening admission for some people. The safer course is to hide them from both others and yourself.[15]

How would you have handled Joachin if you had been his manager in Real World Example 11.9? How would you explain his passivity?

Once you are convinced that it is a passive person you are dealing with, you can take some positive steps to get meaningful feedback from this type of difficult person:[16]

- **Ask open-ended questions.** Don't ask passive people any question that can be answered with a *yes* or *no,* or even with a brief phrase. Develop questions that encourage them to open up. Some examples are: "How do you react to that?" "What thoughts on this subject occur to you right now?" or "What would you do if . . . ?"
- **Develop and use a friendly, silent gaze.** After asking an open-ended question, look directly at the silent person with a quizzical, expectant

expression on your face. This expression should not be unduly threatening, but it should urge a hesitant person to talk. If you are to use this technique successfully, you must be willing to maintain the gaze *beyond the limits of your own comfort.* Sometimes, this technique won't work. If it doesn't, move quickly to another method.

- **Don't fill the space.** A supportive person often is tempted to make enough small talk to fill the uncomfortable empty pauses. If you rescue passive people, you will have enabled them to remain passive.
- **Make statements to help break the tension.** Call attention to what has been going on. Make a statement such as "I expected you to say something, Ignatio, and you're not. What does that mean?" Then return to the friendly, silent gaze. You might also ask, "Can you talk about what you're thinking?" or "What's on your mind right now?"
- **Hold them accountable.** They are responsible for their work. Do not apologize for asking them to be accountable. When passive people hold underlying anger, they may eventually explode; hold your own emotions in check. Don't get pulled into their anger.
- **Set time limits.** Plan in advance how much time you plan to spend dealing with the passive silent person. Tell the person what the time limit is. Often, a great deal will be said in the last few minutes by the silent person who knows that time is short.
- **Help slackers be productive.** Some passive employees are also slackers. Help them plan goals and break tasks into manageable pieces. Sometimes being passive is a means to avoid looking incompetent, and sometimes it is due to a lack of motivation. In the worst case, slackers may turn into ghosts, who never seem to be around and do not contribute. These employees will need extra attention to plan and be held accountable to their work plans.

Snipers and Intimidators

When employees take a more aggressive approach to making others in the office look bad, they may become a sniper, who attacks you behind your back; or an intimidator, a workplace bully.[17] Here are some ways to combat snipers:

- **Communicate directly to the person about the behavior.** Confront it head on. Ask the person why they need to take control of a meeting, make you look bad, or other damaging behavior. Often they lack confidence in their own work and are trying to make others look bad as a way of looking good. This has to be done in a calm way so as not to escalate the emotions.
- **Ask for solutions to their issues.** If the sniper attack or the bullying behavior is masked by an issue they bring up, ask them to help solve it as a way to disarm them.

- **Plan ahead.** If you are planning a meeting or team assignment, you may be able to predict how they are going to act, and prepare ahead of time for what they might do or say. Hold a pre-meeting when it might give you notice ahead of time about what their issues are, and it may give them a feeling of power in being asked ahead of time for a meeting, which could de-escalate the emotions.

The Grinch and the Gossip

A Grinch is a person at work who is cranky, sulky, cynical, irritable, or unpleasant, every day. The gossip enjoys making others look bad by spreading rumors or sharing enticing bits of scandal (real or imagined). Both of these employee types have the same effect on the workplace at the end of the day. They make it an unpleasant place to be, where lots of time is wasted.[18] And the negativity can be contagious. Stop them with these tips:

- **Model good behavior.** Don't be like the irritable Grinch or the annoying gossip, and don't fall into their web of negativity. Set a high standard at work for productive and positive behavior.
- **Create formal expectations for work.** Set an office policy (or ask administrators to make this happen) so that there is an actual expectation of productive behavior in place for employees. Then you have a document to refer to when gossip and Grinch behavior are going on too long.
- **Stay positive.** Smile! Distracting others from the Grinch's bad mood or the gossip's daily updates by remaining positive and focusing on work creates a reward for those who are maintaining high standards of productivity, and they will be less likely to be drawn into the negative behavior.

Other types of difficult people produce conflict in the workplace. Working effectively with all of them requires patience, good listening skills, and time. Whenever a conflict with a difficult person begins, you must become aware as soon as possible that a difficult person is involved, then plan your strategy accordingly. Once the problem is identified, work toward a solution, attempting to get a commitment from the difficult person.

Pixtal/AGE Fotostock

Because of the nature of difficult people, most of them will never completely stop being difficult. Work cooperatively with their difficulties on an event-by-event basis, realizing the limitations of any conflict management procedure. And remember the old saying, "They can't drive you crazy if you don't give them the keys." You are in control of your own emotions and behavior—don't give up that control.

STRATEGIES FOR SUCCESS

Strategy 11.1 Negotiate Win–Win Solutions

1. Get emotions under control.
2. Agree on ground rules.
3. Clarify all positions.
4. Explore multiple needs and issues.
5. Develop alternatives.
6. Choose solutions that are win–win.

The conflict manager should look for underlying reasons, interests, and needs. Once these areas are identified, the leader should get each side to list them in order of importance. The rest of the negotiation process is a series of exchanges, with one side giving up one issue in order to gain another from the other side. At this point in the process, a creative negotiator can bring off concession bargaining moves that would not occur to a less creative mind. **Concession bargaining** is the process of getting each side in a conflict to willingly make concessions in exchange for concessions (compromises) made by the opposing side.

concession bargaining
The process of getting each side in a conflict to willingly make concessions in exchange for concessions made by the opposing side.

Of course, this process isn't as easy as it sounds. The conflict manager must take the group through a series of steps, following some important guidelines, before the win–win method can work.

more about. . .

Concession bargaining is used frequently by union bargaining teams to negotiate flexible issues, such as salaries, benefits, and employee rights.

1. **Get emotions under control.** If emotions are strong on one or both sides, a conflict manager must put most of the creative effort into calming people down. Leaders should be especially careful that their own emotions are not involved with either side. A good beginning might be "Look, I know you're angry, but if we're going to resolve this, we need to put our feelings aside and try to work on some alternatives. Would you be willing to do that?"[19] The final question is crucial. Press for a commitment to solving the problem, rather than placing the blame.

   People handle their anger in different ways, and the anger itself can become a source of conflict. One side's anger will often feed the anger of the other side until the situation seems hopeless. Both sides may think that the other is not acting in good faith. When you are sitting down to reach a solution, that distrust must be dispelled. Anger *must* be expressed or the other person will not be able to understand the focus of your emotions—yet expressing that anger too strongly (such as with personal insults) can block further communication. If nothing else works, the leader should try getting both sides to explain why they are angry. The focus then becomes the *reasons* behind the feelings, rather than the feelings alone.

2. **Agree on ground rules.** Once the anger has been dealt with, the conflict manager should establish ground rules. He or she should explain that the rules are meant to keep the process running smoothly, not to force either side to conform. To emphasize this, when establishing ground rules, the conflict manager should encourage both sides to suggest rules. The earlier in the process you can get participation, the better. Some of the basic rules could include:[20]
   - Agree to listen as carefully as possible, without interrupting.
   - Agree to control anger, even if someone disagrees with your position.
   - Agree to treat each other with the respect you would like to receive.
   - Agree on the amount of time you will devote to achieving a solution.
   - Resist the urge to force the participants to conform.

REAL WORLD EXAMPLE 11.10

Jeanne was a factory employee who spent virtually all of her free time complaining about her job, personal life, co-workers, or manager. Her favorite word seemed to be "unfair." Everyone was unfair. The job was unfair, especially the pay, and—of course—her manager. Not only did Jeanne cause daily misery for herself, but she made others around her miserable as well.

Once ground rules have been established, they can be used as calming and directive devices if the discussion threatens to get out of control. By reminding each side of the rules they agreed to, the leader has a better chance of retaining control.

3. **Clarify all positions.** When emotions are dealt with and the ground rules are set, it is time to get all of the issues, facts, and opinions out for close examination. When both sides have seen what the problems are from the other's perspective, they can move toward an understanding that makes both feel like winners. Both sides will still push for whatever they want most, but they will also be listening to the needs of the other side.

   Allow both sides equal time for self-expression. If either one is dominating the discussion, the conflict manager should call for more input from the opposition. Some people become suddenly silent during this phase and need to be encouraged to participate. Stay in the *objective mode* as consistently as possible. Everyone involved should take care not to form value judgments.

more about...

The **objective mode** means being neutral and open, not judgmental, and not unduly swayed by feelings or emotions. It is calm and does not let emotions interfere with objective decisions.

4. **Explore multiple needs and issues.** Begin this phase by allowing both sides to explain why they chose their position rather than the other one. Then find multiple interests in the issue and look for the ones that both sides share.
5. **Develop alternatives.** Based on the needs and issues you have uncovered, list each possible alternative to be examined carefully later. This can be done much like a brainstorming session: don't allow any value judgments or editorial comments by either side, and strive for *quantity* of ideas, rather than *quality* at this point.
6. **Choose solutions that are win–win.** Explain carefully what a win–win solution is: one that gives something of perceived value to both sides. Then go through each alternative, asking how it can be seen as a win–win solution. Usually a list of acceptable solutions will evolve by consensus. When that fails to happen, the conflict manager must make the decisions alone, asking for a consensus of the solutions he or she selects.

For these six steps to work as a conflict management model, several requirements must be met. First, everyone involved in the conflict must be willing to go through the steps, desiring a long-term solution rather than merely fighting to win. Second, all must be willing to take the *time* required to carry out the process to its conclusion; the win–win strategy is often abandoned for lack of time. Third, the conflict manager must be flexible, sensitive, patient, and calm under fire.[21]

REAL WORLD EXAMPLE 11.11

An auto dealer who had been forced to reduce his accounting staff heard constant complaints from the head bookkeeper about working with fewer people. He finally asked, "If you can't manage the job with two fewer people, can you recommend someone who can?" The complaining stopped abruptly.

STRATEGIES FOR SUCCESS

Strategy 11.2 Make Collaboration Work

1. Identify the problem.
2. Generate a solution.
3. Identify an action plan.
4. Put the action plan to work.

People using collaboration see conflict resolution as a problem-solving process. This process should include four phases:

1. **Identify the problem.** Make sure that you are dealing with the real issue, not a result of a deeper problem. Otherwise, even a solution that seems to be win–win will be focusing on symptoms, rather than problems.
2. **Generate a solution.** A group can take this step in many different ways, from group discussion to written questionnaires. This method should involve everyone who is directly affected by the conflict.
3. **Identify an action plan.** If possible, get input from both sides in the creation of this plan. Then get an agreement from both sides to follow it.
4. **Put the action plan to work.** Don't forget to follow up on the results. The follow-up is important in preventing future destructive conflict.

STRATEGIES FOR SUCCESS

Strategy 11.3 Stop Conflicts before They Start

1. Define what *is* acceptable behavior.
2. Pick your battles.
3. Compromise.
4. Watch for sparks.
5. Be fair, don't assume the worst.

The best way to handle negative conflict is by preventing it. Of course, no workplace is totally without negative conflict, but both managers and employees can take steps to prevent many conflicts and soften their impact when they happen.

1. **Define what *is* acceptable behavior.** Don't wait for conflict to arise to address it. Many times, conflicts arise when work team members have different understandings of policies and procedures; for example, whether there is a dress code, or how strict or lax the company is on punctuality. Resentment leading to conflict can arise when one team member believes another is intentionally ignoring the rules. Include training on tasks that employees will be doing. Not knowing the correct way to do a job can be mistaken by others as deliberate carelessness or errors.

REAL WORLD EXAMPLE 11.12

Albert, an elderly man, would always shrug and mutter, "Sure, why not?" whenever he was asked to do anything. He showed anger in subtle ways nearly all the time. One reason he was angry was because he had found himself working for a manager who was 20 years younger than he was. The age difference made him feel inferior. His manager found that by asking for his advice, even sometimes when the advice wasn't really needed, the passive anger was reduced.

2. **Pick your battles.** Many disagreements can arise to the level of a conflict when they don't need to. Help employees (or yourself) identify what is really important, and what they can let go.
3. **Compromise.** How important is it that team members do things exactly the way you would like them to be done? What modifications can you live with? You may find that in compromising, the end result turns out better than it would have if you had insisted on having things done strictly your way.
4. **Watch for sparks.** Watch out for sparks that may erupt into a wildfire. Head off a larger conflict by stepping in early, before it has time to disrupt. You may be familiar enough over time with your team that you can step in when tensions begin to rise. That is the time to bring it out in the open, asking team members to air their issues honestly before getting back to the work that needs to go forward.
5. **Be fair, don't assume the worst.**[22] Most people do not have malicious intentions. Encourage communication and collaboration to keep attitudes positive. When you start to assume someone has a negative intent, try to see the issue or the explanation from multiple perspectives. Ask clarifying questions. Give people the benefit of the doubt. Model that mindset, build it into your company culture, and it will become the norm.

CHAPTER ELEVEN SUMMARY

Chapter Summary by Learning Objectives

LO 11-1 Identify the types of conflict. Although conflict is always present in the workplace, it isn't always negative. Conflict can be seen as either functional or dysfunctional. When classified by the actors in the conflict, five types can be found: inner conflict, person-against-person conflict, intragroup conflict, intergroup conflict, and person-against-group conflict.

LO 11-2 List sources of conflict. Conflict usually springs from one of four sources: content conflict, values conflict, negotiations-of-selves conflict, and institutionalized conflict.

LO 11-3 Define conflict analysis. Analyzing the situation is the first step toward resolving a conflict. Ask such questions as: *Who is involved? What is at stake? How important is time?* and *What are the tie-ins with other issues?* Conflict prevention often involves asking these questions early on.

LO 11-4 Give examples of potential solutions to a conflict. The best solution is nearly always win–win, the solution that makes everyone who is involved feel like a winner. Although they usually don't give permanent solutions to conflicts, win–lose and lose–lose can be used as well.

LO 11-5 Compare and contrast styles of conflict management. The Thomas-Kilmann Model shows five different types of conflict management styles for use as strategies in conflict resolution: competitor, avoider, compromiser, accommodator, and collaborator. The best one is collaborator, because it can solve most conflicts when allowed enough time and energy.

LO 11-6 Explain how to deal with special conflict cases. Problem people produce a different type of conflict. Learning to deal with major problem personality types can be helpful in conflict management. Different strategies must be used for low conformers, envious people, whiners and complainers, passive people, Grinches and gossips, snipers and intimidators, and other challenging employees.

key terms

accommodator 321
avoider 320
collaborator 321
competitor 320
compromiser 320
concession bargaining 329
conflict 312
content conflict 313
dysfunctional conflict 312
functional conflict 312
inner conflict 312
institutionalized conflict 317
intergroup conflict 313
intragroup conflict 313
lose–lose strategy 319
low conformers 323
negotiation-of-selves conflict 315
person-versus-group conflict 313
person-versus-person conflict 313
values conflict 315
win–lose strategy 318
win–win strategy 319

review questions

1. What are the major types of conflict in the workplace in terms of who is involved?
2. What are the four major sources of conflict within organizations? Explain each one, using an example.
3. Explain the Thomas–Kilman Conflict Model. What does this model show as the best method of conflict resolution?
4. Is conflict always negative? If so, what are some effective ways of preventing destructive conflict in the workplace?
5. You are trying to negotiate a workplace conflict through to a win–win solution. What steps would you follow? What pitfalls would you need to avoid?

6. What is negotiation-of-selves conflict, and why is this source of conflict probably the most important in the workplace?
7. What should you do when a person who constantly complains confronts you? Why should you avoid being indifferent or ignoring the person? How would reality checks and being a team leader help?
8. How can a manager or employee tell if he or she is dealing with a passive person? What is the best way to deal with a passive, silent person who is determined not to communicate?
9. Have you encountered a Grinch or a sniper at work or at school? What is the best way to handle these problem people in a professional way?

critical thinking questions

1. Try to remember a conflict you have had with someone recently. What were the sources of the conflict? Was the conflict ever resolved? If so, how? Would you resolve it differently if you could replay the event?
2. Have you ever tried to work or study with a difficult person, such as a whiner or envious person? How did you relate to that individual, if at all? Have you ever confronted an envious person? If so, what happened?
3. Conflict can occur at work, in a school setting, among friends, and at home with family. Think of a recent conflict you have experienced, and summarize how a resolution would occur using the different styles of competitor, avoider, compromiser, accommodator, and collaborator.

working it out 11.1

YOUR CONFLICT MANAGEMENT STYLE

School-to-Work Connection: Interpersonal Skills

Instructions: This exercise will help you discover the strategies you use, or would be likely to use, in a conflict situation. In the space next to each statement, write "5" if the statement applies often, "3" if the statement applies sometimes, and "1" if it never applies. (This test will not be accurate unless you strive to be completely honest with yourself in answering.) When I differ with someone:

____ 1. I explore our differences, neither backing down nor forcing my own view.

____ 2. I disagree openly, then invite some more discussion about our differences.

_____ 3. I look for a mutually satisfactory solution.

_____ 4. Rather than let the other person make a decision without my input, I make sure I am heard and also that I hear the other person out.

_____ 5. I agree to a middle ground rather than look for a completely satisfying solution.

_____ 6. I will admit that I am half-wrong, rather than discuss our differences.

_____ 7. I have a reputation for meeting the other person halfway.

_____ 8. I expect to be able to get out about half of what I really want to say.

_____ 9. I will give in totally rather than try to change the other person's opinion.

_____ 10. I avoid any controversial aspects of an issue.

_____ 11. I agree early on, rather than arguing about a point.

_____ 12. I give in when the other person becomes emotional about an issue.

_____ 13. I try to win the other person over to my side.

_____ 14. I work to come out victorious, no matter what.

_____ 15. I never back away from a good argument.

_____ 16. I would rather win than end up compromising.

To score your responses, add your total score for each of the following sets of statements:

Set A: Statements	1–4 _____
Set B: Statements	5–8 _____
Set C: Statements	9–12 _____
Set D: Statements	13–16 _____

A score of 17 or more on any set is considered high. Scores of 12 to 16 are moderately high. Scores of 8 to 11 are moderately low. Scores of 7 or less are considered low.

Each set represents a different strategy for conflict management:

Set A: Collaboration (I win; you win.)

Set B: Compromise (Both win some; both lose some.)

Set C: Accommodation (I lose; you win.)

Set D: Competition (I win; you lose.)

working it out 11.2

RESOLVING CONFLICT

Everyone has a different conflict management style. Consider each scenario that follows. Describe how you would resolve it, using each one of the five strategies described in this chapter. Which one(s) worked better for you? Did some strategies not work as well?

The five conflict management styles include: accommodator, avoider, collaborator, competitor, and compromiser.

1. You are at your college and need to complete an assignment in the computer lab. The assignment is due today in class and your computer at home has crashed. All of the lab computers are in use, and you are waiting for one to become available. Just as you see another student leave a terminal and head toward it, another student pushes past you and sits down at the computer. What do you do?
2. You overhear college classmates laughing at a close friend of yours who is also in the same class, making up insulting names for him and mocking him. What do you do?
3. You are at the small family restaurant where you work part-time making pizzas. You hear some loud voices and commotion coming from one of the tables so you come out of the kitchen to see what is going on. You hear a customer complaining loudly and angrily about the pizza you have made, saying the order is wrong and the quality is terrible. What do you do?
4. You are seated at the family dinner table where your extended family has gathered for a family wedding. Everyone is in a celebratory mood. Then, your uncle makes a joke about a national politician. Some family members laugh, and some scowl; it is obvious there are many differing opinions on politics around the table. You find your uncle's joke particularly offensive as you have strong opinions on the situation and the politician. What do you do?
5. You are assigned to work on a group project in your class with four other people. Two of them have not done any work on the project and the due date is soon. The other two have started work on a direction that you think is headed down the wrong path. There is no specific leader on the project. What do you do?
6. You received a bill in the mail for something you know you did not order. The bill says "past due, final billing." You call the customer service line and cannot get through to a live person. You e-mail the customer service department of the company and do not hear back. Within days, you receive another letter saying your past due account is being

sent to a collection agency. When you call the collection agency, they tell you that they can work with you to make payments over time, but you will have to pay the bill. What do you do?

working it out 11.3

COMPASSIONATE CURIOSITY

Watch the TEDx Talk by attorney and negotiator Kwame Christian, titled "Finding Confidence in Conflict," and then answer the following questions.

1. Describe the three possible reactions to conflict, according to the speaker. Have you experienced these reactions? Explain.
2. Why does the speaker say that conflict can be the most heated part of our personal and professional lives?
3. What is the "cereal-gate" example that the speaker described? Think of a time that you experienced a similar conflict. How did you respond? What would you do differently next time?
4. What is meant by compassionate curiosity, according to the speaker? Use the term in describing a situation you have experienced.
5. What is wrong with being a people-pleaser, according to the speaker? Do you find yourself being a people-pleaser? How does conflict present us with an opportunity?

The video can be found here: www.youtube.com/watch?v=F6Zg65eK9XU.

case study 11.1

Searching for a Win–Win Solution

Scott is an executive director and Juanita is a fundraising manager at Werner Charities. They are trying to create a more effective letter to secure funding from past and prospective donors. Their response from the current letter–and the second–have been disappointing, to say the least. Both Scott and Juanita are acutely aware of the importance of the success of this mailing. Also, each of them has some definitive ideas about how the letter should look and sound.

Scott, the charity's director, believes it is vitally important to address the logical, thoughtful mind of potential donors. He wants the letter to focus on facts, figures, and good works the charity has accomplished. Juanita, the fundraiser, takes the approach that the letter should tug at the heart strings of potential donors. She wants the letter to focus on real life stories of people the charity has helped. Further, Juanita wants to pull in new, younger donors through social media outlets and digital letter delivery who will donate electronically; while Scott wants to retain the older, wealthier, more established donors who prefer a paper letter through the mail with return envelope for sending in checks.

Both Juanita and Scott are known for their expertise in different areas of marketing. Because of company protocol, both of them will need to sign off on this crucial letter and on its delivery method. Also, both have run very successful campaigns in the past.

Right away, tensions started to rise between them. Both of them know that a win-win solution should be their goal. Before anyone could have predicted it, however, they were both raising their voices more than necessary. Both of them were sure that the other one's letter design and delivery would ruin the company.

Case Study Questions

1. What steps should Scott and Juanita take to start making some progress toward a win-win solution?
2. What could they have done to prevent the situation from starting out this way? If you were running this donation campaign, how would you set up the campaign so that conflict would not occur?
3. Would a win-lose approach work in this situation? Why or why not?
4. What additional information should you obtain to be effective in settling this difference of opinion?

Don't Call Him Boss

Lael and Waheid both work for a small software development firm. Both of them have strong résumés and both have about the same number in the "years of experience" column. However, when Waheid was hired, Lael had objected strongly. When she was asked why, she said that Waheid was not qualified for the position. She believed that other applicants who were not hired would have been better in the position.

Six months after Waheid was hired, the manager (Barbara) left to start her own company. As Barbara was leaving, Lael had demanded that it was to be clear that she would not take orders from Waheid. All three agreed.

At first, things seemed calm and workable. After a month had gone by, however, Waheid called a meeting of all seven members of the project team, which included Lael. As Lael saw things, Waheid was usurping power and "trying to run the place." At that meeting, Waheid reviewed everyone's job in detail. He also sent out e-mails, signing himself as project director. The new manager who had taken Barbara's place had not commented on Waheid's signature as project director.

Waheid: Lael, you are all hung up on power issues. Hey, I don't want power. I just want this team to operate efficiently. Just because I sign myself as project director doesn't mean I want to take things over.

Lael: Get real. Just yesterday, two people referred to you as "the boss." And I've heard that from several others.

Waheid: Notice that I didn't ask them to call me that.

Lael: Well, you obviously didn't tell them *not* to, either.

Waheid: I give up.

Case Study Questions

1. These two people seem to be having more than one conflict taking place at the same time. Explain.
2. What could you do to settle the conflict in this case? See if you can come up with more than one solution.
3. What could they have done to avoid this conflict in the first place? What would you have done, as the manager, to set up conditions to avoid a conflict?

CHAPTER TWELVE

12

STRESS AND STRESS MANAGEMENT

LEARNING OBJECTIVES

After studying this chapter, you will be able to:

LO 12-1 Identify the main causes of stress.

LO 12-2 Give examples of external and internal sources of stress.

LO 12-3 Compare and contrast type A and type B personality behaviors.

LO 12-4 Describe the physical effects of stress.

LO 12-5 Explain the cost of stress in the workplace.

LO 12-6 Learn to manage stress in your life.

STRATEGIES FOR SUCCESS

Strategy 12.1 Discard Irrational Beliefs

Strategy 12.2 Change Your Behaviors to Reduce Stress

Strategy 12.3 Take Care of Yourself

In the Workplace: What's Wrong with Me?

SITUATION

Image Source

Stephanie Williams is a lower-level supervisor at a county agency. At first she enjoyed her job, but lately she just can't seem to concentrate at work. She has also been having trouble sleeping, has lost her appetite, and resumed smoking. To top it off, she seems to be getting every cold and flu that goes around.

At home, things have not been easy financially since her divorce last year. Her three children are pretty easy going kids, but over the summer Stephanie missed two weeks of work when her daughter had chicken pox, and several more days this fall when her son fell off the playground equipment at school and broke his arm. Now she has used up all her vacation time and sick leave, and she has even had to take some unpaid leave days. Meanwhile, her ex-husband has fallen behind in his child support payments since losing his job, and she is feeling overwhelmed.

Stephanie's supervisor, Donna Clark, has called her in several times in the past month to talk about Stephanie's performance. She has told Stephanie that the office is getting complaints from clients about poor service in the office, and she wants to know why Stephanie is not handling routine things in her usual efficient manner.

Over lunch, Stephanie tells her friend and co-worker Lakeesha Jones, "I just don't know what's the matter with me. I can't seem to get anything done, I lose my train of thought all the time, I don't feel well half the time, I'm always tired, and I keep snapping at the kids for no reason. Am I going crazy? What's wrong with me?"

DISCOVERY

Lakeesha answers, "I don't know what your problem is, but you'd better snap out of it or you're going to lose your job. I heard that Donna has been looking over files in personnel, and you know what that means! Somebody is going to get the ax!"

"Oh, no!" Stephanie wailed. "Lakeesha, I just *can't* lose my job! What am I going to do?"

THINK ABOUT IT

What seems to be wrong with Stephanie? What kinds of actions could Stephanie take on her own to help herself?

If you were Lakeesha, what would you identify as Stephanie's problem? What would you suggest Stephanie do to help her situation?

Have you had friends or co-workers in similar situations, or have you yourself experienced them? How were they resolved?

» CAUSES OF STRESS

Which of these two situations do you believe would be more stressful?

- During the past year, you were fired or laid off from your job, and a close friend died.
- During the past year, you got married, added a healthy baby to your family, received a big promotion at work, and bought your first home.

The answer may surprise you: stress researchers would say that the second situation is more stressful. This is because the more major life changes you are experiencing, the more stress you are likely to feel. This reasoning will be explored in more detail in this chapter. First, though, is an explanation of what is meant by *stress* and *stressors.*

stress
Any reaction or response made by the body to a new situation.

According to psychologists, **stress** can be defined as *the nonspecific response of the body to any demand made on it.*[1] In other words, any reaction or response your body makes to a new situation is stress. Ongoing situations that seem to be too much for us to handle will also cause stress. The *reaction* is both emotional and physical.

Hans Selye, a Canadian physiologist who researched stress and its effects for 50 years, believed that human bodies are nearly always in some kind of stress. He maintained that some stress is necessary for life, and he distinguished between two kinds of stress. The first is **eustress**, or good stress—the kind of pleasant, desirable stress you might feel when playing tennis or attending a party. The second is **distress**, or bad stress—the kind of stress you might feel during an illness or when ending a relationship.[2] Even though there are positive effects of stress, and some kinds of stressful events are pleasurable, this discussion of stress will actually refer to *distress,* which fits the everyday definition of stress.

eustress
Positive stress, the kind felt when doing something one enjoys, such as playing tennis or attending a party.

distress
Negative stress, the kind felt during an illness or when going through a divorce.

stressor
A situation or an event that causes the body to react (causes stress).

Stress is your *body's reaction* to a new situation, or an ongoing situation that seems overwhelming. A **stressor** is the situation or event itself that caused your body to react. Stress can be caused by major life changes and everyday hassles, as well as many other sources. Stressors can be caused by internal factors, such as a negative or suspicious thinking style, or the kind of worry about ongoing life problems that Stephanie was experiencing in our opening vignette. Stressors can also come from external sources, such as "red tape" or bureaucracy at work or school that is outside your control.

major life changes
Changes in your life, such as divorce or a career change, that increase daily hassles, leaving you stressed and worn out.

daily hassles
The daily annoyances, such as getting stuck in traffic or misplacing your keys, that can cause stress in your life.

Life Changes and Daily Hassles

Any change can be stressful, especially **major life changes**. However, according to some stress researchers, the **daily hassles** that everyone experiences can be very stressful as well, possibly even more so because they happen more frequently and seem to pile up on top of one another.[3]

One day you might be rushing out the door for work and you spill coffee on yourself. You set your keys down, run and change your clothes, only to forget where you put your keys. You finally find them, but by now you are late for work. You drive too fast, get pulled over, and receive a speeding ticket. You make it to work and find there is no place left to park. You finally find a space, grab your belongings from the car and run for the office, but in your haste you drop a set of important papers into a nearby mud puddle—and your workday has not even started yet!

DAILY HASSLES
When daily hassles start to pile up, especially early in the day, they can have a strong effect on you. Even though the stress is short term, the build-up of these multiple smaller stressors can be as intense as some types of long-term stress. *How do you deal with those days when nothing seems to go right?*
Jupiterimages/Stockbyte/Getty Images

Major life changes and daily hassles can go hand in hand—especially when major life changes *cause* daily hassles.

Imagine that you have just gotten a divorce. This is a major life change that can lead to many daily hassles you may not have had before. You may have to move, set up a new child care arrangement, take over a larger share of the housework or yard work, open a new bank account, find a new grocery store, explain your situation repeatedly to friends or acquaintances, and so on. These daily hassles can leave you feeling stressed and worn out.

Even if your stress is due to a pleasant change, such as starting college, daily hassles can occur. You may be very excited to begin your new adventure in college, but the little hassles such as finding parking, finding the bookstore, figuring out which books to buy, finding the library, getting your picture taken for your student identification card, locating your classrooms, and standing in line for registration and admissions or figuring out the online application and registration system can leave you feeling drained and stressed—and you haven't even started your first classes yet!

Chronic Stressors

chronic stressors Inescapable, day-to-day situations or conditions that cause stress.

Chronic stressors are inescapable, day-to-day situations or conditions that cause stress. They are more stressful than daily hassles, but not as stressful as a major life change. Things like poverty, ongoing abuse, and long-term health problems are examples of chronic stressors. Being discriminated against because of issues such as race or ethnicity, gender, age, or religion is also a chronic stressor.

In the past few years, researchers have focused attention on the chronic stress of being a member of a minority group. Even when there is no outright evidence of racism, simply being the only member (or one of the few members) of a particular race or ethnic group in a variety of settings such as work or school can cause stress.[4] Similar stressful experiences occur when you are a female in a male-dominant career, or vice versa; when you speak a different first language from your co-workers; when you have a different religious background; and other factors. Diversity issues will be discussed in more detail in Chapter 14.

more about...

Chronic Stress

"We know that chronic stress can take a toll on a person's health. It can make existing health problems worse, and even cause disease, either because of changes in the body or bad habits people develop to cope with stress. The bottom line is that stress can lead to real physical and emotional health consequences," says the executive director for professional practice for the American Psychological Association.

—Katherine C. Nordal, PhD

Source: American Psychological Association, "Stress in America: Coping with Change," February 15, 2017, http://www.apa.org/news/press/releases/stress/2016/coping-with-change.pdf (retrieved June 20, 2017).

» LIFE CHANGES AS STRESSORS

Extreme change can create tremendous stress and is usually accompanied by a great sense of *loss*. This type of change usually involves something coming to an end–perhaps a marriage or close relationship, your friendships in a town you had to leave, or a job that was extremely important to you. But stress-causing events aren't always negative; they could also include marriage (the end of life as a single person), promotion (loss of a lower position which was well within your comfort zone, and the challenge of new responsibilities), or relocation (loss of familiar surroundings, time and effort needed to learn about the new location).

Holmes–Rahe Social Readjustment Rating Scale (SRRS)
A listing of many kinds of changes, rated from 100 to 0 on the basis of their intensity and the adjustment problems they can create.

Figure 12.1 presents the **Holmes–Rahe Social Readjustment Rating Scale (or SRRS)**. This scale, also known as the Holmes and Rahe Stress Scale, lists examples of major changes that people may experience. These are rated from 100 to 0, high to low, on the basis of their intensity and the adjustment problems they can create. Go through the scale as a self-test. You might find more stress-producing changes in your life than you knew.[5]

What does the score on the Holmes and Rahe Stress Scale mean for you, and what should you know about your personal score after calculating it? You may wonder, first, if these scores really can accurately predict a person's chance of becoming ill. Although the scale was created decades ago, in 1967, it has proven surprisingly valid over time and across different groups of people. The scale is a good predictor of upheavals in life being linked to later illness for males and females, across ethnic groups and religions, across age groups, in international comparisons, and even in comparisons of healthy adults and medical patients.[6]

more about...

Control and Stress

"The greatest weapon against stress is our ability to choose one thought over another."
—Psychologist William James (1842–1910)

But does this mean that the disruptions in your life have doomed you to illness? No, not necessarily. High stress does not inevitably cause illness. The Stress Scale has been tested on thousands of people over several decades.[7] But any time we look at research results from large studies, it is important to remember that results are reported across the groups as a whole, and do not necessarily apply at the individual level. Each person who completes the Stress Scale interprets the questions a little differently.

We all have different circumstances, goals, personalities, and values. Most importantly, we all have different coping strategies and resources. Throughout this chapter, one of the most important messages to remember is that *you* control your interpretation of events, and *you* control your coping mechanisms. Effective coping is a learned response to stress. As you complete this chapter, keep your Stress Scale score in mind, and think about how you can re-interpret stress, build up resources to buffer your stress, and learn successful coping strategies to carry with you.

more about...

Stress and Control

"You may not control all the events that happen to you, but you can decide not to be reduced by them."
—Maya Angelou, author (1928–2014)

Life Events	Score
Death of spouse	100
Divorce	73
Marital separation from mate	65
Detention in jail, other institution	63
Death of a close family member	63
Major personal injury or illness	53
Marriage	50
Fired from work	47
Marital reconciliation	45
Retirement	45
Major change in the health or behavior of a family member	44
Pregnancy	40
Sexual difficulties	39
Gaining a new family member (e.g., through birth, adoption, adult moving in, etc.)	39
Major business readjustment (e.g., merger, reorganization, bankruptcy)	39
Major change in financial status	38
Death of close friend	37
Change to different line of work	36
Major change in the number of arguments with spouse	35
Taking out a mortgage or loan for a major purchase	31
Foreclosure on a mortgage or loan	30
Major change in responsibilities at work	29
Son or daughter leaving home (e.g., marriage, attending college)	29
Trouble with in-laws	29
Outstanding personal achievement	28
Spouse beginning or ceasing to work outside the home	26
Beginning or ceasing formal schooling	26
Major change in living conditions	25
Revision of personal habits (dress, manners, associations, etc.)	24
Trouble with boss	23
Major change in working hours or conditions	20
Change in residence	20
Change to a new school	20
Major change in usual type and/or amount of recreation	19
Major change in church activities (a lot more or less than usual)	19
Major change in social activities (clubs, dancing, movies, visiting)	18
Taking out a mortgage or loan for a lesser purchase (e.g., for a car, TV, freezer, etc.)	17
Major change in sleeping habits	16
Major change in the number of family get-togethers	15
Major change in eating habits	15
Vacation	13
Christmas or major holiday season	12
Minor violations of the law (e.g., traffic tickets, etc.)	11
Total	

Scoring

Less than 150 life change units	30 percent chance of developing a stress-related illness in the next two years
150–299 life change units	50 percent chance of illness in the next two years
Over 300 life change units	80 percent chance of illness in the next two years

figure 12.1

THE HOLMES–RAHE READJUSTMENT SCALE

Read through this scale, and take it as a self-test. Look for events that have happened either to you or to someone close to you. *What does your score show?*

Source: Adapted from T. H. Holmes and R. H. Rahe, "The Social Readjustment Rating Scale," *Journal of Psychosomatic Research* (Pergamon Press, Ltd., 1967), pp. 217–218.

more about...

Stress in College

"Living a stress-free life is not a reasonable goal. The goal is to deal with it actively and effectively."
—Stanford psychiatrist David Spiegel

» SOURCES OF STRESS

In addition to studying major life changes, daily hassles, and chronic stress, psychologists studying causes of stress have identified specific internal and external sources of it in people's lives. While some of these sources of stress are out of your control, remember that your response to these stressors is much more within your control than you may realize.

external stressors
Stressors that include anything from outside sources that causes you pain and discomfort.

frustration
The feeling people get when goals they are trying to attain are blocked.

External Stressors

According to psychologists, **external stressors** generally include those outside sources that cause you pain or discomfort, frustration, or conflict.[8]

1. *Pain or discomfort.* Chronic or even temporary pain can make you feel stressed and lower your job performance. Think of the last time you had a bad toothache or headache and how much that interfered with your concentration. Discomfort (even something as minor as the workroom being too hot or too cold) can have a negative effect on you as well.
2. *Frustration.* The feeling you get when a goal you are trying to attain is blocked defines **frustration**. For example, you might feel frustrated when a co-worker takes credit for your creative ideas, or members of your class project team take credit for your research.
3. *Inner conflict.* Chapter 11 introduced several ways of thinking about conflict. In this chapter, we will examine one of those in more detail, as a source of stress: **inner conflict**. Inner conflict is the kind of pressure you feel when you are forced to make a choice. Even though you feel it internally, it is considered an external stressor because the *source* of this conflict comes from outside. This type of conflict is the feeling you get when you are torn in two or more directions.

MANY SOURCES OF STRESS
Stress can be caused by many different factors: both positive and negative major life changes, as well as smaller everyday problems. *Do you have different ways of dealing with different kinds of stress, whether in the workplace or in your personal life?*
fStop/Getty Images

We all experience several kinds of inner conflict. These include approach-approach, approach-avoid, and avoid-avoid conflict. The first of these, approach-approach, is the feeling of conflict you get when torn between two desirable goals. For example, you may really like your job and enjoy your co-workers, but when offered a promotion, you are also excited about the prospect of making more money. You want to stay in your current job and spend time with your friends at work, but you also want the promotion that would give you more money. You can't have both at the same time.

An approach-avoid conflict occurs when you are drawn toward and away from something at the same time. For example, you may really want that promotion, but it would mean transferring to another state, and you are reluctant to pull up stakes and start over again somewhere else. If you stay, you make less money; if you go, you have the enormous task of moving to another state. Deciding either way causes a push-pull of the approach-avoid conflict.

An avoid-avoid conflict occurs when you are torn between two *un*desirable options. For example, you may not get along with your supervisor and you may dread going to work each day, but at the same time you hate the idea of pounding the pavement looking for a new job. Or you may not want to tackle the huge project assigned in a class, but you do not want the "F" that would result from not turning it in.

Internal Stressors

According to psychologists, **internal stressors** can include your own perceptions or interpretations of a stressor, as well as personality factors.[10] (See Figure 12.2 for examples of both external and internal stressors.)

Every person has a different perception of the same situation or stressor. A major problem to one person may be an exciting challenge to another. Let's take the example of a common event in the business world since the 1980s–downsizing. Two middle managers who are laid off may see their situations quite differently: one sees the layoff as a chance for a new start creating his own business as an entrepreneur, whereas the other sees it as a terrible personal and professional disaster that is unrecoverable. What makes each of them perceive the same events differently? Two basic internal factors are their cognitive appraisal of each situation and their individual personality factors.

Cognitive Appraisal

Cognitive appraisal can be thought of as your "thinking evaluation" of an event or a situation. In the process of making a **cognitive appraisal**, you unconsciously ask yourself two questions. The first one is: *Is this stressor harmful to me in any way?* If the answer to that question is yes, then you also ask yourself: *Do I have the resources (time, energy, and so on) to handle this stressor?* If the answer to that question is no, then you feel stress. These questions and responses are processed in a fraction of a second, usually faster than you are aware.

more about...

Stress in College

College is easily one of life's ultimate stressors. The demands placed upon students to constantly perform at a high academic level, to work constructively with peers from different backgrounds in the classroom and on group projects, to manage the constant barrage of work assignments and tests, and to manage the financial demands of attending college—all while trying to balance a healthy lifestyle outside of academics—can be daunting.

But without some stress, people would not get as much done. The extra burst of adrenaline that helps you finish your final paper, or put the finishing touches on a big project assignment, or prepare for an important exam, is positive stress. In this case, the stress is a short-term physiological tension that promotes mental alertness. Researchers at the University of California, Berkeley, have found that short bursts of stress lasting a few minutes to a few hours can actually be good for you. According to Professor Daniela Kaufer, "Some amounts of stress are good to push you just to your level of optimal alertness, behavioral and cognitive performance." Short bursts of stress push your creativity and productivity. "You always think about stress as a really bad thing, but it's not," says Kaufer.[9]

If you are unable to return to a relaxed state, however, the stress can become negative. Over time, the cumulative changes in your body that stress can cause (such as increased heart rate and blood pressure, and muscle tension) may take their toll on your health and cause you mental and physical exhaustion, and short-term or chronic illness. It is unrealistic to think that we can do away with stress, but identifying it and managing it actively and effectively is key!

inner conflict

Conflict within an individual; it might involve values, loyalties, or priorities; the pressure you feel when you are forced to make a choice.

figure 12.2

EXTERNAL AND INTERNAL SOURCES OF STRESS (EXAMPLES)

Source: Singapore Institute of Mental Health (updated 2012). "Overcoming Stress," Institute of Mental Health, National Healthcare Group, https://www.imh.com.sg/wellness/page.aspx?id=558 (retrieved 6/7/2020).

External	Internal
Bureaucracy, deadlines	Suspicious outlook, over-analyzing situations
Financial problems	Negative thinking and negative self-talk
Unemployment	Chronic worry, dread, depression
Poor health	Poor social skills, poor health habits
Relationship issues	Shy or unassertive personality
School pressures	Aggressive or bossy personality
Problems in the workplace	Hostile, impatient, time-urgent
Loss (grief, bereavement)	Overly competitive, perfectionist
Daily hassles	Calm outside, agitated inside
Unexpected bad news	Poor time management
Organizational rules, policies, red tape	Poor lifestyle choices (lack of sleep, smoking, overeating, etc.)
Physical environment (heat, noise, etc.)	Self-critical, take things personally
Behavior of others (rude, bossy, etc.)	Unrealistic expectations, all-or-nothing thinking, rigid thinking
Major life changes	

internal stressors

Your perceptions of stressors, which may vary depending on personality.

cognitive appraisal

The thinking evaluation of an event or situation that varies from person to person and, for an individual, from day to day.

DEALING WITH EXTERNAL STRESSORS
Stress can be caused by external factors that are both ordinary and out of your control, ranging from an uncomfortable environment to frustration and conflict. *How do you manage the stress caused by factors beyond your control?*
Ingram Publishing

Cognitive appraisal varies not only from person to person, but from day to day with the same person or the same situation. What makes you spend some mornings in rush-hour traffic cursing and shaking your fist at other drivers, while you spend other mornings during the same traffic-filled commute singing along with the radio, smiling with empathy at other drivers? Part of the answer lies in the number of daily hassles you experience: the more stressors you encounter, the more annoyed you feel at new stressors and the more difficulty you have adapting to them. Sometimes you may feel a particular situation is potentially harmful; at other times you may not. Sometimes you *do* feel you have the energy (a resource) to handle a particular situation, but at other times you just *don't* have the energy.

Another part of the answer to why cognitive appraisal varies so much lies in the individual internal factors that make each person unique. Here is a closer look at another specific type of internal factor, the irrational belief system.

Irrational Beliefs

Albert Ellis, a well-known psychologist, argued that one of the internal causes of stress (i.e., stress that you put on yourself) is an **irrational belief system.**[11] These irrational beliefs include such things as believing that everyone must like you, or that you must never make mistakes. At worst, some people **catastrophize**, or turn an irrational belief into an imagined catastrophe. For example, let's say that in Zena's weekly department meeting, her co-worker made a remark that sounded innocent enough, but which made

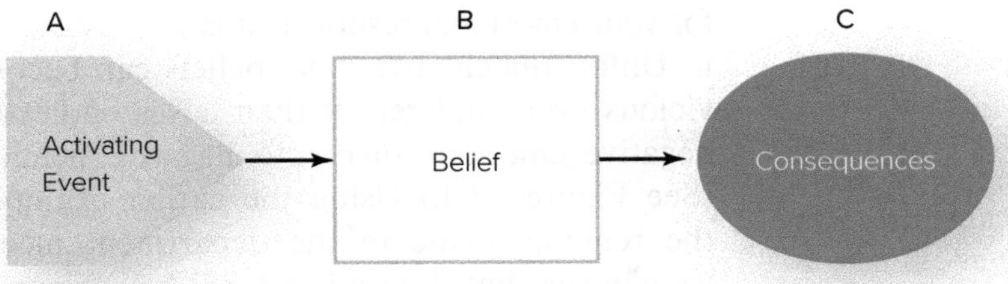

figure 12.3

ELLIS'S ABC APPROACH TO STRESS

This ABC formula illustrates how stress develops inside of people. An *activating event* triggers people to form a *belief* about it, which in turn shapes the *consequences. How much can your beliefs affect the outcome of stressful situations?*

irrational belief system

A way of thinking that causes internal stress by substituting a realistic belief with one that is destructive, illogical, and largely false.

catastrophize

To turn an irrational belief into an imagined disaster.

the co-worker look very industrious, while it made Zena look a little incompetent: "I noticed that Zena wasn't able to finish the accounts receivable forms in time to ship out yesterday, so I went ahead and finished those up last night. You can thank me by buying me lunch, Zena!" Other people in the meeting just smile or chuckle, but Zena is thinking, "I will never make a good impression with these people. I am never going to get ahead in this company. I'll probably just get demoted for the rest of my life. And I can't work anywhere else, because no one here will give me a good recommendation. I might even get fired. They'll probably turn my friends and family against me too, because they won't want to be around me after I get fired. Why can't I ever do anything right?" Zena turned one event into a catastrophe with her irrational beliefs.

According to Ellis, it can be understandable to believe things should turn out better than they actually do. However, it is irrational to *expect* that they will, and irrational to believe that you cannot survive unless they do. Ellis believed that not just stressors themselves, but also people's *beliefs* about stressors, are sources of stress. Using an example in which your supervisor asks you to redo some work, take a closer look at Ellis's ABC approach to stress in Figure 12.3. In this idea, the A stands for an *activating event*–in this case, being asked to do the work over again. The B stands for your *belief* about the activating event–in this case, the irrational beliefs that arise from having to redo the work. The C stands for the *consequences* of the eventual outcome caused by the activating event and your beliefs about it–in this case, the anxiety and misery you feel, and the behavior resulting from those feelings.

Irrational beliefs, then, can lead to catastrophizing an event–a stressor–or blowing it out of proportion. This makes you less able to cope with it, which in turn makes you less able to solve the problem and adds more stress. The biggest culprit in your emotional stress and anxiety, according to Ellis, is the B (or belief) part of the ABC. It is not the event itself that is responsible

more about...

Stress in the United States

The 2020 results of the American Psychological Association's annual survey on stress in the United States found that stress levels have risen in the "time of Covid-19" compared with previous years. The 2020 results find the highest increase in reported stress since the annual survey began in 2007. Stress levels have risen in the past decade, but much more stress has been reported in all aspects of life since the onset of the coronavirus, when compared with earlier years.

The effects of the pandemic are expected to last well into the future, causing serious and long-term impacts on individuals' physical and mental health, education, and employment. The ways in which we work, go to school, and interact with others will continue to evolve, requiring a willingness to adapt to change under stressful conditions. A small example: up to 88% of adults now take normal, routine prevention measures against communicable disease such as Covid-19. This has led to an increase in mask wearing in public spaces and the workplace, and formalized some of the "social distancing" discussed previously in Chapter 6.

Americans are also reporting more stress related to political divisiveness and tension. The survey found that frustration, fear, and anger are on the rise, with an increase in respondents reporting stress related to systemic racism and police actions. Adding to the nation's stress is a degree of political and economic unpredictability that has increased in our society.

Findings from surveys in 2020 with more than 3,000 adults of all ages and varied racial, ethnic, language, and political groups show that Covid-related stress was overwhelming other, more "traditional" stressors. At the time of the survey, respondents reported:

- The **future of our nation** is a significant source of stress (83%), with the majority of those surveyed (72%) responding that this is the **lowest point in history that they can remember.**
- The **coronavirus pandemic** itself is a source of stress (80%).
- Worry is high for **family members or self contracting the coronavirus** (74%).
- Parents report higher stress levels than adults without children, including stress over **basic needs** and **online education, social-emotional development,** and **behavior;** and worry about the **pandemic's long-term effects** on their children (71%).
- Regardless of political party or geographic location, adults report stress related to the **government's response to the pandemic** (about 64%–85%).
- The national **economy** and individual **work** are also sources of stress (70%).
- African-Americans report an increase in stress due to **discrimination** (71%), and believe it is a **difficult time to be a person of color** in today's society (78%).
- More than half of respondents (60%) reported stress from **police violence toward minorities,** as well as stress from **protests over police violence** (60%), and the **government's response to the protests** (64%).
- The majority of respondents, more than 70%, reported stress over the **unpredictability in our nation** and the **current political climate.**

for your emotional response; it is your belief about it. Unfortunately, irrational beliefs can become a vicious cycle and repeat themselves endlessly as negative emotions turn into negative behaviors. (See Figure 12.4.) Using the earlier example of the remarks made in the department meeting, we can see that Zena's irrational beliefs can lead to depression and anxiety, and these lead to low motivation and low energy, which can make her less likely to finish other projects in the future. This just repeats the cycle until she says, "I was right; I can't do this job at all. What's the point of even trying?" And the eventual outcome is that she quits trying.

Is there any hope for reducing the stress of irrational beliefs? Yes, according to Ellis. You can try to reduce the stress of irrational beliefs by changing them yourself, using his principles of "rational-emotive therapy" to improve your own belief system and replace irrational beliefs with more rational ones. In a nutshell, this means changing the B of the ABC. Strategy for Success 12.1 explains this in more detail.

Technology

Is technology itself a stressor? In today's modern world, it is nearly impossible to "unplug," that is, to turn off technology. How much does our connection to technology, including social media, add to our stress levels? Regarding research results: it's complicated.

Technology allows us to stay connected with others for social support. When social media posts are directed to us personally from people we care about, well-being improves. But when ties with others and communication from posts are weak, such as one-click "likes" or photo views, well-being is not improved, and envy and resentment can result. Young adults and adolescents can feel both more connected and very lonely when they rely on social media for personal relationships. Young adults and adolescents are also more likely to experience the stress of cyberbullying than older groups, and they experience this type of bullying more often than in-person bullying.[15]

Harm from technology becomes worse when use is excessive. Using popular social media platforms more than two hours a day is linked to social isolation. Depression, stress, and anxiety can rise when people, especially young adults and teens, rely on social media to express themselves and build their identity, but find that negative feedback erodes their feelings of self-worth. Excessive use of social media is also linked with higher rates of alcohol and drug abuse and eating disorders. The absolute volume of information coming through social media can be overwhelming, adding to stress levels.[16]

Can social networking overuse become an addiction? Many social scientists say it can. "Social network users risk becoming more and more addicted to social media platforms even as they experience stress from their use," say researchers at Lancaster University. The researchers find that when stress from technology use builds, people do not turn it off–they usually just move to a different activity on the same platform.[17] Rather than coping, use becomes even more excessive. How common is this type of addiction? Estimates are 5 to 10 percent of us meet the definition, including an uncontrollable urge to use social media, to the point of interfering with other aspects of our lives.[18] Fortunately, treatment is available, and people can return to normal usage and a healthier, less stressful connection with technology.

Technology is here to stay. Digital devices have made our lives easier in countless ways. But as with any tool, a good understanding of it is essential. The American Psychological Association reminds us that to be good consumers of technology, we need to:

1. *Never use phones when behind the wheel.*
2. *Turn off devices to get enough sleep.*
3. *Turn notifications off, check when you have time.*
4. *Manage your expectations online.*
5. *Make good choices with social media.*
6. *Be present in the moment rather than online at all times.*
7. *Take time to unplug and restore yourself.*[19]

How do survey results on stress in the United States differ from 2019 to 2020?

- In 2019, top sources of stress named included **mass shootings** (71%) and **health care** (69%).
- The **political climate** (62%) was named as a stressor, with more than half (56%) of respondents believing this is the lowest point in our nation's history.
- **Work** (64%) and **money** (60%) were also named as significant stressors.
- Additional stressors named include **terrorist acts** (64%)**, violence and crime** (64%)**, climate change** (56%), and **sexual harassment** (45%).
- **Immigration** as an issue was listed as a stressor (48%), as was the wish that respondents could do more to **help immigrants** (58%).
- **Discrimination** was listed as a stressor for one fourth of respondents (24%), but the majority of respondents of color named discrimination as a stressor (63%).
- The majority of respondents (72%) agreed that **the media** blows things out of proportion, and more than half (54%) say they want to follow the news but it causes them stress.
- On a more positive note, respondents understand the **value of social support** in reducing stress, with three in five (59%) saying they would like more support.

Sources: American Psychological Association, "Stress in America 2019,™ November 2019, https://www.apa.org/news/press/releases/stress/2019/stress-america-2019.pdf (retrieved April 4, 2020).

American Psychological Association, "Stress in the Time of COVID-19, Vol. 1," (May 2020). https://www.apa.org/news/press/releases/stress/2020/stress-in-america-covid.pdf (retrieved Oct. 1, 2020).

American Psychological Association, "Stress in the Time of COVID-19, Vol. 2," (June 2020). https://www.apa.org/news/press/releases/stress/2020/stress-in-america-covid-june.pdf (retrieved Oct. 1, 2020).

American Psychological Association, "Stress in the Time of COVID-19, Vol. 3," (July 2020). https://www.apa.org/news/press/releases/stress/2020/stress-in-america-covid-july.pdf

REAL WORLD EXAMPLE 12.1

A working mother was having a rough morning, full of hassles and feeling overwhelmed. Rushing to finish breakfast with her son, she spilled her coffee on her black sweater. Her young son said to her, "Mommy, you should always wear black clothes, because then no one can see the coffee you spill on yourself and you don't have to change your clothes." Children have a way of seeing our stressors with a fresh perspective!

figure 12.4

IRRATIONAL BELIEFS AND STRESS

Irrational beliefs can cripple people facing stress because they make them fear outcomes that do not actually exist. Most of these irrational beliefs take situations to extremes—even though that can create more problems and stress. *What are your irrational beliefs, and what do they do to your stress level?*

Ten Irrational Beliefs

Although everyone has irrational beliefs, according to Albert Ellis (1913–2007), each person has a different set of them. Ten of the most common irrational beliefs can be summarized as follows. As you read this list, ask yourself (honestly!) how many of them you believe or have you believed.

Irrational belief #1:	I must have love or approval from all of the people who are important to me.
Irrational belief #2:	I must prove myself to be thoroughly competent, adequate, and achieving at something important.
Irrational belief #3:	When people act obnoxiously or unfairly, they should be blamed for being bad, rotten, or wicked individuals.
Irrational belief #4:	When I am seriously frustrated, treated unfairly, or rejected, I must view the situation as awful, terrible, horrible, and catastrophic.
Irrational belief #5:	Emotional misery comes from external pressures and I have little ability to control or change my feelings.
Irrational belief #6:	If something seems dangerous or fearsome, I must preoccupy myself with it and make myself anxious about it.
Irrational belief #7:	It is better to avoid facing my difficulties and responsibilities than it is to use self-discipline to obtain rewarding things.
Irrational belief #8:	My past experiences remain all-important. Since something once strongly influenced my life, it has to keep determining my feelings and behavior today.
Irrational belief #9:	It is awful and horrible if I do not find good solutions to life's grim realities.
Irrational belief #10:	I can achieve maximum happiness by inertia or inaction or by passively and uncommittedly "enjoying myself."[12]

type A and type B personalities

Two standard personality-related sets of behaviors. Type A behaviors are characterized by impatience, hostility, perfectionism, and a sense of time urgency. Type B behaviors are characterized by flexibility, the ability to relax and delegate work, and a minimal sense of time urgency.

» TYPE A AND TYPE B PERSONALITY BEHAVIOR

So far in this discussion of the internal stressors, you have examined cognitive appraisal and irrational belief systems. Turn your attention now to the third type of internal stressor, personality factors—also known as **type A and type B personalities**.

This personality theory has become so popular that most people are already familiar with it. According to this theory, people can be categorized into either of these two personality types on the basis of their behaviors and personality styles. Type A people are seen as impatient, hostile perfectionists with a sense of time urgency. Type B people are more relaxed.

The danger of being like Marco in Real World Example 12.2 is that type A people seem more likely to have cardiovascular problems such as heart attacks and strokes. Type B people, on the other hand, are more flexible, more relaxed, better able to delegate work, and less time-urgent.[20] Two bits of folk wisdom are sometimes heard about type A and type B people in the workplace. The first is that top-level executives are likely to be type Bs, with type A assistants frantically running around doing their work for them. This is because type Bs can delegate responsibility, whereas type As are such perfectionists that they have to do all the work themselves and will never get to the top because of this. The second thing heard about types A and B is that the road to becoming a CEO is paved with the dead bodies of type As (presumably dead from heart attacks), with type Bs stepping over the bodies on their way to the top.

Although the type A and type B personality idea has been very popular in recent years, psychologists now say it may not be as useful as originally thought. People are not so simply categorized. They may act like a type A one day and a type B the next, or with some issues they act like one type and with other issues the other type. In addition, they may act like one type on the outside but feel completely different inside. The best point to learn from the type A/type B personality theory and stress debate is that it is most important for people to examine their *behaviors*. The truth seems to be that the behaviors of constant anger (sometimes called *toxic hostility*) and, to a lesser extent, time urgency (sometimes called *hurry sickness*) probably have worse health effects than does an overall personality type.[21]

If you recognized yourself in the risky type A behavior profile, relax! These behaviors are just habits; they don't have to be permanent. Later in this chapter you will examine ways to change behavior, or cope with stress in a healthy way. If your behaviors are more

more about...

Survivor Guilt

Research on the *survivors* of mass layoffs and downsizing (i.e., those who kept their jobs) has found that these employees can at times suffer more stress effects than the *victims* of layoffs. Survivors have reported feeling more stress, less control on the job, lower job satisfaction, and "survivor guilt," along with poorer health and quality of life than victims of layoffs who later found jobs. Survivors also missed work more often and reported more drug use. Surveys with survivors of 74 percent report reduced productivity after layoffs of their colleagues.[13]

What can companies do to reduce this guilt? Communicate daily with staff members. Focus on issues within your control. Avoid assigning tasks or meetings that waste time. Focus on meaningful work that adds value to customer service and safety.[14]

more about...

Are You a "Constant Checker?"

An annual survey conducted by the American Psychological Association found that more than four out of five American adults say they check their e-mail, texts, and social media accounts often or constantly. These "constant checkers" also are more likely to experience higher levels of stress. Regarding these "constant checkers," researcher Lynn Bufka says that "while technology helps us in many ways, being constantly connected can have a negative impact on both their physical and mental health." Her recommendation? Take time to unplug. Taking a periodic "digital detox" can reduce the stress of the ever-present technology in our lives.

American Psychological Association, "APA's Survey Finds Constantly Checking Electronic Devices Linked to Significant Stress for Most Americans," February 23, 2017, https://www.apa.org/news/press/releases/2017/02/checking-devices (retrieved April 4, 2020).

REAL WORLD EXAMPLE 12.2

Marco shows type A personality behaviors. He walks and eats quickly and combines two or more tasks to save time. He finishes other people's sentences for them, finishes other people's work if he feels they are too slow, and feels guilty when he is not busy. He also becomes extremely irritated when having to wait for anything such as a traffic light, a dentist appointment, or a meeting.

more about...

Time Urgency

In the final words of Queen Elizabeth I (1533–1603), "All my possessions for a moment of time."

relaxed than hostile, don't gloat! Too much of a good thing is a problem, as well—people who are overly relaxed, to the point of having depressive personalities, also have an increased risk of disease.

To find out if you fit into a type A or a type B personality behavior profile, take the test at the end of the chapter (see Working It Out 12.1). Remember, these are just *behaviors,* which can be changed. Behaviors are not some unchangeable aspect of personality that has been set in stone.

hardy personality

A resilient personality type, characterized by the ability to meet challenges, a sense of commitment, and a feeling of being in control of life.

You may know someone with a different kind of personality than type A or type B, someone who just seems to be a *survivor.* This type of person, in spite of stressors and problems that seem impossible to overcome, manages just fine. Why are some people in stressful situations able to come out smiling, while others fail? Suzanne Kobasa and others in the past three decades have been studying what they call the **hardy personality**, or resilient personality.[22]

Regardless of the situation, people with a resilient personality seem to have three things in common—the "three Cs" of a hardy personality: challenge, commitment, and control. Where others see terrible problems to overcome, they see *challenges* to meet. People with a hardy personality also have a sense of *commitment.* It doesn't matter to what; it could be to their jobs, education, a religion, a political cause, to raising their children, or to a healthier lifestyle for themselves. They just feel a sense of purpose or a mission in life. Finally, they feel that they are in *control* of their lives and in charge of what happens to them, instead of seeing themselves as passive beings with no say in the course of their own lives. This is the idea of the "internal locus of control" introduced in Chapter 2.

HOLDING ON TO SELF-DEFEATING BELIEFS
An important step in getting rid of irrational beliefs is to dispute, or argue against, beliefs that sabotage your ability to stay calm in stressful situations. Think about your beliefs; if any are self-defeating, eliminate them. *How can you get rid of self-defeating beliefs?*
Angela Waye/Alamy Stock Photo

» THE PHYSICAL EFFECTS OF STRESS

You can see that stress can have more than just emotional and psychological effects. It can also have serious, even life-threatening, physical effects. To reduce the harmful effects of stress, you need to understand how this process works.

How Our Bodies Adapt to Stress

In his book *The Stress of Life,* Hans Selye developed and tested a theory about what stress does to people physically. He called it the *general adaptation syndrome,* or GAS. According to this theory, when you are first confronted with a stressor, your body responds with an activation of the sympathetic nervous system. This has come to be known as the *fight-or-flight response.* During the fight-or-flight response, your body quickly (in a matter of seconds) gets ready to confront or to escape the stressor by specific physical and chemical reactions. These include increased heart rate, blood pressure, respiration, stomach acid, tensed muscles, and a sudden release of adrenaline. When the fight-or-flight response is activated, according to Selye, you have entered the first stage of GAS, the *alarm stage.*[23] (See Figure 12.5.)

Once the alarm is sounded, you enter the second stage of GAS, the *stage of adaptation.* You adapt to the stressor and can usually return to normal. As you try to restore lost energy and repair any damage done to your body, your sympathetic nervous system is still activated, but not at the high level it was during the alarm stage. As you successfully cope with the stressor, you activate your parasympathetic nervous system. Heart rate, blood pressure, respiration, and muscles then relax. Most of the time, people at this stage are able to cope with the stressor and soon return to normal.

In some cases, though, you are not able to adapt to a stressor and can end up using up (or exhausting) all of your physical resources. You then enter the third stage of GAS, the *stage of exhaustion.* During this stage, the

LEARNING FROM THE OTHER SIDE

Neither a type A nor a type B personality is free from stress. They both deal with stress in different ways, with benefits and risks to each method. *Why is it important to learn from the opposite type if you classify yourself according to this personality theory? What can you learn by observing others who act differently under stress than you do?*

RuslanDashinsky/iStock/Getty Images

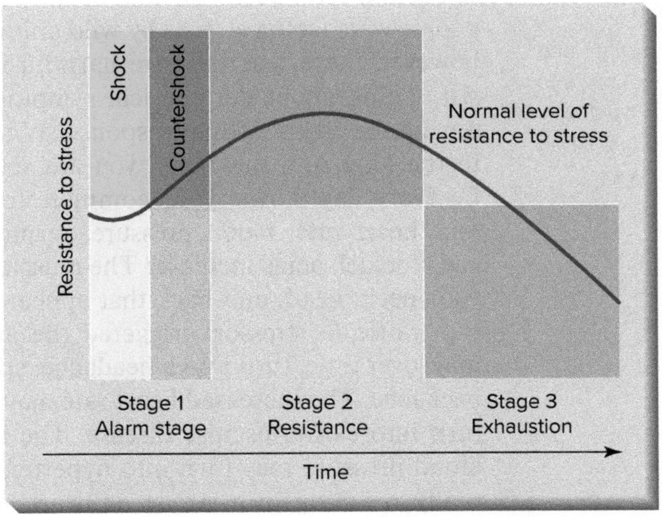

figure 12.5

SEYLE'S GENERAL ADAPTATION SYNDROME

Source: John W. Santrock, *Adolescence,* 7e (New York: The McGraw-Hill Companies, Inc., 1996).

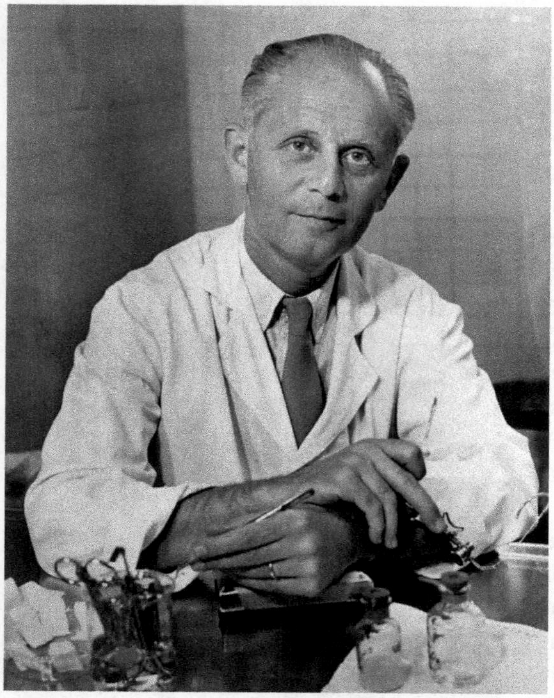

HANS SELYE

Bettmann/Contributor/Getty Images

parasympathetic nervous system is still activated, so you appear relaxed, but the stressor is still present. In this stage, you are unable to cope with the prolonged stressor, and you can become vulnerable to other stressors.

As the school term nears an end, for example, stress increases so that during final exams week many students are using up all their stored energy and physical resources. By the end of the term, students have completely used up their energy and resources, and they enter the stage of exhaustion. Then, instead of enjoying the break between terms, they may wind up catching a cold or the flu, or becoming accident-prone. The same thing can happen at work when employees exhaust themselves trying to get everything finished and out of the way before they go on vacation. Instead of enjoying vacation time, they get sick!

Selye would say these students and employees have succumbed to a *disease of adaptation.* In the most extreme cases, people exposed to prolonged stress may even die. You may know of a case where an elderly friend or relative fell and broke a hip (because balance declines and bones get more brittle with age), entered the hospital for treatment of the broken hip, and died soon thereafter of pneumonia or heart failure. According to Selye's theory of GAS, if the stress of healing the broken hip was prolonged, then the patient entered the stage of exhaustion and fell victim to a disease of adaptation (pneumonia or heart failure).

According to Selye, extreme responses to stress may have been essential in early times when people were facing attacks by wild animals. Today, however, these reactions are harmful if they persist. Think about the physical symptoms present during the fight-or-flight response. What happens in the long run, say, when you are stuck in traffic every day during your commute to work and your heart rate, blood pressure, respiration rate, and stomach acids increase? The muscle tension in your neck, head, and back that appeared because the traffic (a stressor) triggered the alarm stage may, over time, turn into a headache, stiff neck, or backache. The increased heart rate may eventually turn into cardiovascular disease. The increase in blood pressure may turn into hypertension, eventually resulting in a stroke or heart attack. The

more about...

Hans Selye (1907–1982) was a Canadian doctor and medical educator who pioneered research on different types of stress. He began his studies on stress in 1926, during his second year in medical school. He co-founded the Canadian Institute of Stress in 1979, which is still active today, offering training programs and consultations for workplaces and individuals, and reporting findings on stress research. His classic book, *The Stress of Life,* was originally published in 1956 and has been revised over the years.

more about...

Taking Charge

"It is not stress that kills us, it is our reaction to it."
– Hans Selye

increase in stomach acid may turn into heartburn, indigestion, or ulcers.

Remember that in Selye's theory, eustress (stress from positive events) and distress (stress from negative events) both produce the physical and chemical changes of the fight-or-flight response because your body cannot tell the difference between the two. Imagine a friend telling you, for example, that he wasn't able to sleep, had no appetite, felt dizzy and lightheaded, and couldn't concentrate. Without any more information, would you guess that he was coming down with the flu or falling in love? Events that you interpret as good or bad can produce the same physical reactions. They are both stressors because they make demands on your body to adapt or to change. As you have learned, it is adapting to change that is stressful.

Although Selye's original book is more than 60 years old, its theories are supported even more today by the work of health psychologists and medical researchers who study long-term effects of stress and the relationship of stress to the immune system.

In a "meta-analysis" (a study of studies) made public in 2004, researchers examined the results of almost 300 studies that took place over a 40-year span (1960–2000) and included almost 20,000 people. What they found supported Selye's ideas about the GAS's stages of alarm, resistance, and exhaustion. In the short term, stress gets the immune system "revved up" and ready to fight the stressor. In the long term, though, chronic stress wears down the immune system, and immunity begins to break down. This long-term wear and tear makes the immune system much less able to fight new stressors as they come along, or handle continuing stressors. Not surprisingly, these researchers also found that people who were at risk—for example, who were elderly or already ill—had the worst outcomes. This research reminds us of the importance of keeping stressors in check, and finding ways to manage the possible damage of long-term, chronic stress.[24]

more about...

Stressors . . . or Situations?

As one woman said during her treatment for cancer, "Stop feeling sorry for me! I'm not *dying of* cancer, I'm just *living with* cancer!" This rethinking of her diagnosis, she says, helped her fight the disease and eventually recover.

more about...

Adding Fuel to the Fire

Researchers found that one reason people with type A behaviors are more susceptible to coronary artery disease is that they are also more likely to smoke and to eat high-cholesterol fast foods. Reducing stress and learning to relax may reduce the "need" to smoke, and the "need" to buy prepared food rather than cooking nutritious meals, both of which then reduce the risk of heart disease.

Source: From *The Harvard Heart Letter*, President and Fellows of Harvard College, January 1992, p. 104.

Stress and the Immune System

The immune system serves three basic functions. Briefly, these include:

1. Recognizing foreign cells and attacking them.
2. Developing antibodies to recognize foreign invaders in the future.
3. Sending white blood cells and other helper cells to the location of an injury or infection to speed healing.

INCREASE HEALTH BY DECREASING STRESS
By paying attention to factors such as nutrition, exercise, and proper sleep, you can avoid the debilitating long-term effects of most types of stress. *What do you do to strengthen your body against stress?*

Samuel Borges Photography/Shutterstock

Just by having chronic stress, you can actually weaken your immune system and fall victim to an illness that you would normally fight off with ease.

Medical research is finding evidence that even serious chronic illnesses such as cancer are linked to stress as well. Because your immune system is weakened by stress, anything from the common cold to an uncommon cancer is more likely to invade when you are under stress for long periods of time. Other stress-related illnesses can include asthma, ulcers, colitis, skin disorders such as eczema or hives, allergies, strokes, and heart attacks.

Medical research suggests that the effects of stress can strike back as long as 20 years later or even longer. Men who were highly anxious in middle age, studies show, are much more likely 20 years later to have high blood pressure than men who had a calmer outlook on life. Additionally, researchers have found a link between adverse childhood experiences (abuse, neglect, domestic violence) and chronic stress-related health problems (heart disease, obesity, premature death) decades later.[25]

figure 12.6

REDUCING WORKPLACE STRESS

Managers can do a lot to reduce stress in their work environments. The key elements are clear, positive communication and "leading by example" by handling stressful situations with calmness and fairness. *What can your current (or most recent) manager do to reduce stress at his or her workplace?*

Source: Sigmund Ginsberg, "Reducing the Stress You Cause Others," *Supervisory Management* 35 (December 1990), p. 5. See also: Christina Maslach and Michael P. Leiter, "Take This Job and Love It," *Psychology Today*, September/October 1999.

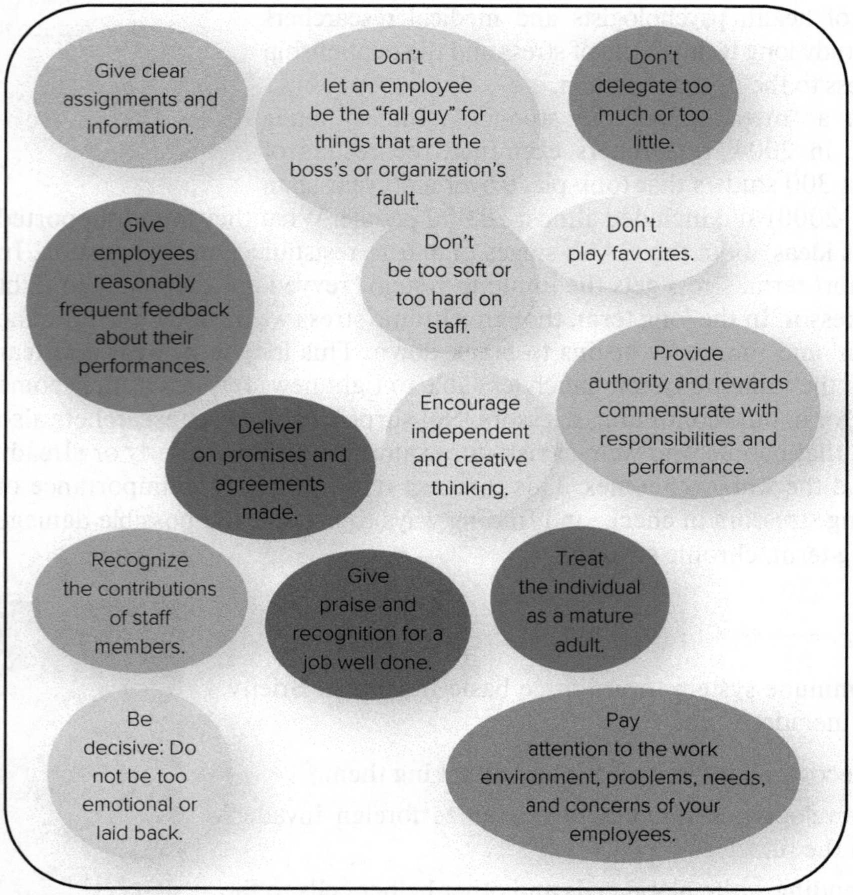

You can probably recognize the fight-or-flight feelings of immediate stressors, but how can you know when you are overstressed? Take the stress self-test in Working It Out 12.2 to find out how much stress you are under. Then review the stress reduction techniques in Strategies for Success 12.2 for ideas that may help you reduce stress levels.

How can you recognize excessive stress in other people? Researchers have found that people under stress may act restless, impatient, competitive, and pressured. They may have had recent changes in work or personal lives that would help explain the excessive stress.[26] See Figure 12.6 for ways managers can reduce workplace stress.

more about...

The Connection between Chronic Stress and Mental Illness

Researchers at the University of California, Berkeley, have found that chronic stress produces long-term changes in the brain that make people more likely to develop anxiety and mood disorders later in their lives, including PTSD (post-traumatic stress disorder). Researchers are still investigating exactly what these changes are, and how these stress levels result in mental illness. Researcher Daniela Kaufman believes one possible explanation is that the connections in the brain that lead to an "alarm" response are strengthened over time with stress, unintentionally strengthening these pathways and making the stress response more likely to occur. The link between chronic stress and physical illness is well documented, and the new direction of research into the link between chronic stress and mental illness will bring an even greater understanding of the damage caused by stress.

Source: Robert Sanders, "New Evidence That Chronic Stress Predisposes the Brain to Mental Illness," *Berkeley News*, February 11, 2014, http://news.berkeley.edu/2014/02/11/chronic-stress-predisposes-brain-to-mental-illness.

» THE COST OF STRESS IN THE WORKPLACE

In this chapter, we have focused on the effects of stress at the individual level. However, there are enormous costs to business and to society because of stress, as well. According to the American Institute of Stress, stress-related problems cost the American economy more than $300 billion every year![27] These costs are an estimate based on lower productivity due to stress, lost days of work, worker's compensation claims, health insurance and healthcare costs, stress management programs, and lawsuits that are a result of stress-related illness or injuries.

The American Institute of Stress has also found in a survey of 800,000 workers in over 300 companies that more than *one million* workers are absent every day due to stress. Estimates are that 550 million lost days of work in the United States each year are due to stress, and one in five of all last minute no-shows are due to job stress. This causes a domino effect across productivity for any companies involved. The annual price tag on stress-related absences for large employers is nearly $3.5 million annually.[28]

Employees increasingly report stress-related headaches, back pain, exhaustion, anxiety, anger, insomnia, and digestive upsets from their jobs. Close to 90 percent of visits to the doctor are for stress-related symptoms. Up to 80 percent of industrial accidents are blamed on stress. In a survey of employees' stress-related symptoms, most employees reported feeling at least three symptoms. About one-fifth of those surveyed had missed work because of stress, and one-third had thought about quitting as a way of relieving stress. Some conditions on the job that employees reported as stressful included crowding, noise, air pollution, poor lighting, and uncomfortable temperatures.[29]

Employees also reported stress from management, including having no say in decisions, too much or too little structure, racism, sexism, frustrating company policies, and low pay. They also reported stressful relationships with supervisors, peers, and other staff members, as well as individual stressors, such as boredom, work overload, too much responsibility, no promotions, and disagreements with management. Psychologically stressed employees reported feeling depressed, anxious, frustrated, fatigued, and bored, with lowered self-esteem. Stressed employees were more likely than non-stressed employees to have accidents on the job, eat or smoke too much, have outbursts of anger, and abuse alcohol or other drugs.[30]

Increasing numbers of employees are seeking help for stress through employee assistance programs or EAPs (discussed in more detail in Chapter 16). Stress-related worker's compensation claims and lawsuits are also on the rise. There is no reason to think that stress and the costs of dealing with stress are going to decrease any time soon. It is up to the organizations to research and implement programs and resources to help reduce workplace stress.

Considering the physical and psychological problems associated with stress, it is not hard to imagine that stress also affects self concept. Stress can make us feel overwhelmed, unable to do what we have to do. Stress makes people less productive and less successful, which lowers self-confidence. These become part of a vicious cycle in which effectiveness and self-concept both sink lower. Stress can also make people turn to poor coping substitutions such as substance abuse. Being caught in a web of substance abuse can reduce self-concept still further. Therefore, stress impacts all areas of people's lives—physical health, mental health, social life, and job performance. Learning to change the things you can change to reduce stress in your life is certainly worth the time and effort! (See Figure 12.7 for ways to alleviate the stress that leads to **job burnout**.)

job burnout

Physical and emotional exhaustion resulting from long-term stress or frustration in one's workplace.

» MANAGING STRESS

Throughout this chapter, you have learned that your attitudes and your cognitive appraisal of a stressor both play a large part in your response to a stressor. Your reaction to a stressor, as we have seen, affects both your physical and your mental health. In this section, we talk about managing the stress in your life to reduce its harmful effects in addition to adjusting your beliefs and behavior.

Stress is an unavoidable part of being human. Some stressors are out of your control, such as the loss of a loved one. Others are within your control, such as getting a speeding ticket. Distinguishing between those in your control and those outside of your control is a first step in reducing stress. Focus on the stressors you can control.

The best way to reduce stress is to prevent it. Better time management (see Chapter 16) is a skill and a habit that can be learned as one way to reduce stress.

Beating Burnout

Employee stress can lead to **job burnout.** Employees who feel insecure, misunderstood, frustrated, overloaded, overwhelmed, undervalued, and alienated often do the bare minimum at work or leave their jobs. Burnout is bad for employees and employers alike. Can job burnout be beaten? Experts Christina Maslach and Michael P. Leiter have interviewed thousands of people about job burnout. They list six key areas for employee happiness and reduced job burnout.

1. **Workload** must be manageable. Employees who feel that they have too much work to do in too little time with too few resources feel burned out. When workload is manageable, employees can meet demands and seek out new challenges.
2. Employees need a sense of **control.** Rigid office policies or chaos in the work environment can prevent employees from finishing work and feeling productive. Employees who are allowed to make decisions, solve problems, and determine the outcomes of their projects are more productive.
3. Employees must have an opportunity for **rewards.** Low pay, little praise, and no recognition leave employees feeling undervalued, unhappy, and resentful. When the work seems valuable to others, employees take pride in their work and work harder at tasks.
4. A feeling of **community** buoys employees. Conflict or tension among co-workers leaves everyone feeling angry, anxious, suspicious, and fearful. Being physically or socially isolated also leaves employees without a sense of community. Being able to share ideas, praise, and humor with co-workers leads to greater cohesiveness, respect, support, and team spirit.
5. Trusting the workplace to be **fair** keeps employees loyal. When some employees feel they do the lion's share of the work while others get the praise, a feeling of fairness is lost. Favoritism isn't fair. Employees are left feeling distrustful, cynical, and disloyal. Respect and justice, along with mutual respect between co-workers, form the basis for fairness in the workplace.
6. Shared **values** promote ethical behavior. Employees who don't share the company's values may do something unethical, or may do something that clashes with their personal values. This leads to employees feeling bad about themselves and their work. Meaningful work that doesn't cause a clash between the organizational norms and personal principles is more satisfying to employees.

figure 12.7

AVOIDING JOB BURNOUT

Managers can beat burnout in themselves and their employees by adhering to these simple principles. *Which of these principles seems most important to you?*

Source: Christina Maslach and Michael P. Leiter, "Take This Job and Love It," *Psychology Today,* September/October 1999. See also: Michael P. Leiter and Christina Maslach, *Banishing Burnout: Six Strategies for Improving Your Relationship with Work* (San Francisco, CA: Jossey-Bass, 2005).

Focusing on health habits is another way to reduce stress. When you feel stress, do you reach for a cigarette, an alcoholic drink, another cup of coffee? These can exaggerate stress effects. Substituting these with non-caffeinated tea, aromatherapy, or 15 minutes of meditation or other mindfulness activities can reduce stress. Rather than reaching for a plate of cookies when stressed, reach out to a friend with a phone call. Knitting, yoga, and exercise can distract your mind from spiraling stressful thoughts.

Why is exercise a stress-buster? In the short term, exercise releases endorphins, or your body's internal painkillers. If you have heard the term "runner's high," it is referring to endorphin release. After about 20 to 30 minutes of

more about...

Stress and Social Support

"Somehow we've come to equate success with not needing anyone. Many of us are willing to extend a helping hand, but we're very reluctant to reach out for help when we need it ourselves. It's as if we've divided the world into 'those who offer help' and 'those who need help.' The truth is that we are both."

—Brené Brown

exercise, endorphins are released along with other brain chemicals (neurotransmitters) such as dopamine, norepinephrine, and serotonin. Together these neurotransmitters, along with the stress hormone adrenaline, regulate mood and stress. In the longer term, exercise contributes to healthy heart and lung function and a healthy immune system to promote physical health.[31] And exercising with others builds social support, another healthy habit.

Brené Brown, well-known social worker and speaker, recommends stress reducing tips that work for her. First, she says, *set boundaries.* Know your limits and know when to say no. We do not need to prove ourselves to others by taking on more responsibilities (and more stress). *Be honest about burnout.* When you feel yourself becoming resentful or judgmental, those are warning signs that stress is rising, burnout is approaching, and it is time to step back and recalibrate. *Make a clearing for yourself.* Find an activity (a nature walk, a swim, writing in a journal) that clears your head and helps you cool down. And remember to get enough sleep![32]

STRATEGIES FOR SUCCESS

Strategy 12.1 Discard Irrational Beliefs

1. Evaluate the consequences of the belief.
2. Identify your belief system.
3. Dispute the self-defeating belief.
4. Practice effective ways of thinking.

Since one of the internal sources of stress is an irrational belief system, to reduce stress you must change your irrational beliefs by replacing them with rational beliefs. Whenever you start thinking along the lines of "I've failed the midterm exam! I'm going to flunk this class and get kicked out of school!" you must stop that irrational thought. Replace it with something more rational, such as "I've failed the midterm exam. If I get a tutor and spend more time studying, I can do better on the next exam and still pass the class."

Albert Ellis believes that for any irrational belief, you can follow these four steps to replace it with a more rational belief:

1. **Evaluate the consequences of the belief.** (Part C of the ABC) Negative emotions as a result of a stressor may seem to be natural, but they aren't inevitable. Ask yourself if these reactions are helping you live effectively, and helping you solve your problems.
2. **Identify your belief system.** (Part B of the ABC) Ask yourself why you are feeling the specific emotions aroused by the irrational belief. Ellis believes that by examining the irrational belief, you can figure out what is causing the negative consequences (negative emotions).
3. **Dispute the self-defeating belief.** After you have identified an irrational belief, you can argue against it.
4. **Practice effective ways of thinking.** Continue to examine your reactions to activating events. Try substituting more real beliefs and imagining more successful outcomes.

STRATEGIES FOR SUCCESS

Strategy 12.2 Change Your Behaviors to Reduce Stress

1. Take charge of your life.
2. Use humor.
3. Compare yourself with others.
4. Take advantage of stress.
5. Learn to live with unavoidable stress.

Remember that one of the internal sources of stress is your personality style or behavior. Changing your personality involves both cognitive (thought-related) and behavioral strategies. You may assume that you cannot change your personality, but you can change your behaviors to more healthy and less stress-producing ones. Learn to recognize and monitor the toxic hostility behaviors and the hurry sickness, which cause you more stress. Use the following strategies to reduce these behaviors:

1. **Take charge of your life.** Think of the three Cs of the hardy personality—challenge, commitment, and control. Tell yourself to think positive thoughts—that the stressor you are facing is a challenge, not a problem, that you are in control of your own life. Take charge! Confront stressors when you can in a thoughtful and assertive way. Stay committed to your goal instead of giving up. Remind yourself to take charge when stress rises.
2. **Use humor.** Learn to see the humor in situations, and increase the amount of humor in your life. An increase of humor reduces stress, because you physically can't feel both at the same time. Humor also makes you feel better, distracts you temporarily from the stressor, and lets you relax.
3. **Compare yourself with others.** Another cognitive strategy is social comparison. By comparing yourself with others who are in a similar situation but worse off, you may feel better about your situation. This does not mean you should listen to the horror stories that well-meaning friends or co-workers delight in telling! You will cope better when you hear encouraging stories about people in situations like yours.[33]
4. **Take advantage of stress.** Pay attention to your stress levels and learn what your optimal level is in order to be productive. Remember, with too little stress or challenge, you may become bored, unmotivated, and unproductive. With too much stress, you will be overwhelmed. Find out how much is right for you.
5. **Learn to live with unavoidable stress.** Finally, as a cognitive strategy for coping with stress, learn to live with the stressors you cannot avoid. This does not mean giving in to stress; it means accepting the fact that some stressors are unavoidable. Learn to think about these stressors in different ways than before.

STRATEGIES FOR SUCCESS

Strategy 12.3 Take Care of Yourself

1. Use relaxation techniques.
2. Increase your fitness: exercise, eat well, and reduce/quit smoking and drinking.
3. Make time for rest and leisure.
4. Maintain social support.

REAL WORLD EXAMPLE 12.3

C. W. Metcalf, a business consultant and entrepreneur, spent more than two decades teaching ways of adding humor to the workplace. Companies across the country have begun to recognize the value of humor, says Metcalf. His workshops for companies during downsizing were successful in preventing possible problems such as sabotage, threats to management, and suicide attempts.[34]

5. Try to reduce stress in the workplace.
6. Manage your time.
7. Stop procrastinating!

According to stress research, some amount of stress is inevitable and even good for you (it keeps you motivated and alive!), so you don't want to eliminate all stress. Your goal should be to reduce or minimize the negative effects of stress by coping with or managing stress.

1. **Use relaxation techniques.** In addition to changing your thoughts, you can use specific relaxation strategies as a way of reducing or managing stress. Since relaxing and feeling stress are not physically compatible, you can't do both at the same time. Forcing yourself to relax means you are getting rid of stress (at least temporarily!). Some simple relaxation techniques include deep breathing, progressive relaxation, meditation or other mindfulness activities, and biofeedback.

   To use *progressive relaxation,* you would close your eyes and imagine your entire body becoming relaxed, slowly, one muscle group at a time. *Meditation* is a relaxation technique that teaches you to focus outward, becoming aware of sensory input around you; or inward, becoming more self-aware.

   Biofeedback requires the use of a machine that gives you information (feedback) about specific biological (bio) processes. By learning to recognize what a change in heart rate and skin temperature feel like, you can actually learn to control such processes as heart rate, respiration, skin temperature, and perspiration. Many people have successfully used biofeedback to treat such stress-related illnesses as asthma, migraine headaches, epilepsy, and high blood pressure, as well as to control other physical processes that were once thought to be out of their control.[35]

2. **Increase your fitness: Exercise, eat well, and reduce/quit smoking and drinking.** Relaxation is one behavioral strategy used to manage stress and increase wellness. Another strategy is to increase general overall fitness. The more physically fit you are, the less negative the effects of stress will be, and the stronger your immune system will be to fight stress-related illnesses. Stay healthy by eating a nutritionally sound diet that is low in fats and sugars and high in fibers. Follow an exercise plan. If you are overweight, lose weight. If you smoke or drink alcohol a great deal, cut down or stop. Avoid long exposure to the sun or to harmful chemicals. If your workplace is excessively noisy, ask for earplugs and use them.

3. **Make time for rest and leisure.** Getting enough sleep at regular times and building leisure activities into your schedule will help you manage stress better. You need sleep to stay healthy. You may be thinking, "I can't add leisure activities to my schedule! I have too much to do already!" If so, you are just the person this suggestion is aimed at. Stop and think about the stress that your behaviors are creating for yourself.

4. **Maintain social support.** Friends, family, or even a support group can help in relieving stress. Examples of social support may include things such as receiving a home cooked meal when you are sick or personal loans when you are low on cash. It also

includes emotional support, such as sympathy and understanding, when you are unhappy or stressed. But remember: Whatever your support network gives you, you will probably be asked to return at some time when others are stressed. Be clear on whether some family members or friends cause more stress than they relieve.

5. **Try to reduce stress in the workplace.** Organizations can help reduce stressors in the workplace, too. One source of stress that employees often mention is rigid work schedules that don't allow for family obligations or emergencies. Companies are increasingly offering flextime, job sharing, telecommuting, and compressed work-weeks. Scheduling that allows employees to meet their needs means less absenteeism and higher productivity. Helping employees cope with stress on the job means lower turnover rates, more commitment and loyalty from employees, higher productivity, and better relationships with co-workers.

   Nationwide, companies are offering services to reduce workplace stress. Services range from counseling (e.g., psychological, nutritional, weight control, and substance abuse counseling) to onsite health and fitness centers and day-care facilities. What, you might ask, does day care have to do with workplace stress? Businesses are realizing that stress at home spills over into stress at work (and vice versa), so the best way to combat workplace stress is to reduce overall stress. Your Human Resources Department or employee assistance program (EAP) will have more information on these.

6. **Manage your time.** One of the easiest and most productive ways to combat stress behaviorally is to learn to manage time better. This will help you know what to expect and how to feel some control over your schedule and your life. Time management can be a problem when you waste time (underutilization), or schedule too many things into one time slot (overload).

   Whether your problem is overload or underutilization, you can take specific steps to learn to manage your time better. Start by making a list of all the regular activities you carry out in a day for work, school, family activities, and even leisure time. Make another list of upcoming events and deadlines. Put together a master time schedule with daily activities as well as dates to remember, filling in each time block with activities scheduled. Keep a daily time plan (an index card will fit neatly into a pocket), but also a monthly calendar for those upcoming events. Plan ahead, but set realistic timetables for getting work done. Allow an extra cushion of time for emergencies or unforeseen events. Reward yourself along the way (but not until *after* you have completed your work!) with activities you like, such as talking to friends, going out to eat, watching television, and so on. Modify the schedule until it is workable. Then stick to it!

7. **Stop procrastinating!** *Procrastination,* or putting things off until later, allows you to avoid things you don't really want to do. Procrastination ultimately increases your stress level! To reduce procrastination, make a specific plan about what you need to do, break large tasks into small chunks, reward yourself for work done along the way, and give yourself credit for a job well done. Reread the material on procrastination in Chapter 2 and see Chapter 16 for more information.

Everyone will have different approaches that work, as well as different types and levels of stress; therefore, you will want to choose what applies to you to suit your needs. Perhaps you plan too much work in too short a time frame. Then, to make matters worse, you procrastinate and fail to meet all of your deadlines. At the same time, your fitness level is high, and you have a large social support network. In a case like this, you would probably want to focus on preceding steps 6 and 7. You probably would not need to focus on steps 2 and 4. You might also want to incorporate the remaining steps in your life to increase overall well-being.

CHAPTER TWELVE SUMMARY

Chapter Summary by Learning Objectives

LO 12-4 Identify the main causes of stress. Stress is a part of everyone's life. Stress is the body's reaction to a stressor, which can be caused by life changes and daily hassles; by chronic stressors; by external circumstances; or by internal cognitions, belief systems, and personality-related behaviors.

LO 12-5 Give examples of external and internal sources of stress. External stressors can include anything from outside sources that cause pain, discomfort, frustration, or conflict. Examples are deadlines, poor health, work or school pressures, or financial problems. Internal stressors can include your own reactions of a stressor, as well as personality factors. They include irrational beliefs, poor social skills, unrealistic expectations, and poor time management, just to name a few.

LO 12-6 Compare and contrast type A and type B personality behaviors. Type A and type B personalities are differing behavior patterns related to personality. Type A behaviors include impatience, excessive time-consciousness, and perfectionism. Type B behaviors include a more relaxed and flexible outlook, with less focus on time and deadlines.

LO 12-7 Describe the physical effects of stress. Stress occurs in three stages as your body sounds the alarm that a stressor is occurring, tries to cope with the stressor, and if coping fails, exhausts its resources and becomes vulnerable to illness due to a weakened immune system.

LO 12-8 Explain the cost of stress in the workplace. Stress-related problems cost the American economy more than $300 billion per year. These costs include lost work, insurance claims and costs, stress management programs, and stress-related lawsuits.

LO 12-9 Learn to manage stress in your life. Take care of your physical and mental health to reduce stress and improve well-being. Focus on diet, exercise, social support, and mindfulness activities, and learn how to change negative thoughts.

key terms

review questions

1. What is meant by stress and stressors? Identify two sources of eustress, and two sources of distress, in your own life.
2. How are major life changes different from daily hassles? How can a major life change lead to daily hassles? Discuss examples of these in your own life.
3. Many major changes are listed in the Holmes–Rahe Readjustment Scale. What characteristics do they all have in common? Explain. What factors would you add or otherwise change in this scale?
4. Suppose that you were really looking forward to going to work one day, but when you left for work you realized your tire was flat. Your stress level increased. Discuss how this situation leads to internal and/or external sources of stress.
5. Are there any chronic stressors in your own life, or the life of someone you know? Describe the stressor, and possible coping strategies.
6. Do you hold any of the irrational beliefs described by Ellis? How do they affect your perception of events?
7. According to Ellis, what is catastrophizing? Do you ever find yourself catastrophizing? In what situations? How can you minimize it?
8. What is the difference between meditation and biofeedback? How can each be used to reduce stress? What other specific suggestions for coping with stress can you incorporate into your own life?
9. Suppose you are driving to work one day on your usual route past the City Zoo, when a giant grizzly bear escapes, runs out of the entrance, growling and roaring, and heads straight for your car. Describe the physical and chemical changes that you would experience, according to the general adaptation syndrome (GAS).

critical thinking questions

1. A life without stress seems like a pleasant and desirable goal. Do you agree with Selye that stress is necessary in order to motivate you and keep you alive? Why or why not? What do you think would happen if you didn't have any stress in your life?
2. Some people say that since everyone is going to die anyway, it would be better to enjoy life without worrying about diet, exercise, and other behaviors that may prolong life while reducing the enjoyment of life. Why do you think these people feel this way? What do you think?
3. What are your personal strategies for reducing harmful stress in your life? After reading this chapter, will you adopt new strategies, or change what you are doing in some way?

working it out 12.1

BEHAVIOR ACTIVITY PROFILE—TYPE A MEASURE

Each of us displays certain kinds of behaviors, thought patterns, and personal characteristics. For each of the 21 sets of descriptions that follow, circle the number that you feel best describes where you are between each pair. The best answer for each set of descriptions is the response that most nearly describes the way you feel, behave, or think. Answer these in terms of your regular or typical behavior, thoughts, or characteristics.

1.	I'm always on time for appointments.	7 6 5 4 3 2 1	I'm never quite on time.
2.	When someone is talking to me, chances are I'll anticipate what they are going to say by nodding, interrupting, or finishing sentences for them.	7 6 5 4 3 2 1	I listen quietly without showing any impatience.
3.	I frequently try to do several things at once.	7 6 5 4 3 2 1	I tend to take things one at a time.
4.	When it comes to waiting in line (at banks, theaters, etc.), I really get impatient and frustrated.	7 6 5 4 3 2 1	Waiting in line simply doesn't bother me.
5.	I always feel rushed.	7 6 5 4 3 2 1	I never feel rushed.
6.	When it comes to my temper, I find it hard to control at times.	7 6 5 4 3 2 1	I just don't seem to have a temper.
7.	I tend to do most things like eating, walking, and talking rapidly.	7 6 5 4 3 2 1	I tend to eat, walk, and talk slowly.

TOTAL SCORE 1–7 ____ = S

8.	Quite honestly, the things I enjoy most are job-related activities.	7 6 5 4 3 2 1	I enjoy leisure-time activities more than job-related activities.
9.	At the end of a typical workday, I usually feel like I needed to get more done than I did.	7 6 5 4 3 2 1	In a typical workday, I feel I accomplished everything I needed to.
10.	Someone who knows me very well would say that I would rather work than play.	7 6 5 4 3 2 1	Someone who knows me well would say that I would rather play than work.
11.	When it comes to getting ahead at work, nothing is more important.	7 6 5 4 3 2 1	Many things are more important than getting ahead at work.
12.	My primary source of satisfaction comes from my job.	7 6 5 4 3 2 1	I regularly find satisfaction in non-job pursuits, such as hobbies, friends, and family.
13.	Most of my friends and social acquaintances are people I know from work.	7 6 5 4 3 2 1	Most of my friends and social acquaintances are not connected with my work.
14.	I'd rather stay at work than take a vacation.	7 6 5 4 3 2 1	Nothing at work is important enough to interfere with my vacation.

TOTAL SCORE 8-14 ______ = J

15.	People who know me well would describe me as hard driving and competitive.	7 6 5 4 3 2 1	People who know me well would describe me as relaxed and easygoing.
16.	In general, my behavior is governed by a desire for recognition and achievement.	7 6 5 4 3 2 1	My behavior is governed by what I want to do—not by trying to satisfy others.
17.	In trying to complete a project or solve a problem, I tend to wear myself out before I'll give up on it.	7 6 5 4 3 2 1	I tend to take a break or quit if I'm feeling fatigued by a project or problem.
18.	When I play a game (tennis, cards, etc.) my enjoyment comes from winning.	7 6 5 4 3 2 1	My enjoyment in playing games comes from the social interaction.
19.	I like to associate with people who are dedicated to getting ahead.	7 6 5 4 3 2 1	I like to associate with people who are easygoing and take life as it comes.
20.	I'm not happy unless I'm always doing something.	7 6 5 4 3 2 1	Frequently, "doing nothing" can be quite enjoyable to me.
21.	What I enjoy doing most are competitive activities.	7 6 5 4 3 2 1	What I enjoy doing most are non-competitive pursuits.

TOTAL SCORE 15-21 ______ = H

Source: John M. Ivancevich and Michael T. Matteson, *Organizational Behavior & Management,* 11e (The McGraw-Hill Companies, Inc.) pp. 240–242.

Impatience (S)	Job Involvement (J)	Hard Driving and Competitive (H)	Total Score (A) S + J + H

The Behavior Activity Profile attempts to assess the three type A coronary-prone behavior patterns, as well as provide a total score. The three types of type A coronary-prone behavior patterns are shown:

Items	Behavior Pattern	Characteristics
1-7	Impatience (S)	Is anxious to interrupt
		Fails to listen attentively
		Gets frustrated by waiting (e.g., in line, for others to complete a job)
8–14	Job Involvement (J)	Focal point of attention is the job
		Lives for the job
		Relishes being on the job
		Gets immersed in job activities
15–21	Hard Driving/Competitive (H)	Is hardworking, highly competitive
		Is competitive in most aspects of life, sports, work, etc.
		Races against the clock
1-21	Total score (A)	Total of S + J + H represents your global type A behavior

Score ranges for total score are:

Score	*Behavior Type*
122 and above	Hard-core type A
99–121	Moderate type A
90–98	Low type A
80–89	Type X
70–79	Low type B
50–69	Moderate type B
40 and below	Hard-core type B

Percentile Scores

Now you can compare your score to a sample of more than 1,200 respondents.

Percentile Score	**Raw Score**	
Percent of Individuals Scoring Lower	**Males**	**Females**
99%	______140	______132
95%	______135	______126
90%	______130	______120
85%	______124	______112
80%	______118	______106
75%	______113	______101
70%	______108	______ 95
65%	______102	______ 90
60%	______ 97	______ 85
55%	______ 92	______ 80
50%	______ 87	______ 74
45%	______ 81	______ 69
40%	______ 75	______ 63
35%	______ 70	______ 58
30%	______ 63	______ 53
25%	______ 58	______ 48
20%	______ 51	______ 42
15%	______ 45	______ 36
10%	______ 38	______ 31
5%	______ 29	______ 26
1%	______ 21	______ 21

working it out 12.2

STRESS SELF-TEST

School-to-Work Connection: Personal Qualities Skills

The Perceived Stress Scale (PSS). How much stress are you under? To measure the degree of stress you feel, take this stress test. Although your total score might not surprise you, a high score might indicate it would be wise to consult your doctor to determine whether you have a health problem that requires medical attention, one that might be contributing to your stress level and your ability to withstand it.

The PSS was created in 1983 and is still one of the most widely used tests available for perceptions of stress, or the feelings that one does not have the ability to cope with stressful situations.

Instructions: Circle the appropriate number for each question and tally your total score.

- Scores ranging from 0–13 would be considered low stress.
- Scores ranging from 14–26 would be considered moderate stress.
- Scores ranging from 27–40 would be considered high perceived stress.

In the last month, how often have you. . .	**Never**	**Hardly Ever**	**Sometimes**	**Fairly Often**	**Very Often**
1. Felt distressed about something unexpected happening to you?	0	1	2	3	4
2. Felt that you were losing control of the main things in your life?	0	1	2	3	4
3. Felt stressed out or anxious?	0	1	2	3	4
4. Lacked confidence that you could handle issues in your personal life?	0	1	2	3	4
5. Felt that things in general were not going as you wanted them to?	0	1	2	3	4
6. Felt overwhelmed about having too many things to do?	0	1	2	3	4
7. Felt that you could not control hassles in your life?	0	1	2	3	4
8. Felt that you were just not getting things done that you need to do?	0	1	2	3	4
9. Felt angry about not being able to handle all the things you need to do?	0	1	2	3	4
10. Felt that problems were adding up to the point you could not handle them?	0	1	2	3	4

Source: Cohen, S; Kamarck T; Mermelstein R. (December 1983). "A global measure of perceived stress". *Journal of Health and Social Behavior.* 24 (4): 385–396.

working it out 12.3

MAKE STRESS YOUR FRIEND

Part One

Watch the TED Talk by health psychologist Kelly McGonigal, titled "How to Make Stress Your Friend," and then answer the following questions.

1. Why should we make friends with stress, according to the speaker? How does this fit with our usual view of stress?
2. What does the speaker say creates a notable difference in illness and death rates, whether they are higher or lower?
3. What is the social stress test as described by the speaker? Why was it done, and what did the researchers find?
4. How important are our beliefs about stress in our health outcomes? What *should* we tell ourselves about physical stress responses, according to the speaker?
5. How does "stress make you social," according to the speaker? Why is this important? After viewing this talk, what will you do differently regarding stress in your life?

The video can be found here: www.ted.com/talks/kelly_mcgonigal_how_to_make_stress_your_friend.

case study 12.1

Bonnie the Bumblebee

James rested his head in his hand and mused as he watched his supervisor, Bonnie, buzz around the office at high speed. He liked to think of her as a giant bumblebee—always moving and often stinging. Bonnie was always in a hurry because she felt she had to do her own work and then redo everyone else's. The stinging came often in the form of criticizing her employees, upper management, her family, and everything else. James, in contrast, preferred a slower, more steady, but thorough pace of work. He didn't see any advantage to constantly being so critical and rushed all the time.

"James, you're going to have to do this spreadsheet all over again. I just don't have time to fix it for you, and the Finance Department will never accept it in this form."

Suddenly, she stopped and looked thoughtful. "You know, James, I'm going to be eligible for early retirement in only eight years. I'll probably be promoted to upper management soon. You're a lot younger than I am, but you should be thinking about your future with this company. I think you're probably capable, yet you just don't seem to have the drive, the aggression, that I had at your age. You're just too *nice* or something. Don't you want to make anything of yourself?"

James only smiled and said, "Well, Bonnie, I'll have to think about that." In fact, James had thought quite a lot about the differences between the two of them. He was quite certain that of the two of them, he'd be more likely to be promoted to upper management.

Case Study Questions

1. Is James correct—will he more likely make it to upper management, or will Bonnie? Why? Which style do you see more often in management? Explain why this might be the case.
2. Thinking of the personality behaviors discussed in this chapter, what characteristics would lead you to categorize Bonnie and James as either type A, type B, or hardy?
3. Does Bonnie seem stressed? If so, from what sources (major life changes, daily hassles, chronic stressors, internal stress, or external stress)? If not, why?
4. Does one of the work behavior styles above describe you? After reading this chapter, are you inclined to make any changes? Explain.

case study 12.2

Overworked, or Just Overstressed?

Rick Russell and Arturo Garcia had been friends since childhood. Last year they both graduated from high school with above-average grades. Now, both are attending their local community college, studying business, and hoping for successful lives. They have talked a lot about transferring to a four-year college in the future, maybe before finishing the two years where they are. Although both did well in high school, Rick seems to be really struggling to keep up with both school and a part-time job.

"Art, how do you handle all the stuff you're doing in your life and still stay so calm? How do you manage to get all those good grades? I can barely keep my C average and keep from getting on academic warning. All these instructors want way too much work from us. They act like we don't have a life outside of school. In fact, they seem to think that their classes are the only things we're doing at all!"

Art looked dubious. "You're always exaggerating, Rick. If you really look at it, we don't have that many more assignments than we had last year, and you seemed to do fine then. What's going on that's so radically different from high school? You played baseball and ran track in high school and you still graduated with a B average. What's changed, anyway?"

"This isn't high school, Art, in case you haven't noticed! The work is a lot harder here, and the instructors never remind us when stuff is due or when exams are going to be. I'm always getting my work in late, and I never feel ready for tests when they come. At least in high school my mom or my teachers would pester me about getting things done. Here, it doesn't seem like anybody cares! A lot of my teachers act like they don't care whether I come to class or not."

"Why are you blaming everybody else?" Art replied. "I saw you hanging out in the student lounge all morning yesterday, and you knew that we had a project due in English Comp. You need to learn how to set some priorities and manage your time better. Why can't you get it together?"

Case Study Questions

1. Do you think Rick will ever "get it together"? What are the real causes of his frustration? Why isn't Arturo having the same kinds of problems?
2. What sources of stress would you say Rick is experiencing? What coping strategies does he seem to be using? What would you suggest he change, if anything?
3. If you were to create long-term specific stress management programs for both Arturo and Rick, what would you include?

13

CHAPTER THIRTEEN

YOUR EXTERNAL AND INTERNAL CUSTOMERS

« « LEARNING OBJECTIVES

After studying this chapter, you will be able to:

LO 13-1 Explain how to determine what customers really want.

LO 13-2 Define customer service.

LO 13-3 Describe the internal customer.

LO 13-4 List the two simplest principles of customer service.

LO 13-5 Give examples of issues in customer service.

LO 13-6 Compare and contrast ways to handle a difficult customer.

LO 13-7 Explain the significance of going the extra mile.

LO 13-8 List ways to use strong ethics in customer service.

LO 13-9 Explain the moral of the Poor George story and how it relates to customer service.

« « STRATEGIES FOR SUCCESS

Strategy 13.1 Establish a Bond with the Customer

Strategy 13.2 Support the Customer's Self-Esteem

Strategy 13.3 Handle the Difficult Customer Professionally

Strategy 13.4 Keep Customers Satisfied

In the Workplace: Good Service—the Other Half of Success

SITUATION

natalia bulatova/Shutterstock

Shaun smiled as he sat back after a long, rewarding day. He had always thought of Chopped Carrots as more than just a small meal prep company. He had learned to cook from his grandma as a boy, who had taught him the value of using fresh ingredients and preparing them with love. He'd taken those lessons with him through life, and they'd come in handy as he worked his way up through the restaurant scene, where he was known for his knife skills, among other things.

As busy as he was working others' kitchens, Shaun developed a technique for quickly chopping and preparing fresh produce on his days off, so he could use those fresh ingredients throughout the week for quick, on-the-go meals for himself.

Some of his co-workers caught on, as well as his friends and some of his neighbors. Soon, Shaun was chop-prepping for a dozen people, and then twice that. He soon left the restaurant scene and began his own fresh-chop meal prep company, Chopped Carrots.

DISCOVERY

At the end of his day, Shaun sat reflecting on how his business had grown so quickly. It didn't feel like he was doing anything all that different from his prep work in restaurant kitchens before this. But he did notice a difference in his customers' attitudes when he would interact with them. They didn't just seem to make their purchase and keep it moving. Rather, they would linger, share recipes with him, and they would express how grateful they were for him and his service.

THINK ABOUT IT

Why is Chopped Carrots so popular, when the same "carrots" could be purchased at the grocery store or bought in a restaurant? As much as it is a functional service for hungry people, Chopped Carrots also offers subscribers the *convenience* of eating a prepared meal, extends a *connection* with the person who prepared it, and helps buyers feel as if they are making *healthy lifestyle choices.* Chopped Carrots brings these positive feelings together with its product and approach, creating an experience that people are willing to invest in time after time.

What steps do you think the Chopped Carrots should take to continue its success? What other business outside of the food industry can you think of whose brand brings to mind convenience, connection, or other positive "lifestyle" feelings? How would you describe Shaun's customer service philosophy?

» WHAT DO CUSTOMERS REALLY WANT?

In business circles it is often said that any company's scarcest resource is capital; that is, money to invest. Rather than capital, an increasing number of people running businesses today are realizing that *satisfied and happy customers* are the most crucial resource. Without a good base of customers, any business will fail. Without customers, you don't have a business–or a future.[1]

In *How to Win Customers and Keep Them for Life,* Michael LeBoeuf points out that customers buy only two things: **good feelings and solutions** to problems.[2] Everything that a customer wants from you will fall into one of those two categories. For example:

good feelings and solutions
The only two things customers really buy.

- You don't sell clothes. You sell a sharp appearance, style, attractiveness, comfort, and warmth.
- You don't sell insurance. You sell financial security for people and their families.
- You don't sell toys. You sell happy moments for children.
- You don't sell a house. You sell comfort, contentment, a good investment, pride of ownership, privacy, and space.

Chopped Carrots in the opening vignette doesn't just sell prepared meals; it offers its customers the good feelings associated with a positive lifestyle choice. Every moment you are on the job, think about feelings and solutions. Make those two goals your most important activities. If you do, your relationship with customers should improve as you keep your goals in mind.[3]

What feelings does your customer show when he or she first approaches you? What nonverbal signals can you use as clues to the customer's real feelings? Be sure your own feelings are not getting in the way of understanding–or reacting correctly to–the customer.

The importance of leaving customers with good feelings cannot be overemphasized. High-quality customer service has never been more important than it is today. The most obvious reason for this increased importance is greater competition. Global competition from European and Asian countries with a high customer service emphasis has caused American businesses to look more closely at how they treat those who buy from them.

A second reason for this emphasis is the growth of services in the United States over the past few decades. Today there are many new services available that did not exist several years ago. They might include going to a debt counselor, hiring a webmaster, receiving online healthcare services, shopping for groceries (or anything else) online, or consulting with an aromatherapist. These are just a few examples of the thousands

more about. . .

The Transition to a Service Economy

The American economy began to dramatically shift in the 1990s, at a time when it was dominated by manufacturing and industrial production. In the decades since then, the American economy has made major shifts to become a service economy. Watch an animated gif of the American economy's shift from manufacturing in 1990, to a predominantly service economy in 2013 here: www.washingtonpost.com/blogs/govbeat/wp/2014/09/03/watch-the-u-s-transition-from-a-manufacturing-economy-to-a-service-economy-in-one-gif

Reid Wilson, "Watch the U.S. Transition From a Manufacturing Economy To a Service Economy, in One Gif" *The Washington Post,* September 3, 2014 (retrieved April 15, 2020).

of new services offered today. While the manufacturing economy was the dominant sector in 1990, today the American economy is based on delivery of services.

This final reason for high-quality customer service is the most important one: keeping customers happy and loyal simply makes good economic sense. Maintaining an ever-growing group of satisfied customers is essential to staying in business and making a profit. Without loyal customers, businesses fail—and, sadly, many do fail every day.

SATISFYING THE CUSTOMER

When customers pay for products and services, they buy good feelings or the solution to a problem, too. *Why is it important to recognize the real needs of customers?*

Ariel Skelley/Blend Images

» WHAT IS GOOD CUSTOMER SERVICE?

What is good customer service? Customer service guru John Tschohl says, "You have good service only when customers think you do."[6] He also says that customer service is part of successful selling because satisfied customers come back to be customers again. According to the American Management Association, 65 percent of a typical company's business comes from repeat business by *current* customers.[7]

Have you ever scrapped a purchase or a transaction because of bad service? More than half of Americans say they have. One third say they will consider changing companies after only one experience with bad service. The cost of finding a new customer is considerably greater than the cost of keeping one you already have—between five and 25 times more expensive.[8] Unhappy customers also create a ripple effect for businesses. Across the board, more Americans tell others about bad service (an average of 15 people) than good service (11 people on average).[9]

more about...

Repeat Customers

Surveys over the past several years find that 65 percent of a typical company's business comes from the repeat business of existing customers.[4] Conversely, 90 percent of dissatisfied customers will not return for repeat business.[5]

Good service, which nearly always includes good human relations, is the main reason for repeat business. Good service pays off. Seven out of 10 consumers in the United States have spent more money to do business with a particular company because they know it delivers great service. Treating your customers as the most important part of the organization will pay off in the long run, in terms of both growth and added profits.

Working on improving customer relations is also excellent for your own self-development. Learning what works in the process of satisfying customers can aid you in cultivating your own skills in problem solving for other areas of life. Dealing successfully with customers is a learning process that is ongoing and can always be improved.

Customer relations skills can be transferred to almost any other occupation or profession. If you are an employee who has a vested interest in the success of the company you are working for, the development of customer service skills is worthwhile for you. Also, customer relations presents one of the most challenging aspects of human relations skill development. You will never be wasting your time by learning how customers think, respond, and perceive reality. Any other business you might enter later in life will involve customers in some way. This includes both external customer and internal customers.

» THE INTERNAL CUSTOMER

Businesses have gotten savvy in recent years in understanding their customers' expectations for excellent customer service and a pleasant experience. Treated well, a loyal customer will buy more and spread the good word. Treated poorly, customers will begin to walk away and tell others of their unfavorable experiences. This focus on external customer service is critical for the long-term success of an organization.

Consider for a moment the people who work within and for the company, the so-called "internal customers." These employees have many customer-like interactions within your organization that provide an opportunity—or a risk—to improving their overall employee experience.[10] The term *internal customer* is used to describe the complex interaction among managers, employees, and external customers around a business or organization. When the person who is connected long term to a company is treated the way an external customer should be, the results are predictably positive. One definition of the **internal customer** is the person who depends on the other people in the company to provide the services and products for the external customer.[11]

internal customer

The person who depends on the other people in the company to provide the services and products for the external customer.

Internal customers usually don't walk away when the service is bad. Unlike their external counterparts, they are tied to the company more directly than that. This is exactly why treating them right is really important to the overall success of the business.

more about...

Internal Customers

"Customers will never love a company until the employees love it first."
—Simon Sinek

Management expert Shep Hyken provides an example of an internal customer. In the example, she is a clerk in the payroll department. She depends on the managers throughout the company to give her the information she needs to produce an accurate payroll each week. One manager doesn't get that information to her on time, and when the e-mail does arrive, it contains several errors. This manager has failed an internal customer—his colleague. The manager's responsibility to that payroll clerk is just as important as the responsibility of the company to any single external customer.[12]

As Hyken puts it, "A company that has an excellent service reputation didn't get it without everyone in the company being a part of the service strategy. Someone once said that if you aren't working directly with the outside customer, you are probably working with someone who is."[13]

What is your responsibility to the internal customer? If you are a manager, it's your role to be sure the needs of every person in your area are being met, just as should be the case with the external customer. If you are a work team member, do your best to be the kind of loyal fan you would be of, let's say, a favorite restaurant or some other business where you are a contented repeat customer. The internal customer concept is helpful in creating a company with memorable customer service.

Think about how a business or company functions. Every employee is accountable to someone, whether to outside customers or internal customers. In his article on improving internal customer relations, business consultant Lane Baldwin says, "Make no mistake. Your teammates are as important to your success as the people walking through your door. And the better you serve your teammates, the more they will help you succeed."[14] For the remainder of the chapter, then, when you read the word *customer,* think about customers as those who buy products and services from you, and those who are connected in some way that makes the company's existence possible.

» THE TWO SIMPLEST PRINCIPLES OF CUSTOMER SERVICE

When you are dealing with any type of customer, the **two simplest principles** can help guide you:

two simplest principles
Finding out what the customer needs, and doing whatever is necessary to satisfy it.

1. Find out what the customer needs.
2. Do whatever is possible to satisfy those needs.

By listening carefully to the customer's stated needs, you might discover unspoken needs. In some cases, the customer doesn't have a thorough understanding of what his or her own needs are. Your task in that case becomes one of probing and asking a series of questions to find out what is behind the surface statements.[15]

Although these two principles are very simple, you must remember that besides the immediate needs of the purchase, each customer has basic human needs that all people share. (See Figure 13.1.) Often customers simply

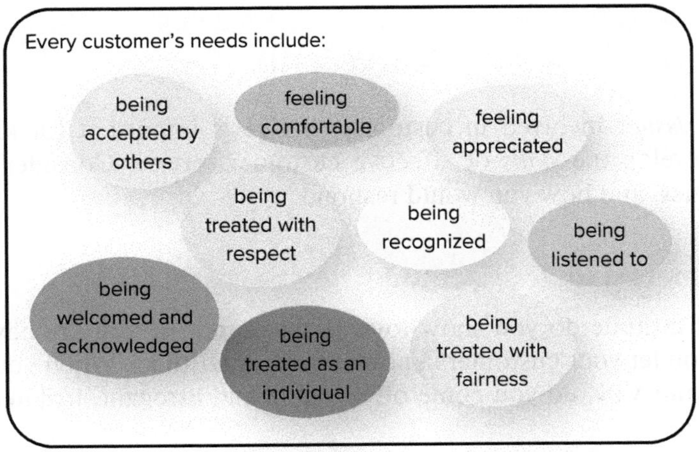

figure 13.1

THE CUSTOMER'S NEEDS—BASIC HUMAN NEEDS

Understanding the customer as a person just like yourself will make it easier to anticipate his or her needs and help to find solutions. *How many of these needs do you feel when you are making a purchase?*

REAL WORLD EXAMPLE 13.1

Luis Alvarez was a department store clerk in a small town. One day, an elderly woman came in to look at the bicycles on display. "My, my," she said. "The bikes seem a lot different than they used to be—more gears, more colors, so many options! The last time I looked at bicycles was more than 30 years ago."

Luis had no idea what this customer really wanted. In fact, he wasn't even sure that she was a customer at all. She spent several minutes telling him about days long ago when her three children had ridden bicycles on the vacant lot where the department store now stood. After asking a few questions about her interest in the bikes, Luis determined that this person simply needed to chat as she was lonely. And he understood that he, Luis, had fulfilled that need by remaining friendly and sympathetic.

Two months later, Luis was surprised when the same elderly woman returned to the store and purchased three new bicycles as Christmas presents for her grandchildren. As it turned out, she had been shopping for the bikes for months all over town and had been struck by Luis' patience and professionalism, when others had hurried her to the cash register or out the door.

For his part, by finding out her real need in their first encounter—to be respected and listened to—he had made a good impression, building a rapport with the woman, which later resulted in three major sales. Luis had followed the two simplest principles. He realized the customer needed to be heard, and he responded to her needs by listening to her. In return, she came back as his paying customer.

want to be noticed, listened to, and taken seriously. Remembering their basic needs could be the only difference between your business and a competitor's. Having quality products alone, without the positive treatment of customers, is simply not enough for a business to succeed.

The wise choice in answer to the question in Real World Example 13.2 is to treat the person with the same cordiality you would treat a paying customer. After all, that person's opinion of your establishment might bring him or her back again. The customer's positive experience might even influence a friend or family member to shop there. The same type of policy is also wise to follow when a nonpaying customer wants to use the restroom facilities in your business, or even one who asks for directions to the location of your competitor. Treating others well is not only good business; it is the right thing to do.

» ISSUES IN CUSTOMER SERVICE

Knowing the *issues* involved in customer service is important for anyone wanting to develop the *skills* of effective customer service. Consider these important issues, and how you would respond.

Your Customers and Your Attitude

What kind of attitude do you show toward customers? If you are having a bad day, do you let your customers know with your attitude? When your day is not going your way, do you come off as smug and arrogant, irritated and

REAL WORLD EXAMPLE 13.2

You are a cashier in a retail store. Someone who is apparently not a customer presents a five dollar bill and asks for change. In fact, it looks like she just walked in from the bus stop outside and needed change for the bus. What do you do?

annoyed, distracted and down, or too humble? Or can you set those feelings aside and bring a winning attitude to your customers? Checking your attitude around customers should be an ongoing practice.

Some people who have contact with customers seem to feel that once they have "landed" a customer, they can move on to bringing in the next deal, and they may begin to start taking the earlier customer for granted. This is a mistake. Whenever you deal with customers, remember to treat them the same way later on as you treated them when you were trying to win them over the first time. Nobody likes to be taken for granted, and customers are no exception.

WHEN YOUR CUSTOMERS ARE OTHER BUSINESSES

When your customers are other businesses, you must not only maintain the same high-level service you would give to individuals, but you must also get to know the business. *How can you learn more about the businesses with which you work?*

Cultura/Image Source

Delivering Bad News

It can be a difficult task to give a customer unwelcome news–especially when they expect nothing but good news from your organization. For example, a loan officer in a bank will have to refuse a certain number of applicants every month. Staff in the box office may need to tell dozens of people that the show is sold out. Or a health practitioner may need to share unwelcome news with a patient about their physical health. Even if you are professional and experienced in your job, it can be hard to say no or break bad news to your customers. Developing sound **bad news skills** can be essential to help make the task less unpleasant.

bad news skills

The skills necessary to deliver bad news to customers but still retain their business and goodwill.

In the Real World Example 13.3, what could Jeffrey have been doing that was so effective? Here's what he did: In a very polite voice, he would say, "I'm really sorry, ma'am (or sir), but our owners have decided that they want to create a clean, smooth transaction at the register, and so we will become a 'cashless' card-only business and stop accepting cash. Our apologies for the change, but this will actually help us become more efficient with our operations, and keep our prices low for you. We do offer the option to pay via phone app, if that might help." A few customers would express dismay, but most would actually say thank you to Jeffrey as they passed him a card or swiped the funds from the screens of their phones.

Notice the steps that Jeffrey took in delivering the bad news to customers. First, *he used a polite tone of voice.* Second, *he didn't dwell on long apologies.*

REAL WORLD EXAMPLE 13.3

At a popular vegan eatery, the owners had decided that they were going to follow the trend and become a "cashless" operation, meaning they would no longer accept cash or checks, only credit or debit cards. The owners had not consulted the managers or staff and had not given much instruction on how to deal with the transition. Nonetheless, the changes went into effect that weekend.

Most of the employees who worked at the café felt unequipped as they interacted with the annoyed customers, who were dumbfounded when they took cash out to pay, but couldn't use it to buy their favorite items. Some employees tried responding to the customers with a halting version of, "I'm so sorry, I don't really know what to tell you, but . . . sorry!" This didn't help soothe some of the grumpier customers.

In contrast, Jeffrey, one of the employees who worked the busy weekend brunch shift, seemed to always work through this awkward part of the transaction without the same level of customer frustration or annoyance. Soon, the others started asking Jeffrey for help every time a customer became agitated by the new policy. After Jeffrey would speak to the customer, he or she would always leave satisfied. Bustling as the café was, some of the employees smiled to themselves as they wondered, "What was Jeffrey doing that was so effective?"

Although he said he was sorry and apologized, his message wasn't an apology: it was an explanation. Third, *he dealt specifically with why the problem existed.* Fourth, *he closed his remarks with a positive statement* as to what could be done to make the situation better for both the business and the customer. Those four rules (as shown in Figure 13.2) can help when giving customers messages that they would rather not hear.

Most customers would rather not hear the word *policy.* "We can't do that because it's against company policy" is one of the weakest explanations companies can use. If you work for a manager who tells you that you must use that line, at least find out the reasoning *behind* the policy so that you can explain it clearly to the customer.

Encouraging Complaints

In some way, every customer has a problem. If nothing else, the problem is that the customer is in need of the goods or services your company provides. Perhaps the problem is dissatisfaction with some part of your operation—or

figure 13.2

GIVING A CUSTOMER BAD NEWS

When giving a customer bad news, focus on explanations and solutions rather than apologies and excuses. A brief apology is almost always necessary, but do not dwell on it; rather, look for a win-win solution. *How can you help customers understand the options available?*

Four Rules for Giving a Customer Bad News

1. **Use a polite tone of voice.** Make it a point to check on this. For many people, vocal tone is mostly unconscious, unless they try specifically to take notice of it.
2. **Don't spend too much time and energy on apologies.** Apologizing is fine, but most customers want *reasons* and *action*.
3. **Explain why the problem exists.** If you don't know, let the customer know that you will find out; then do it. If the problem's cause is impossible to discover, go to step 4.
4. **Talk about what can be done to solve the problem.** If possible, this includes alternatives and suggestions from which the customer can choose. When only one possible course of action is available, *sell* the customer on why that action is the best.

your competitor's. Learn to focus on the problem. Ask yourself: "What can I do to solve the problem *as this person sees it*?"

Don't rely on being told what the problem is. Later in this chapter you will read about an angry customer who yells and screams. Learning how to deal with that type of person is certainly necessary. However, yellers and screamers are in the minority. Most customers are like the **"nice" customer** (see Figure 13.3). These customers would actually be more helpful if they were a bit less nice, because then they would provide better feedback. Many companies today realize that customer complaints are necessary and should be encouraged in every way possible.[16]

"nice" customer
The customer who never complains, but responds to bad service by taking his or her business elsewhere.

The Nice Customer Statement

Some people in businesses make the incorrect assumption that if anything is wrong, the customer will say so. Here's a little statement that is posted on the walls of businesses all across the country:

I'm a nice customer. You all know me. I'm the one who never complains, no matter what kind of service I get. I'll go into a restaurant and sit quietly while the waiters and waitresses gossip and never bother to ask if anyone has taken my order. Sometimes someone who came in after I did gets my order, but I don't complain. I just wait.

And when I go to a store to buy something, I don't throw my weight around. I try to be thoughtful of the other person. If a snooty salesperson gets upset because I want to look at several things before making up my mind, I'm just as polite as can be. I don't believe rudeness in return is the answer.

The other day I waited in line for almost 15 minutes for a cup of coffee while the barista chatted with his old friend. And when he did finally serve my coffee, he spilled some on my sleeve. But did I complain about the service? Of course not.

I never kick. I never nag. I never criticize. And I wouldn't dream of making a scene, as I've seen some people do in public places. I think that's uncalled for. No, I'm the nice customer. And I'll tell you who else I am.

I'm the customer who never comes back!

Author Unknown (but nice)

figure 13.3

THE NICE CUSTOMER

The nice customer may not complain or make a scene, but he or she won't come back, either. You can lose loyal customers without knowing it if you wait for the nice customer to let you know about a problem. The nice customer may also tell many others about his or her bad experience in your establishment, losing you many potential customers. *What is a good way to help the nice customer let you know his or her true feelings?*

more about...

Customer Self-Esteem

"Customer service shouldn't just be a department, it should be the entire company."

—Tony Hsieh, Internet entreprenuer, venture capitalist, former CEO of Zappos

To encourage complaints, you must understand what a customer complaint is. It is not a personal attack, nor is it a signal that your relationship with the customer is broken forever–or even temporarily, in most cases. A complaint is *an opportunity to improve.* Customer complaints inspire improvements to service that would otherwise have gone unnoticed to people in many businesses.

An emphasis on careful listening to complaints sends the signal to customers that yours is a customer-focused business. It says, "We view our customers as partners; we want to build relationships with them."[17] When customers perceive that you are willing to listen, and that you are encouraging their response, they will be much more likely to respond honestly and openly.

When people in a business solicit complaints, they often phrase questions in a way that will encourage a neutral or positive response. For example, you might ask a restaurant customer, "How was everything, was it okay?" or "Was the food tasting great tonight?" and you are likely to get the response, "Yes, it was fine," whether it was really fine or not. However, if you ask, "What one thing could we have done to improve your dining experience?" an honest and helpful complaint is much more likely to result.

If you are in management, do all that you can to make complaining easy for the customer. Put a suggestion box by the register. Offer a space on your website where customers can easily provide feedback. Use various methods of rewarding customers who complain, like offering free food or a chance to win a prize. All of these are ways to reward customers who offer helpful complaints.

Most important of all, make sure that you do all you can to correct the problems customers are complaining about. Without that step, most of the rest is meaningless. With this positive, constructive attitude toward complaints, you'll probably develop a greater mutual respect with your customers. With that, your human relations with them will improve.

An effective way to prevent customer dissatisfaction is to define what your company's brand brings to customers, and then to make good on what you have promised your company will deliver. This is known as a **brand promise.** Figure 13.4 gives examples of the brand promises of some well-known corporations. The brand promise expresses attitudes of value toward customers and the world. A brand promise represents the company's ideas, beliefs, and values. It summarizes the value or experience a company's customers can expect to receive when they interact with the company. The better the company delivers on the promise, the stronger the brand value in the mind of customers and employees.[18]

brand promise

A short statement that tells customers what they can expect from a particular brand.

» HANDLING THE DIFFICULT CUSTOMER

"The customer is always right." Everyone has heard this, but is it true? It's true only in terms of the attitude it expresses. Although the customer may be very wrong, you still need to treat that customer with courtesy and civility.

Brand Promise Examples

1. **Starbucks:** "To inspire and nurture the human spirit—one person, one cup, and one neighborhood at a time."
2. **Coca-Cola:** "To refresh the world. . . To inspire moments of optimism and uplift. . . To create value and make a difference."
3. **Nike:** "To bring inspiration and innovation to every athlete in the world."
4. **Google:** "Organize the world's information and make it universally accessible and useful."
5. **Geico Insurance:** "15 minutes or less can save you 15% or more on car insurance."
6. **Coors Light:**"The world's most refreshing beer."
7. **McDonald's:** "Inexpensive, familiar and consistent meal delivered in a clean environment."
8. **H&M** (Hennes & Mauritz AB clothing retail company): "More fashion choices that are good for people, the planet and your wallet."
9. **Marriott Hotels:** "Quiet luxury. Crafted experiences. Intuitive service."
10. **IBM** (International Business Machines Corporation): "Innovation that matters, for our company and for the world."

figure 13.4

BRAND PROMISE EXAMPLES

As you can see, remembering the customer is the key to each of these examples of a brand promise. *How can these brand promises help you keep the customer in perspective?*

Carrying out such an attitude can sometimes require more than a little self-discipline. It may also require some courage.

Remember two things when dealing with an unreasonable, angry, or overly demanding customer. First, stay focused. The success of the company depends on satisfying your customers, no matter how unreasonable they might seem. If you can remain focused on those long-term needs, rather than on a short-term need to express your own anger or frustration, you will be the winner. Remember, there will actually be very few difficult customers; stay focused and remember how most customers are reasonable and easy to deal with.

more about...

Customers

"The customer may not always be right, but they are the customer. So, let them be wrong with dignity and respect."

—Shep Hyken

Second, avoid the **self-esteem trap**. The customer is probably upset about something that has little to do with you directly. Even if the problem is the result of one of your own mistakes, don't take the attack personally, and especially don't let it affect your own self-esteem. Don't allow a customer's emotional outbursts to make you have negative feelings about yourself.

self-esteem trap

The circumstance that comes from taking a customer's attack personally and letting it affect your self-esteem.

Sometimes, the only way to get a customer to communicate with you is to help him or her calm down and cool off. Instead of using your energy to show that you are right and that the customer is wrong, put your energy into getting the customer calmed down. Some obvious exceptions to this rule would be customers who are sexually harassing or physically assaulting employees, as well as customers who are involved in other illegal activities.

more about...

Using Empathy to Diffuse a Difficult Situation

Empathy is the ability to share and understand others' emotions. A recent survey of 150 CEOs showed that over 80 percent recognized empathy as key to success.[19] Using empathy at work to deal with an upset customer can help remind us that, "This is just business; it's not personal!"

REAL WORLD EXAMPLE 13.4

Bob Farrell (1927–2005), motivational speaker and restaurant entrepreneur, often repeated the story of a new waitress he hired. A customer who had been coming to this same restaurant for a few years asked the new waitress why the customary pickle wasn't in his hamburger. The waitress replied, "A pickle will cost you extra." As you might expect, this answer irritated the customer greatly. When Farrell heard the story, he coined a phrase that he used often when he spoke in public: "Give them the pickle!" Farrell urged all companies to figure out what their "pickle" is, and give it to customers.

figure 13.5

BUSINESSES GOING THE EXTRA MILE

Many successful businesses go the extra mile by offering customers free services to ensure goodwill. *When did a company "going the extra mile" make you want to stay their customer?*

Ways to Go the Extra Mile

- The local coffee shop has a loyalty rewards program. When customers buy nine drinks, they get the tenth free.
- A large furniture and home goods store provides a safe place for children to play while the customer is shopping.
- An auto parts store posts free online tutorials online for its customers that explain how to do various car repairs.

» GOING THE EXTRA MILE

"Giving the customer the pickle," or not charging extra for small requests, is simply good business. If this has ever happened to you as a customer, you might remember how it felt when you asked for a small "extra" with your order and the employee handed it over with a smile, without charge. A different, opposite example to that might be if you stopped into a store to ask for some change, only to have the cashier tell you, "Sorry, we don't make change unless you're buying something." When you do need to make a purchase, will you come back to that store? Probably not. Will you likely tell some of your friends and family about the incident? Probably so. By refusing you the small extra, the store may have lost a dozen future sales.

None of the examples discussed in Figure 13.5 would cost a company much money, and the payback is well worth it. When a company gives customers small "extras" as a way of showing appreciation, it is called **going the extra mile**—and it nearly always pays for itself.

going the extra mile
When a company gives customers small extra products or services as a way of showing appreciation for their business.

» CUSTOMER SERVICE ETHICS

Acting ethically is essential in all manners of business and customer engagement. When deciding on the ethical approach to a situation, ask yourself, "Would I want all of my procedures to be made public knowledge?"

The customer service ethics of a company or organization help to define the quality of the services the customer will receive. With this in mind, a strong, well-trained customer service staff is the "face" of the business, but the culture of the business is dictated by managers' support for their staff (and their adherence to strong ethical standards in delivering customer service). Sometimes, working under stress can bring out the best–and worst–in an organization's employees' delivery of customer service.

Christopher MacDonald, a business ethics consultant and professor at Duke University and Ryerson University, suggests that workplace ethics are a crucial dimension of customer service, noting several ways that customer service can become *unethical.* Dr. MacDonald has found that:

- Front-line service representatives can do unethical things like lose orders, lie to customers, or even sabotage their own work.
- Managers may say they commit to providing "post-sale" quality service, but then provide fewer resources than needed for this important customer service function.
- Senior management may make policy decisions that result in unethical customer treatment, such as making it difficult for customers to request warranty service, or limiting the amount of time and attention devoted to each customer's needs.

Unethical customer service can result in victimized customers, or may create a frustrating gap between the service that the customer expects and actually receives, and can negatively affect a business's reputation through negative online reviews and plain old word-of-mouth.[20]

So how does a company ensure the highest standards of professionalism and ethics in its delivery of customer service? Most simply, by promoting its desired values (ethics), and making sure frontline workers follow the rules (compliance). This takes the form of being truthful to customers, safeguarding sensitive information, and displaying empathy and concern to customers with problems.[21] By making sure that customers know that their satisfaction is guaranteed, and by following the philosophy that the

more about...

Many organizations and companies, especially those that deal extensively with the public, have adopted a formal, written "Customer Service Code of Ethics" (see the example that follows). Have you noticed this kind of formal policy at places you do business, or where you've worked?

Customer Service Code of Ethics

"We promise to provide value-added customer service through:

1. Polite and courteous service.
2. Handling requests in a timely manner with consistent follow through and communication.
3. Mastering knowledge of Human Resources laws, rules, policies, and concepts and ongoing issues within the organization.
4. Proactive problem solving and guidance.
5. Offering confidentiality and an open door policy.
6. Facilitating positive change through employee relations programs, services, and consultation.
7. Encouragement of a high level of employee morale through recognition and effective communication.
8. Promoting learning and personal growth to increase individual success and the overall value of the organization.
9. Operating with integrity and promoting accountability.
10. Providing a safe and healthy working environment."

Source: State of Oregon, Department of Public Safety Standards and Training, Human Resource Division, 2013.

more about...

An excellent guideline for **ethical customer service** is the Golden Rule: Are you treating the customer the way you would like to be treated in a similar situation?

customer's needs are of the greatest importance, much of the ethics issue will take care of itself. Both employees and managers, though, must bear in mind the ethical issues when considering overall needs of their company. You will learn more about ethics in Chapter 15.

» POOR GEORGE STORY

YOUR CUSTOMER'S SELF-ESTEEM

To succeed with customers, you must learn to bolster their self-esteem. When customers are uneasy about purchases, your ability to reassure them will help them trust you and your product or service. *How can you tell if a customer's self-esteem is interfering in his or her interaction with you? What are ways to support a customer in that case?*

Moxie Productions/Blend Images LLC

Who is the running the business? As this chapter ends, one final point must be emphasized: you must set limits as to the extent to which you will allow a customer to run your business. Regardless of how important the customer is, he or she must never be allowed to undermine company decisions. Les Schwab, Inc. is a successful tire store chain in the western United States. When the founder, Mr. Schwab, was still alive, he used the following story at training sessions for tire store managers. He called it the "Poor George Story."

George was a very likable, hardworking owner of a small tire store. One day John, a trucker, came into George's store and asked, "George, I need four tires for my pickup. How much?" George glanced quickly at his price sheet and replied, "The tires are $60 each. Do you want 'em balanced?"

"Of course, I want 'em balanced," was the answer.

"Well, $240 for the tires and $20 for the balancing–that's a total of $260."

"Oh, man! That's too much," countered John.

At this point George thought to himself, "I would hate to lose this sale; and, besides, business hasn't been very good lately." So without even doing the math, he said to John, "Tell you what, I'll throw in the wheel balance for nothing." George had made his first big mistake: He gave in, letting his customer know that his prices were variable.

Seeing that he could bargain, John came back with, "Make it $225, and you have yourself a deal."

George did some quick arithmetic and noticed that by selling the tires for $225, he would still have a profit margin of $33. Since business was so slow, he replied, "Okay, John, we'll put them on."

To run a tire store, the cost is 25 to 26 percent of sales, but George lowered himself to 14.7 percent. He wouldn't have to make this mistake many times before going broke.

Once the tires had been mounted and balanced, John asked if he could send him an invoice later for the tires since he didn't have his wallet with

REAL WORLD EXAMPLE 13.5

Junko is a receptionist at an insurance company. On Friday afternoon, her boss says, "I'll be out the rest of the day. Hold my calls." Thirty minutes later, an irate customer asks to see Junko's boss and tells her, "I have a 3:00 appointment, and this claim has to be handled today, or I'll lose everything!" What should Junko do? What would you do in the situation with this angry internal customer?

him. George said yes, but he had always assumed that since his operation was so small, he didn't need a formal policy on charging interest, collecting past-due amounts, or dealing with chargebacks.

John received his bill from George for $225 within a couple weeks. John thought to himself, "Good old George, he won't mind if I skip him this month." When he received a second bill, John figured that he should at least pay part of the bill. He gave George $50 and acted as if he were doing George a big favor. Five months later, the purchase was finally paid off.

FINDING A BALANCE

Although keeping your customers satisfied is an essential part of good business, attention to customer service needs to be balanced with firm leadership—including ethics and perspective—in order for a business to succeed. *How can customer service sometimes conflict with ethics, or let a customer run your business?*

Juice Images/Glow Images

After a few years, George went into bankruptcy. Hearing about the sad occurrence, John told his friends, "I sure do miss old George; he was a great guy. I guess he just wasn't a very good businessman." The next time John needed tires, he went to a chain store. There, the clerk quoted him the price, charged him $10 per tire for the wheel balance, and required a credit check and a long credit application form to fill out and sign. Although they charged him 18 percent interest, John didn't argue at all. And he didn't even think of trying to bargain them down to a lower price.

At the end of the story, George is broke. He goes to work for the same chain store that sold John his new tires. He sells tires at listed prices; he doesn't bargain; he charges interest; and he gives credit only to customers who qualify and will pay promptly. The moral of the story is: respect your customers and give them only the highest-quality service, but *never let your customers run your business.*

STRATEGIES FOR SUCCESS

Strategy 13.1 Establish a Bond with the Customer

1. Understand the customer's real needs.
2. If your customer is another business, learn about that business.
3. Provide exceptional service.
4. Avoid taking your special relationship for granted.

relationship selling

Forming meaningful relationships with your customers, which makes them much more likely to return and buy from you again.

Few factors will create more impact on overall and repeat sales than *bonding* with the customer. If you form meaningful relationships with your customers, they are much more likely to return and buy from you again. This practice is also known as **relationship selling**. When you have established a relationship with a customer, service is usually perceived more positively. For example, an attorney or real estate agent's services will be seen in a better light if they establish trust with their clients.[22]

Here are four principles that will help you form a bond of trust with your customers:

1. **Understand the customer's real needs.** Careful listening to the customer can compensate for a great number of drawbacks in a company. Think about your relationship with someone who is trying to sell you a product or service, or an internal customer on your work team you'll be working with on future projects. We would all rather work with someone who listens to our needs and preferences.
2. **If your customer is another business, learn about that business.** Customers will be more likely to want to work with you if you show a genuine understanding of their business and what it means to them both personally and professionally. Read annual reports, trade journals, and newspaper and magazine articles to acquaint yourself with the business you are dealing with, including knowledge of their competitors. Learning about the "business" of a customer includes learning about the functions and processes of other departments in your own company, who may be internal customers.
3. **Provide exceptional service.** Exceptional service yields a strong bond in a business relationship. Providing exceptional service isn't always up to you completely, and even as a manager you might not have as much control over the quality of service as you would like. You can be creative, and it is usually possible to innovate.
4. **Avoid taking your special relationship for granted.** Don't ever misuse the working relationship you have created. As mentioned earlier in the chapter, avoid ever getting to the point where you take the customer for granted. Remember, the customer includes your co-workers and other internal customers as well. The bond you have worked hard to create is a precious commodity; treat it—and your customers—accordingly.

STRATEGIES FOR SUCCESS

Strategy 13.2 Support the Customer's Self-Esteem

1. Put the customer at ease.
2. Put yourself in the customer's place.
3. Make the customer feel understood.
4. Make the customer feel important.
5. Praise the customer appropriately.

As with all parts of the human relations process, the customer relations issue has a great deal to do with self-esteem—in this case, the self-esteem of the customer.

You probably have a favorite store, bar, or restaurant where you feel welcome, where you feel comfortable and at ease. That feeling of ease cannot be packaged and sold as a commodity. Yet it is very real—and extremely important to customers of any business, in any place.

When you work with customers, you need to be always aware that their self-esteem is an issue, and it may be a big issue. However, many people in business ignore their customers' needs. Instead, they get wrapped up in trying to impress customers with the things they are selling, or with their own part of the company's tasks—and with themselves. Focusing on the customer will make the customer interested in your products and more likely to want to continue a positive working relationship.

Here are some steps you can take to build up your customers' self-esteem:

1. **Put the customer at ease.** Getting your customer to relax, and to feel comfortable with you and your company, is the most important first step. Smile with a genuine smile, not a phony one. Use the customer's name—but be careful about using it too soon, especially the customer's first name, because certain customers do not like being called by their first name by people they don't know very well. Stand close enough to the customer to have a conversation, but not too close; avoid invading personal space. (See Chapter 6.) Try to use a similar tone of voice, rate of speaking, and body language as the customer. These details are subtle, but customers tend to identify with people who have mannerisms like their own.[23]
2. **Put yourself in the customer's place.** *Empathy* is the ability to imagine yourself in the other person's place. Develop empathy by asking yourself, "If I were this customer, with the needs she has, how would I feel?" This habit can be difficult to form and cultivate. But if you begin thinking this way, it will improve all areas of your human relations, not only customer relations.
3. **Make the customer feel understood.** Like all other people, customers need to feel they are communicating successfully. Be sure to interpret what they say correctly. Asking a question that starts out with "Do you mean . . . ?" or "It sounds like you are saying . . . " can go a long way toward letting the customer know that you care enough to listen and understand what he or she is saying. If you are at all unclear about what the customer means, ask questions until you are sure.[24]
4. **Make the customer feel important.** One of the worst things you can do is to allow distractions (such as phone calls or other interruptions) to pull your concentration away from the customer. While you are working with a customer, act as though nothing else is as important. Let people know you are focused on being with them. To the customer, you are the whole company—so do all you can to make that feeling go both ways.
5. **Praise the customer appropriately.** You don't have to try too hard when praising a customer. Has the customer accomplished something special recently? Congratulate him or her specifically. But do so in the framework of authentic caring. This is another habit that will likely help in relationships outside of work, too. Praise is a powerful human relations tool, but use it wisely. Insincere praise can be much worse than none at all.

   Be sure to make the praise specific. A generalized compliment can leave the customer wondering, "What did that really mean?"[25] Don't just say that Mr. Johnson asks good questions that show he knows the product; tell him sincerely that you admire that quality in a customer! If your only knowledge of the quality you want to praise is general, ask a specific question in a nonthreatening way. A specific question shows real interest and often leads to a point where you can offer sincere praise.

STRATEGIES FOR SUCCESS

Strategy 13.3 Handle the Difficult Customer Professionally

1. Let the customer vent.
2. Get the facts.
3. Understand the customer's feelings.

4. Suggest a solution.
5. End on a positive note.
6. Don't expect to win them all.

Here are some easy-to-follow guidelines for dealing with a customer who is already angry.[26]

1. **Let the customer vent.** You should allow an angry customer to speak his or her mind. This approach might be difficult, but being a good listener (even to an angry, perhaps ranting customer) is still the best approach. Cutting the customer off usually does more harm than good. Let the customer know that you sympathize and care enough to hear everything. Have you ever noticed your anger disappearing after you have gotten somebody to listen to you? Quite possibly, the customer mainly needs the chance to express some strong emotions on the issue; all you need to be is the sounding board.
2. **Get the facts.** If possible, have all available information on the case right in front of you. If the customer is wrong, be sure that your sources are correct. Ask questions to verify what the customer is telling you. If two or more versions seem to contradict each other, ask questions until you are satisfied that you have found the truth. If the customer is wrong, don't say so directly. In all cases, focus on what can be done to solve the problem, rather than to place blame.
3. **Understand the customer's feelings.** A great deal of expressed anger can confuse you when you are trying to listen. Are you sure you understand the main issue in the mind of the customer? What you see as the main issue might not be what the customer thinks it is. Only when you have completed this step and know what the customer thinks is wrong can you find out how to make it right. Remember also that among the most common emotions you will encounter from customers will be insecurity and fear. Identifying the source of the emotions is an important step in solving a clash with an upset customer.
4. **Suggest a solution.** Be specific and clear. Be careful not to make promises that the company might not let you keep. If the solution you can offer isn't what your customer wanted, clearly explain why you have to offer this solution instead. Avoiding using "company policy" as an excuse. If you must use that phrase, explain the reasons for the policy as best you can.
5. **End on a positive note.** Once you have agreed to a solution, thank the customer for his or her patience and for bringing the problem to your attention. Don't apologize too much. Instead, focus your attention on the future. Mention steps that can be taken on both sides to prevent such problems from happening again. Don't hesitate to include things you will do personally to prevent future occurrences. Your main purpose now is to keep the customer's future business.[27]
6. **Don't expect to win them all.** You can be as patient, empathetic, helpful, and efficient as possible, and still have a percentage of customers who will remain angry and/or fearful. Some customers simply are difficult people, and they will stay that way no matter what anyone does. Again, don't take their words or actions personally. If possible, ask your manager for help.[28]

When the time arises to use these six steps in the workplace, do the best you can. If you don't remember all of them, at least remember to do everything you can to keep an angry customer's complaint from turning into an argument. It takes two people to make an argument. As the representative of the company, you must refuse to become that second person. You may have to suppress the desire to answer back defensively. In the end, though, your self-control will pay off because you'll have kept your cool—and demonstrated to yourself and others around you that you can handle stressful situations.

STRATEGIES FOR SUCCESS

Strategy 13.4 **Keep Customers Satisfied**

1. Personalize the customer's experience.
2. Utilize technology.
3. Provide seamless access.
4. Talk to customers.
5. Use social media.

To reduce the loss of unhappy customers—both internal and external—to competitors, keep current customers happy. Considering that our largest economic sector is the service sector, and that online shopping for both goods and services is on the rise, remember technology in your customer service. Keeping up with social media and modernizing applications will help retain satisfied customers.

1. **Personalize the customer's experience.** Address the customer by name, maintaining respect. Find out what the customer wants and expects in the way of service. Personalize and customize the customer's experience.
2. **Utilize technology.** Go mobile where possible. Use mobile applications for convenient access and services for customers where available.
3. **Provide seamless access.** Create easy access for customers to move between sales channels. Provide sales and services that make the customer experience easy.
4. **Talk to customers.** Ask customers what types of technology they use and invest in the services and applications that will support those technologies.
5. **Use social media.** Use technology to gather immediate data for decision making for your business. Find customer preferences for sales and services through social media channels. Advertise up to the minutes with social media.

Source: Ira Sager, "Angry Customers Cost Companies $5.9 Trillion," *Bloomberg,* October 22, 2013, https://www.bloomberg.com/news/articles/2013-10-22/angry-customers-cost-companies-5-dot-9-trillion (retrieved June 20, 2017).

CHAPTER THIRTEEN SUMMARY

Chapter Summary by Learning Objectives

LO 13-1 Explain how to determine what customers really want. No matter what business you are in, customers really want only two things: good feelings and solutions to problems. By listening to the customer, you can discover the customer's needs in these two categories.

LO 13-2 Define customer service. You have good service only when the customer thinks you do. Good customer service always includes good human relations.

LO 13-3 Describe the internal customer. The internal customer is the person who depends on the other people in the company to provide services and products for the external customer.

LO 13-4 List the two simplest principles of customer service. (1) Find out what the customer needs. (2) Do whatever is possible to satisfy those needs.

LO 13-5 Give examples of issues in customer service. Major issues in customer service include: (1) your customers and your attitude, (2) delivering bad news to customers, and (3) encouraging complaints. All three are very important in creating a customer-friendly business.

LO 13-6 Compare and contrast ways to handle a difficult customer. When dealing with an unreasonable, angry, or overly demanding customer, stay focused and avoid the self-esteem trap. When customers are already angry, let them vent. Find out the facts, making sure that you also understand the customer's *feelings;* then suggest a solution. End as positively as possible. Don't expect success in all cases; some difficult customers will remain difficult no matter what you say or do.

LO 13-7 Explain the significance of going the extra mile. Going the extra mile means giving customers those little extras to show your appreciation of their business. These little "perks" are inexpensive and have a tremendous potential payoff in customer satisfaction.

LO 13-8 List ways to use strong ethics in customer service. Good ethics in treatment of customers nearly always comes back as customer satisfaction.

LO 13-9 Explain the moral of the Poor George story and how it relates to customer service. The Poor George story illustrates how someone in business can keep the customer from running the business. Treat your customers well, with great respect and deference, but never let the customer make business decisions for you. That is, don't let the customer run your business.

key terms

bad news skills 383
brand promise 386
going the extra mile 388
good feelings and solutions 378
internal customer 380
"nice" customer 385
relationship selling 392
self-esteem trap 387
two simplest principles 381

review questions

1. Explain what it means to say that customers really want *feelings* and *solutions,* rather than products and services. When you are a customer, what does that mean to you?
2. Define the term *internal customer.* Why is the concept of *internal* customer service important to an overall understanding of customer service?

3. Why is an understanding of the "nice" customer of great importance in improving customer service? Have you ever known or been someone like this "nice" customer, who is unhappy but only leaves and never returns rather than voicing concerns to the business?
4. What are the "two simplest principles" of customer service? What importance does listening play in the use of those principles? Have you ever seen them violated?
5. Explain the importance of forming a relationship or bond with the customer. How does one go about establishing such a bond?
6. What are the four steps in giving the customer bad news? Explain each step.
7. What are some steps one can take to build the customer's self-esteem? Which step, in your opinion, is the most important? Explain.
8. What is meant by "going the extra mile"? Provide an example from your life of either serving customers or being a customer. How did your experience affect you? Was there ever a time when someone didn't go the extra mile?
9. What is a danger in allowing clients too much power in making decisions in working with you? How would you explain the "Poor George" idea versus the old saying that "the customer is always right?"

critical thinking questions

1. Try to recall if you can identify a businessperson who was able to establish a relationship or bond with you or one of your family members. How was this accomplished?
2. Have you ever been the victim of a company's poor customer service policy, as either an external or internal customer? What specifically occurred? How did this treatment make you feel? What would you have changed in that situation if you had the power to do so?
3. Have you been in a situation where you witnessed a difficult customer? Explain. What would have calmed the situation?

working it out 13.1

THE DIFFICULT CUSTOMER

School-to-Work Connection: Interpersonal Skills

Scenario: A customer at the pharmacy inside the larger drugstore where you work has come to pick up a prescription, but there is no prescription order in her name. She tells you that she has been a customer at this store for years. You try to track down the order, but cannot find any records for her. You also cannot find any record of her ever having been a customer at all. She is becoming increasingly upset. She does not believe that you cannot find the records and says you are not looking hard enough. She says that you are trying to make her health condition worse. She demands that you call her doctor (she can't quite remember the doctor's full name) and her insurance company (she doesn't remember the name of the company and she has not brought her insurance card with her) to make sure her medications, once they are ordered, will be covered. Meanwhile, a line of customers is forming behind her. The longer the conversation takes, the louder and more flustered she becomes. The more flustered she becomes, the more concerned customers and store employees become. Your manager is on a lunch break while this situation is occurring. You have a feeling she is in the wrong drugstore pharmacy.

Instructions: What should you do? Place an X on the line next to the actions that are the most appropriate responses to this difficult situation.

____ 1. Frown and show how irritated you are with the request to figure out her doctor's name and insurance company.

____ 2. Laugh at the customer and act as though she is joking.

____ 3. Respond in a calm and patient tone.

____ 4. Show empathy by saying you have been in a situation when you could not find your health insurance card and you understand her frustration.

____ 5. Walk away and tell her that you have some important things to do.

____ 6. Look at your watch and ask how much longer this is going to take.

____ 7. Tell her you are not paid enough to handle this situation, and she should have asked for a manager.

____ 8. Explain in detail how your pharmacy is highly rated among its competitors and tell her she is lucky to be able to get her medications there at all.

____ 9. Ask her to be reasonable and consider the needs of customers waiting in line behind her.

____ 10. Thank her for her understanding and cooperation.

Answers: 3, 4, and 10 are the most appropriate choices. All of the other choices could make the situation worse by increasing the customer's negative experience, which could damage your customer relations in the long term.

working it out 13.2

ROLE-PLAYING THE CUSTOMER

School-to-Work Connection: Interpersonal Skills

Purpose: To experience the difficulties in dealing directly with customer problems.

Procedure: Two students should volunteer to play the parts of a customer and an employee, role-playing the following situation.

Ron (or Rhonda) works in the men's fashions department in Bernstein's, a large department store. Delmar Wiggins, a customer, places three shirts and a sweater on the counter. In a friendly voice, he jokes, "I guess this is all I can afford." When Mr. Wiggins offers his Bernstein's charge card, Ron (or Rhonda) quickly runs a computerized check for the approval. The card is denied. Ron (or Rhonda) excuses himself for a moment and reaches for a phone out of earshot from the customer. His call to the office confirms that Mr. Wiggins hasn't paid a cent on his already-large account for over four months.

Instructions: The student who plays Ron (or Rhonda) should proceed with the plan for fair treatment of Mr. Wiggins. Remember that Ron (or Rhonda) needs to keep Mr. Wiggins as a cash customer in the future, and hopefully, for this sale as well. Mr. Wiggins should act innocent, as though he has no knowledge of a bad account, but he also should be willing to comply with whatever reasonable suggestions Ron (or Rhonda) comes up with.

The student who plays Mr. Wiggins may decide to deny the fact that payments are overdue. In this case, Ron (or Rhonda) needs to find other ways of dealing with the customer. He or she could say something like, "It appears that they have not received your most recent payments. I am sure that there is some misunderstanding. Would you like me to put you on the line with them so that you can confirm your most recent payments?" Mr. Wiggins, knowing that no such payments have been sent, will probably back down and agree to another method of payment.

working it out 13.3

THE RESILIENCY QUIZ

Watch the TEDx Talk with author and CEO Jenn Limm, titled "Delivering Happiness," and then answer the following questions.

1. What does the speaker mean by saying we are "hard wired" for happiness, but we have a hard time knowing how to achieve it?
2. Why would a major shoe company, Zappos, have a CEO in charge of happiness? Who is being served, the internal customers or the external customers?
3. How does the speaker describe the purpose of Zappos? How does this fit with what you have learned in this chapter?
4. What does the author mean by saying that "success does not create happiness, but happiness creates success" in life?
5. What are the factors in the "happiness framework" described by the speaker? How do these fit (or not) with your own work and life journey?

The video can be found here: www.youtube.com/watch?v=1be5QdcwM34.

case study 13.1

The Car Salesman Who Lost the Sale

Jody had been out of high school for two years when she landed a good office job with opportunities for advancement. This week was the one-year anniversary of getting that job. As she had promised herself, she was taking some time off work to fulfill her long-held dream of buying a brand-new car.

She had done some research. Not only had she spent weeks poring over online brochures that her older brother had sent her, she also had read *Consumer Report* articles on all of the cars within her price range. At the first dealership, she was snubbed by three salespersons who seemed to be too busy to talk to her, so she left. The second dealership she visited was about the same. She decided that was okay, since she did not see the car she wanted at the first dealership or the second anyway. By the time she had approached the third car lot, she had begun to lose some of her initial enthusiasm.

But that was where she found the car of her dreams. It was exactly what she had been looking for. After the test drive the salesman, Kyle, asked her to make him an offer. "Any offer; just whatever you think is reasonable," he said. Jody knew that she could bargain. She started with a very low figure–about $3,000 below the price on the sticker. "Well, I'll see what I can do," Kyle replied. "I'll have to ask the boss; I hope he's in a good mood."

Twenty minutes later, Jody walked to the back of the showroom to the candy machine. She had heard a familiar voice ask someone: "Well, d'ya think I've stalled this one long enough?" It was now clear that Kyle was not busy discussing this offer with the boss. Jody asked one of the customer people the whereabouts of the sales manager, Kyle's boss. "He's gone for the day," was the reply.

Quickly, Jody returned to Kyle's office. When Kyle walked in a minute later, he said without pausing, "Well, I'm sorry; the boss just won't go for it, but let's see if we can work out a deal that will be almost as good." Kyle was startled when Jody answered, "No thanks, you've wasted enough of my time."

With that, Jody walked out of Kyle's office and left the dealership.

Case Study Questions

1. What procedures and attitudes covered in this chapter could have helped Kyle make the sale to this would-be customer, Jody? (Remember, this was to be the car of her dreams.)
2. Years ago, a number of car dealerships tried to change the traditional methods of selling cars in the United States (most notably, the Saturn Corporation). As a potential customer, what advice would you give them to aid in their attempts?
3. Specifically, what suggestions would you give car dealers who use Kyle's tactics, if they want to boost return business?
4. What suggestions would you make to Kyle in terms of the internal customers at the car dealership?

International Business Calling

An automotive parts manufacturer in Michigan is part of a larger supply chain that extends from the United States, to Canada, Mexico, and back. Emma Wilson, the manager at the main plant outside Detroit, is responsible for customer care–that is, dealing with her international customers when they have problems with orders and shipments. She has been distracted on this particular morning resolving an issue with a shipment to Mexico–the client is waiting for an immediate shipment of 10,000 replacement mirrors due to a defect, which is nowhere near ready to ship. This means she will have to authorize overtime for staff to complete the rush order, and then find the budget to cover the cost of expedited shipping to Mexico due to their delay. She has not counted on any of this.

When the phone rings and she recognizes the voice of her Canadian colleague from Toronto on the line, she is already annoyed and begins immediately, "Ugh, what's up, Asha? I don't really have time to help you right now. Can't you just handle your problems yourself this time, and I will call you later in the week?" Asha, a little taken aback, has not had a chance to tell Emma that one of their clients is actually with them on speakerphone and is now very angry, cursing in Canadian French. The client on speakerphone had his request for a full refund for a recent damaged shipment denied, and now he is livid, ready to cancel all future orders with the company. Asha had called Emma to have her help calm the client down and preserve their business relationship, which is now at serious risk.

Meanwhile, Asha is now caught in the middle. On top of being unable to satisfy the client's business demands, she has now also lost the client's respect as Emma's attitude toward her made her "lose face." The client, who now feels insulted, has launched into an angry tirade. Emma is also angry, thinking that Asha should have warned her ahead of time that a client was also on the line. And Asha is embarrassed by the whole incident.

Case Study Questions

1. Does this situation have more to do with external customer relations, with internal customer relations, or both? Explain.
2. What should Emma do to resolve the situation on all fronts? What should Asha do to keep the client happy and to develop a better working relationship with Emma?
3. Explain how this company could encourage complaints in the future to avoid such situations. What types of complaints and solutions would you anticipate management receiving in the company?

PART FOUR

thriving in a changing world

14 Human Relations in a World of Diversity

15 Business Ethics and Social Responsibility

16 A Productive Workplace and Success

Every time you scan the news workplace issues appear in the headlines. You have probably read about the nationwide shift to a service economy, diversity and globalization, corporate ethics, and the challenges in balancing home, career, and family life. How can we use human relations skills to handle these and other workplace issues? Part Four offers some answers.

Chapter 14 covers the trend of increasing diversity in the workforce, and offers strategies on ensuring cooperation and fairness in a diverse environment. Chapter 15 explores ethics and ways to maintain an ethical workplace. Chapter 16 looks at personal issues that affect the work experience and affect individual productivity.

14

CHAPTER FOURTEEN

HUMAN RELATIONS IN A WORLD OF DIVERSITY

LEARNING OBJECTIVES

After studying this chapter, you will be able to:

LO 14-1 Describe the current trends in labor force participation, and how they are creating more diverse, inclusive workplaces.

LO 14-2 Explain the benefits of diversity and inclusion in the workplace.

LO 14-3 Identify barriers to creating a diverse organization.

LO 14-4 List different types of discrimination in the workplace.

LO 14-5 Define cultural intelligence and its importance, and how to increase it.

LO 14-6 Describe the connections among stereotype, prejudice, and discrimination.

LO 14-7 Give examples of how to promote a more diverse workplace.

STRATEGIES FOR SUCCESS

Strategy 14.1 Build Your Cultural Intelligence

Strategy 14.2 Assess Your Knowledge

Strategy 14.3 Reducing Sexual Harassment

In the Workplace: In the Minority

SITUATION

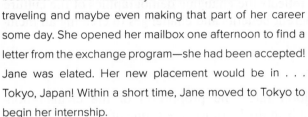

Gorodenkoff/Shutterstock

Jane applied to spend her last semester of college in an internship exchange program overseas. She had grown up not far from her college in the midwest, where she was majoring in business. But she had always dreamed about traveling and maybe even making that part of her career some day. She opened her mailbox one afternoon to find a letter from the exchange program—she had been accepted! Jane was elated. Her new placement would be in . . . Tokyo, Japan! Within a short time, Jane moved to Tokyo to begin her internship.

"This way please, Miss Halstead." Jane chuckled at being called "Miss" and looked around with amazement as her new boss, Mr. Takahashi, led her through a quick tour of the office. This new job would be her first time in a professional work environment. She had worked summers at the lake, but that was mostly just a way for her to hang out with her high school friends who were also working there, and make some money at the same time.

But this new office in the middle of the metropolis of Tokyo was a whole different experience! As she walked toward her new office, she passed dozens of her new co-workers already busy at work. Even though this was a large financial organization with offices around the world, Jane was a little surprised to see that most of the employees were men, and appeared, by their mannerisms and styles, to be Japanese. This puzzled her; the type of ethnic and social diversity she had grown used to back in her college town was absent here. She began to feel a little lost, then brushed this thought aside, thinking, "This will be great, and I am going to make the best of whatever happens!"

DISCOVERY

As Jane continued to walk through the maze of offices, smiling and shaking hands or being greeted with a head nod or a traditional bow, she thought, "This is different, but it's going to be amazing! I've got so much to learn about my new colleagues!" She looked forward to getting started.

THINK ABOUT IT

Jane had become accustomed to the diversity of her college town. How might the apparent lack of diversity in her new environment affect her on a day-to-day basis? What other types of diversity might she expect to encounter? What specific tools and skill sets might she need to develop to work successfully with her new co-workers? How can finding yourself in a new role or environment help you better understand yourself and others?

DIVERSE WORKPLACE
Hero Images/Image Source

» A DIVERSE SOCIETY

American society has become more racially and ethnically diverse during the past few decades, and Americans like Jane will find that the workforce reflects this growing participation of older employees, women, racial or ethnic minorities, and immigrants across a wide spectrum of job sectors. Diversity also appears in languages and religious traditions among employees. As companies from Wall Street to Silicon Valley seek to shape their companies in a way that reflects the changing demographics of the culture around them, there are inherent benefits and challenges to creating an inclusive, diverse workplace.

A Changing Labor Force

The labor force participation rate—"the proportion of the civilian non-institutional population that is in the labor force"—is one of the key measures of labor market activity in a country's economy. Each age, gender, race, and ethnic group exhibits a different socioeconomic trend and so a different labor force participation rate. Demographic trends in the workplace are worth noting because they describe a labor force and workplace that is changing with the times. These changes include an aging and more diverse population that will continue growing, but at a slower rate. Ultimately, these changes will impact the growth of the U.S. economy and its ability to create goods and services.[1] The following labor force trends have been observed in recent years:

- The size of the overall labor force is contracting, with automation increasing.
- Women will continue to enter the labor force at a faster pace than men.
- Baby Boomers (people born between 1946 and 1964) are exiting the labor force in large numbers. The leading edge of the Baby Boomers turned 65 in 2011 and became eligible for Social Security retirement benefits. Since then, large numbers of them have been leaving the labor force every year.
- While many Baby Boomers are retiring, a significant number are not. This means that the proportion of older employees in the workplace may increase, in part because older workers may increasingly choose to remain in the workforce past the traditional retirement age.
- Racial and ethnic minorities have assumed an increasing presence in the labor force, and the result can be seen in the growing diversity of the workforce.
- Hispanic or Latinx employees will continue to expand their workforce participation; their share of the labor force is projected to double from 15 percent in 2010 to 30 percent by 2050.

- African Americans and Asian Americans will continue to increase their labor force participation at a faster rate than non-Hispanic whites.
- The number of American companies engaging directly in competition with overseas companies will rise, and the importance of the global marketplace will continue to increase.
- Younger people are entering the job market later because they are staying in school longer to be able to obtain better paying jobs in the future. As a result, they are beginning their careers at a slightly older age.

And while not explicitly included in the demographic numbers, people with disabilities are more visible in the workplace today, as are people with diverse religious beliefs. The overall diversity of the American workplace will continue to increase due to broad labor force trends like the ones described previously, as well as companies' own internal focus on creating inclusive, diverse workplace for their employees.

Positive Attitudes about Diversity in the Workplace

The Pew Research Center is a nonpartisan American think tank based in Washington, D.C., that provides information on social issues, public opinion, and demographic trends shaping the United States and the world. In its 2019 Report, *Americans See Advantages and Challenges in Country's Growing Racial and Ethnic Diversity,* Pew researchers found that most Americans value workplace diversity, with at least half saying that it is very important for employers to promote workplace diversity.[2] Consider the highlights from the survey that follow (see Figure 14.1):

- A majority of Americans (57 percent) say the fact that the U.S. population is made up of people of many different races and ethnicities is very good for the country, and another 20 percent say this is somewhat good.
- More than 6 in 10 Americans (64 percent) say that the fact that the U.S. population is made up of people of many different races and ethnicities has a positive impact on the country's culture; just 12 percent say it has a negative impact; and 23 percent say it does not make much difference.
- Three-quarters of Americans say it is very important (49 percent) or somewhat important (26 percent) for companies and organizations to promote racial and ethnic diversity in their workplace. African Americans are particularly likely to say this is very important: 67 percent say this, compared with 52 percent of Hispanic or Latinx respondents, and 43 percent of white respondents.
- Most Americans (75 percent) say it is somewhat or very important for companies and organizations to promote racial and ethnic diversity.

figure 14.1

RESEARCH ON DIVERSITY IN THE WORKPLACE

Source: "Americans See Advantages and Challenges in Country's Growing Racial and Ethnic Diversity," Pew Research Center, May 8, 2019. https://www.pewsocialtrends.org/2019/05/08/americans-see-advantages-and-challenges-in-countrys-growing-racial-and-ethnic-diversity

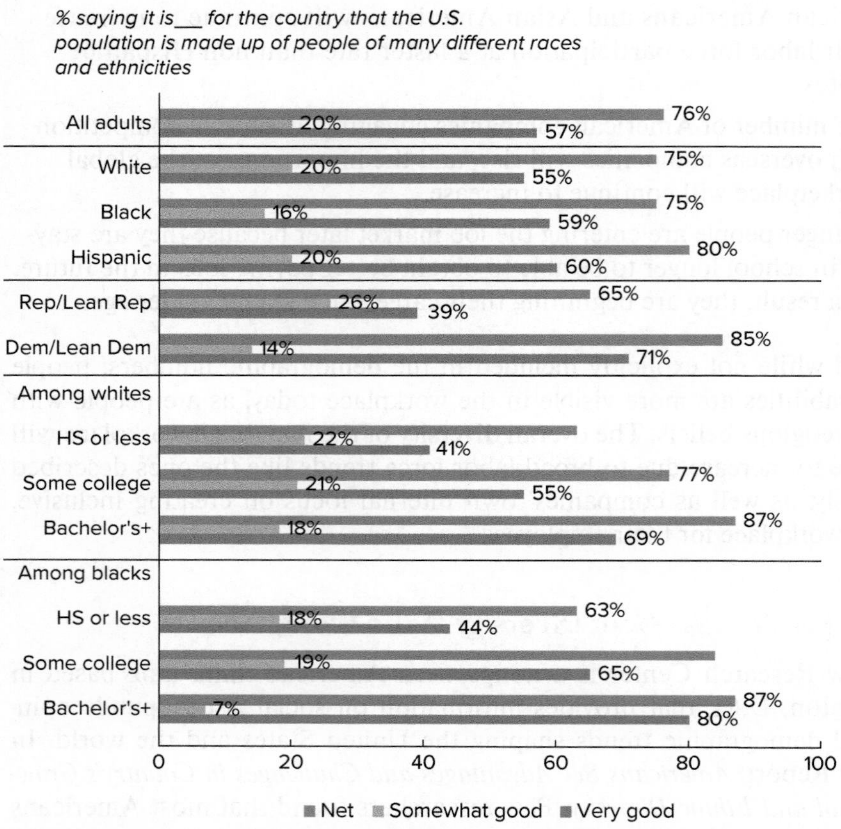

(a) More than half of respondents say racial and ethnic diversity is very good for the country

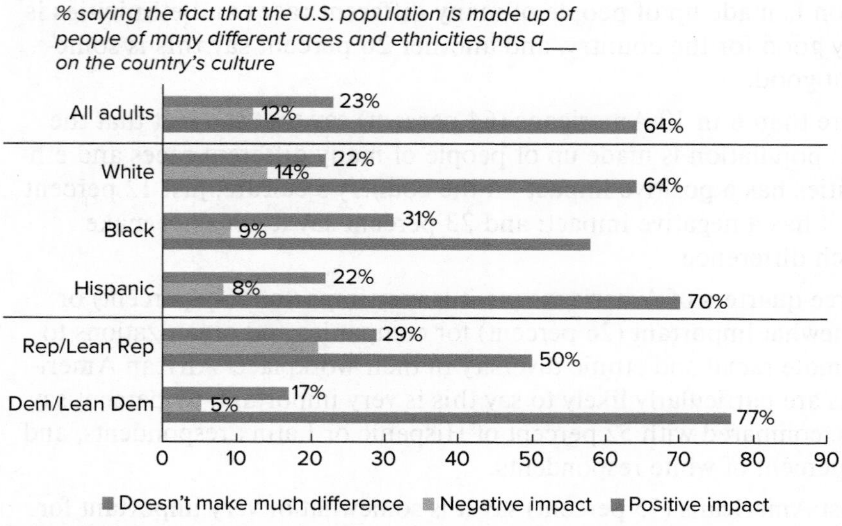

(b) Most see diversity as having a positive impact on the country's culture

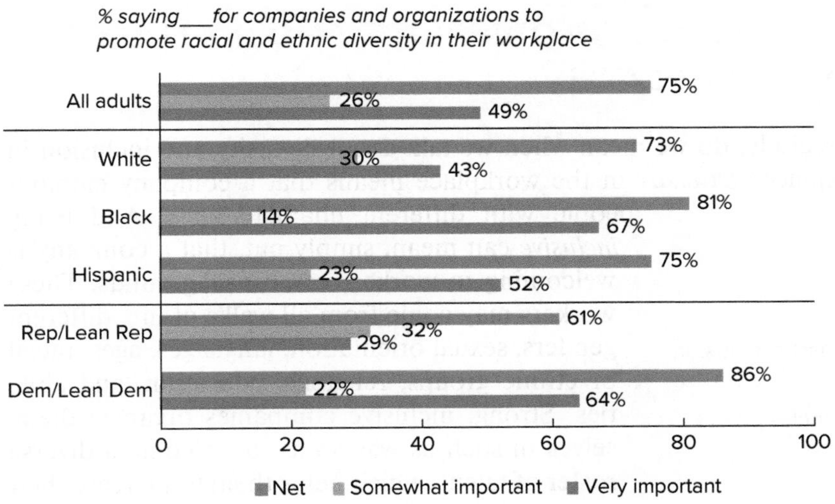

(c) There is broad support for workplace diversity

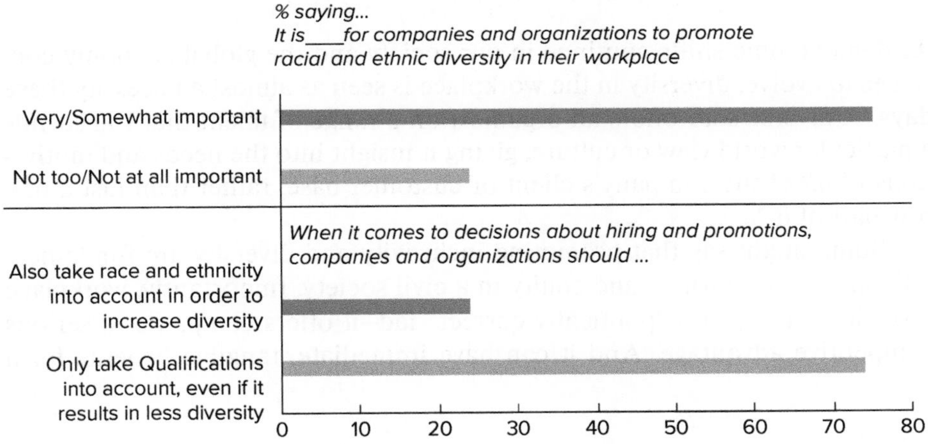

(d) Many say applicants' race and ethnicity should not be a factor in hiring and promotions

About one in four (24 percent) say that, in addition to their qualifications, a person's race and ethnicity should be considered in decisions about hiring and promotions in order to increase diversity.[3]

Consider the survey findings presented here, which describe varying attitudes about diversity in the workplace. What trends do you notice? Based on your own individual experience, how would you have answered the survey questions?

more about...

Corporate Diversity Policies

Companies often publish their diversity policies in statements on their websites under links titled "Corporate Social Responsibility" or "Corporate Ethics" or "Company Values." Take a look at the websites for companies you do business with, or any large organizations you are familiar with. Can you find such a link? What information does each company include?

» THE BENEFITS OF DIVERSITY AND INCLUSION IN THE WORKPLACE

What, precisely, do we mean when we talk about diversity and inclusion in the workplace? *Diversity* in the workplace means that a company employs people with different characteristics. And being *inclusive* can mean, simply put, that a company is welcoming to workers of all backgrounds. These workers may come from all walks of life, different genders, sexual orientation, languages, ages, racial or ethnic groups, religions, education, and abilities. Strong, inclusive companies organize themselves in such as way so as to welcome a diverse roster of talent, which helps them to increase their competitive edge in the marketplace.

more about...

Diversity and Inclusion

"Diversity is being invited to the party; inclusion is being asked to dance."

—Verna Myers, Diversity and Inclusion Expert

Why Is Workplace Diversity Important for Businesses?

As demographic shifts continue in our society and the global economy continues to evolve, diversity in the workplace is seen as almost a necessity these days. A diverse staff offers an organization a range of talent that transcends a particular world-view or culture, giving it insight into the needs and motivations of *all* of the company's client or customer base, rather than just a narrow part of it.[4]

Some might say that promoting inclusivity and diversity are fundamentally matters of fairness and equity in a civil society. Importantly, workplace diversity is not just a "politically correct" fad—it offers companies a serious competitive advantage. And it can have immediate, tangible benefits for a

more about...

Making the First Move—Say Hello!

Here are 50 ways to say hello around the world.

Language	Greetings: "Hello"
Arabic	Marhaba
Bavarian and Austrian German	Grüß Gott
Bengali	Namaskar
Bulgarian	Zdraveite
Catalan	Hola
Chamorro	Hafa adai
Chinese	Nǐ hǎo
Croatian	Dobro Jutro = Good morning Dobar dan = Good day Dobra većer = Good evening
Danish	God dag

Language	Greetings: "Hello"
Dutch	Hoi = Hi Hallo = Hello
Finnish	hyvää päivää
French	Bonjour
Gaeilge	Dia dhuit
German	Guten tag
Greek	Yasou
Hebrew	Shalom
Hindi	Namaste
Hungarian	Jo napot
Icelandic	Góðan dag
Igbo	Nde-ewo
Indonesian	Selamat siang
Italian	Salve
Japanese	Konnichiwa
Korean	Ahn nyong ha se yo
Latin	Salve
Lithuanian	Sveiki
Luxembourgish	Moïen
Maltese	Bonġu
Nahuatl	Niltze
Nepali	Namastē
Norwegian	Hallo
Persian	Salam
Polish	Cześć
Portuguese	Olá
Romanian	*Bună* ziua
Russian	Zdravstvuyte
Serbian	Zdravo
Slovak	Ahoj
Spanish	Hola
Swahili	Hujambo
Swedish	Hallå
Tahitian	Ia orna
Thai	*Sawasdee*
Tsonga	Avuxeni
Turkish	Merhaba
Ukrainian	Zdravstvuyte
Urdu	Assalamo aleikum
Vietnamese	xin chào
Welsh	Shwmae
Zulu	Sawubona

Source: Twin English Centres, "Learn to Say 'Hello' in 50 Languages," https://www.englishcentres.co.uk/blog/learn-to-say-hello-in-50-languages (retrieved April 17, 2020).

company's bottom line. Consider the following benefits that workplace diversity can offer to businesses:[5]

- *Variety of perspectives.* Differing viewpoints become highly beneficial for planning and executing a business strategy.
- *Increased creativity.* People with different backgrounds can offer different experiences and different perspectives. Exposure to a variety of perspectives and views can lead to higher creativity.
- *Higher innovation.* According to corporate HR talent management and leadership strategist, Josh Bersin, inclusive companies are *1.7 times more likely* to be innovation leaders in their markets.[6] When employees from different backgrounds and perspectives interact, this can open the door to innovation.
- *Faster problem solving.* Employees from different backgrounds bring different solutions to the table. In fact, *Harvard Business Review* found that diverse teams are able to solve problems faster than cognitively similar people.[7]
- *Better decision making.* Researchers have found that when diverse teams made a business decision, they outperformed individual decision-makers up to 87 percent of the time.[8] When working together, employees with different perspectives and backgrounds come up with more solutions, which leads to more informed and improved decision-making processes and results.
- *Increased profits.* Companies with greater workplace diversity achieve greater profits. They make better decisions faster, achieve better business results, and reap more profit.
- *Higher employee engagement.* The link between workplace diversity and employee engagement is straightforward—an employee who feels included will be more engaged.
- *Reduced employee turnover.* Diversity and inclusion in the workplace help all employees to feel accepted and valued. When employees feel accepted and valued, they are also happier in their workplace and stay longer with a company. As a result, companies with greater diversity in the workplace have lower turnover rates.
- *Better company reputation.* Workplace diversity can enhance the company's reputation and brand, making it easier for many different people to relate to the company and its brand. Companies that are dedicated to building and promoting diversity in the workplace are seen as more human, and more socially responsible organizations.
- *Improved hiring results.* When a company has a reputation for being diverse and inclusive, it can be seen as a more desirable place to work, making it easier to attract top-notch talent from the region, and beyond. According to Glassdoor, 67 percent of prospective job seekers

identified a diverse workforce as important when considering new job offers.[9]

DIVERSITY AIDS EMPLOYEES

Monkey Business Images/ Shutterstock

Why Is Diversity Good for Employees?

As just discussed, creating a more diverse workforce is increasingly important for businesses in today's economy. It has become a critical factor for employees on the job, as well. Whether they are new hires or brought together on internal teams to accomplish the organization's professional goals, employees value a diverse workforce for many reasons, including the promotion of mutual respect at work, gains in economic power, conflict reduction, improved business reputation, build-up of business assets, and increased exposure to people of other groups. These reasons are discussed as follows in more detail:[10]

- Diversity in the workplace *promotes mutual respect among employees.* Creativity flows when groups or teams comprised of co-workers with different work styles, who represent different cultures, genders, or generations, come together to perform essential tasks. Co-workers may begin to better recognize their colleagues' varied strengths and talents, increasing their mutual respect for one another.
- Diversity in a workplace *increases economic empowerment of marginalized workers.* A hard reality of the American economy is that different members of the workforce have historically been marginalized (or treated as insignificant) due to racism, ageism, discrimination against people with disabilities, and other factors. Such discrimination is, of course, unethical and illegal. It also has serious economic consequences for these groups experiencing discrimination. When people from diverse backgrounds are able to find meaningful work in their chosen field, their standard of living can improve, creating stronger, financially secure employees (and their families). This economic empowerment of marginalized workers can have wider benefits in the community, city, and region.
- *Conflicts can be resolved and reduced* with diversity in groups. When employees from diverse backgrounds and skill sets come together for a common task, individual differences can be minimized and conflict can be reduced. Respect for co-workers can both reduce the likelihood of conflict and give employees the tools to resolve conflict on their own. This focus on conflict resolution can minimize employee complaints and litigation. And it can enhance the quality of employees' interactions with their supervisors and co-workers.
- A company's *business reputation is enhanced* with a diverse staff. A business organization known for hiring a diverse roster of employees

can attract a wider pool of talent. This diversity in the workplace is critical for employees because it can enhance the business's reputation, attracting new customers who choose to do business with companies whose practices match their own socially responsible worldview. And a company's diversity can breed loyalty—both from employees within the organization and its external customers.

- *Employee development can be used to build business assets.* With the rise of global markets and a supply chain that can stretch across the globe for even a small-sized business, the importance of workplace diversity cannot be overstated when it comes to an organization's work in foreign countries or with foreign suppliers. Conversely, a diverse roster of employees can appreciate and perhaps better respond to the challenges that working within a global marketplace presents.
- Diversity in the workplace *brings exposure to different kinds of people.* Employees are people, and people are inherently social creatures. A diverse workplace creates an environment where employees can interact with others and be exposed to the ideas from different cultures and backgrounds. This can be particularly rewarding for employees when they are placed in multigenerational work environments, where important, foundational ideas from the past can be interpreted through the lens of younger, more tech-savvy workers.[11]

more about...

Diversity

"We become not a melting pot but a beautiful mosaic. Different people, different beliefs, different yearnings, different hopes, different dreams."

—Jimmy Carter, former U.S. President

» REMOVING BARRIERS TO A DIVERSE WORKPLACE

Despite the best of intentions, many businesses and organizations may not always recognize internal barriers that could be hindering their path toward an inclusive, diverse workplace. They may have the talent in place, be legitimately interested in creating a work environment that reflects the larger society, or be otherwise civic-minded. But it is essential to recognize—and address—the barriers described below when they occur.

Some organizations will have regular diversity training programs, workshops, and other resources for their employees. Larger size employers may even make a commitment to hiring diversity officers as part of the administrative team, and they may have established policies of working only with suppliers who have similar policies.

Attitudes that Create Limitations

All attitudes have three parts: what you *think, feel,* and *do.* These three parts of an attitude exist whether you are talking about the NBA playoffs, state politics, or creamed spinach. For example, you may *think* to yourself, "Creamed spinach is green," then *feel* a negative reaction to that particular color of green: "That color reminds me of slime. Gross!" As a consequence, you *do* something (or in this case choose to *not* do something) by not eating the creamed spinach.

In talking about diversity in the workplace, you can think of prejudice against other people as part of a specific, often harmful attitude. Like other attitudes, this one is composed of three parts. **Stereotypes** are your *thoughts or beliefs* about specific groups of people. **Prejudice** is how you *feel* as a result of those thoughts or beliefs. **Discrimination** is your *behavior,* or what you do (or intend to do, or are inclined to do) as a result of your stereotypes and prejudice. A closer look at these components follows.

HANDLING PREJUDICE
Everyone needs to know how to handle prejudice when it's encountered, and everyone needs to know how to eliminate prejudice within himself or herself. This applies especially to people whose jobs involve working with the public. *How can someone's prejudiced attitude affect others when working with the public?*
Terry Vine/Blend Images/Getty Images

Stereotypes

A stereotype is a thought or belief about members of a given group. That belief may be positive, negative, or neutral; and it is usually oversimplified, exaggerated, and/or overgeneralized. Whether it is a positive belief ("Asians are good students and employees") or a negative one ("senior citizens are too old to be good employees"), it is potentially damaging because it lumps everyone into one group without recognizing their individual characteristics.

People also stereotype tasks and jobs: a manager's job has often been stereotyped as "a man's job," whereas clerical or secretarial duties are labeled "women's work." Or people may group entire occupations in gendered groups, as still seems to happen with firefighters and nurses. Stereotypes hurt minorities, women, men, and members of other groups—they are harmful to everyone and to the organizations itself. Hiring, promotions, and job evaluations are areas where stereotypes can affect who is accepted or passed over.

A study of stereotyping and prejudice on the job uncovered these examples:

- "My supervisor follows me to the restroom, lunchroom, telephone, or whenever I am away from my work area. I think it's because I'm the only minority there."
- "She scrutinizes my work closer than she does the white employees. She gives me orders in a derogatory way."
- "He constantly makes vulgar remarks about me, such as calling me the 'entertainment and recreation committee.'"
- "She always shakes her finger in our faces when she doesn't like something we did."[12]

In each of these cases, the stereotyping has resulted in feelings of prejudice and discriminatory behavior against an employee.

stereotypes
Your thoughts or beliefs about specific groups of people.

prejudice
The outcome of prejudging a person. Prejudice in communication is the unwillingness to listen to members of groups the listener believes are inferior, such as other ethnic groups or women; it can also take more subtle forms; how you feel as a result of the stereotypes you believe in.

discrimination
Your behavior, or what you do (or intend to do, or are inclined to do) as a result of your stereotypes and prejudice.

Prejudice

Prejudice is another type of attitude. *Prejudice* means "to prejudge" or make a judgment without knowing a person beforehand. It sums up the negative feelings or evaluations about people and groups that are stereotyped. Prejudice causes **bias**, which is a tendency to judge people before you know them, basing the judgment only on their membership in some group or category of people. This type of conscious or obvious bias is also known as **explicit bias**. Explicit bias can be negative or positive; that is, we may consciously lean *toward* or favor a person or group, or lean *away from* or disfavor a person or a group.

bias
A tendency to judge people before knowing them, basing the judgment only on their membership in some group or category of people.

explicit bias
Attitudes and beliefs individuals hold on a conscious level, related to a person or a group. This type of bias often arises as the direct result of a perceived threat.

unconscious bias (implicit bias)
Social stereotyping about certain groups of people that individuals form outside their own conscious awareness; also known as *implicit bias*.

Bias can also happen at the unconscious level. **Unconscious biases** are social stereotypes about certain groups of people that individuals form outside their own conscious awareness. This type of *unconscious* thinking is also known as **implicit bias**. We all carry our own unconscious beliefs regarding different social and identity groups, and these biases stem from our innate human tendency to organize the things in our social worlds by categorizing.

Unconscious bias occurs with much more prevalence in the workplace than explicit, conscious bias does; and it is often incompatible with one's conscious values. Certain scenarios can activate unconscious attitudes and beliefs, such as when multitasking or working under time pressure.[13]

Everyone has certain prejudices, whether conscious or otherwise, and whether you believe it or not. Even people who consider themselves unprejudiced often have certain *strong* likes and dislikes based on categories of people. Prejudice undermines human relations, and impacts productivity. It is disruptive and causes low morale in the workplace or in any other place where it occurs unquestioned.

Origins of Prejudice

For American society to eliminate prejudice, it needs to know where prejudice comes from. For decades, psychologists and sociologists have been very interested in studying what causes prejudice. Although they do not agree on any one cause, there are a few theories that can be summarized. In general, the origins of prejudice can be divided into three broad categories: social causes, cognitive (thinking) causes, and emotional causes.[14] (See Figure 14.2.)

Social Causes of Prejudice

Many theories have been put forth about how social factors cause prejudice. One theory is that people form prejudices to try to increase their own feelings of self worth, such as when climbing the career or social ladder. It's easier for people to feel superior when they are able to identify other groups of people as inferior. This unequal status leads to prejudice. It also becomes a vicious cycle when people then use the fact that they are higher up on the status pole to justify their prejudice and discrimination toward people they view as lower status.

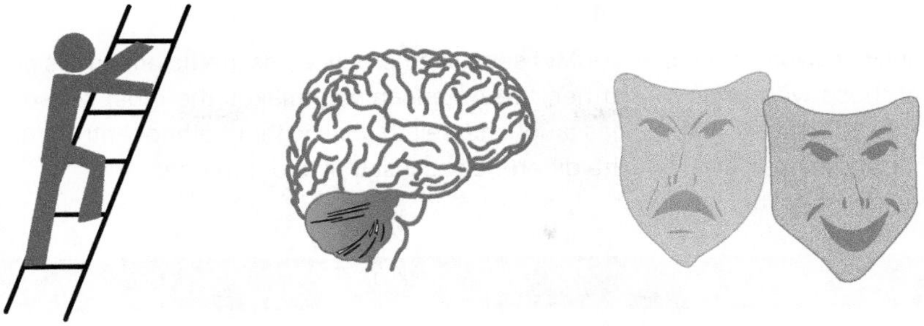

Social
- Status
- Self-esteem
- Us vs. them
- In group/out group

Cognitive
- Thinking
- Reasoning
- Categorization
- Boxes

Emotional
- The "right way"
- Habit
- Ethnocentrism
- Competition

figure 14.2

THE ORIGINS OF PREJUDICE

The three origins of prejudice are social ones (the need to feel higher in status than others), cognitive (the need to categorize and stereotype people), and emotional (such as habit, or ethnocentrism). *Which type of prejudice can be most damaging?*

Another social theory is that prejudice helps people define themselves and feel socially accepted. When people belong to a group and feel accepted, they tend to rate other groups as inferior. Conforming to a group's standards also helps people feel more accepted, and many groups encourage *us-versus-them* feelings and behaviors. For example, a new university student in a strange city may join a fraternity or sorority to make friends, but this could mean missed opportunities to form friendships outside of the group. In this example, prejudice may be used to reduce the student's anxiety, insecurity, and inner conflict. These same feelings are also social causes of prejudice.

A final social theory of prejudice looks at institutional support systems, or the way organizations and society itself unintentionally create institutional racism, sexism, or exclusionary policies. For example, men and women make up about equal proportions of the population, but men are still highly over-represented in films and television shows as main characters, narrators for commercials, and authority figures.[15] This has the effect of promoting the idea that men really are authority figures who know much more about kitchen floor wax or dog food than women know about such things.

more about...

Scapegoating is *the practice of unfairly blaming others (such as ethnic groups) when something goes wrong.* The term originated from an ancient biblical custom of sending a goat into the wilderness to escape after the sins of the community were placed upon its head, taking the group's sins with it.

scapegoating
The practice of unfairly blaming others (such as ethnic groups) when something goes wrong.

All it takes to create prejudice is for people to identify themselves as part of a group (the in-group) while they see others as part of a different group (the out-group). If that seems too simple to be true, try this easy experiment on your own: go to any high school football or basketball game and actively cheer for the visiting team while sitting with the home team spectators. Note how you feel—and how the home team spectators behave toward you.

Cognitive Causes of Prejudice

cognitive categorization
A process in which the mind quickly sorts information into categories to function efficiently.

Cognitive causes have to do with thinking and reasoning processes. Some psychologists believe that prejudice originates with a process called **cognitive categorization**, in which the mind quickly sorts information into categories

REAL WORLD EXAMPLE 14.1

SooMei and Tracey are American businesswomen who often work in Argentina. They respect those who stick to schedules because punctuality is a shared value in their culture. However, when they work in Argentina, where an appointment might take hours—or days—to be kept, SooMei sees such practices as inefficient and is annoyed; to her, the American way makes the most sense. Tracey has taught herself to think without ethnocentrism and sees the difference as just that: a difference.

to function efficiently. Cognitive categorization is generally a necessary skill; for instance, if every time you walked into a classroom you had to take the time to figure out all over again which objects to sit on and which objects to write with, you would fail in school and in life. The problem is that cognitive categorization also allows you to categorize people quickly, and this can lead to prejudice.

Think about how you do this. When someone is walking toward you on the sidewalk, for example, you quickly and unconsciously notice some characteristics about the person: young, male, sagging pants, and carrying a skateboard. You feel able to understand, without figuring out each characteristic separately, what *type* of person this is. Cognitive categorization goes too far, however, when you assign people to cognitive *boxes,* then negatively evaluate them based on the boxes you've put them in.[16]

Emotional Causes of Prejudice

ethnocentrism

The belief that one's ethnic group is more normal than others; an emotional source of prejudice because of people's gut-level feelings about how right their group is—and, in turn, how wrong they think other groups are.

Ethnocentrism is the cause of a great deal of prejudice that people experience. Human beings tend to see their own ethnic groups as the most normal, and they believe their way of seeing and doing things is *the* right way. Ethnocentrism is an emotional source of prejudice because of people's gut-level feelings about how right *their* group is–and, in turn, how wrong they think other groups are.

Ethnocentrism exists everywhere, not just in the United States. Most societies are ethnocentric. This phenomenon is not intentional; the familiar way of doing things just seems right to most of us. If what is familiar is right, then by extension, many people feel that what is unfamiliar must be wrong. People are creatures of habit, and if it is their habit to live a certain way, doing otherwise may be strange or unusual.

Another theory about the emotional causes of prejudice is that people look for a target to blame when they are frustrated. When members of two groups are competing for scarce resources (such as jobs in an area with high unemployment), this competition can lead to frustration, followed by aggression, prejudice, and discrimination.[17]

Sample Sexual Harassment Policy Statement

Sexual harassment of employees or applicants for employment will not be tolerated in this company. Any employee who feels that he or she is a victim of sexual harassment by a supervisor, co-worker, or customer should bring the matter to the immediate attention of (name and title of person). An employee who is uncomfortable for any reason about bringing the matter to the attention of his or her supervisor should report the matter to the human resources department.

Complaints of sexual harassment will receive prompt attention and will be handled in as confidential a manner as possible. Prompt disciplinary action will be taken against persons who engage in sexual harassment.

figure 14.3

EMPLOYER'S SEXUAL HARASSMENT POLICY STATEMENT

Every employer needs to have a policy on how to deal with this issue, then inform each employee about it. Such an action will help prevent occurrences, as well as give employers guidance on how to act on complaints. *What are the components of an effective sexual harassment policy?*

Source: Robert K. McCalla, "Stopping Sexual Harassment Before It Begins," *Management Review,* April 1991, p. 46.

Sexual Harassment

The phrase **sexual harassment** was coined by Lin Farley, author of *Sexual Shakedown,* in the late 1970s. What is sexual harassment? The answer is spelled out clearly by EEOC guidelines: "Unwelcome sexual advances, requests for sexual favors, and other verbal or physical conduct of a sexual nature. . . ." Sexually harassing behaviors include forced fondling, slurs, and unwelcome flirting; it also includes sharing or posting suggestive pictures or material where others can see it.[18] (See Figure 14.3.)

The problem of sexual harassment in the workplace goes back to the time when men and women first started working together, especially in professional settings outside of the home, but people such as Farley have called attention to this long-ignored problem. You have already seen in this chapter how much the workforce is changing. Record numbers of sexual harassment (and sexual assault) reports now being made public remind us of the seriousness and the enormous extent of this unacceptable behavior. As women and men work together more and more, this problem of sexual harassment will need to continue to be examined, addressed, and resolved to prevent it from getting worse. The U.S. Equal Employment Opportunity Commission (EEOC) provides resources to help individuals and companies recognize and prevent such behavior, as well as other forms of discriminatory behavior.[19]

more about...

Hostile Environments

When sexual harassment relates to indirect actions such as posting pornography or talking about sex in a manner that makes others uncomfortable, this is called creating a **hostile environment**. It is considered equally as serious as direct harassment.

A hostile work environment is one in which behavior within a workplace creates an environment that is difficult or uncomfortable for another person to work in, due to discrimination.[20]

sexual harassment

Behavior that is defined by the EEOC as "unwelcome sexual advances, requests for sexual favors, and other verbal or physical conduct of a sexual nature."

The EEOC reports that the most common type of harassment consists of unwanted sexual teasing, jokes, remarks, and questions.[21] The AFL-CIO, or American Federation of Labor and Congress of Industrial Organizations, is the largest federation of unions in the United States. According to the AFL-CIO, "sexual harassment occurs in virtually every workplace, in every industry and at every level within organizations."[22] They report that the majority of people do not come forward to report the harassment, mostly due to fear of retaliation and job loss. Strict company policies that are publicized and followed can reduce this serious issue in the workplace.

Sexual harassment is not limited to male supervisors harassing female employees; anyone can become a victim of sexual harassment. In college settings, female professors have been harassed by male students and male professors, as well by female students and colleagues. While fewer reports are filed by men, sexual harassment can occur between people of either—or the same—sex. (See Figure 14.4.)

What can you do as an employee when someone sexually harasses you? The best way to stop harassment is to prevent it in the first place. But for

figure 14.4

IS THIS SEXUAL HARASSMENT?

While reading these instances, make sure that you ask yourself if all of the key elements to sexual harassment are present. *Are any elements missing in any of these?*

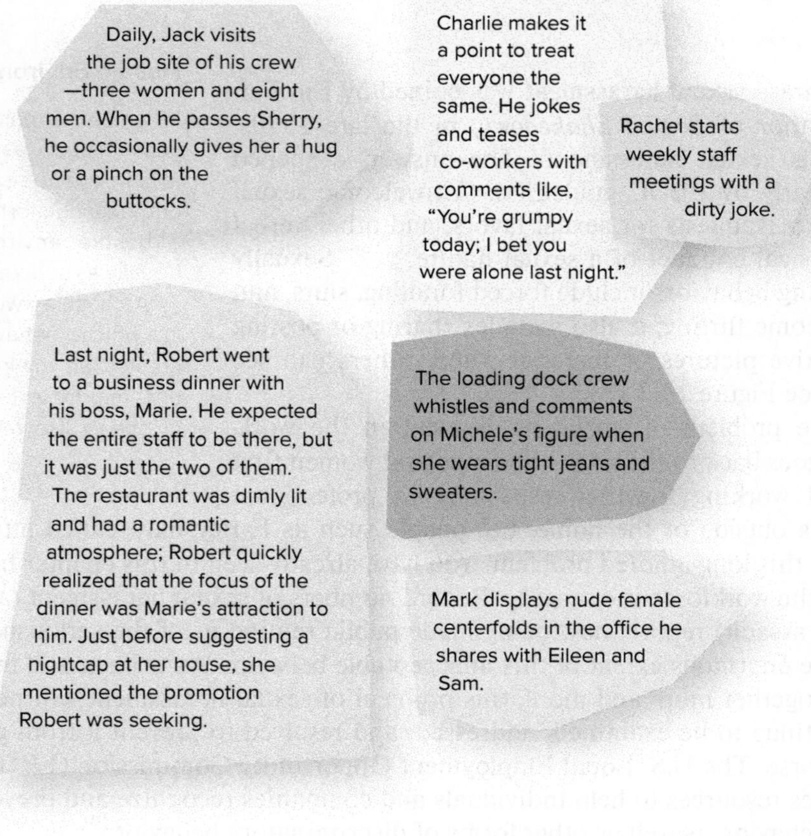
Daily, Jack visits the job site of his crew—three women and eight men. When he passes Sherry, he occasionally gives her a hug or a pinch on the buttocks.
Charlie makes it a point to treat everyone the same. He jokes and teases co-workers with comments like, "You're grumpy today; I bet you were alone last night."
Rachel starts weekly staff meetings with a dirty joke.
Last night, Robert went to a business dinner with his boss, Marie. He expected the entire staff to be there, but it was just the two of them. The restaurant was dimly lit and had a romantic atmosphere; Robert quickly realized that the focus of the dinner was Marie's attraction to him. Just before suggesting a nightcap at her house, she mentioned the promotion Robert was seeking.
The loading dock crew whistles and comments on Michele's figure when she wears tight jeans and sweaters.
Mark displays nude female centerfolds in the office he shares with Eileen and Sam.

employees who are harassed, the best advice is to *actively respond.* The most important first step is to ask or tell the person to stop. According to a 2016 survey by the U.S. Merit System Protection Board (MSPB) of federal employees, this tactic was used by 61 percent of the employees who tried it. Telling officials about the problem (36 percent of employees), or threatening to do so (35 percent), were also tactics widely used. Less often, employees filed a formal complaint (11 percent). Just remember that *the worst response is no response:* ignoring the problem and hoping it will go away hardly ever works, and will only cause you a higher level of stress.[23] And, while you may find yourself in the uncomfortable position of facing a harasser, the MSPB reminds us, "the onus should be on the harasser not to subject others to harassment and on the organization to hold harassers accountable."[24]

more about...

Stopping Sexual Harassment

Telling the harasser to stop is the best way to make sure the person knows the behavior is *unwanted.* Failing to let the person know the behavior is unwanted makes it more difficult to convince the supervisor or a trial judge that harassment occurred. Keep a dated notebook of occurrences and your responses. Tell a supervisor what is going on. If the harasser *is* your supervisor, report the situation to the next higher manager.

Some critics claim that the spotlight on sexual harassment over the past few decades has changed the workplace into a sterile environment. Is this true? Is today's workplace one in which no one feels relaxed, feels free to chat or exchange jokes with co-workers, or can compliment a co-worker? Some people claim so, and report feeling stifled, uncertain, timid, and resentful of the new rules. These claims, though, are usually greatly exaggerated—often by people resentful of women entering the workforce or of women's rights in general.

Good advice for both men and women is to adopt the slogan, "Don't Be a Jerk at Work." That is, use common sense—those who are thin-skinned should be less so; those who are obnoxious should stop being so.[25] Follow the commonsense guide in Figure 14.4 to recognize what types of behaviors will lead to sexual harassment complaints. With modified wording, these situations could apply to both men *and* women, and to all types of offensive behavior. They could also serve as examples regarding general ethical or unethical behavior, which you will learn about in the next chapter. If you're still in doubt as to whether or not particular words or actions would be seen as sexual harassment, use your own reaction as a guide: ask yourself, "Would I want someone saying or doing this to my spouse, my parent, my sibling, or someone else I care about?" If the answer is no, then others would probably see it as sexual harassment, too.

On both individual and company-wide levels, sexual harassment can best be prevented by people who know what it is, know the laws forbidding it, and know what to do when it happens. This chapter has provided an introduction to the issue. For more information, your public library and numerous law-related websites are full of information on sexism and sexual harassment.

In 2017, *Time* magazine selected the "silence breakers" of the #MeToo movement for their "Person of the Year" award, recognizing the importance of coming forward when sexual harassment and assault occur. Racism, sexism, sexual harassment, and other forms of discrimination are a serious issue

more about...

The Beginning of Civil Rights

The civil rights movement's first major victory came 10 years earlier than the Civil Rights Act of 1964 with the passage of *Brown v. the Board of Education,* a 1954 U.S. Supreme Court case that outlawed school segregation based on race.

in today's workplace, involving even the highest levels of corporate and political leadership. Everyone must take these issues seriously in order to combat them and create a productive and collegial work environment where employees are respected and treated with dignity.

Discrimination

Discrimination is acting or intending to act, or being inclined to act, on a prejudicial attitude. Prejudice is a feeling; discrimination is an act. Not all feelings of prejudice result in acts of discrimination, but individual acts of discrimination usually come from prejudicial feelings.

Discriminatory acts that are not caused by prejudice include discriminatory policies in the workplace that are not intentionally set to exclude members of specific groups or to treat them differently, but that have that effect anyway. These policies are referred to as **institutional prejudice**, or exclusionary policies.

institutional prejudice

Prejudice that is caused by policies in the workplace that are not intentionally set to exclude members of specific groups or to treat them differently, but which have that effect anyway.

One of the saddest dangers of discrimination is its tendency to become a **self-fulfilling prophecy**, which occurs when a victim believes that prejudice against him or her is deserved and then becomes what the stereotype states. In other words, a lifetime of discrimination can have devastating effects for individuals and their families.

self-fulfilling prophecy

The tendency for a prediction to actually occur once it is believed; for example, when a victim believes that prejudice against him or her is true, then fulfills these negative expectations.

A step toward eliminating discrimination in the workplace came with the passing of the Civil Rights Act of 1964. This law makes it illegal to discriminate against anyone because of race, color, religion, sex, or national origin. Title VII of this law covers any employer who does business between states and who employs at least 15 people for at least 20 weeks per year. This definition of *employer* also includes governments and other public institutions, schools and colleges, unions, and employment agencies. The Civil Rights Act was amended in 1972. In that year, the **Equal Employment Opportunity Commission (EEOC)** was established to monitor these laws.

Equal Employment Opportunity Commission (EEOC)

A federal agency established to monitor the laws set in place by the amended Civil Rights Act of 1964, as amended in 1972.

Discrimination comes from any number of different sources and can be aimed at a variety of different targets. The following section explores ways that discrimination can negatively affect different groups in the workplace, and offers some solutions to improve discriminatory conditions.

» RECOGNIZING DISCRIMINATION

Discrimination comes from any number of different sources, and can be aimed at a variety of different targets. Here we explore some major types of discrimination that may be targeted at certain groups.

Racism

racism

Prejudice and discrimination based on race.

Racism, which is prejudice and discrimination based on race, is one of today's most important social topics. This topic is filled with emotion and controversy and has been at the heart of many conflicts throughout history. Many people who lived through World War II or through the 1950s and 1960s expected that by the 21st century, racism in America would be a thing of the past. Sadly, they were wrong. Ethnic and racial minorities in the United States still experience widespread discrimination and prejudice. For many months beginning in May, 2020, protests and counter-protests exploded in the United States and around the world, sparked by events based on racial conflict.

HOW THE MEDIA CREATES PREJUDICE
Advertisements often portray men as authority figures and women as sex objects for no reason other than prejudice. *Are these images meant to portray reality, or are these models given roles by misguided advertisers? How can you identify institutional prejudice?*
Lars A. Niki

There are indications that the issue remains a serious problem in our time. For example, *genocide,* which is the systematic murder of an entire racial, ethnic, or national group, continues around the world. In the 1990s, genocide occurred in Rwanda and the former Yugoslavia. In the 2000s, the location was Darfur when in 2004 the U.S. government declared genocide to be occurring in this area of the Sudan.[26] In 2017, horrific actions in Myanmar against the Rohingya minority have been labeled "ethnic cleansing" by the United States and by the United Nations.[27] Unfortunately, these are just a few of the examples of widescale racism that continue to have devastating impacts on large groups of people.

Racial prejudice has proven difficult to overcome, and many people in the United States are still not accepted as part of mainstream society. Ethnocentrism is one of the factors in this problem, but certainly not the only one. Prejudice is another major reason. Racial and ethnic groups such as African Americans, Asians, Hispanics or Latinx, Native Americans, Jews, and other groups still strive for equal status in American society.

For example, America's history of racial inequality has created large gaps in education and employment that are still very real today. Data for 2019 (as an example) reveal such differences. The economic fallout of the COVID-19 pandemic will certainly create long-term unemployment effects on the U.S. economy, but prior to 2020, the economy was healthy and unemployment was low. While 2019 was a year of record unemployment, differences by race did emerge:

- Total U.S. unemployment rate in 2019: 3.5 percent
- Unemployment rate for white Americans: 3.0 percent
- Unemployment rate for African Americans: 5.7 percent
- Unemployment rate for Asian Americans: 2.7 percent
- Unemployment rate for Americans of Hispanic origin: 4.1 percent[28]

If these percentages don't seem drastically different to you, remember that they represent thousands of people. The most striking difference is the unemployment rate for African Americans, which is more than twice as high as the rate for Asian Americans and nearly twice as high as the rate for white Americans. Counted in this statistic are all those who are actively looking for work (seeking work). This is important because when a person *feels* his or

more about...

Black Girls Code

Black Girls Code (BGC) is a nonprofit organization created in 2011 in San Francisco, California, to help African-American youth, mainly girls, learn computer programming and coding, as well as website, robot, and mobile application building. The goals of this organization are to provide African-American youth "with the skills to occupy some of the 1.4 million computing job openings expected to be available in the U.S. in 2020, and to train one million girls by 2040" and to create community leaders and STEM (science, technology, engineering, math) teachers. BGC has now grown to several states and at least one other country, South Africa. Thousands of youth have now learned coding skills through BGC. Other organizations with similar goals include Girls Who Code, Native Girls Code, and I Look Like an Engineer. Within one organization, Black Girls Code is addressing three of the major types of discrimination addressed in this chapter—racism, sexism, and economic discrimination.

See: Black Girls Code, http://www.blackgirlscode.com.

her chances at securing a job are severely diminished, he or she may stop looking for work and will no longer be added to the data. This means that unemployment figures are always certainly higher than reported.[29]

Research has shown that African-American employees tend to be recommended for promotions less often and are less satisfied with their careers than white employees, in large part because of the stigma that arises when employees belong to a minority group.[30] In STEM fields (science, technology, engineering, and math) and in healthcare settings, these employees report incidents of discrimination, including receiving lower pay, facing hiring disadvantages, being treated as less competent, and being excluded from critical social networks.[31]

What many employers fail to realize is that by discriminating against employees because of their racial prejudices, these employers are damaging their own productivity (by reducing morale) and not capturing the skills and talents of these employees. With the historic two-term presidency of Barack Obama, American voters showed a willingness to set aside racism and select an African American to lead our nation. However, lingering perceptions about his ethnicity and Arabic name affected his acceptance and may have contributed to slowed legislative progress. Persistent national struggles about race during and after Obama's time in office indicate that we are by no means at the crossroads of a new, "post-racial" society.

Economic Prejudice

economic prejudice
Prejudice and discrimination toward people who are poorer or wealthier than you are.

Economic prejudice, which can be defined as the struggle and resentment between the *haves* and the *have-nots,* is an ancient and often ugly battle. The American Revolution in 1776, the Russian Revolution in 1917, and India's independence from Britain in 1947 are a few historical examples of these struggles. In these situations, the have-nots—who were at first powerless—joined together against their oppressors and won their freedom.

One of the theories of prejudice is that competition leads to frustration and aggression. In the United States, when economic times are hard, prejudice can focus on groups—often ethnic groups—that are seen as taking something away from "ordinary Americans," even if members of these ethnic groups *are* Americans. When the economy sagged in Michigan several decades ago, Japanese Americans were singled out because of auto employees' anger at Japanese auto manufacturers for hurting the American car market.

The discrimination against people of Japanese descent was so great that in some cases even people of other Asian national origins, such as Chinese, were violently discriminated against. This led directly to the murder of Vincent Chen in Michigan in 1982.

As with all prejudice, economic prejudice goes both ways. Not only do the poor resent the rich and stereotype them as selfish and uncaring, but the rich often look down on the poor and stereotype them as lazy or worthless. Many of those who live a middle-class or above existence are fond of reminding others that the United States is still a land of opportunity, where "you just have to work hard enough." They may believe that the have-nots simply refused the golden opportunity that was there for them. However, such an oversimplification is another example of how cognitive categorization leads to prejudice. (See Figure 14.5.)

more about...

History Repeats Itself

Just as Japanese Americans were unfairly blamed for the slump in American auto manufacturing, they were also blamed decades earlier for Japan's involvement in World War II. They were deprived of their belongings and sent to internment camps until the war ended. It was not until 1989 that the U.S. government repaid them for some of their losses.

Sexism

The term *male chauvinism* was coined during the 1960s to describe a feeling of male superiority over females that is quite similar to ethnocentrism. This is also known as **sexism**. Because a man may have attitudes and stereotypes of women in society, he may choose to see them as being of less worth—in other words, he may devalue women's contributions, or may even objectify (treat as non-human objects) or dehumanize women (treat as less than

sexism

Prejudice and discrimination based on gender.

DISCRIMINATION: THREE PROBLEM ISSUES

Type	Issues to Consider
Racist	Acceptance of minorities
	Assimilation versus separation
	Educational opportunities
	Cultural biases
	Hiring and recruitment policies
Economic	Power struggles
	Resources
	Resentment
	Competition for limited opportunities
Sexist	Male chauvinism and male advantage
	Gender roles
	Wage discrepancies
	Educational opportunities
	Tradition versus innovation

figure 14.5

PRIMARY FORMS OF DISCRIMINATION

Although there are many forms of discrimination, the three primary ones are racism, economic discrimination, and sexism. *How can employers fight each of these?*

REAL WORLD EXAMPLE 14.2

The employees at the distribution center had begun to kick it into high gear as the first truck of the night rumbled up to the loading dock. This was an experienced team, equal numbers men and women, and they were essentially interchangeable in their roles. With all the pallet jacks in use, several on the team had begun to hand-carry items off the truck. When Ivan saw Jessica transferring a heavy load onto the conveyor belt, he called out, "Hey Jessica, don't worry about that! It's heavy, and besides, I don't want you to mess up your outfit—let me get it for you!" Jessica, a high school wrestling champion who could deadlift more than most men her size, laughed off the suggestion. She had seen this subtle form of gender bias before, but refused to buy into the notion that she should have diminished responsibilities because of her gender.

human). This can happen in different ways. For example, one type of man sees females as inferior, not really worth listening to, and needing a man to be complete. Another type puts women on a pedestal. This sounds better, but it can be at least as frustrating to women as the first behavior. If a woman is placed on a pedestal, she is still not being seen as a fellow human being, and this distortion easily translates into numerous forms of inequality because she is expected to fulfill unrealistic expectations that the man has determined for her. This less direct form of male chauvinism is difficult to deal with because this man may honestly think he is treating women very fairly and kindly. Consider the case of Jessica, a worker in a distribution center, in Real World Example 14.2.

Women in most societies are expected to be feminine, a term associated with disempowering behaviors such as dependence, instability, emotional insecurity, a willingness to take orders but not give them, and passivity. When these expectations toward women exist in a workplace, so does prejudice; an obvious paradox occurs when a woman in such an organization becomes a manager or assumes another role of authority. (See Figure 14.6.)

Women have made significant strides since the 1950s in promoting inclusion and equality with their male counterparts. Despite these gains, American society still contains a number of areas where very little progress has been made. For example, consider the highest levels of the United States government. Since 1789, of the more than 2,000 senators in the history of United States Congress, only 50 have been female. And with more than 10,000 members of the House of Representatives since its inception, just 288 members have been female. During the 1992 election year, jubilantly dubbed "The Year of the Woman," only 2 women were elected to the Senate (out of 100 senators), and just 28 women (out of 435 members) to the House of Representatives. And while many countries in the world have elected women to the highest position of power (e.g., president or prime minister), the United States has not.[32]

Workplace Conditions for Women

Although women find it possible to be promoted to the supervisory level (the lowest level of the management structure), many report great difficulty in

Gender Prejudice in the Business World

Man	Woman
A businessman is aggressive.	A businesswoman is pushy.
He is careful about details.	She's picky.
He loses his temper because he is so involved in his job.	She's bitchy.
He's depressed (or hung over) so everyone tiptoes past his office.	She's moody, so it must be her time of month.
He follows through.	She doesn't know when to quit.
He's firm.	She's stubborn.
He makes wise judgments.	She reveals her prejudices.
He's a man of the world.	She's been around.
He isn't afraid to say what he thinks.	She's outspoken and opinionated.
He exercises authority.	She's a tyrant.
He's discreet.	She's secretive.
He's a stern taskmaster.	She's difficult to work for.

figure 14.6

HOW TO TELL A BUSINESSMAN FROM A BUSINESSWOMAN

Although men and women bring the same traits into the business world, many prejudiced employers and co-workers continue to perceive these traits as positive in men and negative in women. *Why do these prejudices persist?*

Robert Fulmer, Practical Human Relations (Homewood, IL: Richard D. Irwin, Inc., 1983), p. 360. McGraw-Hill Education. Used by permission.

getting into middle- and upper-level management, where the major decisions are made. In the 1990s, very few chief executive officers (CEOs) of publicly held corporations were women, and not much has changed in the decades that have followed. One reason may be that women are perceived by men as not being able to handle power when they get it. In fact, many women who are promoted to upper management positions succeed, and some feel this is because they had to work harder to be accepted. Some who fail in higher positions may do so because of indifference, scapegoating, or hostility from their male colleagues; not because they are incapable of succeeding.

Women's average income has been rising in recent years, but women still do not make as much as men do, even in the same occupations. Compared to non-Hispanic white men, white non-Hispanic women are paid 81 cents on the dollar and Asian women are paid 88 cents on the dollar. By contrast, this *gender wage gap* is much larger for Black and Hispanic women, who are paid only 65 cents and 59 cents on the dollar, respectively, compared with white males. In terms of the impact on women's paychecks, this means that relative to the typical white man, Black women take home $7.63 less per hour and Hispanic women take home $8.90 less per hour.[33] This adds up to a startling amount over an individual's career. According to the AFL-CIO, "The wage gap costs the average full-time U.S. woman worker between $700,000 and $2 million

more about...

Girls on the Run

Girls on the Run is a nonprofit organization found in all 50 states with the goal of teaching girls aged 8 to 18 confidence and life skills. "Running is used to inspire and motivate girls, encourage lifelong health and fitness, and build confidence through accomplishment." The program began in 1996 in Charlotte, North Carolina, and has now served more than one million youth.

See: Girls on the Run, https://www.girlsontherun.org.

MORE COMPLICATED THAN IT LOOKS
When women enter the U.S. workforce, they earn less on average than men, a phenomenon known as the *gender wage gap*. Added to lower earnings, women in the workforce are more often the primary caregivers in the home. Gender effects can sometimes blend with ethnic prejudices and have a doubly powerful impact on the groups in the workplace who are experiencing prejudice. *What are some ways to get at the real causes of prejudice, in order to stop it?*
Image Source

over the course of her work life."[34] In an annual survey by the AFL-CIO of more than 23,000 women, economic discrimination (lack of equal pay for equal work) was listed as a major workplace concerns named by respondents.[35]

The Fast Track versus the Mommy Track

Another problem women often face in the workplace is being expected to choose between the *fast track* and the *mommy track* when climbing the career ladder. Since women still shoulder most of the housework and child rearing in traditional American homes, if they choose the fast track they will have to forego at least some of these domestic responsibilities. In the fast track, employees are expected to work extra hours, ask for extra work, and work nights and weekends. The fast track seems to ask women to forget that they have families, or place families second in importance after jobs, rather than helping families balance home and work responsibilities.

What happens in the mommy track is just the opposite. When women try to balance family responsibilities with work responsibilities, they receive fewer promotions or raises and are often stuck in low-wage jobs. What most women want (and what many employers are slow to give) is a compromise: a job that offers satisfying work and a chance for advancement, with enough flexibility to allow for raising a family, too. This can be offered through flextime, manageable workloads, the option to telecommute all or part of the week, setting up onsite child care, and through other ways that reflect an employer's understanding of employees' personal needs.

By not allowing this kind of flexibility, many employers are restricting women with families from certain jobs, which is another type of discrimination. Not only are these employers shortchanging women who would like to have had such jobs, but they are also shortchanging their own businesses by not employing (or by under-employing) a large pool of potential employees with a high degree of talent and skills.

The three categories of discrimination just discussed (racism, sexism, and economic inequality) easily come to mind when considering prejudice and discrimination in the workplace, but there are other types of prejudice that don't fall neatly into one of those categories.

Overweight People

Court cases over the past decade have repeatedly ruled against prejudice against overweight people, at least where hiring and firing are the issues. In a landmark 1989 case, flight attendant Sherry Cappello, a 25-year veteran of American Airlines, was fired for being 11 pounds overweight. Because of a lawsuit Cappello filed, American Airlines was forced to change its weight-requirement policies.[36]

Although one might see Cappello's victory as a small one, prejudice against overweight people is still an issue today. In the words of Dr. Albert

Stunkard, a physician who specializes in obesity, "The extent to which overweight people have difficulty in obtaining work goes far beyond what can be justified by medical data and must be due to discrimination."[37] This issue will be critical in years to come—as the nation struggles with increasing obesity rates, will the stigma of obesity recede? At the same time, a backlash against "body shaming" has become more vocal in recent years, promoting acceptance for all body types.

more about...

According to the Centers for Disease Control (CDC), more than 70 percent of Americans are overweight, and more than 40 percent of this total is obese—a trend that continues to escalate into one of America's most serious ongoing crises. The health consequences of obesity can affect an organization if workers must take time from work to address health issues, and resources and workplace dynamics can be strained. Across the wider economy, absenteeism due to obesity or other health issues can impact national healthcare spending and the economy as a whole.

Source: "Obesity and Overweight," Center for Disease Control and Prevention, https://www.cdc.gov/obesity/data/adult.html (retrieved October 2020).

The LGBTQ Workforce

An emerging topic in the workplace has been the creation of a more open work environment for people who may not identify with traditional gender or sexuality roles. Where this topic was once highly controversial, even taboo in the workplace, the inclusion and full participation of non-binary, gay, queer and other ways in which people might identify themselves, has now become more widely accepted. In fact, the emphasis seems to have shifted from accommodating the individual worker, to creating an inclusive, inviting work environment for people of all backgrounds. This includes individuals who identify as lesbian, gay, bisexual, transsexual, or anyone who is non-heterosexual or non-cisgender (where cisgender means that personal identity and gender do correspond with birth sex).

Many current employment policies in the private sector forbid discrimination on the basis of *sexual orientation* (a person's sexual identity in relation to the gender to which they are attracted) or *gender identity* (a person's perception of having a particular gender, which may or may not correspond with their birth sex). And a growing number of states, counties, and cities have passed laws to make such discrimination illegal.[38]

more about...

Anti-Discrimination Complaints

In states that have anti-discrimination policies in place, LGBTQ (Lesbian, Gay, Bisexual, Transgender, Queer) complaints are equivalent to the number of complaints filed based on sex and fewer than the number of complaints filed based on race.

Source: "The State of the Workplace: for Lesbian, Gay, Bisexual, and Transgender Americans" (PDF). Human Rights Campaign. Retrieved July 2017.

A Supreme Court ruling in 2020 became a landmark action for the growing national consensus that LGBTQ workers should be protected from discrimination. Until June 2020, no federal law protected the rights of LGBTQ employees in the United States. Title VII of the Civil Rights Act of 1964 did not include sexual orientation in its protections. Although every Congress since 1974 introduced legislation to include sexual orientation, it took 46 years to pass.

Although this ruling created federal changes, at the time of the ruling, there were no specific, state-level protections for sexual orientation in 28 of the 50 U.S. states. There is no state-level gender identity protection in 30 of the 50 U.S. states. Employees can be fired for being transgender.

more about...

LGBTQ and EEOC

The U.S. Equal Employment Opportunity Commission (EEOC) is responsible for enforcing federal laws that make it illegal to discriminate against a job applicant or an employee because of the person's race, color, religion, sex (including pregnancy), national origin, age (40 or older), disability, or genetic information. While Title VII does not include gender identity and sexual orientation as components of protection from sex discrimination, the EEOC and federal circuit courts have taken the position that they should be included. The EEOC resolved 2,013 charges and recovered $7 million for LGBTQ individuals who filed sex discrimination charges with EEOC in fiscal year 2019 alone, with the data showing a steady increase in the number of charges filed and monetary rewards over the seven years since the agency began collecting LGBTQ charge data. From fiscal year 2013 through fiscal year 2019, more than 10,000 charges were filed with EEOC by LGBTQ individuals alleging sex discrimination, and the EEOC recovered $29.2 million for victims of discrimination.

Source: "LGBT Based Sex Discrimination Charges," EEOP, https://www.eeoc.gov/eeoc/statistics/enforcement/lgbt_sex_based.cfm.

more about...

"Shooting" Down Stereotypes: The San Diego Splash

It should not surprise anyone that women have their own basketball teams, but not many teams are made up only of women in their 80s and 90s. The San Diego Splash plays 3-on-3, half-court games. They stay fit, both mentally and physically, and have fun doing so. "We play to win," says one team member. These athletes challenge our stereotypes about the abilities of aging adults.

Source: Enjoli Francis, "For This Group of Seniors, It's Basketball over Bingo Any Day," *ABC News*, June 30, 2017, http://abcnews.go.com/Sports/group-seniors-basketball-bingo-day/story?id=48379676 (retrieved July 1, 2017).

A mixed pattern of more protection and less protection exists among states, in cities, in other municipalities, and in workplace policies.[39]

While individual states and the national government wrestle with policies protecting LGBTQ workers, they will continue to debate quality of life issues, such as on-the-job harassment, benefits for life partners the same as for legally married spouses, and other issues. Discussions around the issue will continue to evolve. For example, the U.S. military's so-called "Don't Ask Don't Tell" policy was instituted in 1993, then overturned in 2011. The "Don't Ask Don't Tell" official U.S. policy prohibited military personnel from discriminating against or harassing "closeted" homosexual or bisexual service members or applicants (those who had not made their sexual orientation public), while barring openly gay, lesbian, or bisexual persons from military service. In 2017, a ban was imposed on transgendered people serving in the military, but this ban was immediately challenged in court and has not yet been formally implemented, although in 2018 was considered to be in place. Attitudes about equal protection for same-sex couples have stirred debate even at the highest levels of government, including the U.S. Supreme Court.

The Elderly

Until 1967, no law protected older people from discrimination. Many employers justified such discrimination on the grounds that older people are slower and less healthy, and therefore don't perform as well as younger employees. In 1986, President Reagan signed an amendment to the 1967 law, making it illegal to discriminate against anyone over 40.

Specifically, the Age Discrimination in Employment Act (ADEA) protects employees and job applicants from being discriminated against because of their age in hiring, promotions, discharge, pay, terms or conditions of employment, and privileges given by the employer. It also abolishes mandatory retirement for some employees (including federal employees) and raises the mandatory retirement age for others from age 55 to 70. Because of the ADEA, setting a mandatory retirement age is allowed now only when it is necessary to maintain normal business operations; for example, firefighters and law enforcement officers can still be forced to retire at a certain age.

Recent studies show that **ageism**, or negative attitudes toward older people, is still very much alive.[40] A 2019 investigation by the AARP (originally the American Association of Retired Persons), an advocacy group for elderly people, found that ageism at work is widespread, tolerated, and even viewed as the "last acceptable bias."[41]

The AARP study found that age bias occurs in three basic areas: *hiring,* in which employers target younger job applicants; *on-the-job situations,* in which older workers may be harassed or held back from advancement due to due to misperceptions about their skills; and *firing,* whereby older workers may be targeted for early retirement or dismissal because of false perceptions about their pay levels and contributions.[42] The AARP research also found that large employers tolerate age bias because the laws that protect older workers are much weaker than those prohibiting other forms of discrimination.

Currently, employees age 40 and older are covered under ADEA. This is a huge group of employees, and as the Baby Boomers (those born between 1946 and 1964) age, it will grow even more. As you can see, this is an important law, not to be ignored. We all should also remember that *this is the one group everyone will belong to some day.*

PREJUDICE AGAINST HOMOSEXUALS
Does a person's appearance reveal sexual orientation? You cannot tell a person's sexual orientation by appearance alone. Nonetheless, prejudice, hostility, and general misunderstanding of homosexuality continue. *How can you deal with homophobia in the workplace?*
JUPITERIMAGES/Comstock Images/Alamy Stock Photo

ageism
Prejudice and discrimination toward older people.

People with Disabilities

As of 2019, more than 13 percent of the U.S. population in the 18 to 64 age group was identified as having a disability.[43] Many of those who could be working, and would like to work, are not. This waste of talent is concerning.[44] The greatest barrier to the hiring of these would-be employees is prejudiced attitudes that, like most others, are based on largely inaccurate information. Think of this misinformation as myths; then read the information in Figure 14.7 to determine whether you are harboring any of these myths.

Employees who are disabled are also protected by law from discrimination, originally under the Rehabilitation Act of 1973. That law was not greatly effective because the courts struggled with the definitions of *handicapped* and *disabled.*[45] The remedy to this issue came in July 1990, when the Americans with Disabilities Act (ADA) became law. The overall purpose of this law is to allow people with disabilities to enjoy most of the benefits that everyone else enjoys.

figure 14.7

MYTHS ABOUT HIRING PEOPLE WITH DISABILITIES

Many people still hold on to myths about the reliability and talents of people who have disabilities. The unfortunate result is that as many as 85 percent of all working-age people with disabilities are unemployed. *How are people with disabilities better employees than most people think?*

Source: George E. Stevens, "Exploding the Myths About Hiring the Handicapped," *Personnel*, December 1986.

Disabled people are unreliable. The fact is that statistics prove the exact opposite is true. As a group, the disabled have a rate of missed work that is well below the average of all employees. They also quit jobs much less frequently and tend to be much more concerned about doing a good job at whatever task they are assigned.

Disabled people can't do very many jobs. In today's workplace, especially with the increasing use of technology, there are relatively few jobs that a disabled employee *can't* do. Also, there are very few companies of any size in which a disabled employee couldn't be placed somewhere meaningful.

Disabled people will make other employees feel uncomfortable. The truth is that once other employees become acquainted with a disabled employee as an individual, the discomfort goes away. Plus, the more disabled people you spend time with, the more comfortable you will tend to feel around others like them.

The ADA prohibits discrimination by companies in any of the following areas: employment, public transportation, telecommunication, and other privately owned services to the public (hotels and motels, restaurants and bars, public gathering places). Also, the law requires that benefits and opportunities for people with disabilities must be of the same quality as those offered to everyone else, if possible. This law continues to be modified and refined, but because of it, access has improved for those with disabilities.[46]

Religious Groups

The experience of prejudice and discrimination based on religion goes back millennia, and a shared history of religious persecution goes back to the very founding of our country. Many of the Pilgrims who arrived in the New World came to escape religious intolerance, and were followed by hundreds of thousands of others who came for the same reason. Based on this history, Americans should not be prejudiced when religious differences are involved—but are they?

The EEOC reports a steady increase in complaints based on religion over the past 20 years. In fiscal year 2007, the EEOC reported 2,880 charges of religious discrimination and had recovered $6.4 million in monetary benefits for people bringing the charges. By 2011, the number of charges of religious discrimination had climbed to 4,151, the highest number during the 20-year period from 1997 to 2016, with $12.6 million in monetary benefits recovered. The total number of charges was down slightly in 2017, with 3,436 reports and $11.2 million in settlements, and has remained relatively slightly lower since then.[47]

In recent years, members of Muslim groups have found themselves increasingly discriminated against in the United States and elsewhere. The facts show that members of religious groups often find themselves the objects of discrimination both at work and in social circles. Title VII of the Civil Rights Act of 1964 forbids discrimination against members of any religion. Employers are generally required to accommodate employees who express a need to practice religious beliefs at work, but they do have some flexibility in how these accommodations will be made.[48]

more about...

Faith Communities Extend a Hand

In early 2017, arson fires in two different parts of the country destroyed mosques and threatened to divide communities, but local faith communities offered assistance. When the Islamic Center of the Eastside in Bellevue, Washington, was destroyed by arson, the Bellevue Stake of the Church of Jesus Christ of Latter-Day Saints (LDS) opened their doors to the displaced mosque members. The LDS church has sat next door to the Islamic Center for decades, but with shared space the two faith communities have drawn closer together. In Victoria, Texas, after the Victoria Islamic Center was burned down, members of the B'Nai Israel temple opened their synagogue for mosque members to gather and pray. In both cases, several local churches also offered assistance. Concern and compassion across religions can change social norms, in concert with legislation to change behaviors.

Sources: Gabe Cohen, "Church Takes in Bellevue Muslim Community After Arson," *KOMO News*, January 20, 2017, http://komonews.com/news/local/church-takes-in-bellevue-muslim-community-after-arson (retrieved July 2, 2017); and Madeline Farber, "How Jews and Christians in This Texas Town Are Helping Muslims Whose Mosque Burned Down," *Time*, February 2, 2017, http://time.com/4657876/texas-mosque-fire-jewish-christian-communities-help (retrieved July 2, 2017).

Pregnant Women

The issue of pregnancy has been reexamined numerous times as women's roles have grown in an increasing number of workplaces. Through the 1970s a female job applicant was routinely asked if she was pregnant or planning to become pregnant, and what her employment, child care, and other plans would be if she were to have children. These types of questions are now illegal because they have been shown to severely affect hiring decisions and hurt women's chances for employment and advancement. Even today, a visibly pregnant woman runs such risks of discrimination–although it will probably be left unsaid by her employer.

» CULTURAL INTELLIGENCE

There is an important theory of intelligence in addition to those we have talked about previously (see Chapter 8). This theory relates to our ability to think beyond our own cultural perspective. It is known as cultural intelligence, or CQ (cultural quotient). **Cultural intelligence (CQ)** is the ability for people, organizations, and businesses to relate to culturally diverse situations and work effectively in them.[49] In order to do business across cultures, people need to understand what is important to people in other cultures, and why they behave in ways they do that may seem unfamiliar or strange.

cultural intelligence (CQ) The ability for people, organizations, and businesses to relate to culturally diverse situations and work effectively in them.

CULTURAL INTELLIGENCE
kzenon/123RF

Global collaboration is now a norm in the business world, and productive and successful workplaces are those that know how to communicate effectively with clients and other business with whom they work. While a focus on cultural intelligence can cost time and money for a business, as well as being complicated since each country or region may need a different cultural approach, it is worth the investment in the long run. Corporations that invest in cultural intelligence have a better corporate reputation and can achieve better results cross-culturally. They can increase the innovation and creativity in a company as they pull together diverse resources and make good use of multicultural perspectives. They may have a more competitive edge and can adapt more quickly and easily to a changing environment.[50]

Corporations that sell products internationally may take a "glocalization" (global + local) approach in which they tailor products to fit the tastes of local consumers around the world. Many fast food and grocery corporations have glocalized successfully, including KFC, Subway, Starbucks, PepsiCo, and many more. Glocalization does not have to cross international borders, though, as regional taste may vary within a country. For example, hungry travelers who dine only at McDonald's may order grits with their breakfast in southern U.S. states, have a burger and fries for lunch in Los Angeles, then arrive in Hawai'i in time for dinner with a dessert of hot taro (a root plant) or haupia (coconut pudding) pie.

What is cultural intelligence, or CQ, at the individual level? What does it include, and how can we develop it? One way to understand CQ is in three parts or dimensions: cognitive, motivational, and behavioral.[51]

Cognitive CQ includes knowledge about a culture: its customs, the political, economic, social, environmental, and legal systems that form the culture. This knowledge can be gained with informational searches widely available.

Motivational CQ is the empathy or "heart" of really understanding another culture. While information on what is important to members of another culture can be gained in general information searches, this type of CQ takes genuine interest to really gain appreciation for another culture. A positive emotion of wanting to understand a new culture in a positive and interested frame of mind, rather than a negative emotion of judgment, makes up this element of CQ.

Behavioral CQ is the bodily, verbal, and nonverbal practices that are distinct among cultures. An example is the contrast between a handshake

more about...

Culture and Grasshoppers

"You see them at international airports like Heathrow: posters advertising the global bank HSBC that show a grasshopper and the message 'USA—Pest. China—Pet. Northern Thailand—Appetizer'."

In this quote from the *Harvard Business Review,* we are reminded that cultural norms and values can vary around the world. In this example, a grasshopper takes on the symbolic value of each country for comedic effect. Our workplaces are more productive and efficient when we remember to suspend our cultural lenses when working with others whose experiences and beliefs are different from ours.

Source: P. Christopher Earley and Elaine Mosakowski, "Cultural Intelligence," *Harvard Business Review,* October 2004, https://hbr.org/2004/10/cultural-intelligence.

or nod as greeting in the United States and a traditional bow in Japan. Behaviors across cultures take physical practice to learn and understand, more than reading a description. The best way to practice these behaviors is in conversation and coaching with someone from the culture or someone who has experienced it first hand.

« STRATEGIES FOR SUCCESS

Strategy 14.1 **Build Your Cultural Intelligence**

1. Be interested and curious in learning about people from other cultures.
2. Become aware of yourself in relation to others.
3. Start with a mental clean slate.
4. Become aware of your existing biases about other cultural groups and their traditions.
5. Go where people from other cultures are present.

Cultural intelligence, or CQ, is not something we are born with, or are born lacking. Everyone can work to develop higher CQ.

1. **Be interested and curious in learning about people from other cultures.** Ask questions, appropriately and respectfully. Be open and willing to learn from what you observe in people from other cultures. View situations and behaviors from another perspective outside of your own.
2. **Become aware of yourself in relation to others.** Think about your own cultural background and the experiences you have had in your lifetime. How did they frame your perspectives? How would these be different from, or similar to, people in other cultural groups?
3. **Start with a mental clean slate.** Be objective, avoid judging others. If you find yourself becoming judgmental, stop your inner conversation with this statement: "That is different, and it is interesting. I want to know more." Be aware that differences in generations and economics mean that not all people from one culture are the same.
4. **Become aware of your existing biases about other cultural groups and their traditions.** Think about your own biases. Confront them, and ask yourself what you can do to break away from them. For each one, work to develop a clean slate.
5. **Go where people from other cultures are present.** Attend cultural events or volunteer for activities that give you first-hand experience about people from other cultures. While you are there, practice the first four strategies in this list.

Source: Simma Lieberman, "Five Ways to Build Cultural Intelligence," *Alan Weiss*, December 7, 2012, https://alanweiss.com/five-ways-to-build-cultural-intelligence (retrieved March 11, 2020). See also: David Livermore (2015), *Leading with Cultural Intelligence*, AMACOM.

» LOOKING AHEAD

What can be done to reduce feelings of prejudice and acts of discrimination in the workplace? Consider from what we know about cognitive categorization (introduced earlier in this chapter) that prejudging others seems to be a natural human trait. When a member of a group acts in a way we expect, our stereotype is confirmed. When the person acts differently from the way we expect, we may decide that he or she is the exception to the rule. These negative ideas are hard to get rid of! Does this mean there is no hope for reducing prejudice and discrimination? The good news is that some negative feelings and behaviors can be permanently eliminated. The bad news is that there is no simple cure.

Although the federal government has taken solid steps to define and forbid discrimination in the workplace, there are still steps you can take individually and in your organization as well. A key ingredient for people to begin to understand and appreciate members of other groups is contact; but communication as a result of contact is crucial to understanding others. Employees need the opportunity to interact and communicate with each other, because **proximity** (physical closeness) and exposure to other people generally increase the chance that they will come to better know, understand, and like each other.[52] It will also reduce any tendency to stereotype groups of people; after all, you wouldn't be likely to prejudge the group to which your best friend and her family belong.

proximity

Physical closeness; here, it refers to contact between members of a diverse workplace.

Contact by itself is not enough. Recall that one of the causes of prejudice and discrimination is unequal status. If this is the case, prejudice will not diminish. Businesses can take steps to hire employees who are frequent targets of discrimination into all levels within the company. The second necessary ingredient in reducing prejudice and discrimination, then, is ensuring **equal status** for everyone.

equal status

The condition that occurs when companies hire employees who are frequent targets of discrimination into all levels within the company.

A third important ingredient in reducing prejudice and discrimination is *cooperation* instead of competition among members of "different" groups. Psychologists have discovered that when members of different groups not only must cooperate but also must depend on each other to reach common goals—also known as **interdependence**—conflict is greatly reduced.

interdependence

A relationship in which members of different groups not only must cooperate but also must depend on each other to reach common goals.

Practicing your cultural intelligence skills is a good start to reducing prejudice and discrimination in the workplace. Working together works!

STRATEGIES FOR SUCCESS

Strategy 14.2 Assess Your Knowledge

How much do you know about the issue of sexual harassment? Take the following true-false quiz to assess your knowledge.

1. **True–False Test**

T F 1. Offering someone an award, bonus, promotion, or other job benefit on the condition of sexual contact is an example of sexual harassment.

T F 2. Sexually suggestive teasing, jokes, or pranks directed toward someone in a sexually suggestive way, are not definitions of sexual harassment.

T F 3. Sexually suggestive remarks have to occur in person, sexual harassment cannot occur by e-mail.

T F 4. If I make sexual comments to someone and that person asks me to stop, then my behavior is not welcome and I have to stop.

T F 5. Sexual harassment can occur between people of the same sex, the harasser can be a man or a woman, and the harasser can be a supervisor, co-worker, or even a non-employee who works with the company.

T F 6. Posting sexually offensive or demeaning pictures, cartoons or other materials at work is a type of sexual harassment.

T F 7. A sexually harassed man does not have the same legal rights as a woman who is targeted for sexual harassment.

T F 8. Verbal abuse of a sexual nature toward a colleague that occurs off-duty, even if it is unwelcome, by definition does not affect the workplace so it is not sexual harassment.

T F 9. Accidentally standing too close to someone or brushing up against him or her is not a type of sexual harassment.

T F 10. Leaving someone unwanted objects that are sexual in nature or giving sexual gifts fit the definition of sexual harassment.

Answers: 1—True, 2—False, 3—False, 4—True, 5—True, 6—True, 7—False, 8—False, 9—True, 10—False

Source: Test questions based on "Sexual Harassment Policy," Office of Civil Rights, U.S. Dept. of State, https://www.state.gov/key-topics-office-of-civil-rights/sexual-harassment-policy/ (retrieved July 10, 2020).

« STRATEGIES FOR SUCCESS

Strategy 14.3 Reducing Sexual Harassment

1. Develop a corporate policy statement, post it in a public place, and talk about it.
2. Set expectations for appropriate employee behavior.
3. Train employees on how to file a complaint if necessary, and how to intervene if they see harassment occurring.

How do you prevent sexual harassment? Understand that the problem is serious, and that related cases are costing U.S. corporations, governments, and small companies millions of dollars per year. Effects on victims are impossible to measure. The toll that sexual harassment takes on company morale, productivity, and employee well-being is too high to let such behavior continue. Merely pointing to a policy, or conducting a one-time training session with employees, is not enough to change behavior in a company. A change in culture to one that does not accept this behavior is essential to a productive and successful workplace.

1. **Develop a corporate policy statement, post it in a public place, and talk about it.** If you are in a management position, you may be responsible for making sure such a policy is written, posted, and discussed. If this is not your area of responsibility but you cannot find a policy posted or it is never discussed, ask about it. Many resources are available to decide what should be included in this policy. A good place to start is the Office for Civil Rights, U.S. Department of State.[53]

2. **Set expectations for appropriate employee behavior.** As with the policy itself, setting expectations starts at the top of the corporate structure. But everyone contributes to a corporate culture. Become part of a culture that does not engage in sexual harassment, does not turn a blind eye to it, and takes employee concerns seriously. Setting expectations that all employees are responsible for a healthy working environment increases their sense of responsibility and the likelihood that bystanders will speak up and report harassment when it occurs.
3. **Train employees on how to file a complaint if necessary, and how to intervene if they see harassment occurring.** Employees are much more likely to come forward as targets of sexual harassment and as bystanders who have witnessed the harassment if they know the steps to filing a complaint or bringing a concern forward to managers. Training increases a sense of accountability for all employees. Effective training may include pre-training, the training itself, and follow-up post-training. An anonymous survey as the pre-training step can be used to find out the extent of harassment, specific issues employees are facing, and questions they may have. The training itself is most effective with interactive, authentic scenarios; but videos, discussions, and role play exercises can also be effective. The post-training activities can include knowledge assessments and scheduled refreshers to make sure employees understand the training should be taken seriously.

If a sexual harassment case from your company gets to court (or even to the attorneys for an out-of-court settlement), a central question will be whether or not your company had a clear, well-defined policy against sexual harassment, and authentic and effective training for employees. Changing a corporate culture to one that does not accept sexual harassment of any kind may take work and time, but will go a long way toward preventing sexual harassment at work.

Source: Brendan L. Smith (Feb. 2018). "What it Really Takes to Stop Sexual Harassment," *American Psychological Association, Feb. 2018, Vol. 49, No. 2. Print version: page 36.* https://www.apa.org/monitor/2018/02/sexual-harassment (retrieved July 10, 2020).

CHAPTER FOURTEEN SUMMARY

Chapter Summary by Learning Objectives

LO 14-1 Describe the current trends in labor force participation, and how they are creating more diverse, inclusive workplaces. Labor force trends are shaping diversity in the workplace, with more women, people of color, and elderly employees. Inclusivity is found in the full acceptance of differing lifestyles and personal attributes. The challenge to human relations is to make this mixture of people an asset, rather than a liability.

LO 14-2 Explain the benefits of diversity and inclusion in the workplace. A diverse staff offers an organization a range of talent that transcends a particular world-view or ethnicity, giving it insight into the needs and motivations of all of the company's client or customer base, rather than just a narrow part of it.

LO 14-3 Identify barriers to creating a diverse organization. Stereotypes, bias, prejudice, and other forms of unequal treatment can be barriers to an organization's stated goals of an inclusive, diverse workplace.

LO 14-4 List different types of discrimination in the workplace. The major types of discrimination in today's world include racism, sexism, religious prejudice, economic prejudice (one of the oldest prejudices in the world), and ageism. Prejudice against others based on sexual and gender orientation, weight, and disabilities are also too common.

LO 14-5 Define cultural intelligence and its importance, and how to increase it. Cultural intelligence is the ability for people, organizations, and businesses to relate to culturally diverse situations and work effectively in them. In order to do business across cultures, people need to understand what is important to people in other cultures.

LO 14-6 Describe the connections among stereotype, prejudice, and discrimination. Prejudice can be defined as the way one feels as the result of the stereotypes one believes. It can also be seen as the unwillingness to give credibility to others of different backgrounds, and seeing them as inferior. Discrimination is one's behavior based on that person's stereotypes and prejudices.

LO 14-7 Give examples of how to promote a more diverse workplace. Recruiting the most talented, diverse workforce possible requires an openness to hiring individuals with different skill sets, experiences, and backgrounds. Crating a fair, open workplace enhances a business' reputation, and can help promote diversity within an organization.

key terms

review questions

1. What are the three components of an attitude? Describe the three components of a prejudiced attitude.
2. What individuals and groups can you think of who are likely targets of prejudice and discrimination? Do you fit into any of these groups that are likely targets? Have you ever found yourself a target of prejudice or discrimination as a member of this group? Explain.
3. Discuss some of the sources of prejudice. Within these sources, can you think of a particular prejudice that you have and how it arose? Explain your personal example.
4. Discuss the negative effects of discrimination in the workplace, both on the individual and on the business organization. Have you seen any discriminatory acts occurring in your workplace? Explain.
5. Describe steps that can be taken in the workplace to reduce or prevent sexual harassment.
6. How is institutional racism or institutional sexism different from open racism or sexism?
7. What is meant by the term *self-fulfilling prophecy*? Think of an example in your life or someone else's where a self-fulfilling prophecy (either positive or negative) arose. Explain your personal example.
8. What are some of the common myths about people with disabilities in the workplace? What is being done to protect employment for this group?
9. What are the elements or cultural intelligence or CQ? How strong are your CQ skills? In what ways might you improve in these factors of CQ?

critical thinking questions

1. Under what circumstances is it acceptable to treat co-workers or employees differently because of their differences? Should you be blind to differences between co-workers or employees, or recognize them openly?
2. People today talk a lot about "tolerance." Is there a difference between *tolerance* and *acceptance* of differences, whether they are cultural, gender-related, religious, or other? Explain the differences.
3. Thinking of your workplace or college, do you see more efforts happening to promote *diversity* or to promote *inclusion*? Explain. If you were to be tasked with promoting inclusion, what plans and actions would you put into place?

working it out 14.1

IMPRESSION FORMATION: ARE PERCEPTIONS INFLUENCED BY ETHNICITY?

School-to-Work Connection: Interpersonal Skills

Purpose: Do people hold generalized perceptions of others just because of their ethnicity? This project will help you discover that for yourself.

Instructions: First, decide on two ethnic groups or nationalities you would like to study (as a class or as an individual project). They may include African Americans, Native Americans, Japanese, French, Italians, Swedes, Costa Ricans, or any other ethnic or national group. Next, each student should approach at least two people and ask them to take part in a study on impression formation. If this is a class project, decide with your classmates what two groups you want to study. Those who agree to participate should be asked to conjure up an image of members of a particular ethnic or national group and then describe their characteristics on the rating scale that follows. Half the participants should be asked to describe a member of the second ethnic or national group chosen for the study. The data collected from all the students will allow you to compare the participant's perceptions as influenced by awareness of a person's ethnicity or nationality.

Part One: The person you have in mind is (ethnic or national group).

Describe this person using the rating scale in the table at the end of these instructions.

1. When you think about people in this group, what is the first thing that comes to mind?
2. What is most characteristic of members of this group?
3. What is most definitely not characteristic of them? (What would be surprising or unexpected to see?)
4. What characteristic do you think most people assign to members of this group?

Part Two: Now do the same for the second person and ethnic or national group. Examine your results. Are you surprised by any of these results? Do you hold certain perceptions about people just by being aware that they belong to a specific group? If so, what can you do about it? How can you reduce your stereotypical beliefs about members of certain ethnic groups?

Part Three: Try this exercise again, substituting male and female for the two ethnic or national groups, or young person and elderly person, or physically able and physically challenged, and so on.

RATING SCALE

Dominant	1	2	3	4	5	6	Submissive
Warm	1	2	3	4	5	6	Cold
Unambitious	1	2	3	4	5	6	Ambitious
Stupid	1	2	3	4	5	6	Smart
Clean	1	2	3	4	5	6	Dirty
Disliked	1	2	3	4	5	6	Liked
Poised	1	2	3	4	5	6	Unpoised
Unaggressive	1	2	3	4	5	6	Aggressive
Insensitive	1	2	3	4	5	6	Sensitive
Active	1	2	3	4	5	6	Passive

Source: Adapted from Ayala Pines and Christina Maslach, *Experiencing Social Psychology: Readings and Projects,* 3rd ed. (New York: McGraw-Hill, Inc., 1993), pp. 203–205.

working it out 14.2

GENDER STEREOTYPES IN THE MEDIA

School-to-Work Connection: Interpersonal Skills

Purpose: Much of what people learn about men and women comes from the way they are portrayed on television and in movies, online, and in magazines. How are men and women portrayed differently in the media? This is the question you will try to answer in this project.

Instructions: Pick one type of medium: your favorite online news source, magazine, TV program (a news program, a soap opera, cartoons, music videos, situation comedy, etc.), or radio programs (news format, rock music, sports, etc.). Decide on your research sample gathering (a week, seven issues, 10 hours, etc.) and the particular material you are going to observe. Record your results.

1. What was your source (what type of medium)?
2. What were you looking at (advertisements, cartoons, music lyrics, or other)?
3. How did you collect your data (at what times, how often, and so on)? What exactly did you observe (what programs and how many hours, or what magazine and how many issues)?
4. What themes around gender did you discover? Were there any surprises in what you found? Is the media's portrayal of men and women accurate? How powerful are the media's messages on gender?

Source: Adapted from Ayala Pines and Christina Maslach, *Experiencing Social Psychology: Readings and Projects,* 3rd ed. (New York: McGraw-Hill, Inc., 1993), pp. 203–205.

working it out 14.3

GETTING SERIOUS ABOUT DIVERSITY AND INCLUSION AT WORK

Watch the TED Talk by business consultant Janet Stovall, titled "How to Get Serious About Diversity and Inclusion in the Workplace," and then answer the following questions.

1. What is Project '87?
2. Why does the speaker say that business is the best entity to dismantle racism, especially compared with college and religion?
3. What are the three things that business can borrow from Project '87 to dismantle racism?
4. What are the advantages to businesses to dismantle racism? What are the consequences of ignoring diversity and inclusion?
5. What is the difference between "diversity" and "inclusion?" Why is this important? What is the tipping point into inclusion?

The video can be found here: www.ted.com/talks/janet_stovall_how_to_get_serious_about_diversity_and_inclusion_in_the_workplace.

case study 14.1

It's None of Your Business

More than 30 years ago, well after the Civil Rights Act made discrimination in hiring illegal, a professor with a PhD was interviewing for a research job at a university in California. Although many of the questions asked by the interviewer were clearly not allowable, the interviewer persisted. Some of those questions were:

- How old are you?
- Are you married?
- Do you have any children?
- How old are they?
- What type of day-care arrangement do you have?
- What type of backup day-care arrangements have you made?
- Are you planning on having more children?
- What kind of car do you drive?
- Is your car reliable?
- How will you get to work if you have car trouble?

Case Study Questions

1. Thinking about the questions, if you were considering hiring someone and wanted to be sure that you were hiring a reliable employee, these are things you might want to know as well. So why can't you ask these questions? What is inherently wrong with wanting to know these things about a potential employee—why is it illegal, when not directly related to job tasks?
2. Using the skills you have learned in previous chapters and the information you have learned in this chapter, what would you have said to this interviewer during the interview, in order to end these personal questions?
3. Let's say the interviewer continued this line of personal questions, even after you said something. The interview ended, and you were not hired. Would you have felt bias had occurred in this hiring? Would you have taken further action? Explain.

case study 14.2

Sparkle Sunshine Cleaning Service

Alexandre is the owner of a successful cleaning and home-organizing company in the suburbs outside of a major city. The company has been around for a few years now, and has slowly grown into an operation of eight employees working throughout the week. Business has been steady, but for some reason, morale seems a little low lately. Alexandre has grown concerned about the well-being of the company's employees and fears that any major internal problems could hurt the company in subtle ways, including its bottom line.

Calling the two shift managers into the office, Alexandre soon hears what the problem is. "Yeah, I've been giving the easier jobs to Jackie and Phillip lately. You know, because they're older and slower," Mario explains, innocently. Alexandre hears from the other shift manager, Lucinda, that she has been grouping the teams together by which islands in the Caribbean they come from. And when Mario admits that he has been sending some of the company's younger and lighter-skinned employees to certain customers because, "Well, you know how customers can be in those areas," Alexandre realizes that there are serious internal problems afoot and quick action is needed to get ahead of any major repercussions.

Alexandre understands that the managers are only human, and that it is the owner's job to set expectations in the workplace. Later that week, an expert in workplace discrimination is brought into the office. "Team, I have some great news," Alexandre tells the employees of the company at their weekly team meeting. "My friend Carlos will be joining us shortly for some required training. Don't worry, no one's in trouble and I think you'll get a lot out of it." With that, Carlos enters the room, turns on his projector, and begins his presentation.

Case Study Questions

1. Which prejudices will Alexandre need to address for morale to improve and for the business to run smoothly again?
2. Should Alexandre fire (or at least discipline) the shift managers Mario and Lucinda? Explain.
3. Let's say you have been called in as the expert, Carlos. After you turn on your projector, what will you communicate to the group? What steps will you take? On what principles will you base your presentation?

CHAPTER FIFTEEN

15

BUSINESS ETHICS AND SOCIAL RESPONSIBILITY

LEARNING OBJECTIVES

After studying this chapter, you will be able to:

LO 15-1 Define ethics.

LO 15-2 Explain the importance of a code of ethics.

LO 15-3 Describe the process of rationalizing unethical behavior.

LO 15-4 Explain ethics in the context of the U.S. workplace.

LO 15-5 Describe the influence of group goals on ethics.

LO 15-6 Give examples of global ethics issues.

LO 15-7 Define social responsibility.

LO 15-8 Describe the process of whistleblowing.

STRATEGIES FOR SUCCESS

Strategy 15.1 Making Ethical Decisions: A Quick Ethics Test from Texas Instruments

Strategy 15.2 Navigating the Ethics of Global Business

In the Workplace: An Unethical Pile-Up

SITUATION

Somos Images LLC/Alamy Stock Photo

Chloe loved her job as the HR manager at a local advertising firm. She had been with the company for three years. During the past year, however, things had begun to change. It had started when the Marketing director resigned to go back to college. Chloe's supervisor told her that since there was some similarity in duties between the HR and Marketing positions, it would be great if Chloe would expand her current role to help manage the Marketing division. As if that weren't enough, the head of the Finance division was soon to begin her maternity leave, and Chloe's supervisor told her that since she was really good at understanding data, it would be great if Chloe could take on that job, as well, for a while.

Chloe was overwhelmed. When she heard a rumor that yet another employee in the research department would be retiring from the company, Chloe gathered her thoughts and prepared herself before her supervisor stopped by her office. He began the conversation:

"So I guess you heard J.J. is retiring. I think it would be great if . . . "

"Hold on," said Chloe, "if you are going to ask me to take J.J.'s job too, you're going to have to find me an assistant or maybe two, give me a raise, and a new title. I cannot take on another full-time job on top of the extra work you have already given me."

Her supervisor, Chuck, was surprised. "But I thought you loved this company and wanted to help it succeed! Why would you turn down a chance to help us out? Besides, you're so good at what you do, I'm sure this extra work won't be too much of a burden. You're efficient, you can handle it. And don't forget, your job description does say 'other duties as assigned.'"

DISCOVERY

Chloe held firm. "I cannot take on another person's full-time job in addition to my own and the other jobs you have given me. I can't be good at all these jobs when I'm stretched so thin."

Chuck held firm, too. "The company cannot hire extra people right now; you know how the budget looks. If you are refusing a job assignment, then that is insubordination. I will have to write you up, and begin a progressive discipline process."

THINK ABOUT IT

What are Chloe's options now? What would you do if you were in her place? Do you believe an ethical standard has been violated here? Explain.

» WHAT IS ETHICS?

ethics

The expression of the standards of right and wrong based on conduct and morals in a particular society.

morality

A system of conduct that covers all broadly based, mostly unwritten standards of how people should behave and generally conform to cultural ideals of right and wrong.

Ethics refers to the standards of conduct and morals in a particular society; in short, ethics expresses standards of right and wrong. However, ethics and morality are not identical concepts, although both relate to "doing the right thing." **Morality** is how an individual's behavior should generally conform to cultural ideals of right and wrong. It represents broadly based, mostly unwritten standards of how people should behave. Ethics is more precise and is often based on written guidelines. Ethics also often addresses deeper issues of fairness, equity, and compromise.[1]

In this chapter, you will examine the complex issue of ethics in the workplace. You will learn about the many ways ethics plays a part in your relationships with others on the job. You will also learn about specific actions that both managers and employees can take to develop stronger ethical conduct on the job.

Business in every sense brings many benefits to society. The business world has provided jobs for millions, created a high standard of living, and given many people an opportunity to achieve the dream of business ownership. However, businesses do not always uphold the highest ethical standards. Highly publicized scandals damage the public image of many businesses, and because of the alarming number of scandals in the global financial sector in recent years and in the corporate world in general, a new awakening to the issues of business ethics has emerged.

Surprisingly, though, this renewed interest in learning about ethics in recent years seems to be coming from college students themselves, as much as by corporations or business schools. In a 2016 survey sponsored by the United Nations of nearly 1,700 business students from 40 countries, researchers found that 75 percent of students believed that businesses have a social responsibility that goes beyond making a profit and that businesses have a responsibility to society and for the environment.[2] An additional global survey sponsored by LinkedIn found that 74 percent of students want to work in a job where their work matters. And a survey by Heartland Monitor found that Millennials placed the value of making a difference in society above making money.[3] Given the importance of intrinsic motivation we learned about in Chapter 5, this should not come as a surprise. (See Figure 15.1.)

In addition to being different from morality, ethical standards are also different from *law,* which is another code of conduct. Although both ethical standards and laws are generally agreed upon within specific cultures, laws are different because they are always set down in writing, and descriptions of them are available to the public. Ethics violations are not always punishable, but violating the law carries specific penalties: in other words, laws have *teeth.*

In contrast, it is difficult to pin down when ethics violations have occurred and what, if anything, the penalties for such violations should be. This is because although ethical standards are often in writing, there are

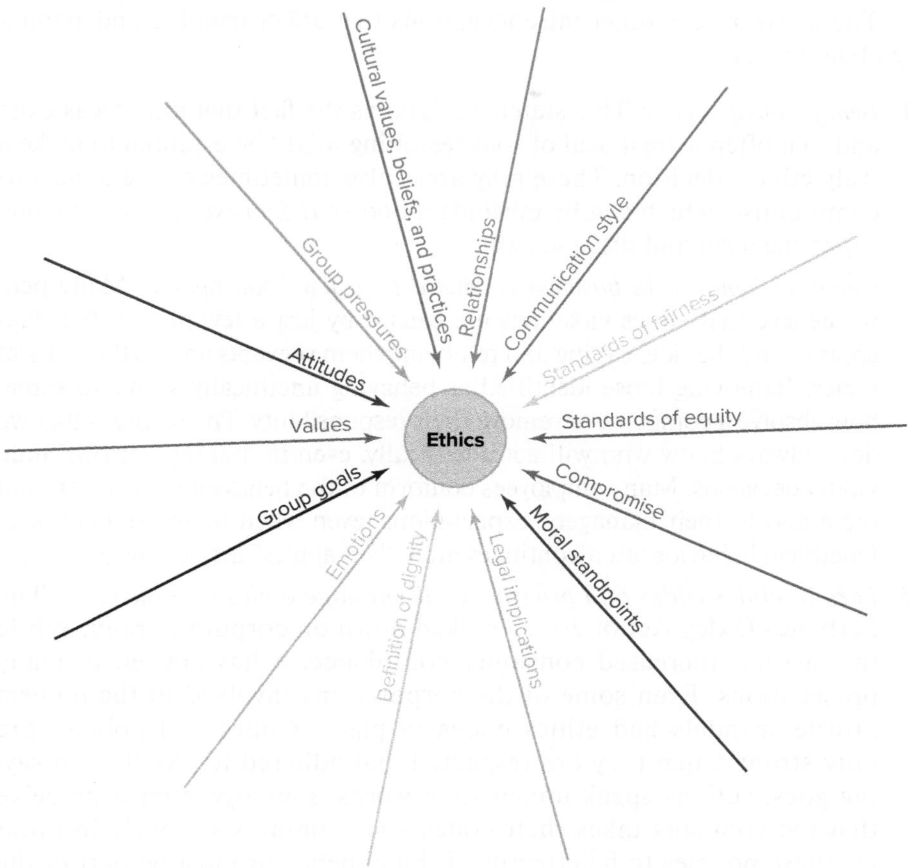

figure 15.1

FACTORS INFLUENCING WORKPLACE ETHICS

Several personal and professional factors influence a person's ethics on the job. Furthermore, personal ethics can be greatly reshaped by the ethical standards already in place at a company, and counteracting forces may simultaneously push a person toward unethical conduct and pull him or her away from it. For instance, a salesperson may be tempted by financial incentives to lie to a customer about services or products, but a fear of getting caught or being punished in some way or loss of self-respect may change that person's mind. *Do your personal ethics stay the same at your job, or do they change somewhat from home to work? Why?*

usually no written guidelines on how to respond when these same ethics are violated. Some organizations have addressed this issue, though, by creating guidelines on punishing and terminating employees who violate established ethical guidelines.

more about...

Ethical Policies in Organizations

Few professions have strict and enforceable **ethical policies**. The medical profession and the legal profession are two exceptions—both have procedures to discipline members who behave unethically.

One common public perception is that *business* and *ethics* are terms that can hardly be used in the same sentence. That perception is based on the misunderstanding that profit and morality simply do not mix, and that one can't make money without becoming corrupt. A quote by former Harvard Business School ethics professor and sociologist Amatai Etzioni sums up this belief many people have that ethics and business do not mix: "If we want businesses to maximize profits for shareholders, it is incompatible with ethics, because ethics calls you to make sacrifices for the common good."[4] In Etzioni's view, though, this belief is a false perception, as working toward the common good is imperative in a society.

The following are other misconceptions that affect people's understanding about ethics:[5]

1. *Being ethical is easy.* This statement ignores the fact that gray areas exist and that often a great deal of soul-searching might be essential to make a truly ethical decision. These gray areas also sometimes create a need to compromise, which can be misunderstood as indecisiveness to someone expecting a cut-and-dried answer.
2. *Unethical behavior in business is caused by a few "bad apples."* Many people believe that ethics violations are caused by just a few people, the "bad apples," and that identifying and removing them prevents any further ethical issues. Removing those identified as behaving unethically seems to somehow absolve a company, or remove their responsibility. The reality is that we don't always know who will act unethically, even in making our own individual decisions. Many employees conform to the behavior they see around them and to their managers' expectations, even when these are unethical. Unethical behavior often continues after "bad apples" are removed.
3. *Formal ethics codes and programs will manage ethics in a business.* The Sarbanes-Oxley Act of 2002 cracked down on corporate fraud. While the law has increased consumer confidence, it has not led to many prosecutions. Even some of the corporations involved in the highest profile scandals had ethics codes in place. Codes and policies are only strong when they are respected and adhered to. As the old saying goes, actions speak louder than words. Employees must perceive that the company takes their codes and programs seriously in order for these policies to be effective. Ethical behavior must be part of the corporate culture.
4. *Ethical leadership is determined by the leader's integrity.* Having integrity or being perceived as a moral person is important, but it is also important to be seen as a moral leader who expects everyone in the company to act ethically. Remaining silent on ethics can be seen as not caring much about others. Ethical leaders need to demonstrate ethical behavior.
5. *People are less ethical than they were in the past.* Public scandals about corporate ethics bring the problem into our minds and can make it seem that this is a new issue. But the oldest writings from philosophy and religion talk about ethics. This issue has probably been around as long as people have been on earth.

Even the most ethical person should be willing to admit that all of us are sometimes faced with ethical and moral dilemmas. The most ethical course of action isn't always clear-cut and obvious. For example, suppose that you were a buyer for a retail chain, and you told a supplier company, "We can't continue to pay the $26 per unit any longer. If you can't cut your cost by at least $3 per unit, we'll buy from someone else." Not realizing that you are bluffing, the supplier gives in and drops her price. Once you've done the math, you are now able to report to your manager that you just saved the company $32,000 per month. Your manager is ecstatic and gives you a raise.[6] You have helped both your manager and your company. Have you done something unethical? If you aren't quite sure, hopefully by the end of this chapter you will have some tools to help you make such a judgment.

Ethics and the Internet

One of the stickiest ethical issues today is how to behave ethically on the Internet. You would most likely feel violated if a police officer searched your house without cause or permission, or if your company tapped your office phone. Yet every day companies legally monitor employee e-mails and track online usage, looking for the personal misuse of company property. While we may think of ourselves online as anonymous or our information as confidential, it is nearly impossible for complete anonymity and confidentiality, as well as privacy in general, to be maintained online.

In what many see as another invasion of privacy, online merchants regularly purchase confidential information about people's buying habits that has been provided by electronic profilers (also called *cookies*). This issue has caused conflict since the beginning of online commerce, because consumers often resent having their personal information sold without their consent. Many people also see this as a threat to their privacy. Companies now create policies and guidelines to address these issues before lawsuits and bad publicity create irreversible damage. The use of data that was collected by big data firms has led to heated debates among the public and legislators as policies and laws are created to address data usage.

Privacy, confidentiality, and anonymity are often named as serious ethics issues related to Internet usage. These are not the only serious issues, however. Among the most serious ethical issues related to Internet usage is the spread of **disinformation**, which is deliberately false information spread to damage the reputation of a rival power, person, issue, or other entity. The largest social media sources are now in the midst of disinformation controversies and lawsuits as we adjust to changing ethics rules online. The judgment of what information is disinformation, and what is truth, is often difficult to discern. We are all responsible for checking resources and facts before we spread disinformation unintentionally.

Cyberbullying and *cybercrime* are also ethics issues related to Internet use. **Cyberbullying**, or targeted intimidation or demeaning messages meant to bully a person, became a major cause for concern during the past decade. Highly publicized cases have come to light of cyberbullying incidents, where the targets of the bullying, especially among young teens, have committed suicide. While many schools and municipalities have rules or laws against bullying in person, cyberbullying is less often defined into law. It has been more difficult to track and to stop, and laws have not kept up with advances in technology.

ETHICS AND TECHNOLOGY

How has widespread use of the Internet created new kinds of ethical dilemmas? What strategies would you suggest for making ethical decisions in Internet-related ethical issues?

Image Source, all rights reserved.

disinformation
Intentionally false and misleading information, including propaganda issued by a government organization, to damage the reputation of a rival power or media source.

cyberbullying
Using electronic communication to bully a person, typically by sending targeted intimidating, threatening, or demeaning messages.

cybercrime
Criminal acts carried out online.

Cybercrime simply refers to criminal acts that are carried out online. One Internet ethics issue related to cybercrime is copyright infringement, where online businesses have been caught using, distributing, and even selling copyrighted materials such as text, images, and music. One of the first issues that brought this to light was an early music file-sharing site, Napster, which offered free MP3 downloads of copyrighted music. A lawsuit brought against Napster forced them to stop their distribution of copyrighted materials. However, in the wake of Napster's shutdown, peer-to-peer file sharing, including use of various "bit-torrent" sites and streaming sites, has been much harder to control. While the Napster lawsuit occurred more than 20 years ago, its legal and ethical impacts are still felt in the music and entertainment industry today.

digital divide
The gap between those who have available access to technology and computers, and those who do not.

Another ethics issue relates to who does, and does not, have access to the technological advances available to society. This idea is referred to as the **digital divide**, or the gap between those who have computers and Internet and those who do not. It is probably easier to imagine the digital divide in comparing highly developed countries with those countries that are just now developing; however, the digital divide occurs in developed countries as well. In the United States, it is not difficult to find families or specific areas of a city or in rural areas where families and communities are not able to access some of the technology that many of us take for granted.

net neutrality
The idea that Internet service providers should make access available to all content and applications regardless of the source, and without favoring or blocking specific products or websites.

An additional issue related to who has access to what information online is **net neutrality**. This is the idea that Internet traffic should be treated equally, with no Internet service provider (ISP) having the power to prioritize one source over others by blocking, slowing down, or requiring payment to access sites or to use faster search speeds. Currently, legislation on net neutrality is in flux as some ISP corporations work to strengthen their hold on the Internet market in a system where net neutrality is not legislated or enforced.

Since the widespread use of the Internet, many ethical issues have arisen, often faster than laws or society can address them. Spamming, hacking, online pornography, use of bots (robots), malware (harmful software), online vandalism of others' websites, intellectual property issues, plagiarism, and many more issues arise in reference to ethical behavior online.

All of these examples illustrate some of the countless ways in which the Internet challenges the ethics of employees and businesses, creating new debates and raising new questions about ethics.[7] As we go about our daily lives, the Internet has become an integral part of everything we do.

» CODES OF ETHICS

ethical codes
Formalized sets of ethical guidelines developed by some companies for use at all levels of an organization.

If ethical issues aren't the same as moral or legal issues, how can you judge them? Some companies have developed specific **ethical codes** that are accepted and abided by in all levels of the firm.

REAL WORLD EXAMPLE 15.1

In March 2013, Internet users across the globe faced an unprecedented slowdown of the Internet resulting from the biggest cyber attack in history up to that time. Computer systems around the world had slowed or become disabled by collateral damage from the deliberate actions of just one group of hackers set on dismantling the website of The Spamhaus Project, a European spam-fighting group that had blacklisted a major spam-hosting site called CyberBunker. Spamhaus serves as a clearinghouse of information on illegal spamming, and may be responsible for up to 80 percent of all spam that gets blocked. For its part, CyberBunker maintained that Spamhaus continually overstepped its bounds and had unfairly targeted its data-storage company in its spam-fighting efforts. As a result of the feud, the cyber attack slowed Internet traffic to a crawl for several days.

This event raised a number of alarming ethics questions, including: Is it ethical to send spam? And what are the ethics of slowing or disabling the entire Internet in order to attack your business rival and make your point? While many serious and damaging cyber attacks have happened since then, the later attacks were clearly illegal, while the Spamhaus/CyberBunker incident focused on ethics.

Texas Instruments (TI), a global powerhouse for innovation and new ideas, is one such company. With groundbreaking inventions such as the first semiconductor, the handheld calculator, the microchip, and DPI projection systems, TI has a long history of putting ethics into action, pairing its commercial success with praise for its ethical approach to business. In fact, TI has consistently been ranked as one of the most ethical companies in the world for their culture of accountability, based on the core values of integrity, innovation, and commitment–values that are applied both internally and externally.[8]

In the 1980s, TI became one of the first to codify its ethical values when it published a manual for managers called *Ethics in the Business of TI.* The manual described the company's overall philosophy of business, noting that "good ethics and good business are synonymous when viewed from moral, legal, and practical standpoints."[9] Since then, TI has continued to refine its ethical approach across its global business practice through its frequently updated manual, *Code of Conduct: Our Values and Ethics,* and its internal *Corporate Citizenship Topic Brief on Ethics,* which is frequently updated for internal distribution.[10]

While large companies like Texas Instruments and Johnson & Johnson are well-known as active leaders in promoting professional ethics, what if you find yourself in a more local, average workplace, one that does not provide such well-known guidelines? How do you know whether you are on the right track regarding your ethical decisions? The ethics test in Strategy for Success 15.1 at the end of this chapter, which was developed by Texas Instruments, can be helpful.

more about...

Another Well-Known Ethical Code

Johnson & Johnson has published a well-known ethical code directed to their consumers, employees, communities, and stockholders. This multinational medical and pharmaceutical manufacturing company is more than 130 years old and employs more than 130,000 people today. Link to www.jnj.com/about-jnj/jnj-credo to read their full credo.

STAYING ETHICAL ON THE JOB

Some jobs present strong temptations to be unethical, such as by cheating customers. An employee must avoid unethical shortcuts. *How have you responded to pressures to behave unethically on the job?*

James Lauritz/Photodisc/Getty Images

Codes of ethics like that of Texas Instruments are usually based on one of the following ethical principles: utilitarianism, universalism, rights/legal, justice, virtue, common good, and ethical relativism approaches.[11] These are often identified as among the most (but not the only) common ethical philosophies. They can be used to guide individual, organizational, and stakeholder behavior.

principle of utilitarianism

An ethical philosophy that holds that all decisions should do the greatest good for the largest number of people.

1. The **principle of utilitarianism** means making decisions that promise to do the greatest good for the largest number of people. That is, the ends justify the means. Using utilitarianism, a manager would lay off 50 employees now to provide several hundred new jobs in the future. Someone who lives by this principle would have little problem sacrificing hundreds of soldiers in a war effort to help the overall good of the country, especially if the country were populated with tens of millions of citizens.

principle of universalism

An ethical philosophy that all human life has value, and ethical decisions should protect all.

2. The **principle of universalism** takes the view that all human life has value. All risks and all people involved are considered when making ethical decisions. Rather than sacrificing a few to save many, as utilitarian principles would do, the universalism principle would find the move that saves all. A manager in this case might decide that rather than laying off 50 people to save 300 jobs, she will not lay off anyone, and instead will ask all employees to take a pay cut to save everyone's jobs.

rights or legal principle

An ethical philosophy that legal rights determine the ethical decision to make.

3. The **rights or legal principle** sees the legal or moral stand as most important. In this principle, individual rights are important, and decisions may be based on, for example, the U.S. Constitution and the Declaration of Independence. Conflict can arise, though, when

two competing sides each base their stand on legal or moral rights. And some individuals may selfishly base their actions on legal rights. Whose rights should be upheld, for example, when one person claims free speech rights to spew hatred, and another claims the right to be free from hate speech?

4. The **principle of justice** focuses on making sure that all decisions are consistent, unbiased, and based on fact. For example, a manager using this principle would want to be certain that he or she had all of the facts in a given case before making a decision. The judicial systems of most countries are based on the principle of justice, including that of the United States. In applying this principle to a moral dilemma, ask yourself about the decision you are making: Is it fair? Is it right? Who gets hurt? Who has to pay for the consequences?
5. The **principle of virtue** believes that one's character traits of wisdom, truth, and moral goodness should be used to make ethical decisions. A question to ask in this philosophy is "What would my best self do?" Altruism is found in this principle, and virtuous decisions will lead people to well-being and flourishing in their lives. One question that can arise in this principle is how is virtue defined, and by whom?
6. The **principle of the common good** is based on a belief that decisions should be made that benefit everyone, now and into the future, for our own families, societies, and the broader social environment. This belief takes a long-term viewpoint, also considering the later impact of decisions we make now. The common good focuses on the intent and the effects of decisions and actions.
7. **Ethical relativism** is a belief that each person should make the best ethical choices based on their own self-interests, values, moral standards, and culture. This approach is quite common and can lead to decisions made without facts and with selfish intents. At the societal level, leaders with this belief system can become dictatorial. The most ethical decisions using this belief system should be made carefully and thoughtfully.

Does one of the ethics principles listed–utilitarianism, universalism, rights/legal, justice, virtue, common good, and ethical relativism–seem the most appropriate to you in making ethical decisions? Additional principles in use are listed in Figure 15.2. Some choices are better and some more popular than others. Which choice or combination of choices seems most appropriate to your values? Which choices are the most useful for the workplace?

principle of justice
An ethical philosophy that holds that all decisions should be consistent, unbiased, and based on fact.

principle of virtue
An ethical philosophy that stresses decisions that are wise, true, and lead to one's best self.

principle of the common good
An ethical philosophy that decisions made for the common good affect the best choices for individuals and societies, in the present and the future.

ethical relativism
An ethical philosophy that believes that each person should make their best decisions based on self-interest, values, morals, and culture.

more about...

"Don't be evil, and if you see something that you think isn't right—speak up!"

The ethical credo for Alphabet, the parent company for Google, was summarized very simply in 2000: Don't be evil. To explain, the preface of their longer document began with:

"'Don't be evil.' Googlers generally apply those words to how we serve our users. But 'Don't be evil' is much more than that. Yes, it's about providing our users unbiased access to information, focusing on their needs and giving them the best products and services that we can. But it's also about doing the right thing more generally—following the law, acting honorably, and treating co-workers with courtesy and respect."

In 2018, the corporation widened its slogan to "And remember . . . don't be evil, and if you see something that you think isn't right—speak up!"

Alphabet, Inc., "Google Code of Conduct," https://abc.xyz/investor/other/google-code-of-conduct, last updated July 31, 2018.

REAL WORLD EXAMPLE 15.2

Luis, a maintenance manager, offers a day off with pay to his employee Monica to thank her for not reporting an accident on the job. Luis tells himself that he never *saw* any written code saying that this was not allowed—but he never looked for one, either.

figure 15.2

WHAT IS YOUR DEFINITION OF ETHICAL?

Ethics can be hard to define because many people's personal ethics are summed up by their feelings and gut instinct, which are hard to quantify. Also, answers like "What my feelings tell me to do" may be acceptable for someone in a specific context or culture, but completely unacceptable for another individual in a different context. *What is your definition of the word* "ethical"?

What Does Ethical Mean?

Possible answers include:

- What most people around me consider appropriate behavior.
- Whatever reflects the Golden Rule.
- Whatever is not against the law.
- What my feelings tell me to do.
- Whatever is in line with my religious beliefs.
- Whatever is customary in my society.
- Whatever would be approved of by a neutral panel of people in my line of work.
- Whatever doesn't hurt other people.
- What does the most good for the most people.

rationalize

To justify unethical behavior with excuses.

» RATIONALIZING UNETHICAL BEHAVIOR

Even people with a good knowledge of ethical principles can fall prey to the temptation to justify or **rationalize** unethical behavior. Management experts warn that unethical behavior in the workplace often starts with one or more of six basic rationalizations:[12]

1. *Rationalization error:* We justify our behavior because we think that we are more ethical than we actually are. We want to believe we are good people at heart, and this lends itself to quick–and often unethical–decisions.
2. *Obeying authority:* We become more willing to act unethically when someone more senior tells us to do so.
3. *Conforming:* When we believe that everyone else is behaving unethically, we are more likely to do so.
4. *Time pressure:* Unethical behaviors are more likely when we act under a time pressure.
5. *Fatigue:* Unethical behaviors are more likely when we are tired.
6. *Lack of transparency:* Unethical behaviors are more likely when we know that no one is watching.

Whenever you are expected to make a work-related decision, be aware of these rationalization behaviors. When you are justifying a decision that seems unethical, ask whether you are being honest with yourself in your rationalizing. Since rationalization is often done without conscious thought, you must be alert to the use of this mental manipulation of the facts.[13]

REAL WORLD EXAMPLE 15.3

At Matco Plastics, the head of the production department is being promoted to vice president. Hoping to be her replacement, the eight supervisors employed under her spend the three months before she leaves both massaging the boss and undercutting one another. They now work in an environment that is negative for all of them.

As with many of the topics presented in this book, a person's sense of self plays an important part in this discussion. For example, people with high self-esteem are more likely to feel good about themselves, which allows them to not seek the short-term gains of unethical behavior and not engage in rationalization to justify it. Likewise, a person focused on using a growth mindset is likely to focus more on learning and development than rationalizing failures. This, in turn, can promote healthy connections with others around them, and create an organizational climate in which people are more likely to act in a socially responsible way.

more about...

Rationalizing

Rationalizing is a term that means finding an excuse for behavior that causes embarrassment, shame, anxiety, or pain. It is one of the defense mechanisms described by the late psychoanalyst Sigmund Freud.

» ETHICS IN CONTEXT

In Chapter 3, you learned about the importance of using self-disclosure and being honest in your relationships with others. This can become an ethical issue when people act insincerely in their relationships with other people in order to achieve their own ends. Loss of trust is the result, and, as you learned in Chapter 1, trust is the basic element of relationships. In a business setting, as in personal relationships outside of the office, trust can be earned, and it can be lost. To gain trust with your work team members or those you supervise, put into practice these four simple statements: *I understand you. I appreciate you. I have your back. I tell you the truth.*[14] Get to know people in order to understand them. When you know people, you can show them authentic appreciation. Supporting them builds trust and helps to define roles and responsibilities. Being honest with each other allows difficult conversations to take place in a respectful environment.

Politics exist in any company, and gaining political power isn't in itself an unethical behavior. However, when people compromise their own integrity to succeed at getting ahead in the company, an important ethical line has been crossed. In the United States, there is a widespread belief that if you are agreeable and easy to get along with, your job will remain secure. The idea seems to be that, although unpleasant and dishonest, the practice of **boss massaging**, is a necessary price one must pay for success. Most people do not judge those who play this game because it is a common practice. Many times, this game includes competition among co-workers.

boss massaging
The practice of currying favor, or kissing up, with a manager to achieve your own goals.

The employee wishing to rise above this disharmony can have trouble remaining detached from it. If you find yourself in such a position, remember that *no one can force you to act unethically.*

REAL WORLD EXAMPLE 15.4

Tina will retire in a few months. The company wants to hire an internal replacement. Josh and Denise both report to Tina, they are the only internal candidates, and they both want the position. Josh begins to spend a lot of time helping people in the division finish their work, taking people to lunch, and especially volunteering for anything Tina needs to have done. Denise spends her time working hard on her own projects, and expects to be judged on her own merits. She feels that Josh is acting unfairly to gain an advantage. When she calls him on it, he acts surprised and says he thought they both just wanted the same thing—for the company to be successful. Tina tells others that Josh is really "stepping up" and should get the position. *Is anything unethical going on? Would you be more like Josh or like Denise in this scenario? Why?*

If you are the boss who is being massaged, an honest look at the power realities should show that you are free to take many actions to discourage such behavior. Be a manager who makes it clear that your employees' performance is based on merit, and be consistent in the application of that philosophy.

» THE INFLUENCE OF GROUP GOALS

The biblical story of the Good Samaritan tells of a Samaritan (person from Samaria) in ancient times who came upon a man who had been beaten and robbed by criminals. Though a stranger, the unnamed Samaritan bandaged the victim's wounds and paid for food and lodging until the man had healed.[15] This parable has served for centuries as an example of how an individual should act when finding a helpless person in great need. However, often, the exact opposite occurs: when encountering someone in need, many people look the other way because other people's goals or a group's pressures override the need. This creates an ethical conflict: even when people have learned helping behavior in their families and communities, they sometimes find themselves unable to transfer those behaviors to the workplace.

Research by social scientists shows that many people change their ethical standards between home and work. In a study with 250 people, researchers found that most people see themselves as having similar traits and behaviors in different situations, and most people see themselves as behaving morally and ethically across all situations. This thinking helps a person to preserve their concept of themselves—whether accurate or inaccurate. As the researchers explain, "If I tend to think about myself the same way from one identity to the next, then if I do something that's going to make me feel bad about myself, it's likely that I'll feel bad about myself across all of my identities."[16]

Remaining positive and sticking to a growth mindset can help people avoid taking on a negative self-image, and it can motivate people to behave more ethically. People who compartmentalize their self-identities more easily, seeing themselves as having some traits in one context and another set of

REAL WORLD EXAMPLE 15.5

Mara, an electronics engineer in a computer company, stole an innovative idea for software from a competing company. She assumed that she would be expected to take any steps that could help the company compete in the software market. After all, her manager, her department, and the whole company would benefit. Instead, when she brought the idea to her supervisor, she was reprimanded and placed on disciplinary leave of absence.

traits in another (e.g., "I'm this way at work, and I'm a different other way at home"), can more easily justify acting unethically or immorally in a work setting. Do you see yourself as one person with one traits across all situations, or different "selves" depending on the context?[17]

Perhaps someday you will work for a company that encourages you to leave your ethics at the door when you come to work. Such companies do exist; however, the perception that management wants you to behave unethically is often more imagined than real. Make sure that you are interpreting your company and its management fairly, and that you do not assume that unethical actions are required of you that actually are not.

Whatever the company attitude, everyone who works for a company should closely examine how his or her personal ethics fit into the ethics of the firm. If compromise is necessary to continue as an employee, make sure that the compromise does not force you into areas of ethical choice where you would be opposing your own values. Few situations cause more stress than compromises with your own conscience.

» GLOBAL ETHICS ISSUES

As trade expands, interconnecting people and supply chains across the globe, successful organizations recognize differing ethical views in other nations and acknowledge these differences with an attitude of acceptance. American values, beliefs, and practices are not the only ones in this world. American values have their roots in the ancient cultures of Greece and Rome, as well as that of the British Empire. Judeo-Christian religious influences have also been a large factor, as are the U.S. Constitution and Bill of Rights. Other nations have value systems that may come from very different—though equally valid—sources.[20]

A Historical Perspective

The values and customs of other countries are not inferior, primitive, or degraded. They have different origins, evolutions, and applications through history. They are based on differing histories and cultural memories. Practices that might seem unethical to Americans often have cultural histories that go back thousands of years.

Consider bribery, or the payment of "kickbacks," or even insider trading in stocks. While these are mostly illegal and frowned-upon in the United

REAL WORLD EXAMPLE 15.6

Harley-Davidson Company has an ethical code based on the company's definition of "healthy working relationships." It contains five points: being truthful, practicing fairness, keeping promises, respecting others, and encouraging intellectual curiosity.[18] The company also has a 12-point philosophy of "financial ethics" that all employees and managers have to read and sign.[19]

figure 15.3

ETHICAL STANDARDS

Although many basic ethical standards are practiced throughout humanity, their application varies from culture to culture. What is considered politeness, hospitality, and punctuality can vary greatly, even within regions of the same country. *Which of these propositions do you agree with most?*

Source: Adapted from Gene R. Lacznick and Jacob Naor, "Global Ethics: Wrestling with the Corporate Conscience," *Business*, Summer 1985, pp. 8–9.

Ethical Propositions for the Global Business Climate

- There are diverse standards of ethical behavior around the world.
- Enforcement of law, not existence of law, often determines behavior.
- You cannot be too ethical.
- Multinational corporations have high ethical responsibility and accountability.
- The likelihood of ethical misjudgments is relatively high.
- A country's concern with ethics increases with its economic well-being.

States, they are common practice in some parts of Latin America, Asia, and the Middle East. In some countries in Africa and other parts of the world, age-old traditions that *require* payoffs are rooted in a communal heritage, and an entire tribe or village benefits from such payoffs. If the community is the enforcer of law, one can easily see why tradition would overcome any written law in most cases. (See Figure 15.3.)

In sum, there are differences in the history and practice of ethical standards among different countries and cultures. And while most governments do have laws concerning bribes and payoffs, the implementation of these laws in some countries or regions can be lax; any law is only as effective as its enforcement. If you do business with foreign companies, especially in developing countries or those that are less Westernized, you should work to understand three concepts, introduced here: The Inner Circle, Future Favors, and Gift Exchange. While norms and standards change rapidly in our globalizing world, these practices remain commonplace in different parts of the world.[21]

The Inner Circle

inner circle

A clique of trusted family members, tribal members, or friends (depending on the culture) who are at the center of power or influence.

Most communal societies make a strong distinction between insiders and outsiders. Those who are in the **inner circle** are, depending on the culture, family members, tribal members, or trusted friends. In China an inner circle might include people who speak the same dialect. In India members of an inner circle would likely be from the same historical caste or social class. In many cases, a skillful American or other Westerner can become sufficiently trusted to break into the inner circle, but such acceptance can require great skill and patience. The possibility of unjust treatment toward outsiders is always a consideration,

REAL WORLD EXAMPLE 15.7

By paying a cash bribe and gaining a million-dollar customer, sales manager Ron thought that even if he were caught, the company would thank him for landing the account. "After all," he thought, "this is how they do business in this area." Instead, he was fired for this unethical behavior, which had left the company legally vulnerable and damaged its reputation as a company with integrity.

and outsiders should watch carefully for this. In some inner circles, fairness and kindness to those outside the circle are not considered to be necessary.

WORKING IN THE GLOBAL MARKET

Even everyday events such as buying dinner can be very different in other countries, and American businesspeople who want to succeed internationally have to be flexible and open-minded to such differences. *How might a different cultural situation cause problems for someone used to American ethics?*

SetsukoN/Getty Images

Future Favors

Within these inner circles, one will find the assumption of **future favors**. Traditional Japanese call it *inner duty;* in Kenya, it is known as *inner relationship,* and for traditional Filipinos is it known as *inner debt.* The practice can be found in nearly any traditional culture that respects the inner circle concept. It translates into *I owe you; I pay you off. Now you owe me.* The trading back of favors can go on for years, even generations. When a typical American says, "I owe you one," the seriousness with which such an expression is both meant and understood is much less than in most developing countries. It is also worth remembering that while global traditional cultures are becoming more Westernized in many ways, remnants of older beliefs can still be found.

future favors

A practice commonly seen in developing countries based upon mutual obligation and resulting in the exchange of favors over years and even generations; also used in some industrialized countries such as Japan and South Korea.

Gift Exchange

Americans who witness a **gift exchange** in another country may suspect bribery, but such an accusation would horrify most people who practice this custom. In some cultures, this tradition of exchanging gifts goes back to ancient times. In today's global marketplace, the tradition often becomes a standard tool of business. Although gift exchange does exist in the Western world, the sense of obligation related to it (based on future favors) is not nearly as strong. This tradition is related to the concept of the inner circle, too, as the gift exchange is often the rite of passage into that circle.

gift exchange

A strong tradition in many cultures, in which giving gifts creates a future obligation to the receiver; it can also be a rite of passage into an inner circle.

REAL WORLD EXAMPLE 15.8

The rapid growth of global trade relationships with China has already taught other countries some hard lessons on differing attitudes about what is ethical. Consider this example: Marketing executives at Japanese automaker Toyota decided to repurpose an old Chinese proverb that says, "When you get to the foot of the mountain, a road will appear," by creating a new advertising campaign that cleverly spun-off from the original proverb: "Wherever there is a road, there is a Toyota." Most of us would admit that the statement isn't literally true, and most other cultures—including the United States—are used to that sort of hyperbole (sometimes straining credibility, even) to get the customer's attention. Not the Chinese. Chinese government authorities saw the slogan as highly unethical, and accused Toyota of false advertising.[23]

When we think of global ethics challenges, there are many more besides the previous examples that will arise. These issues include insider trading, child labor, quality control, discrimination, worker safety, environmental protection, truth in advertising, employee misconduct, gender issues, and more. How do we keep up with the changes in laws and norms and the differences in expectations around the world? Three best practice ideas to keep in mind come from Thomas Donaldson in the *Harvard Business Review:*

- Respect core human values, which provide you and your company with the moral threshold for all business activities.
- Respect local traditions.
- Remember that the situation and the context matter when you are deciding what is right and what is wrong.[22]

ETHICAL OR PERSONAL CONFLICT?

Sometimes in intercultural business settings, you will be asked to agree to things that make you feel ethically uncomfortable. You need to determine if these requests reflect genuine cultural traditions of the people with which you are working, or if an ethical conflict is occurring. *How can you determine whether a situation is truly unethical, or if it is just your personal discomfort with the issue?*

alvarez/Getty Images

» SOCIAL RESPONSIBILITY

Social responsibility means putting ethical standards to work in all areas of the global community in which you live. Being socially responsible is acting ethically while understanding that your actions are part of the larger, interactive picture of the workplace, the community, and the world. Social responsibility includes acting ethically with customers, co-workers, suppliers, competitors, and the community in which you live.

What types of social responsibilities does a typical workplace have? Every workplace has an obligation to make choices or decisions about issues such as environmental pollution, discrimination, employee safety and health, dishonesty, and community commitments such as volunteerism. The growing awareness over the past few decades of such obligations has prompted many companies to become more socially responsible. (See Figure 15.4.)

Here are just a few of the thousands of examples of corporate social responsibility:

Starbucks, the Seattle-based coffee company, has been working to improve local communities since 1997, when it launched a literacy program. The company has provided matching grants to help nonprofit agencies, to improve youth job skills training, and to provide clean water access to people in developing countries.

AT&T has developed technology that reduces pollution and shares this technology with other companies.

Gap Inc. (which also includes Old Navy, Intermix, Athleta, and Banana Republic) has worked to improve factory conditions worldwide, to help provide access to clean water, and to meet sustainability goals in manufacturing sites. They have also supported job training in local communities and provided incentives for their employees to volunteer for local area efforts.

Levi Strauss & Co., one of the world's largest clothing companies and a global employer, has donated millions of dollars and incentivized employee volunteer efforts to improve living conditions for refugees, to reduce stigma to members of the LGBTQ community, and to help reduce climate degradation and provide clean water access.

Ben and Jerry's Homemade, Inc., though taken over by corporate giant Unilever, has remained socially responsible. In 2004, the company supported research on sustainable dairy farming practices and on new eco-friendly refrigeration technology that could have great environmental impact in the future. Their mantra "business has a responsibility to the community and environment" has not changed as they continue to support local and global communities, and their own employees, in efforts to be socially responsible.

Merrill launched a $2 billion pledge to support charities that address critical issues, including education and employability, cultural understanding, and environmental sustainability. They have supported and provided incentives for employees to volunteer for local efforts.

figure 15.4

COMPANIES THAT CARE

Thousands of companies give back to their communities in different ways every year. The key to effective social responsibility is to consider the entire community when business decisions are made, and to give back things that the community wants and will appreciate. *What is your favorite example of corporate social responsibility? (It doesn't have to be from this list.)*

Sources: "Starbucks Social Impact," Starbucks, https://www.starbucks.com/aboutus/csr.asp; "Society," AT&T, https://www.att.com/about/community; "Sustainability," Gap Inc., https://www.gapinc.com/content/gapinc/html/sustainability.html; "Social Impact," Levi Strauss & Co., https://www.levistrauss.com/values-in-action/social-impact; "Our Values," Ben & Jerry's, https://www.benjerry.com/values; and "About Us," Merrill, https://www.ml.com/about-merrill-lynch.html. All retrieved April 7, 2020.

Of all the companies that do give back to their communities by matching gifts, the organization Re:Charity ranked at the top of 17 companies. These included BP (British Petroleum), Merck (pharmaceuticals), Disney, Soros Fund Management, State Farm, Grainger, MBIA (Municipal Bond Insurance Association), Noble Energy, Starbucks, The Home Depot, General Electric, Coca-Cola, Bristol Myers Squibb, ExxonMobil, Johnson and Johnson, Capital Group, and American Express.[24] Look around your own community. What companies do you see contributing to the community? What corporate sponsors do you notice contributing to your college or university?

One of the difficulties in deciding whether or not a company is socially responsible is that there is disagreement about just *whom* the company should be responsible *to.* Corporate social responsibility in a traditional view says that a corporation is responsible to

social responsibility

The practice of acting ethically while understanding your actions are part of the larger, interactive picture of your workplace, community, and world.

more about...

Social responsibility is also demonstrated at the individual level. People who volunteer for coastal clean-up activities, recycling centers, adopt-a-highway programs, child mentoring activities, hospice care facilities, and so on, are acting in a socially responsible manner.

REAL WORLD EXAMPLE 15.9

The administrative board of a nonprofit organization started a mentoring program for at-risk children in a semi-rural community. Shortly afterward, another organization opened an after-school program for at-risk children. These two organizations had the same goals and served similar populations, and so they began competing for grants and contributions from the same sources. Hard feelings and conflict arose until both organizations were able to secure enough funding to continue without financial worries. Might there have been a more optimal, ethical path for the two nonprofits?

itself, its stakeholders, and the public. These are also referred to as the traditional (or classical) view, stakeholder (or accountability), and affirmative (or public) social responsibility.[25]

1. *Traditional social responsibility* says that a company or organization is responsible only to itself and to making a profit. In this view, the government and general public, not companies, are responsible for solving social problems. In an organization, though, any decision that does not directly benefit shareholders is considered irresponsible. This view of social responsibility is based mostly on materialistic ideals that emerged with the Industrial Revolution in the late 1880s when large corporations were first formed. Today it is still practiced worldwide but is often criticized as selfish and destructive.
2. *Stakeholder social responsibility* holds that companies are responsible to **stakeholders**–that is, to any group they interact with as a business. In this view, a company is responsible not just to make a profit, but also to answer to customers, competitors, unions, suppliers, consumer groups, government agencies, and so on. This view emerged in the 1930s during the Great Depression, when views on employee rights and human relations underwent significant progress. This perspective goes beyond what is good for the company and commits a company to having ethical responsibilities.
3. *Affirmative (or public) social responsibility* is the most broadly based of the three perspectives. In this view, companies are not just responsible to their profit margin and their stakeholders, but they are also responsible to the general public and society at large. Companies in this view would be expected to avoid creating social problems such as pollution and poverty, and to work toward goals that improve conditions for everyone. This view came about in the 1960s, when social unrest escalated and disapproval of business practices became more publicized. It is based most heavily on ethical principles, in particular those of moral rights and justice.

stakeholders

Any group that a business interacts with, such as customers, competitors, unions, suppliers, consumer groups, and government agencies.

A Few Cautions about Social Responsibility

Just as there are many difficult questions regarding ethics, there are also many difficult questions regarding social responsibility. For example, what

REAL WORLD EXAMPLE 15.10

Several years ago, a small-town physician announced publicly that he would offer an incentive of $40 a month to all the teenagers in his community who did *not* get pregnant while in high school. This offer on his part was meant to help curb the spiraling rate of pregnancies among young teens in his particular community. His offer was subsequently interpreted by some members of his community as promoting contraception with a pro-abortion hidden agenda. He became the target of criticism and controversy, in an effort to be socially responsible.

happens when a company can no longer afford to support charities or organizations that have become dependent on them? A move to protect the company's economic health by cutting charitable funding may seem selfish to outside observers.

How does a company choose to support specific organizations while not helping others? Choosing among equally important organizations can create hard feelings among nonprofit organizations or charities, although this may not be obvious to corporate donors.

Companies or individuals may also find that their acts of social responsibility are misunderstood and resented by the community. As well, differences in political views among the general public mean that some corporate social responsibility activities are seen as desirable and valuable by some people, while being viewed as undesirable and inappropriate by others.

These examples are not meant to discourage you from becoming socially responsible. They are only meant to show you that social responsibility–just like the larger issue of ethics in general–often contains a lot of gray areas and difficult choices.

more about...

Corporate Social Responsibility

Forbes magazine reported findings from a survey conducted in 2019 by Reputation Institute, a global company based in New York. About 230,000 people in 15 countries named the corporations they believe to have the best reputations for international corporate social responsibility. Here are the top 10:

1. The LEGO Group
2. Natura
3. Microsoft
4. Google
5. The Walt Disney Company
6. Bosch
7. Havaianas
8. Intel
9. Lavazza
10. Ikea

Source: Vicky Valet, "The World's Most Reputable Companies for Corporate Responsibility 2019," *Forbes*, September 17, 2019, https://www.forbes.com/sites/vickyvalet/2019/09/17/the-worlds-most-reputable-companies-for-corporate-responsibility-2019 (retrieved April 4, 2020).

» BLOWING THE WHISTLE

What do you do when you have found unethical conduct taking place in your company? Most strategies involve **whistleblowing**–turning in the offending person or people and exposing the truth. As defined by the U.S. Government Accountability Project, whistleblowing happens when an employee brings to light information that is "evidence of illegality, gross waste or fraud, mismanagement, abuse of power, general wrongdoing, or a substantial and specific danger to public health and safety."[26]

whistleblowing
Turning in or otherwise exposing people who behave unethically in your company.

THE NEED FOR WHISTLEBLOWING

When companies behave unethically, the answer might be to "blow the whistle." Companies such as this can cause severe environmental or financial damage that affects human health and lives. *What are the possible costs of not blowing the whistle on unethical corporate behavior?*

ColorBlind Images/Blend Images LLC

The first law passed to protect whistleblowers was the Lloyd–La Follette Act of 1912, which protected federal employees who gave information to Congress.[27] Wider protection for those who blow the whistle on dangerous, fraudulent, or unethical practices in their workplace has been in existence since the 1970s. Although free speech rights are guaranteed under the First and Fourteenth Amendments to the Constitution, retaliation against whistleblowers was so widespread that enacting specific laws became necessary. The Whistleblower Protection Act was passed in 1989 and strengthened in 1994. In addition to federal laws, many individual states also have their own whistleblower protection laws. Nevertheless, the Government Accountability Project states that "Every year, thousands of Americans witness wrongdoing on the job . . . [that] may jeopardize the health, safety, or lives of others . . . [and] most employees remain silent in the face of such misconduct" for various reasons, such as fears of retaliation and the belief that there is nothing they can do to stop the misconduct.[28]

In 2006, the U.S. Supreme Court ruled against whistleblowers when the court voted *not* to protect government employees from retaliation after they have blown the whistle on employers. In May 2007, the first "Whistleblowers Week" event was held in Washington, D.C., to encourage the U.S. Congress to pass stronger protective laws for whistleblowers in both the private sector and the government. The Whistleblower Protection Enhancement Act of 2007 was introduced into Congress but wasn't signed into law for another five years, until November 2012, likely due to the complexity of the issue of whistleblowing.

more about...

Protection for Whistleblowers

The Government Accountability Project was established in 1977 to help employees who blow the whistle on unethical corporate practices. They provide legal help and advocacy for such employees.

The person facing the difficult moral decision to become a whistleblower should first consider the situation from different perspectives. These include the individual's motives, the timing, objectives, commitment to action, and possible steps to take. A thorough consideration will include:

- *Pick your battles.* What will happen if you don't blow the whistle? How high are the stakes? What exactly is at stake? If stakes are high, you may need to blow the whistle.
- *Check your motives.* Be honest with yourself about your motives. Are you trying to become a hero, take revenge on someone, prove you are indispensable, want to be noticed, want to be validated, or want to teach someone a lesson? Are you setting the company up to fire you because you don't want to resign? If those motives are the case, then you should not blow the whistle.
- *Check the timing.* Will the situation play itself out if you do not blow the whistle? Or is there something happening that is so critical that it must be stopped now? Responses to these questions may lead to different decisions.

- *Consider your place.* If it is your responsibility to speak directly to a person whose behavior needs to be stopped, then do that instead of blowing the whistle. If it is not your place to address the person, you may need to blow the whistle.
- *What are your objectives?* Are you trying to bring attention to an issue, or stop something from happening? Be prepared to explain your intended outcomes.
- *How far will you go?* How far are you willing to go, how many steps up the chain of command, to see results? If the company refuses to address the problem, are you willing to go outside of the company to authorities?
- *Who will you talk to?* Begin with your supervisor, unless your supervisor is the one causing the problems that need to be addressed. Report issues to Human Resources, then Human Resources administrators, and finally if no action is taken, to the company CEO. Some whistleblowers choose to go to the media, which may be a reasonable decision if the company refuses to address an extremely critical issue.
- *Maintain a positive perspective.* Assume a mistake was made unintentionally, rather than assuming malicious intent. Remain non-judgmental, unemotional, and frame the issue in a "helping" tone, rather than an accusatory tone.
- *Maintain accountability.* As you move up the chain of command, ask what steps will be taken to resolve the issue, and ask to be informed when corrections occur. Document your steps and the company's response.[29]

more about...

Hacktivism

"Hacktivism" (hack + activism) is a newer form of whistleblowing that uses computers and computer networks to promote political rights, free speech, human rights, and freedom of information ethics. Considering their actions a form of civil disobedience, hacktivists have targeted foreign governments with spotty human rights records, religious organizations, multinational corporations, and even the United States government. In a notable case of "hacktivism," Army soldier Bradley Manning (now Chelsea Manning) allegedly provided whistleblowing website WikiLeaks with sensitive U.S. military data that has embroiled the soldier and the founder of WikiLeaks Julian Assange in scandal for years. In another example, the hacktivist group called Anonymous has brought attention to global issues in several hacktivist acts. Dozens of hacktivist acts have caught international attention in recent years, and more are sure to come.

Hopefully, you will never find yourself in a situation that calls for whistleblowing. But if you do, considering these points will help you be more effective with this difficult task.

For reasons that remain unclear, people have traditionally looked down on the person who "tells on" someone else, especially in some areas of life. In grade school, for example, being a tattletale or a "snitch" is not respected. As adults, most people don't like busybodies who seem to be prying into other people's business. For these reasons and others, even many otherwise moral and ethical people are afraid of blowing the whistle. After all, one's job might be at risk, or the whistleblower might be excluded from the informal work group. Other, less rational fears include losing one's nerve at the last minute, not having the courage to follow through once the accusations have been made, or worrying that one's good intentions might be mistaken for backstabbing.

REAL WORLD EXAMPLE 15.11

In 1997, at the Hanford nuclear plant in Richland, Washington, seven pipefitters became concerned and spoke out about tank farm pipes that didn't meet safety standards. These "tank farms" hold millions of gallons of nuclear waste and had been leaking into the surrounding community. When asked to attach a valve to the system that they felt was unsafe, they refused. All seven were fired. Two months later, by court order, they were all rehired. However, in 1998 five of the seven were fired again.

Years of legal struggling went by. Finally, in 2005, they had their day in court, along with four others who became involved later, and won the lawsuit. A Department of Energy contractor was ordered to pay damages.[30] The 11 have sworn that they blew the whistle only because they were afraid of potential physical harm to themselves and the rest of the community.[31]

The federal government has since taken the Hanford danger seriously, by authorizing the Government Accountability Project in early 2008 to set up a nonprofit organization, Hanford Challenge, to oversee cleanup of the site. By 2013, the Department of Energy, which oversees Hanford (regarded as the nation's most contaminated nuclear site), confirmed that eight tanks have been leaking an estimated 1,150 to 1,300 gallons of toxic, radioactive waste a year, and that an additional 14 more tanks may also be leaking nuclear waste into the ground.

These types of fear are not unfounded, even with current whistleblower protection in place. It is a sad reality that many companies punish whistleblowers in various ways for their honesty. A new movement encourages whistleblowing in a few U.S. companies by providing rewards. Such a system, though, may only create distrust among employees if it leads to a perception of spying.

The best solution to addressing difficult moral and ethical choices is the kind of leadership that makes whistleblowing unnecessary. The ethical tone of an organization nearly always originates in top management and moves downward. Thus, top management is in an ideal position to create an ethical environment for everyone who works in the company.

Management can also create low ethical standards by making the following managerial mistakes:

- Favoritism occurs when one employee is given extra privileges and allowances. This creates resentment among other employees and the impression that they, too, are entitled to these same extra privileges—even if they are unethical.
- "Fudging" with the expense budget–allowing employees to use company expense budgets for items of doubtful use to the company or for obvious personal use–is unethical treatment. Managers should also be careful not to do the same, thus setting a bad example. This behavior may also be illegal, setting employees and their managers up for possible legal ramifications.
- Lying to or otherwise manipulating other departments or offices within one's company creates an atmosphere of distrust, which erodes team spirit.

Most people will face ethical dilemmas during their lives. Knowing one's own values and standards (as covered in Chapter 4) is essential; but some

REAL WORLD EXAMPLE 15.12

Sonia is the president of a mid-sized firm. When one of her friends, William, asked her about an open vice-president position, she encouraged him to apply. The company had strict rules about hiring in order to prevent nepotism or other ethical dilemmas: a screening committee would send forward finalists for Sonia to interview, and she would select the final candidate from among those sent up from the committee. In this case, Sonia's friend William did not make the semi-finalist list. She directed the committee to keep sending more semi-finalists, until William's name finally appeared. Then she hired him.

Was this a breach of ethics? If you agree that it was, what would you do? Would you be a whistleblower? If so, to whom would you report the ethical issue?

situations, such as the one about the unethical treatment of an experienced employee in this chapter's opening story, are still difficult to navigate. There are no easy answers to offer here. Hopefully, though, you now have a heightened awareness of the issues surrounding ethics in the workplace after studying this chapter.

STRATEGIES FOR SUCCESS

Strategy 15.1 Making Ethical Decisions: A Quick Ethics Test from Texas Instruments

1. Is it legal?
2. Is it consistent with the company's stated values?
3. If you do it, will you feel bad?
4. How would it look in the news?
5. Do *you* think it's wrong?
6. If you're not sure—ask.
7. If you don't get a clear answer, keep asking until you do.

Texas Instruments, a giant manufacturer of electronics and computer chips, teaches its employees to run through these seven steps whenever they have a question about whether a business action is ethical.

1. **Is it legal?** If not, then don't do it, even if it's borderline.
2. **Is it consistent with the company's stated values?** Texas Instruments has a clearly stated set of corporate values. Actions that don't fit with them shouldn't be undertaken.
3. **If you do it, will you feel bad?** If so, there's probably something wrong.
4. **How would it look in the news?** If having people "find out" through public sources—including social media—will be embarrassing, there's a problem.
5. **Do *you* think it's wrong?** If so, don't do it.
6. **If you're not sure—ask.** Never feel you have to make a decision on ethics by yourself. Get help from others.
7. **If you don't get a clear answer, keep asking until you do.** Don't gloss over an ethical problem by saying you "tried" to get help but couldn't. Keep asking—the boss, the company's lawyers, and human resources personnel—until you get a clear answer.[32]

STRATEGIES FOR SUCCESS

Strategy 15.2 Navigating the Ethics of Global Business

1. Know the laws in your home country for doing business.
2. Agree to follow international business guidelines.
3. Develop one consistent strategy ahead of time.
4. Be clear in communications and understand differences.
5. Practice your company's guidelines.
6. Understand and acknowledge differences.

International business ethics change constantly, and you as an individual and your company as a business need to be ready to navigate these business ethics. Cultural tradition, language, and history are different everywhere, and businesses need to adapt to these differences.

Business owners and the employees who represent them have the responsibility to follow laws, including U.S. law (if based in the United States), local laws, and customs. Here are six points to remember in preparing to do business ethically in the global marketplace.

1. **Know the laws in your home country for doing business.**
   Even though cultural traditions in some countries expect a bribe, for example, the U.S. Foreign Corrupt Practices Act of 1977 bans businesses and their representatives from bribing foreign government officials to do business. This law also directs businesses to comply with specific accounting practices.
2. **Agree to follow international business guidelines.**
   The Organisation for Economic Co-operation and Development (OECD) is a think tank that makes recommendations on global business issues. Nearly 40 countries are members, including the United States. The OECD provides standards on many international business practices including child labor, environmental protection, and worker safety, among many more difficult issues.
3. **Develop one consistent strategy ahead of time.**
   Before you or your company begin business overseas, develop consistent policies and procedures to navigate the many differences that will arise. The company headquarters or a branch office in other countries should have this code of conduct on hand and follow it to be sure the company's fundamental guiding principles are in place to use for employee decision making. Behavior will need to be adapted for different areas of the world, but guiding principles should stay in place. For example, if your company sets a standard that it will not use child labor, this needs to be followed consistently. Levi Strauss found itself in this position several years ago and had to cut ties with producers in some countries.
4. **Be clear in communications and understand differences.**
   Intercultural communication is critical for global business success. Successful businesses maintain their ability to communicate verbally and non-verbally, understanding the importance of all forms of communication. As an example, doing business in the Middle East means being very clear in communication—repeating messages so that all angles are covered. In these regions, the business partners may not want to ask clarifying questions so as not to lose face, so your communication needs to be very clear.
5. **Practice your company's guidelines.**
   Once your business has its values and code of conduct in place, the next step is to ensure the implementation of those policies. Each employee should learn the guidelines and understand what is expected of them and how to conduct themselves as workers for the company.

6. **Understand and acknowledge differences.**
   Without compromising the company's core values, it is possible to embrace certain cultural differences as long as those actions aren't against the law in the United States. In some countries, bribes are allowed and are tax deductible as a business expense, according to the Justice Department.

Source: Linda Doell, "6 Tips to Navigate the Ethics of Global Business," *American Express*, October 30, 2012, https://www.americanexpress.com/en-us/business/trends-and-insights/articles/6-tips-to-navigate-the-ethics-of-global-business (retrieved April 4, 2020). See also: Thomas Donaldson, "Values in Tension: Ethics Away from Home," *Harvard Business Review*, September–October 1996, https://hbr.org/1996/09/values-in-tension-ethics-away-from-home (retrieved April 4, 2020).

CHAPTER FIFTEEN SUMMARY

Chapter Summary by Learning Objectives

LO 15-1 Define ethics. Ethics refers to the standards of conduct and morals in a particular society. In short, it expresses the standards of right and wrong as accepted among a specific group of people.

LO 15-2 Explain the importance of a code of ethics. Codes of ethics vary from person to person and from company to company. Codes of ethics provide agreement and documentation for the manner in which the company sees itself ethically operating. While there are many principles of ethics that are used to develop codes of ethics, this chapter addresses utilitarianism, universalism, rights/legal principle, justice principle, virtue principle, common good principle, and ethical relativism.

LO 15-3 Describe the process of rationalizing unethical behavior. Rationalization is the use of reasonable-sounding excuses to explain unethical conduct. Common reasons to rationalize our unethical behavior include rationalization error, obeying authority, time pressure, conforming, fatigue, and lack of transparency.

LO 15-4 Explain ethics in the context of the U.S. workplace. A major ethical issue in the United States is the issue of "boss massaging." Anyone working here, or in some other countries, must look carefully at this practice and decide on its integrity, or lack of it.

LO 15-5 Describe the influence of group goals on ethics. Many people with strong personal ethics find themselves unable to carry their values into the workplace; this can be from the pressure of the larger group. The Parable of the Good Samaritan and the Parable of the Sadhu (in the end-of-chapter Working It Out 15.2) are used in this chapter to explore that issue.

LO 15-6 Give examples of global ethics issues. When doing business in other countries and cultures, you must become sensitive to the differences in ethical definitions and attitudes. Be certain that you understand the thinking of the other culture before acting or jumping to conclusions. Especially remember these three concepts: the inner circle, future favors, and gift exchange.

LO 15-7 Define social responsibility. Social responsibility means putting ethical standards to work in all areas of work and life. Three common views of social responsibility are responsibility to the company itself, to stakeholders, or to the public; also referred to as traditional (or classical), stakeholder (or accountability), and affirmative (or public) social responsibility.

LO 15-8 Describe the process of whistleblowing. If you discover unethical behavior in your own organization, you will likely consider whistleblowing. Consider all aspects of the situation while making a decision to blow the whistle. Knowledge of your own ethical standards will help greatly in any decision involving ethical choices.

key terms

boss massaging 457
cyberbullying 451
cybercrime 452
digital divide 452
disinformation 451
ethical codes 452
ethical relativism 455
ethics 448
future favors 461
gift exchange 461
inner circle 460
morality 448
net neutrality 452
principle of justice 455
principle of the common good 455
principle of utilitarianism 454
principle of universalism 454
principle of virtue 455
rationalize 456
rights or legal principle 454
social responsibility 462
stakeholders 464
whistleblowing 465

review questions

1. Briefly define *ethics*. Give your own definition of ethics as the term applies to your own values. Do you think it is a good idea to base your decisions on what "feels" right? Are there any outside forces that influence your behavior?
2. What is a code of ethics? In your opinion, how effective are such codes?
3. Evaluate Alphabet's Codes of Ethics and other examples in the "Codes of Ethics" section in this chapter. What is the key to their popular appeal?

4. Define the term *rationalizing.* What role does rationalization play in making bad ethical decisions? Thinking back, have you ever rationalized a bad ethical decision? Explain.
5. Explain the ethical problems involved in boss massaging. When is this practice a good idea? When is this practice a bad idea? Explain what may occur when employees are involved in boss massaging.
6. What major ethical issues are likely to confront someone who is doing business in a foreign country? Give some specific examples. What are some strategies for becoming culturally aware of ethical conduct in foreign countries?
7. How does the Internet create new ethical issues? Do you believe it is unethical for a company to share your data to help tailor what you see online? Explain.
8. What is your attitude toward whistleblowing? Would you ever be a whistleblower if the situation merited such action? Why or why not?

critical thinking questions

1. There are times when people feel they must act unethically in the short term in order to benefit the greater good in the long term. Can you think of a time or a situation that you are familiar with in which this has happened? Is it *ever* acceptable to act unethically?
2. Ethical standards often are made into laws over time. In many states, children under age 16 must wear helmets when riding bicycles. Several years ago, this was only an ethical standard that some parents chose and others did not. Do you think that all ethical standards should have "teeth" in the way that laws do? Who would govern codes of ethics? Or should some or all codes of ethics be made into laws so that they carry more weight?
3. Consider the ethics of "hacktivism." Is former Army soldier Chelsea Manning a hero for trying to promote open, transparent government, or a traitor who gave military secrets to a whistleblowing website? With regard to the Internet battle between CyberBunker and Spamhaus—who was right or wrong in this case? And finally, who is in charge of the Internet; that is, who is in charge of its content and for policing unethical behavior?

working it out 15.1

ETHICAL OR NOT?

School-to-Work Connection: Interpersonal Skills

Objective: This exercise will help you clarify differences in a group's opinions of what *ethical* means.

Instructions: Divide into groups of four or five. Using the criteria listed as follows, arrive at a group consensus as to what is meant by the term *ethical.* The suggestions below can be combined, changed, or ignored by group consent. Avoid democratic voting if possible, and instead seek consensus agreement. Next, as a group, create a story illustration—either factual or made up—that illustrates the group definition of ethics you have created.

As the last step, all groups will share both definitions and story illustrations with the rest of the class. Discuss the differences and the reasons for them.

Ethical is:

______ what most people around me consider appropriate behavior.

______ whatever does the most good for the greatest number of people (the *utilitarian principle*).

______ whatever action reflects the Golden Rule.

______ whatever is not against the law.

______ what my feelings tell me to do.

______ whatever action is in line with my religious beliefs.

______ whatever is customary in the society I am in.

______ whatever action would be approved of by a neutral panel of people in my line of work.

______ whatever doesn't hurt other people.

working it out 15.2

THE PARABLE OF THE SADHU

School-to-Work Connection: Interpersonal Skills

Objective: This parable will help you better understand the conflict between individual and corporate ethics.

Instructions: Break into groups of four or five. Read the following parable: while the biblical story of the Good Samaritan is well known in Western culture, a parable of another kind comes from the article "The Parable of the Sadhu," written by Bowen McCoy of *Harvard Business Review.*

McCoy tells of a trip to Nepal in which he walked 600 miles through 200 villages in the Himalayas. At a high elevation, one of the members of a party of New Zealanders who had joined him discovered an Indian holy man—called a *sadhu*—nearly naked and unable to walk. No one wanted to step forward from the group and help him, at least not to the point of helping him down the slope to warmth and safety. He was given some clothing, but since he was unable to walk, his likelihood of surviving without help was very small. In the end, the group left him, presumably to die.

The arguments for and against this lack of action were debated afterward at length. McCoy's friend Stephen summarized the dilemma by saying, "I feel that what happened with the sadhu is a good example of the breakdown between the individual ethic and the corporate ethic. No one person was willing to assume ultimate responsibility for the sadhu. Each was willing to do his bit just so long as it was not too inconvenient. . . ."

All of the travelers who ignored the sadhu were intent on the goal of reaching an 18,000-foot mountain pass to get to a village on the other side. Partly because of the importance of this goal in everyone's mind, the suffering individual was all but forgotten. In other words, an unethical action that an individual in other circumstances would not have taken became possible because of group pressures and group goals. These same forces of goals and the pressures to reach them exist in business. The parable thus asks this question: to what extent can an employee or manager of a company ignore the intense needs of a suffering individual in order to achieve the goals of the larger group?[33]

Most importantly, the parable of the sadhu illustrates the conflict of the individual's personal ethics versus the ethics of the group. Most people learn their moral and ethical values from their families or communities, but for various reasons, they don't always transfer those same values to the other groups (such as the workplace).

Discussion: After you have read the parable of the Sadhu in your small group, begin discussing this topic. In your group, come to consensus on the relevance of this parable to ethics in the workplace. How could your workplace be improved with an awareness of the lesson in this story?

What do you think *you* would have done if you had been the one to come across the sadhu? Have you experienced any situations in which you have been faced with helping—or not helping—someone in distress? What did you do? What did others around you do? Why do you think these people chose the actions they did?

working it out 15.3

ETHICS IN THE WORKPLACE

Part One: What would You Do?

Ethical behavior is not always as easy as it seems. Instead of black and white, there are often gray areas. Do you consider yourself an ethical person?

Read each scenario that follows and answer, honestly, what you think you would do. There are no right or wrong answers. What do you believe would be the most ethical response? The least?

1. Your work colleague asks you to cover for her so she can sneak out of work early. She says she will do the same for you the next time you want to leave early. What do you do? If you say no, and she leaves anyway, would you alert your supervisor?
2. You are about to sign a new client to a high dollar deal. Your supervisor is under pressure to increase sales. He calls you in to his office and tells you that his job is on the line, which means your job may also be on the line. He wants you to include the new deal into a sales report claiming that it is already signed and done. It is not signed, but it probably will be soon. Do you comply?
3. Two of your colleagues are very good friends and often take lunch breaks together. You have noticed that these lunch breaks are quite extended at times, as they return up to an hour later than they should. Others in the department shrug it off and cover for them. What do you do?
4. Your company policy does not allow co-workers to become romantically involved with each other. You work in a small town and often run into someone at work, get to know the person better, and find yourself attracted to the person. Do you take the friendship to the next level and keep silent about it, or just stay casual friends?
5. One of your co-workers has a second job of legal online sports betting. He does not keep it a secret and excitedly shares stories of big wins. Because your work spaces are near each other, you know that much of his betting activity occurs at your job, where he is supposed to be working, and should not be using the company technology or company time for his side job. Is his behavior unethical? What do you do?
6. Your best friend is a manager at another company. Your two companies sometimes do business together. You take her out to lunch just to catch up on personal lives, family, and so on. You pick up the check and claim this as a "business lunch" so that you can submit the receipt for reimbursement as a business meeting. Is this ethical?
7. While you are in the break room getting a cup of coffee, you overhear your supervisor on his cell phone saying that two employees are going to be laid off next month, naming their departments and titles. These two employees are friends of yours. Do you tell them they are about to lose their jobs?
8. You work really hard on a project with the three members of your work team. After finishing the project, you deliver the results to your supervisor. He presents the work to the company management as his own work,

and receives high praise and a bonus in return. He tells you that without his leadership, your work team would not have produced anything valuable. Is this unethical? What do you do?

9. The newest employee in your area is completely unproductive: coming in late, leaving early, distracting others who are working, and not following through with his work. You talk to your supervisor about him, but you are told that the new employee is related to one of the company's top administrators. You are told to leave the new employee alone, and make him look good by "improving" his performance reviews and work reports. Do you comply?

10. Your closest friend at work has three school-aged children and a lot of family debt. She often takes little things home with her for her children to use for school: a stapler, pens and pencils, folders, paper clips, paper, and so on. They do not add up to a large dollar amount, and your company can afford to lose them. Do you consider these to be thefts and something to be concerned about, or nothing important? What do you do about this?

Part Two: Unethical Behavior?

Were the previous workplace situations easy to resolve ethically? Outside of the workplace, do you believe you behave ethically most of the time? Now, consider the situations below that occur outside of work.

Have you ever:

- . . .lied to avoid hurting someone's feelings?
- . . .lied so you would not have to go to a social event?
- . . .cheated a little on an income tax deduction?
- . . .taken a sick day when you weren't really sick?
- . . .blamed a family member for a mistake you made?
- . . .lied to a creditor ("I paid that already")?
- . . .put pressure on others to do something you knew they did not want to do?
- . . .downloaded copyrighted music or movies?
- . . .received extra change at the store and kept it?

Did you find yourself answering the workplace scenarios differently from the non-work scenarios? Did any of the scenarios seem *more* or *less* serious in their ethical consequences? After completing this exercise, do you think of ethics any differently? Explain your responses.

Source: Frank Bucaro, "What Would You Do?" *Corporate Compliance Insights,* April 5, 2017, https://www.corporatecomplianceinsights.com/what-would-you-do (retrieved March 22, 2020).

working it out 15.4

WHISTLEBLOWING: WOULD YOU BLOW THE WHISTLE?

Watch the TED Talk by Professor Kelly Richmond Pope, titled "How Whistle-Blowers Shape History," and then answer the following questions.

1. What is whistleblowing? How does it help a company, and a society?
2. Why are people reluctant to blow the whistle? What do you think you might do in any of the situations described by the speaker?
3. Describe an example given by the speaker of when whistleblowing shaped history. What might have been a logical course of events if someone had NOT blown the whistle?
4. How is whistleblowing related to the material in this chapter on ethics, in general? In your opinion, is it ever more ethical to *not* blow the whistle? Explain.
5. What advice does the speaker give on traits we need to encourage in people to encourage whistleblowing?

The video can be found here: www.ted.com/talks/kelly_richmond_pope_how_whistle_blowers_shape_history.

case study 15.1

Life Over Profit

The following scenario is adapted from a classic ethics test developed by psychologist Lawrence Kohlberg more than 50 years ago. Read the ethical dilemma presented and then answer the Case Questions that follow.

A woman living in Europe was near death from a rare kind of cancer. The doctors knew of only one drug that might save her, a type of radium that a druggist in her town had recently developed. The drug was expensive to make, but the druggist was charging patients 10 times the cost of producing it. He paid $200 for the radium but charged $2,000 for a small dose of the drug.

The sick woman's husband, Heinz, went to everyone he knew in an attempt to borrow the money, but he could only get about half of the $2,000 he needed. He told the druggist that his wife was dying and begged him to sell the drug cheaper, or to extend some credit. But the druggist insisted, "No! I discovered the drug, and I'm going to make money from it." Heinz became desperate and broke into the store to steal the drug to save his wife.[34]

Case Study Questions

1. Was the husband's behavior excusable under the circumstances? Was it ethical?
2. If you were a police officer in the town, would you have arrested the husband for theft?
3. Should the druggist who made the drug face any penalty? Were his actions ethical?
4. If you were Heinz, would you have stolen the drug? If not, why not? What would you have done instead?

case study 15.2

No Sense of Humor?

Cecilia is the CEO of a mid-sized company. One of Cecilia's favorite expressions is "If people don't like working here, we'll help them leave." She has been at the company only a year, and people are not sure how seriously to take her. But in the past year, Cecilia has identified several top managers she thought were "not a good fit" with the company, and she "helped them leave." Many of the remaining managers are now nervous about losing their jobs, and are careful not to say or do anything to confront her.

Cecilia meets weekly with her 10 top-level managers. During these meetings, she often makes fun of other staff who are not present, or the members of the Board of Directors, mocking them and imitating them in an unflattering way.

During these times, some of the managers laugh at her antics, while others look down at their notes, sneaking looks at the other managers at the table to try to gauge their reactions. Early on, when the CEO had just joined the company, one of the managers asked a pointed question about the ethical boundaries of the company. She became angry and accused him of having no sense of humor. He was demoted soon thereafter. Since then, no one at the company has felt comfortable speaking up, or calling her out on her mockery of staff and Board members. No one wants to go over her head and tell the Board of Directors what is going on. So Cecilia just continues this behavior, and now people expect it of her and see it as normal. Some of the managers who report to her also now engage in the same mocking and demeaning behavior.

Case Study Questions

1. How does this situation present an ethics issue? How is the scenario related to the myths of ethics in the workplace?
2. Is this situation tied to each person's sense of self? Explain.
3. How does this situation tie in to the concept of the internal customer, as explained in Chapter 13?
4. If you were one of the managers at the table, what would you do?

16

CHAPTER SIXTEEN

A PRODUCTIVE WORKPLACE AND SUCCESS

LEARNING OBJECTIVES

After studying this chapter, you will be able to:

LO 16-1 Understand factors that create and maintain a productive workplace.

LO 16-2 Learn methods of improving morale and appraisal techniques.

LO 16-3 Learn strategies to improve your use of time.

LO 16-4 Recognize substance abuse and other behaviors that reduce workplace productivity.

LO 16-5 Know what employers and employees can do to address substance abuse as well as other personal or financial problems.

LO 16-6 Explore the concept of success and the attainment of goals.

LO 16-7 Focus strategies to increase and maintain your personal success.

STRATEGIES FOR SUCCESS

Strategy 16.1 Goals for Success

Strategy 16.2 Make an Inventory of Your Skills

Strategy 16.3 Define Your Goals

In the Workplace Company (Dys)Function

SITUATION

Ingram Publishing

Jennifer and Saroja were supposed to be finishing up a report that their manager had asked for the previous day, but they had much more important things to do first. They had to compare notes on their winnings from online card games, read their e-mail, respond to text messages, and get fresh coffee from the coffee place down the block. Jennifer had to check breaking news headlines on Facebook and watch a couple of cute videos on TikTok, while Saroja had a few quick tweets to post to her Twitter account. They both then had to look through new profiles of single men on Tinder, and Jennifer had to quickly (or so she said) look for new profiles on LinkedIn.com while Saroja checked Craigslist to find a new couch. Jennifer needed to check the New York Stock Exchange for some details to add to the report, but then decided to check the progress of her own stocks while she was thinking about it. Saroja waited for her to finish up while reading the *Los Angeles Times* online, just to keep up on current events.

Before they knew it, an hour had gone by, and then another one. When the deadline neared for turning in the report that afternoon, they had barely begun it. Their stress level rose as they felt the urgency of the deadline approaching.

DISCOVERY

"This place is unreasonable! Way too much pressure!" complained Jennifer. "How do they expect us to get our work done on such short notice? Now I'll have to stay late again tonight to finish up! That's going to cause problems with the babysitter, and I can't afford her overtime fees again anyway."

Saroja nodded in agreement, and added, "The stress level for what they pay us is not worth it! They should get a better idea of how long things take before they hand out deadlines. It's just ridiculous that they don't give us enough time for the projects we have to do!"

THINK ABOUT IT

Has there been a time when a friend or family member has had time management issues or personal problems that affected his or her performance at work? Have you had such problems yourself? Does your employer have resources to help with such issues? Do you sometimes notice that people are doing things to reduce their own productivity that they don't seem to see in themselves?

» A PRODUCTIVE WORKPLACE

productivity

The ratio of an organization's inputs, or its resources, to its outputs, or the goods and services it produces.

What does it mean to say a workplace is productive? We can define **productivity** as a ratio of *inputs* (that is, an organization's resources) to its *outputs* (that is, the organization's goods and services produced). Given today's business competition and our global economy, it is essential to maintain high productivity in the workplace.

Productivity can be increased, in general, by focusing on input and output separately. By becoming more efficient, an organization may be able to improve the production process and gain more output for the same input, achieve the same output as before with less input, or increase input slightly for greater output. There are many ways to improve efficiency in productivity. Many of these strategies are out of the individual control of the employee. These include long-term and complex processes such as improving the research and development arm of an organization, or buying new equipment, buildings, or machinery. The organization can simplify its products, or improve the production process. Another way to improve productivity is to increase the efficiency of employees at the individual level. This last strategy is under our individual control, and it is the focus of this chapter.

Increasing Morale to Boost Productivity

It is traditional in the field of human relations to point out that *morale* and productivity are closely related. *Morale* is defined in Chapter 5 as "the overall mood of an individual or a group based on attitudes and satisfaction." When morale is low, productivity inevitably suffers. This lowered productivity includes everything from a slower pace of work to an increase in accidents.

Employees with high morale are not just more productive—they also perform better and stay longer with a company, reducing turnover rates. In a time of crisis, employees with high morale are more likely to work hard to help the company survive and meet its goals.[1]

Companies with high employee morale will find it easier to recruit and retain good employees, since people want to work in a pleasant environment. Employees want to work for companies that care about employee well-being. Employee surveys have found that companies using employee programs to improve morale report 223 percent higher customer loyalty and an increase of 26 percent in annual revenues.[2]

What can be done to improve the morale of your workplace? A check on morale should not be a one-time event—it should occur regularly. An exit interview with employees leaving the company is one way to get information on morale. If you or your managers have taken the pulse of morale at your workplace and found that it is low, here are some suggestions to improve it:

1. *Develop trust.* Treat co-workers with respect, and make decisions with integrity. If employers and employees have made work-related agreements, follow through. If you are a manager, be transparent. Allow employees to

know what decisions are being made, especially those that affect them. Employees who are part of the team should listen to decision-making processes with an open mind, not with skepticism. Remember that trust works in both directions.

2. *Set goals in the group.* Get everyone in the organization involved in goal setting, both individually and collectively. Lack of direction and poorly identified goals are big factors in lowered morale. Everybody needs a sense of accomplishment and direction to create a connection that helps them feel good about their company. Increasing the individual level of involvement by employees leads to feelings of personal investment and accountability. Individuals will be more productive with higher morale where they have committed to a goal they helped design.
3. *Encourage professional development, and promote from within.* If you are a manager, let employees know that the company is dedicated to helping them succeed and to be promoted, if that direction is desired. Few factors hurt morale more than a feeling that the company is somehow working against the people in it, or not allowing individuals to move up in their careers. Nurture creativity and encourage innovation. If you are not a manager, take advantage of professional development opportunities offered by your company.
4. *Encourage communication.* Set up avenues for communication between employees, among departments, and within teams. It's been said that it is impossible to over-communicate in these settings. Within any reasonable limits, the more communication you have in a given company, the better. In addition to exit interviews, managers should conduct "stay interviews" to ask employees "What keeps you here, what do you like about working here?" Recognize accomplishments and hard work.
5. *Promote* **work–life balance**. Supervisors should show employees they are valued. Employees will be more productive when they have a healthy measure of time outside of work. This may mean encouraging people *not* to work overtime, or allowing telecommuting. For all employees, set aside time for personal interests, avoid letting work get in the way of family needs, and take a vacation where you unplug from work.[3]

work–life balance
Equilibrium between professional life, personal life, and family life.

In Chapters 5 and 7, we covered the concepts of organizational climate and the corporate culture. In those earlier chapters, the weather of the workplace and the cultural norms of an organization are discussed in terms of groups and teams, with the responsibility seen as belonging to management to make the workplaces a positive place to be. But in thinking about your own work experience, you, as an individual, also have the responsibility to contribute to the climate and the culture of your work experience. The attitudes you bring to work and the effectiveness of your communication will partially determine the morale around you, and will play a part in overall company morale. *You* are a piece of the puzzle in the big picture of morale and productivity.

Several other factors encourage a productive workplace. One factor is the manner in which employees and managers are appraised (evaluated). The traditional once-a-year **employee appraisal** in which all of the negatives are saved up and thrown at the employee in one giant toss has become a thing of the past at many companies. Creative appraisal systems stimulate productivity by encouragement, two-way communication, and motivation. The more ongoing the appraisal system is in any company, the better. A manager should never have to tell an employee during an appraisal anything negative that has not already been addressed—there should be no surprises in evaluation meetings.

employee appraisal
Feedback to an employee from supervisors on how he or she has performed over a given period.

more about...

An **effective employee appraisal system** will use something like the SMARTS system. To help improve morale and productivity, an appraisal system should be:

- **S**pecific
- **M**easurable
- **A**chievable
- **R**esults-oriented
- **T**ime bound
- **S**tretchable

All of these are fairly self-explanatory except the last one, "stretchable," which is probably the most important of the six. A "stretch goal" in an appraisal or evaluation process refers to a goal that should "stretch" the employee, giving him or her new goals and new horizons to grow into a new comfort zone.[4]

Productivity and Task Maturity

Another way to encourage productivity is to match an individual to the jobs that need to be done—in other words, to consider an employee's **task maturity**. Someone with task maturity has the skill set for the job at hand, is able to set and meet realistic goals, and can take on the necessary responsibility for the task. Task maturity does not refer to an employee's age or seniority on the job, and a person can be mature in other life areas but possess poor task maturity. Meeting goals and taking responsibility are skills that can be developed over time. Individual job performance can be increased by discovering and reducing behaviors we do to sabotage our own performance, including managing time better.

Avoiding Self-Sabotage

task maturity
Having the skill set necessary to complete a job, as well as the ability to set and meet realistic goals and the ability to take on responsibility for the task.

self-sabotage
Damaging your own credibility or competence.

procrastination
Putting off until later the things a person should be doing now.

Self-sabotage means damaging our own credibility or competence. There are many reasons we sabotage our own efforts, in large part tied to fear or apprehension, insecurity, or lack of motivation. In researching the most common ways people sabotage themselves, procrastination is in the top three.[5] **Procrastination** is the act of putting off until later the things we should be doing now.

Procrastination is not only a form of self-sabotage; it is also a major source of stress. As we know from Chapter 12, stress is damaging both physically and mentally. If procrastination is stressful and ultimately damaging, then why do we do it? The obvious benefit is that we can put off an unpleasant task until some later time. We may find the task too large and overwhelming. We may have waited too long to begin and have now run out of time. We may be afraid of failing, or we may be perfectionists who cannot complete a task if it is not possible to complete it perfectly.

Hidden benefits of procrastination exist as well. These may benefit the procrastinator, and also cause others to suffer in the process. They include being able to get back at people who are making demands on us, being able to avoid unpleasant tasks if others get tired of waiting and complete the work for us, being assigned less to do if others decide we are overwhelmed by existing tasks, and perhaps getting to work on other things we like better and shifting responsibility for unpleasant tasks onto others.

EMPLOYEE APPRAISALS

Appraisals are important for employees, so that they can get feedback on their job performance, make changes if necessary, and become more productive in the process. *When has an appraisal helped you to change your working style to become more productive?*

John Lund/Marc Romanelli/Blend Images/Getty Images

Steps to Stop Procrastinating

Procrastination is an intentional choice. Because we have made a choice to procrastinate, we can also make a choice to stop procrastinating. The following suggestions can help us get started on those tasks we put off:

1. *Get going on the task.* Don't wait for motivation to appear on its own, as if by magic. When you get started with a task or project, the motivation will begin to come to you. It doesn't take long to get on a roll or build the momentum to keep going and complete the task.
2. *Make a plan.* It is easier to say to ourselves that we will get a task started "one of these days" or "later" than it is to actually begin the task. Instead of putting it off, make a plan. When will you start it? Today? At what time? What pieces of the project will you do today? How much time will you spend on each part that you've planned for today?
3. *Reduce the task to smaller components.* Break big projects or jobs down into smaller parts. Start with, say, 30 minutes of work on a project before switching to something else. You don't need to do it all at once. When you look at a task in its entirety, chances are you may feel too overwhelmed to get started. Plan the smaller piece you will do today, finish that part, and then you can decide either to quit for the day, or go ahead and work on another part.
4. *Think positive.* What negative thoughts are you having about yourself and this task? Think about why you are putting it off. Does not completing the project make you feel you are a failure? Do you feel insecure in worrying that others will belittle your work? Are you afraid your work will be wrong? Concentrate on replacing negative thoughts with more reasonable and positive thoughts. Adopt the growth mindset that you learned about in Chapter 2. With a growth mindset, the possibility of failure seems less scary. This is the opposite of the fixed mindset where you see your abilities as limited and then sabotage yourself so your weaknesses won't be clearly exposed. In a growth mindset, tell yourself, "I can do this. It is taking a longer time than I wanted, but I'll practice and get even better at it."
5. *Reward yourself along the way.* Give yourself a small reward after finishing each smaller task–there is no need to wait for the entire project to be finished first. You will find a boost to productivity when you give yourself

an incremental reward. This can be as simple as a self-congratulation, a short break, taking a walk, watching a movie you've been waiting to see, or serving up a treat from the kitchen. Chipping away at a large task successfully also builds confidence, reducing one reason to procrastinate.

6. *Give yourself credit.* Pat yourself on the back for a job well done. You need not have completed the entire project in order to give yourself some credit; you can still recognize the parts of the job that you did finish. Congratulate yourself for managing your time efficiently. And give yourself credit for not procrastinating!

» TIME MANAGEMENT

time management

Making effective use of available time.

overloading time

Planning too many activities into one time slot.

underutilizing time

Making poor use of available time.

Time management refers to making effective use of available time. This sounds simple, but it does take planning. We often **overload** our time by planning too many activities into one time slot. At other times we may **underutilize** time by making poor use of available time that we do have. Procrastination is one cause of underutilization of time.

Considering again the ways that people sabotage themselves, at least one of these—procrastination—can be overcome by more efficient use of time. Using time more efficiently can also reduce the likelihood of acting impulsively, getting distracted or losing focus, taking on too many things at once, having unrealistic expectations, not asking for help when needed, rushing through things, worrying too much, and not finishing what was started.

setting priorities

Deciding ahead of time which tasks are the most, and least, important.

Making use of a time analysis tool enables us to examine our time effectiveness in an ongoing process. Taking a look at how we use our time can allow us to see in print how long we spend on activities. We often spend too much time on unimportant activities while not allowing enough time for more important tasks. Seeing such a pattern in time use can help us manage time better and set priorities. **Setting priorities** means you decide ahead of time which tasks are the most important, and which are the least important. The most important tasks must be completed first. If all tasks seem equally important, go through the list again and decide which are most urgent, and which can be put off until a little (or a lot) later.

to-do list

A list of what you need to do, when, and where.

Creating a **to-do list** by keeping lists of what you need to do, when, and where, will take a little time. The time you save in efficiency, however, will more than make up for the time you spend. Once you have prioritized your tasks by importance and by deadlines, write them down, or make use of a digital task list if you prefer. The most important tasks and those with upcoming deadlines should be entered first and completed first. Those less important should be listed last. Grouping the tasks together by location will allow you to save time by going to each location only once. Some tasks will seem much larger than others. Larger tasks, or projects, can be broken down into smaller parts, so that each smaller task can be completed without a feeling of being overwhelmed by too large a task.

REAL WORLD EXAMPLE 16.1

At the small rural airport he manages, Fredo is tasked with making sure his employees complete their quarterly training on time. They have three months to complete eight hours of online training. Despite his frequent reminders, cajoling, nudging, and serious conversations, staff members cannot seem to make the time to complete the training. He often hears "I forgot it was the deadline" or "I ran out of time" or "I can't remember how to log in" or "My home computer wouldn't run the program." Failure to complete the training on time means the individual staff members fall out of compliance, and this pulls the entire station out of compliance. It is not until the airlines cancels their performance-based bonuses that staff members stop procrastinating.

Your to-do list can work better for you if you start with something you enjoy doing. This can motivate you to keep going. Delete or check off items on your list after completing them. You may be surprised how rewarding this can be! Remember to reward yourself along the way as you complete difficult individual tasks.

more about...

Time analysis tools are available to help us analyze our use of time so that we can see where we can become more efficient in time management. Many of these tools are available online, or as apps on our smartphones. These time-tracking tools help us to analyze how well we are making effective use of time by keeping track of activities over a period of several days, or a week. Think of this as a scaled-down version of a personal journal. Activities can be recorded electronically or by hand. Construct a template to keep a log of all activities. Include column headings such as activity, location, and purpose. Under each column, note how long each task took, with a brief note on location and purpose.

» BEHAVIORS THAT REDUCE WORKPLACE PRODUCTIVITY

Troubling personal situations can arise for anyone. How you decide to handle them can affect not just your personal life, but also your work, your co-workers, and your prospects for career advancement in the future. Individuals who don't handle these situations very well can affect the overall well-being and productivity of their workplace. In a productive workplace, morale is high, relationships between co-workers are positive, and self-perceptions are healthy.

time analysis
Tools available to help with analyzing your use of time so that you can see where to become more efficient in time management.

When employees bring personal problems to work, these problems can affect the entire workplace. When employees abuse alcohol or drugs, have conflict in their marriage or family life, or have financial difficulties, their struggles (although not necessarily their fault) can create problems on the job. These problems do not always happen alone; many people experience combinations of them, sometimes because one problem triggers another.

Employees, managers, and entrepreneurs are all responsible for handling situations in their personal lives effectively. The problems addressed here are serious, but can be overcome with determination and effort, and for some issues, commitment to a program of professional help. They do not need to diminish the productivity of any workplace, and they do not need to ruin people's careers or lives!

REDUCED PRODUCTIVITY AT WORK

Even though you may do your best at a job, sometimes situations out of your control can affect your productivity, and it's up to you to handle them successfully. *When you had a situation that reduced your productivity at a task, what steps did you take to correct it? What advice would you give to a friend with a similar situation?*

Chris Ryan/age fotostock

substance abuse

The continued use of a psychoactive substance even though it is causing or increasing problems in a person's life.

Substance Abuse: Alcohol and Other Drugs

Substance abuse is one of the most common–and expensive–employee problems that companies face. Abuse of alcohol and other drugs together costs the American economy an estimated *$442 billion per year* in lost workdays and lowered productivity (mistakes on the job, accidents, illness, incomplete work, tardiness).[6] Healthcare costs also add to this amount (emergency room visits, treatment for overdoses, mental health problems, alcohol-related heart disease, stroke, or cancer). Crime-related costs, motor vehicle crashes, and early deaths also add to this amount. What does this mean at the individual level? Each of us pays out more than $1,000 each year for these damaging effects of other people's substance abuse.[7] Every day, nearly one out of 10 full-time workers on the job is abusing alcohol or drugs.[8] The rates for alcohol abuse are about the same as they were 20 or more years ago, and they are continuing at about the same rate; rates for prescription and illicit drug abuse, on the other hand, have shown a steady pattern of increase.[9]

Among the most costly forms of substance abuse–in terms of dollars spent and lives lost–is the opioid epidemic. Estimates are that it costs the United States $179 billion per year. Of that, $72.6 billion is estimated for overdose deaths, including lost earning potential for people who die of overdoses. Healthcare costs alone account for more than $60 billion, including treatment for addiction and treatment for babies born addicted.[10] Who becomes addicted to opioids? People of all ages and from all walks of life, all income groups, and every area of the country can become addicted. Some begin with prescription painkillers after an injury or surgery, and others are introduced while abusing other drugs. Nearly 50,000 people per year in the past few years have died of opioid overdoses, with no guaranteed successful treatment or prevention in sight yet.

Alcohol abuse is a long-standing problem in the workplace and in people's personal lives. Since at least 80 percent of heavy drinkers work, and 76 percent of people who abuse illegal drugs work part- or full-time, no business can consider itself immune to the problems of employee substance abuse.[11] These statistics can be overwhelming to digest. Perhaps a more important point to remember is that everyone pays for these costs when tax dollars pay for government services such as highway safety, criminal justice services, and medical and education resources for babies damaged prenatally by drugs or alcohol. Everyone also pays more consumer dollars when the costs of goods and services increase due to reduced productivity.

Recognizing Alcohol Abuse in the Workplace

Who is likely to be an alcoholic? Alcoholics may be difficult to identify because they can be found in all occupational groups; they can be any age, gender, race, or ethnic group. Changes may arise in the person's appearance (e.g., unsteady walking, or smelling of alcohol) or behavior (e.g., slurred speech, missing work, reduced productivity, taking long breaks, irritability). Not all alcoholics will show these changes.

REAL WORLD EXAMPLE 16.2

Kathleen's marriage was falling apart. It was easier to join co-workers at a local bar than go home at night and argue with her husband. At first she went to Happy Hour twice a month, but gradually this increased to four times per week. Her work performance began to drop, and she was no longer saving any of her paycheck. Her arguments with her husband became more serious: He accused her of abandoning their children and becoming an alcoholic. He threatened to take custody of the children, which caused her already low opinion of herself to drop further. As a result, she drank even more.

One night, just before leaving work, Kathleen contacted her company's confidential Employee Assistance Program (EAP) and explained her situation. They gave her a consultation the next evening, during which they recommended family counseling and Alcoholics Anonymous (AA) meetings. Kathleen went home and talked to her husband. To her surprise, he was supportive and not only agreed to the counseling, but also agreed to accompany her to her first AA meeting. As Kathleen began to piece her life back together, she realized that she could have sought this help at any time; it was there for anyone in her company who needed it.

Employee Drug Abuse and Dependency

When people think of drug abuse, they often think of illegal drugs such as cocaine or heroin. However, legal drugs can also be abused, including prescription drugs such as tranquilizers or painkillers that add to the opioid crisis (for example, fentanyl, oxycodone or hydrocodone) and over-the-counter drugs, such as diet pills.

Some form of legalized marijuana exists in more than half the states in the country, whether medical, recreational, or both. Recently, recreational marijuana has become legal in several states. Although legalization has been many Americans' dream come true, it has also created new problems, including driving under the influence, potential use by minors, regulations for growers, and so on.

Substances that aren't normally thought of as drugs, such as nicotine and caffeine, can also be abused. Any substance that affects a person's judgment, behavior, mental processes, mood, conscious experience, or perceptions is referred to as a psychoactive drug. What qualifies as drug abuse is really determined by the user's dependence on the drug and how the substance affects his or her behavior.

The Effects of Substance Abuse in the Workplace

Substance abuse is a very expensive employee problem for the employee with the problem, but also for everyone else. There is no way to quantify the loss to employee morale and group unity when employees are

more about...

Opioid Addiction: An American Epidemic

In 2011, the national Centers for Disease Control and Prevention (CDC) first made it official: opioid addiction had reached epidemic levels in the United States. Since that date, the rate of addition has risen even higher. Oxycodone and hydrocodone, painkillers, remain among the most abused. Nearly 450,000 people died from overdoses involving any opioid, including prescription and illicit opioids, from 1999 to 2018. Another opioid, fentanyl, is considered more deadly than heroin, and has recently taken center stage as fentanyl deaths increased over 540 percent in the three years between 2013 and 2016. Fentanyl has included in its wake the lives of numerous high-profile celebrities, and torn apart the lives and families of countless others addicted to, or killed by, the drug. Treatment options have not been able to keep pace with rates of addiction.

Source: Centers for Disease Control and Prevention, "Prescription Drug Overdoses: An American Epidemic," February 18, 2011, https://www.cdc.gov/cdcgrandrounds/archives/2011/01-February.htm (retrieved July 3, 2017).

See also: "Opioid Data Analysis and Resources," (March 19, 2020). CDC, https://www.cdc.gov/drugoverdose/data/analysis.html. Retrieved Oct. 10, 2020.

See also: Josh Katz, "The First Count of Fentanyl Deaths in 2016: Up 540% in Three Years," *The New York Times*, September 2, 2017, http://www.nytimes.com.

REAL WORLD EXAMPLE 16.3

Joe began taking a prescription painkiller after a back injury. Soon he realized that it helped him to relax from the pressures of his fast-paced career as an assistant district attorney. It worked very well—so well, in fact, that he requested a larger prescription and began taking it nightly. Soon he found that he was running out of energy at work, getting sick more often, and not sleeping as soundly as before. He tried reducing the dosage and instantly felt withdrawal symptoms. Frightened, he called his doctor for help. His doctor recommended an inpatient drug treatment program over several weeks.

Joe almost laughed; he didn't need a drug treatment program—he wasn't a drug addict. Or was he? Slowly he realized that he needed the program, and he agreed to it. It wasn't easy taking the time off from work, especially on such short notice, but if he didn't, he would end up even more dependent—and the results could eventually be fatal.

more about...

Alcoholism is a chronic disease with genetic, psychosocial, and environmental factors in its development and outcomes. This disease is often progressive and fatal. About 10 to 20 million Americans are alcoholics. About half of high school students say they drink. Alcohol is involved in about half of all murders and domestic violence incidents, about one-third of suicides, one-quarter of accidental deaths, and about half of all highway deaths in the United States. In fact, the American Medical Association lists alcohol as *the most dangerous and physically damaging of all psychoactive drugs.*[12]

substance abusers, or when non-abusing employees work with substance abusers. Employees without substance abuse issues may resent the abusing employee's lost time or productivity, they may feel obligated to pick up the slack, or may even feel obligated to protect the substance-abusing coworker from getting into trouble. Non-abusing employees may also feel less safe, especially if substance-abusing employees are operating machinery. A substance-abusing employee may also go into withdrawal at work, which can cause distress for everyone in the workplace.

Marital, Family, and Other Personal Problems

Employees often bring family difficulties to work, whether they are marital conflicts, separation or divorce, difficulties with child care or elder care, financial problems, or other family-related issues. These can reduce workplace productivity when employees miss work, have accidents at work, make poor decisions, pay poor attention to detail, have conflicts with co-workers, or relate poorly to customers. Job instability, housing instability, and relocation by employees all affect the workplace. These effects along with lost productivity and increased turnover that occur in less productive workplaces can cost American businesses in the billions. Family fragmentation alone—divorce and other family problems—are estimated to cost the American economy $120 billion a year.[13]

How can managers spot employees who are troubled by family or other personal conflict? Some warning signs include excessive tardiness or absenteeism, unusual behavior such as crying or losing one's temper, a decline in the quality of work or work performance, trouble concentrating, signs of physical harm or unexplained injury, and a decline or change in appearance. For their part in keeping the workplace productive, managers can create a culture of trust and non-acceptance of issues such as violence or substance abuse, and create training sessions to raise awareness of the issues and of available assistance.

The end of a marriage or a relationship can lead to depression, with problems in sleeping (too much or too little) or eating (loss of appetite and weight), inability to work, and feelings of hopelessness. Even people who have been unhappy in their marriages and asked for the divorce or separation may still become depressed. Because it is considered more acceptable for women to openly express feelings such as depression, they are more likely to seek help for their problems, while men may feel too humiliated or embarrassed to do so. For men, the marriage may have been the major (or only) source of social support, and nationally, men are three times more likely than women to become depressed due to divorce. Family situations such as divorce may also lead to poor health habits, financial problems, and to other problem behaviors, such as substance abuse. The most alarming finding in research on the effects of divorce finds that divorce is associated with earlier age of death, and at much higher rates for men than women.[14]

FUNCTIONING ALCOHOLICS

Eighty percent of heavy drinkers work, and many are highly functional; they perform well at their jobs and conceal their problem successfully. *When should an employer intervene with an employee's suspected alcoholism?*

Stockbyte/Getty Images

family violence

Violence that can be defined as physical, emotional, verbal, or sexual violence against another family member.

Family violence, which can be defined as physical, emotional, verbal, or sexual violence against a family member, is another problem that spills over into the workplace. About one out of every four women, and one out of every nine men, will be abused at some time in their lives.[15] Intimate partner violence involves a weapon in almost 20 percent of cases. About 9 out of 10 victims are women abused by men.[16] Current estimates are that domestic violence costs American businesses more than $10 billion a year in absenteeism, lower productivity, and healthcare costs.[17] When costs for emergency shelters, police and court costs, foster care, and so on are added in, the costs to the American economy can more than double.[18] In addition, substance abuse may be linked to family violence and abuse problems.

Employees affected by family violence may also have conflicts with co-workers, and may become so preoccupied with their problems that their productivity suffers. To make it worse, the employee often feels too ashamed or embarrassed to admit the abuse or seek help. If the employee is the abuser, he or she may be afraid to ask for help for fear of possible legal action. To add to the problem, co-workers may be fearful of violent acts occurring in the workplace because of the employee's situation, either as a victim or as an abuser.

more about...

Domestic violence can occur between married or unmarried partners. Child abuse occurs in 30 to 60 percent of family violence cases. About one-third of female murder victims were killed by partners. For more information, see the U.S. Department of Health and Human Services, www.hhs.gov.

Financial Problems

Employees who are under severe financial pressure may experience difficulties, such as lowered productivity

REAL WORLD EXAMPLE 16.4

Tim, Viraj, and Sandra worked in the same department for five years as an interdependent team that created and distributed important monthly reports for a large IT firm. Over the last year, Tim started showing signs of substance abuse. He came to work every Monday bragging about the heavy partying he had done all weekend. His previously near-perfect work was full of errors, such as running the wrong reports or including the wrong data. One night, after Tim had left 45 minutes early to meet some friends, Viraj and Sandra had to stay late and rerun reports Tim had done incorrectly.

"It's not just that I'm getting tired of this," Viraj said to Sandra. "It's that he's getting worse, and soon we won't be able to cover for him even if we wanted to."

"I know," she admitted. "People have been noticing the change in him and asking me about it. I don't feel good lying to them by glossing over things. This has to stop. Let's talk to Tim tomorrow; if that doesn't work, let's talk to management."

and increased stress levels. Financial problems can also make the employee susceptible to stealing from the company in some way (time or resources).

Financial pressures may be tied in with other problem behaviors as well, such as substance abuse, or even domestic violence. For example, stress from financial problems may cause an employee to start using drugs, and the resulting dependency can lead to financial problems because the employee needs more and more money to pay for the substance.

compulsive gambling
The inability to control one's betting habit.

Some employee financial problems may transition into, or may arise from, **compulsive gambling**. Compulsive gamblers are not the same as the 95 percent of the general population who occasionally play state lotteries, bet on football pools, or play bingo or the stock market; compulsive gamblers are unable to control their betting. They may also become depressed and have relationship problems in their personal lives or at work. They may borrow huge amounts of money from friends and family, co-workers, or themselves (borrowing against credit cards, life insurance policies, their own home, or credit unions). By some estimates, somewhere between 2 and 20 million Americans, both male and female, are compulsive gamblers,[19] and their costs to the U.S. economy are enormous in terms of lost productivity, criminal acts, lost jobs, bankruptcy, bailout costs, and even suicide.

» RESPONSES TO SUBSTANCE ABUSE AND OTHER NONPRODUCTIVE BEHAVIORS

When supervisors or co-workers suspect substance abuse is a problem, they should not directly accuse employees of having such problems. Not only is denial a very likely response, but there may also be legal issues that result from making those kinds of serious accusations. A supervisor's main responsibility when handling any employee problem behavior is to make the employee understand that his or her job performance is not acceptable. The employee needs to understand that performance is the focus of the supervisor's concern, and whatever the cause of the problem, the employee is accountable for

REAL WORLD EXAMPLE 16.5

Manuel noticed that his brightest junior accountant, Therese, seemed to be changing. She was late for work almost every day, she took long lunch breaks, and she was alienating her clients. In fact, one just called him to say that she showed up late for a meeting, and when she did show up, she was belligerent and her breath smelled of alcohol. He called Therese into his office and repeated the client's story to her. Therese denied it immediately, and said the odor was from mouthwash. Manuel genuinely cared for Therese, and wanted to try to offer her some advice, but he knew that he was not a trained counselor and his efforts could backfire.

Instead, he reached into his desk and handed her a card. Therese read it; it was for the firm's Employee Assistance Program (EAP). "It's your choice, Therese," he said levelly, "but your work performance is beginning to fall below average, and I suggest you think about what needs to be done."

poor job performance. *Supervisors should not try to counsel or advise employees themselves.* Since most supervisors are not trained in counseling, they should refer employees to the appropriate resource, such as an Employee Assistance Program or EAP, community counseling center, or substance abuse professional.

Employee Assistance Programs

employee assistance programs (EAPs) Company-sponsored programs that treat employees with substance abuse problems, marriage and family conflicts, and financial difficulties.

Employee assistance programs, *or* **EAPs**, have been around since the 1940s, when large companies (together with Alcoholics Anonymous) first started them as alcoholism treatment programs. In the 1960s, these programs expanded to treat employees with other life issues, such as marriage and family conflicts or financial difficulty. Today, about two out of three EAP referrals are for help with personal or family problems that are not directly related to substance abuse.

In order for EAPs to work, supervisors must be able and willing to observe employees and watch for problems. They must be willing to approach employees who appear to be having problems, refer these employees to the EAP, and follow through. They must be willing to listen to employees who come to them for help. Employees who are referred to EAPs are usually told that their involvement is voluntary, and that they are free to reject the help. With or without the EAP's help, though, their job security will depend on improving their job performance; therefore, without receiving help for their problems, they could lose their jobs. EAPs can help employees with:

- Abuse of alcohol and other drugs
- Mental health and illness issues
- Financial problems
- Legal issues
- Poor physical health
- Stress, depression, anxiety, and other emotional issues

figure 16.1

EAPS: HOW MUCH CAN THEY HELP?

Many companies find that EAPs not only save them money, but they also create a healthier, happier, and more productive work environment. *What kind of services do you think a company should offer its employees?*

Sources: "Employee Assistance Programs," March 1999, http://www.workplace.samhsa.gov/WPResearch/EAP/FactsEAPfinal.html, Division of Workplace Programs, U.S. Department of Health and Human Services, Substance Abuse and Mental Services Administration; "Why Does Your Company Need an EAP?" 2003; http://www.psychworks.com/benefits.html, PsychWorks, Inc., "Benefits of an EAP," 2004; http://www.advocareeap.com/learn/benefits/saved.html, Advocate EAP.

How Well Do EAPs Help Companies?

- Abbott Laboratories reported a 6-to-1 return on dollars spent for the EAP, and noted that employees who utilized the EAP spent $10,000 less over three years for inpatient medical costs than employees who didn't use EAPs.
- Virginia Power reported medical costs were reduced by 23 percent for employees using the EAP.
- Campbell Soup Company saved 28 percent in mental health costs alone with employee use of their EAP.
- Chevron has identified savings of $50,000 per case from reduced turnover due to EAP use, and improvement of 50 percent for employees referred to EAPs by supervisors.
- Caterpillar Inc. reports a cost savings over 18 months for mental health issues alone of $3.5 million.[22]

- Grief and loss support
- Family and marriage conflict
- Other personal problems or concerns

When an employee problem involves substance abuse, EAPs have the advantages of informing the employee that a problem exists and providing a chance for rehabilitation. Rehabilitation improves employee attendance and safety practices, while reducing healthcare costs for the company. EAPs give an employer the opportunity to reduce and prevent serious problems in the workplace. They are also cost-effective: employers can save from $5 to $16 for every dollar they invest in an EAP, according to the U.S. Department of Labor.[20] The cost of an EAP varies depending on what type of assistance program is used and what benefits it includes, but the average cost is estimated in the range of $12 to $28 per employee annually, with an average cost of $22.[21] (See Figure 16.1.)

Workplace Substance Abuse Policies

Before taking any action regarding employee substance abuse, employers must develop a company policy on substance abuse and put it into place. The policy should clearly state all testing and search procedures (if applicable). It should also outline any possible disciplinary actions that the company may take against employees who are abusing alcohol or other drugs. Supervisors will need training in what symptoms to look for, and will also need to be aware of what EAPs are available to employees, so that they can direct employees toward those resources.[23]

Regarding workplace substance abuse policies, companies must determine their stand on substance abuse with input from human resources representatives, as well as medical, security, safety, and legal staff. With that input, companies will write an EAP policy explanation. This policy explanation will be shared among employees. It should explain what the employee assistance program provides in terms of services, how to access the services, why the EAP programs are being offered, and privacy and confidentiality protections. Employees (and their families, when possible) should have available drug awareness education.[24]

For larger companies, substance abuse policies that include health plans, education, and drug testing may be cost-effective within a short time, but what about small businesses? Within a small business, substance abuse can cause a financial drain that means the difference between economic survival and collapse. Because of this issue, the Department of Labor, the Small Business Administration, and the Office of National Drug Control Policy can provide resources to help small businesses deal with substance abuse policy problems.[25] In addition, local Chambers of Commerce, assisted by the U.S. Chamber of Commerce, can provide information and services to local businesses.[26]

more about...

Treatment Options: The 12-Step Program

Alcoholics Anonymous (AA) created the **12-step program** to help recovering alcoholics. Modified versions of the 12-step approach can also work for drug addiction and various psychological problems.

What Else Can Be Done for Employees?

Managers often feel they should not get involved with an employee's personal problems. They may feel that problems at home are too private to discuss with employees, but when these problems affect the employee's job performance, the manager must take action. Again, since most managers are not trained counselors or psychologists, their role is to intervene for the employee without trying to offer advice and counseling.

What can be done for employees facing serious financial problems, whether these are caused by compulsive gambling, poor money management, divorce, a medical emergency, substance abuse, or other temporary crisis? EAPs can steer employees toward the appropriate resources for help. Those with credit management problems can consult consumer credit counseling services, usually with no charge to the person using the service. These companies help people with huge credit debts to stop getting deeper into credit debt and to consolidate debts into a manageable load (see Figure 16.2).

EAPs can also steer those with temporary and financial emergencies to an appropriate resource, such as a credit union. Employees facing temporary emergencies may not be aware of outside help and services that are available to them. Depending on the type of emergency, employees may find much needed help with housing, food, or medical emergencies, or even temporary shelters in the case of domestic violence.

The issues discussed in this chapter relating to reduced workplace productivity are highly personal, and good human relations skills are needed to identify, confront, and solve these realities—challenges to workplace productivity that you will probably witness on the job sometime during your career.

REAL WORLD EXAMPLE 16.6

Jenna noticed that her assistant Cynthia had been showing signs of abuse. Once, Jenna noticed a large bruise on her upper arm. Another time, she heard Cynthia crying in the restroom. She had also heard Cynthia tell another assistant that she was afraid of her boyfriend's temper. Jenna wanted to do whatever she could to help Cynthia, but she knew that she wasn't an experienced counselor, and she was afraid of saying the wrong thing. Instead, she took Cynthia out for lunch, where she expressed her concern for her health and offered her several options—most came from literature she received from the company's EAP. Cynthia seemed surprised, but grateful. She took the information, entered counseling, and after a time was able to leave the abusive relationship.

figure 16.2

FINANCIAL COUNSELING AND CONSUMER CREDIT COUNSELING SERVICES

People can have financial crises for any reason, and that is usually when they seek financial counseling. However, these counseling services are good for everyone—and sometimes using them before an emergency can help prevent one. *How might a credit counselor help you?*

Consumer Credit Counseling Services: Not Just for Emergencies!

Even people who are not facing serious financial problems can benefit from the services of a consumer credit counseling service. These organizations can teach you strategies to better manage credit, including:

- Figuring out a budget you can afford.
- Setting aside some money each payday.
- Avoiding debt when possible.
- Planning for purchases instead of buying on impulse.
- Paying for items with cash instead of credit.
- Trying to arrange and invest your finances so that you will gradually increase your net worth.
- Figuring out your own debt repayment plan before a financial crisis occurs.

Maintaining a productive workplace is rarely easy. As you have seen in this chapter, many factors, both negative and positive, must be carefully monitored to make it all work. Productivity is a human relations issue precisely because productivity's biggest enemy is negative or nonexistent interpersonal relationships. Whether you are a manager or an employee, watch for all of these factors in your workplace and notice how productivity is affected by them. Most of all, make sure you are a part of the solution, rather than part of the problem.

» HUMAN RELATIONS IN YOUR FUTURE

Many changes will undoubtedly take place in the next several years in typical home life and in the workplace. How you respond to those changes in your work and personal environment will be up to you. Regardless of the circumstances surrounding your life, the final reality you live with will be the one you create. With that in mind, how can you fit successfully into a changing business world? The following section discusses ways to increase your individual success in the workplace.

Your Definition of Success

Until recent years, success in the business world was often defined as the *bottom line,* or the profit margin. Employees themselves often defined their individual success simply by their paychecks and individual wealth. In return, employers expected their employees to be loyal to their companies and not change jobs. The 1980s were called the "Me Decade" because amassing more and more material goods was usually the main motivation for individual business success. Now, in the 21st century, many Americans define success in a different way.

In today's definition of success, employees should be able to feel a sense of self-satisfaction and fulfillment at work, and also have the time and freedom to lead a satisfying family life or to spend time on hobbies or outside interests. The successful balance of work and family life is not just a topic that all of us in the general public are interested in. Work–life balance, introduced in the beginning of this chapter, is also of ongoing interest to business leaders, policy makers, and social scientists, as well.[27] This is partly because of the increasing diversity of the workforce, especially with women working at all levels in greater numbers than ever before, and with the many different compositions of family that exist today (see Chapter 1). Employers need to attract and keep good employees. Recognizing that employees' priorities are changing is one way to do that. Work–life balance for employees is linked to lower stress and less job burnout (see Chapter 12). Employers will need to be more flexible to accommodate changing needs for employees to meet balance in their work and home lives.

NEW DEFINITIONS OF SUCCESS IN THE 21ST CENTURY

Changing values and business conditions have contributed to a shift in how Americans define success, which now often includes an emphasis on satisfaction both at work and outside of it. *How do you define success?*

Amble Design/JGI/Jamie Grill/Shutterstock

The rapid growth of Internet commerce is making flexibility increasingly possible in terms of work locations. More people than ever before are now able to work from home, from a hotel room, a coffee shop, a car, or a commuter train. Corporations are more often acting on the knowledge that to attract valuable employees, they have to keep up with changes to American families and make benefits packages more attractive and useful to them.

With more than half of all American mothers in the workforce, and with the general aging of the U.S. population, employees today often need **intergenerational care**, which is day care not only for children but also for elderly family members. The U.S. Department of Labor estimates that nearly one-third of working adults are caring for an aging parent or other family member, and they expect this number to rise to more than half of working adults in the coming years as the American population ages. These workers may require some flexibility during their workweek to accommodate family responsibilities. Some caregiving activities are required daily (providing help with bathing, dressing, and cooking), and nearly half of caregivers say they spend 40 hours per week in such activities.[28]

intergenerational care

Day care not only for children but also for elderly family members.

REAL WORLD EXAMPLE 16.7

When a son of one of the authors of this text was in middle school (junior high), he wandered into the living room one day where his mother was reading the newspaper, and said "Hey, mom, what do Chinese people call Chinese food?" She replied warily, "I don't know, what do they call it?" expecting either a bad joke or an offensive remark, one that would require a discussion of appreciation for diverse world cultures. He responded, "They just call it food. You see? It's just their regular food to them, so they wouldn't call it *Chinese* food, right? It's just food," and he wandered away again. She was both relieved and pleased. With this brief conversation he showed that he could take another perspective, a "world view" that would serve him well in preparing for future employment—and life—in a world of diversity. For the generations of Americans preparing to enter the workforce, the ability to take a global perspective is not just an afterthought, it is a daily reality.

sandwich generation
Middle-aged adults who are taking responsibility for both dependent children and parents at the same time, and being sandwiched by these obligations.

This **sandwich generation**, as introduced in Chapter 1, is the term used for middle-aged adults who have both children and elderly parents they may be taking care of at the same time. Among those in the sandwich generation, nearly half (44 percent) of working adults aged 45 to 55 have an elderly living parent and a child under 21. About half (48 percent) are providing some financial help to an adult child, with more than one-quarter of those (27 percent) providing the primary support. About one adult in seven (15 percent) is supporting both an adult child and an elderly parent at the same time. Two-thirds of caregivers are women.[29]

By the year 2030, about 70 million Americans will be over age 65, and many of these aging adults will need part-time or full-time care, adding even more adults to the sandwich generation.[30] By the year 2050, this number will rise to nearly 90 million. That means that about 20 percent of people in the United States–one out of five–will be elderly. This "graying of the population" means that we will need to reconsider what the workplace looks like, what benefits are offered to employees, and what services are available to all ages.

About two-thirds of the members of the sandwich generation work outside the home, either full-time or part-time. Most of those caring for two generations feel more squeezed than stressed, mostly just pressed for time. Adding to the feeling of being squeezed, about one-fourth say that they also provide significant emotional support to aging parents. This is in addition to financial help and time spent helping with daily living tasks such as taking the family member shopping or to medical appointments, cleaning house, cooking, and handling financial matters. Overwhelmingly, people say that their family is the most important thing in their life–a fact that employers need to remember when making extra demands on employees' time or pressuring them to make a decision that may feel like an ultimatum. Caregiving is not all stress and strain, however: 84 percent of caregivers say that they are happy in their role as a caregiver.[31]

Issues of cultural diversity and inclusivity, along with age-related family obligations, arise when talking about work and family balance. White non-Hispanic Americans have the lowest rates of sandwich generation responsibilities, but there are more of them in total numbers. Hispanic Americans usually have more children and living parents requiring care. They also are more likely to be taking care of additional older relatives (aunts, uncles, family friends) and children (nieces, nephews). The kind of care they perform includes both financial help and personal care. Asian Americans report providing even more care, taking parents to appointments, and doing other time-consuming tasks. They are also more likely to feel stress from the time pressures, and guilt over feeling they should be able to do more. African Americans also report facing stressful situations, but are more likely to say they have family networks (siblings, cousins) to share in the tasks. They are more likely than other groups to ask for help from doctors or agency resources. When thinking about *your* future success, keep in mind the value of being welcoming toward diversity and inclusivity (see Chapter 14). In other words, these statistics remind us that when we talk about "diversity issues in the workplace" we are really just talking about people, who are members of families, with lives not too different from our own.

Overall, most people in all groups say they are optimistic about their futures and their ability to handle their sandwich generation duties. As our nation's life expectancy rates rise or fluctuate near their current high, employers should expect even higher numbers of these sandwich generation employees.[32] Companies will need to be flexible in allowing employees to find innovative ways to meet these complex responsibilities. As an employee, you may be thinking about—or even facing—such issues at a time when you thought your focus would be just on your own career.

Over the past few decades, companies have been getting creative in providing care for employees' dependents. Some companies offer day care for dependents regardless of age (from infants to the elderly), and some offer a cafeteria-style benefits package in which employees can choose only the benefits they want. Other companies offer intergenerational care where children and elders are cared for in the same facility. The Stride Rite Shoe Company was the first to offer employee-sponsored, onsite day care decades ago. Patagonia now has a 30-year history of offering onsite child care, and they report that some children of employees who attended child care are now adults, parents themselves, and employees at Patagonia. Both companies report great success with their programs, saying that everyone—even the community—benefits.[33]

Should your definition of success include success as a family member? Ask yourself this question the next time you contemplate what success really means to you.

Self-Perception, Confidence, and Success

In this text, you have learned about the importance of self-perception and self-esteem as a beginning point for effective human relations skills (see Chapter 2). A key to building a positive self-perception is developing confidence in yourself and your decisions. Confidence is something that has to

REAL WORLD EXAMPLE 16.8

Danita had trouble arriving to class on time, and her grades were beginning to slip. After doing worse than she had expected on her midterms, she started telling herself, "I am a good student, and I arrive on time for my classes." Over a short period of time, she made this a part of her inner belief system, and it became a new habit.

come from within you, but you can build it up with positive self-talk. You can tell yourself that you are making the best decision you can based on the evidence that you have, then avoid criticizing yourself if things do not work out. People who act in a self-confident way on the outside, whether they feel it or not on the inside, are often described and evaluated by others as being capable and competent. Because they are treated as if they are competent, they begin to feel and act that way more than before. Their behavior becomes a self-fulfilling prophecy: by acting with self-confidence, they become more self-confident.

self-discipline

The ability to teach or guide yourself to set up and carry out your goals and plans.

Self-Discipline and Success

Self-discipline is the ability to teach or guide yourself to set up and carry out your goals and plans. This is important to your future success because in order to carry out the plans you have made and to meet your goals, you must teach yourself strategies to keep working toward those goals. Self-discipline allows us to break bad habits and replace them with new ones. This can be accomplished through positive self-talk.[34]

The kind of self-talk we do creates our self-image—either better or worse. The choice is ours. If we tell ourselves that we *can't* do something, then we won't be able to do it. Use positive self-talk and a growth mindset (see Chapter 2) to build on successes. When you find you are slipping back into self-defeating internal messages ("It's no use; I just can't do it"), use self-discipline to demand from yourself that you switch to positive self-talk. Giving up is easy. Sitting down and figuring out what you need to do to start a pattern of behavior that builds toward a goal takes a lot more effort.

If you're stuck in negative self-talk and having trouble thinking of things that are *right* with you, try writing a list of your professional and personal assets. List your skills, experiences, potential, and talent. That is, write down what you're good at. This list can become your script for your future self-talk; refer to it often. When you have an important task or meeting coming up at work, close your eyes and picture yourself succeeding at the task, or running the meeting successfully in a professional manner. This visualization technique is the same one used by successful athletes at the highest levels of competition. It works!

SELF-DISCIPLINE IN YOUR LIFE
You can teach yourself self-discipline, then use your self-discipline to develop and maintain healthy habits. Although some habits may not feel good at first, their lasting effects will contribute to your overall success. *What are the main characteristics of self-discipline?*
Stockbyte/Getty Images

Use this same self-discipline to help you meet your goals. Once you have identified these goals and prioritized them, you will need to muster your self-discipline in order to put a plan of action into place. Start each day by asking yourself, "What will I do today to make the best use of my time to lead me closer to that goal?" Refer to (and revise) your goals often enough that you are aware of them and they help guide your actions. When faced with a decision, ask yourself, "Which choice will better lead me toward meeting my goals?"

Don't be afraid to ask for advice and to learn from others. Get to know people who have goals similar to your own. Find out what their action plan is like, and how they overcame setbacks. Aim high! You may not reach your highest goal, but you'll achieve a lot more than you will when you aim low.

Taking responsibility is an important part of self-discipline. Be accountable to yourself and your own actions. Feel the control you have of your life, the power to change things, and feel comfortable about doing so. Taking responsibility does not include trying to change or control other people, but it means that they don't control you, either.

"I just don't feel like exercising right now; I'd rather watch television," or "I don't have time to cook a good dinner–I'll just grab a snack and eat something healthy later." Do these statements sound familiar? Another component of self-discipline is to make conscious choices that lead to a more healthful and productive life. Chapter 12 discussed the harmful effects of stress, the need for maintaining a healthy lifestyle, strategies for stress reduction, the importance of building in leisure time, and maintaining a support system of friends and family. These ideas all relate to long-term success because they promote health and happiness. Remember that it takes self-discipline to maintain a healthy lifestyle and healthy habits as you work toward reaching your goals.

» SELF-MOTIVATION, SELF-DIRECTION, AND SUCCESS

Psychological studies show that the strongest kinds of motivation come from internal rewards, not external ones. Self-motivation is central to this idea of intrinsic motivation (see Chapter 5) and **self-direction**, which is the ability to set short-term and long-term goals for yourself.

The more specific your goals, the clearer they seem, and the better they work. **Short-term goals** are the specific plans of action for things you would like to accomplish right now or in the immediate future, such as finishing a specific course or work assignment. **Long-term goals** are those things you decide to work toward after developing a life plan for the future, such as moving up the corporate ladder in accounting after you have completed your accounting degree, or starting a family. Both short- and long-term goals are important to individual success; breaking long-term goals into manageable short-term ones is a way of creating a ladder of success that increases your

self-direction
The ability to set short-term and long-term goals for yourself.

short-term goals
The specific plans of action for the things you would like to accomplish right now or in the immediate future.

long-term goals
Those things you decide to work for after developing a life plan for the future.

more about...

Success and Goal-Setting Quotes

"A goal is a purpose, a reason to be in the race." (Russ von Hoelscher)

"What you get by achieving your goals is not as important as what you become by achieving your goals." (Zig Ziglar)

"Setting goals is the first step in turning the invisible into the visible." (Tony Robbins)

"Discipline is the bridge between goals and accomplishment." (Jim Rohn)

"I don't focus on what I'm up against. I focus on my goals and I try to ignore the rest." (Venus Williams)

"You need to overcome the tug of people against you as you reach for high goals." (Gen. George S. Patton)

"I think goals should never be easy, they should force you to work even if they are uncomfortable at the time." (Michael Phelps)

"What keeps me going is goals." (Muhammad Ali)

"Our goals can only be reached through the vehicle of a plan, in which we must fervently believe, and upon which we must vigorously act. There is no other route to success." (Pablo Picasso)

"You control your future, your destiny. What you think about comes about. By recording your dreams and goals on paper, you set in motion the process of becoming the person you most want to be. Put your future in good hands—your own." (Mark Victor Hansen)

"When it is obvious the goals cannot be reached, don't adjust the goals, adjust the action steps." (Confucius)

chances of future success in the long term. The time analysis tools referred to earlier in this chapter can also be used to set up a time schedule that includes short-term and long-term goals.

» FEAR: THE ENEMY OF SUCCESS

Fear is a negative emotion that can stop you from carrying out your plans and working toward your goals. In order to fight fear, you must first identify your fears and then work toward eliminating them. One of the most common fears in the business world is the **impostor phenomenon**, in which successful people are afraid that they did not really succeed because of their own talents and hard work. They are afraid that they are not smart, hard-working, or talented enough to continue to succeed, and that someone will find them out as impostors. They may feel that they have been lucky, or have gotten away with something, or that other people have just made a mistake about them, and they live in dread of the mistake being discovered. This feeling is common enough that you may have felt it yourself—estimates are that 70 percent of people have felt it at some time.[35]

impostor phenomenon
A feeling successful people experience when they are afraid that they did not really succeed because of their own talents and hard work.

Another common fear is **fear of failure**, which occurs when people are afraid of looking bad in front of others. People with extreme fear of failure may stop trying to achieve anything, or stop trying anything new in order to avoid the possibility of being criticized. After learning about the human relations principles discussed throughout this book, some people are reluctant to put these principles into action: they fear failing and then being judged in a negative way. Although it does seem easier to not "rock the boat" by putting new principles into place, it is actually harder to live your life without focusing on self-confidence, success, and more effective communication skills. Try these new ideas, and you will not only find less failure than you probably expected, you may be surprised at how well they work!

People who have **fear of success** may have not experienced much success in their lives, so they feel they do not deserve it. They may feel that they will not live up to the reputation that goes along with success, and that others will reject or demote them. They may find the feeling of success so unfamiliar or fleeting that it is painfully uncomfortable.

REAL WORLD EXAMPLE 16.9

When the oldest son of one of the authors of this text was seven years old, he asked his mother why she was in college (she was in graduate school at the time). They had a long talk about the importance of college, different types of colleges, preparing for college, strategies in paying for college, and so on. He announced at that time that he was definitely going to college, and if he didn't have any money, then he would find a way for his favorite activity—basketball—to pay for his expenses. His mother nodded earnestly, but had a hard time keeping from laughing. Ten years later, this son signed a National Letter of Intent to play basketball at one of the top academic universities in the country, an NCAA Division I school. Just a coincidence? Not really. During those 10 years, he had joined every school, playground, and traveling basketball team he could find. He played ball four or five hours a day, rain or shine. He kept his grades up, stayed involved in leadership activities at school, and worked hard to be the kind of student athlete sought by college recruiters. In other words, his strong self-direction allowed him to set short-term and long-term goals, and he was self-disciplined enough to remain motivated through the years it took to meet these goals.

How can people eliminate these fears? One key is to practice emotions that are just the opposite, such as courage and self-confidence. It is physically impossible to feel two opposite feelings such as anxiety and relaxation at exactly the same time, so you can probably outweigh the fear with something more positive. Talking about the situation with a friend or a mentor can help. In some cases, the fear may be so powerful that counseling or psychotherapy may be the best way to eliminate it.

more about...

If your goals include **material success,** that is fine, but be careful that your possessions do not end up possessing you.

» POSITIVE PSYCHOLOGY

Fear can be a barrier to success, as we have just discussed. Can that barrier be overcome? Can we potentially train children–and adults–to avoid such barriers, and reach the levels of success they have set as goals? Many psychologists would say "yes." One of the newest and most exciting developments in psychology is a movement called **positive psychology**.[36] This new area came about as a result of some leading psychologists thinking that psychology is too focused on what's *wrong* with people, rather than what is *right* with us. Martin Seligman, whom you remember from Chapter 4 with his ideas about learned optimism, is credited with moving this field to the mainstream of psychology. In Seligman's view, when we focus only on what makes people unhappy or mentally unhealthy and on how to treat those problems, we miss half the picture of what it means to be human. The other half, says Seligman, is the part of humans that is joyful, satisfied with life, and maintains healthy self-esteem. This healthier side of humans holds the traits and strengths that lead to success.

Positive psychologists believe that we all have strengths that can overcome barriers to healthy self-development. These barriers include low self-concept and low confidence, for example, along with their related fears. The strengths

fear of failure

The fear that occurs when people are afraid of looking bad in front of others.

fear of success

The fear that occurs when people who have not experienced much success in their lives feel they do not deserve it.

positive psychology

A subfield within psychology that focuses on experiences, individual traits, and institutions that create happiness and hope, rather than focusing on mental illness.

that protect against poor outcomes in mental health include optimism, good interpersonal skills, courage, good work ethic, perseverance, honesty, and ability to think toward the future. These strengths can be learned by practicing a growth mindset. And when people begin using them, such ideals become a type of self-fulfilling prophecy. Building these strengths can not only improve poor performance and raise self perception, but also prevent such problems from happening in the future.

The first step in learning to be positive, says Seligman, is to stop thinking in terms of catastrophes and defeat. Learn to see bad events as temporary, not permanent crises. Get into the habit of disputing beliefs you hold, or even statements by others, that one rejection determines a person's lack of ability forever. Keep positive psychology in mind when applying for internships or jobs: Very few people are offered the most wonderful job in the world with their first job application. The likelihood of being offered a job is higher for those who appear confident than for those who present themselves as failures, so remaining positive is crucial to future success. Incidentally, says Seligman, what really makes people happy is not tons of money, but meaningful relationships and spiritual faith.[37]

finding your niche
Finding the place where you thrive and are most content; includes finding the type of job or career where you will be most satisfied.

» FINDING YOUR NICHE

To be successful throughout your life, you must find a place where you thrive and are most content. This is called **finding your niche**, which includes finding the kind of job or career where you will be most satisfied. Finding your niche and promoting career success requires that you understand what your skills are. Richard Bolles, an expert on job-hunting and career change, describes three "families" of skills:[38]

1. *Skills with information or data* include gathering or creating data, managing it, computing it, storing it, and putting it to use. People with these skills may become data entry technicians, computer programmers, research analysts, or demographers.
2. *Skills in working with people* include helping and serving others, counseling, entertaining, supervising, negotiating, and mentoring. People with these skills may find satisfaction in becoming counselors or psychologists, occupational therapists, physical therapists, teachers, actors or comedians, consultants, sports coaches, or politicians.
3. *Skills in working with things* include specific skills in athletics, in the fine arts, with construction, and with agriculture or farming. People who have these skills may enjoy work as farmers, construction workers, cabinetmakers, dancers, architects, botanists, artists, or professional athletes.

See Strategy for Success 16.2 for more information on these sets of skills.

WHERE IS YOUR NICHE?

Finding your niche means finding what you really enjoy doing and being able to make your living from it. This can include traditional careers, such as teaching or medicine, and it can include careers that never before existed. *Where do you think your niche might be?*
Gorodenkoff/Shutterstock

REAL WORLD EXAMPLE 16.10

Jerome graduated from college with degrees in psychology and philosophy and four years of college basketball experience, but without a firm plan about his career future. After trying an office job and a retail job, Jerome began some serious introspection. He knew that he wanted to work with people, did not want a job sitting in an office and wanted to see the world. For the past five years, Jerome has been working at a job that suits him very well: he works with people as a supervisor for an airline, with free flight benefits that he uses whenever he has time off.

» PREPARE FOR A CAREER CHOICE

Some people seem to know, from very early on, what type of job they will eventually do. They select high school classes and decide on their educational plan (high school graduation, business school, two-year or four-year college or university) on that basis. They select a college major and specific courses in preparation for the career they want. Other people are not so sure what they will "be" when they grow up. They may decide to return to school later, or go through years of education and still not have a career figured out. They may try out several careers before deciding what fits. Still others may decide midway through their employment years that they are ready to change careers and do something new and different.

If you find yourself in either of the "questioning" categories, then you may want to investigate your college's available resources. Does your college have a career guidance center? Does your school offer a career planning class? Take advantage of these resources in your search. If your school offers vocational interest testing, take the tests. There are also thousands of online sites that offer career guidance; some are free, others charge a fee, and the quality varies greatly among all the sites.

> **more about...**
>
> **Niche**
>
> In biological or ecological terms, a **niche** refers to any place that is best suited for a living creature (including a human, animal, plant, or sea life) to survive.

But before investing time and (possibly) money into these career guidance tools, you should first do some introspection—that is, looking inward. It is difficult to know how to get somewhere if you don't know where you're going. So, where are you going with a career plan? If you have never really thought about it before, take some time now to think about what it is you really want out of a career. In the "big picture," what is it that you want to do with your life? What will make you feel fulfilled? Start with some very general questions about what you want to do. Is there something you have always felt passionate about—a career in the arts, data crunching, or a helping profession? Is there a specific type of company you've always been interested in—a *Fortune* 500 company, a local community-based business, or a nonprofit agency? Are you looking forward more to the work itself, or

REAL WORLD EXAMPLE 16.11

During middle school and high school, Jacob liked to cook. When other kids found out, they teased him without mercy: it just wasn't seen as "macho" for a guy to be in the kitchen. But his self-esteem and confidence were healthy enough that he stuck to this interest, in spite of the teasing. He kept on creating and inventing new dishes for his family and friends. By the time he graduated from high school, Jacob had taken every cooking class and every business class his high school offered. He was awarded three scholarships to attend a community college in his state that offered a culinary arts program within its business department. When he completes the program, he'll be in a very good position to be a chef in a top local restaurant, and eventually open his own restaurant someday.

to the paycheck? When you envision your work environment, are you there alone in peace and quiet, or is it a busy and lively place? Taking time to answer these questions will help you begin to frame your answers.

When you do land your dream job, or maybe your good-enough-for-now job, there is a good probability that it will not be your one and only job. The U.S. Bureau of Labor Statistics estimates that we will have about 10 jobs before the age of 40, and up to 15 over our working years, on average. Some of these may be within the same occupation while changing employers, and some may be changes to completely different lines of work.[39] Some will be in the private sector, and some in the public sector. Some careers will take place in formal organizations, and others in a gig economy.

Since you will likely be changing jobs during your career years, it will be to your benefit to prepare. This may mean working as an intern, or completing a formal certificate or degree. It may mean completing extra training to "upskill" (update your current skills or learn new skills). For many workers, the way to build a résumé and move up the career ladder is to take courses online, free or low cost. Some of the most popular online websites for these courses include Khan Academy, edX, Coursera, Udemy, TED-ed, CodeAcademy, and Stanford Online.

lifelong learning

The ongoing, voluntary, and self-motivated gaining of knowledge for personal and professional reasons.

Taking courses from the thousands of online courses available is not just good for your career, it is a good way to pursue personal development and interests. **Lifelong learning** is the ongoing, voluntary, and self-motivated gaining of knowledge for personal and professional reasons. Lifelong learning is something you can do on your own through books or videos, and through colleges that offer community-based interest courses, in addition to taking online courses. Lifelong learning can help you improve your competitiveness and employability. It also helps connect you to your community, and helps you to be an active citizen.

Whatever your path, we (your authors) wish you success in all areas of human relations in your future!

REAL WORLD EXAMPLE 16.12

One day when he was about five years old, another son of one of the authors of this text announced, "When I grow up, I am going to be the trash collector at the zoo." His amused mother asked him why he had chosen that particular occupation. "Because I really like the zoo, and I am good at taking out the trash," he responded with pride. This is such a simple and logical response from a child, but reasoning that we can all learn from: discover what you do well, in an environment you enjoy. In other words, find your niche. More than 30 years have passed since this young man announced his career plans. Turns out he's not the trash collector at the zoo, but he *has* succeeded in finding his niche as an audio-video engineer and entrepreneur.

STRATEGIES FOR SUCCESS

Strategy 16.1 Goals for Success

School-to-Work Connection: Interpersonal Skills, Personal Qualities Skills

Instructions: Write down on a piece of paper 10 to 20 things you really want out of life: your desires, dreams, small and larger goals. Be specific. Number each as you go along. After the number, begin a sentence with "I want . . ." and then write down your dream. Think of things you want for yourself, not items that would make others happy or those you feel you *should* want. After the "want" statement, ask yourself questions that will bring the "want" into focus even better. The more detail you use, the better. Being specific will help you focus on what it is you really want. As you continue to refine your goals into the future, think about the answers to these questions and whether they change.

The following are some examples.

1. I want a job I really like. (*What type? What things about a job will make me really like it?*)
2. I want to see the world. (*What parts of the world? What job or volunteer activities could help me do that? Do I want to be a tourist, or do I see myself actively engaged in work somewhere else?*)
3. I want to be my own boss. (*At what? What kind of self-employment would I like? What is it about working for myself that attracts me?*)
4. I want to spend more time with my family. (*How will I make this happen? What type of job will help me do that? What am I willing to give up to get this—a promotion, a career change?*)
5. I want to retire early. (*At what age? How will I prepare financially to make this happen?*)

Now, arrange them in priority, from "most important to me" to "least important to me." As you do this, imagine yourself achieving each "want." Think about what each one means to you personally.

Over the next few weeks and months, come back to these goals, and rearrange them by importance. Begin to put a plan of action into place for your top "wants" or goals.

Source: Denis Waitley and Reni L. Witt, *The Joy of Working* (New York: Dodd, Mead, and Company, 1985).

STRATEGIES FOR SUCCESS

Strategy 16.2 Make an Inventory of Your Skills

Richard Bolles, author of the best-selling job-hunting guide *What Color Is Your Parachute?,* suggests that you can understand your skills as a way to figure out which careers will make you most happy and successful.

List the kinds of things you are good at, like doing, or do most often in your spare time, then decide what family of skills these fit into.

Major skill types include:

1. Health and physical stamina
2. Quantitative ability and interest level
3. People skills
4. Leadership skills
5. Mechanical ability
6. Musical ability
7. Artistic ability
8. Creativity and discernment
9. Self-assurance
10. Speaking and writing ability

Take some time to list your skills and talents. Sometimes people have trouble seeing these clearly, so the following list of categories should help your self-evaluation process:

1. **Health and physical stamina.** Are you healthier than the average person in your age group? Do you enjoy physical activity?
2. **Quantitative ability and interest level.** Are you good with numbers? Equally important, do you enjoy working with figures?
3. **People skills.** Do you get along well with others? More importantly, do you enjoy spending time with a variety of people?
4. **Leadership skills.** Do others see you as a leader? Do you often find yourself taking charge when a project is undertaken by a group? Do you see yourself as someone others might follow, even if only in certain contexts of your life?
5. **Mechanical ability.** Do you enjoy fixing mechanical or electronic equipment, maintaining it, and learning how it works?
6. **Musical ability.** Do you seem to pick up a tune when you hear it? Do you play a musical instrument or sing?
7. **Artistic ability.** Do you paint, draw, or sculpt? Do you suspect that you could, if you gave yourself a chance?
8. **Creativity and discernment.** Can you often see solutions where others see failure? Have you ever thought of an invention or an improvement of a process, just to find out later that someone else already thought of—and implemented—that same idea?
9. **Self-assurance.** Do you have the self-confidence to believe that your ideas will work, even when others doubt them?
10. **Speaking and writing ability.** Can you express yourself effectively in your speech and writing? Can you speak to a group of people without strong anxiety?

This list is by no means complete, and you can probably come up with several other areas of ability if you give yourself a chance to think about it. However, you most likely have talents in one or more of these given areas.

The next step is to apply the skills you've identified to a specific goal. Find information on careers, but don't limit yourself to the information you find. Often, people have constructed their own niche by inventing a business or product that no one else thought of before. **Entrepreneurship**, which is the risk-taking entrance into your own enterprise, might take you to new and unexplored endeavors.

entrepreneurship

The risk-taking entrance into your own enterprise.

« STRATEGIES FOR SUCCESS

Strategy 16.3 Define Your Goals

1. Consider definitions of goals.
2. Describe which definitions are meaningful to you.
3. Use the definition that best fits with you to create your own goals.

Many famous (and not so famous) people talk about the importance of goals, and have different definitions of goals. Read some of the examples of goals listed in the "Self-Motivation, Self-Direction, and Success" section in this chapter, and decide which one(s) speaks to you the most. Describe why this statement resonates with you. Create a goal for yourself, based on the definition you selected.

1. **Consider definitions of goals.** Select definitions that appeal to you from the "More About Success and Goal Setting" list earlier in this chapter, in the section titled "Self-Motivation, Self-Direction, and Success."
2. **Describe which definitions are meaningful to you.** Which quote(s) did you select? Why?
3. **Use the definition that best fits with you to create your own goals.** Create a small goal, basing its creation and potential for success on the definition you selected. Note over time how well the goal was achieved, and what you might change next time for an even greater level of success.

CHAPTER SIXTEEN SUMMARY

Chapter Summary by Learning Objectives

LO 16-1 Understand factors that create and maintain a productive workplace. Productivity in the workplace is affected by many factors, some at the organizational level and others at the individual level. The factors affecting productivity that you and I can do something about involve increasing the productivity of workers and managers on the individual level.

LO 16-2 Learn methods of improving morale and appraisal techniques. Morale is closely related to productivity. To boost morale, work to develop trust, set goals in the group, encourage professional development and promote from within, encourage communication, and promote work–life balance.

LO 16-3 Learn strategies to improve your use of time. The beginning point in time management is to acknowledge that you have an issue, that improvement is needed. This process can be aided by time use analyses, to-do lists, and priority setting. One also needs to deal with procrastination and other self-sabotaging behaviors.

LO 16-4 Recognize substance abuse and other behaviors that reduce workplace productivity. One of the most common and expensive sources of reduced workplace productivity is employee substance abuse.

Abuse of alcohol and other substances can lead to physiological and psychological dependencies. Several types of substances can be abused, and substance abuse can contribute to an unproductive workplace in several ways, such as lowering employee productivity, creating conflicts stemming from substance abuse, and adding to overall healthcare costs.

LO 16-5 **Know what employers and employees can do to address substance abuse as well as other personal or financial problems.** Employers who have employee assistance programs (EAPs) have a built-in resource for all the types of employee problems discussed in this chapter, including alcohol and drug abuse, divorce, family violence, compulsive gambling, and other financial issues. Employers must have a substance abuse policy in place in order to successfully combat substance abuse.

LO 16-6 **Explore the concept of success and the attainment of goals.** The 21st century promises many changes both in the workplace and society. Whatever happens to change those factors, the burden is on you to fit the changes meaningfully into your life. A new definition of success focuses on satisfaction on the job and at home, not just on the bottom line. Many corporations are realizing that they will have to restructure to fit new definitions of success.

LO 16-7 **Focus strategies to increase and maintain your personal success.** Self-motivation, self-direction, and success are related. Fear is the enemy of success. Understanding yourself and finding your niche by discovering where your skills lie can lead to lifetime individual success.

key terms

compulsive gambling 494
employee appraisal 486
employee assistance programs (EAPs) 495
entrepreneurship 510
family violence 493
fear of failure 504
fear of success 504
finding your niche 506
impostor phenomenon 504
intergenerational care 499
lifelong learning 508
long-term goals 503
overloading time 488
positive psychology 505
procrastination 486
productivity 484
sandwich generation 500
self-direction 503
self-discipline 502
self-sabotage 486
setting priorities 488
short-term goals 503
substance abuse 490
task maturity 486
time analysis 489
time management 488
to-do list 488
underutilizing time 488
work–life balance 485

review questions

1. What is your definition of a productive workplace? List factors that make a workplace productive. Why is productivity an important issue?
2. Briefly explain the importance of positive workplace morale, along with suggestions for improving it. What factors make an effective appraisal system? How are these two concepts related?
3. Do you procrastinate? Can you identify specific tasks or situations that seem to increase your procrastination? Describe steps you can take to reduce procrastination.
4. What are some physical signs of employee alcoholism along with some behavioral or other warning signs? What are some suggestions for statements that should be included in company policies to combat alcohol and drug abuse at work?
5. What are some warning signs that family violence may be occurring to an employee? Why is violence occurring in the home identified here as a problem in the workplace? What other types of workplace issues may be related to family violence?
6. Nearly every strategy for success in human relations that we've discussed in this textbook can be tied in with time management. Thinking about any of the topics to date (e.g., working in teams, conflict management, ethics, stress, and so on), select three, and explain how more effective use of time would result in more effective human relations.
7. Why is the work-family issue considered so important and how are employers dealing with this issue?
8. What is meant by the *impostor phenomenon*? What is one way to eliminate fears such as this? How does a fear of *failure* differ from a fear of *success*? Think of an example for each.
9. What is positive psychology? How is it different from regular psychology—that is, what does it emphasize?

critical thinking questions

1. What is included in the idea of self-discipline? What are some examples of everyday behaviors you are currently engaging in that require self-discipline? Can you succeed without these behaviors?
2. What is meant by finding your niche? What is one suggestion to help you in doing this? What are you doing in order to find your niche?
3. What are your goals for the future? What do you want to accomplish in the short term and in the long term? How do YOU define success? How well does your definition fit with the text's definition?

working it out 16.1

ALCOHOL DEPENDENCY SELF-QUIZ

School-to-Work Connection: Personal Qualities Skills

Purpose: The American Psychiatric Association uses the Diagnostic and Statistical Manual of Mental Disorders (DSM-5) to diagnose troubling behavior. If you are concerned about your own drinking or suspect that someone you know may be drinking too much, try taking the following self-quiz.

In the past year, have you:

1. Had times when you ended up drinking more, or longer, than you intended?
2. More than once wanted to cut down or stop drinking, or tried to, but couldn't?
3. Spent a lot of time drinking? Or being sick or getting over other after-effects?
4. Wanted a drink so badly you couldn't think of anything else?
5. Found that drinking—or being sick from drinking—often interfered with taking care of your home or family? Or caused job troubles? Or school problems?
6. Continued to drink even though it was causing trouble with your family or friends?
7. Given up or cut back on activities that were important or interesting to you, or gave you pleasure, in order to drink?
8. More than once gotten into situations while or after drinking that increased your chances of getting hurt (such as driving, swimming, using machinery, walking in a dangerous area, or having unsafe sex)?
9. Continued to drink even though it was making you feel depressed or anxious or adding to another health problem? Or after having had a memory blackout?
10. Had to drink much more than you once did to get the effect you want? Or found that your usual number of drinks had much less effect than before?
11. Found that when the effects of alcohol were wearing off, you had withdrawal symptoms, such as trouble sleeping, shakiness, restlessness, nausea, sweating, a racing heart, or a seizure? Or sensed things that were not there?

Scoring: According to the American Psychiatric Association, The presence of at least two of these symptoms indicates **Alcohol Use Disorder (AUD).** The severity of the AUD is defined as:

- **Mild:** The presence of 2 to 3 symptoms
- **Moderate:** The presence of 4 to 5 symptoms
- **Severe:** The presence of 6 or more symptoms

If you answer "yes" to two or more of these questions, you are probably dependent on alcohol. If you or someone you know does appear to have alcohol dependency, contact your Employee Assistance Program (EAP) or any Alcoholics Anonymous (AA) group in your area for more information on getting help, or talk with your family doctor.

Source: National Institute on Alcohol Abuse and Alcoholism (NIAAA), https://www.niaaa.nih.gov (retrieved April 4, 2020).

working it out 16.2

WORKPLACE HEALTH

School-to-Work Connection: Interpersonal Skills

Purpose: This role-playing exercise will help you gain a better understanding of the behavior of employees with a substance abuse, family, or medical problem and understand how to communicate with them to develop an intervention plan.

Procedure: Divide into groups of three students. One student will play the role of a supervisor, another will play the role of an employee, and the third will play the role of referee. The employee will act as a person with a substance abuse problem, a financial problem, or a family problem, and will display the appropriate symptoms. The employee will not tell the others ahead of time what problem is being acted out, since a part of their role is to figure out what is affecting this employee. One problem at a time should be role-played, and after each problem is role-played, students should switch roles so that everyone has a turn. The supervisor will be responsible for communicating to the problem employee what is wrong with the employee's performance at work and what plan of action will be taken to correct it. The referee will oversee the dialogue and make necessary suggestions.

working it out 16.3

PRACTICE YOUR INTERVIEW SKILLS

Interview Preparation

Pair with another student in class. One will serve as the job applicant, and the other as the interviewer. After 5 to 10 minutes, switch roles. The interviewer should invent a company and an open position for the applicant.

As you prepare for your roles, take note of your body language. What is your nonverbal behavior saying? Both roles have similar goals—to convey confidence and a calm demeanor. Make appropriate eye contact (not staring and not looking away). Sit up straight, smile, walk at an even pace, and control any nervous jitters. Begin by introducing yourself. Shake hands or use another appropriate greeting. When the interviewer/applicant introduces himself or herself, repeat the name (e.g., "Good to meet you, Ms. Jones."). Be friendly and positive.

Interviewers: Be organized. Have questions ready ahead of time. Sample questions are included as follows. Do not ask questions that discriminate on any basis. Do not ask personal background questions. While the applicant tries to present why he or she would be a good employee, the interviewer should also present the company as a good place to work.

Applicants: Be organized. In a real interview, you would do your homework ahead of time to familiarize yourself with the company. Use examples in your answers to show you have researched the company ("I see that Acme Fittings doubled the sales force last year, I am looking for a fast-paced environment in a company that is growing its impact."). Bring a copy of your résumé. Most word-processing programs include templates for creating résumés so that you are not starting from scratch. Practice responses beforehand. Dress appropriately for the position you are seeking.

Arrive at the interview on time or a little early. Turn your cell phone off and put it away. When answering questions, be sure to answer all parts of each question. Stay on track, do not veer off into anecdotes or jokes. Find out how much time you have for the interview and pace yourself accordingly. If you have an example to give for a question that shows the interviewer that you have relevant experience, include it in your answer. When the interview is finished, thank the interviewer for the opportunity.

INTERVIEW SAMPLE QUESTIONS

1. How have your education and experience prepared you for a position as a(n) _____?
2. What attracted you to this position at _____?
3. Tell me about a time where you had to deal with conflict on the job. How did you resolve it?
4. How will you work to create an environment that is welcoming, inclusive, and increasingly diverse?
5. If I were your supervisor and asked you to do something that you disagreed with or thought was wrong, what would you do?
6. Describe a time that you felt you went above and beyond the call of duty at work.
7. Describe your ideal working environment.
8. If you were interviewing someone for this position, what traits would you look for?
9. What are your long-term career goals?
10. Is there any additional information you would like to add to this interview?

If you have the opportunity to ask questions of the interviewer, some questions you may want to ask include:

1. What do you expect from team members in this position?
2. What is a typical day like at _____?
3. What are the growth opportunities in this position?
4. What are the next steps in the hiring process?

After both students have played the applicant and the interviewer, evaluate the interview you experienced for each role. What would you do differently? In your role as the applicant, would you want to work for this company? In your role as the interviewer, would you want to hire this applicant?

working it out 16.4

CAREER PLANNING: SHORT TERM AND LONG TERM

School-to-Work Connection: Interpersonal Skills

Purpose: Will you change careers during your lifetime or keep the same job for your entire career? Nearly half of people will change to completely different careers over their worklives.[40] Most of us will change jobs a dozen or more times over our careers.[41] Job changes and job choices will be more successful when time is taken to plan and prepare before making decisions. Career planning should focus on both short- and long-term transitions. Each of these has different tasks, but both should be done with some careful thought and honest reflection.

Short-Term Planning

Short-term planning is aimed at just the next few years. For some people, roadblocks set up unintentionally may slow down their progress, including personal traits such as procrastination and lack of motivation. Additional roadblocks include family pressures and peer pressure to work in a certain occupation, or to avoid some occupations. A realistic evaluation of how you will clear roadblocks, as well as how much job preparation you will need and whether you can complete it in the short term, will also help in short-term planning. Remember, just as you grow and change during your lifetime, your career goals may develop and change as well.

The following are some suggestions to get you started with short-term career planning:

1. **Lifestyle.** Think about your lifestyle now and lifestyle goals in the future. Are you happy with it? Do you want to change it, or keep it the same? Does your current job allow you to have the lifestyle you want? Does another career fit better with the lifestyle you want?

2. **Activities.** Think about the activities and tasks in your job, and how much you like or dislike doing them. What tasks do you enjoy, both at work and away from work? What activities do you not look forward to? How well does your job fit with these likes and dislikes? Would another career be a better fit?

3. **Passions and excitement.** What are you passionate about in your job, what excites you at work? What gives you energy and "flow" at work? Do you experience this passion, excitement, or flow in your current job? Would another job or career better kindle your career passions?

4. **Strengths and challenges.** What skill set do you bring to your job? List your strengths and challenges from the perspective of an employer. What skills and abilities, knowledge and training, talents and personal strengths do you have? What do you find challenging? Are you working in a job that plays to your strengths? Would another career fit better?

5. **Success.** How do you define success? While some people link success to power or to wealth and lifestyle, others may consider success as fulfillment or satisfaction instead. Are you able to achieve your vision of success in your current career path? Would another career path help you achieve your vision of success?

6. **Personality fit.** Who are you, in terms of your personality? Are you more extraverted or introverted? Are you happier working outside, or in a comfortable office cubicle? Do you like to be constantly challenged, or prefer a predictable routine? Does your personality fit with your current job? Is a different job a better fit?

7. **Ideal job.** What is your dream job? Have you had a lifelong dream of a particular career? What makes a job seem ideal to you? Has this class revealed anything to you about careers and occupations that might interest you?

Think about your current situation in terms of your responses to these questions. What types of careers fit with your personality, your ideals, preferences, and so on? Be realistic, but begin to define some goals to work toward. With the information you have gathered in answering these questions, you can work toward those goals. Narrow down your career choices after doing additional research about the careers you are considering. Identify additional training you will need. Develop a timeline and an action plan for meeting your short-term career planning goals.

LONG-TERM PLANNING

Long-term career planning requires that you think 5 years, 10 years, or longer into the future. The guidelines for this planning are broader and more general and include:

1. **Core skills.** Technology and the workforce itself are changing fast, so you may have job skills now that won't be needed in the future. Identify

core skills that will always be in demand, and work toward strengthening them. Communication skills, creativity, teamwork, problem solving, and many of the skills discussed in this textbook are core skills.

2. **Employment trends.** Examine employment trends and future job predictions. The "Occupational Outlook Handbook" published annually by the Bureau of Labor Statistics (BLS) is a good place to start (the updated handbook is readily available online at www.bls.gov/ooh).
3. **Keep current.** Stay current in your short-term career planning. Keep up on newly emerging industries, technologies, and occupations. Keep an open mind (stay in the "open mode") while you creatively explore new ideas. Don't get locked into one idea; you can always change your mind as new information comes along.

Whether you love your job and want to keep it forever, or can't wait to find the next one, short-term and long-term career planning can help. You can put yourself in a better position to advance in your career, or begin a completely new occupation, with some strategic planning. Think of career planning as an interesting journey. Take your time, and be willing to head to a new adventure in a different direction if one should arise.

Source: Randall S. Hansen, "Developing a Strategic Vision for Your Career Plan," *Quintessential Careers,* www.quintcareers.com.

working it out 16.5

THE NEW ERA OF POSITIVE PSYCHOLOGY

Watch the TED Talk by positive psychology founder Martin Seligman, titled "The New Era of Positive Psychology," and then answer the following questions.

1. Why does the speaker say that the state of psychology is "not good enough?" What is the difference between psychology as a field and positive psychology specifically?
2. How do extremely happy people differ from the rest of us? Does this mean that those of us who do not fit these factors will never be happy?
3. What are the "three happy lives" that the speaker describes? Where do you fit with these three types?
4. What are the "positive interventions" that the speaker describes? Have you found yourself using these on your own? If not, which of them do you see yourself doing?
5. What is the difference between "less miserable" and "more happy" according to the speaker? Why is this important?

The video can be found here: www.ted.com/talks/martin_seligman_the_new_era_of_positive_psychology.

case study 16.1

Whose Job Is It?

Sanjay Patel was walking quickly through the office building on his way to a meeting with the other managers when his assistant, Robyn, ran up behind him. "Mr. Patel, I know you're busy, but I just can't figure out how to finish this budget report. I know it's due by tomorrow, do you think you could help me with it?"

"Sure, Robyn, let me take a look at it. I'll get back to you later today."

A few moments later, Phil, a sales associate in Sanjay's division, stopped him. "Sorry to bother you, but I didn't get those sales projections finished. I know I said I could probably finish them by today's meeting, but I couldn't find the information from the Midwest locations."

"All right, I can get that information for you this afternoon. I'll get back to you on it," Sanjay answered.

That afternoon, Phil called. "Did you have a chance to finish the sales projections? I'd like to get them over to the head office today."

"I'm still working on it," was Sanjay's reply.

About an hour later, Robyn came by Sanjay's office. "How is it going? Did you finish the budget report for me?"

At about that time, it occurred to Sanjay that something was not right with this situation. How did he, as the manager, become responsible for reporting back to his own assistant and others who should have been working for him?

Case Study Questions

1. Explain the type of time use issue that has become problematic in this case. How could this situation, if left to continue, lead to even more interference with workplace productivity in the future?
2. Who has a greater time management problem: Sanjay, or the two other employees who report to him? What would you suggest Sanjay do to improve the situation and increase productivity? What should Robyn and Phil do differently?
3. Has a situation like this ever happened to you? What did you do at the time? What would you do differently if it happened to you again?

case study 16.2

No Direction Known

Ivy had graduated six months ago with an associate of arts degree in general science, but really did not know whether she should transfer to a four-year university, or decide on a career and move forward to pursue it. In the meantime, she went through a compressed summer session to complete a course in EMT-Basic so that she could work part-time while she figured out her future. Today, she has an interview with a local biotechnology research firm looking for a laboratory technician. She is not sure she wants this job, but then she is not really sure what direction she is going in her career, or her life in general. She meets the minimum qualifications for the lab tech position with her AA degree and her emergency medical tech experience. She was instructed to arrive 20 minutes early so that she could preview the interview questions.

As Ivy looks over the interview questions, she has a moment of panic. The questions she is going to have to answer in the interview are exactly the same questions she has been asking herself, and she still doesn't have the answers:

- Tell us about yourself, and why you want this position.
- What are your long-term career goals? What do you see yourself doing in five years?
- What are your greatest professional strengths?
- Describe your dream job.
- How has your education prepared you for your career?
- What are the most important rewards you look for in a job? In your career?

Case Study Questions

1. Have you been in a similar situation as Ivy? If so, how do you answer these questions?
2. If Ivy asked for your advice, what would you tell her about goals, motivation, direction, career preparation, and finding her niche?
3. Suppose you are Ivy's career counselor. Set up a short-term plan and a long-term plan that she can use to develop the next step in her future, whether her future direction is a job, going back to school, or another option.

glossary

accommodator Someone who wants to avoid conflict by engaging in positive thinking.

achievement needs Occur in people who are goal oriented and take personal responsibility for achievements.

active listening Listening with greater concentration, less tolerance for distractions, and more feedback to the speaker.

affiliation needs Occur in people who want to be accepted and liked by others.

ageism Prejudice and discrimination toward older people.

aggression Hurting others and putting them on the defensive.

Aslan phenomenon A circumstance that exists when people make rules, then follow them even after the situations to which they originally applied no longer exist.

assertiveness Standing up for your rights without threatening the self-esteem of the other person.

attitude An evaluation of people, ideas, issues, situations, or objects.

authority The vested power to influence or command within an organization.

autocratic leaders Leaders who make all the decisions and use authority and material rewards to motivate followers.

autonomy Independence, the ability to act and make decisions on one's own without undue interference from management.

avoider Someone who would rather not be around conflict at all and values neutrality highly.

bad news skills The skills necessary to deliver bad news to customers but still retain their business and goodwill.

beginning The *last* of three general steps in the acceptance of personal loss. This is where "experimenting" and "completion" take place. (See **ending** and **neutral zone.**)

behavior modification The process of changing behavior because of a reward or lack of a reward.

bias A tendency to judge people before knowing them, basing the judgment only on their membership in some group or category of people.

blind pane The pane in the Johari Window that contains everything other people can see about you, but you can't see yourself.

boss massaging The practice of currying favor, or kissing up, with a manager to achieve your own goals.

brainstorming A type of spontaneous group discussion to help find multiple solutions to problems.

brand promise A short statement that tells customers what they can expect from a particular brand.

bureaucracy A formal organization in which each person has specific duties and responsibilities and is assigned to only one supervisor.

catastrophize To turn an irrational belief into an imagined disaster.

charismatic power Power that is based on the attractiveness a person has to others.

chronic stressors Inescapable, day-to-day situations or conditions that cause stress.

cliché conversation The level of communication with the least amount of self-disclosure, including niceties such as, "Have a nice day."

coercive power Power that depends on the threat of possible punishment.

cognitive appraisal The thinking evaluation of an event or situation that varies from person to person and, for an individual, from day to day.

cognitive categorization A process in which the mind quickly sorts information into categories to function efficiently.

cognitive dissonance The emotional state that results from acting in ways that contradict one's beliefs or other actions.

collaborator Someone who brings both sides together for discussion and not only is most likely to bring about a win-win solution but is actually necessary for it.

collective habits of thought Ways of thinking that occur when groups have own beliefs about *what* should be done and *how* it should be done.

communication The giving and receiving of ideas, feelings, and information among people.

compensating The use of a strength to make up for a real or perceived weakness.

competitor Someone who is most likely to try a win-lose approach to conflict resolution, especially if he or she is personally involved in the conflict.

compromiser Someone who uses his or her skills to blend differences and form a workable alternative.

compulsive gambling The inability to control one's betting habit.

concession bargaining The process of getting each side in a conflict to willingly make concessions in exchange for concessions made by the opposing side.

conditional positive regard Acceptance of individuals as worthy only when they behave in a certain way.

conflict A Friction or opposition resulting from actual or perceived differences or incompatibilities.

conformity Behaving in a way that meets a specified standard, in coordination with a group.

consultative leaders Leaders who tend to delegate authority and confer with others in making decisions, but who make the actual decisions independently.

content conflict Conflict that tends to focus on disagreements over what a statement or concept means.

context A point of reference (or a place from which to begin) when communicating.

creative process The way in which creativity helps you develop ideas and solve problems.

creativity The ability to produce ideas or solutions to problems that are unique, appropriate, and valuable.

cultural Intelligence (CQ) The ability for people, organizations, and businesses to relate to culturally diverse situations and work effectively in them.

culture stories Stories that illustrate the values of the people who make an organization work.

cyberbullying Using electronic communication to bully a person, typically by sending targeted intimidating, threatening, or demeaning messages.

cybercrime Criminal acts carried out online.

daily hassles The daily annoyances, such as getting stuck in traffic or misplacing your keys, that can cause stress in your life.

defensiveness The inappropriate reaction to another's behavior as though it were an attack.

denial Failure to confront your problem; characteristic response by an alcoholic.

digital divide The gap between those who have available access to technology and computers, and those who do not.

discrimination Your behavior, or what you do (or intend to do, or are inclined to do) as a result of your stereotypes and prejudice.

disinformation Intentionally false and misleading information, including propaganda issued by a government organization, to damage the reputation of a rival power or media source.

displays Gestures that are used like nonverbal punctuation marks, such as pounding your fist on the table.

distancing The distance of physical space you maintain between other people and yourself.

distress Negative stress, the kind felt during an illness or when going through a divorce.

dysfunctional conflict Destructive conflict.

economic prejudice Prejudice and discrimination toward people who are poorer or wealthier than you are.

eight intelligences Eight separate areas in which people put their perceptiveness and abilities to work.

either/or fallacy When you see only one of two extremes as a possible solution, while ignoring the endless number of creative choices that might exist between the extremes.

emblems Gestures that are used in a specific manner because they have a specific meaning, usually one understood by both sender and receiver; the peace sign is an example.

emotional competence A learned capability based on emotional intelligence; results in outstanding performance at work.

emotional intelligence (EI) The ability to see and control your own emotions and to understand the emotional states of other people.

emotional mind A powerful, impulsive, sometimes illogical awareness; an ability to perceive emotions.

employee appraisal Feedback to an employee from supervisors on how he or she has performed over a given period.

employee assistance programs (EAPs) Company-sponsored programs that treat employees with substance abuse problems, marriage and family conflicts, and financial difficulties.

ending The *first* of three general steps in the acceptance of personal loss. This is where "emotional standstill," "denial," and "anger" take place. (See **neutral zone** and **beginning.**)

entrepreneurship The risk-taking entrance into your own enterprise.

Equal Employment Opportunity Commission (EEOC) A federal agency established to monitor the laws set in place by the amended Civil Rights Act of 1964, as amended in 1972.

equal status The condition that occurs when companies hire employees who are frequent targets of discrimination into all levels within the company.

ERG theory A refinement of Maslow's hierarchy that includes only three needs areas: existence (mostly physical needs);

relatedness (needs linked to relationships); and growth (internal esteem needs and self-actualization).

esteem needs Fourth level of Maslow's hierarchy of needs; includes recognition from peers and colleagues.

ethical codes Formalized sets of ethical guidelines developed by some companies for use at all levels of an organization.

ethical relativism An ethical philosophy that believes that each person should make their best decisions based on self-interest, values, morals, and culture.

ethics The expression of the standards of right and wrong based on conduct and morals in a particular society.

ethnocentrism The belief that one's ethnic group is more normal than others; an emotional source of prejudice because of people's gut-level feelings about how right their group is–and, in turn, how wrong they think other groups are.

eustress Positive stress, the kind felt when doing something one enjoys, such as playing tennis or attending a party.

expectancy In *expectancy theory,* the likelihood that if a person tried, the result would be better performance.

expectancy theory Developed by Victor Vroom to explain human behavior in terms of people's goals, choices, and the expectation that goals will be reached.

expert power Power that comes from a person's knowledge or skill in areas that are critical to the success of the firm.

explicit bias Attitudes and beliefs individuals hold on a conscious level, related to a person or a group. This type of bias often arises as the direct result of a perceived threat.

external locus of control When people feel they have no control over the events in their lives.

external stressors Stressors that include anything from outside sources that causes you pain and discomfort.

extraversion Characteristic of a happy attitude in which a person's behavior is directed outward, toward others.

extrinsic rewards or motivators External factors intended to provide motivational incentives, including salary, bonuses, promotions, praise, or high grades in classes.

family violence Violence that can be defined as physical, emotional, verbal, or sexual violence against another family member.

fear of failure The fear that occurs when people are afraid of looking bad in front of others.

fear of success The fear that occurs when people who have not experienced much success in their lives feel they do not deserve it.

feedback Information given to people either on how well they are performing a task, or on how clearly they are being understood.

filtering A method listeners use to *hear only what they want to hear,* which may result in failing to receive messages correctly.

finding your niche Finding the place where you thrive and are most content; includes finding the type of job or career where you will be most satisfied.

first-, second-, and third-degree games In transactional analysis, categories of games based on intensity of play. First-degree games are relatively harmless; second-degree games are moderately harmful; third-degree games are extremely damaging.

fixed mindset The belief that talents and abilities are inborn and unchangeable.

flow The feeling of oneness with an activity that allows an individual to uniquely experience an event or activity by becoming totally engaged in the process; term was coined by Mihalyi Csikszentmihalyi.

force field analysis A model in which the status quo is like a battlefield being fought for by two armies: the driving force and the restraining force.

free-rein leaders Leaders who set performance standards, then allow followers to work creatively to meet standards.

frustration The feeling people get when goals they are trying to attain are blocked.

frustration regression principles A principle that says that someone who fails to reach a higher need level will sometimes become frustrated and regress (go back) to a lower need level, and stay there for some time–perhaps forever.

functional conflict Constructive conflict.

future favors A practice commonly seen in developing countries based upon mutual obligation and resulting in the exchange of favors over years and even generations; also used in some industrialized countries such as Japan and South Korea.

game An encounter between two people that produces a "payoff" for the one who starts the game, at the expense of the other player.

gift exchange A strong tradition in many cultures, in which giving gifts creates a future obligation to the receiver; it can also be a rite of passage into an inner circle.

goal setting Employees set their own goals.

going the extra mile When a company gives customers small extra products or services as a way of showing appreciation for their business.

good feelings and solutions The only two things customers really buy.

grapevine A network within the informal organization that communicates incomplete, but usually somewhat accurate information.

group A collection of two or more individuals who interact, share certain characteristics, and coordinate their participation in the group around some shared idea or goal.

group dynamics The set of interpersonal relationships within a group that determine how group members relate to one another and that influence task performance.

groupthink A problematic type of thinking that results from group members who are overly willing to agree with one another because of time pressure, stress, and low collective self-esteem.

growth mindset The belief that our basic abilities can be developed and improved through dedication and hard work.

growth mindset The belief that abilities can be developed with work and practice.

gut-level communication Level of communication in which feelings are expressed honestly.

hardy personality A resilient personality type, characterized by the ability to meet challenges, a sense of commitment, and a feeling of being in control of life.

Hawthorne Experiment A five-year study conducted at the Western Electric plant in Hawthorne, Illinois, that showed that workers performed better when someone was paying attention to them.

hidden agendas The secret wishes, hopes, desires, and assumptions hidden from the group. People often try to accomplish hidden agendas while pretending to care about the group goals.

hidden pane The pane in the Johari Window that contains information and feelings that you are hiding from other people.

high-context culture A culture in which the *social context* surrounding a written document is far more important than the document itself. One must be very careful about cultural norms, nonverbal behaviors on both sides, and anything else involving the overall atmosphere of the communication.

higher self-esteem When individuals have healthy feelings about themselves and are therefore more likely to succeed in personal and career goals.

Holmes–Rahe Social Readjustment Rating Scale (SRRS) A listing of many kinds of changes, rated from 100 to 0 on the basis of their intensity and the adjustment problems they can create.

horizontal communication Messages that are communicated between you and your equals in the formal organization.

human relations The skill or ability to work effectively through and with other people.

hygienes (also called "dissatisfiers") The qualities in the workplace that are outside the job itself (examples: company benefits, policies, job security). When these factors are weak or missing, motivation will fall; however, when they are high, motivation will not be strong or long term.

ideal self The way you would like to be or plan to become.

ideas and judgments Expressed through conscious thoughts, opinions, and theories in level three of Powell's five levels of communication.

illustrators Gestures that are used to clarify a point, such as pointing when giving directions.

impostor phenomenon A feeling successful people experience when they are afraid that they did not really succeed because of their own talents and hard work.

informal organization The ever-changing set of relationships and interactions that are not formally put together; they form naturally in the workplace.

information overload The type of listening that happens when a listener is overwhelmed with incoming information and has to decide which information will be processed and remembered; this is a common cause of poor listening skills.

inner circle A clique of trusted family members, tribal members, or friends (depending on the culture) who are at the center of power or influence.

inner conflict Conflict within an individual; it might involve values, loyalties, or priorities; the pressure you feel when you are forced to make a choice.

inner critic An inner voice that attacks people and negatively judges their worth.

inner saboteur Negative inner voices that form mental habits that sabotage our actions, keeping us from reaching our full potential.

institutional prejudice Prejudice that is caused by policies in the workplace that are not intentionally set to exclude members of specific groups or to treat them differently, but which have that effect anyway.

institutionalized conflict Conflict that occurs when a conflict factor is built into the structure of the organization.

instrumental values Values that reflect the ways you prefer to behave leading toward larger life goals.

instrumentality The likelihood that something good (or bad) will come from an increase in effort.

intelligence Traditionally seen as reasoning ability, as measured by standardized tests.

intensity The degree to which an individual shows serious concentration or emotion; another dimension of nonverbal communication.

interdependence A relationship in which members of different groups not only must cooperate but also must depend on each other to reach common goals.

intergenerational care Day care not only for children but also for elderly family members.

intergroup conflict Conflict that occurs when already-formed groups have conflicts with each other.

internal customer The person who depends on the other people in the company to provide the services and products for the external customer.

internal locus of control When people feel they are in control of the events in their own lives.

internal stressors Your perceptions of stressors, which may vary depending on personality.

intragroup conflict Conflict that occurs when two groups form and take sides.

intrinsic motivators or intrinsic rewards Factors that motivate a person from within, such as the joy and excitement of the discovery process. In *expectancy theory,* the internal factors related to the value of work, including the amount of creativity allowed, the degree of responsibility, and the satisfaction of helping others.

intuition Direct perception or insight.

irrational belief system A way of thinking that causes internal stress by substituting a realistic belief with one that is destructive, illogical, and largely false.

job burnout Physical and emotional exhaustion resulting from long-term stress or frustration in one's workplace.

job enrichment The upgrading of a job that makes it more interesting, meaningful, or rewarding and provides long-term motivation.

Johari Window A composite of four panes that shows you ways of relating to others: the open, blind, hidden, and unknown panes.

Kaizen Literally, "to become good through change." The concept of *Kaizen* is one of restructuring and organizing every aspect of a system to ensure optimal efficiency.

leadership The ability to influence others to work toward the goals of an organization.

legitimate power Power based on the position a person holds in an organization that is effective only when followers believe in the structure that produces this power.

Lewin change model A workplace change model with three steps; unfreezing the status quo, making changes, then refreezing to the previous work mode.

lifelong learning The ongoing, voluntary, and self-motivated gaining of knowledge for personal and professional reasons.

locus of control The perceived location of the control you feel you have over events that happen to you; this control is perceived to be located within the individual (internal locus of control) or is attributed to external factors (external locus of control).

logical incrementalism A model that acknowledges that bringing about changes in a large organization is usually time-consuming and complicated, and presents a method of simplifying the process.

long-term goals Those things you decide to work for after developing a life plan for the future.

looking-glass self The self you assume others see when they look at you.

lose–lose strategy A strategy in which everyone gives up something, and the focus is on compromise.

love and belongingness needs Third level of Maslow's hierarchy of needs; includes complete acceptance from family and friends.

low conformers Individuals who think independently, solve problems creatively, and often cause some conflict in the process.

low-context culture A culture in which a written agreement, such as a contract, can be taken at face value.

lower self-esteem When individuals are unable to see themselves as capable, sufficient, or worthy; or believe they have little value to offer the world.

major life changes Changes in your life, such as divorce, that increase daily hassles, leaving you stressed and worn out.

manifest needs theory Developed by David McClelland to show that all people have needs that motivate them in life and on the job. These three needs include power needs, affiliation needs, and achievement needs.

Maslow's hierarchy of needs Model that shows that people tend to satisfy their needs in a certain order: first, physiological needs; then safety and security, belongingness and love, esteem; and finally, self-actualization.

mentor A person who acts as a guide or teacher for another, leading that person through experiences.

morale Overall mood of an individual or group, based on attitudes and satisfaction.

morality A system of conduct that covers all broadly based, mostly unwritten standards of how people should behave and generally conform to cultural ideals of right and wrong.

motivation The force of the need or desire to act.

motivators (also called "satisfiers") The factors in Herzberg's theory that cause real, long-term motivation, usually containing *intrinsic* motivation factors (examples: interesting and challenging tasks, advancement, achievement, growth).

mutual respect The positive consideration or regard that two people have for each other.

negotiation-of-selves Conflict that is involved in the process of defining yourself to others and responding to their implied definitions of themselves.

net neutrality The idea that Internet service providers should make access available to all content and applications regardless of the source, and without favoring or blocking specific products or websites.

networking power Power that is attained by gaining contact and knowing the right people.

neutral zone The *second* of three general steps in the acceptance of personal loss. The neutral zone is the area where "helplessness" and "bottoming out" take place. (See **ending** and **beginning.**)

"nice" customer The customer who never complains, but responds to bad service by taking his or her business elsewhere.

nine-dot puzzle A puzzle that is used to show people's respect for rules that don't exist. Participants are asked to connect nine dots using only four straight lines, without lifting the pen off the paper. Most fail because they feel the need to stay "inside the box" formed by the nine dots.

nominal group method An exercise that encourages creativity within a group framework by allowing everyone to offer ideas individually.

nonconversation A way to describe the amount of actual conversation in cliché conversation.

nonverbal communication Communication that allows you to understand and interpret meaning in context.

nonverbals Ways of communicating without speaking, such as gestures, body language, and facial expressions.

norm A standard of behavior expected of group members.

OD change agent A company's formal change agent; often an outside consultant who specializes in planned change or organizational development (OD).

OD intervention Training tools that teach members of the organization how to solve problems they face or make needed changes to organizational development (OD).

open mode A state of mind where you are relaxed, expansive, less purposeful, and more fun than in the everyday closed mode.

open pane The pane in the Johari Window that contains information that you know about yourself and that you have no reason to hide.

optimal experience The pleasure in performing the process of an activity itself, rather than achieving the goal.

organizational change Change that a group of people must learn to accept and implement.

organizational citizenship behavior An attitude of willingness to go above and beyond the behaviors that are generally associated with life in the workplace.

organizational climate The emotional weather within an organization that reflects the norms and attitudes of the organization's culture and affects worker morale, attitudes, stress levels, and communication.

organizational communication Oral and written communication in an organization. It has formal and informal dimensions and travels vertically and horizontally.

organizational development (OD) A planned, companywide, systematic method of achieving change in an organization.

organizational or corporate culture An organization's network that includes the shared values and assumptions within it.

overloading time Planning too many activities into one time slot.

participative leaders Leaders who encourage the group to work together toward shared goals.

passive Accepting or allowing what happens or what others do, without active response or resistance.

peak communication Communication characterized by complete openness and honest self-disclosure. It happens rarely.

perception The way in which a person views the world.

person-versus-group conflict Conflict that occurs most often when a member of a group breaks its rules, or norms.

person-versus-person conflict Conflict that involves two people who are at odds over personality differences, values conflicts, loyalties, or any number of issues.

personal competence The ability to be self-aware, motivated, and self-regulated.

personal control The power people perceive they have over their destinies.

persuasive leader Leaders who make the final decision but are open to persuasion.

physiological needs The most basic level of Maslow's hierarchy of needs; includes the satisfaction of physical needs, including food and shelter.

positive attitude A position resulting from healthy self-esteem, optimism, extraversion, and personal control.

positive psychology A subfield within psychology that focuses on experiences, individual traits, and institutions that create happiness and hope, rather than focusing on mental illness.

positive self-talk A method of building self-esteem by thinking and speaking positively about yourself.

power The ability of one person to influence another.

power needs Desired by individuals who want to control and influence other people.

prejudice The outcome of prejudging a person. Prejudice in communication is the unwillingness to listen to members of groups the listener believes are inferior, such as other ethnic groups or women; it can also take more subtle forms; how you feel as a result of the stereotypes you believe in.

principle of justice An ethical philosophy that holds that all decisions should be consistent, unbiased, and based on fact.

principle of the common good An ethical philosophy that decisions made for the common good affect the best choices for individuals and societies, in the present and the future.

principle of universalism An ethical philosophy that all human life has value, and ethical decisions should protect all.

principle of utilitarianism An ethical philosophy that holds that all decisions should do the greatest good for the largest number of people.

principle of virtue An ethical philosophy that stresses decisions that are wise, true, and lead to one's best self.

procrastination Putting off until later the things a person should be doing now.

productivity The ratio of an organization's inputs, or its resources, to its outputs, or the goods and services it produces.

proximity Physical closeness; here, it refers to contact between members of a diverse workplace.

psychological contract An agreement that is not written or spoken but is understood between people.

quality circles Process that bring employees and managers together to brainstorm and find ways to improve quality and performance.

racism Prejudice and discrimination based on race.

Rath Test Finds out if the values you think you have are the ones you truly have.

rational mind An awareness of reality, which allows you to ponder and reflect.

rationalize To justify unethical behavior with excuses.

real self The way you really are when nobody is around to approve or disapprove.

red flag words Words that bring an immediate emotional response (usually negative) from the listener, generally because of strong beliefs on the subject.

regression Slipping backward to an earlier stage of growth; it can be either temporary or permanent.

regulators Gestures that are used to control the flow of communication; eye contact is a common type of regulator.

reinforcement theory Explains human behavior in terms of repetition. Behavior that is rewarded enough times will be repeated, whereas behavior that repeatedly receives no reward will probably discontinue.

reinforcers Incentives such as awards, bonuses, promotions, gifts, and even compliments.

relationship selling Forming meaningful relationships with your customers, which makes them much more likely to return and buy from you again.

repress To block off memories that may cause pain, embarrassment, or guilt.

reverse brainstorming A group problem solving method that begins with how to cause a problem, and reverses those ideas to solve the original problem.

reward power Power that comes from the user's ability to control or influence others with something of value to them.

rights or legal principle An ethical philosophy that legal rights determine the ethical decision to make.

role model A person to whom an individual can look for guidance by example, but who isn't necessarily actively interacting with the individual.

rumor mill A gossip network that produces mostly false information.

safety and security needs Second level of Maslow's hierarchy of needs; includes physical safety from harm and the elements as well as financial security.

sandwich generation Middle-aged adults who are taking responsibility for both dependent children and parents at the same time, and being sandwiched by these obligations.

SCAMPER A strategy, created by Bob Eberle, to release your creative mind.

scapegoating The practice of unfairly blaming others (such as ethnic groups) when something goes wrong.

scientific management A system based upon scientific and engineering principles.

script In relationship transactions, a psychological script like a movie or theater script, with characters, dialogue, etc., that most people heard as children.

second right answer Refers to a method of decision making in which people get rid of the stumbling block that prevents them from looking for more than one solution.

selective listening The type of listening that happens when a listener deliberately chooses what he or she wants to pay attention to.

self-actualization Highest level of Maslow's hierarchy of needs; occurs when one has fulfilled his or her potential.

self-awareness The knowledge of how you are being perceived by others.

self-concept The way you picture yourself to be.

self-direction The ability to set short-term and long-term goals for yourself.

self-discipline The ability to teach or guide yourself to set up and carry out your goals and plans.

self-disclosure The process of letting other people know what you are really thinking and feeling.

self-efficacy The confidence an individual has in his or her ability to deal with problems when they occur and to achieve goals.

self-esteem The regard in which an individual holds himself or herself.

self-esteem trap The circumstance that comes from taking a customer's attack personally and letting it affect your self-esteem.

self-fulfilling prophecy The tendency for a prediction to actually occur once it is believed; for example, when a victim believes that prejudice against him or her is true, then fulfills these negative expectations.

self-image The way you honestly see yourself.

self-justification Explaining your behavior so that you feel it is correct.

self-perception What and how you believe yourself to be.

self-respect Positive self-image with high self-esteem.

self-sabotage Damaging your own credibility or competence.

setting priorities Deciding ahead of time which tasks are the most, and least, important.

seven major life changes Loss, separation, relocation, a change in relationship, a change in direction, a change in health, and personal growth.

seven stages of personal change Emotional standstill, denial, anger, helplessness, bottoming out, experimenting, and completion.

sexism Prejudice and discrimination based on gender.

sexual harassment Behavior that is defined by the EEOC as "unwelcome sexual advances, requests for sexual favors, and other verbal or physical conduct of a sexual nature."

short-term goals The specific plans of action for the things you would like to accomplish right now or in the immediate future.

skill variety The opportunity and ability to use numerous different skills in one's position at work.

social competence Empathy for others combined with sensitivity and effective social skills.

social responsibility The practice of acting ethically while understanding your actions are part of the larger, interactive picture of your workplace, community, and world.

stakeholders Any group that a business interacts with, such as customers, competitors, unions, suppliers, consumer groups, and government agencies.

status The rank an individual holds within a group.

stereotypes Your thoughts or beliefs about specific groups of people.

stress Any reaction or response made by the body to a new situation.

stressor A situation or an event that causes the body to react (causes stress).

substance abuse The continued use of a psychoactive substance even though it is causing or increasing problems in a person's life.

task identity The worker's perception of the meaningfulness of a job, often based upon the worker's permission to start a job and see it through to completion.

task maturity Having the skill set necessary to complete a job, as well as the ability to set and meet realistic goals and the ability to take on responsibility for the task.

task significance A worker's perception that the task directly affects other people's work or lives.

team The relationship among employees with different skill sets who work together to create value for a business or organization. Workplace teams can be short term or have a long-range purpose.

team building The process of creating and encouraging a group of employees to work together toward achieving group goals and increased productivity.

ten "mental locks" Rules or beliefs that keep people from being as creative as they otherwise could be.

terminal values Values likely to maintain a high priority throughout your life.

Theories X and Y Theory X managers see workers as lacking ambition, disliking work, and wanting security above all else. Theory Y managers see workers as enjoying work, able to assume responsibility, and being creative.

time analysis Tools available to help with analyzing your use of time so that you can see where to become more efficient in time management.

time management Making effective use of available time.

to-do list A list of what you need to do, when, and where.

Total Quality Management (TQM) A management organizational philosophy that was very influential in the 1980s and 1990s, which stated that quality must be present in the product or the service produced, and in the process itself of producing the goods or service. **See quality movement.**

triarchic (three arches) theory Intelligent behavior arising from a balance between analytical, creative, and practical abilities, where these abilities function together to allow people to achieve success within their social and cultural contexts.

trust Firm belief in the reliability, truth, ability, or strength of someone or something.

two simplest principles Finding out what the customer needs, and doing whatever is necessary to satisfy it.

type A and type B personalities Two standard personality-related sets of behaviors. Type A behaviors are characterized by impatience, hostility, perfectionism, and a sense of time urgency. Type B behaviors are characterized by flexibility, the ability to relax and delegate work, and a minimal sense of time urgency.

unconditional positive regard The acceptance of individuals as worthy and valuable regardless of their behavior, usually applied to parental acceptance of children.

unconscious bias (implicit bias) Social stereotyping about certain groups of people that individuals form outside their own conscious awareness; also known as *implicit bias*.

underutilizing time Making poor use of available time.

unknown pane The pane in the Johari Window that contains unknown talents, abilities, and attitudes, as well as forgotten and repressed experiences, emotions, and possibilities.

valence The value a person places on a reward.

value systems Frameworks people use in developing beliefs about themselves, others, and how they should be treated.

values The worth or importance you attach to different factors in your life.

values conflict Conflict that occurs when one set of values clashes with another, and a decision has to be made.

vertical communication Messages that are communicated according to an organization's chain of command by flowing both upward and downward.

whistleblowing Turning in or otherwise exposing people who behave unethically in your company.

win–lose strategy A strategy that allows one side of a conflict to win at the expense of another.

win–win strategy A strategy that leads to a solution in which both sides feel they have come out on top.

work team A group of employees with shared goals who join forces on a work project.

work–life balance Equilibrium between professional life, personal life, and family life.

references

Chapter 1

[1] Richard Baran, "Interpersonal Relationship Skills or How to Get Along for Productivity and Profit," *Personnel Administrator,* April 1986, p. 12.

[2] Janette Moody et al., "Showcasing the Skilled Business Graduate: Expanding the Tool Kit." *Business Communication Quarterly,* March 2002, p. 23.

[3] U.S. Census, Population, Projections of Size and Composition of the U.S. Population, https://www.census.gov/content/dam/Census/library/publications/2015/demo/p25-1143.pdf (retrieved May 11, 2017).

[4] Mihalyi Csikszentmihalyi, published on July 1, 1996, last reviewed on June 9, 2016, "The Creative Personality," *Psychology Today,* https://www.psychologytoday.com/articles/199607/the-creative-personality (retrieved June 20, 2017).

[5] http://reports.weforum.org/global-gender-gap-report-2015/report-highlights/ (retrieved May 13, 2017).

[6] Mitra Toosi, "Projections of the Labor Force to 2050: A Visual Essay," *Monthly Labor Review,* October 2012, pp. 3–14.

[7] W. Richard Plunket, *Supervision: The Direction of People at Work* (Dubuque, IA: W. C. Brown, 1983), p. 161.

[8] M. R. Hansen, "Better Supervision for A to W," *Supervisory Management,* August 1985, p. 35.

[9] https://venturebeat.com/2011/12/27/ocean-marketing-how-to-self-destruct-your-company-with-just-a-few-measly-emails/ (retrieved May 13, 2017).

[10] Fyodor Dostoevsky, *The House of the Dead* (London: JM Dent & Sons Ltd., 1933).

[11] Nancy E. Roberts, "Most Managers Fail; Here's Five Reasons Why." http://EzineArticles.com/?expert=Nancy_E_Roberts (retrieved March 27, 2013).

[12] Anon., "The Importance of Human Relations in the Workplace." http://avaha1978.hubpages.com/hub/The-importance-of-human-relations-in-the-workplace (retrieved May 28, 2013).

[13] Suneel Ratan, "Why Busters Hate Boomers," *Fortune,* October 4, 1993, pp. 57–70.

[14] Philip Bump, "Here Is When Each Generation Begins and Ends, According to Facts." March 25, 2014, *The Atlantic.* https://www.theatlantic.com/national/archive/2014/03/here-is-when-each-generation-begins-and-ends-according-to-facts/359589/ (retrieved May 13, 2017).

[15] "China GDP Annual Growth Rate," *Trading Economics,* https://tradingeconomics.com/china/gdp-growth-annual (retrieved October 20, 2017).

[16] Robert Kaplan, "How We Would Fight China," *Atlantic,* June 2005, pp. 49–64. http://www.bloomberg.com/apps/news?pid=20601013&sid=av1phRnqSgCM&refer=emergingmarkets (retrieved March 27, 2013).

[17] Jeff Poor, "Life Expectancy Increasing or Decreasing, Depending on What Day It Is." Business and Media Institute. http://www.businessandmedia.org/printer/2007/20070913152112.aspx (retrieved March 27, 2013).

[18] Caleb Hannan, "Management Secrets from the Meanest Company in America," *Bloomberg Businessweek* January 7, 2013, pp. 46–51.

[19] Eriq Gardner, "Dish Network's Charlie Ergen Is the Most Hated Man in Hollywood." *The Hollywood Reporter,* April 2, 2013 (accessed April 4, 2013 at http://www.hollywoodreporter.com/news/dish-networks-charlie-ergen-is-432288).

[20] Paul R. Timm and Brent D. Peterson, *People at Work: Human Relations in Organizations* (Minneapolis/St. Paul, MN: West Publishing, 1993), pp. 122–123. See also "William Ouchi on Trust," *Training and Development Journal,* December 1982, p. 71.

[21] Stephen R. Covey, *The Seven Habits of Highly Effective People* (New York: Simon and Schuster, 1989), pp. 66–67.

[22] Mary Ellen Guffey and Dana Loewy, *Essentials of Business Communication* (Mason, OH: Cengage Learning, 2013), p. 7.

[23] John R. Dickman, *Human Connections* (Englewood Cliffs, NJ: Prentice Hall, 1982), pp. xi–xii.

[24] Michael Drafke, *The Human Side of Organizations* (Upper Saddle River, NJ: Pearson Prentice-Hall, 2006), pp. 211–214.

[25] David Krech, Richard Crutchfield, and Egerton Ballachey, *Individual in Society* (New York: McGraw-Hill, 1962), pp. 527–529.

[26] Peter F. Drucker, *The New Realities* (New York: HarperCollins, 1990).

[27] James R. Lowry, B. W. Weinrich, and R. D. Steade, *Business in Today's World* (Cincinnati, OH: South Western Publishing, 1990), p. 243.

[28] L. K. Frankel and Alexander Fleisher, *The Human Factor in Industry* (New York: Macmillan, 1920), p. 8.

[29] Ibid., pp. 10–28.

[30] Max Weber, *The Protestant Ethic and the Spirit of Capitalism,* trans. Talcott Parsons (New York: Scribner, 1930), pp. 121–156.

[31] Max Weber, *The Theory of Social and Economic Organization,* ed. and trans. A. M. Henderson and T. Parsons (Oxford University Press, 1947), pp. 22–57.

[32] Frederick W. Taylor, *The Principles of Scientific Management* (New York: Harper and Brothers, 1923), pp. 35–38.

[33] Daniel Nelson, *Frederick W. Taylor and the Rise of Scientific Management* (Madison, WI: University of Wisconsin Press, 1980).

[34] Daniel A. Wren, *The Evolution of Management Thought* (New York: Ronald Press, 1972), pp. 158–168.

[35] Henry C. Metcalf and L. Urwick, eds., *Dynamic Administration: The Collected Papers of Mary Parker Follett* (New York: Harper and Row, 1942), pp. 20–38.

[36] Elton Mayo, *The Human Problems of an Industrial Civilization* (New York: Macmillan, 1933).

[37] John G. Adair, "The Hawthorne Effect: A Reconsideration of the Methodological Artifact," *Journal of Applied Psychology,* May 1984, pp. 334–345. See also Mitchell Cohen, "The Hawthorne Studies, Another Look." http://nyc.indymedia.org/en/2010/10/112886.html (retrieved March 30, 2013).

[38] George T. and John W. Boudreau, *Human Resource Management* (Homewood, IL: Richard Irwin, 1991), pp. 605–609.

[39] Mary Walton, *The Deming Management Method* (New York: Putnam, 1986), pp. 3–21. Also, John Hunter, "Eliminate Sales Commissions: Reject Theory X and Embrace Systems Thinking," *The W. Edwards Deming Institute Blog,* http://blog.deming.org/2012/11/eliminate-sales-commissions-reject-theory-x-management-and-embrace-systems-thinking/ (entered November 1, 2012; retrieved March 28, 2013).

Chapter 2

[1] Joseph L. Massie and John Douglas, *Managing: A Contemporary Introduction,* 5th ed. (Englewood Cliffs, NJ: Prentice-Hall, 1992).

[2] Samuel E. Wood and Ellen Green Wood, *The World of Psychology* (Boston, MA: Allyn & Bacon, 1999). See also Kimberly Fulcher, "Envisioning Your Ideal Self," SelfGrowth.com, www.selfgrowth.com/articles/Fulcer2html (retrieved March 16, 2008).

[3] Samuel E. Wood and Ellen Green Wood, *The World of Psychology* (Boston, MA: Allyn & Bacon, 1999). See also "How Do You Talk to Yourself?" Norwich University Online, www.leadersdirect.com/talkself.html (retrieved March 15, 2008).

[4] Mary Pipher, *Reviving Ophelia: Saving the Selves of Adolescent Girls* (New York: Ballantine Books, 1994).

[5] Carolyn M. Ball, *Claiming Your Self-Esteem* (Berkeley, CA: Celestial Arts, 1990), p. 138.

[6] Stanley Coppersmith, *The Antecedents of Self-Esteem* (San Francisco: Freeman, 1967).

[7] Amy L. Gonzales and Jeffrey T. Hancock. "Mirror, Mirror on my Facebook Wall: Effects of Exposure to Facebook on Self-Esteem" *Cyberpsychology, Behavior, and Social Networking,* Volume: 14, Issue: 1–2, 2011, pp. 79–83.

[8] Wayne Weiten and Margaret Lloyd, *Psychology Applied to Modern Life: Adjustment at the Turn of the Century,* 6th ed. (Belmont, CA: Wadsworth, 1999).

[9] Spencer Rathus, *Psychology,* 6th ed. (Fort Worth, TX: Harcourt Brace Jovanovich, College Division, 1998).

[10] Ibid.

[11] Alfred Adler, *The Individual Psychology of Alfred Adler* (New York: Basic Books, 1956), p. 48.

[12] Hertha Orgler, *Alfred Adler: The Man and His Work* (New York: New American Library, 1963).

[13] Julian Rotter, "External Control and Internal Control," *Psychology Today,* June 1971, pp. 37–42, 58–59 [13]. See also Samuel E. Wood and Ellen Green Wood, *The World of Psychology* (Boston, MA: Allyn & Bacon, 2006), pp. 339–340.

[14] Matthew McKay and Patrick Fanning, *Self-Esteem* (Oakland, CA: New Harbinger, 1987), p. 181.

[15] Adapted from Matthew McKay and Patrick Fanning, *Self-Esteem* (Oakland, CA: New Harbinger, 1987).

[16] Stephen R. Covey, *The Seven Habits of Highly Effective People* (New York: Simon & Schuster, 1989).

[17] Ibid. See also Neil A. Fiore, *The Now Habit* (Los Angeles, CA: Jeremy P. Tarcher, 1989), pp. 6–26.

[18] Denis Waitley, *Psychology of Success: Developing Your Self-Esteem* (Homewood, IL: Richard D. Irwin, 1993), p. 76. See also B. David Brooks and Rex K. Dalby, *The Self-Esteem Repair and Maintenance Manual* (Newport Beach, CA: Kincaid House, 1990), p. 55.

[19] Robert Rosenthal and Lenore Jacobson, *Pygmalion in the Classroom: Teacher Expectations and Pupils' Intellectual Development* (Norwalk, CT: Irvington Publishing Co., 1992). See also Cecilia Elena Rouse, and Lisa Barrow, "U.S. Elementary and Secondary Schools: Equalizing Opportunity or Replicating the Status Quo?" Opportunity in America, Volume 16, Number 2, Fall 2006. Future of Children: A Collaboration of The Woodrow Wilson School of Public and International Affairs at Princeton University and The Brookings Institution, www.futureofchildren.org/information2826/information_show.htm?doc_id=392628 (retrieved March 14, 2008).

[20] Victoria Clayton, "Are We Raising a Nation of Little Egomaniacs? Debate Erupts Over Whether Kids Get Too Much Praise or Not Enough," MSNBC, 2008 MSNBC Interactive, Mon., April 2, 2007, /www.msnbc.msn.com/id/17821247/ (retrieved March 14, 2008).

[21] Lilian Katz, "How Can We Strengthen Children's Self-Esteem?" KidSource Online, www.kidsource.com/kidsource/content2/Strengthen_Children_Self.html (retrieved July 30, 2005). See also Robert W. Reasoner, "Review of Self-Esteem Research," National Association for Self-Esteem, posted 2004, www.self-esteem-nase.org/research.php (retrieved March 15, 2008).

[22] Lisa Firestone, PhD, in "How to Tame Your Inner Critics," *Psychology Today,* posted April 11, 2016 (https://www.psychologytoday.com/blog/compassion-matters/201604/how-tame-your-inner-critic). See also Robert Firestone, Lisa Firestone, Joyce Catlett, and Pat Love (2002) *Conquer Your Critical Inner Voice: A Revolutionary Program to Counter Negative Thoughts and Live Free from Imagined Limitations* (Oakland, CA: New Harbinger Publications).

[23] Ibid.

[24] Ibid.

[25] Ibid.

[26] References with further characteristics of the scale: Rich Crandal, "The Measurement of Self-Esteem and Related Constructs," in J. P. Robinson and P. R. Shaver, eds., *Measures of Social Psychological Attitudes,* rev. ed. (Ann Arbor: ISR, 1973), pp. 80–82; M. Rosenberg, *Society and the Adolescent Self-Image* (Princeton, NJ: Princeton University Press, 1965) (Chapter 2 discusses construct validity); E. Silber and Jean Tippett, "Self-Esteem: Clinical Assessment and Measurement Validation," 16 *Psychological Reports,* pp. 1017–1071 (discusses multitrait-multimethod investigation using RSE), 1965; Ruth C. Wylie, *The Self-Concept,* rev. ed. (Lincoln, NE: University of Nebraska Press, 1974), especially pp. 180–189.

Chapter 3

[1] Carl Rogers, "What It Means to Become a Person," in Clark E. Moustakas, ed., *The Self: Explorations in Personal Growth* (New York: Harper & Row, 1956), pp. 195–211.

[2] Marie Lundquist, *Holding Back: Why We Hide the Truth About Ourselves* (New York: Harper & Row, 1988), p. 5.

[3] Ibid.

[4] Joseph Luft, *Group Process: Introduction to Group Dynamics* (Palo Alto, CA: National Press, 1970). See also Phillip C. Hanson, "The Johari Window: A Model for Soliciting and Giving Feedback," in *The 1973 Annual Handbook of Group Facilitators* (San Diego, CA: University Associates, 1973), pp. 114–119.

[5] Sam Keen and Anne V. Fox, *Telling Your Story: A Guide to Who You Are and Who You Can Be* (New York: Signet, 1973), pp. 22–24.

[6] This list is based on Marie Lindquist, *Holding Back*, p. 26.

[7] Maxwell Maltz, *Psycho-Cybernetics* (New York: Simon & Schuster, 1960), pp. 165–167.

[8] Roy F. Baumeister and Dianne M. Tice, "Four Selves, Two Motives and a Substitute Process Self-Regulation Model," in Roy F. Baumeister, ed., *Public Self and Private Self* (New York: Sprinter-Verlag, 1986), p. 63.

[9] Lisa Rosh and Lynn Offerman, "Be Yourself, but Carefully," *Harvard Business Review*, October 2013.

[10] Michal Kosinski, David Stillwell, and Thore Graepel "Private traits and Attributes Are Predictable from Digital Records of Human Behavior," from the *Proceedings of the National Academy of Sciences in the United States of America*. Edited by Kenneth Wachter, University of California, Berkeley, CA, and approved February 12, 2013 (received for review October 29, 2012).

[11] This list of disadvantages is based on Marie Lindquist, *Holding Back*, pp. 27–33. Also see John Powell, *Why Am I Afraid to Tell You Who I Am?* (Allen, TX: Argus Communications, 1969), pp. 77–83.

[12] The following five levels come from John Powell, *Why Am I Afraid to Tell You Who I Am?* (Allen, TX: Argus Communications, 1969, pp. 50–62; republished by Thomas More Association, 1990).

[13] John Powell, (1969, 1999), *Why Am I Afraid to Tell You Who I Am?* p. 58.

[14] This is a terrific oversimplification of Maslow's point. For further reading, see Abraham Maslow, "Lessons from the Peak Experiences," *Journal of Humanistic Psychology*, February 1962, Vol. 2, pp. 9–18. Also see Abraham Maslow, *Religions, Values, and Peak Experiences* (Columbus: Ohio State University Press, 1964).

[15] John Powell, *Why Am I Afraid to Tell You Who I Am?*, p. 62.

[16] Ibid., p. 77.

[17] Ibid., p. 80.

[18] These three advantages of "gut level" communications are based on John Powell, *Why Am I Afraid to Tell You Who I Am?*, pp. 79–85.

[19] R. D. Laing, *Knots* (New York: Perennial Press, 1972). See also R. D. Laing, H. Phillipson, and A. R. Lee, *Interpersonal Perception* (New York: Perennial Press, 1972).

[20] This list of fears is based in part on Susan Jeffers, *Feel the Fear and Do It Anyway* (New York: Ballantine, 1987), pp. 11–18, and on Marie Lindquist, *Holding Back*, p. 155.

[21] Dale Carnegie, *How to Stop Worrying and Start Living* (New York: Pocket Books, 1953).

[22] Virginia Satir, *Peoplemaking* (Palo Alto, CA: Science and Behavior Books, 1972), pp. 75–79.

[23] L. Miller, R. Archer, and J. Berg, "Eliciting Self-Disclosure," *Journal of Personality and Social Psychology*, vol. 44, 1983, pp. 1234–1244.

[24] Ibid.

Chapter 4

[1] Lucian Ghinda, "54 Sources of Happiness" Ghinda.com/blog/2010/54-Sources-of-Happiness/ (retrieved February 8, 2013).

[2] David G. Myers, "The Secret of Happiness," *Psychology Today*, 25 (July/August 1992), p. 38–45.

[3] Martin Seligman, *Learned Optimism: How to Change Your Mind and Your Life* (New York: Simon and Schuster, 1990).

[4] O'Connor Anahad, "Really? Optimism Reduces the Risk of Heart Disease," *New York Times*, www.nytimes.com (posted April 23, 2012).

[5] C. S. Carver, C. Pozo, S. D. Harris, V. Noriega, M. F. Scheier, D. S. Robinson, A. S. Ketcham, F. L. Moffat, Jr., and K. C. Clark, "How Coping Mediates the Effect of Optimism on Distress: A Study of Women with Early Stage Breast Cancer," *Journal of Personality and Social Psychology*, 65 (1993), pp. 375–390.

[6] William J. Chopik and Ed O'Brien, "Happy You, Healthy Me? Having a Happy Partner Is Independently Associated With Better Health in Oneself," in *Health Psychology*, 2017, Vol. 36, No. 1, 21–30.

[7] M. F. Scheier, J. K. Weintraub, C. S. Carver, "Coping with Stress: Divergent Strategies of Optimists and Pessimists," *Journal of Personality and Social Psychology*, 51 (1986), pp. 1258–1264.

[8] Andrew Steptoe, Samantha Dockray, and Jane Wardle (2009), Positive Affect and Psychobiological Processes Relevant to Health. *Journal of Personality*, 77: 1747–1776 .

[9] Diener, E., & Chan, M. Y. (2011). "Happy People Live Longer: Subjective Well-Being Contributes to Health and Longevity," *Applied Psychology: Health and Well-Being*, 3, 1–43.

[10] S. A. Everson, D. E. Goldberg, G. A. Kaplan, R. D. Cohen, E. Pukkala, J. Tuomilehto, and J. T. Salonen, "Hopelessness and Risk of Mortality and Incidence of Myocardial Infarction and Cancer," *Psychosomatic Medicine* 58 (1996), pp. 113–121.

[11] Carl Jung, *Psychological Types* (Princeton, NJ: Princeton University Press, 1971).

[12] Amanda Enayati, "Workplace happiness: What's the Secret?" CNN, Living. www.cnn.com (posted July 10, 2012).

[13] Huffington Post, "Happiness: Study Suggests Large Circle of Friends Is Key to Well-Being in Midlife." www.huffingtonpost.com (posted August 22, 2012, retrieved March 4, 2013).

[14] CIFAR Knowledge Circle, "Real-Life Friends Make You Happier." http://knowledgecircle.cifar.ca/exchange (Issue No. 3, February 13, 2013).

[15] Judith Rodin, "Aging and Health: Effects of the Sense of Control," *Science* 233 (1986), pp. 1271–1276.

[16] David G. Myers, "The Secret of Happiness," pp. 38–45.

[17] Michael W. Kraus, "The Happiness Chronicles I: The Dark Side to Happiness?" *Psychology Today.* Posted March 23, 2012. (https://www.psychologytoday.com/blog/under-the-influence/201203/the-happiness-chronicles-i-the-dark-side-happiness).

[18] Webster's New World Dictionary, (World Publishing Co., 1972), p. 513.

[19] Frances Merrit Stern, "Getting Good Feedback—and Giving Back in Kind," *Training/Human Resource Development,* April 1982, p. 34.

[20] Dow Scott and Stephen Taylor, "An Examination of Conflicting Findings on the Relationships between Job Satisfaction and Absenteeism: A Meta-Analysis," *Academy of Management Journal,* 28 (1985), pp. 599–612.

[21] Edwin A. Locke, "The Nature and Causes of Job Satisfaction," in *Handbook of Industrial and Organizational Psychology,* Marvin D. Dunnette, ed. (New York: John Wiley & Sons, 1983), pp. 1332–1334.

[22] Edward E. Lawler and Lyman W. Porter, "The Effect of Performance on Job Satisfaction," *Industrial Relations,* October 1967, pp. 20–28.

[23] Mark Ehrrant and Stephanie Nauman, "Organizational Citizenship Behavior in Work Groups: A Group Norms Approach," *Journal of Applied Psychology,* December 2004, pp. 960–972.

[24] *The Wall Street Journal,* January 12, 1988, p. 1, and Tom W. Smith, *Job Satisfaction in the United States* (April 2007) NORC/University of Chicago (retrieved March 2013 from www.news.uchicago.edu).

[25] Marcia A. Finkelstein, "Individualism/ Collectivism and Organizational Citizenship Behavior: An Integrative Framework," *Social Behavior and Personality,"* Vol. 40 (October 2012).

[26] Paul Thagard Ph.D., "What Are Values?" *Psychology Today,* https://www.psychologytoday.com/blog/hot-thought/201304/what-are-values (retrieved May 21, 2017).

[27] Daniel Yankelovich, "The New Psychological Contracts at Work," *Psychology Today,* 11 (May 1978), pp. 46–50.

[28] Daniel Yankelovich and John Immerwahr, *Work in the 21st Century* (Alexandria, VA: American Society for Personnel Administration, 1984), pp. 16–17.

[29] Best College Reviews, "Cheating in College: The Numbers and Research" http://www.bestcollegereviews.org/cheating/ (retrieved May 20, 2017).

[30] Schroeder, Peter, "Harvard Students Withdraw after Cheating in 'Intro to Congress' Course." The Hill. www.thehill.com (posted February 2, 2013).

[31] David Callahan, *The Cheating Culture: Why Americans Are Doing Wrong to Get Ahead* (Orlando, FL: Harcourt, 2004), pp. 44–107.

[32] Milton Rokeach, *The Nature of Human Values* (New York: Free Press, 1973), pp. 3–12.

[33] Leon Festinger, *A Theory of Cognitive Dissonance* (Stanford, CA: Stanford University Press, 1957). See also: Robert Levine, *The Power of Persuasion: How We're Bought and Sold* (New York: Wiley, 2003).

[34] Ibid. See also: E. Aronson, "Dissonance, Hypocrisy, and the Self-Concept" in E. Harmon-Jones and J. S. Mills, *Cognitive Dissonance Theory: Revival with Revisions and Controversies* (Washington, DC: American Psychological Association, 1998).

[35] John Tierney, "Go Ahead, Rationalize. Monkeys Do It, Too," *New York Times,* Science. http://www.nytimes.com/2007/11/06/science/06tier.html?_r=1&oref=slogin (posted November 6, 2007).

[36] Martin Seligman, *The Optimistic Child* (Boston, MA: Houghton Mifflin, 1995), pp. 219–223.

[37] Ibid.

[38] From *Time,* October 2, 1995, pp. 60–68. These suggestions are thoroughly revised but generally inspired by: Elwood N. Chapman, *Your Attitude Is Showing* (New York: MacMillan, 1991), pp. 23–25.

[39] Harry Levinson, "What Killed Bob Lyons?" *Harvard Business Review: On Human Relations* (New York: Harper & Row, 1979), pp. 332–333.

[40] Source: Maxwell Maltz, *Psycho-Cybernetics: A New Way to Get More Out of Life* (New York: Simon & Schuster, 1960), pp. 91–93.

[41] Louis Rath, Merrill Haron, and Sidney Simon, *Values and Teaching* (Columbus, OH: Charles Merrill Publishers, 1976).

Chapter 5

[1] Peter Drucker, *Management: Tasks, Responsibilities, Practices* (New York: Harper & Row, 1974), p. 455.

[2] C. H. Deutsch, "Why Women Walk Out on Jobs," *The New York Times,* April 29, 1990, p. F27.

[3] Spencer Rathus and Jeffrey Nevid, *Adjustment and Growth: The Challenges of Life,* 7th ed. (New York: Harcourt Brace College Publishers, 1999).

[4] Edward Hoffman, *The Right to Be Human: A Biography of Abraham Maslow* (Los Angeles: Jeremy P. Tarcher, 1988), p. 154. See also Laurie Pawlik-Kienlen, "Self-Actualization in Action: How to Apply Maslow's Hierarchy of Needs to Your Life," *Suite101.com,* posted March 21, 2007, http://psychology.suite101.com/article.cfm/fulfill_your_potential (retrieved May 1, 2008).

[5] Abraham Maslow, *Motivation and Personality* (New York: Harper & Row, 1970), pp. 46–65.

[6] Robert Tanner, "Motivation—Applying Maslow's Hierarchy of Needs Theory," https://managementisajourney.com/motivation-applying-maslows-hierarchy-of-needs-theory/ (posted January 2, 2017; retrieved May 25, 2017).

[7] Richard M. Steers and Lyman Porter, *Motivation and Work Behavior,* 3rd ed. (New York: McGraw-Hill, 1983), pp. 3–5.

[8] Clayton Alderfer, *Existence, Relatedness, & Growth* (New York: Free Press, 1972), pp. 12–26.

[9] See www.netmba.com/mgmt/ob/motivation/erg. Accessed May 1, 2008.

[10] David C. McClelland, *Human Motivation* (Glenview, IL: Scott, Foresman, 1985).

[11] David C. McClelland and David Burnham, "Power Is the Great Motivator," *Harvard Business Review* 54 (March–April 1976), pp. 100–110.

[12] Ibid., pp. 102–110.

[13] S. M. Klein and R. R. Ritti, *Understanding Organizational Behavior* (Boston, MA: Kent Publishing, 1984), pp. 256–258.

[14] A. Kukla, "Foundations of an Attributional Theory of Performance," *Psychological Review,* 79 (1972), pp. 454–470.

[15] David C. McClelland, *Human Motivation.* See also R. B. McCall, "Academic Underachievers," *Current Directions in Psychological Science* 3 (1994), pp. 15–19.

[16] Sibin Wu and Grace K. Dagher, Management Research News, "Need for Achievement, Business Goals, and Entrepreneurial Persistence," *Management Research News* 30(12): 928–941. November 2007 (https://www.researchgate.net/publication/241674423_Need_for_achievement_business_goals_and_entrepreneurial_persistence, retrieved May 25, 2017).

[17] Frederick Herzberg, "One More Time: How Do You Motivate Employees?" *Harvard Business Review,* Winter 1979, pp. 101–121. See also Frederick Herzberg, *Work and the Nature of Man* (New York: Harper & Row, 1966).

[18] Frederick Herzberg, "Workers' Needs: The Same Around the World," *Industry Week,* September 21, 1987, pp. 29–31.

[19] J. R. Hackman and Gene Oldman, *Work Redesign* (Reading, MA: Addison-Wesley, 1980).

[20] Ibid.

[21] Andrzej Marczewski, (April 2012). *Gamification: A Simple Introduction* (1st ed.). p. 3. ISBN 978-1-4717-9866-5. https://trends.google.com/trends/explore?date=all&q=gamification, retrieved May 28, 2017.

[22] Jane McGonigal, *Reality Is Broken: Why Games Make Us Better and How They Can Change the World* (New York: Penguin Books, 2011).

[23] Brian Burke, "How Gamification Motivates the Masses," *Forbes,* https://www.forbes.com/sites/gartnergroup/2014/04/10/how-gamification-motivates-the-masses/#7bf7beb25c04, retrieved May 28, 2017. http://www.chicagotribune.com/lifestyles/ct-tribu-play-at-work-story-20111010-story.html, retrieved May 28, 2017.

[24] http://www.enterprise-gamification.com/mediawiki/index.php?title=Target_-_Checkout_Process_at_the_Cashier, retrieved June 4, 2017.

[25] Jane McGonigal, *Reality Is Broken: Why Games Make Us Better and How They Can Change the World* (New York: Penguin Books, 2011).

[26] http://www.gartner.com/technology/research/gamification/, retrieved May 28, 2017.

[27] Victor H. Vroom, *Work and Motivation* (New York: John Wiley & Sons, 1964), pp. 170–174.

[28] Hina Raheel, "Leadership and Motivation: The Effective Application of Expectancy Theory," *Journal of Pioneering Medical Sciences Blog,* August 17, 2013. http://blogs.jpmsonline.com/2013/08/17/leadership-and-motivation-the-effective-application-of-expectancy-theory/.

[29] Barry M. Staw, *Intrinsic and Extrinsic Motivation* (New York: John Wiley & Sons, 1976). See also Uco J. Wiersma, "The Effects of Extrinsic Rewards in Intrinsic Motivation," *Journal of Occupational and Organizational Psychology* 65 (1992), pp. 101–114.

[30] B. F. Skinner, *Beyond Freedom and Dignity* (New York: Alfred A. Knopf, 1971).

[31] Eric Berne, *Games People Play* (New York: Grove Press, 1964), pp. 34–37.

[32] Michael LeBoeuf, *The Greatest Management Principle in the World* (New York: Berkeley Publishing, 1987), pp. 12–27.

[33] B. F. Skinner, *Beyond Freedom and Dignity,* pp. 17–48.

[34] R. A. Katzell and D. E. Thompson, "Work Motivation: Theory and Practice," *American Psychologist* 45 (1990), pp. 144–153.

[35] Leong Teen Wei and Rashad Yazdanifard, "The impact of Positive Reinforcement on Employees' Performance in Organizations," *American Journal of Industrial and Business Management,* 2014, 4, 9–12 Published Online January 2014 (http://www.scirp.org/journal/ajibm) http://dx.doi.org/10.4236/ajibm.2014.41002 (retrieved May 25, 2017).

[36] Jack Falvey, "To Raise Productivity, Try Saying Thank You," *The Wall Street Journal,* December 6, 1982, p. 26.

[37] Joel Brockner, *Self-Esteem at Work: Research, Theory, and Practice* (Lexington, MA: Lexington Books, 1988), pp. 159–161, 192. See also Matthew McKay and Patrick Fanning, *Self-Esteem* (Oakland, CA: New Harbinger Publication, 1987), pp. 159–189.

Chapter 6

[1] Frank K. Sonnenberg, "Barriers to Communication," *Journal of Business Strategy* 11 (July/August 1990), pp. 56–58.

[2] Sandra Hagevik, "Just Listening," *Journal of Environmental Health* 62 (July 1999), pp. 26–32.

[3] Sonnenberg (1990), "Barriers to Communication," p. 56.

[4] Lyle Sussman and Paul D. Krivonos, *Communication for Supervisors and Managers* (Easton, PA: Alfred Publishing Company, 1979), pp. 66–68.

[5] Anthony Allesandra, quoted in *The Power of Listening,* Revised Edition (firm) (CRM Films, 1987).

[6] John Stewart and Carole Logan, *Together: Communicating Interpersonally* (New York: McGraw-Hill, 1993), pp. 246–247.

[7] Edward T. Hall, *The Silent Language* (Greenwich, CT: Fawcett Books, 1959), pp. 51–53.

[8] Albert Mehrabian, *Nonverbal Communication* (Chicago, IL: Aldine-Atherton Company, 1972), pp. 23–38.

[9] "The Anatomy of a Message," *Ford's Insider* (1981), pp. 4–9.

[10] Paul Ekman and Wallace V. Friesan, "Hand Movements," *Journal of Communication* 22 (1972), pp. 353–358.

[11] Based on Edward T. Hall, "Proxemics: A Study of Man's Spatial Relationships," from *Man's Image in Medicine and Anthropology* (New York: International Universities Press, 1963).

[12] William M. Pride and O. Jeff Harris, "Psychological Barriers in the Upward Flow of Communication," *Atlanta Economic Review* 21 (March 1971), pp. 30–32. See also "Organization Charts as a Management Tool," http://management.about.com/cs/generalmanagement/a/orgcharts_2.htm. Accessed May 3, 2008.

[13] Keith Davis, "Management Communication and the Grapevine," *Harvard Business Review* 31 (September–October 1953), pp. 45–47.

[14] O. Jeff Harris and Sandra J. Hartman, *Human Behavior at Work* (New York: West Publishing Company, 1992), pp. 270–271.

[15] Karan Ronin, "5 Common Body Language Mistakes on International Business Trips," January 22, 2014. http://www.executive-impressions.com/blog/5-body-language-mistakes-international-business-trips.

[16] Edward T. Hall, "How Cultures Collide," *Psychology Today* 10 (July 1976), pp. 66–74. See also Edward T. Hall, *Beyond Culture* (Garden City, NY: Doubleday, 1976).

[17] Based on Dulek, Fielden, and Hill, "International Communication," pp. 21–22.

Chapter 7

[1] Jon L. Pierce and John Newstrom, *Leaders and the Leadership Process* (Burr Ridge, IL: McGraw-Hill Irwin, 2008), pp. 158–163.

[2] G. E. Myers and M. T. Myers, *The Dynamics of Human Communication* (New York: McGraw-Hill, 1973), pp. 125–127.

[3] V. W. Tuchman, "Developmental Sequences in Small Groups," *Psychological Bulletin* 63 (May 1965), pp. 384–399.

[4] Ibid., pp. 386–389. See also A. C. Kowitz and T. J. Knutson, *Decision-Making in Small Groups: The Search for Alternatives* (Boston, MA: Allyn & Bacon, 1980).

[5] Feldman, "Development and Enforcement of Group Norms," pp. 49–53.

[6] https://highered.mheducation.com/sites/dl/free/0073010189/228359/groupthink2.html (From the First Edition of *A First Look at Communication Theory* by Em Griffin, © 1991, McGraw-Hill, Inc.)

[7] Robert R. Blake and Jane S. Mouton, "Don't Let Group Norms Stifle Creativity," *Personnel* 62 (August 1985), pp. 28–33.

[8] J. Richard Hackman and Charles G. Morris, "Improving Group Performance Effectiveness," in *Advances in Experimental Social Psychology,* ed. Leonard Berkowitz (New York: Academic Press, 1975), p. 345.

[9] Peter Piven, "Increasing Your Project Team's Effectiveness." Coxe Leadership Group, 2008. www.coxegroup.com/articles/effectiveness.html (retrieved May 4, 2008).

[10] These three categories are based on Dr. Marlin S. Potash, *Hidden Agendas* (New York: Dell Publishing, 1990), p. 56. See also Roberta Shaler, "The Queen and Her Bobble-Heads: Uncovering 'Hidden' Agendas," http://hodu.com/queen.shtml (retrieved May 4, 2008).

[11] Richard L. Daft and Dorothy Marcic, *Understanding Management,* 5th ed. (Mason, OH: Thompson South-Western, 2006), pp. 412–413.

[12] Warren Bennis and Burt Nanus, *Leaders: The Strategies for Taking Charge* (New York: Harper & Row, 1986), pp. 19–26.

[13] Rosabeth Moss Kanter, "The New Management Work," *Harvard Business Review,* November/December 1989, pp. 85–92.

[14] Robert R. Blake and Jane S. Mouton, "A Comparative Analysis of Situationalism and 9.9 Management by Principle," *Organizational Dynamics,* Spring 1982, pp. 20–43.

[15] Afsaneh Nahavandi, *The Art and Science of Leadership,* 4th ed. (Upper Saddle River, NJ: Prentice Hall, 2007), pp. 99–112.

[16] Gary A. Yukl and C. M. Falbe, "The Importance of Different Power Sources in Downward and Lateral Relations," *Journal of Applied Psychology* 76 (1991), pp. 416–423. See also Gary Yukl, *Leadership in Organizations,* 6th ed. (Upper Saddle River, NJ: Prentice Hall, 2005).

[17] Nahavandi, *Art and Science of Leadership,* pp. 184–190. See also John P. Kotter, *John P. Kotter on What Leaders Really Do* (Boston, MA: Harvard Business Review Books, 1999), pp. 143–172.

[18] Harvey Robbins and Michael Finley, *The New WHY TEAMS DON'T WORK: What Goes Wrong and How to Make It Right* (San Francisco, CA: Berret-Kohler Publishers 2000). See also Rosemary Batt, "Work Organization, Technology and Performance in Customer Service and Sales," *Industrial and Labor Relations Review* 52 (July 1999), pp. 539–563 (retrieved July 15, 2005), http://www.hrzone.com/articles/teams_tqm_or_taylorism.html. See also "Work Team Skills and Productivity," Center for Collaborative Organizations (Center for the Study of Work Teams), University of North Texas (retrieved May 18, 2008). http://www.workteams.unt.edu/research.htm.

[19] These defining factors are based on E. Thomas Moran and J. Fredericks Volkwein, "The Cultural Approach to the Formation of Organizational Climate," *Human Relations,* January 1992, p. 20.

[20] Stewart R. Segall, "Reflections of Your Management Style," *Supervisory Management* 36 (February 1991), pp. 1–2.

[21] E. Thomas Moran and J. Fredericks Volwein, pp. 22–47. See also: R. M. Guion, "A Note on Organizational Climate," *Organizational Behavior and Human Performance* 9 (1973), pp. 120–125.

[22] Sharon L. Kubiak et al., "Making People an Organization's Most Important Resource," *Business* 40 (October–December 1990), p. 33.

[23] For more on stories in corporate cultures, see Thomas J. Peters and Nancy K. Austin, A *Passion for Excellence* (New York: Random House, 1985), pp. 278–293.

[24] Paul Hellman (1992), op. cit., p. 63.

[25] Edgar Schein, "How Founders/Leaders Embed and Transmit Culture" (retrieved July 12, 2005) http://www.tnellen.com/ted/tc/schein.html. See also: Edgar Schein, *Organizational Culture and Leadership,* 3rd ed. (New York, Jossey-Bass, 2004).

[26] These qualities of the "New Corporate Culture" are based in part on: Joseph D. O'Brian, "The 'New Corporate Culture': Mainly Just Common Sense," *Supervisory Management* 39 (January 1992), p. 9.

[27] Marshall Sashkin and Richard L. Williams, "Does Fairness Make a Difference?" *Organizational Dynamics* 19 (Autumn 1990), pp. 56–58.

[28] For information on the psychological contract, see Edgar Schein, *Organizational Psychology* (Englewood Cliffs, NJ: Prentice Hall, 1980).

Chapter 8

[1] Daniel Goleman, Paul Kaufman, and Michael Ray, *The Creative Spirit* (New York: Dutton, 1992), pp. 72–79.

[2] Daniel Goleman, *Emotional Intelligence* (New York: Bantam Books, 1995), p. 34.

[3] Goleman, *Emotional Intelligence,* pp. 8, 291–296.

[4] Allen Farnham, "Are You Smart Enough to Keep Your Job?" *Fortune,* January 15, 1996, pp. 34–42. See also "Leading by Feel: Be Realistic," *Harvard Business Review,* January 2004, p. 28.

[5] Goleman, *Working with Emotional Intelligence,* pp. 26–28.

[6] Robert Sternberg, *Successful Intelligence* (New York: Simon & Schuster, 1996), also retold in Daniel Goleman, *Working with Emotional Intelligence* (New York: Bantam Books, 1998), p. 22.

[7] Ibid., pp. 24–27.

[8] Mark Daniel, *Self-Scoring Emotional Intelligence Tests* (New York: Sterling Publishing, 2000), pp. 1–2.

[9] Daniel Goleman, Richard Boyatzis, and Annie McKee, *Primal Leadership: Realizing the Power of Emotional Intelligence* (Boston: Harvard Business School Publishing, 2002). pp. 105–109.

[10] Richard E. Boyatzis, "Developing Emotional Intelligence Competencies," in Joseph Ciarrochi and John Mayer (eds.), *Applying Emotional Intelligence* (New York: Psychology Press, 2007), pp. 29–30.

[11] Cf. Boyatzis, pp. 30–31.

[12] Goldman, Boyatzis, and McKee, *Primal Leadership,* pp. 107–118.

[13] Matthew McKay, Martha Davis, and Patrick Fanning, *Thoughts and Feelings: Taking Control of Your Moods and Your Life* (Oakland, CA: New Harbinger Publications, 2007), pp. 233–234.

[14] These four characteristics of anger are based on Gilian Butler and Tony Hope, *Managing Your Mind,* 2nd ed. (New York: Oxford University Press, 2007), pp. 171–173.

[15] Daniel Goleman, *Emotional Intelligence* (New York: Bantam Books, 1995), p. 65.

[16] These steps were drawn in part from Butler and Hope, *Managing Your Mind,* p. 178.

[17] Jim Tamm, *Radical Collaboration* (New York: HarperCollins, 2005), pp. 123–159.

[18] Shirzad Chamine, "Positive Intelligence," http://www.positiveintelligence.com/ (retrieved June 2, 2017).

[19] Marina Krakovsky, "Shirzad Chamine: How to Defeat Your Internal Saboteurs," Stanford Graduate School of Business, posted September 9, 2013, https://www.gsb.stanford.edu/insights/shirzad-chamine-how-defeat-your-internal-saboteurs (retrieved June 2, 2017).

[20] "Positive Intelligence and PQ," Sources of Insight, http://sourcesofinsight.com/positive-intelligence-and-pq/ (posted 2012, retrieved June 2, 2017).

[21] Lydia Dishman, "How to Quiet the Negative Thoughts That Are Killing Your Career," *Fast Company,* posted June 12, 2012, https://www.fastcompany.com/1839905/how-quiet-negative-thoughts-are-killing-your-career (retrieved June 2, 2017).

[22] Muriel James and Dorothy Jongeward, *Born to Win* (Reading, MA: Addison-Wesley, 1973), op. cit., pp. 69–70.

[23] Gerald M. Goldhaber and Marylynn Goldhaber, *Transactional Analysis* (Boston, MA: Allyn & Bacon, 1976), p. 180.

[24] Maurice F. Villere, Thomas S. O'Connor, and William J. Quain, "Games Nobody Wins: Transactional Analysis for the Hospitality Industry," *The Cornell University H.R.A. Quarterly* 24 (November 1983), p. 72.

[25] "Of Frogs and Princes," http://frogsandprinces.dawntreader.net/games.html, accessed July 12, 2005. See also Ian Stewart and Vann Joines, *TA Today: A New Introduction to Transactional Analysis* (Chapel Hill, NC: Lifespace Publishing, 1991).

[26] Villere, O'Connor, and Quain, "Games Nobody Wins," p. 75.

[27] This example is adapted from Linda L. Phillips, *Film Guide for "Transactional Analysis"* (New York: McGraw-Hill, Films, 1977), p. 6.

[28] Villere, O'Connor, and Quain, "Games Nobody Wins," p. 77.

Chapter 9

[1] Robert M. Fulmer, *Practical Human Relations* (Homewood, IL: Richard Irwin Company, 1983), pp. 292–293.

[2] Edward A. Charlesworth and Ronald G. Nathan, *Stress Management: A Comprehensive Guide to Wellness* (New York: Ballantine Books, 1985), pp. 178–181.

[3] Shad Helmstetter, *You Can Excel in Times of Change* (New York: Simon & Schuster, 1991), p. 46.

[4] Bernadine Kreis and Alice Pattie, *Up from Grief: Patterns of Recovery* (New York: The Seabury Press, 1969), pp. 11–23.

[5] William Bridges, *Transitions: Making Sense of Life's Changes* (Reading, MA: Addison-Wesley, 1980), pp. 90–99.

[6] Gail Sheehy, *Pathfinders: Overcoming the Crises of Adult Life and Finding Your Own Path to Well-Being* (New York: William Morrow, 1981), pp. 313–314.

[7] Bridges, *Transitions,* p. 112.

[8] Kreis and Pattie, *Up from Grief,* p. 36.

[9] L. John Mason, *Stress Passages: Surviving Life's Transitions Gracefully* (Berkeley, CA: Celestial Arts, 1988), pp. 230–232.

[10] These six steps are based on Helmstetter, *You Can Excel in Times of Change,* pp. 145–180.

[11] Prosci, "What Is Change Management?" https://www.prosci.com/change-management/what-is-change-management (retrieved June 2, 2017).

[12] John Paul Kotter, *Leading Change* (Cambridge, MA: Harvard Review Press, 1996, 2012).

[13] Kurt Lewin, *Field Theory and Social Science* (New York: Harper and Row, 1964), especially Chapters 9 and 10.

[14] Ibid., p. 10.

[15] Leonard D. Goodstein and W. Warner Burke, "Creating Successful Organizational Change," *Organizational Dynamics* 19 (Spring 1991), pp. 9–11.

[16] Ibid., p. 10.

[17] Peter B. Vaill, *Learning as a Way of Being: Strategies for Surviving in a World of Permanent White Water* (San Francisco: Jossey-Bass, 1996), pp. 47–78.

[18] Kurt Lewin, "Group Decisions and Social Change," in *Readings in Social Psychology* (New York: Holt, Rinehart & Winston, 1952); and Kurt Lewin, "Fronteerism Group Dynamics: Concept, Method, and Reality in Social Science," *Human Relations* 1 (1974), pp. 5–41.

[19] Ibid.

[20] James Brian Quinn, *Strategies for Change: Logical Incrementalism* (Homewood, IL: Richard Irwin, 1980). Cf. "Logical Incrementalism," www.12manage.com/description_logical_incrementalism.html (accessed May 18, 2008).

[21] James Brian Quinn, "Strategic Change: 'Logical Incrementalism,'" *Sloan Management Review* 30 (Summer 1989), pp. 45–59.

[22] For more information on the role of the leader in organizational change, see David A. Nadir and Michael L. Tushman, "Beyond the Charismatic Leader: Leadership and Organizational Change," *California Management Review* 32 (Winter 1990), pp. 77–97.

[23] Brendan McGuigan, "What Is Kaizen?" published by Conjecture Corporation, November 29, 2012 (accessed March 17,

2013 at www.wisegeek.org). Norman Bodek, *How to Do Kaizen: A New Path to Innovation—Empowering Everyone to be a Problem Solver* (Vancouver, WA, US: PCS Press, 2010). https://en.wikipedia.org/wiki/Kaizen (accessed 3/17/2013).

[24] Stephen P. Robbins and Tim A. Judge, *Organizational Behavior: Concepts, Controversies, and Applications* (Englewood Cliffs, NJ: Prentice Hall, 2007), pp. 665–691.

[25] Harry Levinson, "Easing the Pain of Personal Loss," *Harvard Business Review* 50 (September–October 1972), pp. 80–88.

Chapter 10

[1] Ross L. Mooney, "Groundwork for Creative Research," in Clark E. Moustakas (ed.), *The Self: Explorations in Personal Growth* (New York: Harper & Row, 1956), p. 264.

[2] Mihalyi Csikszentmihalyi, *Creativity: Flow and the Psychology of Discovery and Invention* (New York: HarperCollins Publishers, 1996).

[3] "On Creativity," *Omni* 11 (April 1989), pp. 112–119.

[4] L. Terman and M. H. Oden, *Genetic Studies of Genius:* Vol. 5. *The Gifted Group at Mid-Life* (Stanford, CA: Stanford University Press, 1959).

[5] Arthur Koestler, *The Act of Creation* (New York: Macmillan, 1964), pp. 124–145.

[6] Jacob Bronowski, *The Ascent of Man* (Boston, MA: Little, Brown, 1973), pp. 118–119.

[7] Ibid., pp. 137–141.

[8] Edward Hoffman, *The Right to Be Human: A Biography of Abraham Maslow* (Los Angeles: Jeremy P. Tarcher, 1988), p. 238.

[9] James L. Adams, *Conceptual Blockbusting: A Guide to Better Ideas* (Cambridge, MA: Perseus Books, 2001), pp. 25–33.

[10] From Samuel Wood and Ellen Wood, *The World of Psychology,* 3rd ed. (Needham Heights, MA: Allyn & Bacon, 1999).

[11] Graham Wallas, *The Art of Thought* (Orlando, FL: Harcourt Brace, 1926).

[12] Ibid.

[13] Roger von Oech, *A Whack on the Side of the Head: How You Can Be More Creative* (New York: Business Plus, 2008), p. 142.

[14] Graham Wallas, *The Art of Thought.* (London: Jonathan Cape, 1926), pp. 80–81.

[15] Daniel Goleman, Paul Kaufman, and Michael Ray, *The Creative Spirit* (New York: Dutton, 1992).

[16] L. Juang, D. V. Krasikova, and D. Liu. (2016). "I Can Do it, So Can You: The Role of Leader Creative Self-Efficacy in Facilitating Follower Creativity." *Organizational Behavior and Human Decision Processes,* 132, 49–62. DOI: 10.1016/j.obhdp.2015.12.002.

[17] Siân Harrington, "Exclusive: Employees Want Financial Rewards for Innovation but Employers Are Slow on the Uptake," *HR Magazine,* July 29, 2010, http://www.hrmagazine.co.uk/article-details/exclusive-employees-want-financial-rewards-for-innovation-but-employers-are-slow-on-the-uptake.

[18] Laurie Tarkan, "Work Hard, Play Harder: Fun at Work Boosts Creativity, Productivity," FoxNews.com, Health @ Work (http://www.foxnews.com/health September 15, 2012; accessed March 18, 2013).

[19] For a full discussion of the brainstorming process, see Adams, *Conceptual Blockbusting,* pp. 160–173.

[20] Teresa M. Amabile, "The Motivation to Be Creative," in Scott G. Isaaksen (ed.), *Frontiers of Creativity Research* (Buffalo, NY: Bearly Press, 1987), pp. 229–230.

[21] Ibid.

[22] Cleese, "And Now for Something Completely Different," p. 50.

[23] Parachin, "Seven Ways to Fire Up Your Creativity," pp. 3–4.

[24] von Oech, *A Whack on the Side of the Head,* p. 21.

[25] Jimmy Calano and Jeff Salzman, "Ten Ways to Fire Up Your Creativity," *Working Woman* 14, July 1989, pp. 94–95.

[26] Ibid., p. 95.

[27] von Oech, *A Whack on the Side of the Head,* p. 93.

[28] Teresa Amabile, *The Social Psychology of Creativity* (New York: Springer-Verlag, 1983).

[29] Robert Epstein, "Capturing Creativity," *Psychology Today,* July/August 1996, pp. 29, 41–43, 75–78.

[30] Reprinted by permission of Warner Books/New York. From Roger von Oech, *A Whack on the Side of the Head: How You Can Be More Creative* (New York: Business Plus, 2008).

[31] Bob Eberle, "Scamper On," in *Gifted Education: A Resource Guide for Teachers,* Ministry of Education, British Columbia, Canada, 1987, posted 2007, www.bced.gov.bc.ca/specialed/gifted/process.htm (retrieved May 31, 2008).

[32] Epstein, "*Capturing Creativity,*" p. 3.

[33] 3M Corporation, "Post-it, the Whole Story," www.mmm.com/us/office/postit/pastpresent/history_ws.html (retrieved June 1, 2008).

Chapter 11

[1] Coalition of Services Industries, Jobs Across America: Services Lead Employment 2016, https://servicescoalition.org/jobs/ (retrieved June 20, 2016).

[2] Peter Coffee, "Service Economy Brings New Technology Demands," *E-Week.Com,* December 13, 2004, pp. 1–3, www.eweek.com (retrieved August 20, 2008).

[3] L. L. Putnam and M. S. Poole, "Conflict and Negotiation," in F. M. Jablin, L. L. Putnam, K. H. Roberts, and L. W. Porter (eds.), *Handbook of Organizational Communication: An Interdisciplinary Perspective* (Newbury Park, CA: Sage Publications, 1987), pp. 549–589.

[4] Stephen P. Robbins, *Organizational Behavior: Concepts, Controversies, and Applications* (Englewood Cliffs, NJ: Prentice Hall, 1993), p. 445.

[5] Much of the material on sources of conflict is adapted from John Stewart and Carole Logan, *Together: Communicating Interpersonally* (New York: McGraw-Hill, 1993), pp. 347–377.

[6] These questions are excerpted and adapted from Stephen Goldberg, Eric Green, and Frank Sander, *Dispute Resolution* (Boston, MA: Little, Brown, and Company, 1985), pp. 545–550. See also Howard Raiffa, *The Art and Science of Negotiation* (Cambridge, MA: Belknap Press, 1982), pp. 14–22.

[7] Edward Glassman, "Selling Your Ideas to Management," *Supervisory Management* 36 (October 1991), p. 9.

[8] Barry L. Reece and Rhonda Brandt, *Effective Human Relations in Organizations* (Boston, MA: Houghton Mifflin Company, 2005), pp. 313–314.

[9] Gini Graham Scott, *Resolving Conflict with Others and Within Yourself* (Oakland, CA: New Harbinger Publications, 1990), p. 159.

[10] Edward Glassman, "Understanding and Supervising Low Conformers," *Supervisory Management* 35 (May 1990), p. 10.

[11] Ibid.

[12] This section is adapted from Teresa Brady, "When a Jealous Co-Worker Is Giving You a Hard Time," *Supervisory Management* 36 (June 1991), p. 5.

[13] Robert M. Bramson, *Coping with Difficult People* (Garden City, NY: Anchor Press, 1981), p. 70.

[14] Ibid., pp. 71–72.

[15] Adapted from ibid., pp. 72–76.

[16] Graham Scott, *Resolving Conflict with Others and Within Yourself,* pp. 160–161.

[17] Joseph T. Straub, "Dealing with Complainers, Whiners, and General Malcontents," *Supervisory Management* 37 (July 1992), pp. 1–2.

[18] Adapted from ibid., pp. 161–163.

[19] Reece and Brandt, *Effective Human Relations in Organizations,* pp. 313–314.

[20] Andrew E. Schwartz, "How to Handle Conflict Between Employees," *Supervisory Management* 37 (June 1992), p. 9.

Chapter 12

[1] Hans Selye, "The Stress Concept Today," in I. I. Kutash et al. (eds.), *Handbook on Stress and Anxiety* (San Francisco, CA: Jossey-Bass, 1980).

[2] Ibid.

[3] Allen Kanner, James Coyne, Catherine Schaefer, and Richard Lazarus, "A Comparison of Two Models of Stress Measurement: Daily Hassles and Uplifts Versus Major Life Events," *Journal of Behavioral Medicine* 4 (1981), pp. 1–39.

[4] Deborah L. Plummer and Steve Slane, "Patterns of Coping in Racially Stressful Situations," *Journal of Black Psychology* 22 (1996), pp. 302–315. See also American Psychological Association Press Release, "Racial Discrimination Has Different Mental Health Effects on Asians Depending on Ethnic Identity, Age and Birthplace, Study Shows," posted May 8, 2008, www.apa.org/releases/asianhealth0508.html (retrieved June 1, 2008).

[5] Spencer Rathus, *Essentials of Psychology* (Fort Worth, TX: Harcourt College Publishers, Inc., 2001), Chapter 11.

[6] Daniel Sanders, "Researchers Find Out Why Some Stress Is Good for You," Berkeley News, http://news.berkeley.edu/2013/04/16/researchers-find-out-why-some-stress-is-good-for-you/Posted April 16, 2013. Retrieved June 20, 2017.

[7] Ibid.

[8] Albert Ellis and R. A. Harper, *A New Guide to Rational Living* (Hollywood, CA: Wilshire, 1975). See also Albert Ellis, "The Basic Clinical Theory of Rational-Emotive Therapy," in A. Ellis and R. Grieger (eds.), *Handbook of Rational-Emotive Therapy* (New York: Springer, 1977); Albert Ellis, "Cognition and Affect in Emotional Disturbance," *American Psychologist* 40 (1985), pp. 471–472; and Albert Ellis, "The Impossibility of Achieving Consistently Good Mental Health," *American Psychologist* 42 (1987), pp. 364–375.

[9] The Albert Ellis Institute, http://albertellis.org/.

[10] Kay Devine, Trish Reay, Linda Stainton, and Ruth Collins-Nakai, "Downsizing Outcomes: Better a Victim Than a Survivor?" *Human Resource Management,* Summer 2003, pp. 109–124, www.gpworldwide.com/quick/oct2003/art5.asp (retrieved July 18, 2005). See also Joanne Sujansky, "The ABC's of Employee Trust," KeyGroup.com, www.keygrp.com/articles/article-abcoftrust.html (retrieved July 18, 2005); and "Stress in the Workplace," TheStressClinic.com, www.thestressclinic.com/news/Display.asp?ArticleName=StressAtWork (retrieved July 18, 2005).

[11] Ibid.

[12] Ibid.

[13] Ibid. See also Salvatore Maddi, "The Story of Hardiness: Twenty Years of Theorizing, Research, and Practice," *Consulting Psychology Journal: Practice and Research* 51 (2002), pp. 83–94. See also American Psychological Association Help Center, "The Road to Resilience" and "Resilience in a Time of War," www.apahelpcenter.org/featuredtopics/feature.php?id=6 (retrieved May 29, 2008).

[14] Hans Selye, *The Stress of Life* (rev. ed.) (New York: McGraw-Hill, 1976). See also Hans Selye, *Stress Without Distress* (New York: Harper & Rowe, 1974).

[15] Suzanne C. Segerstrom and Gregory E. Miller, "Psychological Stress and the Human Immune System: A Meta-Analytic Study of 30 Years of Inquiry," *Psychological Bulletin* 130 (4), American Psychological Association, posted July 4, 2004, www.apa.org/releases/stress_immune.html (retrieved July 19, 2005).

[16] Jamie Talan, "Stress Can Strike Back 20 Years Later," *The Bend Bulletin/Newsday,* Bend, OR (November 26, 1993).

[17] James Brodzinski, Robert Scherer, and Karen Goyer, "Workplace Stress," *Personnel Administrator,* July 1989. See also Nick Nykodym and Katie George, "Stress Busting on the Job," *Personnel,* July, 1989, pp. 56–59.

[18] Ibid. See also Robert Epstein, "Stress Busters," *Psychology Today,* March/April, 2000; and "Workplace Stress: It's Enough to Make Your Employees Sick," in *Success Performance Solutions,* www.super-solutions.com/RisingHealthCareCost_workplacestress.asp (retrieved June 1, 2008).

[19] Ibid. See also Ken Frenke, "Stress: An Economic Issue," Money Matters Online, Crown.Org., posted June, 2005, www.crown.org/newsletter/default.asp?issue=328&articleid=396 (retrieved July 19, 2005).

[20] Shelley Taylor, Lisa G. Aspinwall, Traci A. Giuliano, Gayle A. Dakof, Kathleen K. Reardon, "Storytelling and Coping with Stressful Events," *Journal of Applied Social Psychology* 23 (1993), pp. 703–733.

[21] Shari Caudron, "Humor Is Healthy in the Workplace," *Personnel Journal,* 1992, p. 71. See also C. W. Metcalf and Roma Felible, "Humor: An Antidote for Terminal Professionalism," *Industry Week,* July 20, 1992; Nykodym and George, "Stress Busting on the Job"; and Richard Maturi, "Stress Can Be Beaten," *Industry Week,* July 20, 1992.

[22] Spencer Rathus, *Essentials of Psychology.*

[23] Nykodym and George, "Stress Busting on the Job." See also Richard Maturi, "Stress Can Be Beaten," and Brodzinski, Scherer, and Goyer, "Workplace Stress."

[24] Edwin Locke, *A Guide to Effective Study* (New York: Springer Publishing Company, 1975). See also David Burns, M.D., *Ten Days to Self-Esteem* (New York: Quill-William Morrow, 1993).

Chapter 13

[1] Don Peppers and Martha Rogers, "Customers Don't Grow on Trees," *Fast Company Magazine,* July 2005, p. 25.

[2] Michael LeBoeuf, *How to Win Customers and Keep Them for Life* (New York: Putnam, 1987), pp. 38–40.

[3] Ibid., pp. 39–40.

[4] Matt Mansfield, *Small Business Trends,* "Customer Retention Statistics—The Ultimate Collection for Small Business" https://smallbiztrends.com/2016/10/customer-retention-statistics.html (posted October 25, 2016; retrieved June 20, 2017).

[5] Michael Roennevig, *AZCentral,* "The Top Reasons Why Customers Give Repeat Business," http://yourbusiness.azcentral.com/top-reasons-customers-give-repeat-business-7098.html (retrieved June 20, 2017).

[6] John Tschohl, "Customer Service Importance," *Supervision,* February 1991, p. 9.

[7] Ibid., pp. 9–11.

[8] Jerry Plymire, "Complaints as Opportunities," *The Journal of Service Marketing,* Spring 1991, p. 39.

[9] William B. Martin, *Quality Customer Service: The Art of Treating Customers as Guests* (Los Altos, CA: Crisp Publications, 1987), p. 9.

[10] Donna Earl, "What Is Internal Customer Service? A Definition and a Case Study," Donna Earl Training, 2008, www.donnaearl-training.com/Articles/InternalCustomerService.html (retrieved June 14, 2008).

[11] Shep Hyken, "Internal Customer Service," www.hyken.com/Article_10.html (retrieved June 14, 2008).

[12] Shep Hyken, "Internal Customer Service," *Shep Hyken: Create a Customer Service Culture,* 2008. www.hyken.com.

[13] Lane Baldwin, "Serving Internal Customers," Business Solutions, http://customerservicezone.com/cgi-bin/links/jump.cgi?ID=821 (retrieved June 14, 2008).

[14] Steven A. Eggland and John W. Williams, *Human Relations at Work* (Cincinnati, OH: South-Western Publishing, 1987), pp. 152–153.

[15] Norm Brodsky, "How to Lose Customers," *Inc.,* July 2005, pp. 49–50.

[16] Much of the following material on getting customers to complain is based on Oren Harari, "Nourishing the Complaint Process," *Management Review,* February 1992, pp. 41–43. See also Jerry Plymire, "Transforming Complaints into Opportunities," *Supervisory Management,* June 1990, pp. 11–12.

[17] Bill Gates, *Business at the Speed of Thought* (New York: Warner Books, 1999), pp. 267–271.

[18] Plymire, "Transforming Complaints into Opportunities," pp. 11–12.

[19] National Ethics Association, *Customer Service Ethics: Beware the Dark Side,* December 9, 2011 (accessed March 21, 2013 at http://www.ethics.net).

[20] Don Knauss, "The Role of Business Ethics in Relationships with Customers," January 19, 2012 (accessed March 21, 2013 at www.forbes.com).

[21] Andrew J. DuBrin, *Contemporary Applied Management Skills for Managers* (Burr Ridge, IL: Richard D. Irwin, 1994), p. 134.

[22] LeBoeuf, *How to Win Customers and Keep Them for Life,* pp. 48–49.

[23] Martin, *Quality Customer Service,* p. 37.

[24] LeBoeuf, *How to Win Customers and Keep Them for Life,* pp. 48–50.

[25] Debra R. Levine, "Diffuse the Angry Customer," *Transportation and Distribution,* January 1992, p. 27.

[26] Ibid., pp. 27–28.

[27] LeBoeuf, *How to Win Customers and Keep Them for Life,* p. 95.

[28] These examples are based on Martin, *Quality Customer Service,* p. 63.

Chapter 14

[1] Lennie Copeland, "Learning to Manage a Multicultural Work Force," *Training* (May 1988), pp. 48–56.

[2] Ann C. Wendt and William M. Sloanaker, "Confronting and Preventing Employment Discrimination," *Supervision* 52 (March 1991), pp. 3–5.

[3] David Myers, *Social Psychology,* 6th ed. (New York: McGraw-Hill, 1999), Chapter 9.

[4] Claire Renzetti and Daniel Curran, *Women, Men, and Society,* 5th ed. (Boston, MA: Pearson Education Co., 2003). See also Linda Lindsey, *Gender Roles: A Sociological Perspective,* 4th ed. (Upper Saddle River, NJ: Pearson Prentice Hall, 2005) and Margaret L. Anderson, *Thinking About Women,* 6th ed. (Boston, MA: Allyn & Bacon, 2003).

[5] Ibid. Myers, *Social Psychology.*

[6] Ibid.

[7] Jon Corzine, "Corzine, Brownback Renew Call to End Genocide in Darfur, Introduce 'Darfur Accountability Act.'" Press release of Senator Jon Corzine, posted March 2, 2005, http://corzine.senate.gov/press_office/record.cfm?id=232683 (retrieved July 20, 2005). See also "Darfur Conflict," Wikipedia.com, http://en.wikipedia.org/wiki/Darfur_conflict (retrieved July 20, 2005).

[8] United Nations News Centre, "Attacks Against Rohingya 'A Ploy' to Drive Them Away; Prevent Their Return—UN Rights Chief," http://www.un.org/apps/news/story.asp?NewsID=57856#.WiWsnVWnHX4 (published Oct. 11, 2017, retrieved Dec. 4, 2017).

[9] Bureau of Labor Statistics, U.S. Department of Labor, "Unemployment Rates by Age, Sex, Race, and Hispanic or Latino Ethnicity," February 2013 at: http://www.bls.gov/opub/ted/2013/ted_20130312.htm (visited July 2017).

[10] See "Employment Situation Summary," compiled by the Bureau of Labor Statistics, U.S. Department of Labor, www.bls.gov/news.release/empsit.nr0.htm (retrieved June 15, 2008).

[11] Jeffrey H. Greenhaus, Saroj Parasuramam, and Wayne M. Wormly, "Effects of Race on Organizational Experience, Job Performance, Evaluations, and Career Outcomes," *Academy of Management Journal,* March 1990, pp. 64–83. See also Joan Ferrante, *Sociology: A Global Perspective,* 5th ed. (Belmont, CA: Thomson Wadsworth Publishing, 2003).

[12] Resume of Congressional Activity, United States Senate, http://www.senate.gov/pagelayout/reference/two_column_table/Resumes.htm (retrieved April 1, 2013).

[13] Liz Roman Gallese, "Why Women Aren't Making It to the Top," *Across the Board,* April 1991, pp. 18–22.

[14] "Black and Hispanic Women Are Paid Substantially Less Than White Men," Economic Policy Institute, by Elise Gould and Jessica Schieder, March 7, 2017. Visited July 2017 at http://www.epi.org/publication/black-and-hispanic-women-are-hit-particularly-hard-by-the-gender-wage-gap/

[15] Andrea Sachs, "Excess Baggage Is Not a Firing Offense," *Time,* March 25, 1991, p. 50.

[16] Ibid.

[17] "Give Me Shelter: Discrimination Against Gay & Lesbian Workers," *Nolo's Legal Encyclopedia* (Nolo.com, Inc., 2000), www.nolo.com/encyclopedia/arYmp/gay_les.html.

[18] http://www.catalyst.org/knowledge/lesbian-gay-bisexual-transgender-workplace-issues#footnote12_8dqqet7 (visited July 2017).

[19] Michael R. Carrell and Frank E. Kuzmits, "Amended ADEA's Effects on HR Strategies Remain Dubious," *Personnel Journal,* May 1987, p. 112.

[20] Paula C. Morrow, James C. McElroy, Bernard G. Stamper, and Mark A. Wilson, "The Effects of Physical Attractiveness and Other Demographic Characteristics on Promotion Decisions," *Journal of Management,* December 1990, pp. 724–736.

[21] Irene Pave, "They Won't Take It Anymore," *Across the Board,* November 1990, pp. 19–23.

[22] Zachary A. Dowdy, "Fired Workers Awarded 6.7M," *Boston Globe,* Boston Globe Online (Metro Region, p. B01, September 24, 1998), www.civiljustice.com/fired_wo.html.

[23] A "U.S. Equal Employment Opportunity Commission: An Overview," U.S. Equal Employment Opportunity Commission (1999), www.eeoc.gov/overview.html.

[24] Age Discrimination in Employment Act (includes concurrent charges with Title VII, ADA and EPA) FY 1997–FY 2012, accessed April 4, 2013, from http://www.eeoc.gov.

[25] Patricia M. Buhler, "Hiring the Disabled—The Solution to Our Problem," *Supervision,* June 1991, p. 17. See also "Disability Facts," Courage Center, www.courage.org/about/tips.asp?id=9 (retrieved July 20, 2005).

[26] George E. Stevens, "Exploding the Myths About Hiring the Handicapped," *Personnel,* December 1986, p. 57.

[27] Mary W. Adelman, "Does Your Facility Comply with the Disability Act?" *Management Review,* June 1992, pp. 37–41.

[28] U.S. Equal Opportunity Employment Commission (EEOC), "Religion-Based Charges FY 1997–FY 2016" accessed at http://www.eeoc.gov/eeoc/statistics/enforcement/religion.cfm on April 4, 2013.

[29] Barbara Kate Repa, "Religious Discrimination: Keeping the Faith at Work," *Nolo's Legal Encyclopedia* (Nolo.com, Inc., 2000), www.nolo.com/encyclopedia/articles/emp/emp10.html (retrieved June 15, 2008).

[30] Ibid.

[31] Kelly Flynn, "Protecting the Team from Sexual Harassment," *Supervision,* December 1991, pp. 6–8. See also www.mspb.gov/sites/mspb/pages/Public%20Affairs.aspx (retrieved June 16, 2008).

[32] Ibid, pp. 6–7. See also Steve Nelson, "Message from the Chairman," Silver Anniversary Edition, a publication of the U.S. Merit Systems Protection Board, Office of Policy and Evaluation, posted Summer 2004, www.mspb.gov/studies/newsletters/04sumnws/04sumnws.htm#Sexual (retrieved July 21, 2005).

[33] Barbara Kate Repa, "Equal Pay for Equal Work," *Nolo's Legal Encyclopedia* (Nolo.com, Inc., 2000), www.nolo.com/encyclopedia/articles/emp/emp11.html.

[34] Alan Deutschman, "Dealing with Sexual Harassment," *Fortune,* November 4, 1991, pp. 145–146.

[35] Barbara Kate Repa, "Much Ado About the Sterile Workplace," *Nolo's Legal Encyclopedia* (2000), www.nolo.com/encyclopedia/articles/emp/sterile.html.

[36] Gordon Allport, *The Nature of Prejudice* (Garden City, NY: Anchor Books, 1954), p. 139.

[37] Ibid.

[38] Myers, *Social Psychology,* Chapter 9.

[39] Kathryn E. Lewis and Pamela R. Johnson, "Preventing Sexual Harassment Complaints Based on Hostile Work Environments," *SAM Advanced Management Journal,* Spring 1991, pp. 21–26.

[40] Robert K. McCalla, "Stopping Sexual Harassment Before It Begins," *Management Review,* April 1991, p. 46.

Chapter 15

[1] Joseph Massie and John Douglas, *Managing: A Contemporary Introduction* (Englewood Cliffs, NJ: Prentice Hall, 1992), p. 78.

[2] T. J. Murray, "Ethics Programs: Just a Pretty Face?" *Business Month,* September 1987, pp. 30–32. See also Sandra Salmans, "Suddenly Business Schools Tackle Ethics," *New York Times,* August 2, 1987, pp. 64–69.

[3] Robert A. Cooke, *Business Ethics: A Perspective* (Chicago, IL: Arthur Anderson and Co., 1988).

[4] Don A. Moore, Daylian M. Cain, George Loewenstein, and Max Bazerman, *Conflicts of Interest: Challenges and Solutions in Business, Law, Medicine, and Public Policy* (New York: Cambridge University Press, 2005), pp. 37–88.

[5] PC Computing, www.zdnet.com/pccomp. Accessed June 15, 2008.

[6] Ibid.

[7] Texas Instruments, Inc., *Ethics in the Business of TI* (Dallas, TX: Texas Instruments, 1977).

[8] George A. Steiner and John F. Steiner, *Business, Government, and Society* (New York: Random House, 1985), pp. 150–151.

[9] G. F. Cavanaugh, Dennis J. Moberg, and Carlos Moore, "The Ethics of Organizational Politics," *Academy of Management Journal,* June 1981, pp. 363–374.

[10] Justin Longenecker, Joseph McKinney, and Carlos Moore, "Egotism and Independence: Entrepreneurial Ethics," *Organizational Dynamics,* Winter 1988, pp. 64–77.

[11] Immanuel Kant, "To the Metaphysic of Morals," in *The Critique of Pure Reason and Other Ethical Treatises* (Chicago, IL: University of Chicago Press, 1988), pp. 392–394.

[12] Bernard Williams, *Ethics and the Limits of Philosophy* (Cambridge, MA: Harvard University Press, 1985), pp. 61–64.

[13] Saul W. Gellerman, "Why 'Good' Managers Make Bad Ethical Choices," *Harvard Business Review,* July–August, 1986, p. 88.

[14] See David Callahan, *The Cheating Culture: Why More Americans Are Doing Wrong to Get Ahead* (Orlando, FL: Harcourt, Inc., 2004).

[15] Robert Levering, "Can Companies Trust Their Employees?" *Business and Society Review,* Spring 1992, pp. 8–12.

[16] O. C. Ferrell and Gareth Gardiner, *In Pursuit of Ethics: Tough Choices in the World of Work* (Springfield, IL: Smith Collins, 1991), pp. 79–80.

[17] *Life Application Bible* (Wheaton, IL: Tyndale House Publishers, 1991), p. 1823 (Luke 10:30–35).

[18] Ferrell and Gardiner, 1991, *In Pursuit of Ethics,* p. 28.

[19] Robert A. Cooke, "Danger Signs of Unethical Behavior: How to Determine if Your Firm Is at Ethical Risk," *Journal of Business Ethics,* 1991, pp. 249–253.

[20] Kent Hodgson, "Adapting Ethical Decisions to a Global Marketplace," *Management Review,* May 1992, p. 54.

[21] Courtland Bovee and John Thill, *Business in Action,* 3rd ed. (Upper Saddle River, NJ: Pearson Prentice Hall, 2005), pp. 53–56.

[22] Silvia Olivares, *Harley Davidson blogspot,* "Ethics and Social Responsibility," http://harleydavidsonus.blogspot.com/2012/09/chapter-3-ethics-and-social.html (posted Sept. 18, 2012; retrieved June 20, 2017).

[23] Harley-Davidson Home Site, http://investor.harley-davidson.com/downloads/CG_financialcodes.pdf. Accessed June 20, 2017.

[24] Don Hellriegel and John Slocum, *Management,* 7th ed. (Mason, OH: South-Western Publishing Company, 1996).

[25] Courtland Bovee and John Thill, *Business in Action,* 3rd ed. (Upper Saddle River, NJ: Pearson Prentice Hall, 2005), p. 75.

[26] Lloyd–LaFollette Act, MedLibrary.Org, http://medlibrary.org/medwiki/Lloyd-La_Follette_Act (retrieved June 15, 2008).

[27] Survival Tips for Whistleblowers," Government Accountability Project, www.whistleblower.org/www/Tips.htm.

[28] Adapted from Richard P. Nielsen, "Changing Unethical Organizational Behavior," *Executive,* May 1989, pp. 123–130.

[29] Government Accountability Project, "Program Highlight: Pipefitter Case Ends in Triumph," posted September 2, 2005, www.whistleblower.org/template/page.cfm?page_id=68 (retrieved June 15, 2008).

[30] Matthew L. Wald, "Nuclear Waste Believed Threat to River," *New York Times,* October 11, 1997. See also "The Hanford Pipefitters' Story," Government Accountability Project, www.whistleblower.org/template/page.cfm?page_id=134 (retrieved July 2005).

[31] David Ewing, *Freedom Inside the Organization* (New York: McGraw-Hill, 1977).

[32] Sally Seymour, "The Case of the Willful Whistle-Blower," *Harvard Business Review* January/February 1988, pp. 103–109.

[33] Glenn Coleman, "Ethics Communication and Education," Texas Instruments; printed in *Bottom Line/Business,* September 1, 1995. See also Mary Ellen Guffey, www.westwords.com/guffey/ethitest.html.

[34] Andrew W. Singer, "Ethics: Are Standards Lower Overseas?" *Across the Board,* September 1991, pp. 31–34.

[35] Bowen H. McCoy, "The Parable of the Sadhu," *Harvard Business Review,* September/October 1983, pp. 103–108.

[36] This story is adapted from Lawrence Kohlberg, "The Development of Children's Orientations Towards a Moral Order: I. Sequence in the Development of Moral Thought," *Vita Humana,* 1963, pp. 18–19.

Chapter 16

[1] University of Pennsylvania, "Performance and Staff Development Program," http://www.hr.upenn.edu/staffRelations/performance/Default.aspx (retrieved June 24, 2008).

[2] eHow Business Editor, "How to Improve Company Morale without Spending Money," www.ehow.com/how_2045950_morale-without-spending.html(retrieved June 24, 2008).

[3] Dan Neuharth, "Top 20 Self-Sabotaging Behaviors," Secrets You Keep from Yourself, http://www.secretswekeep.com/the_self-sabotage_top_20.htm (retrieved June 24, 2008).

[4] Jeff Nesbit, *US News and World Report,* "The Staggering Costs, Monetary and Otherwise, of Substance Abuse," https://www.usnews.com/news/at-the-edge/articles/2016-12-19/drug-and-alcohol-abuse-cost-taxpayers-442b-annually-new-surgeon-generals-report-finds (posted Dec. 19, 2016; retrieved July 3, 2017).

[5] "Alcoholism and Drug Dependence Are America's Number One Health Problem," National Council on Alcoholism and Drug Dependence, Inc., posted June 2002 (retrieved June 22, 2008), http://www.ncadd.org/facts/numberoneprob.html#10.

[6] National Drug-Free Workplace Alliance, http://www.ndwa.org/statistics.php (retrieved July 3, 2017).

[7] Ibid.

[8] "Reducing Substance Abuse in the Workplace," Work Drug Free, Oregon Department of Human Services, retrieved July 23, 2005, http://www.workdrugfree.org/reducingSubstanceAbuse/reducingSubstanceAbuse.asp. See also "The U.S. Department of Labor Drug Free Workplace Conference Briefing Book," U.S. Department of Labor, July 10, 2003 (retrieved July 23, 2005), http://www.dol.gov.

[9] Ibid.

[10] Mario Alonso, "When an Employee Has Personal Problems," *Supervisory Management,* April 1990, p. 3, and see also David G. Schramm, Ph.D., *The Family in America: A Journal of Public Policy,* "Counting the Cost of Divorce: What Those Who Know Better Rarely Acknowledge," http://familyinamerica.org/journals/fall-2009/counting-cost-divorce-what-those-who-know-better-rarely-acknowledge/#.WVqXdYTyvX4 (retrieved July 3, 2017).

[11] Katarzyna Wandycz, "Divorce Kills," *Forbes,* October 25, 1993.

[12] Jennifer Joseph, "HMOs Target Family Violence," ABC News (November 12, 1999), http://abcnews.go.gom?sections/living/DailyNews/domesticviolenceplans.html. See also "Costs of Intimate Partner Violence Against Women in the United States," U.S.

Department of Health and Human Services, Center for Disease Control and Prevention, Injury Center, posting reviewed August 5, 2004 (retrieved July 22, 2005) http://www.cdc.gov/ncipc/pub-res/ipv_cost/02_introduction.htm.

[13] National Domestic Violence Hotline, http://www.ndvh.org/ndvh2.html. See also "Costs of Intimate Partner Violence Against Women in the United States," U.S. Department of Health and Human Services, Centers for Disease Control and Prevention, Injury Center, posting reviewed August 5, 2004 (retrieved July 22, 2005), http://www.cdc.gov/ncipc/pub-res/ipv_cost/02_introduction.htm.

[14] Deborah Amos, "Victims of Violence: Victims of Domestic Violence Now Get Help from Employers," ABC News (June 5, 2000), http://abcnews.go.com/onair/WorldNe. . .05_CL_domesticviolence_feature.html. See also: "Costs of Intimate Partner Violence Against Women in the United States," U.S. Department of Health and Human Services, Centers for Disease Control and Prevention, Injury Center, posting reviewed August 5, 2004 (retrieved July 22, 2005), http://www.cdc.gov/ncipc/pub-res/ipv_cost/02_introduction.htm. See also: Robert Pearl, M.D., "Domestic Violence: The Secret Killer That Costs $8.3 Billion Annually," *Forbes,* https://www.forbes.com/sites/robertpearl/2013/12/05/domestic-violence-the-secret-killer-that-costs-8-3-billion-annually/#d6a6b234681f, (posted December 5, 2013; retrieved July 3, 2017).

[15] National Domestic Violence Hotline, http://www.ndvh.org/ndvh2.html.

[16] Los Angeles County Sheriff's Department, "The Domestic Violence Handbook . . . A Victim's Guide," http://walnut.lasheriff.org/women.html.

[17] Janet Deming, "Rescuing Workers in Violent Families," *HR Magazine,* July 1991.

[18] Kay James, Commission Chair, "National Gambling Impact Study Commission Final Report," National Gambling Impact Study Commission, revised August 3, 1999 (retrieved July 22, 2005), http://govinfo.library.unt.edu/ngisc/index.html.

[19] U.S. Department of Labor, Bureau of Labor Statistics, http://stats.bls.gov/ (May 24, 2000). See also: "Employee Assistance Programs," U.S. Department of Health and Human Services, and Substance Abuse and Mental Health Services Administration, Clearinghouse for Alcohol and Drug Information, posted November 9, 2000 (retrieved June 22, 2008), http://www.health.org/workplace/fedagencies/employee_assistance_programs.aspx.

[20] Ibid.

[21] VITAL Work-Life Inc., "Why Offer an EAP?" http://vitalworklife.com/fororganizations/offer-eap/ (retrieved July 3, 2017).

[22] Ibid.

[23] Christy Marshall, "Getting the Drugs Out," *Business Month,* May 1989.

[24] Harris Sussman, website articles, "Diversity Questions and Answers column," "The Next Big Thing: People Over 60," and "Review of Workforce 2020," postings updated July 11, 2005 (retrieved July 25, 2005), http://sussman.org/.

[25] Lynn Martin, "Drug-Free Policy: Key to Success for Small Businesses," *HR Focus,* September 1992, p. 23.

[26] Roger Thompson, "Anti-Drug Programs Tailored to Small and Mid-Sized Firms," *Nation's Business,* September 1992, p. 12.

[27] National Caregivers Library, "Fast Facts About Working Caregivers," http://www.caregiverslibrary.org/for-employers/fast-facts.aspx (retrieved July 3, 2017).

[28] Kim Parker and Eileen Patten, *Pew Research Center,* "The Sandwich Generation: Rising Financial Burdens for Middle-Aged Americans," http://www.pewsocialtrends.org/2013/01/30/the-sandwich-generation/ (posted Jan. 30, 2013; retrieved June 20, 2017).

[29] Karen Matthes, "A Coming of Age for Intergenerational Care," *HR Focus,* June 1993, p. 10. See also Roger Crisman, media contact for Work Life Benefits, "The Sandwich Generation Is in a Pickle," Accor Services, posted April 9, 2002 (retrieved June 22, 2008). http://www.wlb.com/en/worklifebenefitsnews/pressreleases/2002/04_09_2002.asp; Belden, Russonello, and Stewart, "In the Middle: A Report on Multicultural Boomers Coping with Family and Aging Issues," Research/Strategy/Management, American Association of Retired People, posted July, 2001 (retrieved June 22, 2008), http://www.aarp.org/research/housing-mobility/caregiving/Articles/aresearch-import-789-D17446.html.

[30] Ibid.

[31] Denis Waitley, *Psychology of Success* (Boston, MA: Richard D. Irwin, Inc., 1993). See also Denis Waitley, *Seeds of Greatness: The Ten Best-Kept Secrets of Total Success* (New York: Pocket Books, 1983), Denis Waitley and Reni L. Witt, *The Joy of Working* (New York: Dodd, Mead, and Company, 1985), Denis Waitley, *Empires of the Mind* (New York: William Morrow and Company, Inc., 1995), and current articles posted on Waitley's website at http://www.deniswaitley.com.

[32] Ibid.

[33] Joan Harvey, and Cynthia Katz, *If I'm So Successful, Why Do I Feel Like a Fake?* (New York: St. Martin's Press, 1985).

[34] Martin Seligman, *Authentic Happiness* (New York: The Free Press, 2002). See also the "Reflective Happiness" website at http://www.reflectivehappiness.com/, or the "Positive Psychology" or "Authentic Happiness" websites at http://www.authentichappiness.org/; Lisa G. Aspinwall and Ursula M. Staudinger (eds.), *A Psychology of Human Strengths: Fundamental Questions and Future Directions for a Positive Psychology* (Washington, DC: The American Psychological Association, 2003); Claudia Wallis, "The New Science of Happiness," *Time,* January 17, 2005 (also linked to http://www.reflectivehappiness.com/).

[35] Richard Bolles, *What Color Is Your Parachute?* (Berkeley, CA: Ten Speed Press, 2005). See also Bolles' online supplements at http://www.jobhuntersbible.com/ (retrieved August 20, 2013).

[36] American Psychiatric Association, *Diagnostic Manual of Mental Disorders,* 4th ed. (Washington, DC, 1994).

index

Pages with examples are indicated with *e*, footnotes and reference notes are indicated with *n*, and figures are indicated with *f*.

A

B

D

H

I

N

T